PERSONALITIES OF THE OLD TESTAMENT

HALE LECTURES

PERSONALITIES OF THE OLD TESTAMENT. By the Rev. Fleming James, D.D., Ph.D. 1938.

THE CHURCH IN JAPAN. By the Rt. Rev. Henry St. George Tucker, D.D. 1937. (Published under the title "The History of the Episcopal Church in Japan.")

THE PRAISE OF GOD. By the Rev. Winfred Douglas, Mus. Doc. 1935. (Published under the title "Church Music in History and Practice.")

THE SOCIAL IMPLICATIONS OF THE OXFORD MOVEMENT. By the Rev. William George Peck, S.T.D. 1933.

PASTORAL PSYCHIATRY AND MENTAL HEALTH. By the Rev. John Rathbone Oliver, M.D., Ph.D. 1932. (Published under the title "Psychiatry and Mental Health.")

CHRIST IN THE GOSPELS. By the Rev. Burton Scott Easton, Ph.D., S.T.D. 1930.

NEW HORIZONS OF THE CHRISTIAN FAITH. By the Rev. Frederick C. Grant, D.D., Th.D. 1928.

SOME ASPECTS OF CONTEMPORARY GREEK ORTHODOX THOUGHT. By the Rev. Frank Gavin, Ph.D. 1921.

THE ETHIOPIC LITURGY. By the Rev. S. A. B. Mercer, D.D., Ph.D. 1915.

BIOGRAPHICAL STUDIES IN SCOTTISH CHURCH HISTORY. By the Rt. Rev. Anthony Mitchell, D.D. 1913.

THE NATIONAL CHURCH OF SWEDEN. By the Rt. Rev. John Wordsworth, D.D., LL.D. 1910.

CHURCH HYMNS AND CHURCH MUSIC. By Peter C. Lutkin, Mus. D., A.G.O. 1908.

THE HALE LECTURES

PERSONALITIES
OF THE OLD TESTAMENT

By

FLEMING JAMES

Professor of the Literature and Interpretation of the Old Testament
BERKELEY DIVINITY SCHOOL

Affiliated with
YALE UNIVERSITY DIVINITY SCHOOL

With a Foreword by
PROFESSOR JULIUS A. BEWER

CHARLES SCRIBNER'S SONS · NEW YORK
CHARLES SCRIBNER'S SONS · LTD · LONDON
1949

DILECTO IN DOMINO

FREDERICK CLIFTON GRANT

FOREWORD

The Old Testament has never been better understood than it is today. The amazing advance in philology, archaeology, and history has shed so much light on the material and political, the social and religious life of Israel, and on the influence of the culture of the centres of civilization upon it that the Old Testament has become an entirely new book, full of interest, throbbing with life. The unfolding of the story of Israel among the nations, and especially the development of her religion from the lowly beginnings of the ancestors to the heights of the ethical monotheism of the prophets, is one of the most wonderful and significant chapters in the history of the world. It is indeed so interesting in itself and we may become so much fascinated by the ever fresh insights as to forget that it has a contribution to make to our own spiritual life. We may study, e.g. even the most devotional book of the Old Testament, the Psalter, as an ancient hymnal and prayer book used in the worship of the temple or at home, we may see the interesting processions and services as we reconstruct in our imagination the whole picture of this ancient religious life with the various experiences, glad or sad, out of which these psalms arose, we may derive intense intellectual satisfaction and joy from it all and yet feel not the slightest stirring of our spiritual nature in response. Similarly, we may read the prophets, especially the great ones, and be carried away with admiration for their moral and spiritual grandeur, their intellectual greatness and literary and oratorical power, and yet miss the essential significance of these spokesmen of God.

This is due to some extent at least to the critical and historical method of study which has freed us indeed from the dogma of the infallible inspiration of every word of the Old Testament but has also taken the divine aura from it by making us read it as we do other literature. Thus we have come to see too clearly its many imperfections, crudities and cruelties, to regard it in its entirety as morally or spiritually binding upon ourselves, and we are led to ask whether it still has any spiritual value for us. Does it still speak to us so that we today may perceive God addressing us

vii

personally, searching our hearts and consciences, convicting us of sin, calling us to faith and trust, awaking in us love, inspiring us with hope, illumining us with insight, strengthening us for our tasks, in short, making us aware of Himself and of His profound interest in each one of us?

In the chapters of this present book Professor Fleming James has seized upon this element and has shown that it is in the personalities of the Old Testament that the truth becomes instinct with life and power, and that we must read the Old Testament, as he himself does, with genuine sympathy and inward participation if we are to secure the spiritual values we seek for ourselves in it. We must put ourselves into the various situations with inward participation. They must become so real to us, that we seem to live them all over again ourselves, just as we do in other great literature, when we feel intensely with the heroes or heroines. This takes time, for it needs brooding over the pages of history, poetry or prophecy. But it is abundantly worthwhile, when the solemn hush of God's own presence falls on our spirit as we stand with Isaiah in the temple; when the psalmist's cry of grief and longing wakens an echo in our hearts or the trust of the singer fills us with confidence and joy; or the sting of rebuke is felt by us too as we read, "Thou art the man!" and the soul joins in the plea: "Create in me a clean heart, O God; and renew a right spirit within me."

To live with the story-teller, the poet, and the prophet and recreate in our imagination vividly the scenes and experiences portrayed by them, that surely is the first requisite. This is what we must do with all great literature if it is to effect in us what Aristotle called the "purging of the emotions" which it is intended to produce: the chastening, cleansing, illumining, transforming of our spirit. If we read the Old Testament thus with hearts awake, minds alert, imagination actively engaged, many of its stories or poems or prophecies assume a new meaning and they speak directly to our souls.

Our critical study and our modern understanding of the Old Testament, far from making it impossible for us to gain its highest, its spiritual values, actually help us immeasurably in this, if only, with open-minded sincerity, real sympathy, and active inward participation we combine a true desire to know what the Old Testament has to say to ourselves. For by our frank discrimination between the permanent truths, however crudely, strangely, or antiquatedly expressed, and the temporary, lower, morally and religiously unacceptable teachings, however brilliantly and appealingly presented, we are enabled to see the truth clearly and to appropriate it with eagerness and spiritual intensity, and thus to perceive God speaking to us directly in the pages of this sacred literature, which the ages have illumined to its readers more and more as progressive interpretation has accompanied progressive revelation.

JULIUS A. BEWER

ACKNOWLEDGMENTS

The author is indebted to many friends for their good offices in
connection with this present volume: to Professors Johannes Hempel
and Roland H. Bainton, and to Canon Cyril E. Hudson, all of whom
read the manuscript in its earlier stages and encouraged him to go
on with it; to Professors Millar Burrows, George Dahl, Cuthbert A.
Simpson and Charles L. Taylor, Jr., and to the Rev. Neville V. Gor-
ton, for reading the completed manuscript and making valuable
suggestions; to Professor Charles B. Hedrick and Dr. G. Ernest
Wright, for doing the same, and also for contributing each an illuminating note; to Librarian Raymond P. Morris for help in compiling the bibliography; to Professor A. T. Olmstead and to the
estate of Professor F. K. Sanders for the use of maps; to Mrs. Fleming James, Jr., for typing the manuscript and compiling the index
of Bible passages; to Mrs. Ormonde L. Rolls for long continued
assistance, including proof-reading; to the Rev. Kenneth W. Cam-
eron for reading the proofs and giving helpful advice; to the students of the Berkeley Divinity School and the Yale University Divinity School, who through eleven years have enabled the author
to test this material in his teaching; to the Rt. Rev. F. A. McElwain,
D.D., and the Trustees of the Seabury-Western Theological Seminary, for extending to him the invitation to deliver the Hale Lectures; to the Faculty and other members of the Seminary for their
hospitality while the lectures were being given; to Mr. William L.
Savage and other members of the staff of Charles Scribner's Sons
for their untiring labours in bringing out this book; to Professor
Julius A. Bewer for his generosity in writing the Foreword, and
for much excellent advice; to many others who have in some way
rendered assistance; and, finally, to Professor Frederick C. Grant,
whose help can never be measured.

The Bible text used in this volume is (for the most part) that of
the American Standard Edition of the Revised Bible, copyrighted in
1929 by the International Council of Religious Education. The author is grateful to the Council for their free permission to make
citations according to his need.

CONTENTS

CONTENTS

NOTE: The Psalmists are not included here, for they are treated in another volume by the present author: *Thirty Psalmists*, G. P. Putnam's Sons, 1938.

PERSONALITIES OF THE OLD TESTAMENT

Chapter I

MOSES

[13TH CENTURY B.C. (?)]

If we can believe in the possibility of *any* miracles, two facts in the field of history and in the complex world of today may well bear that name. One is the Jewish people. Since 70 A.D. they have had no nation of their own, but have been scattered throughout the earth, mingling with all peoples yet remaining distinct, existing everywhere as sojourners, generally discriminated against and often persecuted; yet everywhere teeming, aggressive, vigorous, brilliant, a force to be reckoned with; today kept under here and there only by violence, and probably not to be kept under long; a phenomenon seemingly unique in history. The second fact is Judaism, the religion by virtue of which this people are what they are. Both facts trace their origin to one man.

There is also a third fact, more astonishing than either, which proceeds from Israel and therefore from this same man: the world-religion of Christianity. We may add a fourth fact. Islam, the religion of the Mohammedan peoples, likewise goes back ultimately to Moses.

Our study of the Personalities of the Old Testament ought to begin with Moses, the founder of Israel and its religion. Without him there would, humanly speaking, be no Old Testament, no Jewish people, no Judaism, and no Christian church; perhaps also no religion of Islam.

The Sources

Our main sources for the study of the man Moses are the two earliest documents of the Pentateuch. There is no need here to remind the reader that (in the judgment of most scholars) the first five books of the Bible are made up of four strands of narrative and other material. Of these, the J document (*c.* 850 B.C.?) and the E document (*c.* 750 B.C.?) [1] contain the earliest traditions regarding Moses.[2]

[1] This is the dating of Wellhausen, which is still widely accepted.

[2] The later documents (D and P) confirm in large part the testimony of

Since, however, Moses lived at the latest about 1250 B.C. the question arises how far these documents, which are separated from his day by four or five centuries, can be expected to give us a correct picture of him. We should remember, of course, that the dates assigned to J and E apply only to their present form. It is recognized that they both contain material that goes back much further into the past. But even so this material was subject to the vicissitudes of oral tradition over a long period and can make no claim (except in a fragment or two) to be contemporaneous with the events it narrates. How far then can they be relied on?

Certainly they can be relied on to *some* extent. Modern scholars mostly agree that they preserve in a general way actual recollections of Moses. In them the man, his work and his characteristics stand out sharply marked. When however we come to the *details* of the J and E tradition these scholars grow sceptical. They reserve to themselves the right to treat such details with the utmost freedom, regrouping, remoulding, rejecting. They continually point out that the traditions are overgrown with legend; are indeed "legends," containing only a "core" of historic fact; which often is not much of a core, and not the same core for all.

The details of the narratives therefore are generally so passed over by scholars that while we read in their books much *about* Moses we seldom see and hear Moses himself. For the truth is (as Gressmann[3] so well perceived) that only in the concrete details of the traditions do we find a living Moses. Unless we can have a Moses who smites the Egyptian, succours the daughters of Jethro at the well, argues with God against the commission thrust upon him, strides in before Pharaoh with his demand, speaks assurance to the people at the Red Sea, converses with Jethro, sits all day judging litigants, ascends Sinai to meet God, dashes in pieces the tablets of stone, grinds the golden calf to powder and administers the fatal drink to its worshippers, intercedes for the people, finds food and water for them, enjoins a perpetual holy war against Amalek, blazes out again and again at rebellion, and the like, we

J and E. Indeed, the mass of their contribution consists of revisions of and additions to the fundamental material of J and E. These documents are conveniently assembled for the reader in such books as C. F. Kent, *The Narratives of the Beginnings of Hebrew History* in *Student's Old Testament*, Scribner's, 1904; and Czarnomska, *The Authentic Literature of Israel*, Macmillan, 1924.

[3] See the historical method employed in his *Mose und seine Zeit* (Göttingen, 1913).

have not after all a Moses of flesh and blood, however nobly and admiringly he may be *described*.

Is there any remedy for this situation? Basically, there is none. Nothing can convert the traditions regarding Moses into dependable historical documents of the sort that we have e.g. for David. In Moses' case we must be content with much less. But we can assume (as contemporary writers agree) that the stories of Moses are not fiction: they go back to real situations, and preserve real traits of the great leader. Nor need we stop there. We may well bear in mind the possibility that often the *setting* in which these traits appear is (on the whole) correctly given. If this is so, then the concrete details of the traditions should be handled with respect —not altered and set aside at will. After all they supply the *only concrete information that we have*. Where they are not obviously incredible they are quite as likely to be true as the reconstructions of modern scholars which however ingenious remain still reconstructions. And where they make too large a demand on our credence, it is often better to let them stand for what they are worth than to attempt a reconstruction of our own. Building on what seem to us probabilities is extremely unsatisfactory, for the reason that we *know* so little of the actual circumstances.

This principle applies not only to the individual narratives, but to their present grouping. In handling what are called "legends" it is customary to assume that originally every individual narrative was an independent unit quite unrelated to other narratives. Any link connecting narratives, therefore, is thought to be of later origin. It is maintained that popular imagination, which always liked to tie events together, could keep forging link after link, until at last a continuous narrative emerged—as for instance, in the cycle of stories regarding Abraham, or, pre-eminently, in the tale of Joseph. There is much truth in this view. But it overlooks the probability that in the case of a leader of supreme importance, like Moses, *some general sequence* of his history might well be preserved in memory. When therefore we find the traditions reporting that he appeared first in Egypt, then went to Midian, then returned to Egypt with a commission from Yahweh, then came to grips with the Pharaoh and succeeded in leading forth the Israelites from Egypt, then experienced the deliverance at the Red Sea: that there was a long sojourn in the desert, centring in two places—Sinai, where Yahweh entered into covenant with Israel, and Kadesh, where a number of incidents occurred: that finally Moses led Israel around Edom to Transjordania, where after defeating the

Amorites he met his death:—when we find this sequence we are justified in regarding it as actual history, and not as the work of later imagination.

A word might be said also regarding the term "legend" which is commonly used to describe the Moses narratives. It signifies "a traditional story popularly regarded as historical" [4] and in this strict sense cannot be objectionable. But unfortunately it carries with it the implication that the tradition thus preserved is not true, or at least has only a core of truth. "Legend" is therefore a question-begging term which we shall avoid, substituting for it the neutral term "tradition" (i.e. what has been handed down). This exactly describes what we possess regarding Moses. These stories were actually handed down and believed through generations until they attained their present form several centuries after Moses' death.

In our study of Moses we shall first review what these J and E traditions have to tell us concerning him in each phase of his life and work. Then we shall ask how far their representation can be accepted as history. Such an appraisal will be everywhere open to error. But since err we must, we shall prefer to err on the side of giving credence rather than of withholding it. And we shall try never to lose sight of the probability that with all their imaginative colouring and legendary accretion these stories, and these stories alone, enable us to see Moses pretty much as he really was.

The Oppression

The story of Moses begins with the oppression of the Israelites in Egypt. If it had not been for this oppression Moses might never have arisen to do his work. It served as the provocation which started him on his course, and it determined the nature of the religion which he was to found. That religion was to be a religion of redemption, and it would always keep in mind the initial fact that Yahweh had delivered His people from "the house of bondage."

Traditions of Genesis had related how the Israelites migrated in time of famine into the land of Goshen and there pastured their flocks under the favour of the Pharaoh. Such admissions of nomads into the land east of the Delta are attested by the Egyptian monuments and scholars generally agree that some time before Moses' day a number of Hebrews did enter Egypt with the royal permis-

[4] *Concise Oxford Dictionary.*

sion, coming perhaps in successive groups. These comprised but a few tribes,[1] perhaps the Joseph tribes of Ephraim, Manasseh and Benjamin,[2] perhaps only the tribe of Levi;[3] and the community they formed was not large. One tradition represents it as later served by two midwives, which would mean at most a few thousand persons.[4] Apparently they fared well in Goshen.

The traditions of Exodus however open with an altered situation. "Now there arose a new king over Egypt, who knew not Joseph" (Exod. 1:8). Perhaps it was a change of dynasty. At any rate, the new Pharaoh had no regard for the pro-Israelitish policy of his predecessors. The increasing numbers and power of these half-nomads[5] within his borders aroused his fear lest in the case of an invasion they might take sides with the enemy. This seems natural enough. Sometime about 1700 B.C.[6] Egypt had been overrun by the Hyksos, apparently a Semitic or partly Semitic people from the East, who had dominated it till about 1600 B.C., when Amosis I, founder of the XVIII dynasty, had at length succeeded in driving them out. The memory of this would keep apprehension alive. At the same time another factor entered in which made it inadvisable to expel the Israelites. The Pharaoh had on hand a building program and these aliens were needed as labourers. To impress them would serve the double purpose of breaking their spirit and getting the work done. "Therefore," the tradition says tersely, "they (the Egyptians) did set over them task-masters to afflict them with their burdens. And they built for Pharaoh store-cities, Pithom and Raamses" (Exod. 1:11). It was the first wave of anti-Semitism to roll over this tragic people. And like its successors it failed of its purpose. "The more they afflicted them"—so runs the exultant record—"the more they multiplied and the more they spread abroad."

[1] Gressmann, SAT, I 2, p. 24. [Note that a complete key to all abbreviations such as SAT will be found on page 585f.]

[2] Leslie, OTR, p. 101. Lods, Israel, p. 171, thinks yet other tribes or parts of tribes may have joined them. Sellin, GIJV, I, p. 54, thinks they comprised, or afterwards united in Canaan with, a single Joseph tribe.

[3] Olmstead, HPS, p. 247. Meek, HO, p. 31f, makes a strong case for his opinion that only the tribe of Levi was in Egypt.

[4] Gressmann, ibid., estimates the number of men as perhaps 2000, at most 5000. Sellin, GIJV, I, p. 74, pictures them as meeting Sihon with about 6000 men.

[5] The Israelites were probably not Bedouin (Bédū), or true nomads, but half-nomads ('Arab), living mostly or entirely in tents yet cultivating land. Cf. Albright, APB, p. 131.

[6] Albright, Haverford Symposium, p. 16.

This seems to preserve a genuine historical recollection. In the modern Tell el-Mashuta, the site of the ancient Pithom, there have been uncovered large granaries whose stones bear the royal stamps of a series of Egyptian kings, the earliest being Ramses II (1301-1235 B.C.).[7] The monuments also mention a certain *p'r* people, a foreign group who under the same Ramses II and his successors were used as forced labour in the building of temples and in stone-breaking, their members being subjects of such temples.[8] These *p'r* (or *Apuriu*) have been identified by some historians with the Hebrews, a larger group of which the Israelites formed part. Israel, indeed, is not mentioned and the identification is not certain. But these Egyptian notices show that the kind of thing depicted in the Exodus story could happen. The story itself is intrinsically probable; nor is it likely (as has often been pointed out) that a proud people like the Israelites would have *invented* the tale of their humiliating servitude.

The oppression of the Israelites, accordingly, is accepted by historians as a fact. It is usually dated in the reign of Ramses II (1301-1235 B.C.),[9] the actual exodus being put under his successor, Merneptah. This dating is not unchallenged. Some think that Thotmes III or his successor was the Pharaoh of the oppression, which would place the exodus 200 years earlier.[10] Still other datings are advocated.[11] For our study the date is unimportant, and we shall adhere to the usual chronology.

The tradition tells how the continued increase of the Israelites led the Pharaoh to further attempts at repression, the last being a command that every male Israelite child be destroyed at birth. All in vain. One child slipped through the net and became the deliverer of his people. But this charming story of Moses' rescue and adoption by the daughter of the Pharaoh is generally regarded as legend. One thing, however, is certain: the name Moses is

[7] Sellin, *GIJV*, I, p. 55.

[8] Kittel, *GVI*, I, p. 304; Sellin, *GIJV*, I, p. 55.

[9] The hypothesis, common a short while ago, that the actual exodus took place under Ramses' successor, Merneptah, is (according to Albright) held by hardly any one now (*RDBL*, p. 30). But Barton *AB*[7], p. 447, still adheres to it.

[10] E.g., Garstang, *JJ*, p. 54.

[11] Albright, *BASOR*, No. 58, p. 16, thinks that in the light of recent excavations of sites in Palestine the exodus should be placed in the year 1290 B.C. or a little earlier, which would still bring it within the reign of Ramses II. Meek, however, *HO*, p. 33, while regarding Ramses II as the Pharaoh of the oppression. puts Moses about 1200 B.C.

Egyptian and indicates that its bearer may have received it in Egypt.

Tradition next presents Moses as a grown man. Though exempt apparently from the hard lot of his fellow-Israelites he was drawn to them by an inner compulsion. "He went out unto his brethren, and looked on their burdens" (Exod. 2:11). In his inspection he came upon a gruesome spectacle—an Egyptian flogging a Hebrew, "one of his brethren." At the sight something flamed up in Moses. Assuring himself that no one was looking, he leaped upon the offender and killed him, hiding the body in the sand which tells no tales. Next day he intervened in a fight between two Israelites to protect the weaker. The bully turned on him with the demand, "Who made thee a prince and a judge over us? thinkest thou to kill me, as thou killedst the Egyptian?" His crime, then, was known! Frightened by the threat of Pharaoh's punishment Moses fled ignominiously from Egypt.

Scholars generally do not treat this story as history, and we ought not to lean heavily upon it. But its representation of Moses' character is certainly correct. Here we see already in the young man traits destined to mark his subsequent career: his identification of himself with his people, his blazing anger at the sight of wrong, his impetuous intervention, his heavy hand, his impulse to arbitrate. One element, however, is conspicuous by its absence: not yet is he the "man of God." He acts on his own initiative, not by divine commission; and his authority is promptly challenged. This lack was now to be supplied.

Moses' Call

Moses' flight brought him to the "land of Midian," in the vicinity of the mountain which in the tradition bears two names, Sinai and Horeb. Just where Sinai was located is an old matter of dispute, some placing it down on the Sinai peninsula, some near the oasis of Kadesh, some on the northeast shore of the Gulf of Akaba, where a number of extinct volcanoes are to be found. No one of course really knows, and for our study it makes no difference which theory is right. These Midianites were a pastoral people akin to the Kenites, who later came into intimate relations with Israel. Tradition reports that Moses found a welcome with their priest, Jethro, through his chivalrous aid of Jethro's seven daughters. Receiving one of these girls in marriage, he settled down as a member of the priest's household and was employed as keeper of his flock.

The romantic features of this story are usually set aside as imaginative and they may well be the creation of popular fancy. But scholars are justified in accepting Moses' connection with Jethro as historic fact. In so doing, they are apt to emphasize one point on which tradition is silent. Since Jethro was a priest, as a member of his household Moses must have come into contact with the practice of the Midianitish religion. Now it is a common hypothesis that the Midianites worshipped a deity called Yahweh, and that Moses derived from Jethro a knowledge both of Yahweh and of the way in which He was to be worshipped. Tradition however asserts that he came to know Yahweh in a different way.

The life of a shepherd in the steppe is a lonely one and Moses had abundant leisure for thought. One thing must have occupied his mind incessantly—the suffering of his brethren in Egypt. His active impetuous nature cried out that they must be rescued, but how? Doubtless he was kept informed of the Egyptian situation, for reliable news from the outside world travels with incredible swiftness across the desert.[1] Finally the report came that another Pharaoh had ascended the throne. Now was the opportunity!

He had led Jethro's flock to the west of the desert "to the mountain of God, to Horeb." Suddenly, tradition reports, he was vouchsafed a theophany (Exod. 3:2ff). Turning aside to see a burning bush which yet did not burn, he heard a voice from the midst of it calling his name: "Moses, Moses, draw not nigh hither: put off thy shoes from off thy feet, for the place whereon thou standest is holy ground." Then the speaking Deity identified Himself. "I am the God of thy father, the God of Abraham, the God of Isaac, and the God of Jacob." Overcome with the awful presence Moses "hid his face; for he was afraid to look upon God."

But this manifestation of the Divine was not for Moses' own enlightenment. God had appeared for a purpose. "I have surely seen the affliction of my people that are in Egypt, and have heard their cry by reason of their taskmasters; for I know their sorrows; and I am come down to deliver them out of the hand of the Egyptians, and to bring them up out of that land unto a good land and a large, unto a land flowing with milk and honey." And this purpose involved Moses. "Come now therefore, and I will send thee unto Pharaoh, that thou mayest bring forth my people the children of Israel out of Egypt."

[1] Kittel, *GMMI*, p. 31.

Tradition has it that Moses shrank back from such a commission. "Who am I, that I should go unto Pharaoh, and that I should bring forth the children of Israel out of Egypt?" But God's answer was ready. "Certainly, I will be with thee; and this shall be the token unto thee, that I have sent thee: when thou hast brought forth the people out of Egypt, ye shall serve God upon this mountain." That is, carry out my charge, and your success will prove me true.

But Moses had another difficulty. "Behold, when I come unto the children of Israel, and shall say unto them, The God of your fathers hath sent me unto you; and they shall say unto me, What is his name? What shall I say unto them?" This was a natural question, for to the antique man the name disclosed the very innermost being of its bearer. Moses then was asking for nothing less than an authoritative revelation of the nature of God. And he received it. God answered, "I WILL BE THAT I WILL BE. . . . Thus shalt thou say unto the sons of Israel, I WILL BE hath sent me unto you. . . . Yahweh, the God of your fathers, the God of Abraham, the God of Isaac, and the God of Jacob, hath sent me unto you: this is my name for ever, and this is my memorial unto all generations."

Thus, according to tradition, Yahweh made Himself known to Moses. Here the religion of Israel began. But Moses still urged difficulties. The people, he said, would not believe that Yahweh had appeared unto him. Yahweh answered by giving him the power to work wonders as proof of his commission. And yet he hesitated—"Oh, Lord, I am not a man of words, neither heretofore, nor since thou hast spoken unto thy servant; for I am slow of speech, and of a slow tongue." But Yahweh said to him, "Who hath made man's mouth? . . . Is it not I, Yahweh? Now therefore go, and I will be with thy mouth, and teach thee what thou shalt speak."

Thus runs the sublime, but very human narrative. On analysis it resolves itself into pieces of the J and E documents which have been fitted together to make the present whole. This lack of original unity, and the distance of the two documents themselves from the time of Moses, forbid us to treat the account as on a par with the descriptions which an Isaiah or a Jeremiah give of their call. Gressmann thinks it totally unreliable and accuses those who would seek its historical core of turning mythological fancies into historical facts.[2] But such a negative view fails to take into ac-

² *Mose,* p. 22. Gressmann believes indeed that it has a historical core, but

count many elements of it which have the ring of reality about
them. It contains a number of those vivid touches which make the
Moses of tradition stand out as a sharply defined, unique figure.
Let us now appraise it as best we can.

We must recognize at the outset that if we possess *any* trustworthy recollections of Moses' call these must go back to Moses
himself, for no other human being was a witness of the transaction. Again, if he had such a call he would be compelled to
relate it to the Israelites in order to prove his divine commission.
Such a narrative would naturally be transmitted along with the
other recollections of the great leader, and it is surely not impossible
that it could have come down without substantial disfigurement
to the J and E writers. The fact that these writers preserve different
versions and varying features of it would not detract from their
credibility. We ought therefore to approach it with an attitude of
credence and abandon this only if we meet with elements that are
manifestly improbable.

First, then, it is not improbable that Moses should have been
vouchsafed a theophany. Such manifestations of the divine are
connected by tradition with Abraham, Isaac and Jacob, and are
quite in accord with the religious experience of those early days.
That Moses' theophany should take the form of a flame within a
bush and a divine voice is what we should expect from the prophets'
accounts of their own visions and auditions.[3] We can think of
Moses therefore as receiving his call in a prophetic ecstasy. His
hearing his name spoken, his answer, his realization that he was
standing on "holy ground," and his hiding his face in fear, are
all normal features of such an experience.

On one point both the J and the E traditions are explicit. The
God thus revealing Himself was not a new God, but the God
of the fathers. This does not harmonize at all with the view
entertained by some scholars, which is that the God of Moses had
nothing to do with the *El* or *Els* then worshipped by the Israelites,
but was taken over by Moses from the Midianites.[4] Those who

this is not any psychological experience of Moses. The fact which lies at its
base is that Moses really did deliver his people out of their Egyptian servitude.
Without this fact of experience the legend of the call could never have arisen
(*SAT*, I 2, p. 33. See also Note 3).

[3] Gressmann, *Mose,* p. 21, draws a sharp line between the theophany to
Moses and those to the prophets, characterizing the former as a mythological
occurrence, i.e., in that the Deity appeared to him in bodily form. His reasons for so doing are not convincing to the present writer.

[4] Or from the Kenites, a clan of Midian.

hold this view maintain that the identification of Moses' God with the God of the fathers is a later trait which did not appear until the Israelites were settled in Canaan. It then stamped itself upon the J and E narratives of Moses' call, obliterating the original form of the tradition.

This theory of the Midianitish origin of Moses' religion is widely spread among scholars and has the support of many weighty names.[5] It is based mainly upon a modern recasting of the tradition recorded in Exodus 18 regarding Jethro's visit to Moses, which will be considered later. In spite of the ingenious arguments employed to sustain it, it remains unsupported by the Exodus tradition, which tells nothing of the God of Midian being introduced into Israel by Moses but asserts that the God who appeared to him was the God of the fathers. The present writer can see no reason why that tradition is an improbable one, and he accordingly accepts it.

The next point to be noticed is that the God who meets Moses is very like Moses himself. He too has been listening to the cry of His people and is *going to do something* about it. "I am come down to deliver them." Here is perhaps the outstanding characteristic of Moses' God. He does not sit placidly in heaven but enters the struggle of earth. He enters it on behalf of the oppressed, to deliver them from their oppressors and bring them into a good land. He is a redeeming God, a lover of the poor, a maker of history.

He also works through men. "Come now therefore, and I will send thee unto Pharaoh, that thou mayest bring forth my people the children of Israel out of Egypt!" So He calls men, not to contemplation, but to work. Not to ease, but to selfless devotion. There is no more authentic note of Israel's religion than this.

He demands faith. When Moses' effort is crowned with success: when he has brought the people out of Egypt and they are here, on this remote mountain, worshipping God, *then* Moses will know that God has sent him. Meanwhile he is to go ahead.

He reveals Himself as Yahweh. Upon no element in the Mosaic tradition are scholars in more complete agreement than upon this,

---

[5] Meek, *HO*, p. 110, who rejects this theory, thinks that Yahweh (originally *Yah* or *Yahu*) was at first a storm god known in southern Arabia, who was later adopted by the tribe of Judah as their god. As such he was known, by name at least, to most if not all of the Hebrew tribes before Moses' time (p. 99). Moses' accomplishment was to get the people in Egypt to put heroic trust in this god of whom they already knew something (p. 92).

that Moses introduced the name Yahweh to Israel. The J tradition indeed declares that long before, in the third generation after Adam, men had begun to call upon the name of Yahweh (Gen. 4:26); and that during patriarchal days this had been the accepted name of the God of Abraham, Isaac and Jacob. The E tradition however seems to imply that it was unknown before Moses, and the later priestly tradition confirms this explicitly. According to both it was a wholly new name,[6] expressly revealed to Moses. Scholars generally accept this E-P tradition. But a number of scholars part company with it in maintaining that the name was not original with Moses, but derived by him from another folk-group, the Midianites. The point of course is not important; for every one agrees that Moses alone put into the name Yahweh the content that made it significant for Israel and for the world.

But what did the name mean to him? Here again scholars disagree. Some think that it was derived from the causative of an Arabic root meaning to *fall* and denoted the *feller,* or the one who strikes down, or again, the one who *blows,* i.e.—the storm-god. Albright, on the other hand, holds that it signified "He who causes to exist what comes into existence." [7] S. A. Cook apparently accepts the meaning (advocated by A. B. Davidson) I WILL BE THAT I WILL BE.[8] This at any rate was what it signified to the Israelites of later days and Moses himself may have used it in this sense.[9] If so, the name fitted in with the trait of intervention Moses ascribed to God. He was always the God about to do, about to be—what He would be!

There are several other lifelike traits in the tradition. One is, Moses' shrinking from his commission. That is a very human weakness, and very credible: yet it is hardly the kind of thing his admirers would invent. Moreover it is out of keeping with his later character, presenting one of those inconsistencies in which actual life delights. Another is, his self-distrust. "Who am I?" "I am not eloquent." We do not hear that note again. It belongs to the hour before he had made the great decision and cast himself on God in faith. A third trait is the anger of Yahweh when Moses finally refuses. This is the first appearance in the tradition

[6] The *name* was new, not the God, whom both E and P represent as the God of the fathers. The reader is reminded that the ancient pronunciation of the name "Jehovah" was probably "Yahwéh."

[7] *APB*, p. 164f.

[8] *The Old Testament* (N. Y., 1936), p. 176.

[9] Gressmann, *Mose,* p. 36, thinks it may have meant "He who is," or "The eternal one."

of the divine wrath which was to blaze so frequently from now on, and to constitute indeed a chief distinguishing characteristic of Moses' God. Incidentally, we have preserved here the recollection (which is not expressly stated elsewhere in the tradition) that Moses was a poor speaker.

Through the entire tradition regarding Moses' call appears an attitude which marked this man's work to a pre-eminent degree. It is, that God is put to the fore as the real doer of what is done. Moses' "Who am I?" is met with no assurance that he is just the man for the task but only with the promise: "Certainly, I will be with thee." When Moses objects "I am slow of speech," God replies, "Who hath made man's mouth?" Thus it was to be to the end. Moses ever withdrew behind Yahweh so that Yahweh got credit for all the exploits. And the amazing thing is that he was able to keep himself in the background, to stamp the movement which he initiated with the divine name and not his own. Alone among the great historic religions of mankind that of Moses is not called after its founder. The creeds of Christianity and Islam each contain two names, but Israel's only one. Supreme as was the veneration paid him by after ages, Moses was never regarded as infallible. And this retiring of the human personality behind the divine was thereafter to characterize all of Israel's men of God—until he came, in whom the human and the divine met. Montefiore was right in pointing out the contrast introduced by Jesus: "Verily, I say unto you." Before that it had been "Yahweh spake unto Moses" and "thus saith Yahweh."

Before we leave the story of Moses' call we must notice one element in it that puts a severe strain on our credence. It is the statement that Yahweh gave him wonders to perform as a sign to the Israelites. We must distinguish however between what we think might have happened and what Moses himself may have thought. Remember, whatever truth there is in this tradition goes back to him. Could he have believed that God endowed him with miraculous power? Assuredly he could. Centuries later the prophet Isaiah offered to obtain for king Ahaz *any sort* of miracle that he might request. "Ask thee a sign of Yahweh thy God; ask it either in the depth, or in the height above" (Is. 7:11). So Moses may well have regarded himself as able, through God's gift, to work wonders.

But *was* he able to do so? We meet many accounts of miracles in the tradition regarding Moses and we might as well face at once the question of their credibility. The present writer believes

in God, and so believing he cannot rule out entirely the *possibility*
that miracles may happen. At the same time he regards them as
highly *improbable*. In the story of Moses he is therefore inclined
to view the recorded miracles as pure inventions or as natural
events which were transformed by imagination into miracles. He
cannot however forget that there was present in the days of Moses
a stupendous wonder of a sort that actually *has* happened, say once
in 2000 years; to wit, the man Moses, or rather Moses plus God.
This means that where Moses came on the scene the accustomed
patterns of man's life may well have been broken, to make place
for patterns unlike any that we who live among ordinary men
have ever known. Stupendous events took place, amazing forces
were unleashed, which in a sense were "natural" enough, but
could best be represented in an earlier age as miracles. One would
even be willing to admit that if miracles ever *have* occurred they
would be likely to have occurred in connection with such a personality. In any case, it would be a pity if in dismissing the *form*
of miracle we should lose the *substance* of wonder, and look back
on the Mosaic age as just like any other.

To the mind of the present writer, then, Moses probably did not
cast his rod down to become a serpent, or thrust his hand into his
bosom to draw it forth leprous, or bring water out of a rock by
striking it with his rod. He did not do "miracles"; but for all
that he did what was incredible, he was himself incredible.

To sum up. The JE traditions of Moses' call seem upon examination to report only what is lifelike and congruous with the portrayal
of Moses found in the rest of the Moses traditions. In using them
therefore we are not "converting mythology into history." Many
features of the story may indeed be the creation of later imagination,
but if so that imagination understood Moses and his religion exceedingly well.

The Contest with the Pharaoh

After receiving his divine commission there was but one thing
for Moses to do. According to the sequence of the JE tradition
he obtained permission of Jethro to return to his brethren and
journeyed thither with his wife and his two sons. Both J and E
report that he was joined by Aaron, either before setting out (E)
or on his arrival (J?). Henceforth the two are generally represented as acting together, although Moses often appears alone.
The first step was to present Moses' credentials, and to that end they
gathered all the elders of the sons of Israel into a council. Ac-

cording to J Aaron acted as spokesman, rehearsing "all the words which Yahweh had spoken unto Moses" and performing "all the signs wherewith he had charged him." The effect was decisive. "And the people believed; and when they heard that Yahweh had visited the sons of Israel, and that he had seen their affliction, then they bowed their heads and worshipped" (Exod. 4:20ff).

Thus lightly does tradition pass over Moses' first momentous accomplishment. He came to these elders as an unknown man, bringing the news that the God of the fathers had revealed Himself to him on a distant sacred mountain and imparting the knowledge that this God was to be called by a new name which they had never heard; bringing also the God's alleged assurance that He would rescue His people; and asking them to take him as their leader in a contest with the massive power of Egypt, relying upon the help thus promised. According to tradition, persuasion was easy for he had the signs to prove his commission. But actually it could not have been easy, and tradition itself still preserves echoes of opposition. After all, they were safe now; why stir up trouble by enraging their masters? Could they hope to fight the Pharaoh and succeed? And now they had plenty to eat. Had they not come to Egypt originally to escape starvation? Why seek it again in the desert? "Let us alone, that we may serve the Egyptians!" (Exod. 14:12). Probably Moses could have made little impression upon them if their situation had not been really desperate. If anything was to help them it must be power from outside; and he came offering such outside aid. But could they be sure of it? Ultimately it must have been the manifest sincerity and blazing conviction of Moses himself that overcame their inertia and misgivings and carried them with him on the bold venture. In him they felt the presence of the God of whom he told them.

This initial step of getting his people behind him was absolutely necessary for the success of his enterprise. How could he go to the Pharaoh if he could not speak in the name of a united group? The traditions so obscure the human factor in this transaction that the reader is apt to forget the essential part played by the rank and file of Israelites in the struggle for liberty.

The next step was to approach the Pharaoh with their demands (Exod. 5:1ff). Tradition represents the two Israelitish leaders as having access to the royal presence at all times. Modern scholars are inclined to doubt that such was the case, and to see in this feature an illustration of the naïveté of the tradition. It is not impossible however that tradition is right. Ancient oriental rulers were much more accessible than kings—or corporation heads— of modern times. To "cry to the king" or to the "palace" was the prerogative of every one who felt himself injured. But even if Moses and Aaron could not see the Pharaoh personally they could certainly get their demands before him, especially since they represented a group which might give trouble. The demands of course were not made in their own name but in the name of the outside divine power on whom they relied; and this was a thoroughly antique trait. "Thus saith Yahweh, the God of Israel, Let my people go that they may hold a feast to me in the desert."

It was apparently the first time that this oppressed group had talked back to the authorities and the latter were incensed. "Who is Yahweh," replied the Pharaoh, "that I should hearken unto his voice to let Israel go? I know not Yahweh, and moreover I will not let Israel go." Turning on these upstart leaders he asked them what they meant by freeing the people from their work. Let them get back to work themselves! So large a group, if their toil were relaxed, would make trouble. In fact, the reason for the present demand was that they were not working hard enough. So orders were given to lay heavier work on them.

This was done, tradition relates, by ceasing to furnish straw for the bricks and yet requiring the production of as many bricks as before. The most frantic efforts of the workers failed to accomplish this and the Israelitish foremen were beaten. Complaint brought the reply: "You haven't enough work to do. That is why you are demanding a vacation."

This had exactly the effect that was hoped for. The "agitators" were discredited. Instead of carrying out their promises they had involved their followers in worse trouble. When the distracted foremen came out from their interview with the Pharaoh and met Moses and Aaron standing in their path they spoke their mind angrily. "Yahweh look upon you, and judge; because ye have made our savour to be abhorred in the eyes of Pharaoh, and in the eyes of his servants, to put a sword in their hand to slay us."

It was the first set-back that Moses had encountered and tradition tells us that he met it with prayer, putting his trouble squarely before Yahweh. Yahweh had failed to make good! Here we see the boldness and freedom which tradition throughout ascribes to Moses' prayer; another trait which imagination would hardly have invented. God responded to the challenge. "And Yahweh said unto Moses, Now shalt thou see what I will do to Pharaoh:

for by a strong hand shall he let them go, and by a strong hand shall he drive them out of his land" (Exod. 5:22ff).

From his prayer therefore Moses emerged in fighting mood. The struggle was on! And note who, according to tradition, were the contestants: Yahweh and the Pharaoh. Not, as is repeatedly said by some modern scholars, Yahweh and the gods of Egypt. The gods of Egypt do not appear in the JE tradition at all.[1] What Yahweh was grappling with was rather the embodiment of worldly power in the person of Egypt's ruler.

The scene just related has all the marks of genuineness. One can hardly avoid comparing it with what has taken place in many a struggle of organized labour for better conditions. First, the organizer comes in from the outside and forms the union; then a committee go to the management with their demands; these are curtly rejected; recognition of the union is denied; punitive pressure is applied to the workers in the form, let us say, of the "stretch-out," where the amount of work expected of each operative is increased; the union is thus proved powerless and the leaders discredited; the charge is made that the workers listen to the agitators because they have not enough to do. The workers then turn on the organizers and demand that they make good, and a grim fight ensues in which power is matched against power. Nor is the analogy fanciful for tradition insists that what Moses undertook to do was to emancipate a group of workers. No one need wonder therefore that throughout the Old Testament the successors of Moses were ever championing the poor, the oppressed, the foreigner. This was the bias which he imparted to Israel's religion and that bias still remains. The flaming social passion of many a modern Jew goes back all unconsciously to the man who dared to face the Pharaoh three thousand years ago.

It was indeed a struggle of powers that followed. Tradition represents the situation very simply. Yahweh, through Moses, brought upon the defiant Egyptians a series of startling natural disasters culminating in the death of the first-born throughout the land, winning repeated concessions from the Pharaoh which were afterwards repudiated, and finally breaking his spirit. All three strands of tradition (J, E and P) agree in this general representation, and each adds its own contribution of plagues. They are unanimous that Yahweh did all the fighting.

Now it is quite possible that the stories of the plagues contain

[1] Only the P document speaks of the gods of Egypt (Exod. 12:12; Num. 33:4).

a true recollection of natural calamities which were interpreted by both the Israelites and the Egyptians as acts of Yahweh. To that extent the crumpling of Egyptian resistance was due to Yahweh's direct intervention. But here, as in instances yet to come, we must not forget that human factors played their part in accomplishing the longed-for result. The giant Moses with his group unitedly behind him and showing fight was a force to be reckoned with. Thus superstitious fears combined with actual danger to modify Pharaoh's first refusal and some final outbreak of pestilence in which his own first-born son perished might well have turned the scale in favour of Israel.

In any case, by whatever means, Moses did finally succeed in leading his people out of Egypt. Tradition connects the institution of the *passover* with their departure. Most scholars think that it did not then first come into existence but was a spring festival which the Israelites had inherited from their ancestors. Moses however seems to have made such use of it at the time of Israel's departure that for all time to come it symbolized that great deliverance. With it was associated another ancestral nomadic institution, *the sacrifice of the first-born* to God. Here we see the practical religious genius of Moses, who realized that his people must have periodic rites in order constantly to refresh their devotion.[2]

Of all the extant JE narratives concerning Moses those that recount the plagues are the least appealing to the modern Bible reader. This is due in part to the prevalence of the miraculous element, but more to the spirit that animates them. They exult in the sufferings of the Egyptians and take pride in the cleverness with which the departing Israelites made off with the ornaments of their Egyptian neighbours under the pretence of borrowing them. Yahweh treats the Pharaoh and his people as aliens for whom He has no concern except to exalt Himself at their expense (9:15f). Here we have a strange contradiction in that Yahweh plainly holds sway over the land of Egypt yet gives it no place in His affection. And this unhappily seems to go back to Moses himself. One cannot attribute it to the J writer, for his earlier Genesis narratives reveal him as a man of wide human sympathies who looked on God as caring for all peoples. Indeed it is not till he comes to tell of Moses that his sympathies seem to narrow and his antago-

---

[2] The feast of unleavened bread, which tradition also associates with Moses (Exod. 13:3ff), was an *agricultural* feast and therefore was probably first observed after the Israelites took up agriculture in Canaan.

nisms to arise; and this indicates that the narrowness and the antagonism lie in the tradition, not in him. For we cannot absolve Moses from the charge of nationalism.[3] His religion began with a fight and had all the vigour and heroism that a fight engenders; but it could not escape the bitterness also. The noblest among his successors tried to banish this legacy of nationalism by substituting the love of all mankind; but the legacy would not give place. To the very end of the Old Testament age it kept coming back, and in 70 A.D. it worked itself out to its tragic conclusion. Since then the better voices in Israel have prevailed and an international Judaism has become one of the world's strong forces for peace. Thus has Moses been transcended.

The Deliverance at the Red Sea

Tradition relates that after the Israelites had been permitted to leave Egypt and had gone some distance on their way towards the desert the Pharaoh experienced a change of mind (Exod. 14:1ff). They must be brought back! A force was therefore dispatched in pursuit and overtook them near a body of water that is called in the Hebrew "the sea of reeds" (*yam súph*) and in the Septuagint "the Red Sea." It is evidently pictured as not far from Goshen, which would mean that those who told the story had in mind either the upper end of the Gulf of Suez or the Bitter Lakes north of Suez. If so, the Israelites had not yet crossed the frontier.

The approach of the pursuers, which would have been indicated by a dust-cloud on the horizon, threw the Israelites into terror. Tradition here introduces a feature which reappears frequently from this point onwards. The people turned upon Moses, whom they held responsible for their oncoming destruction. "And they said unto Moses, Because there were no graves in Egypt, hast thou taken us away to die in the desert? wherefore hast thou dealt thus with us, to bring us forth out of Egypt? Is not this the word that we spake unto thee in Egypt, saying, Let us alone, that we may serve the Egyptians? For it were better for us to serve the Egyptians, than that we should die in the desert."

It was indeed a crisis in which the whole work of Moses and the future of Israel hung in the balance. The JE tradition here records

---

[3] Moses of course must not be *blamed* for this limitation. Probably, in his time and situation, no other attitude would have been possible for him. The marvel is that in so many other respects he rose to true and durable ideas of God's nature.

nothing of his throwing the responsibility upon Yahweh, as he had done before in a similar situation; but from the fact that he now spoke in Yahweh's name it is implied that he must have sought divine aid. His reply to the terrorized people was characteristically militant. "Fear ye not, stand still, and see the victory of Yahweh, which He will work for you today; for the Egyptians whom ye have seen today, ye shall see no more for ever. Yahweh will fight for you, and ye shall hold your peace."

Immediately things began to happen. The E tradition tells how "the angel of God, who went before the camp of Israel, removed and went behind them." The J version is that the pillar of cloud intervened between the Egyptians and the Israelites and kept them apart all the night. It adds that Yahweh caused the sea to go back by a strong east wind all the night and made the sea dry land. What followed in JE has been omitted in favour of the P account, but it evidently related how the Israelites took advantage of the water's recession and crossed the uncovered bed of the sea; and that the Egyptians perceiving this pressed after them. Then Yahweh began His fight. The narrative is very dramatic. "And it came to pass in the morning watch, that Yahweh looked forth upon the host of the Egyptians through the pillar of fire and cloud, and confused the host of the Egyptians; and he bound [1] their chariot wheels and they drove them heavily; so that the Egyptians said, Let us flee from the face of Israel; for Yahweh fighteth for them against the Egyptians." This seems to imply that the Israelites had noticed the plight of their pursuers, bogged in the wet sand, and had turned fiercely upon them. Meanwhile "the sea returned to its strength when the morning appeared." Dawn had brought a cessation of the wind and the water was coming in over the flats. But the panic-stricken foe thought they could get across before it was too late. "The Egyptians fled towards it." In vain! "And Yahweh shook off the Egyptians in the midst of the sea. . . . Thus Yahweh saved Israel that day out of the hand of the Egyptians; and Israel saw the Egyptians dead upon the sea-shore." The effect on the people was irresistible. Forgetting their despair of the previous day they "feared Yahweh; and they believed in Yahweh, and in his servant Moses." All was now enthusiastic faith! "And Miriam the prophetess, the sister of Aaron, took a timbrel in her hand; and all the women went out after her with timbrels and with dances. And Miriam answered them,

[1] So the LXX and Syriac.

Sing ye to Yahweh, for he hath triumphed gloriously;[2]
The horse and his rider hath he thrown into the sea."
(Exod. 15:21)

Thus tradition paints the memorable scene which was to live on forever in the hearts of Israelites. That there is here preserved a
genuine historical recollection is agreed to by almost all scholars.
Not only is this deliverance embedded solidly in tradition, but the
little couplet which celebrates it evidently took its rise in the
event itself. Yet when we come to the details of the tradition
scholarly judgments differ. It contains two supernatural or
"mythical" features, the angel of Yahweh and the pillar of cloud.
On the other hand it ascribes the baring of the sea-bottom to the
force of wind—a thing quite credible; and the bogging of the
chariots, the (implied) furious assault of the Israelites, the panic of
the Egyptians, their flight and overwhelming by the waters, are
probable enough. A common view is that something of this sort
actually did occur in the region indicated, and the sea is identified
with the Gulf of Suez, which in that period seems to have extended northward as far as to take in the present Bitter Lakes.[3]
The emigrating Israelites, confronted by the line of Egyptian
border posts extending along the route of the present Suez Canal,
turned south in the attempt to find a way around them, and were
overtaken at a spot where only an extraordinary natural event
saved them. This event they attributed to Yahweh and praised
Him exultingly. Here once more the faith of Moses received
glorious vindication. As for the pillar of cloud and the pillar of
fire, it is wiser not to attempt to find natural explanations of them.

The Journey to Sinai

After the account of the deliverance at the Red Sea the Bible
narrative inserts three chapters (Exod. 16–18) purporting to tell

[2] This couplet in Exod. 15:21 is universally regarded as contemporaneous
with the event of which it sings. The longer poem (Exod. 15:1ff) however
comes from a much later period.

[3] Gressmann and Sellin, however, are compelled to go more than 150 miles
east of Suez, for they are looking for a body of water in the vicinity of an
extinct volcano (of which more later), and they find it at the northeastern
shore of the Gulf of Akaba. Gressmann also abandons the wind as a cause,
and thinks that the Egyptians were overwhelmed by a huge tidal wave which
the then active volcano had set in motion. Sellin on the other hand retains
the wind. In the opinion of the present writer it is better to adhere to the
actual tradition.

of the journey from the Red Sea to Sinai. The JE traditions which these chapters contain do not seem to be fixed in any firm sequence and many, if not all, of them may belong to a later period which followed the events at Sinai. But we might as well treat them here as elsewhere.

We first encounter a cycle of three stories, all of which have to do with food and drink. These have duplicates in the Book of Numbers, but we can consider the whole food and drink tradition at once. As they stand, the stories in two instances recount miracles: Yahweh provides manna from heaven day by day, and causes water to flow out of a rock at the stroke of Moses' rod. Possibly the manna tradition rests on Moses' use of the sugarlike exudation of the tamarisk tree, which melts in the sun and drips to the earth, solidifying in the coolness of the night. Today the Arabs gather it before sunrise, cleanse it, cook and strain it, putting it into leather bags for keeping. It looks like rubber, has a sweet taste, and is eaten as a relish with bread. On the Sinai peninsula from five to seven hundred pounds of it are gathered yearly, but it is found elsewhere also. The Arabs still call it *"mun."* [1] The story of bringing out water from the rock seems to be a popular attempt to explain the way in which some spring gushed out from the very heart of a cliff, as if a divine stroke had broken a way for it. "The miracle of the quail is the imaginative exaggeration of a natural event. The flocks of quail, which annually pass from north to south and back again, swarm over not only the Sinai Peninsula but also the entire Near East. Of Kadesh [2] we hear that there every year multitudes of quail come in the spring. They are caught with the hand or struck down by thousands with sticks. At this season every Bedouin of today still eats his meat." [3]

However we may seek to explain their origin, it is plain that all of this cycle of narratives rest upon an impressive fact. Somehow Moses did manage to secure food and drink for his followers. They looked to him to do so, and rightly. He had persuaded them against their will to launch forth into the desert and he had thereby undertaken the responsibility of providing for them there. In a sense it was easier to fight the Egyptians than to meet the desert. Moses, trained as he was in desert economy, knew this. He knew also that such movements of a few thousand persons across the steppe could be effected, and he understood the ways in

[1] Gressmann, *SAT*, I 2, p. 85.
[2] Where Gressmann locates all these traditions.
[3] Gressmann, *SAT*, I 2, p. 86.

which enough sustenance could with skill be wrung from its resources to keep body and soul together. The element of miracle which now colours the traditions obscures the prodigious accomplishment of the man. It makes the reader fancy that in all emergencies he had but to seek divine intervention and it was forthcoming. The sober reality was probably much more grim. Faith and prayer indeed he did need; but the answer to prayer must have come to him in the same way in which it comes now, through renewed courage and more illumined resourcefulness, through a heightening rather than a lowering of the human factor.

In thus providing for his people Moses was stamping on the religion of Israel another of its dominant traits. Always after this the ruler of the people would be expected to do the same. He would be regarded as the "shepherd" of a flock for whom he must take care in the economic sphere. This concept was not indeed peculiar to Israel, but prevailed largely in the ancient world. Yet in Israel it became an ideal imposed upon political rulers by Yahweh. It rested upon the fundamental assumption that the poor cannot adequately take care of themselves and so ran counter to a present-day theory that the government should let the poor shift as best they can. It finds its successor however in the actual practice of local and federal "relief."

These food and drink stories contain another feature which is doubtless genuine enough. As in the panic at the Red Sea, so now when supplies ran short, the people blamed Moses for their trouble, recalling fondly the "fish they ate in Egypt for nothing, the cucumbers, the melons, the leeks, the onions and the garlic" (Num. 11:5). We get a glimpse of a great demonstration, the "people weeping throughout their families, every man at the door of his tent" (Num. 11:10). Small wonder that Moses' anger blazed and that he turned to Yahweh, who was Himself indignant, with the demand that he be relieved of such a staggering responsibility. "Have I conceived all this people? have I brought them forth, that thou shouldest say unto me, Carry them in thy bosom, as a nursing father carrieth the sucking child, unto the land which thou swarest unto their fathers? Whence should I have flesh to give unto all this people?" (Num. 11:12f). Moses probably did not use just those words, but he may well have said something very like them.

The second item of tradition reports a fight which Israel had with the Amalekites. On some occasion the followers of Moses came to grips with these fierce roamers of the steppe and Moses is said to have directed the battle through Joshua, of whom we now hear for the first time. By holding up his hands with the assistance of Aaron and Hur, he drew down the power of Yahweh until evening brought victory to Israel. Moses must have resented the attack bitterly, for according to tradition he laid upon his people in Yahweh's name the solemn charge to destroy Amalek at a future day. "And Moses built an altar, and called the name of it *Yahweh is my banner;* and he said, Yahweh hath sworn: Yahweh will have war with Amalek from generation to generation" (Exod. 17:15f). This whole incident moves on a low plane of religion, with its magic-working manipulation and its fierce War-God. It seems only too probable however that its representation of Moses is correct. We meet here the same spirit that characterized the fight with the Pharaoh, only that now there is an actual armed struggle. Moses thus passed on to coming generations the idea of the holy war and the War-God, and we shall find his charge against Amalek bearing its tragic fruit two centuries later under his great successor Samuel.[4]

The third recollection preserved by tradition is of Jethro's visit to his son-in-law. He came to Moses at the mount of God, which must now have been reached, bringing Moses' wife and his two sons, whom the E account pictures as having remained in Midian for safe-keeping. After the courteous greetings were over Moses told the story of Israel's deliverance and Jethro, filled with joy, blessed Yahweh for His evident power. "Now I know," he exclaimed, "that Yahweh is greater than all gods." Jethro then, so tradition relates, "took a burnt-offering and sacrifices for God: and Aaron came, and all the elders of Israel, to eat bread with

---

[4] There was indeed an element of great religious value in the idea of the War-God. Not only did it imply Yahweh's supreme power over all enemies, but it brought home to Israel the sense that only by Yahweh could they gain success over their foes. Hempel sees in this fact an illustration of his favourite idea of "polarity" (see Note 10, p. 34). "The combined senses of distance from God and yet of being bound to Him work here in the religion of war in an entirely similar direction, towards a heightening of faith in Yahweh's power. So strongly does the sense of distance thereby come to effect that the language of the Old Testament has not created a secular word for 'victory.' On the contrary, in accordance with its peculiarity of including both action and result in a single expression, it speaks prevailingly of 'help' and 'abandoning self-help'." This self-despair is fostered also by the sense of the bond between Yahweh and His people, even where, as in the case of the prophets, Yahweh's power was turned against His people, to punish them (*GMAT*[2], p. 43f). Nevertheless, the idea of the War-God did not suit the prophets, for they so changed it that it became unrecognizable.

Moses' father-in-law before God." Next day, after watching how Moses sat all day long to adjudicate disputes among the people, he advised him to delegate much of such work to subordinates, lest Moses exhaust both himself and the people by trying to carry the burden alone. Moses however was to reserve the harder cases for himself, that he might carry them to God for decision. Moses took the advice, and presently Jethro left to return to his own land. The whole story breathes an oriental graciousness which delights the reader (Exod. 18).

This bit of E tradition is variously estimated by historians. On the one hand, Gressmann pronounces it the most reliable memory of Moses that we possess, and on the other Sellin finds it highly elaborated and little to be depended upon. It is in this chapter that Gressmann and the school to which he belongs see evidence that Moses got from Midian not only the knowledge of Yahweh but the initiation into the rites of His worship. Originally, they maintain, the tradition told that Jethro here taught the Israelites for the first time how to perform sacrifice to Yahweh, and likewise instructed Moses in the use of the sacred oracle. To wrest such a meaning from it they are compelled to remould it quite drastically, for as it now stands it seems to indicate that Jethro had not known the true power of Yahweh until he heard Moses' story, and that he sacrificed to Yahweh to show his gratitude and to entertain his hosts. His advice to Moses regarding the oracle is presented as a suggestion how Moses might better employ what he is already using. Gressmann's recasting of the story is not convincing. Yet the tradition as it stands seems to preserve a genuine recollection.

Especially to be relied on is the depiction of Moses as judge. It was inevitable that he should be compelled to perform this function, which in the ancient east naturally devolved upon any chief. Only by deciding between disputants could he preserve the peace that was essential to the success of the common venture. But in exercising this office he did not draw upon his own wisdom only; for greater matters he had recourse to God, that is, to some sort of oracle or revelation. So once more we see him mediating between God and the people and in his decisions handing on to them the divine teaching or *torah* regarding human duties. We shall speak presently of Moses in this capacity of law-giver.

The story illustrates three traits of Moses: his devotion to the people, his readiness to take advice, and his willingness to delegate authority. The conscientious judge who sits for hours listening to disputes which have no personal concern for him is in all cultures an example of unselfish dedication to the public good. He who takes criticism constructively will be ever learning new and better methods. And he who knows how to turn over to others work which is within their powers will build up an organization of loyal helpers and multiply his effectiveness many fold. Such a leader was Moses.

The Covenant at Sinai

With chapter 19 of the Book of Exodus we come to a great block of material extending to chapter 10 of the Book of Numbers, all purporting to tell what took place at mount Sinai. Most of this belongs to the priestly document, which seems to have supplanted the earlier JE tradition in important matters such as the making of the ark and the tabernacle; but there still remains a substantial amount of both J and E. It is this of course that will concern us. But we shall find it at once more confused and more coloured by the miraculous than what has preceded; for at its centre looms the sacred mountain, with its continuous theophanies heralded by portentous phenomena and the solitary Moses going up and down between God and the people.[1] Here if anywhere we shall despair of arriving at any clear historic picture of what took place; and yet here more than elsewhere the traits of the man Moses and the massive outlines of his religious thought stand out bold and sharply marked. The Sinai tradition then constitutes the very heart of the narratives concerning Moses.

At the beginning of chapter 19 the Israelites encamp at last before the mount. Moses' faith and energy have fulfilled the sign that God held out before him on the day of his call. What follows is a weaving together of the J and E accounts.

The E tradition tells how after Israel encamped Moses was called by God to ascend the mount and meet Him. He then directs Moses to prepare the people for a theophany and Moses does so. On the third day, amidst awe-inspiring volcanic phenomena, Moses brings the people to the foot of Sinai, and as the voice of the supernal trumpet waxes louder and louder Moses speaks and God answers him. It is then that God delivers to Moses the precepts of the Decalogue (Exod. 20:1ff).

The J tradition begins with Yahweh's proclamation of His choice of Israel. "Ye have seen what I did unto the Egyptians, and how I bare you on eagles' wings, and brought you to myself. Now there-

[1] The confused state of the narrative is graphically brought out by Berry, *Higher Criticism and the Old Testament* (Hamilton, N. Y.), 1937, p. 44.

fore, if ye will obey my voice indeed, and keep my covenant, then ye shall be mine own possession from among all peoples: for all the earth is mine: and ye shall be unto me a kingdom of priests, and a holy nation." This is one of the most beautiful utterances of the Pentateuch, and enunciates a lofty ideal for Israel. As the priest is separated from the common life and consecrated to God, so this nation will be marked off from all other nations and serve God as His priests. Who will deny that this conception may go back to the great founder himself? For it is worthy of his genius. It forms a happy contrast to the many passages in which the Israelites are painted in dark colours.

Moses then assembles the elders of the people and puts before them all Yahweh's commands; what these are the J tradition does not for the moment state. The people, perhaps after being consulted by the elders, agree to keep them. This is the initial step of the *covenant*. Both sides bind themselves of their own free will. Yahweh, on receiving Moses' report of the people's action, announces that He will appear in a theophany to Moses, making His voice audible to the people, that they may believe Moses forever.

This will take place on the mountain on the third day. The whole area of the mountain is now marked off as sacred and not to be touched on pain of death. Here we see the primitive idea that "holiness" in extreme quantity is deadly. It infects the person who touches a holy thing or person, and he in turn must not be touched lest his holiness pass over into the one who touches him. Yahweh then descends in fire upon the mount, which throws up a great column of smoke, quaking violently. He calls to Moses and warns him of the danger of the people if they "break through to gaze." The Godhead is indeed visible, but must not be looked upon. Yahweh is here pictured as like a high-voltage dynamo the flash of which will annihilate the incautious. Here again it is likely that these primitive ideas go back to Moses, who did not indeed invent them but believed them and passed them on.

Next comes a block of E tradition which tells how God revealed His will in the form of what we call the Decalogue. God introduces Himself by name: "I am Yahweh thy God, who brought thee out of the land of Egypt, out of the house of bondage." After the ten commandments are promulgated the people in terror ask that God speak to them through Moses, and not directly, lest they die. Moses reassures them by declaring that God's "coming" is not to hurt, but to test them, and has as its aim such a truly religious attitude on their part as shall keep them from sin. He then goes alone into the thick darkness to meet God. There God imparts to him the provisions of the so-called Book of the Covenant.

The narrative is resumed in chapter 24 by a mixed J and E tradition, or (according to Oesterley and Robinson) by E only. Moses is commanded to select certain men to come up with him into the mount, apparently to represent the people, who remain afar off. Those accompanying Moses go nearer, but still pause far from Yahweh, while Moses alone draws close to Him.

Moses returns and puts before the people the demands of Yahweh. They agree to keep them. Moses then writes them down. He builds an altar at the foot of the mountain and erects twelve pillars or *massebôth,* representing the twelve tribes. Young men now offer to Yahweh the covenant sacrifices. The rite that follows is significant. Half of the blood is sprinkled by Moses on the altar, which stands for Yahweh. He then reads the "book of the covenant" to the people, and when they again agree to obey Yahweh's words he sprinkles them with the "blood of the covenant." This blood evidently unites the two parties in an indissoluble bond.

The feast celebrating the covenant is now held. It is spread apparently by God Himself on the mount, and is partaken of by Aaron, Nadab and Abihu and seventy other chosen representatives, who see the God of Israel unharmed. "And there was under his feet as it were a paved work of sapphire stone, and as it were the very heaven for clearness." God is plainly thought of as having a body, and the whole story reflects naïve ideas of the divine nature. We must remember however that the prophets also seem to have pictured God in bodily form.

After this Moses and Joshua, "his minister," who is here mentioned for the second time, go up into the mount to receive stone tablets engraved by Yahweh Himself with the law and commandments. Moses leaves the elders behind, and gives Aaron and Hur authority to hear and decide cases of dispute in his absence. He remains on the mount forty days and nights, evidently under the instruction of Yahweh. Unfortunately the earlier account of that instruction has been superseded by the later priestly version, which runs on for seven chapters.

In chapter 32 we return to the JE tradition. While Moses is on the mount with God the people, disturbed by his long delay, approach Aaron with the request that he make them gods to replace the leader whom they think they have lost. Aaron complies, constructing out of their ear-rings a golden calf which is proclaimed as the gods (or god) responsible for bringing the Israelites out of Egypt. The next day is set apart as a feast for Yahweh, who in the story is plainly identified with the image; and it is observed with sacrifices, eating, drinking and playing.

According to one version Moses receives warning from Yahweh on the mount as to what was taking place. Another tradition pictures him as first learning of it from the sound of revelry that met his ears as he came down the mountain with Joshua. Joshua mistakes the uproar for the clamour of a battle, but Moses sets him right. When Moses gets near enough actually to see the calf and the dancing, anger flames up in him, and hurling down the tablets of the law he breaks them beneath the mount. Seizing the calf he first burns it, then grinding its metal part to powder mixes it with water and compels the Israelites to drink the potion. The implication is that this is an ordeal, in which those guilty of worshipping the calf will die.

Aaron he faces with indignation. "What did this people unto thee, that thou hast brought a great sin upon them?" Aaron in his fright pleads that the people compelled him to make them gods. He had merely asked for their gold, then thrown it into the fire; "and there came out this calf!" What ensues is not told, for the J tradition breaks in here to tell of another punishment of the people and perhaps of another sin. Seeing that the people have "broken loose" Moses stands in the gate of the camp and demands, "Who is on Yahweh's side? To me!" The "sons of Levi" respond in a body. He orders them to go through the camp and kill right and left, brothers, companions, neighbours, indiscriminately. Three thousand men thus fall. As a reward, the Levites are consecrated to a privileged office, undoubtedly that of priest.

In spite of the severity here ascribed to Moses tradition represents him as interceding for the people with Yahweh, who apparently wishes to destroy them outright. The J narrative contains a beautiful passage to this effect. Next day Moses says to the terror-stricken people: "Ye have sinned a great sin: and now I will go up unto Yahweh; peradventure I shall make atonement for your sin. And Moses returned unto Yahweh and said, Oh, this people have sinned a great sin, and have made them gods of gold. Yet now, if thou wilt forgive their sin—; and if not, blot me, I pray thee, out of the book which thou hast written. And Yahweh said

unto Moses, Whosoever hath sinned against me, him will I blot
out of my book."

It is time now that we pause to ask how much of this narrative
can be regarded as historical. First, there is pretty general agreement among scholars that Moses did bring the people into a
covenant with Yahweh at Sinai.[2] In no other way can we account
for the unanimity with which the Israelites from now on regarded
themselves as belonging to Yahweh. And the fact that this relationship rested on a covenant had a marked effect on Israel's
attitude towards God. The nations about Israel looked on themselves as bound to their deities by a *natural* tie, like that uniting the
members of a clan. But Israel was always conscious that Yahweh
had taken the nation to Himself by *free choice*. Quite voluntarily
He had set His love upon it and called it. This ever tended to
elicit feelings of gratitude and humility and to keep alive the sense
that Yahweh's continued favour depended upon an ethical condition: Israel must obey His will.

A second historical element is that at Sinai Yahweh was revealed as a God of fire and storm and volcanic action.[3] This does
not mean that the thunders, lightnings and thick cloud upon the
mount, the smoke ascending as the smoke of a furnace, the whole
mountain trembling greatly, the voice of the trumpet waxing
louder and louder, actually took place as described. But the
Israelites were somehow made to feel so vividly that Yahweh's
nature corresponded to these phenomena that the impression did
not wear off for several centuries. It is this aspect of the narratives
that has led Gressmann, Sellin and others to locate Sinai on the
shore of the Gulf of Akaba, where alone in that general region
extinct volcanoes are to be found. But if, as Kittel and Lods for
example think, Sinai lay near Kadesh, then we must suppose that
violent electric storms sweeping over the summit produced the
same effect, the purely volcanic features being added by later
imagination. The same would be true if Albright [4] and Montet [5]
are correct in adhering to the traditional site, well down on the
Sinai peninsula, for no extinct volcanoes are to be found in that
region. Whatever be the cause, the fact remains that the Yahweh
of Moses had a storming, blazing, thunderous, blasting aspect which
differentiates Him sharply from the more placid God of the Genesis

[2] E.g. T. H. Robinson, *HI*, I, p. 93ff.
[3] T. H. Robinson, *HI*, I, p. 93, adds, a mountain-God, and a warrior-God
[4] *RDBL*, p. 30.
[5] *Histoire du Peuple d' Israël* (Paris, 1926), p. 43.

tradition; and that this aspect was particularly associated with mount Sinai, where He was believed to dwell. Such was Moses himself, and so he thought of God.

Once more, it is very possible that Moses gave Israel a shorter form of the ten commandments. Such is the view of Gressmann, Sellin, Kittel, Volz, Jirku, and there is good reason to accept it.[6] Now it may be that these commandments were not enunciated at Sinai but at some other place, say Kadesh. Yet since tradition associates them definitely with Sinai and the covenant they probably belong here. In any case, if they go back to Moses they show decisively where he laid the emphasis in human duty. Of the ten only two have to do with ritual obligations, the remaining eight being concerned with moral relations between man and God and man and man. Moses seems to have realized the value of ritual and religious institutions, and he probably believed that God desired a certain number of these, not only because they were good for men, but because He prized them in themselves. But in the main what God wanted was truth and mildness and chastity and integrity. The later prophets therefore were right in declaring that in the days of Moses God asked of Israel not sacrifices but righteousness. In nothing perhaps is the greatness of Moses seen more than in this.

By forbidding the making and adoring of any image Moses seems also to have taught the spiritual nature of God. The physical objects which he associated with deity, such as the ark and the bronze serpent, were only symbols, never *likenesses* of the Divine. Yahweh was too high for such representation.

The giving of the ten commandments agrees with the persistent tradition that Moses gave laws to Israel. We have already seen him judging the people, and in judging decisions must be rendered which become the basis of future adjudication, become in fact law. The Elohist ascribes to him the Book of the Covenant (Exod. 20:22–23:33), and the J tradition the so-called J decalogue of Exod. 34:17–26. These blocks of law, unlike the ten commandments, bear marks here and there of having originated in an agricultural civilization, and so probably cannot be attributed to Moses.

[6] T. H. Robinson, *HI*, I, p. 96, who cites these scholars, takes a neutral ground. "Of this theory it can only be said that it seems to be capable neither of proof nor of disproof, and even some of those who find it impossible definitely to ascribe the written documents to Moses would agree that at least it represents the general moral standard set before Israel during the nomadic period." Quoted by permission of The Clarendon Press.

But they may of course contain some prescriptions which go back to Moses, and the generally humane spirit of the Book of the Covenant (as well as of the early codes found in Leviticus [Lev. 17–26] and Deuteronomy [Deut. 12–26; 28]) is a legacy of the first law-giver. Moses did not indeed originate such a spirit, for we find it in the Code of Hammurabi and it seems to have been a part of the world culture in his day; but he reinforced it with his own burning passion for right and infused it into the laws of future Israel for all time.

The Decalogue however tells us yet more regarding Moses' religion; for it seems to inculcate monotheism. Israel is to have no God but Yahweh. Such exclusive devotion does not necessarily imply monotheism; it may mean only henotheism, or the worship of one God among many. It is usual for scholars to hold that Moses had never thought through to the conviction that there is only one God in heaven and earth, and they may be right. In a matter where so few data are available one cannot be dogmatic. But it is a striking thing that in all the early traditions regarding Moses there is no hint that he took other gods than Yahweh into account. Perhaps he was more consciously monotheistic than scholars think. At least we can. say that what he gave Israel was a practical monotheism, out of which the later theoretical monotheism of a Second Isaiah naturally grew.

The traditions regarding the golden calf present historians with a problem that seems yet to remain unsolved. Bull worship belonged to the agricultural civilization of Canaan, and it is unlikely that it would have tempted the Israelites in the desert.[7] Critical ingenuity has exhausted itself in separating the different layers of this story and reconstructing what actually took place.[8] One turns in despair to the narrative as it stands and generalizes. At Sinai there was some "breaking loose" of the people in the sphere of worship, outraging Moses and compelling him to punitive measures of extreme harshness. The significant element is its portrayal of Moses; and here we get a superlative instance of the point men-

---

[7] T. H. Robinson, *HI,* I, p. 108f, thinks that the story of the making of the bull-image was originally told with a favourable complexion at Bethel and possibly other bull-sanctuaries, and that *Moses,* not Aaron, was represented as the caster of the image, which by divine action came out in bull form of itself.

[8] E.g. Meek, *HO,* 133ff, gives an interesting view. The tribe of Ephraim brought in the bull worship to Palestine, and Jeroboam only revived the ancestral religion which had been suppressed temporarily in favour of Yahwism. The bull-priests were the Aaronites. "Baal" meant the divine bull.

tioned in the introduction, that uncertainty as to the details of the setting does not obscure the characteristics of the leader which the setting presents. Eloquently does Gressmann bring this out.

"The legend before us, with its powerful passion and its extremely effective contrasts, belongs to the pearls of the Moses-garland. A sea of passion floods through the master, who in blazing wrath dashes the tablets in pieces, or in exaltation of love throws his own life into the balance on behalf of his sinful people. The lofty idea of righteousness animates Yahweh, who knows no pity and desires no sacrifice, but punishes guilt where he finds it, even in His own people. While Moses tarries with Yahweh to gain authentic teaching, the impatient people act on their own account, and wilfully, after human fashion, make themselves a god. In the moment when the dissolute actions of the Israelites reach their climax, Moses returns. What a contrast between this people and the master, who in the solitude of the mountain height, alone with his God, has laboured assiduously forty days and forty nights, not for himself but for the people!" [9]

The trait of Moses which most stands out in this story is not his wrath, which we have often met before, but his intercession. Several other illustrations of this appear in tradition, and it may be well to consider it here. Before doing so, however, it will be necessary to conclude our review of the Sinai narratives. Chapter 33 begins with J and E traditions pieced together in a somewhat confused fashion, and even the J tradition which follows uninterruptedly from v.12 through chapter 34 is not consistent. It begins by telling how Yahweh, being angry at Israel's disobedience, commands Moses to proceed without Him. He will not go up in their midst for fear that their rebellion may cause Him to consume them in the way. At these evil tidings the people mourn and abstain from putting on their ornaments. Moses however obtains by intercession from Yahweh the assurance that His presence (face) will accompany them. Moses also asks Yahweh to show him His ways, and Yahweh grants the petition; but since no man can see God's face and live Yahweh arranges that Moses shall see only His back after He has passed by. This is carried out. At Yahweh's command Moses hews two tables of stone and goes up to the mountain alone, carrying them. Yahweh descends in a cloud and stands with him while Moses calls upon the name of Yahweh.

[9] *SAT*, I 2, p. 70.

"And Yahweh passed by before him and proclaimed, Yahweh, Yahweh, a God merciful and gracious, slow to anger, and abundant in lovingkindness and truth; keeping lovingkindness for thousands, forgiving iniquity and transgression and sin; and that will by no means clear (the guilty), visiting the iniquity of the fathers upon the children, and upon the children's children, upon the third and upon the fourth generation" (Exod. 34:6f).

Moses prostrates himself in awe, and pleads with Yahweh to go up in the midst of Israel: "Pardon our iniquity and sin, and take us for thine inheritance." Yahweh's response is a declaration that He is making a covenant with Israel and a promise that by terrible deeds, such as have never been known hitherto, He will drive out the inhabitants of Canaan before them. Israel on their part are to make no covenant with the Canaanites. There follow a series of ordinances in which many scholars find the so-called ritual, or J decalogue (Exod. 34:17–26).

The E tradition injects into this narrative a notice as to the tent of meeting, but otherwise does not contradict it. The story is obviously not sober history but its picture of Moses as intercessor and its amazing summary of the character of Yahweh may well be genuine parts of the Mosaic legacy. Along with it should be taken the other great passage in which Moses is represented as pleading for Israel with Yahweh after the people have rejected the divine command to invade Canaan (Num. 14:11ff).

The persistent tradition that Moses interceded for the people exhibits a loving side of this stern passionate man. Ruthlessly as he struck down rebellion, his heart yet cried aloud for pity. For after all he cared for Israel as perhaps few men in all history have cared for any one. So he prayed intensely for their forgiveness and wrested it from a seemingly unwilling God. In these narratives Yahweh appears in a less favourable light than His great servant, for Moses has to stand between Him and Israel, lest He destroy them. Yet (if there be here any genuine recollection) Moses knew that Yahweh's love for His people was even greater than his own. A God of storm and wrath He might be, but not in His innermost being. For when His name is proclaimed love comes first. In Moses' conception of God therefore two seemingly incompatible elements united—severity and compassion [10]—and compassion had

[10] This union in God of traits inspiring fear and traits calling forth loving trust created in the religion of Israel what Hempel calls a "polarity," which is its peculiar characteristic. "It is not pure fear, yet at the same time it is

the first and last word. Such at least is the way in which Moses'
successors, the prophets, looked on God, and they were not conscious of anything new in the idea. It was because of their sense of
God's fundamental kindness that they also interceded for the Israel
of their day. Moses left behind him no nobler inheritance than
this.

Before we take leave of the Sinai cycle we must say a word
regarding the ark and the tent of meeting. The JE tradition does
not indeed mention the ark in connection with Sinai, but this,
as has been said, is probably because its account of the ark gave
place to that of P.[11] The true nature of the ark is a matter of
dispute,[12] but there can be no doubt that it was an emblem of
Yahweh's presence, not a representation of Yahweh. It seems to
have been housed in the tent. Here Moses would repair to meet
God and to obtain the divine direction, or *torah*, probably through
manipulation of the sacred lot (the *urim* and *tummim*), in which
the *ephod* played a part. The ephod may have been a vestment
in whose pocket the apparatus of the lot was kept. Such practices
belonged to the institutional or sacramental side of religion, and
there is every reason to believe, as has been said already, that Moses
embraced this and taught it. Here too we may place the *sabbath*,
for which he took care in the fourth commandment, and *sacrifices*.[13]

not a limitless longing to become one with God; it is a feeling of being far
from God and yet being bound to him—all in one (*Abstands- und Verbun-
denheitsgefühl in einem. GMAT²*, p. 29f).

[11] T. H. Robinson, *HI*, I, p. 109f, thinks that the ark goes back to Moses
and that the earlier belief was that it contained the very presence and person
of Yahweh Himself. Later tradition located this in the stones it contained.

[12] There are two main views: 1) That it was a "sacred box" containing a
stone fetish (Meyer); or a bull-image of Yahweh and an image of His con-
sort Anatyahu (Gressmann); or an oracle-lot (Arnold); or a sacred stone, or
stones (Oesterley and Robinson). Leslie seems to follow Arnold's view.
Both Arnold and Gressmann thought that there were a number of arks, at
different shrines. 2) That the ark was an empty throne of God (Meinhold,
Dibelius, and recently Eichrodt). Hölscher dismissed all speculations as to
its nature and contents as "suspended in air." "Ancient Israel," he says,
"viewed the ark as the numinous, magically-working embodiment of God"
(*GIJV*, p. 22).

A number of scholars (e.g. Hölscher, Arnold, Leslie) think that the ark
did not exist in the Mosaic period but was adopted after the Israelites came
into Canaan. The present writer agrees with Eichrodt, Oesterley and Robinson and others that it goes back to the wilderness wanderings.

[13] The ordinances regarding sacrifice in the Book of the Covenant (Exod.
20:24ff) are probably later than Moses' time, but it is likely that he approved
and regulated so universal an expression of the religion of his day.

It is likely also that he provided a priesthood in the Levites, as the J tradition hints (Exod. 32:29).

But the tradition regarding the tent of the meeting points beyond ritual to something more immediate and personal. "Yahweh," it declares, "spake unto Moses face to face, as a man speaketh unto his friend." This was more like the way in which revelation came to a prophet, yet it transcended even that. Another passage contrasts it explicitly with the vision and dream in which Yahweh spoke to the prophets. "My servant Moses is not so; he is faithful in all my house: with him will I speak mouth to mouth, even manifestly, and not in dark speeches; and the form of Yahweh shall he behold" (Num. 12:6ff). Moses then was remembered as more than a prophet; and yet that very judgment implies that he *was* a prophet. So Hosea thought of him: "By a prophet Yahweh brought Israel up out of Egypt" (Hos. 12:13).

Moses thus united in his person functions identified later (if not in his day) with both priest and prophet. The fundamental idea of both these offices was their reception of a divine instruction or message which was to be imparted to others for their guidance. God "spoke" to both: to the prophet at irregular intervals and as it were of His own initiative; to the priest through mechanical means such as the lot, which might be employed when the need arose in the expectation that a divine "answer" would be forthcoming. There is no recollection preserved, however, of Moses' uttering the sort of prophetic message that later became usual. He was, tradition reports, slow of speech and of a slow tongue (Exod. 4:10). His work was primarily not to preach but, as Hosea said, to "lead" and "keep" Israel. Upon him lay a staggering practical responsibility which the prophets never knew. They stood in a sense outside affairs and announced to king, judges, priests and people what Yahweh would have them do. Moses had to see that it was done. Here also he transcended them.

The Years in the Desert

Between the narratives we have just considered and the next JE traditions there intervenes an immense tract of priestly writing which tells how Moses carried out Yahweh's injunctions in erecting the tabernacle (Exod. 34:29–40:38); imparted extensive ritual legislation (mixed in with some ethical ordinances from an earlier source, the "Holiness Code," Lev. 17–26) making up the Book of Leviticus and four chapters of the Book of Numbers; numbered the people (Num. 1–4) and finally broke up camp at Sinai. We wish in vain for the JE material which this displaced. We come upon our early traditions again in Num. 10:29ff.

They open with the departure from Sinai and recount a chain of incidents purporting to belong to the time succeeding Israel's sojourn at the holy mount. But as was said before, the sequence of these narratives cannot be depended upon. Gressmann thinks that they and the previous desert narratives of Exod. 16–18 cluster about Kadesh, where in the general opinion of scholars the Israelites lived during the desert sojourn.[1] Some of these narratives we have already considered but we must now run briefly over the rest, fixing our attention on those which throw light upon the personality and work of Moses.

Attached to the narrative of the quail is a tradition that Yahweh gave Moses helpers to share his responsibility as leader. "I am not able to bear all this people alone," he had pleaded to Yahweh, "because it is too heavy for me." Yahweh responded by ordering him to bring seventy elders of Israel to the tent of meeting. "And I will come down and talk with thee there: and I will take of the Spirit which is upon thee, and will put it upon them; and they shall bear the burden of the people with thee." This having been done, the elders manifested their reception of the Spirit by prophesying; that is, by passing into an ecstasy, which however did not continue. Yet not all of the selected elders were present, two having remained in the camp; and the Spirit seized both of these where they were. When news of this was brought to Moses (the story runs) Joshua, his minister, urged him to forbid their ecstasy. Moses' reply to his overzealous subordinate is one of the loveliest touches in the whole tradition. "Art thou jealous for my sake? would that all Yahweh's people were prophets, that Yahweh would put his Spirit upon them" (Num. 11:16ff).

This narrative, so highly coloured by prophetic hands, may be a variant of the tradition telling how Moses appointed subordinate judges. In any case it illustrates the same quality of Moses, his readiness to share responsibility with others. That must have been one of his actual traits; and indeed one would have to presuppose

[1] Kadesh-barnea has long been identified with a large oasis to the south of Palestine discovered by the Rev. J. Rowlands in 1842, one of whose springs still bears the name 'Ain Qadis (holy spring). Dr. H. Clay Trumbull, who visited it later, has described it at length in his book *Kadesh-Barnea* (1884). Albright, *RDBL*, p. 30, declares, however, that this identification has now been completely upset by Woolley and Lawrence, and he locates Kadesh at the oasis of 'Ain el-Qudeirat instead.

it if one believes that he built up a vigorous and enduring organization. But of this more presently.

Another tradition tells of an attack upon Moses by Miriam and Aaron. Their complaint is differently reported, one variant declaring that they disliked "the Cushite (Negro) woman whom he had married," the other that they wanted recognition of the fact that Yahweh had spoken by them as well as by Moses. Yahweh intervenes on Moses' behalf in words we have already noted, and Moses must intercede for Miriam that her punishment of leprosy be taken away. In this story a famous quality of Moses is expressly mentioned: "Now the man Moses was very meek, above all the men that were on the face of the earth" (Num. 12:1ff). The Hebrew word signifies humility rather than mildness, and so does not contradict the tradition that Moses was prone to wrath. It means that Moses did not care for himself or his own prestige, but only for Yahweh and the people's good. Personal attacks he would not repel and Yahweh must take his part.[2]

A third tradition records the people's refusal to invade Canaan from Kadesh. The JE narrative tells how Moses sends spies into the territory around Hebron, a town situated in about the centre of the region that later belonged to Judah, to bring back a report of the country, its people, defences and resources. On their return they are enthusiastic about the land, and exhibit its marvellous products; but they declare that its inhabitants are so formidable and their cities so well fortified that invasion is not to be thought of. Caleb however contradicts his fellow-spies on this point, asserting that conquest is perfectly possible. His words are unheeded and a serious revolt against Moses ensues. The people will not attack Canaan and bring death on their wives and children. Better go back where they came from! "Let us make a captain and return into Egypt."

Yahweh now intervenes, proposing to Moses that He punish and disinherit the present Israelites and make of Moses a greater and mightier nation. Here we come upon another noble story of Moses' intercession. He argues with Yahweh, pleading His interest, reputation and character as grounds for pardon. Yahweh accedes, but condemns the present generation to spend their lives

[2] "The setting of the statement makes clear its meaning: not lack of the capacity for righteous indignation is implied, but a sublime superiority to personal resentment. . . . He was meek in the sense that he had no petty concern for his own position" (Burrows, *Founders of Great Religions*, p. 146).

in the desert, ironically assuring them that their little ones, for whose safety they had been so concerned, should inherit Canaan.

Announcement of this sentence immediately arouses repentance and a resolve to invade at once. Turning a deaf ear to Moses' warnings the people attack the Amalekites and Canaanites to the north of them and sustain a severe defeat (Num. 13–14).

This tradition implies that the stay at Kadesh was no longer possible. Doubtless, as Gressmann [3] supposes, the growth of the population had rendered the oasis too small to support them all. Moses boldly ordered an advance, but the people were not ready. A few may have found their way northward, perhaps the Calebites, but the rest managed to stay on somehow in the desert. The portrayal of Moses here harmonizes with that of the other traditions.

A different sort of revolt is recorded in a fourth tradition. It is said to have been headed by three men, Dathan, Abiram and On, who directly attack what they declare to be Moses' pretensions. Moses summons them to appear before him and they refuse to obey. "We will not come up. Is it a small thing that thou hast brought us up out of a land flowing with milk and honey, to kill us in the wilderness, but thou must needs make thyself also a prince over us? Moreover thou hast not brought us into a land flowing with milk and honey, nor given us an inheritance of fields and vineyards: wilt thou put out the eyes of these men?" This is the only instance recorded where the motives of Moses are impugned; the accusation cuts him to the quick. In burning anger he demands vindication of Yahweh. "I have not taken one ass from them, neither have I hurt one of them." Since they will not come to him he goes to them, accompanied by the elders of Israel, and stakes all on a divine decision; let them be swallowed up alive by the earth! The miracle happens, and his own commission by God is proved. Back of this story lies the fact that in some crisis of the sort he came out victorious through the crushing of his opponents. His conduct here is not inconsistent with the humility attributed to him. If it had been his pre-eminence that was challenged he would have taken it quietly; but a charge of deceit and self-seeking struck at the thing which was absolutely essential to all that he did—his integrity (Num. 16).

The JE traditions of Moses now draw to their close. Israel is on the move at last. Edom refuses leave to pass through its territory, so the people must make the long circuit by the Gulf of

[3] *SAT*, I 2, p. 113.

Akaba. Tradition connects this march with another turning
against Moses, when the punishment of "fiery serpents" is through
Moses' intercession averted by the bronze serpent lifted on high.
In the time of Hezekiah (727–698 B.C.) a bronze serpent had long
been venerated in the temple as a relic of Moses. What its origin
and significance were is an interesting question, but of little importance for our understanding of the man. Arrived east of the
Jordan, Israel under Moses' leadership conquers the Amorite king
Sihon, who earlier had driven out the Moabites and Ammonites
and occupied their territory between the Jabbok and the Arnon.
Tradition ascribes to this time a second victory, over Og, king of
Bashan. Here we see Moses representing the War-God concept
of Yahweh, and vigorously directing military measures.

The last recorded scene of Moses' activity is a melancholy one,
full of foreboding for the future of his people (Num. 25:1ff).
While encamping in Shittim east of the Jordan the Israelites are
said to have made the acquaintance of Moabitish women, who
invited them to a local sacrificial feast in honour of the baal of Peor.
This was the first time that these men habituated to the desert had
come into contact with the rollicking sensual worship of Canaan's
agricultural deities, which was to prove such an allurement to
them in days to come. Even now, with the great leader standing
jealous guard over them, they succumbed to the temptation. "The
people did eat, and bowed down to their gods. And Israel yoked
himself to the baal of Peor." Then once more the wrath of Moses
blazed and fearful punishment was exacted. Tradition says that
all the chiefs of the people were seized and impaled unto Yahweh
in the presence of the sun. Thus it traces back to Moses the dark
custom of "hanging up to Yahweh" victims whose death He specially desired. It was evidently believed that the sight was pleasing
unto Him. And the harshness seems to have had its effect; for
more than a generation, so a later tradition reports, Israel remained
true to Yahweh (Jud. 2:7).

The last JE notices regarding Moses occur at the end of the
Book of Deuteronomy. There it is recorded that Moses, warned
by Yahweh that his days were numbered, took into the tent of
meeting the man who had been his most trusted helper, Joshua,
the son of Nun, and there appointed him leader of Israel. These
notices regarding Joshua in the Pentateuch are none too reliable,
but there is no reason why we should not believe that the present
story is true in substance. So Moses provided his successor.

And now the time had come for this yet vigorous leader to pass from the scene. About his death tradition has spread a mist of solemn and beautiful legend.

"And Moses went up from the plains of Moab unto mount Nebo, to the top of Pisgah . . . And Yahweh showed him all the land of Gilead, unto Dan, and all Naphtali, and the land of Ephraim and Manasseh, and all the land of Judah unto the western sea, and the South, and the Plain of the valley of Jericho the city of palm-trees, unto Zoar. And Yahweh said unto him, This is the land which I sware unto Abraham, unto Isaac, and unto Jacob, saying, I will give it unto thy seed: I have caused thee to see it with thine eyes, but thou shalt not go over thither. So Moses the servant of Yahweh died there in the land of Moab. . . . And Yahweh buried him in the valley of the land of Moab over against Beth-peor: but no man knoweth of his sepulchre unto this day. And there hath not arisen a prophet since in Israel like unto Moses, whom Yahweh knew face to face" (Deut. 34:1ff).

An Estimate of Moses and His Work

Moses, as we have said, founded the religion and the nation[1] of Israel. In so doing he gave to both the direction they were to take through the ensuing centuries. The first thing to realize concerning him therefore is his amazing success as a leader. This is obscured in the tradition by the frequent notices of popular disaffection, which make it appear as if the people were normally pulling against him. Such was the view of the later Deuteronomic writer, who has him say to Israel: "Ye have been rebellious against Yahweh from the day that I knew you" (Deut. 9:24). But the contrary must have been the case. We have reminded ourselves that unless he could have won over the Israelites in Egypt and so presented a united front to the Pharaoh, he could have accomplished little. The battle with the Amalekites presupposes a unified group, and the victory over Sihon at the close of his life would have been impossible had not a fighting ardour swept the people as one man against the enemy. By that time Moses had succeeded in creating a formidable military force inspired by a "battle-fury" which made Israel, in spite of what must have been its poor equipment, almost resistless.

But the military team-work proceeded from a far deeper unity.

[1] That is, the nation as an ethnic group. It was David who first forged this group into a *state*. See p. 146f.

For Moses had been able to stamp upon his people a pattern of religious faith and ethical relationships which is one of the marvels of history. Our contemporary world furnishes startling evidence of the power of a single man to impress his pattern upon a great nation; and for that reason scholars today ought to be more ready than their forbears to accept the tradition of Moses' leadership.

From the first he knew how to gather leaders about him—Aaron, Nadab, Abihu, Hur, Joshua, the judges he appointed, the elders who received of his spirit, the Levites who stood by him in a desperate crisis. By delegating authority and encouraging wider religious initiative he built up the organization needed for the national life. But the significant thing in the national life so created was the content and direction imparted to it by Moses.

Here we see a gulf between him and the dictators of today. Their patterns are mass-patterns, which may demand much sacrifice but are after all suited to masses; they are broad ways along which millions can be set marching and on the whole enjoy it. Moses' pattern was partly of this sort; its group-enthusiasm for Yahweh, its outward rites of religion, its public spirit, its belligerent temper, its racial consciousness had much in common with the temper of the modern totalitarian state. But it possessed something more, something that went contrary to the natural man, which forced him upward towards surrenders and devotions that he has always found hard, and generally too hard. In this respect it was a narrow way, which few could find. For it was a way that led to life, and life is costly.

If we should attempt to describe this pattern we might say that first of all it was God-centred. Moses looked to Yahweh for everything, and carried this faith to such an extent that (as we have seen) the human factor was almost lost sight of behind the divine. Yahweh could be depended on, and nothing else could be depended on. He was a God who intervened to save His people by mighty acts of deliverance and called men to be His instruments in such saving; a jealous God also, tolerating no rivals, demanding utter loyalty and obedience; a God of fire, storm and volcano, whose holy ground must be respected on pain of death; blazing forth in anger at rebellion; yet a God who cared for Israel, and in the midst of punishment remembered mercy; a God of austere purity, who held His people to truth, chastity and justice; who desired to be worshipped through rites and institutions, but most of all required righteousness; a God who took thought for the poor and the oppressed, who provided food and drink for His people, but as His chief gift imparted to them the knowledge of His holy will. The pattern had indeed its grave faults; it fostered narrowness, ferocity towards enemies, lust of conquest and all the evil brood of the War-God. But it carried within it a strange power to transcend itself, for its God was implicitly the one God of heaven and earth who must ultimately make known His equal love for all peoples.

It was, indeed, a pattern for the few; but the audacity of Moses is seen in that he tried to stamp it on a whole people. He brought *Israel* into covenant with Yahweh. They were to be "a kingdom of priests, a holy nation." When rebellions occurred he swept the guilty away, but the nation he never gave up. Tradition ascribes to him no hint of the despair which later drove the prophets to take refuge in the thought of a *remnant* which would be saved. He wanted no remnant, but Israel, to be Yahweh's.

And during the desert years he measurably succeeded. At least a tradition to this effect lived on, contradicting the other tradition of Israel's constant defection. "I found Israel like grapes in the desert: I saw your fathers as the first-ripe in the fig-tree at its first season." So Hosea (Hos. 9:10); and Jeremiah echoed him: "I remember for thee the kindness of thy youth . . . how thou wentest after me in the desert, in a land that was not sown. Israel was holiness unto Yahweh, the first-fruits of his increase" (Jer. 2:2f).

With Moses' death came a dearth of great leadership for perhaps two centuries. At the same time the allurements of Canaanitish nature-worship made themselves felt. Decadence set in. The pattern was disfigured in this aspect and that. One would have expected it to be lost. But it displayed an astounding ability to persist, to develop presently new strength and purity, to mould leader after leader. Even then for a while it seemed to fail. The prophets thought that Israel as a whole had rejected it. But it still captivated them, haunted and tormented them, refused to let them go. Soon under the hand of the scribes it regained its hold, and in the developed form of Judaism at last possessed the entire people. Its vigour has preserved them through two thousand years, and remains still the strange thing it has ever been, the religion of a race, coterminous with it.[2]

[2] In much that has been said in this chapter the present writer finds himself in agreement with the views of Volz, *Mose und sein Werk* [2] (Tübingen, 1932). A sentence from this fine monograph may well be given here: "We must . . . in accordance with the testimony of the prophets, in accordance

Nor was this all. The Founder of Christianity inherited the pattern, "fulfilled" it, impressed it upon the church, disengaged it from its external framework through Paul his apostle, and in a world-religion began to make its spiritual substance available to mankind.

What a man he must have been who wrought this pattern and stamped it upon a few thousand half-nomads more than three millennia ago! Tradition has preserved him to us—hot, impetuous, an intervener on behalf of the oppressed, an adjudicator, shrinking from his hard commission, slow of speech, rising to the challenge of faith, a worker of miracles, a fighter grappling even with the Pharaoh and prevailing, a bearer of his people in his bosom, a provider, an intercessor, humble, selfless, prodigious in his power to work, never resting, never giving up. Yet none of these qualities, nor all of them, can account for his enduring impress on mankind. There was at work in Moses something more than Moses, something transcending man. The ancient tradition puts it simply and sufficiently: "And Yahweh said unto Moses, Lo, I come to thee in a thick cloud, that the people may hear when I speak with thee, and may believe thee for ever" (Exod. 19:9).

with the testimony of the post-Mosaic, preprophetic period in all its manifestations of struggle and falling away, of heights and depths, and in accordance with the testimony of the historical analysis of all times, posit at the beginning of the Old Testament religion a genius who belonged to the greatest of mankind, who as a messenger of God and of the supersensible world far outstripped his own time, who succeeded in drawing his fellow-countrymen into his own life with God, who towered also over the centuries following, and whose power continued on in the following centuries of hardest struggle. . . . The genius of Moses brought wholly unique new comprehensions, whose consequences were not recognized even by himself. He could reutter the voice of God but he could not, as man, fully understand it. Only in the course of centuries was the divine possession of this genius fully absorbed; until finally his program, newly proclaimed by ever new leaders, became self-evident" (p. 16).

Volz's historical *method,* however, leaves something to be desired. In the opinion of the present writer he bears too heavily on the decalogue as containing the whole substance of Mosaic religion, to the exclusion of the other traditions regarding Moses. He is right in thinking that much can be inferred as to Moses from what we find in the preprophetic and prophetic periods, and from the total spirit of the Old Testament; but he need hardly be so sceptical as to the JE material contained in the Pentateuch itself.

CHAPTER II

JOSHUA

[LATE 13TH CENTURY B.C. (?)]

The Sources

Our sources for the study of Joshua are chiefly the JE narratives in the Book of Joshua, combined with a few notices from the same documents in the Pentateuch. The opening section of the Book of Judges (Jud. 1:1–36), while it purports to tell of the period succeeding Joshua's death, is generally regarded as a parallel account of the conquest of Canaan, and so throws light on Joshua's time. Scholars usually assign it to J.

These narratives are supplemented by several ancient poems which reflect conditions in Canaan shortly after the conquest: the Song of Deborah (Jud. 5), the Blessing of Jacob (Gen. 49:2–27), and the Blessing of Moses (Deut. 33). The two latter are included in the JE material, but ought to be mentioned independently, as they are manifestly older than the present form of the J and E documents. None of them speaks of Joshua, or of the Israel of his day, but they help us indirectly to reconstruct the picture of his time.

In addition to the Biblical sources a rich store of archaeological material is now available, particularly the famous El-Amarna letters, written to the Pharaohs Amenophis III and Amenophis IV (1415–1362 B.C.). Many come from Palestine and Phoenicia, and among these some speak of a people called the *Habiru,* who seem to be gradually making themselves masters of the country.[1] These Habiru are generally identified with the "Hebrews" of the Bible records. The letters also mention a certain *PI-su-ia,* or *Wasuya,*[2] whom Olmstead believes to be the Biblical Joshua; but this identification has not been widely accepted.[3] These letters illuminate the period

---

[1] Barton, *AB*[7], p. 25 and 441ff.
[2] Albright's spelling.
[3] *HPS,* p. 188.

preceding Joshua.[4]   Recent excavations of sites in Palestine, especially of Jericho, Ai, Bethel, Shechem, Lachish, Beth-shemesh,
Kiriath-sepher and the Jordan valley, have also much to tell of the
general period in which Joshua did his work.[5]

In particular they seem to show that a destruction of Canaanitish
towns, accompanied by a sharp break in culture, took place in
southern Palestine between 1230 and 1200 B.C.. The eminent archaeologist W. F. Albright [6] concludes from this and other archaeological data that the Israelites led by Moses may have conquered
Sihon's territory before 1250 B.C. and that their union with the
kindred Hebrew tribes west of the Jordan followed.   The confederated forces were then led by Joshua in his victorious attacks
on the Canaanitish city-states, first around Gibeon, next in the
Shephelah (the lower hill-country of Judah), and afterwards—"if
we can accept the tradition in Joshua"—in Galilee. That there was
an Israelitish confederacy existing in Palestine in 1231 B.C. is indicated by the boast of the Pharaoh Merneptah inscribed on his *stele*
of that year, who declares that in his campaign in Canaan he had
"desolated" and "destroyed" Israel.[7]   It is better for us to accept
this dating of Albright than to follow Garstang, who puts Joshua's
taking of Jericho in 1400 B.C.[8]   Albright, however, places the capture
of Jericho and of Bethel, the latter of which was taken by the
"House of Joseph" (Jud. 1:22ff), in the century before the campaigns
of Joshua, which he dates from ± 1235 to ± 1200 B.C.[9]

With all this material at our disposal it would seem that we
ought to know a great deal about the man Joshua. The contrary
however is the case. We have seen that the JE narratives of Exodus
and Numbers cannot be relied on to give us an exact picture of
Moses. The same uncertainty prevails in what J and E have to
tell us of Joshua. But just here a great difference must be noticed.
In the case of Moses the portrayal of the hero is so rich and vivid
and consistent that we may still see the outline of his personality
through the mists of tradition. But the details supplied us by the
same sources concerning Joshua are few, and though in some instances vivid they do not carry us very far. Even if we could

---

[4] Scholars who place Joshua about 1400 B.C. or a little later regard the El-
Amarna letters as reflecting the conditions of his age.
[5] See the list of Albright's articles on p. 582.
[6] *BASOR*, No. 56, p. 11; No. 58, p. 10ff; No. 68, p. 22ff; No. 74, p. 11ff.
[7] See Barton, *AB*[7], p. 376.
[8] *JJ*, p. 147.
[9] *BASOR*, No. 58, p. 13, 17f.

depend upon them absolutely they would still fall short of giving us an adequate idea of Joshua's personality and religious conceptions. Joshua must therefore remain for us a rather vague figure.

When we pass from the man Joshua to his time and his work we are confronted by almost as great an uncertainty. The information available is susceptible of so many different interpretations that scholars, especially in recent years, have put forth a number of divergent reconstructions. This naturally deepens the perplexity of those who would try to get even a very general idea of Joshua and his work.

We shall have to content ourselves therefore with reviewing briefly the picture of Joshua sketched in the JE narratives and drawing a few broad conclusions as to the man and his religious ideas.[10]

Joshua Succeeds Moses

Five times Joshua comes before us in the traditions regarding Moses, and in each case as one intimately connected with the great leader. When the Amalekites attack Israel Moses commissions him to choose out men and fight with the enemy (Exod. 17:8f). Later at Sinai he accompanies Moses as his "minister" up into the "mount of God," and as they come down after forty days it is Joshua who first detects the uproar in the camp, mistaking the noise of idolatrous feasting for the clamour of war (Exod. 24:13; 32:17). It is the young man Joshua (again called his "minister") whom Moses leaves in charge of the tent of meeting (Exod. 33:11). His devotion to Moses exhibits itself in jealous remonstrance over the unauthorized exercise of prophetic gifts by Eldad and Medad: "My lord Moses, forbid them!" The rebuke that he receives is a kindly one: "Art thou jealous for my sake? would that all Yahweh's people were prophets!" (Num. 11:28f). There can be no doubt that tradition regarded the two as united by a close bond of affection, and depicted the older man as preparing the younger to take up the responsibility of leadership. We are not surprised then to find Moses at the end of his life passing on to Joshua the task of bringing the sons of Israel into the land of promise (Deut. 31:14f, 23).

The Book of Joshua opens with the Israelites still east of the Jordan. Moses was dead, but he had left behind him a compact and enthusiastic people. Garstang pictures them as consisting of

[10] For a survey of several recent views regarding the conquest of Palestine, see note, p. 579ff.

about 1200 to 1500 men, besides women and children, armed with outmoded weapons, and in organization and equipment inferior to the Canaanites. Gressmann however estimates the number of men as between 2000 and 5000 [1] and Sellin puts it as high as 6000.[2] Their camp lay probably on the edge of the plain below the foothills, some seven miles east of Jordan. From it the central range of Palestine was clearly visible, and Jericho in plain sight some twelve miles away.

The land which they were now about to invade was a small country. North to south it ran about 150 miles, while its breadth in the north was roughly 23 miles, in the south 80 miles. It covered approximately 6000 square miles, not more than 1/6 the area of England, and stood midway in size between New Jersey and Connecticut. Physically it was one of the most diversified sections of the earth's surface. The high plateau of Moab, running northward into Gilead, rose 2000 feet above sea-level. From this the Israelites had lately descended into the Jordan valley, which at its lowest point drops to 1290 feet below the Mediterranean. They were now in tropical heat. Westward they saw the great backbone of the central range, extending southwards and northwards as far as the eye could reach, rising a sheer three quarters of a mile into cooler air, attaining an elevation of between 2000 and 3000 feet above the ocean. Westward, out of their sight, it dropped more gently with its tangled valleys to the lower hill-country (Shephelah), then down to the coastal plain and the limitless Mediterranean beyond. Down the Jordan valley, with its disorderly deposits of white marl, the river ran amid a jungle of green to the Dead Sea, whose sapphire waters disappeared southward into a haze of heat-moisture. Northward up the endless valley between parallel mountain walls they could see the white snows of Hermon lying low on the horizon. It was a land in which one could pass in a few hours from the palms of Jericho to the oaks and terebinths of the central range, then down again to the citrus groves of the coastal plain. To their eyes, accustomed to the barren wastes of the desert, it must have seemed a land of marvellous fertility, watered as it was by rains in autumn, winter and spring, and in summer drenched with nightly dews deposited by the damp wind from the Mediterranean when it struck the cooler hills. It had many springs and a few unfailing streams. Over much of the central range spread in that day open forests, but there were

[1] *SAT*, I 2, p. 24. Garstang, *JJ*, p. 121.
[2] *GIJV*, I, p. 74.

many clearings, and villages and towns were numerous. The stony hillsides were terraced with vineyards or ranged over by flocks of black goats and white sheep. Olive and fig trees abounded, and pomegranates also were found. Wheat was raised in level spaces. Northward were fertile valleys rich in grain. Much of the year the sky was generally cloudless, and the hills with their many-coloured rocks stood out brilliant in the sunshine. The people lived in stone houses and enjoyed what to the invaders must have seemed a high standard of living.

It was indeed a motley population that spread itself over the country; remnants of the earlier cave-dwellers, Hittites who had come in from the north, "Perizzites" living in the unwalled villages, "Canaanites" crowding the walled cities. But all shared a fairly homogeneous culture, and, compared to the Israelites, were far advanced in civilization. The use of bronze was general. Skilled craftsmen, especially in the precious metals, wrought abundant articles of luxury; there were dyers and weavers of different-coloured threads; graceful pottery was widely produced. Of late Aegean patterns of pottery from the west had become fashionable. Commerce thrived, caravans from Egypt and Mesopotamia crossed and recrossed on the great roads, which till lately had been well kept up by the Egyptians. Scribes could write letters for officials in Babylonian cuneiform characters on clay tablets. Engineers could drill tunnels for water and erect about cities the high massive walls which (tradition said) had so overawed the Israelitish spies from Kadesh.

The stoutest heart, therefore, might well have shrunk from invading that land, so full of vigorous people, so superior in civilization and armaments, so impregnably fortified. But Canaan had. one fatal weakness; it lacked cohesion. Strictly speaking, it was not a "country" at all, but a congeries of loosely federated areas of villages and groups of city-states, each of which was ruled by its own "king," mutually jealous and incapable even under the stress of invasion of attaining any lasting unity. In the recent past the shadow of Egypt had rested protectingly, if oppressively, on the land, but now it seems to have been lifted. Perhaps in the lines of city-states, those spearheads of Egyptian influence piercing from the coast into the hill-country, its power may still have been felt. But the larger areas of the central range, long independent of Egypt, were weakly organized and probably thinly settled, and lay a prize for a united and determined effort of the invader.[3]

[3] *Cf.* Alt, *Die Landnahme der Israeliten in Palästina* (Leipzig, 1925), p. 33.

The task before Joshua, accordingly, was by no means hopeless. And yet it was not an easy one. The Deuteronomic editor therefore is justified in sounding at the outset the note of courage: Joshua heartened by Yahweh and in turn heartening his fellow adventurers. This is to be a military enterprise, and the kind of God needed for that is the War-God who blows the trumpet and leads His people on to the fray.

The Capture of Jericho

Right in the middle of the path which the invaders must take lay the walled city of Jericho. It stood on its mound close under the western mountain wall that bounds the Jordan valley, overshadowed by the great bulk of the height which today bears the name of Jebel Kuruntul. To modern ideas it was but a small town, covering less than six acres, 230 yards long, 130 yards wide, 650 yards in circumference. The population numbered probably about 1500. It had formidable looking walls, an outer one about 6 feet wide, an inner one 12 feet wide and perhaps 25 feet high; but these were poorly built and rested in many places on a foundation of debris. Apparently there was but one gate, that towards the east, opening out on the town's water supply, the present Ain es-Sultan.[1]

Tradition tells us that Joshua, being informed by spies that the inhabitants were in a panic, and that a certain prostitute named Rahab was ready to betray it to the invaders, ordered an advance. From his observation of the practice of desert peoples today Garstang draws an interesting picture of this march as it probably took place. First came the flocks, spread out over perhaps seven miles; next the herds; then the men of war, followed by the women and children, and last of all by the elders and the chief. Moving thus in a closed V they would get over the eight miles between Shittim and the river by nightfall, and there pitch their tents.[2]

The passage of the Jordan, according to tradition, was made possible by a stoppage of the river; and it may well be that Joshua had anticipated this. Spies might have told him that some sixteen miles upstream a mass of overhanging bank was about to be precipitated into the river—a thing that has actually dammed up the river at least three times in recorded history—and earthquake tremors might have led him to expect such an event very soon.

[1] Garstang, *JJ*, p. 131ff.
[2] *JJ*, p. 135.

However that may be, tradition recorded that the Israelites did get across (apparently at the time of year when the river was so full that the fords could not be used) and encamped near Jericho. It was here, according to tradition, that Joshua was vouchsafed a theophany. Standing opposite the city he suddenly was aware of a man over against him, with his sword drawn in his hand. Joshua strode towards him with the question: "Art thou for us or for our adversaries?" "Nay," was his answer, "but as prince of the host of Yahweh am I now come. . . . Put off thy shoe from off thy foot; for the place whereon thou standest is holy" (Josh. 5:13ff).

The fall of the city is represented in tradition as an act of God, who overthrew the walls after the Israelites had compassed them about seven days in solemn procession. At any rate, tradition says that the city was stormed and everything in it "devoted" to Yahweh, Rahab alone being saved because she had protected the spies. Joshua commanded the *herem* (ban) and saw that it was carried out.

Here for the first time we meet with this terrible religious custom, and we ought to pause a moment to consider its meaning. To destroy all living things and all valuable property in a conquered town was regarded as a specially meritorious act, for thereby the victors were renouncing in favour of the god all the spoils that they might otherwise take to themselves. But there was more in the transaction than renunciation. It was thought to gratify deity. Mesha of Moab, in his famous Moabite Stone, speaks of his killing the inhabitants of a captured town as a sight "pleasing to Chemosh" (his god).[3] There can be little doubt that Joshua, if this story is historical, was actuated by a similar idea, and that he sincerely believed that Yahweh through the *herem* satisfied His loathing of the Canaanites. Moreover, Yahweh was very jealous that nothing of the devoted thing should escape Him; and tradition related how the cupidity of the Israelite Achan in appropriating some of the spoil brought Yahweh's wrath upon the whole people. Only the death of Achan's entire family and the devotion of all his property could regain the divine favour. Such was the plane on which the War-God moved!

In this incident of Achan's sin and punishment, to which a whole chapter is given, we get three of the rare passages in which tradition has depicted personal traits of Joshua. After the capture of Jericho Joshua sends a detachment to take Ai, a town perched on the western edge of the great central range overlooking the

[3] Barton, *AB*[7], p. 460ff.

Jordan valley. To his amazement and horror the expedition fails.
When the fugitives arrive in camp reporting the loss of thirty-six
men a panic falls upon the Israelites. At this crisis Joshua, following the example of Moses, throws himself upon Yahweh in agonized prayer: "O Lord, what shall I say, after that Israel hath turned
their backs before their enemies! For the Canaanites and all the
inhabitants of the land will hear of it, and will compass us round,
and cut off our name from the earth: and what wilt thou do for
thy great name?" Here the picture of the War-God runs true to
form. Apprised by Yahweh that the reason for the defeat is the
theft of Yahweh's property, Joshua proceeds to discover through the
sacred lot who is guilty. When Achan is taken, he addresses him in
a fatherly way: "My son, give, I pray thee, glory to Yahweh the
God of Israel, . . . and tell me now what hast thou done; hide
it not from me." As soon however as the wretched man has made
his confession Joshua turns on him savagely: "Why hast thou troubled us? Yahweh shall trouble thee this day!" Achan and all
belonging to him are ruthlessly stoned to death (Josh. 7).

The Conquest of the Highlands

The tradition relates that the Israelites, freed from divine displeasure, now proceeded to capture Ai by strategy, Yahweh Himself
directing the attack in detail (probably through the sacred lot).
Here the *herem* was modified to permit the victors to appropriate
the plunder of the town, but the inhabitants of whatever age were
killed. The town thus taken, however, can hardly have been Ai,
for recent investigations show that at the time of Joshua's invasion
it had been uninhabited since about 2000 B.C. Since Bethel, which
excavations show to have been destroyed in the thirteenth century,
lies only two miles away, it is possible that this story in Joshua 8
was originally told of Bethel, not Ai.[1]
No difficulty however attaches to the next narrative (Josh. 9),
which in its earlier elements tells how the people of Gibeon resolved

---

[1] This is the view of Albright, who discusses the matter in the *BASOR*, No.
56, p. 11. Noth, on the other hand, holds that the whole story arose in a
later time (say 1000-950 B.C.) from an attempt to explain how the ruins of Ai
("the ruin") came to be there (*Das Buch Josua, HAT,* 1938, p. 25). Père
Vincent believes that the people of Bethel, in order to check the invaders at
the top of the pass, had temporarily occupied the ruins of Ai, which furnished
a ready-made fortification; and that it was this fortification with its supplies
and equipment which was captured and burned by Joshua (*RB,* XLVI. 2,
April 1937, p. 262f).

to make terms with the Israelites and succeeded in negotiating a treaty. Tradition affirms that this was accomplished through deceit, for which the Gibeonites were punished by being put to forced labour; but historians are inclined to think that this is a later embellishment. The truth is probably that the policy of extermination through the *herem,* which is attributed to Joshua at the command of Moses, was carried out in comparatively few instances. The invaders on the whole came to some sort of understanding with the population and in many cases entered into covenant relation with them. This was indeed to their advantage. By the present league Israel gained a strong group of retainers. Garstang estimates that the accession of Gibeon and its confederate towns Chephirah, Beeroth and Kiriath Jearim increased the fighting force of Israel by about 1350 men.[2] The situation of the confederated cities was strategic, for Gibeon stands at the head of the road leading down into the Shephelah through the famous pass of the Beth-horons. The way was thus opened to the territory around Jerusalem (six miles to the southeast) and the lower hill country on the west. Israel also gained enormously in prestige by the alliance, for it proclaimed to the world that the Gibeonite confederacy was backing Israel as the coming power.

Incensed and alarmed (so runs the tradition) five kings of towns to the south and southwest formed a coalition under Adoni-zedek, king of Jerusalem, to punish the Gibeonites for going over to the invaders. The latter summoned Joshua from Gilgal, a place near Jericho where the Israelites had their camp, and in the battle that ensued Yahweh was said to have intervened by casting down great hailstones upon the Canaanites fleeing down the Beth-horon pass. A fragment of ancient verse, bidding the sun and moon to stand still till Israel should be avenged of its enemies, is preserved by tradition in connection with this battle; and the story grew up that at Joshua's command the day had been miraculously lengthened. After completing the slaughter of the enemy, tradition reports, Joshua had the five hostile kings brought out from a cave in which they had taken refuge, and after subjecting them to indignity had them killed and impaled till evening. This was no doubt to give Yahweh pleasure. For the same reason Joshua had impaled the king of Ai after taking that town (Josh. 10).

Tradition recounts (Josh. 11:1ff) a final great battle won by Joshua, this time over a coalition of kings under Jabin, king of Hazor, in the far north above the Sea of Galilee. The Deuteronomic

[2] *JJ,* p. 167.

editor and the priestly writers fill out the JE traditions with statements to the effect that the whole land of Palestine was finally conquered by Joshua and divided among the tribes. Embedded in this
later portrayal of complete conquest however stand notices from the
earlier sources which declare plainly that certain parts of Canaan
were not taken in Joshua's day. These were a line of strongholds
running east and west in the neighbourhood of Jerusalem, and
including that ancient city itself; a powerful chain of cities in the
plain of Esdraelon and the valley of Jezreel; and some enclaves
in what was later called Galilee. The parallel account of the
conquest contained in Judges 1 corroborates this. We must regard
the conquest by Joshua therefore as only a partial one. In general,
the Israelites made good their footing in the central range and in
the hills north of Esdraelon. Other Israelites or, to be more exact,
Judahites and allied clans had already conquered the southern
portion about Hebron; but they were separated from their northern
kinsmen by the row of fortresses on the line of Jerusalem.

Yet even in its incompleteness Joshua's conquest was an imposing
one. He began with a small, ill-equipped force of half-nomads
east of the Jordan and he ended by seeing them masters of most
of the western hills, occupying walled towns, tilling rich fields,
vineyards and orchards, and already on their way through amalgamation with the native population to become a numerous and
prosperous people. It may well be indeed that he and his followers
did not accomplish this unaided. Archaeological discoveries lead
us to believe that long before he entered Canaan other Hebrews
had forced or been granted a settlement there, forming no inconsiderable element in the population. If so, these may well have
welcomed their kinsmen from the desert and made common cause
with them. But in any case the Israelites under Joshua contributed
the dominant tone to the resulting groups, for they had something
to give which far exceeded anything that the older groups possessed.
This was the Mosaic tradition.

The new-comers brought with them the impress of a supreme
religious personality and the heritage of the religion which he had
mediated to them. Of that religion Joshua was, if we may trust
tradition, the faithful and enthusiastic champion. Of course he
did not stand alone. The whole generation who had been trained
under Moses in the long desert years were dominated by it. But
Joshua was the leader, and it was under him that the invaders
were somehow able to bring their Hebrew kinsfolk into their com-

mon religious life, to make them worshippers of Yahweh and disciples of Moses. Nor did the absorption into Yahwism stop with these Hebrews. Even in Joshua's day there must have begun that process of fusion by which ultimately the Canaanite element of the population became worshippers of Yahweh, so that by the time of Saul and David they seem almost to have disappeared as a separate body with separate religious loyalties.

This the most significant accomplishment of Joshua is indicated in the JE tradition by the final scene of the book. Chapter 24, which is generally ascribed to the E source, tells how Joshua, after assembling "all the tribes of Israel" at Shechem, summoned their elders, heads, judges and officers to present themselves before God. After reviewing the mighty acts by which Yahweh had in past days delivered them and brought them to their present home in Canaan, he made a direct appeal to them to fear Yahweh and serve Him honestly, putting away the gods their fathers had served beyond the Euphrates; or else to choose other gods to serve, either those of their fathers, or those of the Amorites of Canaan. For himself, his decision was made. "As for me and my house, we will serve Yahweh." "Far be it from us," replied the people, "that we should forsake Yahweh, to serve other gods . . . for he is our God." Joshua then made proof of their sincerity by reminding them of Yahweh's severity and His jealousy of other gods. When however they insisted on their choice he solemnly called Yahweh to witness their resolution and demanded that they put away the foreign gods which were among them. They agreed, and he thereupon made a covenant with the people, setting them a statute and an ordinance and writing these words in the book of the law of God. He also set up a great stone under the terebinth near the sanctuary of Yahweh as witness, and finally dismissed the people.

Here once more tradition baffles us; for historians cannot agree how far this story reflects an actual event. But we are probably justified in believing that a genuine recollection lies at its base. Joshua did bring the people into a solemn covenant with Yahweh, and it is likely that this took place at Shechem, the central sanctuary of the land, which yet another and later tradition connects with him (Josh. 8:30ff). By this time therefore it must have been in the possession of the Israelites.[3]

A final notice records the leader's death at the age of one hundred and ten years, and his burial in "the border of his inheritance in

[3] For the interesting views of Sellin and Meek regarding this transaction, see p. 58of.

Timnath-serah, which is in the hill-country of Ephraim" (Josh.
24:29f).

Some Thoughts on Joshua's Religion

If our unsatisfactory sources permit us to say anything of Joshua
it is this, that he represents as perhaps no other man in the Old
Testament the conception of Yahweh which we call the War-God.
This was inevitable, for no other conception would have answered
for the task which he undertook. It was to push into an inhabited
and highly civilized district and take possession of it, ousting the
present owners. Such an ugly business could be carried out only
by group ferocity, and in a fanatical people ferocity can best be
produced by the idea of a holy war. It was their enthusiasm for
Yahweh that roused in the Hebrews what T. H. Robinson so well
calls their "battle-fury"; and Joshua's business was to foster this.
He must be full of it himself, and keep his followers full of it.
The fact that he exploited the War-God idea to the utmost accounts
for his success.

Fifty years ago this gave no offence to Bible readers. Many can
remember how Joshua the warrier used to figure as a hero-saint
in sermons and in Bible stories for the young. The present writer
recalls a picture in a Bible for children portraying the general
equipped with Greek helmet and a combination Greek and Roman
suit of armour, kneeling before the Prince of the LORD's host in
front of a very Roman-looking Jericho. That seemed quite as it
should be!

Today however Joshua presents a problem. On the one hand,
we ask whether it was right to take part of Canaan from its owners
and in the process to fight, kill, destroy. On the other, whether
Canaan was not necessary for the future development of Israel's
religion; and if so, whether it could have been got in any other way.

Suppose that instead of Joshua the son of Nun the other Joshua
whom we call Jesus had been Moses' successor; would he have
been as well fitted as his namesake to carry on the religion of
Moses? If not, did God need such an agent as Joshua at that
moment, just as He needed Jesus later? Are we to say that He
sent Joshua to Jericho and Jesus to Capernaum? That there is a
"time for everything" in the divine plan? Or are we to rule out
the conquest of Canaan from the divine plan? And along with
it the whole history of Israel in Canaan?

The present writer holds entirely with those who reject the War-
God concept. To his mind God is not, and never was, what Joshua

thought Him to be. He never led an armed force into Canaan, and He leads no armed force today. He did not rain hailstones on the fleeing Canaanites nor supply angelic succour to the British at Mons. He did not command the slaughter of the people of Jericho nor bless the starvation of Germans by a blockade. He was not with the American colonists who exterminated the Indian nor with the armies that took Texas from Mexico.

At the same time, Joshua remains fixed in the history of our religion. No longer perhaps a hero-saint, but still a real leader, a link in the chain; raising uncomfortable questions which though answered to some extent are never quite completely answered.

Joshua of course was not alone in his idea of the War-God. Nor is he to be blamed for putting it vigorously into practice. Moses had it before him and in pressing it he was but carrying on the Mosaic tradition. If we knew more about him we should doubtless find that he fostered other and more peaceable elements in that tradition also, for it must have been the Mosaic pattern as a whole that he kept going. This, as we have seen, was his most valuable contribution to Israel's religion. A late but credible notice declares that "the people served Yahweh all the days of Joshua, and all the days of the elders that outlived Joshua, who had seen all the great work of Yahweh that he had wrought for Israel." The real test of survival was yet to come, when "all that generation were gathered to their fathers: and there arose another generation after them, that knew not Yahweh, nor yet the works which he had wrought for Israel" (Jud. 2:7, 10).

CHAPTER III

DEBORAH

[*c.* 1150 B.C.]

The Sources

For the story of Deborah we are fortunate enough to have in the Book of Judges two sources. Chapter 4 gives us a narrative in prose, containing excellent historical material; but it is far surpassed by chapter 5, the famous Song of Deborah, a glorious hymn which was composed to celebrate the victory of Israel over their foe. It is therefore a contemporaneous document, and the picture of the situation which it gives can be relied upon absolutely.[1] Parts of it indeed are unintelligible because of corruptions in the text, but on the whole the meaning is quite clear. It is attributed to Deborah and probably came from her hand. Thus in passing from Joshua to Deborah we step from legend to history.

Deborah Saves Israel

Joshua and his generation had been dead for half a century. The confederated tribes of Israel, spread over the hill-country of Canaan and merging from south and north upon the wide plain of Esdraelon, had established themselves firmly in the land. But when the initial ardour of invasion had spent itself and the newcomers had settled down to busy farm life the Canaanites began to show their strength. In the highlands indeed they could do nothing to shake off the Israelitish domination, but down on the plain it was different. There, as we have seen, a strong chain of Canaanitish cities remained untaken,[1] from Harosheth near the Mediterranean to Beth-shan on the edge of the Jordan valley. Their mas-

[1] Its date is somewhere in the twelfth century B.C.
[1] There is archaeological evidence that Megiddo, one of the chief Canaanitish strongholds, was captured and destroyed by the Israelites about 1150 B.C. Albright, *BASOR*, No. 68, p. 25. The present writer is not convinced that Albright is correct in placing this capture *before* the song of Deborah

sive walls and their formidable chariots, which could sweep resistlessly over the level or slightly undulating surface of the plain, had kept the Israelites at a distance. Now these Canaanites began to take the aggressive. Under the leadership of the vigorous Sisera, king of Harosheth, who is credited with having had nine hundred chariots of iron, the "kings of Canaan" turned fiercely upon the intruders.

The resulting distress is vividly described in the Song:

> "The caravans ceased,
> And the travellers walked through crooked ways.
> The villages ceased" (Jud. 5:6).

Not only were the roads rendered unsafe and the vital streams of trade and communication reduced to devious trickles, but the settlements of Israelitish farmers in the regions bordering on the plain to the south and north were harried and the inhabitants forced to take refuge in flight. The Canaanites may well have penetrated far into the hill-country, and become bolder with success. For succeed they did. The Israelites seem to have been incapable of rallying to effective resistance.

The Deuteronomic editor asserts that this supine condition of Israel was the result of its sin; by which he means the worship of the baalim. Possibly he may have some justification for thinking thus. The ubiquitous baalim of Canaan, being local gods, would tend to localize the interests of their worshippers, and the sensuous character of their rites would undermine the warlike virtues. But since neither the prose narrative nor the Song charge the Israelites with defection from Yahweh, it is more probable that their lethargy arose from absorption in farming and from the natural decline of military spirit after possession had once been obtained. Another cause was the isolation inevitable from their widely spread settlements. But most of all they suffered from lack of effective leadership wherewith to oppose the energetic Sisera. This want was now to be supplied.

In the hill-country of Ephraim, between Bethel and Ramah, some eight miles north of the Jebusite fortress of Jerusalem which was one day to become David's capital, there lived a remarkable woman. "Now Deborah, a prophetess, the wife of Lappidoth, she judged Israel at that time" (4:4). Her burning enthusiasm for Yahweh, marked by periods of ecstasy in which she received from Him communications to pass on to others, and her sense of responsibility for the welfare of His people which led her to take their troubles upon her shoulders, caused her fellow-Israelites to turn to her for guidance. "She used to sit under the palm-tree of Deborah . . . and the sons of Israel used to come up to her for judgment" (4:5). Doubtless her influence had been growing over many years, till now in her mature age she was known throughout the tribes.

Upon her heart, as long before upon the heart of Moses in the desert, must have lain the increasing misery of her countrymen. Clearly she saw that it was breaking the spirit of the tribes. Her voice must have gone up passionately with theirs in the "crying unto Yahweh" which the Deuteronomic editor so fondly depicts—and here he could not be mistaken! In her great soul lived a faith worthy of Moses, a faith in a God of action.

Nor was she disappointed. The command of Yahweh came. She "arose as a mother in Israel." "And she sent and called Barak the son of Abinoam out of Kadesh-naphtali, and said unto him, Hath not Yahweh the God of Israel commanded, saying, Go and draw unto mount Tabor, and take with thee ten thousand men of the sons of Naphtali and sons of Zebulun? And I will draw unto thee, to the river Kishon, Sisera . . . with his chariots and his multitude; and I will deliver him into thy hand."

It was the trumpet-call of the War-God, blown by a woman. But the hardy northern chieftain to whom it went hesitated. "And Barak said unto her, If thou wilt go with me, then I will go; but if thou wilt not go with me, I will not go." The presence of the God-woman would guarantee the victory of Yahweh. Deborah rose to his challenge. "I will surely go with thee: notwithstanding, the journey that thou takest shall not be for thine honour; for Yahweh will sell Sisera into the hand of a woman!" (4:6ff). So was his lack of faith rebuked.

What a testimony it is to the position of this woman that Barak required her actual presence on the field of battle. She was indeed "mother" in Israel, a mother who was in the counsel of their God of mountain and storm. Through her poured into the souls of warriors a fiery flood of faith. One is reminded of Joan of Arc riding in front of the French, fresh from angelic visions, borne on by faith.

According to the prose narrative Barak was to summon only the tribes of Naphtali and Zebulon; but the Song shows that a wider call went out, to the "Rachel" tribes of the central highlands, Benjamin, Ephraim and Manasseh, to Issachar on the border of the plain, to Dan and Asher in the far north, to Reuben and Gilead across Jordan. For this was an enterprise of the whole people. And one may be sure that the summons was given in the name of Yahweh, through Deborah and Barak. In stinging scorn the Song tells how some failed to respond: the Reubenites discussing and discussing as they sat among the sheepfolds, the Gileadites safe across Jordan, the men of Dan and Asher absorbed in shipping. But the rest rose as one man to the fray. Barak assembled ten thousand from Naphtali and Zebulon on the broad summit of Tabor, then apparently crossed the plain to meet Deborah at Kadesh, a little village perched on the edge of the central hills between the Canaanite strongholds of Megiddo and Taanach. Thither had come down the men of Ephraim and Manasseh and the Benjamites with their resounding war-cry. Thither the men of Issachar gathered also. Forty thousand in all they mustered, armed with the home-made weapons of farmers, not a sword or a spear seen among them. We may picture Deborah moving in and out through the companies, kindling afresh their combat-fury in the name of Yahweh.

Meanwhile the Canaanites were thoroughly roused. Sisera mustered his chariots and moved across the narrow Kishon to meet his allies and sweep eastward upon the ill-equipped Israelites. True to His promise, Yahweh was drawing unto Barak, to the river Kishon, Sisera with his chariots and his multitude. And Yahweh Himself now came marching out of the field of Edom in a wild thunderstorm rolling northward over the heads of the Israelites out upon the plain.

> "The earth trembled, the heavens also dropped,
>   Yea, the clouds dropped water.
>   The mountains quaked at the presence of Yahweh. . . ."

Down poured the torrents upon the Canaanites, turning the hard, dry ground beneath their feet into a marsh. It was perhaps at this moment that Deborah, pointing at the foe struggling onwards through the rain, gave the signal for the charge: "Up; for this is the day in which Yahweh hath delivered Sisera into thy hand: is not Yahweh gone out before thee?"

Now upon the frightened horses and the chariots bogged in mud rushed the forty thousand furies. Fierce was the combat.

> "On came the kings, they fought;
>   Then fought the kings of Canaan;

In Taanach, by the rills of Megiddo;
The gain of money they took not.
From heaven fought the stars;
From their highways they fought with Sisera."

Yahweh was indeed fighting for Israel. At last the Canaanite
forces broke and fled in confused mass along the now swollen
river, until the river itself pressing close upon the overhanging wall
of Carmel blocked their way. Madly they plunged into it.

"The torrent Kishon swept them off;
It faced them, the torrent Kishon. . . .
Then loud beat the hoofs of the horses;
Off galloped, off galloped his chargers." [2]

Sisera, caught in the tangle of fleeing chariots, took to his feet
and made good his escape, only to meet his death at the hands of
Jael, the wife of Heber the Kenite, who struck him down as he
was drinking a great bowl of milk at the door of her tent.[3] Cruel
was the butchery of the Canaanites whom the river did not overwhelm. "There was not a man left." The last picture that we
get is of Sisera's mother in her palace, surrounded by her maidens,
waiting eagerly for the victor returning with his spoils, while the
terrible news is speeding towards them:

"So let all thine enemies perish, O Yahweh:
But let them that love him be as the sun when he
goeth forth in his might!"

Thus was Deborah's life of devotion crowned by a glorious,
sweeping victory. The power of the Canaanitish kings was
broken,[4] and we hear no more of any molestation. In fact, the
process was now well under way by which Israelites and Canaanites
were becoming a single people. The next enemies came from
without, attacking all the population indiscriminately and compelling them to make common cause.

In Deborah we see the War-God aspect of Yahweh at its best,
a uniting force, breaking down isolation and inflaming to heroic

[2] Burney's translation.
[3] 5:24ff. Here the Song seems to differ from the prose narrative (4:21),
which represents Sisera as murdered in his sleep.
[4] At least one of their important cities, Megiddo, presently became an
Israelitish settlement. Albright, *BASOR,* No. 68, p. 25.

deeds. Though it extols the treacherous act of Jael and gloats over the fallen enemy it also rings the praise of the volunteers and pours contempt on the stay-at-homes. Upon those who would not join in the pursuit it invokes a bitter curse (5:23). Nor can we forget that much of Deborah's activity followed the paths of peace. In her the great pattern of Moses lived on. Among the women of the Old Testament she holds a unique place. Of no other is it recorded that she judged Israel and brought it to victory.

CHAPTER IV

GIDEON

[AFTER 1150 B.C.]

The Sources

The story of Gideon and his family is related in Judges 6–9. There it is told how with Yahweh's help he wonderfully overcame Midianite invaders; how he was made chieftain; how he established a sanctuary at his village of Ophrah, acquired a harem, begat seventy sons and died in a good old age; how after his death one of these sons, Abimelech, killed all his brothers but one, became ruler of Shechem and at least some of the contiguous country, and at last perished disgracefully in the strife he had himself stirred up. This narrative however is not all of one piece, and scholars generally agree that in it there are woven together at least two strands of tradition.[1] The first and more primitive is commonly identified with the J source of the Pentateuch, the second with the E source, which is here and there worked over by a secondary Elohist (E²). Each gives its own account of Gideon's exploits, that of J being perhaps the more reliable. The E source is thought to be coloured by later theological ideas, yet even so it also preserves genuine recollections of Gideon and his work. Taken together they give a sufficiently reliable picture of the man and bring out several features that are unusual and challenging. We must of course always bear in mind that the oral tradition on which both draw may well have been elaborated before it reached these writers, for they lived several centuries after Gideon. Yet, as Eissfeldt reminds us, it is quite possible that this tradition may have been fixed in writing at a much earlier time. If this be so, it is even more dependable.

The separation of these J and E sources is in places difficult, and scholars do not all get the same results. It is therefore better for

[1]Eissfeldt, *EAT*, p. 297, and Oesterley and Robinson, *IBOT*, p. 80, think there are three such strands.

us to follow the narrative as it stands and appraise each section in turn.

The Midianite Outrages

Under the guiding inspiration of Deborah Barak had shattered the power of the Canaanitish cities of the plain, and a long period of peace may well have ensued in which Israelite and Canaanite were learning gradually to live with one another. But this at last was broken by a new terror. Swarms of swift camel-riding Bedouin suddenly began to pour in from the vast stretches of desert lying east of the Jordan, intent on plunder and destruction. The tradition calls them Midianites, and it is probable that they were indeed akin to the people among whom Moses found a refuge over a century earlier. They did not come seeking like the Israelites a permanent home, but only the fruits of the farmer's labour, to be carried off and consumed in their native steppe. Very graphic are the words of the narrative:

"And the hand of Midian prevailed against Israel; and because of Midian the sons of Israel made them the dens which are in the mountains, and the caves, and the strongholds. And so it was, when Israel had sown, that the Midianites came up, and the Amalekites, and the sons of the east; they came up against them: and they encamped against them, and destroyed the increase of the earth, till thou come unto Gaza, and left no sustenance in Israel, neither sheep, nor ox, nor ass. For they came up with their cattle and their tents; they came in as locusts for multitude; both they and their camels were without number: and they came into the land to destroy it. And Israel was brought very low because of Midian; and the sons of Israel cried unto Yahweh" (6:2-6).

The Deuteronomic editor may have touched up this statement here and there, but we should not doubt its substantial accuracy. To show that it need not be exaggerated, the historian Rudolf Kittel cites the report of a modern eye-witness concerning conditions in Palestine under Turkish rule:

"In June and July they (the Bedouin of the Arabian desert) came northward from the desert half dead with thirst. The largest 'birke' (pool) is not sufficient to quench their thirst. Then the tens of thousands of camels with half naked riders mounted on their select delules (riding camels) break through the thin ranks of soldiers, and woe unto the fields over which the hungry hordes

first scatter! Not a stem, not a blade of grass is left, for what they
do not devour is trampled under the broad hoofs of their camels." [1]

To such a swift multitudinous foe the Israelitish farmers felt they
could offer no resistance; flight to their coverts in the hills was
the only course.

This appalling ruin, wrought year after year,[2] could have only
one final outcome: the cultivated land would be abandoned and
the people relapse into a more primitive manner of life (cf. Is.
7:21ff). Small wonder if the despairing peasantry cried unto
Yahweh to save them as He had done in the past. According to
an isolated notice inserted without any connection in the text,
Yahweh responded by sending a prophet to denounce them for
their sin in worshipping the gods of the local population; and this
view is taken up by the Deuteronomic editor as his explanation of
the people's suffering. Perhaps a true recollection is here preserved.
It may well be that the Israelites had indeed been inclining more
and more to the cult of the Canaanitish baals, and that this sensuous, narrowly local worship had let them sink back into section-
alism. Only the common loyalty to Yahweh, the desert-God, seems
to have been able to unite them in military exploits such as the
present situation demanded.

Gideon the Deliverer

Yet Yahweh's real answer, so the early story narrates, was not
denunciation but deliverance. The situation suddenly changed by
the appearance of a God-given leader. In the village of Ophrah,
probably not far from the ancient city of Shechem, lived a chief
of the Manassite clan of Abiezer named Joash, a man of wealth
and position. He had several sons distinguished for their regal
appearance, and not least the youngest whom our sources designate
by two names, Gideon and Jerubbaal. It is possible, as Kittel
thinks, that the latter had been given him at birth in honour of
Yahweh, who was called *Baal,* or *Master* by many Israelites; its
meaning being *Baal fights,* or *Baal is strong;* and that Gideon
(*Smiter,* or *Grim Warrior*) was a title of honour acquired later.[3]

One day this young man was beating out wheat in the wine-press

[1] *GMMI,* p. 61 (quoted by permission of The Macmillan Company, publishers). Kittel is particularly good in his treatment of Gideon.

[2] It evidently took place for several summers, although we can place little
reliance on the editor's statement that it lasted for seven years (6:1).

[3] *GMMI,* p. 65.

to hide it from the Midianites, who were then evidently scouring the countryside. The usual way of threshing wheat was to have it trampled out by farm animals on a flat surface on the summit of a hill where the wind could carry off the chaff. The fact that this work must be laboriously done by hand-flail in the low-lying wine-press, where the marauders perhaps would not think of looking in early summer, shows to what devices even a powerful chief was reduced in order to save something of his crops against the starvation of the ensuing winter. As Gideon threshed, bitter thoughts were teeming in his mind; thoughts not so much of personal hardship as of the prostration of Israel; for he seems to have been one of those public-spirited men in whom Israel was so rich: men whose concern was their people rather than themselves.

Suddenly, under a shady turpentine tree nearby, he caught sight of a seated figure who addressed him with encouragement: "Yahweh is with thee, thou mighty man of valour!" Gideon's answer betrayed his thoughts: "Oh, my lord, if Yahweh is with us, why then is all this befallen us? and where are all his wondrous works which our fathers told us of, saying, Did not Yahweh bring us up from Egypt? but now Yahweh hath cast us off, and delivered us into the hand of Midian." The stranger then looked on him and said, "Go in this thy might, and save Israel out of the hand of Midian: have not I sent thee?" Gideon modestly pleaded his insignificance, but the stranger waved his objections aside, as (tradition said) had been done in the case of Moses. "Surely I will be with thee, and thou shalt smite the Midianites as one man." Gideon made no further plea, but asked the guest only to stay till he should serve him with food. This done the stranger, instead of eating what Gideon had brought, bade him set it out on a rock and pour the broth into cupholes carved out of the stone, as one sees them in Palestine today; for the rock was apparently used for worship. The stranger then touched the food with the end of his staff and fire burst forth to consume it, while he himself vanished from sight. Terrified by this proof that his interlocutor had been divine, Gideon cried out in fear lest death come upon him for beholding the angel of Yahweh face to face. He then built an altar on the spot to Yahweh, calling it *Yahweh is peace*. The writer tells us it was still to be seen in his day (6:11–24).

This narrative is manifestly primitive and is assigned usually to the J source. Thus it was early believed that Gideon had been called by Yahweh Himself to save Israel.

In the story which follows this representation is carried further, for Yahweh begins to give orders to Gideon about explicit steps he must take. He is to destroy the altar of Baal belonging to his father and cut down the asherah, or sacred pole that is by it, using the wood for a burnt-offering which he is to present upon a new altar of Yahweh which he is to erect. This is done by night, for fear of the towns-people. Next morning when the deed is discovered there is a general demand that Joash deliver up Gideon for execution; but Joash refuses, asserting that if Baal is a god he ought to avenge himself. For that reason, it is said, Gideon is given the name *Jerubbaal,* which the writer interprets "Let Baal contend." This story, because of its explanation of the name and its theological colouring, is generally thought to be late, and is assigned to the E source. It may however preserve the true recollection of some stand that Gideon took against the current assimilation of Yahweh with Baal. Even so, it reflects no sense of national apostasy or of sin; and here it agrees with the J narrative, which represents Gideon as resenting Yahweh's failure to save His people without any hint that they were themselves to blame.

The E account now proceeds to relate how Gideon asked of God (with whom he was in constant communication) a sign to assure him of divine help and received this when the fleece spread upon the threshing floor was found to be first wet, then dry, in contrast to the ground around it (6:36–40). Meanwhile the Midianites and their allies had encamped in the valley of Jezreel and Gideon had by summons gathered together a force of 32,000 men from his own tribe of Manasseh, and the northern tribes of Asher, Zebulon and Naphtali. With them he encamped on the slopes of mount Gilboa overlooking the invaders (6:33–7:1).

Now Gideon, directed by Yahweh, acted in a most astonishing way for a military leader. By successive steps he deliberately reduced the men under him from 32,000 to three hundred, giving as his reason that Yahweh wished the victory to be due to His divine power alone. Israel should not later vaunt themselves against Him, saying "Mine own hand hath saved me."

Left with the three hundred Gideon, again at the divine command, went down by night into the Midianite camp with his attendant Purah and, in overhearing a dream related by one of the enemy soldiers and interpreted by another, he received once more Yahweh's assurance of victory. The cake of barley bread (the Israelitish farmer) would soon strike the Midianitish tent and cause it to collapse!

Now ensues a thrilling narrative, which scholars generally think

to be made up of two strands (J and E). Throwing his men around
the enemy camp under cover of night he contrived that at a signal
from him every one should break a pitcher in which he had carried a concealed torch, and waving the torch should shout "For
Yahweh and for Gideon!" Then he should use his sword in deadly
earnest.[4] Such was the tradition preserved by J. E, on the other
hand, tells of trumpets which were blown to arouse terror. Perhaps the two traditions should be combined, and the story accepted
as it stands in the text.[5] Wakened out of deep sleep by the crash
and the shouts, and seeing lights and swords all around their camp,
the Midianite horde plunged into panic and presently broke through
in wild flight towards the Jordan valley. Gideon meanwhile had
sent messengers southward into the hill-country of Ephraim over-
looking the fords of Jordan and when the disordered mass of fugitives reached these fords several hours later they found them occupied by resolute foes. The two princes of Midian were taken and
killed, their heads being brought to Gideon in triumph (7:16–25).
A discordant note sounds at the end. The proud Ephraimites,
flushed with their exploit, angrily found fault with Gideon for not
having summoned them to the fight. This self-conceit was characteristic of the predominant tribe; being the largest in Israel, they
felt their importance. Gideon however knew just how to handle
them. "What have I now done in comparison of you? Is not
the gleaning of the grapes of Ephraim better than the vintage of
Abiezer? God hath delivered into your hand the princes of
Midian, Oreb and Zeeb: and what was I able to do in comparison
with you?" Modesty, good temper and flattery had their effect
and the anger of the Ephraimites was abated (8:1–3). Another
time, with a different man, they were not to come off so well!
(12:1ff).

So runs the present narrative. How far is it history? The stories
of the fleece and the dismissal of the host are generally regarded
as later legend; but they none the less testify to an impression
Gideon made upon his contemporaries. Both illustrate his faith
in God; the first, his reliance on divine indications, the second,
his trust in God's help rather than in numbers. Even the older J
source brings out this latter element for it agrees that he had only
three hundred men with which to confront a host. We shall speak
of this again.

[4] It is usual to emend v.20 to express this idea.
[5] Kittel does this (*GMMI*, p. 68).

The account of the night surprise, on the other hand, is generally
taken as historical in its outlines, although some scholars, following
what they suppose is the J tradition, place the scene in the valley
east of Shechem instead of in the valley of Jezreel. The flight of
the routed Midianites would then have been down the Wadi Fara
and not down Jezreel past Beth-shan. The concluding incident of
the Ephraimite unpleasantness is also thought by most to be historical, although there is some disagreement as to the source to
which it is to be assigned.

But now unexpectedly (8:4ff) the reader finds himself in an
altered situation. Gideon and his three hundred men pass over
Jordan in pursuit, not of Oreb and Zeeb, but of Zeba and Zalmunna,
"the kings of Midian," who have made good their escape with a
following of fifteen thousand. He appeals for food to the elders
of the Israelitish city Succoth, only to be met with a derisive
refusal. "Are the hands of Zeba and Zalmunna now in thy hand,
that we should give bread unto thine army?" The same refusal
is made by the neighbouring city of Penuel. Threatening cruel
vengeance after he shall succeed, Gideon presses along the "way
of the tent-dwellers," corresponding to the present "road of the
nomads," [6] comes up with the fugitives at Karkor, over a hundred
miles southeast of Succoth, falls upon them unawares, routs the
host and captures both Zeba and Zalmunna. Returning with his
prisoners Gideon displays them to the elders of Succoth, of whom
he has obtained a list from a young man of the city just taken
captive, and puts them to death by barbarous torture. The men
of Penuel also are exterminated and the tower of their city broken
down. After this Gideon deals with the captive kings; and here
again the reader meets with a surprise. It seems that they have
killed several of Gideon's brothers at Tabor, the dome-shaped hill
rising on the northeastern edge of the plain of Esdraelon, and that
Gideon in pursuing the marauders has been impelled by the obligation of blood revenge. He now asks them to identify their victims, and they, probably knowing that they are doomed, boast
proudly of their exploit: "As thou art, so were they; each one
resembled the children of a king." "They were my brothers,"
replies Gideon, "the sons of my mother: as Yahweh liveth, if ye
had saved them alive I would not slay you." Following a custom
prevalent among the ancient Arabs, he now calls on his oldest
son Jether to kill the murderers; but the boy draws back in fear.
"Rise thou and fall upon us," demand the intrepid kings; "for

[6] Garstang, *JJ*, p. 321f.

as the man is, so is his strength." So Gideon kills them and takes as spoils the crescents that are on their camels' necks.

Opinions differ sharply as to this narrative. Burney assigns it to E, Moore to J, Eissfeldt to L, his earliest and most reliable source. In any case, it seems to relate quite a different exploit of Gideon from that portrayed in chapter 7. A common view is that after the first victory of Gideon the Midianites, under the lead of the two kings named, swept once more over the plain, capturing and killing at Tabor Gideon's brothers and making good their escape before Gideon could attack them. That was why he had to follow them beyond Jordan. Such is Kittel's opinion. Or, as Meinhold thinks, this exploit may have been the first of the two. The tendency is to treat it as historical, though Burney demurs at the incredibly large numbers in v.10, where the fifteen thousand are said to be the remnant of a horde of 135,000. These figures however may be regarded as inserted by the editor.

Twice, therefore, Gideon seems to have routed the Midianites, and each time with an unbelievably small force. The number three hundred was firmly associated with him in the varying traditions. As a result the Midianites gave up their yearly incursions into Palestine and both Israelites and Canaanites had "rest." We cannot be surprised therefore if the hero who had wrought such deliverance was richly rewarded. After the account of the second victory a bit of the E source is added which tells how "the men of Israel" came to Gideon with a request. "Rule thou over us, both thou and thy son, and thy son's son also; for thou hast saved us out of the hand of Midian." But Gideon refused. "I will not rule over you, neither shall my son rule over you: Yahweh shall rule over you." The writer evidently was speaking of something like the monarchy which later was established in Israel.

This story is generally set aside as legend because it represents all Israel as acting together to make king a man who after all was only a local hero, and also because Gideon's reason for refusing seems to belong to the same theocratic tradition which later tells how Samuel repudiated the idea of setting up another king than Yahweh (I Sam. 8:6ff). It is pointed out moreover that if Gideon actually did refuse he afterwards reconsidered, for we find him from now on established as hereditary chief over Shechem and some of the neighbouring places.

There is much force in these objections to the story, but they are not necessarily decisive. Common action on the part of the tribes was not an impossibility, as the Song of Deborah shows, and

Gideon was not merely a local hero. Nor need disapproval of the
Canaanitish office of king be a late attitude. On the contrary, it
is reasonable to suppose that the Israelites, who took over so many
Canaanitish institutions after their settlement, must have had a
decided prejudice against kingship which prevented them from
adopting it for two centuries. This prejudice no doubt was inherited from their past and represented a conservative position.
Yahweh was king, and that was enough. Again, Gideon's son
Jotham in his famous parable (9:7ff) derides the kingship as a
useless office which appealed only to lower minds and might
easily prove injurious; and Gideon's refusal here seems to reflect
the same aversion, though on religious grounds. Finally, Gideon
never did wield anything like royal power on a nation-wide scale;
whatever office he enjoyed was local and the natural result of his
benefits to the community. One cannot therefore be sure that he
did not decline the kingship. At any rate, such a rejection in
favour of the old-fashioned idea of Yahweh's kingship was associated with him in tradition.

One more story is told of Gideon. Asking as a favour the gold
ear-rings taken from the slain Midianites he made with the immense weight of metal thus procured (about 75 pounds according
to Burney) what was called an *ephod,* which he set up in his home
town Ophrah. "The *ephod,*" says Kittel, "was certainly a concession to Baal worship, or was used in a form of Yahweh worship
similar to the Baal service." [7]

Gideon therefore went along in one important respect with the
current Canaanization of Israel's religion; and in so doing he

[7] *GMMI,* p. 80. It now seems certain that the ephod was originally a stiff
sleeveless cylindrical (almost conical) garment placed upon the image of a
god and also worn by a high priest. Divine images so clothed were used in
very early times in Asia Minor and Syria, as is known to us from reproduc-
tions in Greek and Roman times. In the case of such images the garment
(*ependytes*) was usually made of gold plate over a wooden frame, and was
often set with precious stones. It was also connected with the revelation of
the future through the casting of lots. In the present passage "ephod" is
used for the whole divine image, whose most important part was the golden
garment (cf. Jud. 17:5; Hos. 3:4). Such is the view of H. Thiersch, *Ependytes und Ephod* (Stuttgart and Berlin, 1936), reviewed by V. Müller in
JPOS, XVII, p. 286ff. See also Sellin, "Efod und Terafim," *JPOS,* XIV, p.
1–9, corrected by its author in two points after the appearance of Thiersch's
book, in "Noch einmal der alttestamentlich Ephod," *JPOS,* XVII, p. 236ff.
Sellin differs from Thiersch in holding that the ephod used in the sacred lot
by Saul and David was an image, not a high-priestly vestment, as Thiersch
maintains.

departed from the pattern stamped upon the people by Moses. The editor of a later age is justified in condemning this step. At the same time it is only fair to remember that the *ephod* was not objectionable to the great David, who was from first to last a Yah-weh enthusiast. Gideon, like David, seems to have used it with wholehearted loyalty to Yahweh. After all, practices of Canaan-itish worship did not stand all on the same level. An *ephod* was one thing, an *asherah* quite another; for the latter was associated with sensual excesses. If, as is related, Gideon broke down his father's altar of Baal and cut down the *asherah* that stood by it, he was acting in behalf of a purer form of worship than was then prevalent;[8] and we ought not to allow his erection of an *ephod* to obscure this fact.

A concluding notice tells us that Gideon continued to live in his own house in Ophrah; that he had a large harem, and seventy sons, including one named Abimelech, from a concubine in Shechem; that he died in a good old age, and was buried in the sepulchre of Joash his father in his native town.

Gideon's Significance in Israel's Religion

Broadly speaking, Gideon belongs with those who represent the War-God idea in Israel's religious development. But in one im-portant respect the tradition regarding him is distinctive; for he was remembered as a leader who met the enemy with so absurdly small a force that the victory manifestly came from Yahweh. The dismissal of all but three hundred of the 32,000 is probably a legend; but it is not the *usual kind* of legend told of Israel's military leaders. It reflects, as has been said, something unique in this man. The "day of Midian" became, it seems, a proverb for divine deliverance without man's help (cf. Is. 9:4). So Gideon stood for faith.

Then too, Gideon was believed to have refused the kingship, because Yahweh alone was Israel's rightful ruler. A legend, prob-ably, but once more, not the *usual kind* of legend. It may well rest on a true impression of Gideon's attitude. Taken with the parable of Jotham it gives expression to the theocratic idea with which Israel began.

Ethically, Gideon is on the whole an attractive figure. His cruelty to the men of Succoth and Penuel may indeed shock us, but though aroused by a taunt it proceeded fundamentally from an

[8] This is the view of Leslie, *OTR,* p. 108.

outraged sense of national obligation. He sought and obtained blood-revenge, but in earlier days that was the only way in which men thought the peace of society could be maintained. His large harem, too, is offensive to our taste, though we must remember that in his age this indicated ambition more than lust. Yet over against these blemishes must be set his devotion to Yahweh, his public spirit, his modesty, his brilliance in strategy, his daring, his good temper and magnanimity. As tradition has preserved him he is perhaps the most remarkable and the most pleasing military leader that graces the pages of the Old Testament.

Chapter V

SAMUEL

[c. 1050 b.c.]

Israel After the Judges

The judges had come and gone. They had performed a real service for Israel in rallying the tribes to resist the onslaughts of various enemies. With the exception of the Canaanites under Sisera, these enemies had been for the most part invaders of the land from the east. In defending themselves, the Israelites under the judges had also protected the Canaanites among whom they lived, and gradually there had taken place a sort of amalgamation of the two elements of the population. As a result, the Israelites had increased in numbers and now possessed an undivided country.

But the close of the period brought them face to face with a much more formidable foe than raiders from beyond the Jordan. Already in the narratives concerning Samson (Jud. 13-16) we meet the Philistines. These were probably a fragment of the sea peoples, inhabitants of the coast of Asia Minor and the Aegean Islands, who had been driven out by the great migration of Aryan peoples of which the Trojan War may have been an episode. Having been repelled from settling in Egypt by Ramses III in 1195 b.c. they had, in spite of a defeat at his hands, effected a permanent settlement on the coastal plain of Palestine from Gaza well up to mount Carmel.[1] Though of non-Semitic stock they had quickly adopted the language and customs of their new Semitic neighbours, rejecting only the common custom of circumcision. On the plain they were grouped in five cities, each with its ruler (*seren,* which may be akin to *tyrant*), acting together as one body though retaining

---

[1] "Philistine" pottery first appears in excavated sites about 1150 b.c. and no finds in clearly stratified sites can be dated later than about 1000 (Albright, *Haverford Symposium,* p. 25). S. A. Cook, *OT,* p. 80, points out that the "Philistines" of the Egyptian records soon mingled with other elements of the population to form the mixed and Semitised non-Israelitish Philistines who appear in the Old Testament.

mutual independence. It was apparently not long before they began to press up from the plain into the hills, and there they clashed with the Israelites. The struggle proved unequal. Superior in culture and military art to the Hebrews (as they called them: I Sam. 4:9), and having in their number many "giants" whose physical stature rendered them formidable in hand-to-hand combat, they overcame the nearby tribes of Judah and Dan. "Knowest thou not," the men of Judah said to Samson, "that the Philistines are rulers over us?" (Jud. 15:11.) Thence they pushed on and established their mastery over the territory of Ephraim and Benjamin, making the inhabitants their slaves (I Sam. 4:9).[2]

This created a tragic situation. It seems indeed that the yoke of the Philistines was not excessively heavy, but they had their garrisons stationed in important posts to keep down their subjects and took strong measures to disarm the population, forbidding the Israelites to have any smiths in their territory and thus compelling them to go down to Philistia to get their very farm tools sharpened (I Sam. 13:19ff). Nothing is said of their laying heavy taxes on the country, but however light the yoke of subjection may have been it could not but prove galling. Now all this must have had a depressing effect upon Israel's spirit, and at the same time upon its religion; for that religion had been nourished by heroic warlike exploits in the name of Yahweh. What hold upon them would a Yahweh retain who remained quiescent under foreign overlords?

If a "judge" had now arisen to summon the people to resist their masters, at least temporary freedom might perhaps have been attained; but no leader appeared. Legend has indeed extolled the exploits of Samson, but even legend can attribute to him nothing but personal prowess; he had no ability to lead others. Nor was there any prophet who like Deborah could call forth the slumbering energy of a local chief. And here we come to the most serious element in Israel's trouble. For a long time it had lacked any great religious leadership. With the exception of Deborah no person since the days of Joshua had stood forth in any commanding way to speak to the people in the name of Yahweh. It might have seemed that Moses had left only one successor.

Not that the religion of Yahweh was inactive. On the contrary, there are evidences that it was a real force among the people. At Shiloh a temple had been built—no "tent," but a substantial house with door-posts and bars, in charge of a resident priestly family and kept up by a corps of servants. Here the ark was reverently

[2] Lods, *Israel*, p. 349f.

housed and hither the families of Israel came up once a year for sacrifice and feasting in one of the guest-rooms with which it was probably provided. Such at least is the picture drawn in the early story of Elkanah's family preserved in I Samuel 1. This chapter shows us also that Yahweh could play a living part in domestic life. Prayer was a vital thing to Hannah in her trouble. And the religion so portrayed did not consist of mere ceremonial, but had a strong ethical tone. Eli remonstrated with Hannah when he thought she had drunk too much wine and with his own sons when they had fallen into extortion and licentiousness. The conduct of these two sons roused general resentment; people did not like that sort of thing in Yahweh's priests.

All this shows that there must have been some who took the religion of Yahweh very seriously. A sort of rank and file leadership undoubtedly existed, sufficient to carry on Yahwism in a moderate way. But before the crisis presented by Philistine domination it seems to have been helpless. The need of the hour was for some man of God who could arouse new and prodigious forces in the depressed people and put the whole national life on a higher level. The story of Samuel tells how in the providence of God that need was supplied.

The Sources for the Study of Samuel

Apart from an allusion here and there all our information regarding the outstanding figure of Samuel is contained in the first of the two books that bear his name. The First Book of Samuel opens with the story of Samuel's infancy and youth at Shiloh (1-3), then after three chapters devoted to the fortunes of the ark introduces him again in chapter 7 as a man in middle life or old age living at Ramah and judging Israel. In his capacity as judge, or as man of God, he directs the founding of the monarchy, anointing and commissioning its first king, Saul (8-12). At first he supports the new king, but later breaks with him (13:8ff; 15:10ff); and after anointing David to succeed Saul retires to Ramah, where the last glimpse of him shows him standing over a company of the prophets (19:18ff). Finally a brief notice in chapter 25 records his death.

This narrative of Samuel's activity, which at first sight seems to run along smoothly enough, reveals on further study inconsistencies which have led scholars to find in it the piecing together of at least two sources with quite different points of view.

In 9:1–10:16; 11 (except perhaps vv.12–13); 13–14 we have a narrative which is variously called A, Sa, K. It introduces Samuel as a "seer," [1] who for a small fee gives divinely obtained information to people in their perplexities (9:5ff). He receives an injunction from Yahweh to anoint Saul king, in order that by him Israel may be saved from the Philistines. Saul thus empowered rescues Jabesh-gilead from the besieging Ammonites, is proclaimed king by the people, and gains a victory over the Philistines; just before which a break takes place between him and Samuel. In style this A source is fresh, vivid, life-like, and in outlook manifestly primitive. Its colours are bold and bright, its characters real, its scenes detailed.

Intertwined with it is a second source (B, Sb, K[1]) consisting of 7:3–8:22; 10:17–27; 12, which depicts the aged Samuel as the recognized "judge" and priest of all Israel, summoning them at will to a national assembly, upbraiding them for their sins, prevailing miraculously over the Philistines by intercession, going about in a circuit from his home in Ramah to judge them, and acting as a sort of national priest. Without his consent no important step can be taken. This source differs from A in its attitude to the monarchy, which it regards as a bad thing. It tells how the people demand a king and how Samuel looks on this demand as a repudiation of the kingship of Yahweh, granting it only reluctantly and at the express command of Yahweh. The king is chosen by lot and then Samuel lays down his own office, assuring the penitent people that he will continue to pray for them. In striking contrast to A, the style of B is more homiletical than historical; its Samuel is less a real man dealing with real men than an impressive utterer of theological ideas. In fact, it is theological through and through, saturated with a point of view that in its opposition to the monarchy and the baalim is like that of Hosea.

According to the view of most scholars, these two sources do not stop with the end of Samuel's history but continue throughout the First Book of Samuel. A number are inclined to see in them a continuation of the J and E sources of the Hexateuch, but that is a matter with which we are hardly concerned in our study. A much more pertinent question is, how far are they historically reliable?

As to B the answer of scholars is fairly unanimous: it is not to be depended on for history. Its writer, or writers, deliberately remoulded the past to conform to the point of view of a prophetic

[1] Apparently unknown to Saul living not many miles away (9:6ff).

circle representing (as has been said) such a man as Hosea. It undoubtedly goes back to early tradition, but it has altered this to such an extent that the original facts are obscured. Most historians therefore are very cautious in their use of it, and some reject it entirely. Its date is generally put at about 750 B.C.

The A source, on the other hand, is conceded to be early; it stands incomparably nearer the actual events than does B. This does not mean however that we can accept unreservedly what it tells of Samuel. One cannot, for example, read its opening story (9:1–10:16) without recognizing that the hand of legend has been at work, especially with the figure of Samuel. Moreover at least two scholars, Eissfeldt and Lods, though disagreeing in details, find in its account of the founding of the monarchy two distinct and irreconcilable threads of narrative.[2] And among its later stories are a number of duplications, as we shall see. In the use of such a source scholars naturally differ. Kittel[3] believes a great deal of what it tells regarding Samuel and Sellin[4] may be said to do the same. T. H. Robinson[5] accepts its account in substance but treats it with reserve. Meinhold[6] pictures Samuel as merely one of a circle of priests and seers, while Lods[7] denies him any real importance in the history of Saul.

It remains to consider the sources that tell of the earlier and later acts of Samuel: the story of his birth and his boyhood at Shiloh (1–3 with a glance at 4–6) and the second account of his break with Saul (15), followed by the account of his anointing David (16:1–13), and his final appearance (19:18ff).

The account of the birth and youth is hard to classify. Scholars agree that Hannah's Song (2:1–10) is a late insertion, and the story of the man of God in 2:27–36 is also regarded as secondary. The rest however comprises a vivid and circumstantial narrative which seems to go back to early tradition. Scholars are not agreed as to whether it should be considered part of the B source, or of

[2] Eissfeldt, *EAT*, p. 310; Lods, *Israel*, p. 352ff. Hempel, *AHL*, p. 107f also makes a three-fold division, though a different one; and by the employment of ingenious form analysis he resolves all three very largely into a tissue of legend. Just how much historical value they possess he does not make clear.

[3] *GMMI*, p. 86ff.

[4] *GIJV*, I, p. 147ff.

[5] *HI*, p. 180ff.

[6] *AT*, p. 78f.

[7] *Israel*, p. 353. "It is . . . possible that a seer by the name of Samuel may have had some part arousing the revolt (i.e. against the Philistines) and hence in preparing the way for the kingdom."

the A source, or of neither. How reliable it is none can really tell. Childhood stories of great men should be received with extreme caution; yet its freedom from the miraculous and its life-likeness are in its favour. So solid a historian as Kittel [8] uses it confidently. Lods on the other hand infers from the way in which it plays upon the word "ask" (Hebrew *sha'al*) that it originally was told of Saul (*Sha'ul*); a suggestion which Robinson pronounces "interesting," but apparently rejects as involving changes in very many details.[9] The narrative of the ark (4-6) may well have been incorporated from an early history of the ark; but since it makes no mention of Samuel it throws only indirect light upon our subject.

The narrative of Samuel's break with Saul in chapter 15 is frequently assigned to the B source because of the prophetic strain it contains. When however it is compared with the theologized and unreal B narratives of chapters 7-12 it displays a remarkable life-likeness and human interest. Its Samuel is no mere embodiment of theocratic ideas, but a vivid personality, who becomes enraged, cries passionately to God all night, bursts out upon Saul with wrath, demolishes his excuses, partially yields to his entreaties, and hews Agag in pieces before Yahweh. "Prophetic" indeed it is, but possibly just because it displays a prophet in action. Doubtless later hands have been at work upon it, but they did no more than embellish a credible early tradition.

The same life-likeness characterizes the story of the anointing of David. What is urged against it is mainly that it is not in itself probable; this is just the sort of thing (it is said) that legend loves to create—the future ruler pointed out in his boyhood by a divine foreshadowing. The passage is generally classed with chapter 15 as belonging to the B narratives, although some see in it secondary A material. In either case, it is not taken seriously by historians. Probably it will be well for us to acquiesce in this attitude, though we might enter our demurrer that there still is nothing impossible in what it tells.

Finally, the picture of Samuel standing as head over the company of prophets at Ramah (19:18-24) is generally regarded as later prophetic legend; and it must be confessed that several features of the narrative sound improbable. This however should not hinder us from believing that it has a historic core—the connection of Samuel with the ecstatic prophets.

[8] *GMMI*, p. 106f.
[9] *Israel*, p. 354; *HI*, I, p. 180, n.2.

Our sources for the study of Samuel therefore are of mixed value. The later representation of the B account can hardly be depended upon for sober history although it may contain genuine recollections. The earlier A account, on the other hand, may be regarded as reliable, after allowance is made for the accretion of legendary elements. The scepticism of scholars like Meinhold and Lods is not warranted. So, while we may not be able to attain absolute certainty, yet if we are content with reasonable probabilities we can reconstruct the personality and work of Samuel with a fair degree of confidence. Such will be our endeavour.

Samuel Becomes Known as a Prophet at Shiloh

The story opens in something the same way as the Gospel of St. Luke: with a humble Israelitish home and the sorrow of a childless woman. The home is marred by polygamy and its accompanying jealousies, but glows for all that with the light of love and simple piety. The picture is priceless for the knowledge it imparts of life in a Hebrew village in those early days; but our interest is more concerned with its influence upon the child now to be born there. According to the probable reading of I 1:1 the name of the village was Ramath, or Ramah, a "height," in the hill-country of Ephraim. Tradition identifies it with the modern er-Ram, five miles north of Jerusalem, but the succeeding narrative of Saul's journey to seek the asses (9:4) seems to imply that it was much farther from Gibeah, Saul's home—probably to the north. Elkanah, the head of the household, used to take his entire family once a year to the temple in Shiloh where they made merry over a generous sacrificial feast. One year this was spoiled by the grief of his favourite wife Hannah. The whole scene unfolds before us: the jealous taunts of Peninnah, Elkanah's other wife, his inability to comfort Hannah by his tender solicitude, her flight to the sanctuary, her pouring out her soul to Yahweh, her vow to dedicate a son if God would give one, Eli's misjudgment and sharp rebuke, his sudden understanding and contrite blessing, Hannah's immediate assurance and recovered happiness, the start for home, the coming of the prayed-for child, the mother's joy, the three years of nursing when she had the baby to herself, the return to Shiloh with the little boy and the accompanying presents, the conversation with Eli, the presentation, the brave words of offering, the child's first worship of Yahweh in His temple, the journey back without him, the child ministering in the temple before Eli the priest, the yearly visit thereafter when his mother brings him the little robe she has woven for him during the year, the coming of more children, the growing of the child Samuel before Yahweh (I 1:1–2:26).

Up to this point the central figure of the story has been the mother. Like many another woman of antiquity she had tried to obtain a son by a vow, and having succeeded she made good her promise. "For this child I prayed; and Yahweh hath given me my petition which I asked of him; therefore also I have granted him to Yahweh; as long as he liveth he is granted to Yahweh" (I 1:27f). Thus she lived on in the memory of the people, and there came later to be attributed to her a prayer of exultation (I 2:1–10) whose echoes we still hear in the song of another Mother a thousand years after—the *Magnificat* (Lk. 1:46ff). The second man of God after Moses was therefore believed to have been Hannah's gift to Israel.

Kittel [1] thinks that the prayers of such a mother could not but influence Samuel's whole life; and it is indeed likely that he brought to Shiloh from his early home a deep sense of God's being and character which would be fostered by his mother's yearly visits. He was thus prepared to take his part in the ministry of the temple and to be educated as one of its priests; for such seems to have been the understanding between Hannah and Eli. Today Seilun, the site of the ancient Shiloh, lies in a wide valley surrounded by stony hills, some twenty-five miles north of Jerusalem. Outcropping ledges of grey rock upon the hills blend with soft browns and reds and the frequent dark green of orchards. The bottoms between the hills are cultivated, and many artificial terraces show how grain is raised well up into the hills themselves. Old olive trees and young fig orchards abound in the vicinity. In Samuel's day also it must have presented a lovely scene, especially when the winter rains had brought out a flush of grass upon the hills, or when the spring sun was ripening the grain and scattering a profusion of wild flowers. Here, as we have seen, the Israelites had erected a substantial temple where the ancient tent of meeting had its place. Hither came Israelites to sacrifice and worship, probably in considerable numbers. Samuel was thus at the heart of the religious life of the tribes.

But as the developing insight of boyhood made him aware of what was going on about him he perceived that all was not well in the temple. Eli's two sons, Hophni and Phinehas, were using

[1] *GMMI,* p. 106.

their inherited office of sanctuary keeper for insolent extortion and were practising immorality with the women servants in a way that showed contempt for Yahweh. Complaints poured in to Eli from the people; and (as has been said) we cannot fail to notice here the evidence of a moral sense among the laity which demanded from their priests both probity and chastity. The sacred prostitution which seems to have flourished in Israelitish shrines in later times was evidently not in favour in this more primitive age.

Samuel of course overheard these complaints and saw for himself what was taking place. His mind revolted against the desecration of the divine name, and when the weak Eli, after remonstrating with his sons, failed to take any effective steps to stop their wickedness, he could not but believe that God Himself must intervene. Then the "word of Yahweh" suddenly came to him. How old he was we do not know, for the epithet *na'ar* used to describe him can mean anything from a little child to a young man. Probably Kittel is right in picturing him as about fifteen years of age. The story has always been a favourite with Bible readers. It was his duty to shut the doors at night and sleep in the presence of the ark, where the lamp of God was kept burning by day. In the morning he must open the doors and perhaps rekindle the lamp. On a certain night, when he was lying in the sacred room and the lamp of God was slowly burning itself out, a voice called his name. It was not Eli's, as he first thought, but God's. And it conveyed an awful message of doom to Eli's house. All unwilling, when pressed by Eli next morning, he revealed its purport, which the aged priest meekly accepted (I 3).

The narrator tells us expressly that such messages from God were unusual in those days; "there was no widely spread vision" (I 3:1). All the more did this experience of Samuel, when it became known, excite attention. It was soon followed by others of the same sort. "Yahweh appeared again in Shiloh; for Yahweh revealed himself to Samuel in Shiloh by the word of Yahweh. And the word of Samuel came to all Israel." The notable characteristic of these utterances was their reliability. "Yahweh let none of his words fall to the ground"—that is, fail to come true. So "all Israel from Dan even to Beersheba knew that Samuel was established to be a prophet of Yahweh" (I 3:19-21).

Thus runs the narrative. In spite of the suspicion with which its statements are regarded by many scholars, it may well be true that Samuel did become widely known, not only as a priest, but as a prophet. He may not indeed have been called by the latter title, but rather by that of "seer" (I 9:9), meaning one who saw things specially revealed to him by Yahweh. As such he came to be consulted by people with various needs, many of them perhaps quite trivial; and he seems to have accepted small fees for his services (I 9:7f).

Samuel After the Destruction of Shiloh

The activity of the young Samuel at Shiloh was terminated by a tragic event. Chapters 4–6 recount a crushing defeat of Israel by the Philistines in which the ark, which had been carried to the battle-front as a sort of charm to insure Yahweh's aid, was captured. The doom on Eli's house was fulfilled by the death of Hophni and Phinehas who bore the ark, and Eli himself succumbed on hearing the fateful news. The narrator is so occupied in telling how Yahweh's power compelled the Philistines to send the ark back that he says nothing of the result of the Philistine victory. But it is certain that they obtained a firmer hold on the country than before and probably made their yoke heavier. In particular, they wreaked heavy vengeance on the seat of the deity who had inspired the revolt. Shiloh was wiped out of existence. We can infer this from several things. When the ark was finally sent back, the Israelites did not take it to its former home in Shiloh but to the village Kiriath-jearim, where it found lodgment in a private home. Again, in the narratives that follow, the priests of Eli's house are no longer at Shiloh, but in the village ("city") of Nob, near Jerusalem. In the third place, there existed in a later age the definite remembrance of Shiloh's destruction and loss of Yahweh's presence (Jer. 7:12–15; 26:6; Ps. 78:60ff).[1] Finally, recent excavations seem to show that Shiloh was destroyed about 1050 B.C.[2]

Shiloh, then, was destroyed. What happened to Samuel? Our sources are silent. When next he appears it is as a man in later life. Kittel estimates that he must have been about twenty when the destruction took place,[3] and from fifty-five to sixty when he again comes upon the stage. What of the intervening forty years? From what we find at their conclusion we may infer something, and we may imagine a little more.

The shock of the tragedy must have been severe to the young man who had grown up in the temple as his home, sleeping in

[1] S. A. Cook, *OT*, p. 54, however, thinks that Jeremiah appears to allude to something in the more *recent* past, e.g. 734 or 722 B.C.

[2] Albright, *APB*, p. 160f.

[3] *GMMI*, p. 96.

the room where the ark was kept. All that was dear to him was swept away and Yahweh, in His symbol of the ark, reduced to impotence and dishonour. For it is evident that the people's faith in the ark had been rudely shaken by its capture; else they would have returned it to a central place in the worship of Israel instead of leaving it in the house of Abinadab. The priests of Eli's house took no interest in it, being quite content that Abinadab should sanctify his son Eleazar to keep it (I 7:1). Even Samuel himself paid no further attention to it, so far as our sources tell us.[4]

Samuel's faith in Yahweh however remained unbroken; and for Yahweh he had a work to do. But not in connection with his former associates, the priests. From them he seems to have separated himself at once, for he does not appear in their new home at Nob. Instead, he took up his abode at Ramah, making that the centre from which he worked. One thing seems to have been uppermost in his mind: that Israel should be freed from the Philistines. Kittel may well be right when he thinks of the next forty years as devoted to preparing the people for the throwing off of the foreign yoke. If such was his work, it would necessitate much going about on his part and many talks with the leading men of the nation, the "elders" of cities and of the clans. He could not have been the merely "local seer" which some scholars like to term him. He must have approached more nearly to the national figure depicted in the B account; but to that let us now turn.

Chapter 7:3ff draws back the veil after the hidden years and reveals the aging Samuel as the recognized leader of all Israel, summoning them at will to a national assembly, upbraiding them with their sins, prevailing miraculously over the Philistines by his intercession and putting an effectual stop to their incursions into Israelitish territory for the rest of his life; in testimony of which divine intervention he erects the stone *Eben-ha-ezer*. The chapter concludes with a summary of his life-long activity. "And Samuel judged Israel all the days of his life. And he went from year to year in circuit to Bethel and Gilgal and Mizpah; and he judged Israel in all those places. And his return was to Ramah, for there was his house; and he judged Israel: and he built there an altar unto Yahweh."

Here he is not only a judge, but a sort of national priest. Certainly this is not sober history; but it is probably closer to the facts than the idea of Samuel being a "local seer." If we accept the

---

[4] Kittel's idea, *GMMI*, p. 108, that Samuel was angry at Saul for neglecting the ark seems to have no foundation in the sources.

combined tradition of both A and B that Samuel actually did anoint Saul king over all Israel, then it is probable that he was of more than local importance; and indeed the A narrative itself, as we shall see, assigns to him national significance. That is all we are concerned with for the moment. Later on we shall try to put together the various traits found here and elsewhere into a final estimate of the man and his work for Israel. Only this need be added: his character must have been held in high esteem by his contemporaries and his right to speak for Yahweh undisputed. Here the words of Kittel may well be cited.[5]

"A late tradition tells us that when Samuel came unexpectedly to Bethlehem to anoint David, the elders of the city, trembling in awe and submission, came to him. This is an exaggerated description of admiring posterity. It does, however, reflect the fact that he made a deep and lasting impression even upon his contemporaries. Posterity may make a pious man into a saint and paint a halo about his head, but it seldom makes the mistake of giving a halo to one known to be unworthy. If Samuel travelled about the country, pursuing his priestly office, sacrificing, preaching Yahweh, teaching, blessing, ministering to the people, as is the duty of the true priest, if the people came to him to ask for counsel in their affairs and to know God's will, he was surely a highly respected man, whose word was authority far and wide, at least in all of Ephraim and Benjamin and, probably, beyond their borders. Had it not been so, and even if, at this time, he had not been an illustrious and far-famed personality, would the elders have listened to him, and would his time and posterity have looked upon him as the man who should crown Saul?"

Such was the man who now intervened decisively in the history of his people. Tradition has preserved a remembrance of how he looked: "an old man wrapped in a robe" (I 28:14), the embodiment of revered dignity.

Samuel Gives Israel Its First King

Throughout these forty years the dark shadow of Philistine domination lay heavy upon the land and therefore upon the mind of Samuel. The cry of the people was going up to Yahweh, as it had in many a crisis since the days of Egyptian oppression. Something must be done to save them! And in spite of the difficulties

[5] *GMMI*, p. 95 (quoted by permission of The Macmillan Company, publishers).

Samuel could not waver in his faith that Yahweh would at last hear their cry. For he had inherited from Moses the belief in a God *about to do*. How he must have held up the faith of his contemporaries during the long night of bondage; how he must have kept alive their longing for freedom and prepared them to gain it!

As he prayed to Yahweh, as he thought on the situation and conferred with the elders who likewise had the plight of Israel at heart, something became clear to him and to them: the old way of governing Israel no longer sufficed. If the hold of the Philistines was to be broken two things were required: unity and leadership. The days were gone when a Barak, a Gideon, a Jephthah could summon a following of his own clan or even of a group of tribes and drive out the enemy. Even in their days that method had not proven adequate and there had been attempts to set up local kings, as the stories of Gideon and Jephthah show. But now there was not even a judge! In the last battle with the Philistines which our sources record—the ill-fated fight at Ebenezer forty years before—Israel's forces had been led by no single mind, but by the elders; and the bitter outcome had shown the futility of a joint command by mediocre persons, of warfare under a committee (I 4:3). Perhaps there had been other attempts in the years that followed to throw off the yoke; if so, they had failed. Israel was disarmed and held in contempt by its neighbours (I 13:22; 11:2).

Now, however, the years of waiting were over. Samuel was convinced that the time had arrived for the nation to rise and crush the oppressor; and this could be done in only one way. Israel must have a king. We indeed speak of his reaching this conclusion as the result of deliberation, but neither Samuel nor the elders would look on the matter thus. A clear divine word came to Samuel, disclosing Yahweh's will. So the A source tells us and it is surely more credible here than B, which represents Samuel as opposing the request by the people for a king.

But who should choose the king? Yahweh Himself, of course. And both our sources agree that this took place without any previous selection by human means. B has the story of the casting by Samuel of the sacred lot. A is much more picturesque. At his home (in Ramah?) Yahweh revealed to Samuel what He would do: "Tomorrow about this time I will send thee a man out of the land of Benjamin, and thou shalt anoint him to be prince over my people Israel; and he shall save my people out of the hand of the Philistines: for I have looked upon my people, because their cry is come unto me" (I 9:15f). Of the two accounts, that of A is nearer the facts, but does it tell a probable story? Kittel, who in general lends it more credence than most historians, thinks not. "Kingdoms," he says,[1] "are not distributed in this idyllic fashion." Possibly Samuel had observed the stately nobleman of Gibeah for some time, and had been pleased with him; so that when the messengers of Jabesh-gilead came seeking aid Samuel directed them to Saul.[2]

It must be admitted, as has been pointed out, that A's charming story of the unknown young farmer who went out to seek his father's asses and found a kingdom savours strongly of legend, and it may well be that Samuel and the elders had already agreed upon Saul as Yahweh's choice before Samuel acted. But we are not prepared entirely to give up as fiction its vivid portrayal of the meeting between Samuel and Saul which casts so pleasant a light upon them both. Nor is it at all impossible that they indeed met now for the first time. Modern planners for a nation would scarcely depend upon sudden divine illumination in their choice of a leader, but can we say the same of a man of the Old Testament like Samuel, with his intense belief in Yahweh's personal direction? The story as told is in harmony with the thought-world of ancient Israel, and we can accept much of it as based on genuine recollections.

It tells how Samuel greeted the gigantic Saul with inspired certainty: "On whom is all the desire of Israel? Is it not on thee, and on all thy father's house?" The stranger who came with a quarter shekel fee was royally entertained at the sacrificial banquet. That night the seer talked long with him upon the top of his own house, whither he had taken him to lodge, opening his mind (we may imagine) upon Yahweh's saving purpose for Israel and Saul's place in it. In the dawn of the next day, as Samuel was "going down at the end of the city" with his departing guest, he took a vial of oil and poured it upon Saul's head and kissed him, saying: "Is it not that Yahweh hath anointed thee to be prince over his inheritance?" Then he gave him directions which should be signs. These would reach a climax when Saul met a band of prophets "coming down from the high place, with a psaltery and a timbrel and a pipe and a harp before them"; Saul would then experience a kindred ecstasy and the Spirit of Yahweh would come mightily upon him, changing him into another man. After that

[1] *GMMI*, p. 99.
[2] *GMMI*, p. 101.

he was to do as his hand should find, for God was with him
(I 9–10).

Thus, according to the earlier account, Samuel gave Israel its king.
But at the same time he did more: he impressed upon the king
that he was Yahweh's chosen, and must carry out Yahweh's will
as conveyed through His prophet. In other words, Samuel was
establishing the constitution of the monarchy: it was to be theocratic. Yahweh was still the ruler of Israel, and the king His
vicar. Such at least is the report of the earlier narrator, whom no
one suspects of "prophetic" or theological bias. Indeed, as the
narrative now stands, a much more explicit and even arbitrary
command was added: Saul was to go down before Samuel to
Gilgal and wait till he should come to offer sacrifices and show
the king what he should do (I 10:8). But this is generally
assigned to a later stratum of A, and should not be pressed.[3]

Saul then was to obey the word of Yahweh through Samuel.
In return it is plain that the prophet must have yielded the new
king his whole-hearted devotion. Through the story runs a warm
stream of affection; the cordial welcome, the lavish hospitality, the
bestowal of honour, the talking upon the housetop, the kiss, the
confidence expressed in the final injunction, all indicate that the
tall Benjamite quickly won a place for himself in the love of the
older man. Samuel had staked everything on his choice and he
would back Saul with all the influence he possessed.

Samuel Breaks with Saul

The events that in the A source follow the anointing of Saul
seemed to show that Samuel had indeed chosen wisely. Since we
shall review them in detail when we come to our study of Saul,
we must here pass over them briefly. After his meeting with
Samuel Saul returned to live quietly at Gibeah till his hand should
find something to do. It came when, roused by the appeal of
Jabesh-gilead, he gathered a force and relieved that town. Enthusiastic over his victory, the people who had been summoned
to Gilgal by Samuel "made Saul king before Yahweh" (I 11).
Flushed with triumph, Saul next turned to Israel's capital foe.
Hostilities broke out with the Philistines and presently Saul was
left with a handful of men to meet an overwhelming invasion of
Israel's masters. Here also the power of Yahweh enabled him to

[3] Eissfeldt, *EAT,* p. 308ff, maintains that along with its sequel, 13:8–15, it
formed part of what he calls the J thread of the original narrative.

put the enemy decisively to flight (I 13–14). It looked as if a new day had come for Israel.

One might have expected Samuel to rejoice in Yahweh's evident salvation. Instead, both our sources record a break between him and Saul. In 13:8–15, a paragraph which interrupts the account of Saul's victory over the Philistines, it is told how the king disobeyed Samuel's express injunction (10:8). Finding his men deserting him in the panic caused by the threatened Philistine attack and feeling that something must be done, Saul offered up the sacrifices which preceded the battle without waiting (apparently) till the seventh day had quite run out. No sooner had he done so than Samuel appeared in wrath. For this disobedience, declared the prophet, Saul's kingdom should not continue: "Yahweh hath sought him a man after his own heart, and Yahweh hath appointed him to be prince over his people, because thou hast not kept that which Yahweh commanded thee."

Chapter 15 gives another version. Here Samuel in Yahweh's name lays upon Saul the solemn charge of wiping out an old score against the Amalekites, who had resisted Israel's advance towards Canaan in Moses' day. The terrible *herem* is to be enforced; every living thing must be killed. Saul carries out the expedition with success, but fails to make the *herem* thorough-going; for he and the people spare Agag the king of the Amalekites and the best of the animals, devoting only what was contemned and refuse. Before Saul returns, a divine message to Samuel announces his failure, declaring that Yahweh is sorry He has set up Saul to be king, seeing that Saul has turned back from following Him. Samuel receives the message in anger and cries to Yahweh all night—apparently trying to win from Yahweh a revoking of His harsh sentence. In vain. The morning sees Samuel seeking Saul with the fearful news. In Gilgal he finds him. The scene is a dramatic one. To Saul's effusive greeting and his assurance that he had performed the commandment of Yahweh, Samuel answers: "What meaneth then this bleating of the sheep in my ears and the lowing of oxen which I hear?" Saul's evasive reply is met with the prophet's stern announcement: "Because thou hast rejected the word of Yahweh he hath also rejected thee from being king." Saul then confesses that he has sinned, pleading that the people have compelled him, and asks Samuel to pardon him and turn again with him to worship Yahweh. As Samuel refuses and starts to leave him, the king in anguish seizes his robe to hold him back; it rends, and Samuel, using this as a symbol, declares that

Yahweh has rent the kingdom of Israel from Saul on that day and has given it to a neighbour of his who is better than he. As a last favour Saul importunes the prophet to keep up outward appearances before the elders and before all the people, and to turn again that Saul may worship Yahweh. Samuel consents. He then has Agag brought and hews him in pieces with his own hands "before Yahweh in Gilgal," thus fulfilling the violated *herem*. The chapter concludes with the melancholy words: "Then Samuel went to Ramah; and Saul went up to his house to Gibeah of Saul. And Samuel came no more to see Saul until the day of his death; for Samuel mourned for Saul."

Of the two accounts, if we must choose between them, the latter is by far the more vivid, and seems to preserve a true recollection. That a break did occur between the two leaders can hardly be doubted, and it is impressive that both sources agree as to the reason: Saul violated the fundamental principle of the monarchy. Instead of carrying out the will of Yahweh, Saul followed his own. Our sympathy in both accounts is apt to be with Saul; but we must not overlook the fact that in neither case is he represented as contending for a principle. In sparing Agag, for instance, his motive was not humane but selfish; and by saving out the best of the spoil he and his men were doing substantially what Achan had done at Jericho. When confronted by Samuel he acknowledged his "sin" and made no claim to be acting from any higher impulse.

But granting that he did disobey, was one act of disobedience serious enough to justify the peremptory fashion in which he was set aside? Ought he not to have been given another chance? Kittel feels this difficulty so strongly that he supposes the violation of the *herem* to be the culmination of a series of deeds which displeased Samuel.[1] But when we look at the situation with Samuel's eyes we may well believe that Saul's conduct in the Amalekite raid was serious enough of itself to account for the break. Direct disobedience of the will of God *as one understands it* strikes at the root of religion. Saul maintained that in bringing the sheep and oxen to sacrifice to Yahweh at Gilgal (where they would furnish a splendid feast to the worshippers) he was offering a satisfactory substitute for the *herem*. But Samuel was right in insisting that nothing takes the place of doing the particular thing that one is commanded to do. If this were true of a private man, how much more of a king!

[1] *GMMI*, p. 108.

Samuel's Retirement

If Samuel came no more to see Saul, what did he do at Ramah?
For a time he was inconsolable for he still loved Saul. How
different the sequel from what he had hoped! Then, a late tradition reports, he was upbraided by Yahweh for his brooding and
bidden to anoint a successor to the rejected king (I 16:1–13).
This was none other than the great David, then a lad keeping his
father's sheep near Bethlehem. The beautiful story is generally
looked on as unhistorical. But even if it were true it would confirm the impression conveyed by the end of chapter 15, that Samuel
made no attempt to replace Saul; for it implies that David's
anointing must be kept secret till the time came for him to succeed
to the throne. Saul must have his day. Since he had shut the
door to divine guidance through the prophet, let him go his own
way. For unlike Elijah and Elisha at a later time, Samuel felt
no call to promote a change of rulers. He only waited in the
hope of a better king and a better age.[1]

Another late narrative presents him at Ramah "standing as
head" over a company of ecstatic prophets, but it can hardly be
depended on for facts (I 19:18ff). It may well be however that
he did gather around him a group of these fiery enthusiasts and
perhaps inculcate in them the faith and devotion that had marked
his own life.

The next notice in our sources records his death. It too is late,
and may idealize the respect paid to him. "All Israel gathered to
lament him and bury him in his house at Ramah" (I 25:1).

So passed the great man of God.

Samuel and the Prophets

Twice in the narratives concerning Samuel we catch sight of
bands of "prophets" or ecstatics who are in some fashion connected
with him. It was by his direction that the newly anointed Saul
fell in with the prophets coming down from the high place and
succumbed to their frenzy (I 10:5ff); and at the end of his life,
as we have just seen, he is pictured as standing head over a group
of them at Ramah.

These prophets were by no means peculiar to Israel, being but
local manifestations of a religious phenomenon that was wide-

---

[1] Meek, *HO*, p. 157, seems to regard this choice of David as historical.
"It was then that he (Samuel) turned to David."

spread in the Mediterranean world of that day. What marked the Israelitish prophets was their devotion to the national God. They evidently associated themselves in groups at certain sanctuaries and went about with music and wild dancing, stirring up the religious and patriotic ardour of the people. If (as seems probable) Samuel regarded them as under the influence of Yahweh's Spirit (10:6), he was but showing himself a child of his age. And yet he probably saw beyond his age. For this movement, which now assumed such grotesque shape, had in it the seeds of something far higher. It was destined later, in its noblest exponents, to transmute frenzy into the loftiest passion for righteousness that the world has known.[1] The true course for a religious leader in Samuel's time was to welcome it and mould it; and this Samuel seems to have done. He himself, as has often been pointed out, is not portrayed as falling into frenzy. He remained a "seer," receiving visions and revelations in quieter fashion; passionate indeed, but not losing control over his faculties. In this he was a precursor of the great prophets that followed.

Did he found the prophetic movement? Perhaps in a sense he did. Unquestionably he marks a beginning of some sort in the history of Israel's prophecy. Before him, few recorded appearances of prophets and not one mighty name since Moses, unless it be Deborah. After him, a self-perpetuating movement, more and more outstanding names, increasing ethical purity, till we come to Amos the herdsman of Tekoa. How much of this beginning was due to Samuel we have no means of knowing; but we shall not go far wrong if we see in him at least one who fostered prophecy in its early days and set it forward on its true development.

Samuel was himself before all else a prophet. It was by virtue of his receiving communications from God that he led the nation and finally gave it its first king. As a priest he offered up sacrifices, attributing to them, as did Moses, a value in Yahweh's sight. But he knew that there was something more important:

"Hath Yahweh as great delight in burnt-offerings and sacrifices,
As in obeying the voice of Yahweh?
Behold, to obey is better than sacrifice,
And to hearken than the fat of lambs.
For rebellion is as the sin of divination,
And stubbornness as idolatry and teraphim" (I 15:22f).

[1] Alfred Jepsen (*Nabi*, Munich, 1934, *passim*) maintains that the writing prophets did not arise within this movement, but were a distinct phenomenon.

There spoke the prophet. True, his *application* was still unil-
lumined, for he was enforcing the *herem;* but his *principle* was
destined to find immortal expression in the prophets from Amos
to Christ.

An Estimate of Samuel

In spite of all their vagueness and atmosphere of legend, our
sources give the strong impression that Samuel marks a fresh beginning in the life of Israel. He is the first great man of God
since Moses; for even Joshua stands lower than he in tradition.
He is the second of the mountain peaks that tower above the
nation's history, forming a mighty range from Moses to Christ.
And with him, as we have said, comes something new. Holding
fast the Mosaic tradition, he yet built a structure that had not
existed before. In founding the monarchy he exhibited not a
little of Moses' capacity to meet a changed situation with creative
invention. To prophecy he gave a new impulse, moulding and
perhaps in a sense founding the movement that was to dominate
Israel's religion. When he died Israel was on its way to a better
future.

How was he able to accomplish this? What was there in him
to give him such a high place in Israel's development? In a
sense it is hard to find a satisfactory answer. The details of his
activity scarcely explain the matter. In anointing Saul, did he do
more than Ahijah did to Jeroboam (I Ki. 11:29ff), and Elisha's
emissary to Jehu (II Ki. 9:1ff)? In summoning Saul to save Israel
was he surpassing Deborah, who called Barak to fight Sisera (Jud.
4:6)? In enforcing the *herem* against the Amalekites did he not
exhibit a most primitive trait of the religion of Moses, putting him
on the level of Mesha of Moab rather than of Amos? When he
broke with Saul over the king's disobedience, was he not demanding conduct that more developed thought would pronounce distinctly unethical? Would Hosea have hewed Agag in pieces before
Yahweh? Is not his loftiest prophetic utterance tainted with a
low conception of the character of Yahweh? Devoted as he was
to Yahweh, what is there to show that his zeal moved in the
ethical realm?

Yet somehow we cannot dissociate him from ethics. Kittel is
right in maintaining that the halo of the saint is not unjustly given
him by tradition. We must remember how little of his life
the details just mentioned permit us to see. What was he day in
and day out? For he had the Mosaic inheritance of ethical re-

ligion. If he did go about judging the people he must have applied ethics to their disputes. If we can place credence in the story of his boyhood we there behold him condemning the unethical conduct of Eli's sons. The earlier A account represents him as helpful to the people in their perplexities (9:6), as bearing Israel on his heart (9:16, etc.), as showing affection to Saul. It makes the reader feel that this man is "held in honour" (9:6) not only because of his true predictions but also for something in himself—his religious faith, perhaps, and his character. And the coloured B account surely rests on certain massive facts that were remembered about him, his incorruptibility (12:1ff), his insistence on pure worship (7:3), and particularly his intercession for the people. For he stands out in tradition along with Moses as the second great intercessor (Jer. 15:1), who cries all night to Yahweh to forgive Saul (15:11), and shudders at the thought that he should ever sin against Yahweh by ceasing to pray for Israel (12:23).

And so we may say that he was enabled to do so much for Israel because of what he was himself. His character impressed itself upon his contemporaries in such fashion that we still feel it when we read these scanty and often conflicting narratives. There was about him an austere purity, an uncompromising simplicity and directness, a lofty way of looking at life, a sinking of self in the good of his people, a burning desire for Israel's welfare, a passionate advocacy of its cause before God, a faith, a perseverance, a continuance in service, a willingness in his old age to meet a new situation and to throw himself whole-heartedly into the support of a younger man—that rank him with the chiefest of those men of God who were Israel's unique gift to the world.

Chapter VI

SAUL

[REIGNED 1036(?)–1016 B.C.]

We have already caught several glimpses of Israel's first king, as he comes into the story of Samuel. His is a tragic figure. Samuel broke with him, declaring him rejected by Yahweh; and the Bible record writes him down a failure. Let us try now to form our own estimate of him.

The Sources

The sources for the study of Saul are substantially the same as those which we have reviewed in our survey of the sources for Samuel. We have seen how the A and B narratives give different accounts of the way in which he came to be made king. There follow a number of narratives concerning him, most of which are marked by great vividness and possess all the charm of the Israelitish story-teller at his best. Discrepancies, parallels and doublets show that these do not form a single connected unit, and they are variously divided by scholars between the A and B strands of tradition. But they are all more life-like than the theocratic chapters which constitute the B account of the institution of the monarchy, and the historian is often hard put to it to decide which he will believe and which reject. On the whole we may say that our records of Saul are rich in true recollections, and that in spite of legendary features they do give a correct picture of the man, so far as they go. Yet they are anything but complete, preserving only views of him here and there amid shifting scenes which tend ever to grow more gloomy. It is a question also how far they are just to Saul; for in general they seem to come from admirers of David, who tended to use Saul as a foil for the virtues of their hero. Nevertheless it is possible to gain from them a fairly reliable idea of this remarkable man.

96

Saul Becomes Israel's First King

Saul was the son of a Benjamite of wealth and high position whose home was in Gibeah, a hill (as its name implies) some three miles north of Jerusalem. The modern Tell el-Fûl, on which Saul's village stood, rises abruptly east of the main road to Nablus and commands a fine view of the surrounding country. South by southwest can be seen the buildings of Jerusalem, which in Saul's day was still a Jebusite fortress. Eastward the land plunges into a wide valley which opens down to Jordan. The river with its fringe of green and the upper end of the Dead Sea, deep blue against the purple rampart of the Moabite plateau, are in plain sight. To the north and west a valley encircles the mound, connecting with another valley coming up from the southwest. West by northwest the sky-line is cut by the hill Neby Samwil (some two miles away) adorned with its graceful minaret—perhaps the Mizpah, or Watch-tower associated with Samuel's memory, and bearing his name. Saul must have known it as a venerable "high place." Just north of Neby Samwil rises the mound of El-Jib, the ancient Gibeon, whose inhabitants were to experience harsh treatment at Saul's hands. In every direction in the midst of tilled fields may be seen today tiny villages, with their grey stone houses, dotting the hills; and doubtless it was the same when Saul looked out on the surrounding country from his father's house. Gibeah gives one the sense of elevation, of being on the roof of the land; and it befitted the tall man who grew up there, who could look down on others as from a height. The estate of Kish possibly stretched some distance from the village, but he may have owned land on the hill itself and have had his home there. Above his and the other dwellings rose the village "high place" with its local shrine from which the band of prophets were coming down when Saul met them on the memorable day of his anointing.

At the time his story opens he must have been a man in early middle life, for he had a grown son able to bear arms. Tradition implies that he lived with his father and worked for him upon his farm. His was a well known figure in the neighbourhood, for he towered above every one else from his shoulders upward; and his looks were as striking as his size. He is described as "a choice man and a goodly; among all the sons of Israel there was none goodlier than he." The word "goodly" probably refers to his physical beauty, but it implies also that he possessed charm. We may gather that his bearing was characterized by dignity and reserve; anything like wild enthusiasm or ecstasy was quite foreign to him. Not that he was devoid of feeling, for his later history shows that his temperament was charged with emotion; but he had not been stirred as yet. Respected, liked, admired, he nevertheless did not seem the man to throw himself tumultuously into a desperate cause.

Then he met Samuel, and received from his lips the summons of Yahweh to deliver Israel. That experience changed his whole life. Whatever we may doubt in the story, we may well accept the tradition that when he turned his shoulder from Samuel God "altered his heart into another" (10:9). Something about the man of God, some fire in his words, combined with the solemn anointing, had set Saul's sluggish soul aflame. When presently he encountered the prophets coming down from the high place, the music playing before them, all his inhibitions gave way; the Spirit of Yahweh rushed upon him and he prophesied in the midst of them, joined in their frenzied leaping, dancing and crying. No wonder "every one who had known him before" exclaimed: "What has come to the son of Kish! Is Saul also among the prophets!" From this day onward Saul was a strongly religious man.

When the ecstasy had passed Saul returned home, and the non-committal way in which he avoided his uncle's question showed that he had not lost the power to keep his own counsel. Back to the work of the farm he went, waiting for what his hand should find. One evening, on returning from ploughing, he heard the people of Gibeah wailing over the news of outrage which the messengers from Jabesh had just brought; but no one thought of *doing* anything about it. Once more the Spirit of God rushed upon Saul, and this time the ecstasy did not expend itself in prophesying. It took the form of overpowering, liberating rage. Out went his summons far and wide: "Whosoever cometh not forth after Saul,[1] so shall it be done unto his oxen!" In this summons, enforced by the pieces of mangled beasts, the Israelites recognized that a real leader had arisen. An answering flame swept over the nation; they came out as one man. Swift, decisive were the means taken; in the morning watch the rescuers broke into the sleeping camp and smote the Ammonites till the heat of the day, scattering them till no two were left together. It was a dashing victory. In all minds was but one thought; they took Saul to Gilgal and made him king there before Yahweh. Tradition relates that Samuel

[1] It is customary to omit the words "and Samuel" as a later insertion.

took the lead in this solemn ceremony. The people of Jabesh never forgot their deliverer (I 9:1–10:16; 11).[2]

Now the king's main task confronted him; the Philistines must be dealt with. With this in view Saul chose a small force of three thousand men as a sort of standing army, dismissing other recruits, and divided the command with Jonathan his son. Jonathan's impetuosity soon brought action. Anticipating the interference of the Philistines, he attacked and killed their resident officer (or garrison) in Geba, a village not far from Gibeah. Then every one knew that the struggle was on. Saul blew the trumpet, but as the invaders poured in the accustomed fear of them created widespread panic. Saul and Jonathan were left with a handful of men, while the Philistines ravaged the country at will. Once more Jonathan acted. With the help only of Yahweh[3] and his armourbearer, he impetuously attacked the garrison at Michmash, northeast across the valley from Gibeah where Saul was stationed, and threw them into a panic which speedily became a rout. Saul's forces, swollen by an ever increasing number of now emboldened Hebrew skulkers, joined in the pursuit down the Beth-horon pass which ended only with the halt of the victors at Aijalon, far to the west, at the close of day. So once more the new king had come off triumphant, this time against the dreaded foes who had kept Israel under their heel for a generation (I 13–14).[4]

The chief result of this victory seems to have been its moral effect upon Israel. Not very many Philistines had actually been killed (14:30); and when Saul was determined to follow it by a night attack he was prevented by the impossibility of getting a response from the sacred oracle (14:37). The enemy must have rallied almost immediately; but when they pressed back to regain

---

[2] We have told the story as one finds it in modern histories, most of which take for granted that when Saul sent out his summons he was acting as a new man, and that not until after his success did the people think of him as king. The Bible narrative, to be sure, by piecing together the A and B accounts, relates how he had been already proclaimed king; and how some men had mocked at the idea of his being able to save Israel; and explains the making him king in Gilgal as a renewing of the kingdom. This scheme of events is set aside by modern scholars, however, as an attempt to harmonize two incompatible accounts. But the question arises: How was Saul known when he sent out his summons? What credentials did he have? The probable answer is that like Gideon (Jud. 6:34) he needed none: the manifest seizure by the Spirit of God and the blowing of the trumpet were enough.

[3] Possibly an earthquake occurred at an opportune moment.

[4] It was after this battle that, in the opinion of Lods (*Israel*, p. 352), Saul was made king.

their control they found themselves confronted by a changed people. Led by their gigantic hero-king the hitherto cowed Israelites offered furious resistance. Attacks and counter attacks followed one another for years. "There was strong war against the Philistines all the days of Saul" (14:52). It was apparently not till the great invasion in which Saul lost his life that the Philistines were able to regain their mastery of the country. Although Saul was not powerful enough to crush them he kept them pretty much out of Israel's territory, except for constant inroads (e.g. at Keilah 23:1). In these narratives they appear perennially as attackers, but nowhere as resident lords of the land.

The new situation was due not only to the king's prowess but also to his leadership. For he *was* a leader. We have seen how he could assemble hasty levies and rescue Jabesh. In the story of the battle against the Philistines (chapters 13 and 14) he and his knightly son Jonathan dominate the scene. It was his policy to institute a small standing army (13:2); and he made it his aim to associate with him any man who exhibited marked military gifts: "when Saul saw any mighty man, or any valiant man, he gathered him unto him" (14:52). One of these was David, the man destined later to give the Philistine power its death blow. The result was a fighting force that could contend on equal terms with the well-equipped Philistines. This was supplemented when necessary by a general levy from the population—the army, or "host" as it was called. Over it he set as captain his cousin Abner, who must also have been an unusually able leader, for on Saul's death we find him the real power among the clans that remained loyal to Ishbaal, Saul's successor. Under his training the Israelites at large acquired a military effectiveness which made them formidable.

There was also a new unity in Israel. The nation recognized its king and gave him its allegiance. It is remarkable how seldom the names of the several tribes are mentioned in the accounts of Saul's reign. While he apparently trusted his fellow-clansmen of Benjamin most of all, and kept them closest to him, no discrimination seems to have been made among his soldiers on the basis of clan; they were all Israelites before they were anything else. No trace is seen of the sectional jealousy between north and south which was to flame out even under David and later to break the kingdom in two. If we should look for aloofness from a Benjamite king anywhere, it would be among the men of Judah who seem from of old to have had a feeble sense of kinship with the northern tribes; and yet Saul had right of way in Judah even when he was pursuing the Judahite David. Indeed, the men of Ziph actually helped him in his effort to seize their fellow-tribesman (23:19). As for the great tribes of Ephraim and Manasseh, which formed the bulk of the nation, they remained true to Saul even after his death, and along with them their smaller brother tribes, especially the men beyond Jordan. If there is anything that our sources attest regarding Saul, it is that he was accepted as king by the whole of Israel. The unity of which Samuel and the elders had dreamed was now an accomplished fact.

This does not mean that Saul set up an elaborate central government such as came into existence under David, and still more under Solomon. He continued to live in Gibeah, apparently in real simplicity. We get a glimpse of him there, sitting under a tamarisk tree with his spear in his hand, his Benjamite "servants" standing about him (I 22:6). He did indeed erect a royal fortress of impressive dimensions (52 x 35 metres), and the stone courses of part of its foundation (as excavated by Albright)[5] are still standing massive, square, true—a bit of masonry that does honour to the workmen who laid it a thousand years before Christ. It was a rugged building and immensely strong. So far as is now known, it stood unique among the structures of the Palestine of that day. Its construction, though still primitive, was incomparably better than that seen in the other houses of the period of the judges uncovered by excavations. It seems to have marked a new period of unity and vigour in Israel's history. But it was apparently without luxurious appointments of any sort, and it covered the summit of the mound, leaving no room beside it for a complex of royal buildings. Saul therefore may hardly be said to have had a capital.[6] Nor could he have surrounded himself by anything that might be called a court, in the sense of a hierarchy of officials. He did indeed share a common table with his officers, and his "servants" were continually about him; but everything seems to have been rudimentary and informal. When we compare the list of his officials with that of David's, we are struck with the absence of any "scribe," or "recorder," or "priest" (though a priest was with him in his first battle with the Philistines 14:18); and—most significantly—of any one set "over the men subject to task-work."[7]

---

[5] *Annual, ASOR,* IV, 1924, and *BASOR,* No. 52, Dec. 1933, p. 6ff.

[6] Kittel, *GMMI,* p. 111, thinks he showed his lack of statesmanship in not providing one.

[7] Compare I 14:49ff with II 20:23ff.

Gibeah was more like a garrison town crowded with soldiers for whom many additional stone cottages had been built, than a royal seat with its palaces and officials and "singing men and singing women" and sumptuous banquets.[8] It probably did not possess even a royal chapel, any priestly duties being performed by members of the family of Ahimelech, the descendant of Eli, who had made the nearby Nob the priestly centre of the country.[9] Nor did Saul acquire an imposing harem. Apparently he had only one wife (14:50), though another woman, who may have been only a concubine, bore him two sons (II 21:8).

All this means that Saul was not very expensive to the people. They brought him "presents" (10:27; 16:20) and submitted when in a rough and ready way he laid impositions upon them for his campaigns.[10] But of any machinery to extract money systematically from them for a luxurious court and an ambitious building program, there was nothing. No one was forced to labour on the king's projects. And unlike David Saul seems to have remained accessible to the people down to the end.

Strange to say, nothing is said in our sources of Saul's being appealed to as judge. Such appeals must have been made, for to judge was one of the king's chief duties. Nor have we any record of measures of civil government instituted by him, except his suppression of necromancy.[11] It would be hasty, indeed, to conclude from such silence that Saul did not attempt to exercise civil control over the nation; we have here only an illustration of the scantiness and incompleteness of our sources. But it is probable that he did not go far in this direction, leaving the government largely where it had been before, in the hands of the elders. As we have seen, his chief duty was to "save" Israel from its enemies abroad, not from internal disorder.

In the military field, as has been said, he proved fairly successful. Nor, if a somewhat doubtful tradition is to be credited, were the Philistines the only foes he faced. "Now when Saul," we read, "had taken the kingdom over Israel, he fought against all his

[8] When Saul needed a man to play and sing for him, one must be sought out expressly (16:16).

[9] The site of Nob has not been certainly identified, but it must have been south of Gibeah for David stopped there on his flight towards Judah (I 21:1). Isaiah seems to place it in full sight of Jerusalem and very near to the capital (Is. 10:32).

[10] This is a surmise, for there is no record of any such impositions.

[11] His effort to exterminate the Gibeonites can hardly be put into the class of such measures (II 21:2).

enemies on every side, against Moab, and against the sons of
Ammon, and against Edom, and against the kings of Zobah, and
against the Philistines: and whithersoever he turned himself he put
them to the worse (or 'was saved' LXX). And he did valiantly,
and smote the Amalekites, and delivered Israel out of the hands
of them that despoiled them" (14:48). Allowance must be made
here for exaggeration; names may well have been added. But
that he did vanquish the Ammonites (11) and the Amalekites (15)
we know from good tradition. Nor can we forget that David,
in the elegy whose genuineness no one questions, spoke enthusiastically of the prowess of Saul and Jonathan in war, and of the rich
plunder they brought back for Israelitish women to enjoy (II
1:19ff). David was doubtless exaggerating, but he celebrated real
facts. The gloomy pictures of Saul's pursuit of David and defeat
on Gilboa must therefore not blind us to the probability that he
won many victories and much spoil, which he distributed lavishly
with the generosity that marked his nature. On the whole, then,
it was a good day for Israel when Saul became its king; and Israel
seems to have appreciated the fact.

We cannot leave this glance at Saul's kingly activity without
noticing some interesting indications of his religious attitude, as
revealed in the story of his first battle with the Philistines.[12] When
Saul observed the panic in the camp of the Philistines he ordered
Ahijah the priest to bring the ephod.[13] This shows that he wished
to know the divine will for himself in the emergency. When however matters in the distant camp developed with astounding rapid-
ity he felt he could not wait till the ceremony was completed;
and bidding the priest "withdraw his hand" he rushed to the
attack. Such abrupt turning of his back on the oracle might easily
have seemed an affront to deity; and it shows a certain headstrong
impulsiveness about Saul, a taking of matters into his own hands,
that would clash with humble waiting upon Yahweh for direction.
Early in the same battle he laid a curse upon anyone who should
taste food till evening, in order that the king might be effectively
"avenged of his enemies." The curse was a religious act, intended
to propitiate deity. By fasting the favour of Yahweh would be

[12] We shall defer to the next section consideration of the story of his disobedience to Samuel (13:8–15), which some scholars think does not belong
in this narrative.

[13] See note 7, p. 72. Our English Bible, based on the Hebrew text, reads
"ark"; but since the ark was now in disuse, it is better to follow the LXX
and read "ephod."

invited. At the end of the day the famished victors began to eat
the captured animals with the blood in them, killing them on the
ground instead of ritually. Horrified at the violation of Yahweh's
taboo Saul erected an impromptu altar and ordered every one to
kill his victim on that, draining off the blood. He then proposed
to make a night attack and again consulted the oracle, this time
seeing the ceremony through. In vain; Yahweh would not answer!
Repeated attempts brought no result: the opportunity passed.
Suspecting that some one had violated the taboo Saul now had
recourse to the sacred lot. When Jonathan was found to be the
offender Saul insisted that he must die, although of course he had
not known anything of the curse when he ate the honey during the
pursuit. The people however intervened and ransomed Jonathan,
providing, let us hope, an animal instead of a human victim.

What does this show us of Saul's religion? First, that it was
charged with primitive superstitions—perhaps even more so than
that of the "people." Second, that he was in deadly earnest about
it. Third, that in spite of his earnestness, yes, his fanaticism, he
would yield to pressure and compromise. For compromise he
probably did. In this case his own conscience could not have
been easy when he stopped the ceremony, or let a substitute for
Jonathan be offered. Finally, his religious ideas interfered with
sound military policy. Jonathan criticized his laying of the curse,
declaring that it had prevented any considerable slaughter of the
Philistines (14:30); and he allowed the silence of the oracle to stop
his following up of the victory. Saul was then at once ineffective
because of his superstition and vacillating in carrying out what
he believed to be Yahweh's will.

The grimness of Saul's religious zeal is shown by another action,
which we have already noticed. Necromancy was apparently
widely practised in his time and he resolved to stamp it out
(28:3). He must have done this because of the conviction, which
we meet later in the prophets, that knowledge of the divine purpose
should be sought only through the accredited channels of the
Yahweh religion—dreams, the priestly lot, and prophets (28:6).
Inquiry of the dead was specially wicked because the dead were
looked on as belonging to the unholy underworld, where Yahweh
did not live and work and where doubtless popular superstition
thought that other gods held sway. Saul must have felt more
deeply on this matter than most of his contemporaries, for in
spite of his efforts to kill off all mediums some escaped and con-

tinued to practise their function with the connivance of the people (28:7).

Here we may mention also an instance of extreme racial fanaticism which probably was tinged with religion. Tradition had it that the people of Gibeon were protected by an oath sworn by the Israelites in the days of Joshua (Jos. 9:15ff). They remained a thriving Canaanitish community in the midst of the country, in contrast with other "cities," formerly Canaanitish, where a pretty thoroughgoing process of amalgamation with the Israelites had apparently taken place. Yahweh indeed had found entrance there, if we can with Sellin [14] accept the tradition in II Chron. 1:3, that the ancient tent of meeting from Moses' day was located in Gibeon. Another tradition tells how the young king Solomon just after his accession offered up princely sacrifices to Yahweh on its high place, which enjoyed a special pre-eminence (I Ki. 3:4). But none the less the Gibeonites' racial autonomy roused the resentment of the new king, whose "zeal for the sons of Israel and of Judah" was intense (II 21:2). Disregarding the inherited compact he endeavoured to "liquidate" them, not stopping at executions. Here we see again his characteristic rigour, his religious and patriotic scrupulosity and his self-will in over-riding scruples where they stood in his way.

This leads us up to the religious crisis which seems to have marked a turning point in his career.

Saul is Rejected by Samuel

It was Samuel, as we have seen, who summoned and anointed Saul king; who called forth (under God) that marvellous transformation of Saul into another man; who threw all his vast influence into the support of the new king. Though the prophet made no attempt to attend on Saul as a regular companion, he did pay him visits,[1] and on occasion communicated to him a divine injunction which he had received as to Saul's course. Taking as we do the view that Samuel was a chief person in the nation, known everywhere as a man of God, we must feel that his support of Saul was of the utmost value in establishing him securely in popular esteem. But apart from this it was of supreme worth to Saul personally. His affectionate nature undoubtedly responded with

[14] *IOT*, p. 113.
[1] This may be inferred from the statement that later the visits ceased (15:35).

eagerness to Samuel's warmth and he would cherish for him something of the devotion that younger persons feel towards the one who has awakened them to wonderful new life. Moreover, Samuel stood to him for Yahweh, and the prophet's approval assured him of divine favour. Everything goes to show that Saul was peculiarly susceptible to the influence of those about him and this would be signally true of his relations with Samuel.

Then suddenly, or after growing misunderstanding, came the break which terminated those happy relations forever. We have already reviewed the accounts of it and need not tell the story again. On his return from a brilliant campaign against the Amalekites Saul was confronted with the enraged prophet, who upbraided him for disobedience and announced that Yahweh had rent his kingdom from him, to give it to a more trustworthy neighbour. Saul, after a weak attempt to justify his conduct, acknowledged his "sin" and besought forgiveness. All in vain. The utmost concession he could wring from Samuel was that appearances for the moment should be kept up. We have considered the situation and concluded that Saul's disobedience to the will of God, *as he himself conceived it,* was sufficient ground in a theocratic monarchy for his removal. From the other exhibitions of his character which we have just reviewed we can see that in his case such disobedience was not isolated, but something that might be often looked for.

What concerns us now however is the effect that Samuel's declaration of divine rejection had upon Saul. Outwardly, so far as we can see, it had none at all. Although the break between the two could hardly have been kept secret, Samuel's withdrawal cast no cloud over Saul's relations with his soldiers and his people. They continued to follow him and believe in him as before. Or at least they gave no sign of disaffection.

But with the king himself the matter was very different. A marked change took place in his whole mental condition. "The Spirit of Yahweh departed from Saul," reports tradition, "and an evil spirit from Yahweh terrified him" (16:14). Up to this time, we gather, he had been carried along in his warfare by continued impulses of the same "battle-fury" that had swept him to his first victory. Now these ceased, and in their place came black moods of depression and fear which were attributed by those around him (and doubtless by himself) to Yahweh's hostile action. This transformation, in the case of one of Saul's emotional temperament, is not hard to understand. He seems to have had an unusually active conscience, and its uneasiness over his behaviour, combined with the crushing blow of Samuel's abandonment, made his confidence collapse. He sat in his house, his spear in his hand, plunged in dark thoughts (19:9). From this time onwards the conviction held recurring sway in his mind that he was indeed rejected. His kingdom would not last, his son would not succeed him. For Yahweh was against him. Yet unlike the aged Eli he refused to accept the sentence. A fierce will to succeed struggled constantly against conscience's forebodings. He would take the business into his own hands. Yet he seems not to have drawn the conclusion consciously that he was thereby rebelling against Yahweh. His religious zeal apparently continued to the end. But as one high-handed deed followed another he must have had increasing difficulty in justifying them to himself. From now on Saul seems a man at war with his own conscience.

But we are anticipating our story. Shocked by the altered demeanour of their king his followers suggested bringing in a skilful harp-player to dispel his melancholy. Saul gave consent, thereby showing that he was aware of his condition and able to co-operate in measures for its treatment. The result, according to one strand of narrative, was that David presently stood before him. The meeting marks the beginning of a new and fateful era in the king's history.

Saul and David

Our sources contain two differing accounts of the way in which David and Saul met. The one to which we have just referred represents David, when he was recommended to Saul for his musical ability, as already a man of war, an approved fighter, handsome, able in business and successful. The other tells how, an untried stripling, unknown to any in the king's circle, he overcame the mighty Goliath in single combat and thus gained Saul's notice. Of the two scholars generally take the first as more credible and we shall follow it here, reserving the comparison of the accounts till we come to our study of David.

The effect of David's coming was at first all that had been hoped. The charm which made this young Bethlehemite a favourite with every one worked also upon the unhappy king. It was quite in accord with Saul's warm nature that he loved David greatly—a love which never really left him—and took him into the most personal relation to himself by making him his armourbearer. Jesse's consent was obtained to David's remaining in the royal household. Nor did his musical gift disappoint. Whenever Saul would fall into one of his black depressions David would play his harp and dispel it. The king returned to his occupations with renewed vigour. In the intervals occurring between his attacks he doubtless cast off his prostration and was the old dashing Saul again (16:21ff). He and his armourbearer threw themselves into the frequent clashes with the Philistines and accomplished great things; for David now showed himself a fighter of supreme ability. More than this, David won friends rapidly, among them Saul's own son Jonathan, who recognized in the Bethlehemite a worthy companion in arms.

But the happy relationship between Saul and David did not continue long. Tradition says that the first rift was unwittingly caused by the antiphonal song of jubilant women who, in the fashion of ancient Israel, met the king returning victorious with singing and dancing and timbrels, with joy and with instruments of music.

> "Saul hath slain his thousands
> And David his ten thousands."

This was too much for Saul. "They have ascribed unto David ten thousands," he exclaimed in a rage, "and to me they have ascribed but thousands: and what can he have more but the kingdom?" From that moment David became an object of suspicion; Saul watched everything he did and said (18:6ff).

The first indication of his changed attitude was the severance of personal contact. Saul removed David from him and made him captain over a thousand. This brought him into close touch with the army and gave him more opportunity to show his ability. Everywhere success attended him; Yahweh was with him, as people put it. And he gained universal affection. "All Israel and Judah loved David; for he went in and came out before them" (18:13ff). Presently the king heard that his daughter Michal had fallen in love with the young hero.

All this success of David called forth fear in Saul's mind. It was uncanny the way his rival prospered. Jealousy added to the king's misery by making him dwell on the contrast between his own failure and David's success; he was going, David coming! But of the two fear now became the dominating motive. He proceeded to fumbling plots for bringing about David's death in combat, but David doubled the hundred fore-skins of Philistines which had been asked as a dowry and took Michal to wife while

the king looked on helplessly (18:15ff). Next Saul took open
measures; he spoke to Jonathan and all his followers, urging them
to kill David; but when Jonathan reasoned with him, urging
David's past services and present loyalty, the generous nature of
the king broke through the cloud of his suspicion and he swore
to his son that David should not be put to death (19:1ff). Soon
however came news that David had distinguished himself afresh
in overcoming the Philistines, and the former fear returned. Sweeping aside all concealment he tried to kill David with his spear,
as the younger man was playing before him to dispel his depression; and when David slipped from him he sent to arrest him in
his own house. Had not the resourceful Michal contrived her
husband's escape Saul would undoubtedly have put David to death.
This act of his daughter must have confirmed Saul in his belief
that every one was now working against him to preserve David
(19:8ff).

Hatred of David now became a monomania with the king.
When, according to one strand of narrative, Jonathan made an
experiment to see whether his father was indeed set on David's
destruction, Saul turned on his son with fury. "Thou son of a
perverse and rebellious woman, do not I know that thou hast
chosen the son of Jesse to thine own shame, and unto the shame
of thy mother's nakedness? For as long as the son of Jesse liveth
upon the ground, thou shalt not be established, nor thy kingdom."
The high spirited Jonathan retorted with a demand to know what
David had done to deserve death and Saul hurled at him his ever
ready spear. Plainly, the obsession of the king had reached an acute
stage (20:24ff). The same virulence appears in another scene,
where Saul, sitting in Gibeah under a tamarisk tree, his spear in
his hand, burst forth against his own trusted Benjamites standing
about him. "Hear now, ye Benjamites; will the son of Jesse give
every one of you fields and vineyards, will he make you all captains of thousands and captains of hundreds, that all of you
have conspired against me, and there is none that discloseth to me
when my son maketh a league with the son of Jesse, and there is
none of you that is sorry for me, or discloseth unto me that my
son hath stirred up my servant against me, to lie in wait, as at this
day?" These are not indeed the words of an insane man, for
Saul was acute enough to read the situation: his most loyal friends
were trying to prevent his murder of David, realizing that his
accusations were groundless. But such outbursts reveal a mental
condition that had got far from the normal. And the sequel

confirms this. Learning from the Edomite herdsman Doeg what
no Israelite would have revealed, that David had stopped at Nob
in his flight and been kindly received by the priests of the sanctuary,
Saul ordered Ahimelech and all his family to be haled before
him. When the terrified Ahimelech protested his entire loyalty
(there is no reason why we should not believe him in spite of the
suspicion, occasionally voiced by scholars, that he knew more about
the matter than he cared to reveal) Saul pushed aside his protestations and commanded the "runners" to kill him and his fellow
priests. Aghast at such sacrilege and doubtless convinced of Ahimelech's innocence, the runners refused to carry out the order. But
the compliant Doeg, who had no such scruples, performed the
executioner's task and presently the spectators saw eighty-five priests,
clad in the sacred ephod, lying murdered. Nor did the fury
of the king stop here: Doeg went on to Nob and killed everything
living, men, women, children, babies, oxen, asses and sheep. To justify such a deed against public horror and the resistance of his own
conscience Saul could only plead: "Their hand also is with David;
and they knew that he fled, and did not disclose it to me" (22:6ff).

These violent outbreaks however did not capture David, who
was now at large in Judah at the head of an increasing band of
outlaws. The rest of Saul's story, as recorded in our sources, is
largely taken up with his efforts to apprehend the fugitive. Attended by an armed force he scoured Judah, following up every
rumour of David's whereabouts. Once he thought he would get
him in the walled village of Keilah, which David had entered
after rescuing it from an inroad of the Philistines; and had not
David and his men left it the inhabitants would probably have
given him up to Saul (23:1-13). At another time the men of
the village of Ziph actually sent word to Saul that David was in
their neighbourhood, offering the king every assistance in capturing
him (23:19ff). Saul was touched by their good will, but the plan
fell through.

It was during this breathless time, when David was often near
capture, that there occurred a remarkable incident. It has been
reported to us in two forms, showing that it made a deep impression on the popular mind (24 and 26); but the same features
characterize both stories and are doubtless based on reliable tradition.
Saul fell into David's power, and David let him go. According
to both narratives he and Saul exchanged words of great significance. David made himself known to the king and showed how
he had refused to take revenge; urging that his forbearance proved

him guiltless of the designs against Saul with which he was charged. Saul was overcome. All his old affection for the younger man swept back. "Is this thy voice, my son David?" he exclaimed, breaking into weeping. "Thou art more righteous than I; for thou hast rendered unto me good, whereas I have rendered unto thee evil. . . . And now, behold, I know that thou shalt surely be king, and the kingdom of Israel shall be established in thy hand. Swear therefore unto me by Yahweh, that thou wilt not cut off my seed after me, and that thou wilt not destroy my name out of my father's house" (24:16ff). The other account makes his confession even more explicit: "I have sinned: return, my son David; for I will no more do thee harm, because my life was precious in thine eyes this day: behold, I have played the fool, and have erred exceedingly" (26:21).

The psychological truth of these utterances is beyond question. At bottom Saul was of a generous nature and he really loved David; his jealousy, suspicion and hatred were due to mental disorder, which often causes the sufferer to turn against those he holds most dear. The overwhelming proof of David's magnanimity and the sound of the well remembered voice brought in a flood of healing emotion that for the moment carried the king quite out of his diseased condition. The frankness with which he acknowledged his fault was undoubtedly characteristic. Very real also was the way in which he opened his fears. The picture of David as king "cutting off" the family of his predecessor—a common procedure in a change of dynasty—must have been ever present in his harassed mind. Altogether the revelation of Saul is very touching. We have here a glimpse of what this man's life might have been had he trusted David instead of turning against him. It shows also why it was that people loved him, as unquestionably they did, even in his disfiguring depression. But the generous mood could not last. Both Jonathan (cf. 19:7) and David knew that promises and oaths would never withstand the return of the next black mood. The pursuit of David went on.

Finally, the danger of David became so imminent that David sought refuge with the Philistines. This took him quite out of Saul's grasp and the king dropped the hunt.

Saul's Death

There was now leisure for Saul to contemplate the situation in which he and his people stood. And indeed it needed thought.

Whether or no his efforts to capture David had led the king to drop measures against the Philistines for a time, it is certain that matters had taken an evil turn for Israel. We have seen how the old battle-fury of Saul had suffered an eclipse. This was compensated for to some extent by the rise of a younger group of military leaders, such as David, but Israel's fighting force must none the less have felt a subtle demoralization because of the king's loss of spirit. When David was compelled to flee, the country was deprived of its outstanding champion; and now that it was known that he had gone over to the enemy all his prestige would be cast into the opposing scale. At any rate, the Philistines believed that the hour had come to regain their former domination of Israel. They gathered all their hosts together to fight with Israel (28:1) and pouring through one of the passes from the plain of Sharon they entered the plain of Esdraelon and encamped in Shunem just where it debouches into the valley of Jezreel. Robinson thinks that here they were joined by forces from Beth-shan, farther down the valley. Rumour doubtless had it that David and his men were with them.

Against this formidable army Saul mobilized the Israelitish host, encamping high above the valley on mount Gilboa to the south. But his confidence was gone. Terrified by the strength of the enemy he had recourse to Yahweh as his only hope. What would Yahweh do? Often in days gone by the king had made such inquiry of the priestly oracle; but now the sole survivor of the priestly family had taken the oracle to David. He asked of prophets, but there was no "answer of God" (cf. Mic. 3:7). No dreams came to reveal the divine purpose. In his desperation the distracted king had recourse to one of the mediums whom he had endeavoured to exterminate. The narrative is a vivid one. We see the disguised Saul stalking in the darkness across the valley of Jezreel to the home of the medium at Endor, hear him ask for Samuel, after quieting the fears of the woman, and listen to the words of doom that come to him through the mouth of the necromancer, voicing the forebodings of his own conscience. "Wherefore dost thou ask of me, seeing that Yahweh is departed from thee, and is become thine adversary? . . . Yahweh will deliver Israel with thee into the hands of the Philistines; and tomorrow shalt thou and thy sons be with me." At the fatal words Saul collapsed, falling his great length upon the ground and shaking with terror. Then the woman intervened, urging him with respectful affection to eat. He refused, but his companions added their voice to that of the medium and constrained him. "So he arose from the earth, and sat upon the bed" while the woman made hasty preparations for a meal, giving him the best she had. It is a scene that does honour to these nameless people who stood by the king in his darkest hour, the men knowing that they would share his fate. But perhaps more than they does the king compel our admiration, when he pulls himself together, in spite of his mental sickness, eats and strides out again into the night, tramping the twelve weary miles back to Gilboa and climbing its steep side, perhaps just as the day was breaking, to set the hopeless battle in array (28).

The Philistines were not long in attacking. Pressing up the slopes of mount Gilboa they struck down the men of Israel and "followed hard upon Saul and upon his sons." One by one these fell—Jonathan, Abinadab, Malchi-shua. On came the archers, driving at Saul. Disdaining to be captured he fell upon his own sword, his armourbearer doing the same at his side. Today as one looks up from the valley of Jezreel to the lofty promontory of Gilboa jutting out into the plain, he may well think that it was no unworthy place for the tall king to die.

To the story of the battle there is appended a notice whose simple words need no comment.

"And it came to pass on the morrow, when the Philistines came to strip the slain, that they found Saul and his three sons fallen in mount Gilboa. And they cut off his head, and stripped off his armour, and sent into the land of the Philistines round about, to carry the tidings unto the house of their idols, and to the people. And they put his armour in the house of the Ashtaroth; and they fastened his body to the wall of Beth-shan. And when the inhabitants of Jabesh-gilead heard concerning him that which the Philistines had done to Saul, all the valiant men arose, and went all night, and took the body of Saul and the bodies of his sons from the wall of Beth-shan; and they came to Jabesh and burnt them there. And they took their bones and buried them under the tamarisk tree in Jabesh, and fasted seven days" (I 31:8ff).

An Estimate of Saul

What are we to think of Saul? The Bible brands him as a rejected man. There was in Saul a fatal weakness. With all his zeal for Yahweh he could not be depended upon to obey Yahweh's will. Under pressure he would go his own way rather than the

way he himself conceived to be God's. He lacked the power to
subordinate the impulse of the moment to the long advantage of
the future—lacked the self-control and foresight that so characterized David. He forgot the higher issues involved in the scene
before him, the massive divine purpose controlling man's history.
We may call this trait self-will. For at bottom he did not forget, he
simply disregarded duty or explained it away. But—and here is the
baffling thing about Saul—he could not disobey light-heartedly.
Always there pursued him the spectre of doom, the forebodings
of an evil conscience. He refused indeed to acquiesce, striving all
the more madly to regain the success which he felt to be slipping
from him, giving way to hatred and jealousy, striking out in
paroxysms of fury and justifying his most barbarous acts—but he
could never shake himself free from the sense of impending retribution, never come out into peace.

Obviously he was no man to be entrusted with absolute power:
and absolute, for all its democracy, the monarchy of Israel was.
Samuel saw truly. Yahweh must find a better man for His king.

And yet as we survey his life we cannot write him down a
failure. For one thing, he measurably carried out the work for
which he was anointed. If he could not reduce the Philistines to
powerlessness he taught Israel to stand up to them. At the end
the Philistines did indeed triumph, fastening the headless bodies
of him and his sons in derision to the walls of Beth-shan, and
overrunning Israel as in days gone by. But it was their final hour.
They might have taken an omen from the fact that the bodies
disappeared within twenty-four hours. David, building on Saul's
foundation, quickly disposed of these former oppressors. Never
again did they seriously menace Israel.

Nor was Saul's resistance to the Philistines his only military
accomplishment. After making all allowance for the exaggeration
of our sources, we must attribute to him and to his knightly son
Jonathan brilliant prowess on the field of battle, and many successes.
It was this that David celebrated in his elegy over the fallen
heroes:

"Thy adornment, Israel, upon thy high places is slain!
How are the mighty men fallen! . . .
From the blood of the slain, from the fat of the mighty
The bow of Jonathan turned not back
And the sword of Saul returned not empty. . . .
They were swifter than eagles, they were stronger than lions.

Daughters of Israel, weep over Saul,
Who clothed you in scarlet, with luxuries,
Who brought up ornaments of gold upon your garments!
How are the mighty men fallen
In the midst of the battle!" (II 1:19ff).

And Saul was not merely a warrior. He unified the nation and kept its undivided loyalty to the end. His "servants" did not oppose his outrages but made allowance for him and held to him still. This was due partly to his ability and real accomplishments; but still more to something in the man himself. His must have been a kingly personality. Saul was a stately man, of tall and commanding presence, one to be reckoned with wherever he appeared, tremendous in elemental force, a leader whom people feared and followed and adored. For Saul had the "genius to be loved." And he himself could love. One feels this through all his unhappy story. He loved Samuel, but much more, in spite of his hatred, he loved David. Nor can we forget that Jonathan, the knightly-hearted, held close to his father to the last. Saul made more of a success in dealing with his sons than did David, and this appears specially in the tie between him and Jonathan. The affection of these two volcanic natures was destined to live on in the song of David who knew them both:

"Saul and Jonathan! The lovely and pleasant in their lives!
And in their death they were not divided!" (II 1:23).

As the people gave their loyalty to Saul, so he gave himself to them. His "zeal for the sons of Israel and of Judah" might lead him into lawless measures, but no one doubted its genuineness. In spite of his jealousy for his own house and the excesses to which it drove him, he had something of that power to lose himself in his people that characterized the greater men of Israel. It was some such sense of commitment, some such dumb imperative, that made him pull himself together after the medium had conveyed his final sentence of doom and go out into the night. He would fight through to the end.

Finally, for all his self-will, he never wavered in his devotion to Yahweh. His religion was indeed darkened by superstition; his God was the War-God of fierce primitive days, concerned for *herems,* curses, taboos; and he did not obey Him when it cost too much; but still he was loyal. It was from Yahweh that he got his battle-fury. Even the prophetic writers who condemn him lay against him no charge of baalism. And he was in earnest, as we have said. The conversion which he experienced the day he was anointed did not fade.

The question may well be asked: Was he responsible for his actions? We have not gone far in his story before we become aware that we are dealing with a disordered mind. But was he to blame for the disorder? It is always hard to fix the boundary between responsible and irresponsible conduct. Samuel indeed was not concerned to do so, nor were the later prophetic historians. They assumed that he was to blame, and passed sentence. We, who should like to press behind their judgment, are baffled by the meagreness of our sources and the inconsistencies of the man himself. We must be content to leave him an enigma.

Only it is grateful that the last estimate of Saul in the Bible is given, not by Samuel or the prophetic historians, but by the men of Jabesh-gilead and by David.[1]

[1] The author is indebted to Dr. G. Ernest Wright for the following illuminating comment: "More might be made of Saul from the economic standpoint. It was during his reign that the Philistine hegemony was brought to an end and in all probability the secret of iron-smelting was wrested from the Philistines who had jealously guarded it to this time. This meant that the Israelites learned how to use metal, whereas in the period of the Judges 'there was no smith found throughout all the land of Israel' (I Sam. 13:19). The result was a tremendous boom for the Israelites, and David and Solomon were able to build up standing armies. Not only so, but there were great advances made in agriculture because the Israelites were able to make and use iron tools. The earliest iron ploughshare—in other words, the earliest agricultural implement—found in Palestine was discovered in Saul's fortress at Gibeah (see *Annual, ASOR,* IV, p. 17). Other large ploughshares were found at Beth-Shemesh, of approximately the same period. This shows that agriculture was carried on now with iron tools, which were harder and more satisfactory. It involved quite an economic revolution and advance for the Israelites. It was about Saul's time, or not more than two or three decades later, that the semi-circular iron sickle displaced the use of flint; for flint had been employed from the stone age till now, above all for sickles. Apparently, copper and bronze were too soft to make good sickles. So iron drove out this old, old custom." See also Dr. Wright's article "Iron in Israel" in *Biblical Archaeology,* Vol. I, May, 1938, p. 1ff.

Chapter VII

DAVID

[REIGNED 1016–976 B.C.]

Upon the ruins of the house of Saul arose a king who was destined to bring Israel to the zenith of its power and to found a dynasty that would endure for four hundred years. About the name of David clustered in after times a rich profusion of memories, many of which survive in the documents that have come down to us. We know more about him than about any other man in the Old Testament, except Jeremiah.

The Sources

Our chief source for the life and work of David is the historical narrative contained in the two Books of Samuel and the first two chapters of the first Book of the Kings. We have already seen that in the Books of Samuel, or at least in their early part, two strands of narrative are interwoven, one moulded by prophetic writers and displaying a later point of view, the other much earlier, more vivid and faithful to the actual facts. The former strand (B) continues to appear here and there after the story of Samuel closes, but it ceases to be continuous, and is hard to identify. The A narrative however grows more continuous and detailed, supplying an abundance of stories regarding Saul and David, some of which are doublets. This complexity has led Eissfeldt[1] to divide it into two subsidiary sources, one of which he calls the Lay Source (L)— earlier and more reliable for Samuel and Saul, and partly for David —and the other the Yahwist Source (J), which builds on L but introduces much of the legendary. Most scholars however are content to regard A as a unity, in spite of doublets, some of which indeed they assign to B; and to accept what it tells of David as on the whole reliable. Sellin[2] is but expressing the general opinion

[1] *EAT*, p. 310ff.
[2] *EAT*⁷, p. 71 (*IOT*, p. 114).

when he cites the words of the historian Eduard Meyer:[3] "The narratives concerning David teach incontrovertibly by their content that they come from the time of the events themselves, that their narrator must have been very exactly informed as to the doings at court and the character and intrigues of the personalities involved; they cannot have been put into writing later than the reign of Solomon." This reliability is specially acknowledged in the case of a block of chapters (II 9-20; I Ki. 1-2) which tell of the happenings in David's court. Here scholars find an account so graphic and convincing that it could come only from an eyewitness of the events described.

The B narrative, on the other hand, is regarded with the same caution by scholars when it tells of David as when it portrays Samuel. To it is generally assigned the account of David's killing of Goliath (I 17) and the story of Nathan's forbidding David to build a temple (II 7). Some of the doublets in the history of David's relations with Saul are also included in it, but since these seem no more, or very little more, unreliable than the corresponding "A" doublets, it is better to assign them also to the A tradition. A few unclassified stories, such as Samuel's anointing of David (I 16:1-13) and David's taking refuge with Samuel (I 19:18-24) are (as we have already seen) generally regarded as legendary.

So much for the Samuel-Kings material. Another copious source for the study of David might seem to be the long account of him given in the First Book of Chronicles (11-29). But on examination this is seen to be made up in part of material taken from Samuel-Kings, and in part of narratives which so remake the figure of David as to bear on their face the stamp of improbability. We shall consider them when we come to our study of the Chronicler— and very interesting they are as revealing his point of view; but for the history of David they must be accounted almost if not quite valueless.[4]

David is mentioned frequently in the Bible outside the Books of Samuel and the Kings, but such allusions add almost no new information to what those books tell us. It is from them accordingly that we must gain our picture of the great king and his religion and to them we turn, happy in the abundant and generally trustworthy data with which they supply us.

---

[3] *Die Israeliten und ihre Nachbarstämme* (Halle, 1906), p. 485.

[4] It is now generally recognized that tradition was mistaken in ascribing many of the Psalms to David, and we cannot therefore use the Psalms as a source in our study.

David's Rise to Fame

No more romantic story is to be found in the world's literature than that of the shepherd boy of Bethlehem who won a king's favour, then lost it and became a hunted outlaw, only to be made king himself and to place his little people on a proud imperial height; then sinned deeply and saw nemesis work itself out in his house till he died a heart-broken old man in the midst of the splendour he had created. It is no wonder, as Kittel says, that the minstrels and story-tellers of Israel delighted to tell of him.

Not long before the year 1000 B.C. David was keeping his father Jesse's sheep in the vicinity of Bethlehem. Tradition says that he was the youngest of eight brothers, some of whom had a striking and impressive appearance. David himself is described as "red, a youth [1] fair of eyes, good to look at" (I 16:6ff). Among a people prevailingly dark his red hair and ruddy skin at once distinguished him. He must have possessed even as a lad the unique charm of person and manner that later won friends wherever he went. He had in addition a remarkable gift for music, playing on the *kinnor* (harp, lyre) to the pleasure of all hearers and doubtless singing at the same time songs of his own improvisation—an ability still to be found among the Arabs [2] (I 16:14ff). For warfare he had a natural aptitude, being a ferocious and daring fighter endowed with deadly skill. Even as a shepherd boy, tradition affirms, he displayed this, long before he ever faced an enemy in the field; for a lion or bear that attacked his flock had little chance in the encounter that ensued (I 17:34ff); and we may be sure that robbers learned to let his sheep alone. But the most outstanding thing about David was his mind. He could see into a situation with unerring accuracy and choose just the effective way of meeting it; and his will was strong enough to follow out his chosen course with tenacity and patience as well as with prompt daring when the need might be. Add to all this a deep religious devotion, probably from childhood, and a generous nature which inclined him in spite of his astuteness to open-handed and magnanimous dealings, and we obtain the portrait of a youth destined to make his mark on men.

Of his father Jesse nothing distinctive is known. He must have been a man of some means and position in the rural community of

---

[1] According to a probable reading.

[2] Amos (6:5) seems to preserve a tradition that he invented new musical instruments.

Bethlehem. Tradition says that he was the grandson of Boaz the landholder who had married the Moabitess Ruth "in the days of the Judges," which would give David a strain of Moabitish blood in his veins (Ruth 4:21f). The Bethlehem of that day was probably very different in appearance from the modern Christian town with its noble church and other imposing buildings, but it must none the less have been a fair sight, its stone houses rising one above the other on the graceful hill which can be seen from so many places in the surrounding country. David loved the well by the gate for whose cold water he once expressed a longing in the heat of battle (II 23:15). He must also have made himself at home among the tangled heights and valleys that adjoin Bethlehem, learning how to find water and grass for his sheep in the dry season when the brooks fail and to ward off the attacks of wild beasts and bandits—knowledge which was to prove useful to him in his outlaw days when he and his men made the wilderness of Judah their refuge. From the town itself he could gain a sweeping view across stone-strewn grain fields and pastures of the hills that tumble down to the Dead Sea and of the opalescent rampart of the Moabite plateau on the eastern horizon. This was the northern end of Judah, abutting on the land of Benjamin and only five miles from the Jebusite stronghold of Jerusalem which David was one day to make his capital. For David was a man of Judah, the tribe that had always tended to remain aloof from its northern brethren, preserving more than they the austere customs and traditions of wilderness days. In David's boyhood however it seems to have been giving cordial allegiance to the Benjamite king Saul.

The time came when the young shepherd of Bethlehem attracted the notice of the warrior king. Two different accounts of this survive. The longer and best known is the story of David's fight with Goliath, one of the supreme bits of narrative in the Bible. It tells how the unknown boy, too young as yet to be a soldier, visited his brothers at the front, heard the insolent challenge of the Philistine giant, offered to take it up, was brought before the king and clothed with Saul's own armour for the fray; how he put it off, as untried, met the champion only with his faith in Yahweh and his accustomed sling and struck him down, bringing victory to the Israelites. Because of this feat Saul took him into military service and seeing his success in arms soon put him over the men of war, with the approval of every one. David's exploit also brought him the friendship of Jonathan, Saul's son, who loved

David as his own soul, clothing him with his own garments and fitting him out with his own armour (I 17:1-18:5).

This story is preceded by a shorter account which relates how David was invited to Saul's presence in order to dispel the king's depression by his music. He was recommended by "one of the young men" as "skilful in playing, and a mighty man of valour, and a man of war, and prudent in speech" (perhaps, "understanding business") "and a comely person." Saul thereupon asked his father Jesse to send David his son, who was with the sheep. Jesse complied and David, arriving with a present from his father to the king, won Saul's love and became his armourbearer. His playing also proved a cure for the king's black moods (I 16:14ff).

It is plain that these two accounts cannot be reconciled, unless indeed one follows the lead of the Greek translators of the Old Testament, who saw the contradictions and boldly dropped out of the Goliath story everything inconsistent with the shorter account.[3] But if, as is generally thought, we must take the stories as they stand, we must choose between them. Of the two, the Goliath story is by far the more improbable, especially since what seems to be a reliable notice in II 21:19 attributes the killing of Goliath to another man from Bethlehem, Elhanan. The shorter account is therefore regarded as the earlier. True, it contains an apparent inconsistency; for if David were already approved as a competent warrior how could he have shown himself such unless in the fighting led by Saul, where his prowess would have become widely known at once. And again, why was he with the sheep and not in the army? Some scholars look on the whole account as a bit of romance. Perhaps it is; but the wiser course is probably to treat it as trustworthy tradition, seeing it is early, and fits in with the rest of the narratives very well.

David then exchanged the work of a shepherd for a brilliant military career. He was supremely the kind of man Saul had been gathering about him to form his shock troops, and the king gave him generous recognition by appointing him his armourbearer. Even when Saul's first jealousy led him to transfer David from his personal service to the command of a thousand the change worked for the young man's increasing popularity and fame. Kittel[4]

[3] Of course it is *possible* that they had before them a Hebrew text that contained none of the contradictions, and that this was the original text, the contradictions having been added later. But it is most *improbable* that such was the case.

[4] *GMMI,* p. 116.

paints in glowing colours the irresistible charm of David, who knew how to combine deadliness in combat with the power of improvisation in song and open engaging ways which checked all resentment at his rapid rise. Even the proud princess Michal lost her heart to him and presently, in spite of his own protests of unworthiness, he became the son-in-law of the king (I 18:13ff). He was now at the pinnacle of his early glory.

David as Outlaw

We have already seen the alteration that took place in Saul's feelings toward David when he heard the song of the women giving his armourbearer greater praise than himself, and the steps that he took to rid himself of this favourite in whom he now beheld a pretender to the throne. It was during the perilous days of Saul's concealed enmity that David made full proof of the love of Jonathan towards himself. The prince must have been in a most painful position, for he loved his father and enjoyed pleasant companionship with him; yet he loved David, and believed him innocent of any designs against Saul. If he worked with David—and he seems to have done so—it was not from any disloyalty to his father, though the king's darkened mind could not see this. Our accounts relate only how he strove to protect David, and that was the extent of the "conspiracy" (I 22:8) of which Saul accused him.[1]

The efforts of Jonathan proved vain. David was compelled to escape for his life. And now began for him a period when on no day he could be sure of his life: "there was but a step between him and death" (I 20:3). Reaching his home neighbourhood he took refuge in the "cave of Adullam," one of the limestone cavities in which the region of the Shephelah abounds. It was situated in the hills of Judah some twelve miles southwest of Bethlehem. Thither came men as desperate as himself to join his band. "Every one that was in distress, and every one that was in debt, and every one that was bitter of soul, gathered themselves unto him; and he became captain over them; and there were with him about four hundred

[1] Kittel, *GMMI,* p. 126, indeed thinks that he went further, that perceiving his father's growing incapacity for his office he got David to plan with him for Saul's removal. His aim in that case would have been to assume the kingship, or a sort of regency, with David as his right hand man; or perhaps he would have agreed to David being king of Judah while he himself governed the rest of Israel. But however such a picture may commend itself to us as possible, we must turn from it as a work of the imagination, and confine ourselves to our sources.

men." Among these were "his brethren, and all his father's house," whom David's supposed crime had placed in jeopardy. We may picture the latter as a stalwart group. Perhaps they included in their number three of David's step-nephews, Joab, Abishai and Asahel, the sons of Zeruiah, who were to play so prominent a part in his story. His father and mother he had already provided for by taking them for safe-keeping to the king of Moab, upon whose friendship he could for some reason count (I 22:1ff).

This band of outlaws had two great needs. One was, to avoid capture; the other, to get as best they could food and plunder. For the satisfaction of both they looked to David; and nowhere were his adroitness and leadership more brilliantly exhibited than in his handling of these tough men. They had their families with them and so the burden of providing food and of keeping the women pleased with presents was no light one. David, their captain, however had still a third need. He was building for future leadership on a large scale. In particular he wanted to make himself popular with his own tribe of Judah. This prevented him from preying upon the Judahites; plunder must come from another source. His problem therefore was a complicated one; but he solved it. His band made raids on the enemies of the Judahites and the elders of Judah were given a share in the spoils.[2] To the sheep-owning landholders of southern Judah he extended protection against robbers and could claim contributions for this service (I 25:6ff). He was careful to appear always as a friend. On one occasion he drove off Philistine raiders from the village of Keilah (I 23:1ff). As for the other need, that of safety, David was at first able to prevent capture, though this required constant motion and many were the narrow escapes. It was during these rushings about for cover that Saul unknowingly fell into David's power and experienced his magnanimity (I 24 and 26).[3] Once the same quality was exercised towards a private landholder who had excited his rage by insolently refusing David's request for protection money. The churlish Calebite Nabal came near to paying for his contempt with his life, but the intercession of his gracious wife Abigail averted destruction from the whole household and led to David's marriage with her when she presently became a widow (I 25).

All this while David was moulding his band of outlaws into the

[2] This took place after he went over to the Philistines and there is reason to suppose that it was true of the time preceding (I 27:8ff).

[3] Perhaps, as Kittel seems to think, these chapters are not doublets and the situation indeed occurred twice.

most effective fighting unit that Israel ever possessed, creating the nucleus of a future army which was to know no defeat. In this process his right hand man was Joab, well seconded by his brother Abishai. On them David learned to depend as on no others and they became a potent factor in his later success.

Finally, however, the pressure grew too strong and David felt himself compelled to seek asylum with the Philistines. What an impression it must have made upon these enemies that had so often felt his heavy hand when he and his men appeared as deserters! The four hundred had now grown to six hundred, and with the redoubtable David at their head what terror and consternation would they strike into the minds of the Israelites when aligned against them as enemies! So apparently thought Achish, king of Gath, for he received David cordially. David had an open way about him that won confidence even where he was playing a part.

But his success in gaining Achish's trust could not have obscured from David the desperate situation in which he was now involved. Achish of course expected him to fight against Saul and the Israelites and would see to it that David merited their hatred as a renegade. In particular Achish looked to him to make raids against Judah. Then what chance of ever becoming leader, perhaps king of Judah? David met the problem with a bold fraud. Obtaining from Achish the gift of a remote village, Ziklag, on the very borders of Judah, he was enabled to move his men from Gath where they were under constant observation and settle them at a convenient distance from his overlord. From there he made repeated raids, not upon Judah, but upon the clans friendly to the Philistines, pretending to Achish that he was attacking Judah all the while. In order to preserve secrecy it was necessary for David to kill all his captives. Achish, seeing the spoil and imagining that it meant David's final alienation from his own people, was delighted. Actually however part of the spoil was going as presents to the elders of Judah! (I 27:1ff).

How long David could have continued to throw dust in the eyes of Achish we cannot say; but his raids were presently interrupted by a summons to join the forces of the Philistines in the great concerted attack on Israel in which Saul was to lose his life. David obeyed. Now the crisis could no longer be evaded. He must either fight in battle against Israel or go over to the other side. And if he did that he would fall once more into Saul's power. But David did not have to decide. The marvellous good luck that so often attended him came to his rescue. The other Philistine leaders turned on Achish and compelled him to send David and his men home from the very plain of Jezreel. David's secret joy did not prevent him from lodging an indignant protest, to which Achish responded with a profuse apology! (I 29:1ff). But David must have known that the day of reckoning was only postponed.

What followed marks the lowest ebb of David's fortunes. When he and his men reached Ziklag after two days' exhausting march they found it destroyed and their families gone. The Amalekites had availed themselves of their absence to take revenge for David's raids. For the moment David lost his hold on his men. In their rage and anguish they talked of stoning him. But David remained undaunted. At this hour his religious faith came to his support: "he strengthened himself in Yahweh his God." Some time since, after Saul had wiped out the priestly city of Nob, Abiathar had escaped to David bringing the apparatus of the priestly oracle with him; and David had then begun to "inquire of God" before any important step. The oracle was called into use now, and encouraged by its response David immediately led his men in pursuit of the raiders. These were overtaken and captives and spoils recovered. It was in this hour of success that David opposed the majority of his men and insisted that even those who had been too exhausted to keep up the pursuit should none the less share equally in the spoil (I 30).

Two days after David got back to Ziklag news came that Saul was dead in battle. His period of outlawry had come to an end.

David Made King of Israel

David at once acted with the comprehension and alertness that characterized him. It is plain that he had long been working to gain the headship of Judah, and the death of Saul and three of his sons opened up the prospect of becoming king also over all Israel. One thing seems to have been clear to him: he must identify himself as much as possible with Saul and inherit his "good will." When a young Amalekite came with the news of Saul's death and related how he had killed Saul at the king's own request, David immediately put him to death for destroying Yahweh's anointed. He then made lamentation over the fallen king and princes in a beautiful elegy that, as has been well said, does honour to both him and them. We need not think that these manifestations of esteem and love were feigned. On the contrary, they were natural outpourings of David's affectionate disposition. At the same time they were good policy, and David must have felt this. As in the past, so now, his generosity was his best prompter.

Next, after receiving direction from the priestly oracle, David and his men went up to Hebron, the ancient town identified in tradition with Abraham, in the very centre of Judah. He brought his two wives and his men also brought their households. Thus he announced that he had quit the Philistines and intended to make Judah his home. And now he reaped the fruit of all his previous care to make friends of his own tribesmen. There was a gathering of the men of Judah at Hebron and David by popular choice was anointed king over the house of Judah.

Whatever may have been the purpose of the Judahites in taking this step, it is clear that David's ambition looked beyond Judah. This is seen in his message to the men of Jabesh-gilead, praising and blessing them for their kindness to Saul in burying "their lord" and announcing that he himself intended to requite their kindness. "Now therefore," it concluded, "let your hands be strong and be ye valiant; for Saul your lord is dead, and also the house of Judah have anointed me king over them." David was making a masterly bid for their support of him as a candidate (II 2:1ff).

The time however was not yet ripe. Abner, the captain of Saul's host, quickly set up a surviving son of Saul, Ishbaal, as king over all Israel, and he was able to keep the tribes from Benjamin northward faithful to the dynasty of the dead king. Saul's house was specially strong across the Jordan, whither Abner moved the seat of government, making Mahanaim the centre; but the great tribe of Ephraim and his own tribe of Benjamin also remained loyal. This must have been a severe blow to David's hopes and apparently he did not take it without striking back. At any rate we presently find Joab and a detachment of David's men as far north as Gibeon, where they were confronted by Abner and Benjamite troops. A fight ensued in which Abner, being compelled to flee, struck down the pursuing Asahel, Joab's brother, thus supplying Joab's jealousy with the spur of blood revenge.

This encounter was the beginning of "long war between the house of Saul and the house of David," in which doubtless the former were trying to bring back seceding Judah into an undivided Israel headed by a Benjamite king, and David was trying to break Abner's power. It must have been a bitter time, in which the old antagonism between Judah and the other tribes was deepened. The tide was setting all one way; David grew stronger, Saul's house weaker, as the contest went on.

Historians have of course raised the question, What was the attitude of the Philistines during this time? How did they view David's leaving them to become king of Judah? It is strange that although they had become masters of the country once more by the victory at Gilboa they nowhere appear in the scenes following David's anointing. The answer generally given is probably correct: they regarded David as still their vassal and were glad to see him keeping the house of Saul weak, thus doing their own work for them!

At last, after seven years and a half, during which David built up his royal establishment at Hebron, increasing his harem and begetting more children, Abner made overtures to him. Smarting under a merited rebuke of his puppet king Abner offered to bring over "all Israel" to David. True to his policy of inheriting Saul's "good will," David replied by insisting that his wife Michal, Saul's daughter (who had been given to another man when he fled from Saul), be returned to him before he would negotiate. Abner consented and thus David was once more publicly acknowledged Saul's son-in-law. Abner then managed to persuade the elders of Israel, who by this time must have seen that independence was hopeless, to accept David as king. He was the more able to do this because David in time past had been a popular candidate for the succession, as the one chosen of Yahweh to break the Philistine yoke. So Abner came to Hebron with the kingdom, so to speak, in his pocket, and there was doubtless a good deal of political trading before the matter was finally settled. What David had to promise Abner is not known but the price must have been high.

David however was suddenly freed from his obligation by Joab's treacherous murder of Abner in the gate of Hebron. Joab had his own reasons for getting rid of a threatening rival but to David the deed brought immense relief. He at once disowned it with vigour, honouring Abner with a solemn burial and public mourning and composing over him one of his elegies. However sincere he may have been, he did not punish the murderer, pleading that Joab and Abishai were too strong for him. His plea, his manifest grief and his refusal to eat that day, convinced the people that he was guiltless of complicity [1] (II 3).

With Abner gone, Ishbaal was beaten. Two of his officers promptly murdered him, hoping to gain favour with David the

[1] In Benjamin however the opinion obtained that he was a man of blood, and he may well have been thought there to have had a hand in Abner's murder (II 16:7).

coming man. David at once repudiated their deed and put them
to death. But once more fortune had relieved him of an embarrass-
ing problem (II 4). "All the elders of Israel" soon appeared in
Hebron and made him king of a united nation. After all, they
said, he was their kinsman and had led them in Saul's days; and
had not Yahweh pointed him out as future leader over all Israel?

Thus at thirty-seven David found himself undisputed ruler of
his people. Already he had been king of Judah in Hebron for
seven and a half years, and his reign was destined to continue
thirty-three years longer. He was at the height of his powers,
his mind teeming with plans, his military force able to consummate
them (II 5:1ff).

David's Reign

David's first step was to capture the Jebusite fortress of Jerusalem
and make it his capital, thus avoiding sectional jealousy by selecting
a neutral centre and acquiring an impregnable stronghold for his
seat of government. He doubtless set about improving its fortifications and it is possible that the section of fine wall, flanked by the
bit of sloping glacis, which is still visible on the east side of Ophel
(the ancient Jebus) may belong to David's time.[1] Here, also, with
the assistance of Hiram, king of Tyre, he built himself a royal house
and proceeded to enlarge his harem. With true insight he now
brought the long neglected ark in great pomp to his new city, thus
ensuring that Yahweh would make His home there (II 6). The
idea came to him of building Yahweh a temple to house the
ark, but he was prevented by religious conservatism from carrying
it out: Yahweh, said the prophet Nathan, had always dwelt in a
tent. David's piety however was rewarded by a promise that his
dynasty should be established for ever; in return for which the
king offered up a beautiful thanksgiving. Such at least is the story
as told by prophetic historians at a later time, and it may have
some truth in it (II 7).

It was not long before the new king had to deal with the Philistines. Alarmed by the union of the nation under David they tried
too late to subdue him. But their hour was past. David quickly
disposed of them, reducing them to vassalage. A unique military
opportunity now lay before him. For the moment the great world
powers of Assyria and Egypt were quiescent and the Syrian region
presented a prize to any one of the smaller local states which could
master it. David had the most effective fighting force among them

[1] Albright, *RDBL*, p. 32.

all, and by a series of campaigns he proceeded to bring under his
dominion not only the Philistines but also the Moabites, the Ammonites, the Edomites and the Arameans of the Damascus district.[2]
None could withstand him. Thus the realm of Israel was widened
till it became a miniature empire centring in the "city of David,"
his new capital. Of the way in which this empire was managed
we hear nothing, but the fact that David was able to pass it on
intact to Solomon shows that he kept his hold on it. The transformation must have been indeed a bewildering one, from Saul's
harassed little kingdom to David's secure and imposing domain
sweeping on both sides of Jordan from the Lebanons to the southern desert.

Two results at least took place. One was that the subdued
peoples paid tribute and David became wealthy in a way that had
hitherto been unknown in Israel. This would enable him to
make a material display which could not but impress every one
with the sense of his magnificence. He seems indeed to have kept
his expenditures within bounds, but his court and harem none the
less became regal in splendour and luxury. His city of Jerusalem
doubtless set the pace for other large towns of imperial Israel, and
his luxury would call forth emulation from the leading citizens and
their wives. This was of questionable good for the social morality
of his people, and it may well be that from David's time began
the concentration of wealth in the hands of the few at the expense
of the many which later gave such grave concern to the prophets.
But the worst sufferers from David's swollen income were his own
sons. In the heavy atmosphere of his sumptuous harem, with its
idleness and intrigues, they found little stimulus to acquire the
robust virtues of their father; the more so, as he proved himself
weakly indulgent to their whims and excesses.

A second result was that David's court perforce became some-
what cosmopolitan. He must keep in constant touch with his
dominions and receive as well as send emissaries with frequency.
Through the gates of Jerusalem passed pack-trains bringing tribute.
Phoenician artisans were busy with Phoenician materials building
David's house. The relations between him and Hiram, king of
Tyre, grew extremely cordial (II 5:11; I Ki. 5:1). While yet in
Hebron he had taken as one of his wives the daughter of the neigh-

[2] Assyrian inscriptions show that Zobah (II, 8:3) was situated east of
Antilibanus and north of Damascus. Its king Hadadezer seems to have
conquered Assyrian territory along the upper Euphrates shortly before he was
defeated by David (Albright, *RDBL,* p. 32).

bouring king of Geshur across the Jordan (II 3:3) and a number
of those received later into his harem may have been women highly
connected in adjoining peoples. He seems to have favoured foreign
mercenaries in his army, and his body-guard was made up of
Crethi and *Pelethi,* which may mean "Cretans and Philistines."
Some of these foreigners became his most trusted officers and
served him with devotion.[3] All this tended to mellow Israelitish
narrowness and to make the people more tolerant of foreign ways.
Not that David went to an extreme in his cosmopolitanism, any
more than in his display; but he none the less brought in something
new, something destined to play an increasing part in the national
life and seriously to affect its religion.

How did David govern Israel? Unfortunately our sources are
so occupied with relating his conquests and family experiences that
they give us little information regarding his administration at
home. We do indeed get a glimpse here and there. Faithful to his
oath to his dead friend he treated Jonathan's sole surviving son
with kindness, assuring to him the possession of Saul's lands and
admitting him to his royal table (II 9). Like most of David's
generous acts this was also good policy, for it exhibited David's
magnanimity and at the same time kept Mephibosheth under
David's eye. The rest of Saul's descendants did not fare so well at
his hands. At the demand of the Gibeonites, who wished satisfaction for Saul's unlawful executions, he caused seven of them to
be put to death and hanged up before Yahweh in order to break a
prolonged drought (II 21). At some time in his reign he took a
military census of the population (II 24). Once we see him receiving a suppliant for justice and giving orders for her relief (II
14:4ff). Later in life he seems to have neglected this function of
the king and to have caused great discontent by his failure to provide for the hearing of suits (II 15:2ff). But such neglect hardly
characterized his reign as a whole, for after generations cannot have
been wrong in looking back to it as an era when "justice and righteousness" were executed to all the people (II 8:15). There is no
record of complaint because of taxation, nor indeed of any machinery to collect taxes. One sinister figure however appears in the
list of his officials: "Adoram was over the men subject to task-
work" (II 20:24). Evidently David impressed some of his subjects
to labour on his projects. This Adoram carried on the same work
under Solomon and became a fiercely hated figure (I Ki. 12:18).

[3] Uriah the Hittite (II 11) and Ittai of Gath (II 15:19; 18:2) are well-
known examples.

His employment in such a task shows a despotic feature of David's rule. Other officials of the court were the "recorder" and the "scribe." There must have been offices for the transaction of governmental business over which these presided. But that is all we know.

Power and wealth did not bring happiness to David himself. He seems to have begun to take things easily. Then one day he committed a great crime. While his army was besieging Rabbath Ammon he noticed Bathsheba, the wife of one of his officers, desired and obtained her. Whether or no she herself tried to attract him, his own act remains the same. Presently the husband was sent for to cover up a scandal, but he refused to visit his wife, pleading that he could not indulge in the pleasures of wedlock while his comrades were "encamped in open field." As a result David sent him back to Joab with a letter directing that his death be arranged. The cynical Joab complied and after the conventional mourning was over Uriah's wife became one of David's harem (II 11).

This deed aroused public resentment and "brought Yahweh into great contempt." Nathan the prophet bravely confronted the king with the announcement of divine rebuke and David was man enough to acknowledge his wickedness. Nathan then declared that he was forgiven; but that Yahweh's injured name could only be restored by a terrible act of divine judgment. Bathsheba's child must die; and die it did, in spite of the king's frantic prayer and fasting (II 12).

Nor did the consequences of David's crime cease here. His unbridled act could not but have had its effect upon his sons; at any rate we see an evil genius of lust and murder working itself out in the palace. Amnon desired, forced and then insolently cast off his half-sister Tamar. Her brother Absalom, after biding his time, murdered Amnon and fled to his father-in-law, the king of Geshur. David, who had done nothing to punish Amnon, now refused to permit Absalom's return; but the grim Joab was able to win him over to a compromise. Absalom came back but was shut out from the king's presence. With imperious insistence he broke down this barrier and was reinstated as prince.

But ruthless ambition was in the young man's heart. After four years of display, demagoguery and plotting he broke out into open revolt, causing himself to be proclaimed king. The strength of his following is amazing. David by his aloofness and inaction must have lost much of his hold upon the people for recruits flocked to the rebel standard. David was compelled to flee for his life across the Jordan, where alone he could count on support. The description of his flight is one of the saddest pictures in the Bible. We see the broken-hearted old king toiling up the ascent of the mount of Olives, barefoot, his head covered, weeping as he goes, his men about him weeping. But the gloom is lightened by his humility and magnanimity as well as by the devotion of his followers. When the faithful Zadok and Abiathar came with the ark, intending to carry it along with the fugitive king, he sent it back. When the Benjamite Shimei seized the hour of his abasement to revile and curse him as a man of blood and a man of belial he prevented the incensed Abishai from striking him down. There were touching bits of loyalty displayed by the new-comer Ittai, who declined to leave his lord, and the aged Barzillai, who provided generously for the famished fugitives in Mahanaim. Nor did David's resourcefulness forsake him, for he left his counsellor Hushai behind to defeat the advice of Absalom's infallible Ahitophel (II 15–17).

Hushai succeeded in preventing the immediate pursuit of David which alone could have put him out of the reckoning. Absalom delayed, with fatal results. In a battle across the Jordan David's veterans put the rebel army to disastrous flight and Joab capped his victory by killing Absalom contrary to David's orders. The old king's grief for his son, when he heard the news, banished all joy in his own deliverance; and it was not until Joab had brutally broken in upon him with the threat that his mourning would cause serious disaffection in the troops that he made a show of overcoming it. But the wound made by his son's treachery and unhappy death was never healed. When finally he returned to his capital at the invitation of both Judah and Israel, he entered it (as Kittel says) an old, old man.

His return, like his flight, had its lights and shadows. Against the strenuous protest of Abishai he forgave his reviler Shimei, confirming his pardon by an oath; he contemptuously overlooked the failure of his protegé Mephibosheth to follow him in his flight; he loaded Barzillai with gratitude. But he was not able to prevent a fierce outburst of jealousy between the men of his own tribe of Judah and the men of Israel, who fancied themselves slighted by the king. Revolt started when a Benjamite Sheba blew the trumpet and uttered the ominous war-cry that was to sound with such effect two generations later:

"We have no portion in David, and we have no inheritance in the
    son of Jesse!
Every man to his tents, Israel!"

This time it failed through the prompt measures of David, carried
out by the ruthless Joab. Once more David ruled over all Israel.
But he had needed to use all his skill in intrigue to accomplish
the result, for the invitation to return did not come to him spontaneously; and the sword had to be called in to make his restoration
complete. One particular bit of manipulation ended in tragedy.
Partly in revenge for Joab's killing of Absalom, and partly to
win back the support of the north, David had promised to make
Amasa, Absalom's general, captain of the host instead of Joab. The
change was actually carried into effect; but David found he could
not do without Joab, and the latter once more freed his lord from
an uncomfortable situation by a cold-blooded murder. Amasa soon
lay wallowing in his own blood on the roadside (II 18–20).

Two more scenes of David's career pass before us. One when
he lay in extreme senile decrepitude, the fire of his lust still im-
potently burning, heedless of what was afoot in the realm. Suddenly Bathsheba, prompted by Nathan the prophet, invaded his
vacuity with the news that another son whom he had overindulged,
Adonijah, was seizing the throne which David (so she claimed)
had sworn to hand down to her own son Solomon. Roused to a
flicker of his old vigour the aged king gave orders that Solomon
should be proclaimed his successor, while the faction supporting
Adonijah were holding a great feast down the Kidron valley at
what seems to have been an ancient sanctuary. His orders were
at once carried out by the Solomon faction and Adonijah's guests,
surprised by the uproar coming from the distant city, soon understood that they had been outwitted and sought safety in dispersing.
Solomon was king (I Ki. 1).

The last scene reveals the dying David giving his final charge to
the new king. The Deuteronomic editor has put into his mouth a
noble injunction to walk in the ways of Yahweh, that Solomon
might prosper and inherit the divine promise of an assured dynasty.
Doubtless David may have said something like this. But the words
which follow are all that is preserved of the ancient source. In
them David commanded his successor to show kindness to his benefactor Barzillai and to visit with a bloody death two men whom
for different reasons he himself had not been able to execute—

Joab the murderer of Abner and Amasa, and Shimei the Benjamite reviler who had cursed him (I Ki. 2:1ff).

So he died. With him passed the real builder of the Israelitish state and incomparably the greatest ruler who ever sat upon its throne. We have already reviewed his reign and appraised some of its outstanding features.

But David was more than Israel's supreme king; he was a significant landmark in the development of its religion. Let us now consider some of the things that characterized him as a religious man.

David's Devotion to Yahweh

From first to last David was an enthusiast for Yahweh. On this point our records leave no doubt. It is not only that he kept clear of baal worship, which indeed lies so far below the horizon that it is not even mentioned in the narratives concerning him. His was no mere negative loyalty, but a passionate devotion to a personal Being who had loved him and given him all that he possessed. At every step he acknowledged Yahweh's favour and sought His honour. When Michal upbraided him for dancing before the ark he replied: "It was before Yahweh, who chose me above thy father, and above all his house, to appoint me prince over the people of Yahweh, over Israel: therefore will I play before Yahweh. And I will be yet more vile than this, and will be base in mine own sight . . ." (II 6:21f). When it came to expressing his feeling for Yahweh personal dignity might well be thrown to the winds.

Saul however had done as much as this. David's devotion went further. It took the practical form of seeking constantly to learn Yahweh's will and to follow it when known.

For this purpose he inquired frequently through the priestly oracle. His practice of doing so had already begun before he was compelled to flee from Saul. While still in the service of Saul he had gone a number of times to Nob, the city of the priests, and obtained divine responses through the ill-fated Ahimelech. When later the escaped Abiathar brought the oracle apparatus (*ephod*, I 30:7) into David's camp, there began a period in which David took no important step without first consulting Yahweh by its means. However primitive his belief in the oracle may seem to us, we must realize that by so using it he intended to put himself unreservedly into Yahweh's hands.

This practice seems to have ceased after the ark was placed in Jerusalem, for the narrative makes no more mention of its occurrence. But David's attitude remained unaltered. Two instances are given of commands coming to him through prophets. A famous chapter of the B source tells us that at the word of Yahweh through Nathan David gave up his cherished plan of building a temple for the ark. At another time he obeyed a command given by "the prophet Gad, David's seer," to rear an altar on the threshing floor of Araunah the Jebusite (II 24:18ff).

But David's truest submission is seen in a number of instances where the *ethical* will of Yahweh must be obeyed. These will be presently considered. Here we need only point out that for the most part they did not involve the mediation of oracle or prophet, but were decisions made at the promptings of David's own conscience. For this reason they seem more like our own experience. Moreover to our modern way of thinking they were much more important as evidences of David's desire to obey God than his following of external directions to make this or that military move, to build or not to build a temple.

In general the impression made upon us by the sources is that David's habitual attitude towards Yahweh was one of humble and loving trust. What God desired for him he was content to accept. This does not mean that he waited in idleness for God to work on his behalf. Whatever a man could rightly do to help himself, David did. But he differed from Saul in that he consistently refused to seize a coveted prize before Yahweh was willing for him to have it. This appears plainly in his conduct before he was made king. No one could bide his time better than David. Of course it is possible to see in this only a wise policy; but it probably went deeper than considerations of mere expediency. David was really biding *God's* time. The same trait of surrender is seen in his demeanour during Absalom's rebellion. "Carry back the ark of God into the city," he said to Zadok. "If I shall find favour in the eyes of Yahweh, he will bring me again and show me both it and his habitation: but if he say thus, I have no delight in thee; behold, here am I, let him do to me as seemeth good unto him" (II 15:25-26). Humility was even harder when Nathan came to denounce his crime with Bathsheba. The prophet who approached a king with such a message might well be taking his life in his hand. But to Nathan's "Thou art the man" David answered only, "I have sinned against Yahweh." "Let us fall into the hand of Yahweh," he cried to Gad after what was deemed another transgression; "for his mercies are great; and let me not fall into the hand of man!" (II 24:14).

Finally, his gratitude shows a heart full of adoring love. When after the prohibition to erect a temple David received divine assurance that his dynasty would continue, he "went in and sat before Yahweh" and poured out one of the most beautiful thanksgivings to be found in the Bible. True, it is assigned usually to the B source and so falls under suspicion of having been "touched up" by later hands; but it could well be David's, so genuinely does it harmonize with the whole spirit of his life.

In view of all these evidences of David's devotion to Yahweh we cannot wonder that to after ages he should have stood out as the king "after Yahweh's own heart" (I 13:14).

David Regarded Yahweh as a God of War

Like Joshua, David had before him a task which involved much fighting. It is only natural therefore that to him Yahweh should have worn the aspect of a War-God. Nowhere in the Old Testament do we find a more classical expression of such faith than in David's words to Goliath, as they are given in the legendary account of his battle with that famous champion. "Thou comest to me with a sword, and with a spear, and with a javelin; but I come to thee in the name of Yahweh of hosts, the God of the armies of Israel, whom thou hast defied. This day will Yahweh deliver thee into my hand" (I 17:45-46). Such was the idea that a later time had of David's religion. That it was a true one is borne out by the earlier source. Many of the responses obtained by David through the oracle seem to have had to do with military moves. "Shall I go and smite the Philistines?" (I 23:2) "If I pursue after this troop, shall I overtake them?" (I 30:8) One famous answer of Yahweh is recorded: "Thou shalt not go up. Make a circuit behind them, and come upon them over against the mulberry trees. And it shall be, when thou hearest the sound of marching in the tops of the mulberry trees, that then thou shalt bestir thyself; for then is Yahweh gone out before thee to smite the host of the Philistines" (II 5:23-24). God's leadership and participation in the war could not be more graphically pictured.

Such a faith in the War-God is nothing new in our study. In cherishing it David had behind him an illustrious succession of Israel's leaders from Moses to Samuel. What is more, the history of Israel up to this point seemed to justify it. For through war the tribes had been able to establish themselves in the land of promise and to maintain themselves there. The military enthusiasm roused by a Deborah, a Gideon or a Saul had also done great things for the national character and religion. And now David, by continuing the tradition, was able to bring Israel to the height of its glory, subduing all its enemies and building up an imposing little empire with Jerusalem for its capital. Thus not only was Israel exalted, but the name of Yahweh became feared among the nations. David gave the War-God faith its crowning vindication.

After him a change set in. Solomon indeed preserved at least the semblance of military supremacy. But at his death the empire collapsed and the wars of Yahweh's people became largely fratricidal struggles between the two sections of a once undivided nation. Brief successes over neighbouring peoples did indeed occur and under powerful kings like Omri and Ahab wars seemed for a while to bring glory and wealth. But on the whole the record read otherwise. With the reappearance of Egypt and Assyria on the political horizon all possibility of ultimate accomplishment through arms disappeared and a consistent peace policy became the only wise one. The War-God faith as an effective instrument was played out. Not till the days of Judas Maccabeus did it again get results. And then not for long. Its revival by the Maccabees after centuries of enforced idleness marked the beginning of a movement that at last precipitated the great rebellion against Rome and the fall of the Jewish state. After Bar Cochba's second unsuccessful rebellion Judaism finally gave it up as a practical religious idea. In our day, as a book like Klausner's *Jesus of Nazareth* shows, there are Jews who would like to make it live again.

David Fostered the Worship of Yahweh

The writer of the Books of Chronicles, which we cannot treat seriously as a source of historical information, has drawn a picture of a very ecclesiastically-minded David whose chief concern at the end of his life was to institute a rich worship at Jerusalem and provide for the erection of the temple by Solomon. This representation, combined with the ascription of many of the Psalms to David, is responsible for the traditional Christian idea of him as the sainted churchman *par excellence*. Natural reaction from such a view has driven many scholars to an opposite extreme. They have sought to reduce David's interest in matters of worship (which they call "the cult") to insignificant dimensions. Probably, as Sellin [1] points out, the truth lies between the two opposing ideas.

[1] *GIJV*, I, p. 183.

David, as the oldest source shows, was very much concerned with worship and what pertained to it. We have already marked his reverent treatment of the priestly oracle, which certainly belonged to the cult side of religion. That he took part in the prevalent sacrifices and believed them pleasing to Yahweh is to be accepted as a matter of course.

A reliable narrative describing the bringing of the ark into Jerusalem (II 6) sheds welcome light upon his attitude towards that venerable symbol and exhibits him as practising several forms of cult expression. After Jerusalem had been made his capital he proceeded to give it religious sanctity by housing within it the ark of God. This was indeed a master stroke of statesmanship, for it tied the new monarchy firmly to the ancient Yahweh tradition so that from now on both monarchy and capital became themselves elements in Yahweh's religion. But we may be sure that in taking such a step David had more in mind than its effect upon the people. He believed that he would thus unite his capital and his dynasty *to God*. To him, as to his contemporaries, the ark was so identified with Yahweh that it gathered to itself His presence in a very special way. Where it stayed He stayed also, when it moved He moved with it, whatever happened in its immediate vicinity was His doing, and by coming near to it one came near to Him. In short, it signified to David much what the sacred Host means to devout believers in Transubstantiation. It assured one of the sacramental presence of Deity. When, for instance, it is said (II 7:18) that David "went in and sat before Yahweh" we understand that he entered the tabernacle and took his seat in front of the ark. Here he could be certain that he was speaking to God in an intensely close and intimate way.

When therefore David determined to bring the ark to Jerusalem he carried out the plan with all the manifestations of devotion and worship that were appropriate when one was conducting Yahweh personally to a new dwelling place. "All the chosen men of Israel, thirty thousand," went down with the king as a guard of honour. The ark was placed by the consecrated sons of Abinadab upon a new cart and taken out of the humble home that had housed it for many years. The procession then formed. First came "David and all the house of Israel, playing before Yahweh with all manner of instruments of firwood, and with harps and with cymbals." In the rear, the place of honour, followed the ark, driven by Uzzah and Ahio. On the way an unhappy accident occurred which resulted in the death of Uzzah. David attributed this to Yahweh's anger, roused by the priest's hasty attempt to save the ark from falling by taking hold of it. Immediately the procession was abandoned and the dangerous symbol carried into the nearby house of Obed-edom, a Philistine from Gath. Probably David interpreted the happening as an indication of Yahweh's wish to remain where He was.

Three months later, encouraged by the news that meanwhile Obed-edom's house had prospered, David resumed the procession with great joy. Yahweh, he felt, had signified His willingness to go up to Jerusalem. After the bearers of the ark had gone six paces —evidently a propitious number—he sacrificed an ox and a fatling. The great train now gave itself over to wild expressions of happiness. Trumpets brayed, the air resounded with shouts. David himself, wearing the linen ephod of a priest, "danced before Yahweh with all his might." The ark was carried into the city and "set in its place in the midst of the tent that David had pitched for it." The excited king then offered burnt-offerings and peace-offerings in front of it and blessed the people in the name of Yahweh of hosts. A sacrificial feast followed, in which generous portions were dealt out. After the multitude had eaten their fill and gone home the still elated David returned to bless his own household. We have already seen how he justified his conduct in the procession to the scandalized Michal (II 6).

In this narrative we perceive David in a new rôle. He plans, directs and carries out a supreme act of worship. No one who reads the chapter can doubt that this side of religion seemed to him important. And he loved it. One can see that he threw himself into it and thoroughly enjoyed it. He seems to have been specially interested in the music by which Yahweh was honoured, taking part in it and perhaps leading it. This would be natural in a man whom tradition has celebrated as a skilful player upon the harp, a sweet psalmist, an inventor of musical instruments (I 16:18; II 23:1; Amos 6:5). He also magnified the priestly functions, identifying himself with that order by wearing its vestment and performing its duties. Indeed throughout the whole celebration David merged the king in the priest; or perhaps we might more truthfully say, revealed the priest in the king.[2]

The B source supplements this A narrative by telling that David conceived the idea of building for the ark, that is, for Yahweh, a house as splendid as his own new palace. There is every reason to believe the statement. Such a step would have carried out

[2] David was none the less a *layman,* not a "man of God."

David's attitude to its natural conclusion. By the power of his genius he could easily picture what such a temple would mean to the nation. But a prophetic word forbade the project and it was dropped. Religious conservatism was against it.

In the light of all this we must allow that there is some solid foundation for the Chronicler's portrayal of David as a churchman. His picture indeed is quite wrong in its perspective, for ecclesiastical matters could not have been the main interest of David's declining years; it is also fanciful in its details, incorrect in its atmosphere, and full of anachronisms. But we may well credit the general tradition that David gave much thought to the ordering of the music in the new sanctuary and established its priesthood on a worthy basis.[3] According to the A account his own sons were priests, appointed, we may infer, by himself (II 8:18).

Primitive Traits in David's Religion

The narrative of the ark's removal reminds us that David's religion was by no means free from conceptions of a primitive nature. For one thing, he felt that on occasions Yahweh acted in what we should call an arbitrary fashion (II 6:9). To strike Uzzah dead for steadying the ark was certainly not an ethical action. David attributed the possibility of the same capricious conduct to Yahweh in another situation. When a fugitive from Saul he seems to have wondered at times whether Yahweh was not stirring up Saul against him for some reason David could not fathom. If so, He could be appeased by smelling an offering (I 26:19).

Again, David's dancing before the ark belonged to an ecstatic stage of religion destined to give place to soberer and more ethically coloured manifestations of enthusiasm. We should not forget however that the feeling of utter abandonment to God is something that even developed religion cannot afford to lose (II 6:16ff).

Undoubtedly primitive also was his tying Yahweh to the ark in so mechanical a way. The time was coming when Israel would have to get along without the ark and be better off for the loss. But the idea itself of the sacramental presence of God in a symbol survives with massive power among millions of Christians today. Those to whom it does not appeal may deem it mistaken and injurious, but they can hardly dismiss it as "primitive."

Yet other manifestations of David's religion must be put in this

---

[3] David dedicated silver and gold and vessels for Yahweh's worship (I Ki. 7:51).

category. Here would fall his belief in the priestly oracle and his
crudely anthropomorphic use of Yahweh as the War-God. He
also shared the popular idea that it was a sin to number the fighting
men of Israel (II 24:10). When a plague followed his census
he accepted Gad's interpretation: that it was a punishment for his
impiety in trying to find out what Yahweh wished to remain
hidden, and that it could be stayed by erecting an altar on a particular spot. Indeed, David seems to have felt that Yahweh actually
put the intention to number the host into his mind, in order that
He might have cause to vent upon Israel anger which (for some
unknown reason) He *already* cherished (II 24). Once more, the
story of David's flight from Saul reveals the fact that he and Michal
kept a teraphim in their house, evidently an image large enough
to look like a man under the bed-clothes (I 19:13ff). What it
stood for no one knows. It may have been a representation of
Yahweh, or a survival of the household deities used in pre-Mosaic
times. In any case it cannot be reconciled with Israel's later religious thinking, or even with Mosaism.

But the most sinister emergence of primitive traits is to be found
in David's superstitions concerning blood-guilt. He was convinced
that blood once shed would be "returned" somewhere, if not on
the head of the shedder then on that of the king and his descendants. This idea worked for rude justice with the man who claimed
to have slain Saul and still more with Ishbosheth's murderers. But
when Joab killed first Abner, then Amasa David was not strong
enough to wipe out the blood-debt by the execution of the murderer. The fact that he had left the score unpaid seems to have
troubled him all his life, and on his death bed he commissioned
Solomon to bring down Joab's grey head with blood to Sheol
in order that David's descendants might not suffer in the future
(I Ki. 2:5ff; cf. 2:33).[1] Shimei's curse, in like manner, must have
roused his fears. Unless this old Benjamite should die a bloody
death the curse would not come back to its sender but would continue to follow its object. David's own hands were tied because in
a moment of generosity he had sworn not to put Shimei to death;
but since no such obligation lay upon Solomon David left him a
charge to clear the matter up! (I Ki. 2:8). In a kind of supplement
to the history of David's reign (II 21) we find a peculiarly revolting instance of this superstition. When David "sought the face of

[1] T. H. Robinson, *HI,* I, p. 245, following Benzinger and Stade, suspects
that these parting injunctions of David have been invented to exonerate
Solomon from the guilt of killing Joab and Shimei.

Yahweh" to learn the reason of a prolonged drought he received
the answer that blood-guilt rested upon the land because of Saul's
having put to death the Gibeonites. The Gibeonites, when asked
what atonement should be made, demanded the delivery of seven
of Saul's descendants for the purpose of "hanging them up unto
Yahweh in Gibeah of Saul." David acquiesced and the slaughter
took place, followed by the impaling of the bodies until the drought
was at last broken. In such a circle of ideas did the great king
move!

David's Religion as it Affected his Ethical Conduct

No survey of the primitive elements in David's religion would
be complete without including in it a number of instances in
which he displayed an undeveloped ethical sense. We have already
noticed his ideas regarding blood-guilt. His cruelty to prisoners
of war also shocks the modern reader. So does his readiness to
lie if he found himself in a desperate situation. When he made
Ahimelech think that he was on the king's business his deceit
came very close to downright treachery. What is more, he realized
the probable consequences. "I knew on that day," he declared
later to Abiathar, "when Doeg the Edomite was there, that he
would surely tell Saul: I have occasioned the death of all the persons
of thy house" (I 21-22). Yet David showed no sense of having
done a great wrong. There was no apparent remorse, no plea
for forgiveness. "Abide thou with me, fear not; for he that seeketh
my life seeketh thy life; for with me thou shalt be in safeguard."
That was all he had to say. Towards Achish king of Gath he
pursued a course of systematic perfidy, acting his part with consummate skill. "I know that thou art good in my sight, as an
angel of God," his patron acknowledged, when David protested
against being sent home from the Philistine army (I 27:8ff; 29:9).
David had a wonderful power to win men's trust and he exploited
it without scruple. In taking his word Achish took trash. It was
different of course with his oath, for that brought in Yahweh as
a third party to enforce the engagement. Yet he found a way to
evade his oath to Shimei by passing on to Solomon the task of killing him.

Since now we know that David lied in certain situations we have
the uncomfortable feeling that he might have been lying in others
where we should like to believe him truthful. As one reads his
story one cannot shake off the impression that he was always more
or less playing a game. Take for example his message to the men of

Jabesh-gilead regarding their act of piety towards Saul's dead body: "Blessed be ye of Yahweh, that ye have showed this kindness unto your lord . . . and have buried him. And now Yahweh show lovingkindness and truth unto you: and I also will requite you this kindness, because ye have done this thing. Now therefore let your hands be strong, and be ye valiant; for Saul your lord is dead, and also the house of Judah have anointed me king over them" (II 2:5-7). Was he speaking from a full heart here, or making an astute political gesture? Probably both. In the main, of course, David must have been truthful or he would have lost public confidence. But one could never be sure that policy was not entering in.

We should not indeed blame David for such insincerity, or even for lying. Everyone lied in those days. According to the legend Yahweh showed Samuel how to throw dust in Saul's eyes when he went to Bethlehem (I 16:3). Even Jeremiah lied to the princes of Judah (Jer. 38:27). But in one important respect David seems to have fallen below the standard of truth attained by men like Jeremiah and Samuel. They had after all the fundamental sincerity of unselfishness. They sought, not their own good, but the good of the people. David on the other hand was thinking of himself and his house. Not altogether, but still enough to influence his dealings with others. To him people were never *just* people to be loved and helped, they were to some extent pawns in his game. At least, the reader feels so.

In his family relations David had no very developed concept of duty. Polygamy he practised with a good conscience. Sensuality, so long as it could be indulged within the very wide limits of this institution, was quite legitimate. One cannot forget the revolting picture (drawn in I Ki. 1) of his extreme old age. Towards Michal he acted with harshness, depriving her permanently of her rights of cohabitation because of a single taunt. The concubines violated by Absalom he kept in perpetual widowhood. All quite in conformity with current ideas, of course; but all showing how little right a woman, even a princess, had to live the full life of a woman under polygamy. In fact, throughout the whole story of David's relations with women there is struck not one note of beauty or even dignity, unless it be his words to Abigail (I 25:32ff). His adultery with Bathsheba however need not be included here, for he himself condemned it.

His sons he loved passionately but his affection led him to spoil them. Concerning Adonijah the historian remarks laconically: "His father had not displeased him all his life in saying, Why hast thou done so?" (I Ki. 1:6). What a summary of a boy's bringing up! Apparently the handling of Amnon and Absalom had not been very different. They came to manhood selfish and unrestrained. Even such an outrage as Amnon's crime David left unpunished, merely losing his temper over it (II 13:21). Absalom knew that if he wanted anything done in the matter he must do it himself. He knew also that if he killed Amnon he would probably be taken back into his father's favour after a while. David the resolute was weak as water towards his sons. In this case plainly the failure of David's ethics was not due to low ideals prevailing around him, for public opinion in ancient Israel seems to have been quite awake to the responsibility of a father. His conduct was evidently disapproved of by his biographer.

This painful enumeration of David's deficiencies in ethical insight, however, gives but the lesser half of the story.[1] In our study of Samuel we have reminded ourselves that Israel already possessed in the Mosaic tradition many lofty conceptions of duty. David shared these. What is more, he lived up to them on the whole. "Whatsoever the king did pleased all the people" (II 3:36). How different from Saul, who often shocked them by his deeds of violence.

David was particularly careful not to shed "the blood of war in peace." There are several recorded instances where his religious scruples kept him back from such a step. One is the famous story of his sparing Saul, which has come down to us in duplicate form (I 24 and 26) and must contain some truth, however much legend has been at work on it. Both versions agree that when David got Saul in his power he refused to strike the fatal blow. "Yahweh forbid that I should do this thing unto my lord, Yahweh's anointed . . . for who can put forth his hand against Yahweh's anointed and be blameless?" (I 24:6 and 26:9). On another occasion he held back (under great provocation) from doing harm to Nabal, a private individual, protected by no divine anointing. When the fair and gracious Abigail had prevailed on him to refrain from the bloody deed contemplated David cried out in gratitude: "Blessed be Yahweh, the God of Israel, who sent thee this day to meet me: and blessed be thy discretion, and blessed be thou, that hast kept me this day from blood-guiltiness, and from avenging myself with mine own hand!" (I 25:32–33). Years later when, an old and

---

[1] J. M. P. Smith fails to do justice to David when he speaks as if David's finer traits were inconsiderable as contrasted with his "low ideals and attainments." *The Religion of the Psalms* (Chicago, 1922), p. 48.

broken man, he was fleeing before Absalom he responded to Shimei's cursing with a similar forbearance (II 16:11); and on the day of his restoration, in a burst of generosity of which he seems afterward to have repented, forgave him freely. To the remonstrance of Joab and Abishai he replied: "Shall there any man be put to death this day in Israel? for do I not know that I am this day king over Israel?" (II 19:21ff). David plainly had the idea that Yahweh abominated violence towards fellow Israelites, except of course in time of civil war. Joab and Abishai did not agree with him but, as we have said, most of the people did. Indeed there seems to have been in the Israel of that day a strong aversion from such deeds. Abigail is a good example of this nobler attitude (I 25:26ff).

In other respects likewise David felt bound by his religion to act ethically. He sought out Mephibosheth in order to "show the kindness of God unto him . . . for Jonathan's sake"—thus uniting the religious and the human motive (II 9:3 and 7). "I have sinned against Yahweh," he cried when Nathan brought home to him his crime against Uriah (II 12:13). So the reputation of judging justly must have been earned by David through a long series of decisions in accord with Yahweh's known will: decisions untainted by the suspicion of bribery. Moreover, in spite of his personal and dynastic ambition, David did care for the people. "Lord I have sinned and done perversely," he prayed in the time of pestilence; "but these sheep, what have they done? Let thy hand, I pray thee, be against me and against my father's house" (II 24:17).

Finally, as we have seen, David could love greatly. This trait rightly falls under ethics, for where present it colours a man's whole conduct. Two supreme loves stand forth in his life. The first, belonging to his young manhood, was broken when Jonathan lay dead on mount Gilboa. The other began in the full tide of his vigour and ripened to its tragic close in his old age. "O, my son Absalom, my son, my son Absalom! Would I had died for thee, O Absalom, my son, my son!" (II 18:33). Deplore as we may his fatherly weakness, there is something in that cry that goes very deep. It is akin to what Israel's men of God believed to be Yahweh's own feeling for His rebellious people. "Is Ephraim my dear son? is he a darling child? for as often as I speak against him, I do earnestly remember him still: therefore my heart yearneth for him: I will surely have mercy upon him, saith Yahweh" (Jer. 31:20).

And as he could love, so he possessed an amazing power to win the love of others. Men and women alike were overcome by his charm. This is seen in the beautiful little stories that recall the devotion of his rough soldiery. Joab and Abishai, ferocious and unprincipled though they might be towards others, were true as steel to David. And so were the others. When three of his thirty chief men heard him express a longing in the heat of battle for a drink of water from the well of Bethlehem they broke through the host of the Philistines and got it for him. "But he would not drink thereof, but poured it out unto Yahweh. And he said . . . , Shall I drink the blood of the men that went in jeopardy of their lives?" (II 23:13ff). When advancing years had begun to sap his strength he one day almost fell in battle. Abishai rescued him, and his men "sware unto him, saying, 'Thou shalt go no more out with us to battle, that thou quench not the lamp of Israel'" (II 21:15ff). We have seen how in the hour when the nation seemed to be falling away from him his men stood fast by his side. Ittai the newcomer from Gath refused permission to leave his service: "As Yahweh liveth, and as my lord the king liveth, surely in what place my lord the king shall be, whether for death or for life, even there will thy servant be" (II 15:21). And many others besides his soldiers went with him into exile—or would have gone, had he let them—Zadok, Abiathar, their sons, the aged Hushai, and an unnamed company. Nor must we forget the number who gave their hearts to him when he was young: Michal, Abigail, the men of war, even Saul himself in his lucid moments. But perhaps most of all, Jonathan, whose "soul was knit with the soul of David."

> "I am distressed for thee, my brother Jonathan:
> Very pleasant hast thou been unto me:
> Thy love to me was wonderful,
> Passing the love of women" (II 1:26).

David's Significance for Israel's Religion

No reader of the Old Testament (or indeed of the New) can fail to notice how often the name of David occurs in the writings of those who followed him. Why did he bulk so large in the thought and imagination of his successors?

In a real sense David was the founder of the Hebrew nation. Moses had indeed brought the Israelitish people into existence and given them a common faith in Yahweh their God. But not till the days of David did this people take its place as a nation, with a nation's organization and prestige. Saul had begun this work, but his kingdom for all its unity still retained much of the looseness and formlessness of the days preceding it, nor did it win for itself any convincing place amidst its neighbours. David gave it a capital, a court, a government that could be felt. He himself was a king like the sovereigns of important states round about, maintaining equal magnificence, dealing with them as a peer. His kingdom he raised from dependence and insignificance to imperial glory, making it easily the leading state between Egypt and Assyria. Beginning with David Israel was quite a different entity, with a different self-consciousness, a different national life. In spite of the succeeding split between north and south his work remained permanent. Both of the separated members continued to be kingdoms.

The capital that he bestowed upon Israel moreover was something more than a royal residence or a metropolis, however splendid. It was Jerusalem. Now and then in the history of mankind a city has embodied in itself the spirit of a people, becoming the mystic symbol of their achievements and their dreams, taking on in their thoughts something almost of the divine. Such were Athens and Rome. But neither of these meant to its people what Jerusalem meant to Israel. It is well for us to reflect that before David Jerusalem was not; or rather was worse than nothing from the Hebrew point of view, for it remained an unconquered Canaanitish city in their midst. David perceived that it possessed commanding natural beauty and a military situation which rendered it almost impregnable. He saw also that being hitherto alien it could be made his as could no Israelitish city. All his splendour could be poured about it. Finally, it could become the dwelling-place of Yahweh, His earthly home, the religious centre of His people. So he took it and set about shaping its future. He could not of course guess how vast that future would be; but with the intuition of genius he laid the foundation for it. Quite justly was it called thereafter both "the city of David" and "the city of Yahweh."

To David went back also the conception of Jerusalem's temple as Yahweh's home. Though he was not permitted to carry out this idea, David did take thought (as we have seen) for the worship of the Jerusalem sanctuary, associating with the cult side of Yahweh's religion the influence of his great name. He seems likewise to have fostered the music used in worship, so that the temple singers afterwards looked back to him as their patron. We know how he was regarded as the illustrious prototype of the later psalmists.

But more than all else he became to after ages the Ideal King. As his figure receded into the past its faults were overlooked and its virtues came into their own. People saw in David a king wholly faithful to Yahweh, enjoying a unique place in His favour, able through his merits to avert from the lesser kings that followed and indeed from rebellious Israel itself the full penalty of their sins. Again and again, it was felt, Yahweh withheld His anger "for His servant David's sake." The great king's age appeared in memory as one in which the poor and the oppressed had been protected and justice had flourished on earth. The weakness and humiliation of a later time were contrasted with David's empire, when Israel's hosts went out as conquerors and the heathen round about rendered obedience to Yahweh's anointed.

Thus was born the hope that David would one day come again, in his own person or in a mighty "son" who would deliver Israel and make it head over the nations while at home his reign would bring righteousness and plenty. Too often this dream was tainted with aspirations after military power, and for this we must acknowledge that David himself was responsible. The aspect of his career that appealed to the thirst for material magnificence and military glory was a legacy of doubtful value, keeping alive passions and aspirations which were destined to bear evil fruits. But the other side of David's picture far outshone this. As one traces what we may call the "Davidic expectation" through the Old Testament he finds it in the main charged with aspiration for a better and purer world where the poor shall find a royal friend and God shall be truly known. When blind Bartimaeus heard that Jesus was passing by he "began to cry out and say, Thou son of David, have mercy upon me" (Mk. 10:48). Thus side by side with the memory of the warrior prince of the Psalms of Solomon there lived that of the good king unto whom a thousand years before the needy had "cried" and had not been disappointed.

Chapter VIII

SOLOMON

[REIGNED 976–936 B.C.]

The Sources

The incomparable narrative to which we are indebted for the account of David's reign continues into that of his successor; but unfortunately only a little way (I Ki. 1:49–2:46). At the end of I Ki. 2 it abruptly ceases and we pass to a much inferior source, which tells us all that we know of Solomon after the very beginning of his reign. At the base of I Ki. 3–11 lies a document which in 11:41 is referred to as the "Acts of Solomon," excerpts from which have been preserved to us by the Deuteronomic editor who compiled these chapters. This source did not confine itself to bare annals but told a number of stories regarding the great king, mingling them with lists and other statistics. It may in its turn have drawn upon yet earlier documents, one of which may have been an account of the building of the temple. So far as outward facts are concerned, it is thought by scholars generally to preserve a great deal of reliable material; although allowance must be made for considerable exaggeration in the figures given and for the insertion of legends and other embellishments by the editor. We do know therefore not a little concerning Solomon. But we do not know him as we know David. Instead of the intensely human figure presented by the David narratives, moving amid lifelike scenes and real people, we get a Solomon who is viewed from a distance as a grandiose person, draped in the splendid robes of power, proceeding in stately fashion across a magnificent stage, who remains a stranger to us in spite of all our efforts to become acquainted with him. When we see him act it is through the gleaming mist of legend and his words come to us remoulded into the pious utterances of the Deuteronomic editor. If only the writer of the first two chapters could have gone on to tell us the rest! But he did not, and we must do the best we can to reconstruct the real Solomon from the source at our disposal.

The Beginning of Solomon's Reign

We have seen how when David lay dying his eldest surviving son made an attempt to seize the royal power without his father's authorization. Adonijah, the spoiled boy now become a man, organized a conspiracy in which the chief participants were Joab, David's redoubtable captain of the host, and Abiathar the priest who had accompanied the great king in his varying fortunes. Their impelling motive seems to have been jealousy of their rivals, Benaiah the commander of David's bodyguard, Zadok the priest and Nathan the prophet. These in turn worked on the king through Bathsheba to install Solomon as king while the other faction were holding a feast in the Kidron valley preparatory to seizing the reins of government. Surprised and aghast Adonijah and his followers fled for shelter. The prince himself took refuge at the altar whose horns he refused to unclasp until his younger brother Solomon had sworn to spare his life. This the new king did readily. "If he shall show himself a worthy man, there shall not a hair of him fall to the earth; but if wickedness be found in him, he shall die." Reassured Adonijah went with the guard sent to arrest him, made obeisance to Solomon, and was dismissed to his own house (I Ki. 1:52f).

A like clemency was shown to the priest Abiathar. He was indeed put out from his position as priest in the Jerusalem sanctuary and banished to his land in the small village of Anāthôth, three miles north east of the capital; but no further punishment was exacted. "Get thee unto Anathoth, unto thine own fields," said the king, "for thou art worthy of death; but I will not at this time put thee to death, because thou barest the ark of the Lord Yahweh before David my father, and because thou wast afflicted in all wherein my father was afflicted" (I Ki. 2:26f).

The aged Joab however did not fare so well. Solomon claimed, perhaps truthfully, that David had left an express injunction to put him out of the way and this was done at the royal command by the willing Benaiah, who killed him as he clung to the horns of the altar. As justification for this deed Solomon urged the two murders committed by Joab in time of peace. This blood had now returned upon the murderer's own head, and David's house was free of all guilt (I Ki. 2:28ff).

Nor did Adonijah's security last long. When presently he persuaded Bathsheba to petition her son Solomon to grant him David's concubine Abishag as his wife, the king fell into a rage. It is possible that Adonijah had made this request merely because he desired Abishag; but the probability is that he had in mind a political end. The wives and concubines of a dead king passed to his successor, and if Adonijah could procure one of these he might later have some claim on the succession. Thus at any rate Solomon professed to understand his action. Remonstrating angrily with his mother for taking his rival's part Solomon swore vengeance. "God do so to me, and more also, if Adonijah hath not spoken this word against his own life." Benaiah was immediately sent to execute him (I Ki. 2:13ff).

One more enemy remained to be disposed of. Summoning the vituperative Shimei to his presence Solomon ordered him to build a house in Jerusalem and never to leave it under pain of death. The narrator tells us that Shimei kept within bounds for three years, then broke them to recapture a runaway slave. Solomon at once exacted the penalty, and so the curse of Shimei was at last returned upon his own head. Here again the king claimed to be carrying out David's final injunctions (I Ki. 2:36ff).

"And the kingdom was established in the hand of Solomon." With these words the early source breaks off and the Acts of Solomon (as remoulded by the editor) begins. Inasmuch as this source does not give a consecutive story it is well for us to make no attempt at narrative, but to consider Solomon's life and reign under its several aspects.

Personal Ambition was the Keynote of Solomon's Life

Almost at the beginning of the narratives concerning Solomon stands the familiar story of his choice (I Ki. 3:4ff). The young king went to the ancient high place of Gibeon to sacrifice and while there received an oracle from Yahweh. In a dream Yahweh appeared unto him and said, "Ask what I shall give thee." Conscious of his insufficiency for the task before him Solomon replied: "Give thy servant an understanding heart to judge thy people, that I may discern between good and evil." Pleased with the choice Yahweh made answer: "Behold, I have done according to thy word: lo, I have given thee a wise and understanding heart; so that there hath been none like thee before thee, neither after thee shall any arise like unto thee. And I have also given thee that which thou hast not asked, both riches and honour, so that there shall not be any among the kings like unto thee all thy days."

Scholars as a rule are not disposed to take this as serious his-

tory. But none the less the narrative reflects truly what one may
gather from the rest of our sources to have been Solomon's attitude
towards God and towards life. When Yahweh appeared unto
Moses it was as the giver of a work: "Come now, and I will
send thee unto Pharaoh, that thou mayest bring forth my people
. . . out of Egypt" (Exod. 3:10). Upon the lad Samuel He laid
the burden of announcing Eli's doom—a heavy task to be followed
by many another. What Solomon heard was quite different: "Ask
what I shall give thee." Yahweh had become a dispenser of
benefits. There is a world of difference between the two. Looked
at from man's side it means that Moses and Samuel asked, "What
does God want me to do?" while Solomon inquired, "What will
God do for me?" We have seen that there was a good deal of
this in David's religion also.

Solomon's choice of an understanding heart shows indeed that
he had a sense of responsibility towards God and the people and
desired to be a good judge. We shall try presently to do justice
to him in this respect. But even in so noble an aim we see his
passion for pre-eminence appear. His wisdom was to be a personal
acquirement which would bring him reputation: "so that there
hath been none like thee . . . nor shall any arise like thee."

And immaterial wisdom, however honoured, would not be enough.
God would supply something more substantial, "both riches and
honour" i.e. the kind of honour that wealth gives a man. Here also
we see ambition entering: "so that there shall not be any among
the kings like unto thee all thy days."

That was what Solomon expected to get from God and life;
and that he obtained. He stands out in the Bible as the man
who was most brilliantly successful in using God as the supplier
of good things.

He Won a Reputation for Wisdom

Solomon's first aim in desiring wisdom was, according to tradition, that he might judge the people rightly. A well known story
tells how he exhibited this gift in the case of two harlots who
were contending over the possession of a baby. This is generally
regarded by historians as a legend because in varying forms it
appears in the narratives of other great rulers also. "All Israel saw
that the wisdom of God was in him to do justice" (3:16ff).

Passing from legend to history, his treatment of Adonijah,
Abiathar and Shimei exhibited the moderation and firmness which

should characterize the wise judge. Instead of putting to death the rival claimant for the throne Solomon spared Adonijah on condition of good behaviour. It was only after Adonijah's attempt to obtain Abishag to wife that Solomon, suspecting further plotting, ordered his execution. In spite of David's death-bed charge against Shimei, Solomon allowed that aged malcontent and reviler, perhaps also conspirator, to live quietly in Jerusalem till he violated the condition of his safety. Abiathar he merely deprived of his office and banished to Anathoth. This was carrying out the best Davidic tradition of leniency.

Unfortunately this aspect of the wisdom tradition is like a river which runs into sands and disappears. The reader, who has been led to await its development as the main theme, finds no further mention of it.

Another side of the tradition is Solomon's fame as a composer of proverbs and songs. The proverb had flourished as a developed form of literature for several centuries in Egypt and probably among the Arabian tribes to the east. Solomon turned his hand to it and (we are told) produced three thousand of such pithy observations. The number is very large and may well mean (as Sellin supposes) that these were the work not of the king only but of a galaxy of wise men whom he had gathered about him. In any case he got the credit for them. Along with his "songs" to the number of a thousand and five, belonging probably to the same general class of composition, they brought him wide fame, and put him at the head of the celebrated wise men of other peoples, including the Egyptians. So says one of our sources, no doubt with pardonable exaggeration.

Many of these sayings had to do with plant and animal life. "He spake of trees, from the cedar that is in Lebanon even unto the hyssop that springeth out of the wall: he spake also of beasts, and of birds and of creeping things and fishes." But if we may judge both from the later book of Proverbs and from the Egyptian proverbs of Ptahhotep and Amen-em-ope, Solomon must also have had much to say about human life, not least in its ethical aspect (4:29-33).

With this would have gone his ability to answer questions (10:3). Statecraft would have been included. His material success must have added to his reputation for sagacity. The result of all this fame was that he was much sought after. Visitors came even from other countries to hear his wisdom, including (tradition states) some of royal rank.

However much one may be inclined to discount the claims made by the narratives as to his reputation in his own day, there can be no doubt that he became the father of wisdom-writing for the Hebrews of a later age, just as David became the father of psalmody. The Book of Proverbs is attributed to him. The question naturally arises, Is any of it his work? Scholars usually answer in the negative, but there are some who think that in its oldest section we may still have before us some sayings from his pen, although it is now impossible to identify them.

He Made Himself Famous for his Magnificence

There is nothing upon which the Solomonic tradition loves so to dwell as his wealth and splendour. Here again we must be on our guard against exaggerations; but it is certain that Solomon's luxury and display exceeded that of his father as David in turn had in such matters gone far beyond Saul.

This is seen in the accounts of Solomon's court. So large was it that it consumed in one day "thirty measures (335 bushels) of fine flour, and sixty measures (670 bushels) of meal, ten fat oxen and twenty oxen out of the pastures, and a hundred sheep, besides harts and gazelles and roebuck and fatted fowl" (4:22). The queen of Sheba is reported to have wondered at "the house that he had built, and the food of his servants, and the attendance of his ministers, and their apparel, and his cup bearers, and his ascent by which he went up into the house of Yahweh" (10:4–5). His great harem served the same end of display. We miss the point when we look on his "seven hundred wives, princesses, and three hundred concubines" (11:3) as an evidence of his sensuality. Sensual he doubtless was, as his father had been before him; but hardly to the extent that these figures would indicate. He seems to have had a barbaric love of gold, using it extensively for plating in his buildings and furniture as well as on his table. We are told of three hundred shields covered with this metal which his body-guard carried when he went into the house of Yahweh (10:17 cf. 14:26). Special mention is made of the great throne of ivory overlaid with the finest gold, approached by six steps and embellished by no less than fourteen statues of lions: "there was not the like made in any kingdom" (10:18ff). The picture would not be complete without putting into it also the horses and chariots which Solomon got from Egypt and introduced into the Israelitish army. Hitherto these had been absent: David had won all his victories without them. It is not likely that any new situation had arisen which rendered their employment imperative for Israel; but Solomon, in his ambition to be like the great monarchs of the world, probably thought them necessary. It is said that he had fourteen hundred chariots and twelve thousand horsemen, part of which he kept in Jerusalem near his own person while the rest he distributed among the "chariot cities" which he was compelled to build (10:26).

But the most signal illustration of his striving after magnificence is seen in the huge building program which he planned and carried out. North of the "hill of Zion," the original stronghold of Jebus, which had been used by David for his own house and the tabernacle containing the ark, rose the hill of Moriah. This Solomon selected as the spot for a great complex of structures leading up to the temple as its crowning glory. By filling in the depression between the two hills and throwing out huge retaining walls he was able to obtain an area sufficient for three units of buildings. The lowest of these was also the largest, containing the "house of the forest of Lebanon," the "porch of pillars" and the "porch of the throne," all of which served the purposes of government. Next came his own house, with the "house for Pharaoh's daughter" near it. Finally, in the third enclosure, separated only by a wall from the royal palace, rose the temple surrounded by its court. "All these were of costly stones, even of hewn stone, according to measure, sawed with saws, within and without, even from the foundation unto the coping, and so on the outside unto the great court. And the foundation was of costly stones, even of great stones, stones of eight cubits (twelve feet). And above were costly stones, even hewn stone,[1] according to measure, and cedar-wood. And the great court round about had three courses of hewn stones and a course of cedar beams." These buildings were indeed not large according to the standards of today, the greatest of them (the "house of the forest of Lebanon") being only 150 feet long, 75 feet broad and 45 feet high; but the total program with its massive and finished construction, its expensive materials, its lavish carving and gold plating, would require an enormous outlay (I Ki. 7:1ff). Yet this did not exhaust Solomon's building activity. The military exigencies of his kingdom as he interpreted them demanded the erection of extensive fortifications at Jerusalem and in the regions that commanded the trade routes; to which must be added the "store cities,"

[1] But see Note 2, p. 156f.

the "cities for his chariots" and the "cities for his horsemen" (I Ki. 9:15ff).[2]

Certainly, during the long years of Solomon's reign the appearance of little Palestine was changing. Nothing gives such an air of power and importance to a country as the presence of imposing buildings. The land of farms and villages was coming to seem like a world nation with a proud capital and far flung strongholds. The very process of construction bespoke prosperity and progress. The brilliant spectacle of the court, the prancing of the war-horses, the flash of many chariot wheels, the coming and going of embassies, the visits of foreign dignitaries, all contributed to make the Israelite feel that now at last his king was taking a place among the great ones of the earth. At the centre of the splendour, spinning it about himself tirelessly, exulted its royal creator.

Solomon Provided for Yahweh a Beautiful and Costly House

In the midst of the Solomon narrative stands a block of chapters that tell of the erection of the temple (I Ki. 5–7). It was the first enterprise of Solomon's vast building program. On it he lavished the most painstaking thought and the most liberal expenditure. Modest as its dimensions seem now to us,[1] its construction consumed seven years. One notes particularly the profuse ornamentation with which it was embellished, showing Solomon's interest in carving and sculpture. Its furnishings alone must have cost a great sum.[2]

---

[2] The extent of Solomon's provision for his chariots has recently been shown by the excavations at Megiddo, on the southern edge of the plain of Esdraelon. Here the Oriental Institute has uncovered stabling quarters for at least 500 horses. At Hazor and at Tell el-Hesi (Eglon?) have been found similar groups of stables dating from Solomon's day or shortly afterwards (Albright, RDBL, p. 32).

[1] Its length was about 90 feet, its width about 30 feet, its height about 45 feet (I Ki. 6:2).

[2] For a restoration of the temple see Stade, Geschichte des Volkes Israel (Berlin, 1887), I, opp. p. 328, reproduced in part by Bailey and Kent, History of the Hebrew Commonwealth[2], 1935, p. 132. Watzinger (Denkmäler Palästinas, Leipzig, 1933, I, p. 88f) gives a more recent view, based on archaeological data, of the way in which the temple was constructed. The two pillars, Jachin and Boaz, stood free of the building on the podium, flanking the front steps. The floor of the "oracle" (debir) was raised above that of the "temple" (hekal), thus accounting for the smaller distance between its floor and roof (20 cubits instead of 30, as in the case of the temple). Only

When at last it stood completed Solomon caused the ark of the covenant of Yahweh to be brought from the "city of David, which is Zion" into the new temple. The chapter which describes this ceremony (I Ki. 8) is considered by scholars to have been expanded to such an extent that it must be used with extreme caution. We can however gather this much: the elders of Israel were assembled for a guard of honour, the priests bore the ark and the king with the elders and a great procession of the people went before it. On the way many animals were sacrificed. So they passed up the temple hill through the areas where the other buildings were in process of erection into the temple court, through the porch with its two huge bronze pillars into the temple. Then, while the multitude remained reverently without, the ark was deposited in its resting place, the dark "oracle," and left there under the spreading wings of the cherubim. This being done, and Yahweh (as was thought) having been inducted into His house, Solomon as royal priest uttered a prayer, the opening words of which seem from their poetic form to be original:

"Yahweh hath said that he would dwell in the thick darkness.
I have surely built thee a house of habitation,
A place for thee to dwell in for ever" (8:12f).

After this he turned about and blessed the people, who stood in honour of Yahweh. According to our source there followed a long and beautiful prayer of dedication, in the style of the Deuteronomist, which may have a basis of Solomonic thought if we could but penetrate to it. At its close he again blessed the people and in their name and his own offered further sacrifices. So many were these that he was compelled to hallow the court before the house for the purpose, the brazen altar within "before Yahweh" being too little to receive the offerings of flesh and meal. This was the beginning of eight days of feasting in which the people were generously provided with food and finally sent home "joyful and glad of heart."

We can well believe that this was a supreme moment in Solo-

the foundations and footing of the walls were made of hewn stone, the walls themselves (as universally in the ancient near east) being of brick. Hence their massiveness and their cedar facing. He states also that Phoenician architects were responsible for the general plan of the temple, which was an imitation of Phoenician models because Israel had to that time developed no style for large buildings. The ornamentation likewise was the work of Phoenician craftsmen, who were specially famous for their skill in ivory-carving.

mon's life. The whole enterprise of building the temple had been conceived by him in a genuine desire to honour Yahweh and it must have given him joy to bring it to completion. He was heart and soul a believer in what the temple stood for—the presence of Yahweh and the offering of sacrificial worship to Him. To feel that Yahweh had come to dwell in the house which he had reared with such magnificence must have thrilled him, even if he did not so far forget his dignity as to dance before Yahweh after the example of his father. He must have found it gratifying to stand as priest over the multitudes of his people, to offer and pray on their behalf, to dismiss them with his blessing. We learn that thereafter he offered sacrifices in the temple three times during each year (I Ki. 9:25).

Solomon Carried Cosmopolitanism to Excess

His very aim to surpass the kings of surrounding peoples caused Solomon to fix his eyes upon them and enter into relations with them. They were his circle, and he took on their fashions. Early in his reign he succeeded in gaining the hand of a daughter of the Egyptian Pharaoh. As her dowry he obtained the former Canaanitish stronghold of Gezer, which the Pharaoh took and handed over to him. What he gave in exchange it is not told, but it may have been something in the way of commercial concessions. This Egyptian princess remained ever his chief queen. It was for her that he built the house next his own. Unquestionably her establishment and entourage proved a centre of Egyptian influence which worked upon the king as well as upon his court and capital. The intercourse between Solomon and Egypt seems to have been very close. His wisdom was based upon that of the older country and his constant trade with the Nile valley must have quickened the social, moral and religious influence of Egypt which was such a perennial factor in Palestine throughout the whole Old Testament period.[1]

Later, when about to build the temple, he concluded a commercial treaty with Hiram, king of Tyre, with whom David had already been on friendly terms. From Hiram Solomon obtained timber for his buildings and skilled workmen to cut and deliver it. Phoenician masons assisted in cutting the stone. A famous caster of bronze named Hiram, whose mother had been a widow of Naphthali, was also brought from Tyre to make the two pillars and

[1] Cf. J. A. Wilson, *Haverford Symposium*, p. 220.

the bronze furniture. The plan and details of the temple indeed seem to have been drawn from foreign sources, Egyptian and Phoenician. Its carvings and furniture were all reminiscent of alien religious beliefs and conceptions.[2] In return for his services king Hiram received annually twenty thousand measures (220,000 bushels) of wheat and twenty measures (1800 gallons) of pure oil. Solomon subsequently joined with him in mercantile ventures at sea.[3] After twenty years Hiram was given twenty "cities" of Galilee to make good a deficit in the account. The relationship was long continued and mutually profitable, although Hiram at the end expressed dissatisfaction over the twenty cities. Evidently Solomon knew how to come off well in a business deal.

The narrative of the queen of Sheba's visit (I Ki. 10:1ff) is usually regarded by historians as legendary but it probably has a basis of fact. Distinguished and even royal visitors may have come to Solomon's court from time to time, there to be regally entertained. Solomon's wide business connections with Arabia would make this likely. Tradition lingers over the rare eastern products brought to Israel by the queen, adding regretfully that the like never came again.

Pharaoh's daughter was not the only foreign princess whom Solomon took as wife. After making all allowances for exaggeration, we can see from the late source (I Ki. 11:1ff) that he formed marriage connections with a number of the surrounding peoples. "Women of the Moabites, Ammonites, Edomites, Sidonians and

[2] See Note 2, p. 156f.

[3] I Ki. 9:26ff. Ezion-geber (Elath), Solomon's port at the head of the Gulf of Akaba, on the Red Sea, was excavated in the spring of 1938 by Prof. Nelson Glueck of the American School of Oriental Research in Jerusalem. It was evidently an important place, being not only a seaport but also a centre for the overland caravan routes. In it were manufactured pottery, beads, baskets, mats, ropes, yarn and other objects for home use and commercial purposes. Its chief industry, however, was the refining of copper mined in the Arabah. This "formed the main export article which Solomon sent by ship and caravan to Arabia in exchange for the valuable commodities obtainable there." This trade attained such proportions that in Glueck's opinion it dwarfed Israel's commerce with Egypt and Mesopotamia. "From the time of David on, and particularly during the reign of Solomon, Arabia was not the back door but the front portal of Palestine. . . . Solomon's shipping line evidently made such inroads in the lucrative caravan trade controlled by the queen of Sheba that she hastened to Jerusalem with all manner of presents in order to conclude an amicable trade agreement with him" (I Ki. 10:1ff). Glueck, "Solomon's Naval Base on the Red Sea," BA, Vol. I, No. 3, Sept., 1938, p. 13–16. See also Glueck. BASOR, No. 65, p. 12–13; No. 71, p. 3–18; No. 72, p. 2–13.

Hittites" were to be found in his harem. These would be women of distinction in their own nations, bringing with them a marked foreign atmosphere, opening doors of intercourse between Israel and its neighbours.

Thus the king's court took on an air of cosmopolitan urbanity quite different, we may be sure, from the tone of David's entourage. David married foreign princesses, employed foreign mercenaries for his body-guard and had courteous dealings with Hiram and other surrounding kings; but he did not allow their influence to invade his family life or his court. Solomon however had become a man of the great world and was dragging the hitherto isolated Israelites out into the stream of world culture. We cannot doubt that many of them, especially the young and the fashionable, welcomed this change and like their descendants of pre-Maccabean days took on the outward polish of cosmopolitan ways with alacrity.

Unfortunately such a change, pleasant as it might be, tended to undermine the very thing that Israel had to give to the world. From its birth Israel had been "peculiar"—a nation separated from all other peoples and belonging specially to God. This quality could be maintained only by a continuing aloofness from the rest of the world. Every move towards the adoption of foreign customs, dress and ways of thinking, however innocent these might seem, lessened Israel's isolation and diluted its flavour. The urbane Solomon was deflecting his people from the path of destiny.

And in one respect Solomon's cosmopolitanism exceeded the bounds of what was innocent: it led him to latitudinarianism in religion. Out of a desire doubtless to do the right thing by his foreign wives he erected chapels to various alien deities "on the mount that is before (i.e. east of) Jerusalem" (I Ki. 11:7). Here his several consorts were able to carry on the worship of their home deities—"Ashtoreth, the goddess of the Sidonians," Chemosh, the god of the Moabites, and Milcom or Molech, the god of the Ammonites. Priests of these deities must have formed part of the harem retinue, enjoying honourable social position. They conducted their worship openly with royal approval. The nationals of these countries residing in Jerusalem for trade and other purposes would thus be able to "go to their own church." The Israelitish people would also grow familiar with the presence of such worship as quite a normal and legitimate thing for foreigners. In short, Yahweh was being inducted into the great world and taking

His place (a supreme place, it is true!) among the gods of the earth.

Did Solomon personally participate in any of these foreign rites? The Deuteronomic editor, relying perhaps on an earlier source, declares that he did. "It came to pass, when Solomon was old, that his wives turned away his heart after other gods; and his heart was not perfect with Yahweh his God, as was the heart of David his father" (I Ki. 11:4). What more natural, if these women had a hold on his affections and were disposed to a mild form of proselytizing? They would covet for their own gods the honour of attention from the great king. But Solomon need not have gone so far as actually to worship. The very building of the shrines tended straight towards that deadly peril to Israel's religion against which Moses had striven so fiercely—syncretism, or the mixing in of heathen elements.

We may well imagine that Solomon's policy in this respect would not go unchallenged by upholders of the Mosaic tradition. A reliable source tells how a prophet named Ahijah declared that Yahweh would "rend the kingdom out of the hand of Solomon" (I Ki. 11:31) and give all but one tribe to Jeroboam. Ahijah could not have stood alone. But it is significant that these heathen high places were allowed to remain till Josiah's reformation nearly four hundred years later (II Ki. 23:13f). All that time they stood as silent testimonials of Solomon's religious outlook. Were they in actual use during this period? Our sources make no answer. Probably not. But they must have given the encouragement of Solomon's example to those later kings who brought foreign innovations into Yahweh's worship and even practised the terrible rite of child-sacrifice, to which the cult of Molech seems to have been specially addicted (II Ki. 16:10ff; 21:3ff).

Solomon's Program Compelled Him to Impoverish His People

As we read the accounts of Solomon's magnificence and his ambitious building program we are struck with the fact that he had great resources at his command. He must moreover have been a man of remarkable ability for organization and administration.[1]

[1] "The unique document preserved in I Ki. 4:7–19 gave originally a complete list of Solomon's new administrative districts with their prefects and their geographical extent," though when it came to the editor of I Kings it had been somewhat damaged and its text through frequent copying had become very corrupt (Albright, "The Administrative Divisions of Israel and Judah," JPOS, V, No. 1, 1925, p. 17ff).

Our narratives are not wholly clear as to whence he derived his vast income.

Much must have come from direct taxation. For the needs of his table he divided all of Israel into districts, each under its officer, who saw that the royal larder was supplied for one month of the year. This made for a rough equality of burdens, although Judah was apparently exempted in the arrangement. It also insured thoroughness and efficiency (I Ki. 4:7ff). In addition he seems to have taken large amounts of wheat and oil for export to Hiram (I Ki. 5:11). The most noted feature of his taxation system was the levying of enforced labour to carry out his building projects. In one notice (I Ki. 9:20ff) we are assured that this was applied only to the remnants of Canaanitish population, but elsewhere we read (I Ki. 5:13ff) that it extended to all Israel. Tribute was also exacted from subject kingdoms (I Ki. 4:21).

Commerce too furnished its share. The Israelitish products of wheat and oil were exported to Phoenicia in exchange for labour, timber and gold (I Ki. 5:7ff; 9:14). Solomon carried on an extensive trade in horses and chariots, which he bought from Egypt and sold to the kings of the Hittites and of Syria (I Ki. 10:28-29). The story of the queen of Sheba's exchange of presents with Solomon may be a reminiscence of caravan and shipping trade with Arabia. Finally, there were the business ventures undertaken in conjunction with Hiram on the Red Sea, which were of a peaceful and commercial nature (I Ki. 9:26; 10:11).[2]

But all this would hardly account for Solomon's resources. We are told of an annual income of 666 talents of gold "besides that which the traders brought, and the traffic of the merchants and of all the kings of the mingled people and of the governors of the country" (I Ki. 10:14-15). Evidently the narrator had no distinct idea as to whence it came. Perhaps, as has been conjectured, Solomon may have taken toll from the foreign commerce that passed through his land; or the figures may be grossly exaggerated.

As one reads his story however one cannot avoid the impression that his magnificence and expenditure rested on an unsound economic basis. In spite of what appears to have been its amazing productivity, Palestine was after all a small country, unable to support the weight of the royal program. Moreover Solomon with all his building seems to have done nothing to increase the agricultural output. Nor were his buildings of a sort to promote

[2] Archaeology has thrown much interesting light on Solomon's trading activities. See Albright, *RDBL*, p. 33, and note 3, p. 159.

wealth, unless possibly the fortifications along the trade routes may have done so. At the end of twenty years of building he was compelled to make up a deficit in his trade balance with Hiram by ceding him part of his capital—the twenty cities of Galilee.

Being economically unsound, the program of Solomon set a false economic standard. The kings who succeeded him had always his splendour to look back upon with envy and to strive after as a goal. Witness Rehoboam's pitiful attempt to keep up his father's style by replacing the gold shields with brass! (I Ki. 14:27f). Nor would his example stop short with kings. It must have been imitated in some degree by private persons, thus creating the desire to be rich which was later to work such evil consequences.

But the worst thing about Solomon's program was its social effect: it destroyed the happiness of his people. The heavy taxation, the levy with its enforced removal of men from home and work, the handing over of Israelitish cities to a foreign master—these are the kind of things that in all ages have wrought misery wherever they have been put into practice. We know that discontent gathered among all but the men of Judah. A young man of Ephraim, Jeroboam the son of Nebat, whom Solomon had given "charge of all the labour of the house of Joseph" "lifted up his hand against the king" (I Ki. 11:26ff). Just what the nature and occasion of the attempt may have been we do not know, for in our present source this part of the narrative has been omitted to make room for a Deuteronomic section. But we can infer that he must in some way have taken the part of the Ephraimitish labourers against the king and have been compelled in consequence to flee to Egypt. The state of the public mind is clearly seen in the narrative of what occurred immediately after Solomon's death. This same Jeroboam, who had been sent for by common consent and made the spokesman of all Israel, bluntly demanded of Solomon's son Rehoboam that he lessen the burdens laid upon them by his father. Such was the legacy bequeathed by Solomon to his feeble successor. Rehoboam tried to play the role of the "red-blooded" man who would take no nonsense from inferiors, and so lost Israel (I Ki. 12:1ff).

In the light of these considerations a sober judgment of Solomon's program must pronounce it profoundly unethical. He failed to carry out the first duty of a ruler, to benefit his subjects. To use a metaphor employed by the prophets, he did not feed the sheep entrusted to him. The fact is he was not thinking of his people. His interest lay in his own accomplishments and splendour, especially in his buildings. His mind, like that of many another great builder, was on stones and mortar more than on men and women. The passion for building is apt to reverse the true importance of things and make of people a means rather than an end. It forgets that the important structures are after all immaterial fabrics like national happiness.

His policy was also incredibly shortsighted. It is instructive here to note the contrast between him and David, whose statesmanship seems to have been fundamentally sound throughout. All that David did was in the direction of Israel's normal growth: it was, in a sense, inevitable. It might have been the same with Solomon. Had his great powers and his potential resources been directed towards developing a contented people he would have passed on to his son a nation ripened and unified. As it was, he went on a false course that could end in nothing but disaster.

The irony of the situation from a religious point of view is that Solomon probably looked on all the wealth and splendour and glory obtained by these means as "given" him by God!

Concluding Reflections on Solomon's Reign

Two things of value did Solomon do for Israel: He became the father of its wisdom and he gave it its temple.

In the course of centuries this wisdom was to enlist the service of earnest thinkers and develop a noble teaching literature in which deep thoughts of God and a lofty ethic should find expression. How far it had advanced towards this goal in Solomon's day is not known to us. But it is fair that he should have the credit of having imparted to it something of an original impulse.

The temple undoubtedly came from him. Through it Israel's worship was made more splendid and beautiful. It was destined to eclipse and finally to crowd out of existence the other shrines of the land. Its priests were to make their influence increasingly felt in the direction of a lofty and imageless worship, as against the sensuous cult of the "high places." Whether such a tendency towards purity owed anything to Solomon is a question. But at any rate he created the conditions under which it afterward worked effectively.

For the rest of his work and influence we may say in one word that there was nothing for which he stood that the insight of the prophets did not soon or late condemn.[1] Luxury and display at

[1] Cf. Deut. 17:16ff.

the expense of the poor, the building of great houses and fortifications, the dependence on horses and chariots, the seeking of foreign
alliances, the importation of foreign cults, the neglect of the people's good,—the whole spirit of worldly pride that lifts up itself
over others, and that before God—these (the prophets said) were
hateful to Yahweh. Wisdom itself they at times condemned because it gloried in its own attainments rather than in God. Even
the temple did not escape their denunciation. All its sanctity and
its worship (they said) would not avail to save it unless those
who thronged its courts should wash their hands from blood and
oppression. Indeed, they went so far as to declare that the entire
institution of animal sacrifices to which it was devoted was a
matter of indifference if not of loathing in the eyes of a God who
desired the knowledge of Himself more than burnt offerings.

Chapter IX

ELIJAH

[c. 850 B.C.]

The Sources

The thrilling story of Elijah is contained in a block of chapters in the Books of the Kings (I 17-19; 21; II 1-2). These are taken by the editor from a source that probably originated in prophetic circles somewhere between 800 and 750 B.C. It was written by one of the "sons of the prophets" to glorify the great man of God to whom they looked as their unique leader. Back of it stands oral tradition which had already become mixed with legendary elements. Its fondness for the miraculous obscures to some extent the outlines of Elijah's figure, but scholars are pretty well agreed that it preserves trustworthy recollections of the man and his accomplishments. The religious and political situation is depicted accurately and the chief characters impress the reader as true to life. These narratives however are not all on the same historical level. The story of Naboth's vineyard (I 21) reads like sober history, while the accounts of Elijah's calling down fire from heaven (II 1) and ascending thither in a chariot of fire (II 2) are manifestly pure legend. These last two narratives may proceed from a later hand. In any case we shall not use them in our study, but depend wholly upon the material in I Kings.

In order however to understand the situation which Elijah confronted we must briefly survey the history of the northern kingdom from the death of Solomon to the reign of Ahab; and here we shall avail ourselves of a great deal of excellent historical material drawn by the editor from the sources which he calls the Books of the Chronicles of the Kings of Israel (and Judah). He has also embodied less reliable material from prophetic circles; and has embellished the entire compilation with comments from his own Deuteronomic point of view. But this does not prevent us from getting a correct understanding of the events and their meaning.

Jeroboam the Son of Nebat

In the period that elapsed between Solomon and Elijah one man stands out as exercising a formative influence upon the religious development of Israel. Jeroboam I of the northern kingdom accomplished two things which had deep effect. He led and made permanent the revolt of the northern tribes from Judah and he instituted the worship of the golden bulls.

We have already seen how as a young man he had in some way opposed Solomon, perhaps by taking the part of the Ephraim-itish labourers against their oppressor. He appears in the narrative as a "mighty man of valour" and industrious, displaying such ability that Solomon "gave him charge over all the labour of the house of Joseph" (I 11:28). This office he exercised in such a way as to win the confidence of the people under him. He must have been a man with sympathy for these workers and of great boldness, for one would not lightly face Solomon's wrath. Tradition says that while engaged in this work he was told by a prophet of Shiloh named Ahijah that Yahweh would rend ten tribes from Solomon and give them to him. This must have fired his ambition and encouraged him to withstand his sovereign in such a fashion that he was compelled to flee to Egypt.

On the death of Solomon the leaders of the north immediately sent for him as the one man to whom they might turn in the crisis. It was Jeroboam who, at the head of "all the assembly of Israel" in Shechem, faced Rehoboam as he had faced his father before him (I 12:1ff). The demand laid before the new king was explicit and peremptory: Israel would serve him on condition that he lightened the burdens imposed by Solomon. After three days' consideration the infatuated king gave a rough reply: his little finger would be heavier than his father's loins. Israel's answer was a declaration of independence.

"What portion have we in David?
Neither have we inheritance in the son of Jesse:
To your tents, O Israel!
Now see to thine own house, David!"

Over the new state Jeroboam was made king by popular choice. He entered upon his royal work with vigour by building two strongholds, Shechem in the central highlands and Penuel across the Jordan. Then he was compelled to face a serious problem. How

should the break between north and south be made permanent?
The custom of going up to the temple at Jerusalem, which had
apparently arisen during Solomon's reign, might easily lead to a
healing of the schism and a return to Rehoboam. Jeroboam took
the best advice he could get and decided upon a bold course. A
new religious centre must be set up within the new kingdom to
take the place Jerusalem had begun to occupy. This he accomplished in a thoroughgoing way by establishing two conveniently
located shrines with a new priesthood and ready-made calendar.
The places chosen were already hallowed by long use as holy
places—Bethel in the south and Dan in the far north (I 12:25ff).

It was in connection with this plan to promote disunion that
he introduced the special feature of worship which was for ever
afterwards to be connected with his name. Acting with the advice
of his counsellors he set up in each of the two chosen shrines
golden (or gold-plated) images of a bull. Just what was their
significance is uncertain. They may have been intended as representations of Yahweh [1] or they may have been looked upon as
merely His footstool.[2] It is quite clear in either case that they had
to do with Yahweh alone. Nothing was further from Jeroboam's
mind than to bring in the worship of foreign gods.[3]

Why did he take this step? The answer seems plain—it was
sure to prove popular. What he wanted was to bring the people
to Dan and Bethel and he believed this was the way to do it. The
result proved him correct: the people came; the danger of reunion
was banished. From that time on the golden bulls were firmly
established in the worship of the northern kingdom.

These two accomplishments of Jeroboam are viewed very differently by the Deuteronomic editors who have written their
philosophy of history into our present Book of Kings. The revolt

[1] So, for example, Hölscher, GIJR, p. 89f; Oesterley and Robinson, HR²,
p. 160; Lods, Israel, p. 458; Leslie, OTR, p. 139. Pfeiffer denies that there
existed any images of Yahweh (JBL, XLV, 1926, p. 211ff). Eichrodt (TAT,
p. 52), has the same view.

[2] So Eichrodt, TAT, p. 52. Hempel, GMAT², p. 265, on the other hand, is
undecided, though he inclines to regard them as images of Yahweh.

[3] Meek, HO, p. 158, indeed believes that Jeroboam was re-establishing the
worship of the bull god of the ancient Israelitish confederacy, which had
been superseded by the worship of Yahweh, the god of the southern confederacy, through the missionary efforts of Levitical priests. This recent view
involves the setting aside of the plain testimony of tradition, which represents
Yahweh as the God of north as well as south, from the days of Joshua
onwards. The present writer remains unconvinced by Meek's able arguments.

from Rehoboam has their approval: it was of Yahweh, a punishment for Solomon's religious disloyalty. The setting up of the golden bulls, on the contrary, seems to them a great crime. They look on it as the worship of other gods. To their mind it blighted all the succeeding religion of the northern kingdom, and they shudder to tell how king after king did evil in the sight of Yahweh by "walking in the way of Jeroboam, and in his sin wherewith he made Israel to sin" (I 15:34 and elsewhere).

When we try to penetrate behind these editors to the opinions of Jeroboam's contemporaries we find that the prophet Ahijah (as we have seen) gave Yahweh's blessing upon the revolt from Judah but later turned against Jeroboam. The narrative in I 14:1ff has been so coloured by the editors that we can no longer be sure of the reason for this change in Ahijah's attitude; but it seems likely that it was not very different from the reason now given in the text—that Jeroboam set up the images. Chapter 13, which is plainly legendary, tells of a prophet who was sent from Judah to denounce the new worship: it may have a kernel of truth. Indeed nothing is more likely than that such an innovation, however it might suit the mood of the people generally, would call forth strong denunciation from upholders of the old Mosaic tradition. If as seems probable the decalogue in its shorter form goes back to Moses, then Israel already possessed a definite command prohibiting the making and adoration of images. On the other hand, the institution seems to have given no wide-spread offence. Isolated prophetic denunciation could avail little against the popular craving.

Our estimate of Jeroboam's deeds must be an independent one. First, as to the rebellion. Ahijah's approval of it cannot blind us to the fact that for the whole people it was a supreme political calamity. It meant prostration, weakness, internecine warfare. It swept away in a moment all the slow building up of national unity that had been going on under Saul and David. Who can doubt that Israel's true destiny lay in union? Separatism is generally a step backward in human development and it was emphatically so here.

Northern Israel also lost two definite things by the break. For the firmly established dynasty of David it exchanged that of Jeroboam, which possessed no prestige and was soon to be thrust aside with blood to make way for another and yet another. It also deprived itself of the benefits that it could have derived from the temple at Jerusalem. With all their faults the Jerusalem priesthood did stand in the days that followed for a purer tradition of worship than their fellow-priests of the high places scattered through the land. It was in Jerusalem that an imageless worship centred in the ark. If the centralizing tendency which began in the days of Solomon had been allowed to continue the temple would probably have come more and more to set a higher standard for worship throughout Israel.

Upon Jeroboam's shoulders therefore must rest the responsibility for this disaster with all that it involved. True, Israel might have revolted without him; but he provided the necessary leadership and above all he set effective obstacles in the way of reunion—obstacles that were never overcome.

The introduction of the golden bulls, in the second place, meant a retrogression towards the sensuous in religion. It is hard for us to appraise exactly what its effect was upon the people's idea of God. But we can see in a general way that it must have accentuated all those lower elements in worship which the Israelites had about them in Canaan for centuries. Scholars are agreed that it led to the "baalization" of Yahweh's religion. In themselves the bulls were imported symbols, bringing with them from whatever source they came a whole complex of heathen associations. The population of the north moreover was far from being purely Israelitish. So much absorption of Canaanitish blood had been going on that the result must have been a mixed race with mixed traditions. They would take all the more kindly therefore to these "nature" aspects of worship—feasting, drinking, carousing, sacred prostitution. By giving them what they craved Jeroboam was doing a very serious thing. He was putting the stamp of royal approval upon lower customs against which a king should have contended.[4]

After Jeroboam nothing of special interest is recorded until we come to a second royal name which is written in lurid letters upon the story of Israel's religion.

Jezebel's Attempt to Supplant Yahweh by Melkart

In the history of the two kingdoms our attention for the first hundred years is fixed on northern Israel, which was at once the more vigorous and the more influential. After several violent changes of dynasty its throne was seized by a remarkable man who was destined to bring it to a high state of prosperity. Omri, a military commander proclaimed king by his soldiers, after insur-

[4] Cf. Leslie, OTR, p. 140.

ing his throne set about building up his kingdom in so effective a fashion that it came from thenceforth to be known in the Assyrian records as the "house of Omri." Little is told of him in the Books of the Kings, except that he purchased the hill of Samaria and built upon it a new capital called by this name. The beauty and military strength of this city, as well as the fact that it was unhampered by past associations and jealousies, showed Omri's genius in choosing it. Although hard pressed in his wars with Damascus he was able to establish Israelitish dominion over the transjordanic land of Moab, deriving yearly therefrom a large tribute in the lambs which were the special product of the country. He revived Solomon's policy of making marriage alliances with surrounding states by obtaining for his son Ahab the hand of Jezebel, the daughter of Ethbaal king of Sidon. After a reign of twelve years he was succeeded by Ahab, who seems to have inherited his father's ability as ruler (I 16:23ff). And now arose suddenly a new and alarming crisis in Israel's religious history.

Hitherto the kings of Israel had gone on in the path marked out for its religion by their predecessors, "walking in the way of Jeroboam." In other words, they had promoted the inherited worship which in spite of its sensuous character held closely to Yahweh only. Ahab took a new step. He built for his Sidonian wife a "house of Baal" in the new capital and therein "reared up an altar for Baal." The particular baal thus honoured was Melkart, the god of the Sidonians, whom Jezebel worshipped. In doing this Ahab was following the precedent set by Solomon a century earlier in Jerusalem. But for the northern kingdom it was an innovation. And it was probably opposed by enthusiasts for Yahweh just as Solomon's shrines for foreign deities had called forth prophetic disapproval in his day. If however nothing more had come of it than followed from Solomon's policy, the temple to Melkart might have taken its place among the institutions of Samaria without causing any serious disturbance to the national religion. Jezebel and her household might have worshipped there quietly, and after her death the foreign rites would probably have been allowed to lapse through lack of interest.

But Jezebel was of a very different nature from Solomon's foreign wives. Everything that we know about her shows her to have been a woman born to dominate, a very fountain of burning energy, passionate, self-willed, determined, stopping at nothing to effect her ends. To all this was added a religious devotion bordering on fanaticism. For her it was impossible that her god Melkart should remain modestly in the background, tolerated as a guest and ignored by all save the few Sidonians who might be living in Samaria. No! He must at least take an equal place with Israel's God, if he did not thrust Yahweh quite to one side. To this end she imported four hundred and fifty prophets of Melkart and four hundred prophets of "the Asherah," which was evidently closely bound up with Melkart's worship. These she made part of her retinue and supported at the public expense. Nothing definite is told us of what followed but we can legitimately infer that these devotees of Melkart set about making as much impression as possible upon the people. They would naturally be opposed by the prophets of Yahweh and sharp conflicts must have ensued. At any rate we learn that Jezebel began to "cut off the prophets of Yahweh." That would have been her next step. Something like a thoroughgoing effort to sweep away the leaders of Yahweh's religion seems to have taken place. Many were killed. We read of one hundred finding a miserable refuge in a cave where Obadiah, the faithful steward of Ahab's household, kept them alive with bread and water. The places of Yahweh's worship were also attacked and His altars thrown down (I 18:13ff; 19:14).

Ahab's attitude at this juncture is not quite clear. He appears to have allowed Jezebel to carry out her desires without resistance; it is possible that he even helped her with zest. The compiler declares that he himself worshipped Baal (Melkart); but of this we cannot be certain. The puzzling thing is that elsewhere Ahab is portrayed as an adherent of Yahweh. He gave his three children names compounded with that of Yahweh (Athaliah, Ahaziah, Jehoram); and later we find him to be on good terms with "prophets of Yahweh" (I 20:13; 22:5ff). In fact we see him at the end of his life consulting four hundred of these (I 22:5ff); and this has led some scholars to maintain that the notices in chapters 18 and 19 of a destruction of the prophets of Yahweh are erroneous. But the probability is that Ahab's policy did not remain consistent. After the crisis which we are now describing was over he seems to have held on the whole to Yahweh, but for the present he was with Jezebel. We need not be surprised at this for she was just the woman to carry even a strong man like Ahab off his feet. He was evidently devoted to her and had implicit confidence in her leadership.

The people generally appear to have taken no firm stand for or against Yahweh. Our prophetic source describes their conduct in the crisis as a "limping between two sides" (I 18:21). Most of them were ready to pay homage to Melkart by kneeling before him and kissing his symbol, yet on the other hand they still kept up the traditional adherence to Yahweh. No help could be looked for from them to protect the persecuted prophets of Yahweh; indeed, they are spoken of as actually taking part in their destruction (I 19:14). So far as they were concerned Jezebel might have her way. It was an inglorious role that they played but one quite characteristic of the rank and file of Israel in early days.

The very existence of Yahweh's religion in the northern kingdom, therefore, was threatened by this one determined woman. What might have been the issue if she had been permitted to proceed unchallenged, no one can say. But she was not so permitted. Suddenly, in the midst of her victorious course, she was confronted by a foeman greater than herself.

Elijah Brings about a Reaction in Favour of Yahweh

At some moment in the onward march of Jezebel's policy Ahab found himself face to face with a champion of Yahweh who appears in our prophetic narrative with the briefest of introductions: "Elijah the Tishbite, who was of the sojourners of Gilead." Whether or no his contemporaries already knew him we can only guess. But it is plain that to them as to us he was a man of mystery, appearing and disappearing with a suddenness that baffled and perplexed them. From his home across the Jordan among the more primitive element of the people he had come to "sojourn" in western Israel. Tradition has preserved something of his appearance—wearing a garment of hair, girt with a girdle of leather about his loins (II 1:8), a man of the rough pasture lands bordering on the wilderness, who could live on the scantiest food and could run ahead of horses for eighteen miles (I 18:46)—a man of God, whose proper haunt was solitude, moving among the scenes of civilization as one apart, shrouded in solemnity and awe. He it was who now arose to fling down before Ahab the gauntlet of Yahweh's defiance. "As Yahweh, the God of Israel liveth, before whom I stand, there shall not be dew nor rain these years, but according to my word" (I 17:1).

Whether Ahab sought to arrest the bold combatant we are not told. At any rate he made good his escape and for two years nothing was heard of him. Meanwhile the doom pronounced took effect. A long drought brought the land to the verge of desperation. As the suffering increased the king's wrath burned ever hotter against the man who was responsible for it. Search was made for Elijah in vain. At last after two years he faced Ahab once more. "Is it thou, thou troubler of Israel?" cried the enraged monarch. "*I* have not troubled Israel," came the answer, "but thou and thy father's house, in that ye have forsaken the commandments of Yahweh, and followed the Baalim" (I 18:18). Then came a demand: Ahab was to gather at mount Carmel "all Israel" to meet Elijah, and along with them all the prophets of Baal and the Asherah. Ahab complied. Then ensued one of the most dramatic scenes of the Bible. On the wooded headland that rose high above the Mediterranean the solitary prophet of Yahweh met His people with the challenge to choose (once for all) between Yahweh and Baal. Legend has been busy with the story but through its obscurities we can still discern the fact that some test whereby decision should be made was agreed upon and successfully met. The people shouted "Yahweh, *He* is God! Yahweh, *He* is God!" The foreign prophets were dragged down to the Kishon, which flows along Carmel's base, and slaughtered remorselessly at Elijah's command. The long drought was broken and Ahab was forced to drive home to Jezreel in the midst of a great storm of rain.

Yahweh's victory was indeed not yet complete. The undaunted Jezebel, on learning from Ahab what had taken place, sent to Elijah a threat that caused him to flee for his life. The account of his flight (I 19) is one of the supreme chapters of the Bible. Sustained by heavenly food he journeyed (tradition said) forty days and forty nights to Horeb the mount of God, and lodged there in a cave. Presently came an awful theophany. Yahweh passed by in a great and strong wind. The wind was followed by an earthquake, the earthquake by a fire. But Yahweh was not in any of these. At last, after the fire, came a still small voice; and Elijah, wrapping his face in his mantle, went out of the cave to meet God.

"And behold, there came a voice unto him, and said, What doest thou here, Elijah? And he said, I have been very jealous for Yahweh, the God of hosts; for the children of Israel have forsaken thy covenant, thrown down thine altars, and slain thy prophets with the sword; and I, even I only, am left; and they seek my life, to take it away."

Elijah was a beaten man. But Yahweh had only just begun to fight!

"And Yahweh said unto him, Go, return on thy way to the wilderness of Damascus; and when thou comest, thou shalt anoint Hazael to be king over Syria; and Jehu the son of Nimshi shalt thou anoint to be king over Israel; and Elisha, the son of Shaphat, shalt thou anoint to be prophet in thy room. And it shall come to pass, that him that escapeth from the sword of Hazael shall Jehu slay; and him that escapeth from the sword of Jehu shall Elisha slay."

So the apostates would all perish. But not the faithful.

"Yet will I leave me seven thousand in Israel, all the knees which have not bowed unto Baal, and every mouth which hath not kissed him."

However we may interpret this theophany, there can be little doubt that it stamped itself forever upon Elijah's mind. He had been sent back again to renew the struggle by a God who knew no defeat. Just what further measures he took is not recorded; but he now had come to see that there were at least "seven thousand" in Israel who had remained true to Yahweh. Feeling no longer alone and sure that Yahweh would make good His cause through terrible measures of vengeance he went on with his work in confidence.

As a matter of fact the tide had turned. We read of no further attempts of Jezebel to put down the religion of Yahweh, while Ahab now showed himself an adherent of Israel's God. The worship of Melkart still went on and years later there were enough of his declared followers in Israel to fill his temple (II 10:21). But Jezebel seems not to have replaced the great retinue of prophets which she had kept about her at first. Prophets of Yahweh began to utter their messages boldly; their numbers multiplied till four hundred could be found to prophesy at one time before Ahab (I 22:6).

The reason for this change must be found in Elijah's resolute and effective intervention. It was he who so "brought" the people's "heart back again" to Yahweh (I 18:37) that even Jezebel realized the fruitlessness of further efforts to supplant His worship by that of Melkart. The danger of national apostasy passed, never to reappear. Nor must we forget that this had been accomplished at the risk of the prophet's own life. If he had failed that day on Carmel his fate would have been the same as that he meted out to the defeated prophets of Baal.

Elijah Seals the Doom of the House of Ahab

When Elijah had come face to face with Yahweh at Horeb (so said tradition) he had received a command to supplant the royal house of Ahab with a new king, Jehu the son of Nimshi (I 19:16). He was also to anoint Hazael to be king over Syria (v. 15). Since he seems to have made no attempt to carry out either of these injunctions it is possible that they were read back into his story from the traditions concerning Elisha, who is reported to have fulfilled them both (II 8:7ff; 9–10). But whether or no he returned from Horeb with the determination to root out the dynasty of Ahab, the time presently came when he declared war upon it.

Next to the palace of Ahab in Jezreel there was a vineyard owned by a citizen named Naboth. This Ahab wanted for a vegetable garden and approached its owner with a fair offer of purchase or exchange. To Naboth however the thought of alienating any of his ancestral heritage seemed almost sacrilegious, and he gave the king a decided refusal. Ahab, well acquainted with the right of a citizen to dispose of his land, took the refusal as final and returned to his palace in a sulk. When the fiery Jezebel learned the reason for his ill humour she asked scornfully whether he governed Israel or not! "Arise, and eat bread, and let thy heart be merry: I will give thee the vineyard of Naboth the Jezreelite!" Ahab weakly acquiesced and with characteristic vigour she arranged a "frame-up" which led to the execution of Naboth on a false charge involving apparently the confiscation of his estate. Flushed with triumph she came to Ahab. "Arise, take possession of the vineyard of Naboth . . . which he refused to give thee for money; for Naboth is not alive, but dead."

Ahab accordingly rode down to look at his new property, accompanied by two officers who were afterward to play a tragic part in the history of his house, Bidkar and Jehu. His gratification must have been troubled by an uneasy conscience for Jezebel's high handed deed had outraged the traditions of Israel. Suddenly he saw before him a well known figure. "Hast thou found me, O mine enemy?" he cried. Elijah made answer: "Thus saith Yahweh, Hast thou killed, and also taken possession? . . . In the place where dogs licked the blood of Naboth shall dogs lick thy blood, even thine."

What must have been Jezebel's disgust when her husband came back from his new vineyard a broken man! For when Ahab heard the words of Elijah "he rent his clothes and put sackcloth upon his flesh and went softly." So her enemy had triumphed once more! But at the sight of Ahab's repentance the harsh prophet softened. "The word of Yahweh came to Elijah the Tishbite, saying, Seest thou how Ahab humbleth himself before me? because he humbleth himself before me, I will not bring the evil in his days; but in his son's days will I bring the evil upon his house" (I 21).

The doom then was postponed. Elijah disappears from Ahab's path forever. Not so however another prophet, Micaiah ben Imlah, who had likewise set himself against the king. In another source, which apparently does not belong to the Elijah narratives, we learn how Ahab—headstrong as always—constrained king Jehoshaphat of Judah to join him in an attempt to recover from the Syrians the town of Ramoth in Gilead. The pious Jehoshaphat, who seems to have complied only because he was a vassal of Ahab's, demanded that the will of Yahweh be first ascertained. Four hundred prophets of Yahweh were then summoned and one and all assured the kings of success. When Jehoshaphat remained still unconvinced Ahab at last consented to call Micaiah, warning Jehoshaphat that Micaiah would prophesy evil, not good. He always did; that was why Ahab hated him. The scene that follows is among the most dramatic of the Bible, but there is no space to describe it. Micaiah stood his ground against the four hundred prophets of victory and Ahab, defying him, went up to Ramoth-gilead only to meet his death there (I 22).

So Elijah survived Ahab; but Ahaziah his son succeeded to the throne, and the indomitable Jezebel remained entrenched as queen mother in the palace. The prophet was not destined to witness the carrying out of the doom upon the condemned house. His remaining history is sketched for us in two scenes, both of which are densely veiled in legend. The first shows him calling down fire from heaven to consume the soldiers sent out by Ahaziah to arrest him (II 1). The second is the famous narrative of his assumption into heaven by a chariot and horses of fire appearing in a whirlwind. Thus, according to tradition, he passed from earth without experiencing death, letting his mantle fall upon Elisha as he departed.

It is now time to inquire concerning the religious ideas of this prodigious man who in Israel's memory was to rank second to none but Moses.

In Elijah the Religion of Moses Lived Again

The study of Elijah's religion is rendered difficult by the meagreness and legendary nature of our sources. We must however do our best to gather it from the fleeting and uncertain glimpses that we get of him in the narratives.

In the main we perceive that he was faithful to the traditions of Moses. Yahweh had not yet become fully naturalized in Canaan. Though Elijah had most of his dealings with God in that country he seems to have felt that Horeb, the mountain on which Moses received the law, was Yahweh's home. Thither he journeyed in the hour of deepest discouragement and from a cave on its slopes he was summoned to receive a theophany. Yahweh was therefore pre-eminently a God of the desert, of the barren silent wastes over which Israel had wandered in its nomadic stage.

To his mind this Yahweh was a Being of transcendent majesty and power. The mystery that surrounded Elijah himself bespoke this. Like prophet, like God. The Lord before whom such a man as Elijah "stood" must be very high above the companionable nature-deity in whose presence people could gorge themselves with food and drink and sport with sacred prostitutes. He was too great to be contained in the wind, the earthquake or the fire (I 19:11f). Only in the sound of gentle stillness could one find Him, and then one must go out to meet Him with one's mantle wrapped about one's face.

Yahweh was to Elijah a jealous God, tolerating no rivals. It was this certainty that lent such passion to his contention that Israel could follow only one God. To "limp between two sides" was to do outrage to Yahweh. How different this exclusiveness of Elijah from Solomon's easy-going cosmopolitanism or Ahab's complaisance. "Go," he cried to the messengers of Ahaziah, "turn again unto the king that sent you and say unto him, Thus saith Yahweh, Is it because there is no God in Israel that thou sendest to inquire of Baal-zebub, the god of Ekron?" (II 1:6).

Jealousy involved wrath. "Therefore," concluded the message to Ahaziah, "thou shalt not come down from the bed whither thou art gone up, but shalt surely die." If Jezebel murdered the prophets of Yahweh, Elijah felt that Yahweh could retaliate in kind. "Take the prophets of Baal; let not one of them escape!" "Him that escapeth from the sword of Hazael shall Jehu slay; and him that escapeth from the sword of Jehu shall Elisha slay" (I 19:17). It was Elijah's dealing with Ahaziah's officers that the

sons of Zebedee seem to have had in mind when they asked Jesus'
permission to call down fire from heaven upon the inhospitable
Samaritan villagers (Lk. 9:54). To Elijah as to Moses Yahweh
was passionate, volcanic, death-dealing.

He was also a fighter—impetuous, aggressive, acknowledging
no defeat. To Elijah's despairing request that he might be permitted to die Yahweh replied with a peremptory "Go, return . . ."
(I 19:15). He was the Intervener, the God about to do, the God
with a plan, summoning His servant to carry it out against the
world.

Yet to Elijah as to Moses Yahweh was also a God of love. Back
of the drought which He visited upon Israel lay the desire to
bring His people to a better mind that He might bless them. He
commanded the ravens to feed His servant and supported him
on his long journey to Horeb with supernatural nourishment. He
sent him to bless the Sidonian widow and heard his prayer to
restore her child to life. Upon the penitent Ahab He had mercy
(I 21:29). His grim prophet who uttered threats of woe was after
all the nation's truest helper; "the chariot of Israel and the horsemen thereof" (II 2:12).

Like Moses, Elijah believed that Yahweh was pleased with sacrifices. The cult side of religion held a high place in his thought.
Tradition relates that the test he proposed to the people in deciding
between Yahweh and Baal had to do with an act of sacrifice. The
question was, which offering would be accepted by heaven—
Elijah's or his opponents? With his own hands he repaired the
overturned altar of Yahweh (I 18:30). A chief item of his charge
against Israel was that they had "thrown down" these same altars
(I 19:14).

Along with offerings Yahweh demanded righteousness. Here
again Elijah kept true to Moses. It happened indeed that his main
struggle was directed against Baal worship, in which questions of
ethics were only indirectly involved. But tradition has preserved
one splendid instance in which he intervened to avenge a deed
of high handed oppression. The story of Naboth's vineyard leaves
only one thing to be criticized in Elijah's conduct. Why could he
not have arrived on the scene in time to prevent Naboth's murder?
Vengeance was a poor substitute for the protection which Moses
gave to the oppressed of his day.

We are also reminded of Moses by the atmosphere of the marvellous which surrounds Elijah in our sources. It has been often
noted that the miracles recorded in the Old Testament are not

distributed equally through its narratives but are more or less concentrated in certain periods. They cluster about Moses and Joshua
in profusion, then appear but thinly through the next four centuries, only to burst forth in renewed abundance in the path of
Elijah and Elisha. This cannot be attributed entirely to the different view-point of the historical writers; it must go back to the
oral traditions from which the writers drew. For some reason
Moses, Elijah and Elisha attracted the marvellous to themselves.
Why? Partly because they accomplished astonishing results which
we moderns would have explained differently but would have
found astonishing also. They were super-men, if we may use that
hackneyed term. A power lived in them that is seldom found
among men, a power whose source was the unseen world. The
question arises naturally, Did they believe in their own capacity
(by virtue of God's endowment, of course) to work miracles? Our
answer must be yes. Unless all the indications of our sources are
deceptive, Elijah must have been convinced that God wrought
wonders by his hand. This need not surprise us. If Isaiah could
challenge Ahaz to ask any sign he might wish "either in the depth
or in the height above" (Is. 7:11) the more primitive Elijah might
well have proposed the test of fire from heaven to the people
assembled on mount Carmel.[1]

In saying this of Moses and Elijah one is but saying that they
were men of faith. Not faith of the usual kind but of the sort
that once in a while comes to tabernacle in humanity. They lived
so completely with God that for them the impossible did not exist.
It was all perfectly simple. What God wanted done would be
done. Why not?

Therefore Elijah, like Moses, was a man of prayer. "Standing"
as he did before God he naturally asked what he felt was necessary
to the carrying out of God's will. He might also present a personal
request, as when he prayed for the restoration of the dead child
to life. In either case he was dealing with a "living" God, who
could, and probably would, give him what he sought. No scene
in the Bible brings absolute faith in prayer before us more vividly
than Elijah bowed down on the top of Carmel with his face between his knees. He was, we gather, asking for the rain. "And
he said to his servant, Go up now, and look towards the sea. And
he went up and looked and said, There is nothing. And he said,
Go again seven times. And it came to pass at the seventh time,
that he said, Behold, there ariseth a cloud out of the sea, as small

[1] See the similar discussion regarding Moses, p. 13f.

as a man's hand. And Elijah said, Go up, say unto Ahab, Make ready thy chariot and get thee down, that the rain stop thee not" (I 18:43–44).

A final point of resemblance between Elijah and Moses is that both were practical monotheists. We have already seen that while Moses is frequently described by scholars as only a "henotheist" [2] he acted as if the gods of Egypt, for instance, did not exist. So it was with Elijah. Yahweh might be the God of Horeb but He ruled also in agricultural Canaan and in commercial Sidon (cf. I 17:8ff). When Elijah put before the people the alternative between Yahweh and Melkart it was in this form: "If Yahweh be God, follow him; but if Baal, follow him." He did not say, "Israel's God," but simply "God" (I 18:21). "Cry aloud," he called mockingly to the prophets of Baal, "for he is a god; either he is musing, or he is gone aside, or he is on a journey, or peradventure he sleepeth and must be awakened!" (I 18:27). One who speaks thus has little belief in the reality of such a deity. It is hard to see any difference here between Elijah and Amos. The reader must therefore again be warned against taking too seriously the "evolutionary" view of many scholars, that Amos marks a great step forward in the direction of monotheism.

We cannot conclude the comparison of Elijah and Moses without calling attention to a striking difference between them that perplexes historians. Moses forbade the making and adoration of images. Tradition represented him as destroying Aaron's golden calf and punishing those who worshipped it. Elijah, on the other hand, seems to have made no protest against the golden bulls which were still a feature of Israel's worship in his day. Two ways out of the difficulty have been found. One is to deny that Moses gave Israel the second commandment and to ignore as late and untrustworthy the story of Aaron's calf. The other is to maintain that Elijah was so much occupied in the fight against Melkart that he had no time to attack the calf-worship. Of these two theories the second seems more satisfactory. The history of religion will show other instances of a zealous reformer giving so much attention to certain

[2] Albright however, *APB*, p. 167, on the basis of archaeological findings holds that monotheism emerged with the Mosaic movement of the 13th Century B.C. and not with the prophetic movement of the 8th Century. For an examination of the literary testimony see James, "Was there Monotheism in Israel before Amos?" *Anglican Theological Review*, Spring, 1932, p. 130ff. On the other hand, Balscheit (*Alter und Aufkommen des Monotheismus in der israelitischen Religion,* Berlin, 1938) takes the usual position that monotheism was not completely attained in the Mosaic period. See also p. 32.

abuses that he seems blind to others. In fact that is what reformers generally do—and not only in the domain of religion!

Elijah Led on to the Writing Prophets

It would be a mistake to suppose that because Elijah brought about a revival of Mosaism he therefore had his face turned towards the past. On the contrary, he belonged also to the mighty men of God who a century later were to follow him.

There were features of his religious outlook, to be sure, that belonged to a more primitive stage of development than theirs. None of the great prophets, for example, would have gone on a pilgrimage to Horeb in order to get nearer to Yahweh. They would have known that they could come as close to Him in Palestine. Nor would they have felt quite at home—despite their living faith—in Elijah's atmosphere of the marvellous. On the whole they saw God working through natural phenomena and through history rather than by what we call miracles. They would not—to say the least—have exalted the cult side of religion as did Elijah, for their emphasis was ever on righteousness as the one thing for which Yahweh supremely cared. Nor, finally, would they have used violence to accomplish Yahweh's ends. Much as they might proclaim wrath and vengeance upon the wicked, they left it to Yahweh to carry out the sentence. We never find them causing the death of any person or instigating rebellion against an evil king. That sort of activity had happily been eliminated from the prophetic work by the time Amos appeared.

After making all allowance for these differences however we still find much in Elijah that was presently to emerge in the prophets. To begin with, his very faithfulness to Moses links him to them. For the prophets themselves belonged to Moses and shared most of the Mosaic ideas that we have just been reviewing. But we can also note in him certain features which one might call particularly characteristic of the prophets.

Elijah was distinguished from the rest of men by his peculiar relation to Yahweh. He "stood before" Yahweh, as trusted officials stand continually before a king, giving his whole time and self to carrying out his Lord's commands. Thus he was in the counsel of Yahweh, receiving information as to what Yahweh intended to do and directions as to his own part in carrying it out. He looked on the "word of Yahweh" which he was commissioned to utter as a force able to effect results, such as the drought and the rain

(I 17:1). He was given on several occasions a definite promise or threat to impart to those whom it concerned (I 17:14; 21:17ff, 27ff). He was also subjected at least once to the peculiar state of religious exaltation and possession which is described by the phrase "the hand of Yahweh was upon him" (I 18:46).

To Elijah God was everything and man nothing. Kings did not overawe him, perils from men were of no account. True, he quailed once before Jezebel, but only for a moment. Presently he was "returning on his way" to face and defeat her. This capacity to see God as the only factor worth paying attention to in history— to feel intensely that with God all things are possible—to throw oneself upon God as the single effective reality and expect results of astounding nature; this was truly prophetic.

He was one with the prophets also in viewing natural calamities as a sign of God's wrath. The drought came as Yahweh's direct, personal response to Ahab's apostasy. Elijah indeed was the agent through whom Yahweh introduced it but he disclaimed all responsibility for the suffering that ensued. "I have not troubled Israel," he replied to Ahab, "but thou and thy father's house." Here was a point on which the prophets were time and again to clash with their contemporaries. People saw in public woes like war, pestilence and famine every meaning but what the prophets maintained to be the right one—that Israel had brought these things upon itself. They persistently misunderstood the prophets who uttered predictions of evil, refusing to perceive that the prophets were not the enemies of Israel but its truest friends, in warning it of the consequences which its sins would entail.

Elijah had already left behind the attitude of mere nationalism. To his mind Yahweh was not against foreign opponents of Israel, like Damascus, but rather against that portion of Israel itself which had "forsaken his commandments." Indeed, the prophet was commissioned to anoint Hazael to be king over Syria in order that with his invading sword he might carry out Yahweh's punishment upon apostate Israelites (I 19:15ff). This takes us at once into the thought-world of the prophets. It marks great progress from the old concept of Yahweh who marched at the head of the armies of Israel to defeat the Philistines. He is now on His way to become the world Judge who will exact of Israel a higher standard of conduct because of its very privileges (cf. Amos 3:2). So, as Christ pointed out, Elijah was sent to bless a widow, not of Israel, but of Sidon (I 17:8 cf. Lk. 4:26).

In this connection we discover a final point where Elijah leads on to the prophets. He seems to have been the originator of the doctrine of the "remnant." The plan of Yahweh's action sketched in the theophany at Horeb took as its starting point the fact that Elijah was not alone in his loyalty. "Seven thousand"—a mystic number—had likewise refused to bow the knee to Baal. Upon these the future Israel must be built. After the elimination of all apostates they would be "left" as the nucleus of a faithful people. The word is the same as appears in the term "remnant," so prominent in Isaiah's thinking. On its negative side this doctrine is crude indeed. Elijah felt apparently that if one could only kill enough sinners Israel's wickedness would disappear. We shall discuss this further when we come to study Isaiah's religion. We need only remind ourselves now that it has a positive side of real value—the unquenchable confidence that in the darkest hours one can depend on the "seven thousand" to whom belongs the better future (I 19:15-18).

Elijah's Contribution to Israel's Religion

If now we turn to the Elijah narratives as a whole and ask what he did for Israel we shall find that his service lay not so much in any definite accomplishment as in the impulse that he gave. He was one of those rare men through whom the elemental power of God bursts afresh into humanity. He was above all things else a man of God. That is what we still feel as we read of him. When he enters, the familiar scenery of man's world falls away and God appears. Winds begin to blow from out the deep, breaking in pieces the rocks before Yahweh. Earthquake and fire follow. Historians may lament that the sheer miraculous in these narratives thrusts aside the sober reality. But deeper reflection will perhaps convince us that this atmosphere of the supernatural *must* surround the figure of Elijah if we are to see him as Israel felt and knew him—yes, as he really was. After all, those writers of a credulous childlike age who have painted him thus understood him. The Spirit of Yahweh that conveyed him hither and yon; the "word" that shut or opened the storehouse of the rain and kept the widow's meal and oil from failing; the prayer that restored the dead child to life and called down fire from heaven; the angel that ministered unearthly sustenance to the weary sleeper; the theophany with its wind, earthquake, fire and sound of gentle stillness; the mantle that parted Jordan; the chariot and horses of fire that whirled him at last forever from man's sight—these are indeed legend, but they are something else also. They are the bold primitive outlines and colours wherewith natural artists portrayed a reality which would otherwise escape us. For in this man actuality was *not* sober. God was there! This was what he made men feel. He "turned their hearts back again." That was his greatness.

What is more, with him began a succession of great men of God in Israel. Moses before his death had provided a captain who should lead Israel into Canaan. Samuel had given Israel a king to deliver it from the Philistines and make of it a nation. Elijah insured a different kind of succession. "Elisha the son of Shaphat . . . shalt thou anoint to be prophet in thy room" (I 19:16). Over Elisha he cast his mantle as he was ploughing in the field, and to him he let his mantle fall from the chariot of fire (II 2:13). Somehow he was able to pass on to this lesser man a measure of the power that he himself had won from God. It was indeed a "hard thing" that Elisha asked as his master's parting gift—"Let a double portion of thy spirit be upon me." In accomplishing it Elijah met the final test of greatness. When the "sons of the prophets" watching from Jericho cried out, "The spirit of Elijah doth rest on Elisha," they were marking something that was to be thereafter in Israel. One great man of God would henceforth follow another in a steady succession for two centuries till the work of the prophets should be accomplished and the future of Yahweh's religion assured to mankind.

Nor must we forget these "sons of the prophets" who enter the story as humble adherents of the man of God, yielding him an awe-struck devotion. They were evidently living in communities as persons set apart for the service of Yahweh, though we are left pretty much to our own ingenuity to picture to ourselves what was the nature of their work. We are justified in thinking that, however little mentioned, they must have played a necessary part in the activity of Elijah. No leader, however supreme, can operate in a vacuum. He must have some who follow him, absorb his inspiration and mediate it in a wide way to others. In a word, he must have disciples. By attracting to himself the "sons of the prophets" Elijah was providing the spiritual ancestors of those circles of disciples who gathered about Isaiah and his colleagues and passed on to posterity both their utterances and their impulse.

It is significant that the late prophet whom we know as Malachi, longing for and believing in the speedy "coming" of God in history, turned instinctively to this man as the one best fitted to prepare

Israel for the divine intervention. "Behold, I will send you Elijah the prophet before the great and terrible day of Yahweh come. And he shall turn the heart of the fathers to the children, and the heart of the children to their fathers; lest I come, and smite the earth with a curse" (Mal. 4:5-6).[1]

In the time of Jesus Elijah had come to be associated in the mind of Israel with the Messiah, as his forerunner. Some thought that Jesus was Elijah. Our Lord himself saw Elijah in John, the greatest among them born of women. On the mount of transfiguration Peter and James and John saw two men of the Old Dispensation talking with Jesus: Moses who had founded the religion of Israel, and Elijah who had ushered in its consummation.

So lived on the man of God.

To this day the Jews at the Passover feast set a cup of wine for Elijah and at a certain moment open the door to see if he is not standing without.

[1] Many scholars, however, regard these verses as a later addition to Malachi's book. See p. 421.

CHAPTER X

ELISHA

[AFTER 850 B.C.]

The Sources

The narratives which tell of Elisha join on to the Elijah narratives and are contained in I Ki. 19:19–21; II Ki. 2–7; 8:1–15; 9:1ff; 13:14–21. They emanate from the same prophetic circles but exhibit an individuality of their own. In the first place, they give no connected story but are a series of independent narratives loosely strung together. Again, they fail to rise to the heights that characterize the sublime stories of Elijah. Finally, they are even more replete with the miraculous than those which tell of Elijah.

So full indeed of miracles is the Elisha tradition that the reader might be tempted to set it all aside as historically worthless. Such an extreme procedure however is not warranted. Elisha is unquestionably a historical personage and in the reliable narrative of Jehu's rebellion he appears firmly fixed as its instigator (II 9:1). Nor need one doubt that the rest of the Elisha stories preserve a broadly correct idea of the man and his activity. We know indeed even less of him than of Elijah, but we can still perceive the general outline of his figure as it lived on in the memory of the "sons of the prophets" whose lot he shared and for whom he did so much.

Elisha Carried on Elijah's Tradition of Loyalty to Yahweh

Elisha looked on himself as the humble follower of Elijah. He never aspired to be ranked with his great master, but was content if only he might receive the first-born son's portion of the father's spirit. This he obtained, as the sons of the prophets acknowledged. It is natural therefore that he should strike out on no new course for himself. What Elijah stood for was enough.

We first catch sight of him ploughing with twelve yoke of oxen: evidently he was the son of a well-to-do farmer. Elijah passed by and cast his mantle over the young peasant and immediately Elisha

left home and family to go after Elijah and minister unto him
(I 19:19ff). Years after he was known as the man who had
"poured water on the hands of Elijah" (II 3:11). Next we see
him with his master at Gilgal, fully aware that Elijah was about
to be taken from him yet refusing to leave him till the end. When
finally the elder prophet had been whirled away in fire his first
thought was of his own bereavement: "My father, my father, the
chariot of Israel and the horsemen thereof!" But after he had rent
his clothes for grief he took up Elijah's mantle and began his long
life-work alone (II 2:1ff).

This was, as he conceived it, to make the name of Yahweh great.
Like Elijah, he "stood before Yahweh" to do His service (II 3:14).
In his day however no supreme crisis arose such as Elijah had
faced on mount Carmel. The battle fought there had left Yahweh
in possession of the field. But there was need that a "man of God"
wholly devoted to Yahweh should set forth before the people His
power and beneficence. Thus only could the impression made by
Elijah be deepened and rendered permanent.

Such was Elisha. "Behold now," said the woman of Shunem to
her husband, "I perceive that this is a holy man of God" (II 4:9).
She was but voicing what all felt. They believed that he walked
close to Yahweh, understood His purposes, and had great influence
with Him. When Elisha predicted anything by the word of
Yahweh, it surely would come to pass; whether it had to do with
feeding a hundred men or a city's deliverance (II 4:43; 7:1). When
Elisha prayed, he obtained what he sought—the restoration to
life of a dead child or the bewilderment of enemies sent to take
him (II 4:33; 6:18 and 20). When the prophet went to Damascus
even the heathen Benhadad sent to "inquire of Yahweh by him"
whether or no he would recover from his sickness (II 8:8). He so
brought home Yahweh's majesty and might to Naaman that the
Syrian commander burst forth unsolicited into an acknowledge-
ment which reads like a monotheistic creed: "Behold now, I know
that there is no God in all the earth but in Israel. . . . Thy servant
will henceforth offer neither burnt-offering nor sacrifice unto other
gods, but unto Yahweh" (II 5:15 and 17).

Small wonder then that in the popular faith he was guarded by
special provision of God. "Fear not," he said to his terrified servant
when the morning light disclosed the Syrian forces surrounding
Dothan to take him; "for they that are with us are more than they
that are with them." And when in response to Elisha's prayer
Yahweh had opened the eyes of the young man "he saw; and

behold, the mountain was full of horses and chariots of fire round about Elisha" (II 6:14ff). Nor is it surprising that tradition has bathed the figure of Elisha in the light of the marvellous, although in a different way from that of Elijah. The miracles attributed to the humbler successor were less sublime and catastrophic. He did not summon drought or rain or call down fire from heaven. His wonders belonged on the whole to a more familiar and humanly beneficent order. None the less were they believed to be marvels proceeding from Yahweh and revealing His presence in His prophet.

One particularly significant feature of Elisha's work for Yahweh was his close connection with the "sons of the prophets." Here he seems to have gone beyond Elijah. Elijah won their awe-struck devotion but remained aloof from their communities, inhabiting the solitudes from which he emerged from time to time as from another world. Such at any rate is the impression conveyed by our sources. Elisha, on the other hand, became a household figure among these groups, looking out for their food-supplies (II 4:38), advising them as to building new houses, providing for their widows (II 6:1; 4:1), helping them in their difficulties (II 6:6), making himself in a very intimate way their "master" (II 6:5). Thus he insured the widening and perpetuating of his own influence on behalf of Yahweh. For we must remember that these "sons of the prophets" were committed body and soul to Yahweh's cause. However they or their successors might fall short in the interpretation of His moral will, none of their later prophetic critics accused them of abandoning Yahweh for other gods. And as the main object of Elisha's life was to promote loyalty to Yahweh he could throw himself whole-heartedly into their activity and feel that through it his own was being multiplied.

We may note finally that Elisha seems to have found no fault with the use of the golden bulls in Yahweh's worship. Like Elijah he maintained silence on the matter. He lived on good terms with a king like Joash who is condemned by the Deuteronomic compiler for retaining these images (II 13:11, 14ff). It was apparently enough for him that Joash's grandfather Jehu had stamped out the worship of the Sidonian Baal in blood (II 10:18ff).

Elisha Took an Active Part in Political Affairs

Elisha was a national figure. That fact stands out repeatedly in the traditions. Again and again we find him intervening in political affairs with no uncertain hand. Elijah had bequeathed him an undying enmity towards the dynasty of Omri. "What have I to do with thee?" he replied to Ahab's son Jehoram when the latter came to him in an hour of need; "get thee to the prophets of thy father and to the prophets of thy mother" (3:13). It was apparently a king of this house whom on another occasion he described as the "son of a murderer" (II 6:32). In fact, he was committed to bringing about the downfall of Ahab's family and the extirpation of its members, especially Jezebel, who as queen mother still retained her attitude of defiance.

The story of how Elisha accomplished this is full of horror to the modern reader. Joram, the king of Israel, had renewed the perennial attempt to capture Ramoth in Gilead from the Syrians. It was in such an adventure that his father Ahab had met his death twelve years earlier. As then Ahab had been aided by king Jehoshaphat of Judah, so now Joram secured the assistance of Jehoshaphat's grandson Ahaziah. This was the easier of accomplishment because Ahaziah was a son of Athaliah, Joram's sister; for the house of Ahab had by marriage secured control over the Davidic dynasty of Judah. In the fighting Joram was wounded and returned to Jezreel for treatment, leaving the army in command of his officers. His nephew Amaziah later followed to visit him.

It was at this moment, when the army was free from the presence of the two kings, that Elisha saw his opportunity. Calling one of the sons of the prophets he despatched him to the camp at Ramoth-gilead with orders to seek out one of the officers there named Jehu and anoint him secretly to be king of Israel. The charge which Elisha sent to the new king has been coloured by the Deuteronomic editor but there can be little doubt that it was a command to wipe out the whole house of Ahab. Elisha must have known this officer beforehand and have selected him because of his energy and ruthlessness. He may not indeed have foreseen to what savage lengths Jehu would go but he cannot be cleared of responsibility for what followed.

Jehu, acclaimed king by his fellow officers, acted promptly. Driving furiously to Jezreel he surprised and killed the two kings and trampled to death the aged Jezebel who met him with unyielding defiance. But he did not stop there. Seventy sons of Ahab who were being cared for in Samaria were murdered at his behest. Forty kinsmen of Ahaziah whom he met on his way to Samaria encountered the same fate at his hands. Arrived at the capital he killed all survivors of Ahab's house remaining there. His final act was to wipe out all the worshippers of Baal whom he could identify (II 9–10).

This reign of terror had the approval of a Yahweh fanatic like Jonadab, the son of Rechab (II 10:15), and doubtless also of Elisha and the sons of the prophets. For it was indeed a carrying out of the program left by Elijah. But instead of bringing in an era of Yahweh's favour it seriously weakened the kingdom and occasioned darker days than Israel had known under Ahab's dynasty. Its very fearfulness also caused a reaction in earnest minds and discredited the prophetic policy which was responsible for it. A hundred years later Hosea was to look back on the "blood of Jezreel" as a crime to be atoned for only by the fall of Jehu's house (Hos. 1:4). Such a view however was too advanced for Elisha. No word of censure from him is recorded in our sources and his relations with the kings of Jehu's dynasty were continuously cordial.

It was on behalf of these monarchs that he employed his supernatural gifts to effect military results. After the king of Syria had determined to place his camp in a certain place Elisha sent to the king of Israel and warned him not to pass by that way. So marked were the results of this and similar counsels that the Syrian king began to suspect treachery among his own servants. How else would his plans become known beforehand? (II 6:8ff). When he sent men to seize the prophet, Elisha contrived to bring these into Samaria where they were made captives. The kings of Israel came to lean upon him. "My father, shall I smite them?" asked one concerning these same captives, and when Elisha advised mercy, he gave heed. "My father," cried Joash with tears as he visited the prophet on his death-bed; "my father, the chariot of Israel and the horsemen thereof." It was the same title that Elisha had once applied to Elijah. Joash felt that the chief stay of Israel was being taken away. Elisha's reply was to bid him shoot "Yahweh's arrow of victory" out the open window and to smite upon the ground with the victory-giving arrows (II 13:14ff).

Another glimpse of his helpfulness is given in the story of Naaman. "Wherefore hast thou rent thy clothes?" he sent to inquire of the perplexed king. "Send him unto me, and he shall know that there is a prophet in Israel" (II 5:8).

On the other hand we find him visiting Damascus in order to anoint Hazael king in place of the feebler Benhadad. He did this, tradition says, with his eyes open to the disastrous consequences it would bring upon his own people. "Why weepeth my lord?" asked the astonished Hazael. "Because," replied Elisha, "I know

the evil that thou wilt do unto the children of Israel" (II 8:11ff).
This was a strange rôle for the "chariot of Israel" to be playing!
Yet the incident, if true, probably belongs to the early days when
the condemned dynasty of Ahab was still on the throne. Elisha
was here carrying out another aspect of Elijah's program of vengeance. In any case however it shows him intervening in political
matters in a very practical way.

We have already pointed out in the study of Elijah how such
intervention marked a difference between him and the later prophets. However an Isaiah or a Jeremiah might admonish king and
nobles as to the course of public action demanded by Yahweh, they
kept personally aloof from any manipulation of politics. That
method had been given up. When the priest Amaziah sent to king
Jeroboam, saying, "Amos hath conspired against thee in the midst
of the house of Israel" (Amos 7:10), he was uttering a palpable
untruth. Conspire the prophets did not. Nor did the prophets
give advice as to military measures. Their only counsel along this
line was that Israel should rely on Yahweh alone and renounce all
warlike efforts. No one could have called them "chariots of Israel"
in the old sense.

And yet there was in this political activity of Elisha an element
which must command our admiration. It was in fact but a part
of something larger, something that characterized his whole life.

Elisha Lived among the People as their Friend and Helper

Nothing distinguishes Elisha from his mysterious predecessor
more than the way in which he lived among the people. No Spirit
of Yahweh was wont to carry him whither men knew not (I 18:12).
On the contrary he was always at hand. "This is a holy man of
God, that passeth by us continually," the Shunamite said of him
(II 4:9). Our sources reveal him moving constantly from place
to place, a well-known figure everywhere. We find him now with
the army, now in Samaria, now at Carmel, now at Gilgal, now in
Dothan, now in Jericho. His whereabouts at any particular moment could easily be ascertained. The Shunamite in her hour of
need knew exactly how to reach him.

Her story also shows the kind of thing that people had come to
seek from Elisha. They went to him for help in the common
troubles of life. It is remarkable how one golden thread runs
through most of the legends told concerning him—the thread of
human helpfulness. Discount as we must the miraculous element

in these narratives, we cannot set aside their common aspect of service. Elisha must have been a servant of man or these stories never would have come to cluster around his name. One might indeed sum up the total impression he made upon his contemporaries in words used of a Greater than he: "he went about doing good" (Acts 10:38).

People loved to tell how he purified the water-supply of Jericho (II 2:19ff); how he provided for the widow and her sons (II 4:1ff); how he prayed effectively that the Shunamite might have a son, and by his intercession brought this same child back to life again (II 4:16ff); how he healed Naaman the Syrian (II 5) and restored a lost axe-head to a poor man who had borrowed it (II 6:6). He seems to have had a special care for those who were hungry. "Set on the great pot, and boil pottage for the sons of the prophets," he said to his servant once, when in a time of dearth a group of these were sitting helplessly before him (II 4:38ff). "Give unto the people that they may eat," he commanded at another time, as a present of food was brought to him (II 4:42).

He stood always at the beck of the needy. "What shall I do for thee? Tell me" he asked of the widow that cried unto him. Then very practically he inquired further: "What hast thou in the house?" (II 4:2). "Behold, yonder is the Shunamite," he said to Gehazi as he caught sight in the distance of the bereaved mother. "Run, I pray thee, now to meet her and say unto her, Is it well with thee? is it well with thy husband? is it well with the child?" Then when she had caught hold of his feet and Gehazi tried to push her away, he intervened: "Let her alone, for her soul is vexed within her" (II 4:25ff).

Nothing indeed shows more clearly what Elisha could be to people than the whole narrative of his dealings with the Shunamite. Here we see him stopping as familiar yet revered guest in a home, enjoying the chamber reserved for his comfort, seeking how he might repay this gracious hospitality, taking an interest in the family, obtaining for them what they most desired, succouring them in trouble, advising them to move before famine came and in general showing himself their friend (II 4:8ff; 8:1ff).

It was in this spirit, we may well believe, that he befriended the often hard-pressed kings of Israel. Such was his nature. And in thus helping small and great he must have made people feel that Yahweh Himself was helpful also. He brought God home to them where they lived—in the midst of their anxieties, struggles, sorrows, joys, hopes and fears.

An Estimate of Elisha's Religion

If our sources are to be trusted, Elisha stood on no very high plane of religious development. The narratives are full of incidents that reveal the primitive nature of his religious ideas. Elijah's mantle, wherewith he smote and divided the waters of Jericho (II 2:14); his staff which he commanded Gehazi to lay upon the dead child's face (II 4:29); the arrow of victory which he bade Joash shoot, the striking of the other arrows on the ground three times to insure three victories (II 13:14ff)—these approach the magical. The miracle stories abound in further touches of the same feature.

In chapter 3 Elisha appears as a genuine "ecstatic." It is there told how he asked for a minstrel to play before him that the music might bring him into the psychic condition necessary to call forth prophecy. It is however in the content of the word of Yahweh thus received that we perceive the most offensively primitive feature of the narrative. Yahweh is seen as God of war in a particularly cruel aspect. He not only gives directions as to military operations but He enjoins the ruining of the enemy's land. "Ye shall fell every good tree, and stop all fountains of water, and mar every good piece of land with stones" (II 3:19). In a less objectionable way the concept of the War-God runs through later narratives of Elisha.

As is often the case, one finds the most striking evidences of primitive ideas in the domain of ethics. Elisha cursed the boys who made sport of him and caused their death by the two she-bears (II 2:23f). According to the more likely reading he bade Hazael report a lie to his master and pointed the way to his committing murder (II 8:10). He was responsible to a real extent for Jehu's savage measures of extermination (II 9–10). Add to this the fact that the narratives nowhere exhibit him as imparting ethical teaching to the people. We do not see him rebuking their vices or pointing them to nobler ways. Perhaps that was why he got on so well with them! Yet we must always allow for the insufficiency of our sources and the external nature of their portrayal. Perhaps Elisha was quite different in this respect from their representation.

Nor must we forget that his life of service was in itself the most powerful of sermons. By example, if not by definite precept, he showed that the religion of Yahweh meant doing good to one's fellows. And in this connection we find a trait that unites him to the truly great men of God in Israel: he was not seeking his own advantage. Willing indeed he was to take free-will offerings from grateful persons (II 4:10ff, 42ff) and share these with his adherents. He and the sons of the prophets seem to have got their livelihood by this means. But when Naaman pressed him to accept the more splendid rewards sent by the king of Syria, he refused. "As Yahweh liveth, before whom I stand, I will receive none" (II 5:16). Upon the covetous Gehazi, who surreptitiously salvaged some of the rejected wealth, he turned with what is perhaps his single recorded outburst of moral indignation: "Is it a time to receive money, and to receive garments, and oliveyards and vineyards, and sheep and oxen, and men-servants and maid-servants? The leprosy therefore of Naaman shall cleave unto thee and to thy seed for ever" (II 5:26-27).

CHAPTER XI

A PIONEER THINKER OF EARLY ISRAEL

THE YAHWIST

[*c.* 850 B.C.]

About the time when Elijah and Elisha were doing their work [1] in the northern kingdom there lived in the kingdom of Judah a remarkable man, who, though his name is nowhere mentioned in the Bible, stands out today as one of the supreme thinkers of ancient Israel.

This man is a discovery of modern scholarship. He swam into vision, like a new planet, when the Mosaic authorship of the first five books of the Bible was given up and Moses the writer dissolved to disclose in his stead the composers of the several documents that make up the Pentateuch. Of these the earliest is the Yahwist (J).[2] He was in all probability a single personality. Many scholars, it is true, find two or more strands of narrative in the J material (J^1, J^2, etc.),[3] each having its own distinct point of view; while yet others regard the document as the product of a long process of tradition in which all contributions of individuals have been so merged as to be no longer distinguishable. But the J narrative *taken as a whole* is so vivid and colourful, so fresh and full of power, that we can hardly go far wrong in believing it to be the work of a single great mind.[4] Where it manifests inconsist-

---

[1] I.e. about 850 B.C. This is the date generally assigned to J by the Wellhausen school. Oesterley and Robinson, *IBOT*, p. 61, place J and E between 900 and 750. There is a tendency in some quarters to lower these dates. Eissfeldt, *EAT*, p. 222, 224, places L (his oldest source, containing much material usually assigned to J^1) between 900 and 750, J about 750. On the other hand, Sellin, *EAT*⁷, p. 36, assigns J to the time of David or Solomon.

[2] So called from his use of the name *Yahweh* for God.

[3] Eissfeldt uses the symbols L (lay source) and J.

[4] This is the view of Sellin, Kittel and others. Hempel, *AHL*, p. 117, who divides the J material into three layers (J^1, J^2, J^3), thinks that the name "Yahwist" ought to be reserved for J^3, the writer of the story of the beginnings (Gen. 1–11), since it was he who put into its essentially final form the strand of narrative which was given its fundamental tone by J^1.

encies these are best explained by supposing that the Yahwist found them in the material which he took over from tradition and was either unwilling or unable completely to eradicate them.

Of the Yahwist we know only what we may gather from his own pen. What was his name, his home, his position in society remains shrouded in mystery. From the fact that he tends to make a great deal of the patriarch Judah and places the home of Abraham in Hebron it has been inferred that he lived in the southern kingdom. Some have imagined that they could guess his family and even his name but such speculations are without solid foundation.

But the obscurity that covers the outward facts regarding the Yahwist serves well to set off by contrast the brilliant inward revelation of the man as he speaks to us in his own stories. Here we can feel confident that we know him. Indeed, he is one of the most sharply-marked personalities of the Bible. And yet even here we are confronted with difficulties.

They arise from the fact that the Yahwist was not a free composer, creating his narrative out of his own imagination. He employed earlier material and embodied much of it in his work. We can never be sure therefore whether what he has written gives his own view or merely that of his material. When we find him, for example, speaking of God in a very childlike fashion are we forthwith to pronounce him crudely anthropomorphic in his conception of deity? Perhaps he himself was not nearly so naive as these expressions would lead us to infer.

This difficulty increases when we come to his narratives of the patriarchs. Scholars who believe that these contain almost no genuine recollections of the patriarchal period find in them the Yahwist's own ideas or at least those of his age. Wellhausen and his school regarded these stories as reflections of the customs and beliefs of the time of the monarchy. But if, as seems more likely, they preserve much tradition from an earlier time, they cannot be treated as the free creations of the Yahwist. Much more is this the case with the narratives concerning Moses.

If now the Yahwist had written his history in the fashion employed later by the historians of the Deuteronomic school who have given us the Books of Judges, Samuel and Kings, we should be able to distinguish with a fair degree of certainty between his conceptions and those of his characters. These writers insert their own reflections between blocks of more primitive material in such a different style that separation is easy. But the Yahwist by the fires of his genius has fused his material and himself into one glowing whole.

A final difficulty presents itself as we pass to the Book of Numbers. From that point onward the work of the Yahwist becomes so blended with that of the Elohists that a scholar like Dr. Driver gave up the effort to disentangle the two. Obviously we cannot draw with any certainty upon these JE sections for information regarding the ideas of the Yahwist alone.

It seems likely therefore that the portion of the Yahwist's writings which gives the clearest conception of his ideas concerning God and man is that which narrates the beginnings of the world and of mankind. Here his material was probably more elastic, more susceptible of being moulded according to his own forms of thought. At any rate we may believe that what we find here is not likely to clash in any important particular with his own conceptions. We shall therefore use as our chief source the J sections of Genesis 1–11,[5] having regard at the same time to the material contained in the patriarchal and Mosaic history.[6]

Yahweh is the Only God

As he looked back upon the beginnings of nature and of history the Yahwist saw only one divine power at work—Yahweh. Whatever was done was done by Him. He made earth and heaven (2:4b). He brought into existence the father of the human race, the vegetation of earth, the animals, and finally man's help-meet

---

[5] Gen. 2:4b–4:26; 6:1–8; 7–8 (in part); 9:18–27; 10 (in part); 11:1–9, 28–30.

[6] A different view is held by Professor C. A. Simpson, who has long been making a special study of the documents of the Hexateuch. "I am very doubtful," he writes to the author, "whether you can safely reconstruct the Yahwist's religion and theology from the opening chapters of Genesis. I am convinced that the material in these chapters is not due to his own unfettered choice, but to the fact that certain Canaanite and Babylonian legends and myths had become part of the cultural heritage of Israel, and that the Yahwist set to work to purify these and to incorporate them into the Yahweh tradition. I very much doubt whether he intended Genesis 3 to account for the entry of sin into the world. I do not think that he regarded the work of Tubal as sinister. The story of the marriage of the sons of God, in my opinion, came in J after the flood. I do not think he regarded Cain, a fugitive and a wanderer, as a nomad, but rather as one reduced to a cultureless existence, from which the sons of Lamech rose when they inaugurated nomadism. Genesis 4:23f is, I am sure, a secondary addition to J, certainly not from the same hand as the Cain and Abel story." The reader should remember that in the ensuing treatment of the Yahwist he is moving in the region of opinions rather than of proven facts.

woman (2:7ff). In all the subsequent developments of the story nature, animals and man had to do with Him alone.

It is true that other superhuman beings appear now and then. We read of "sons of God" who took them wives of the daughters of men (6:1ff). We hear Yahweh addressing heavenly companions: "Come, let us go down . . ." (11:6ff). We find Him visiting Abraham in the company of two "angels" (18). But all these are plainly His servants. He alone remains the Sovereign. There is no hint of any other god.

Now this silence is significant for the ancient material in which the Yahwist worked had once been steeped in polytheism, as we can see from the Babylonian originals of some of his stories. When therefore we find him ignoring the existence of other gods we can attribute it to but one cause: he was a monotheist. True, he nowhere declares expressly that Yahweh is the only God. Such was not his way of teaching. He preferred, in this and other matters, to tell his story and let it make its own impression. But he must have known exactly what he was doing.

The God of the Hebrews, then, was the God of creation. The Yahwist employs His name boldly in his narrative of the world's origin and asserts that in the second generation after Adam this name came into use in human worship (4:26). Here of course he follows a different tradition from E and P, both of whom say that it was first revealed through Moses. They were probably right in the matter but his very throwing back of the name into primaeval time shows how vividly the Yahwist identified Israel's national God with the universal God.

His Conception of God's Nature

Probably the first thing that impresses the reader in the Yahwist's portrayal of God is its anthropomorphism. The Creator is represented as a very human sort of Being. He "moulded" man out of dust and "blew" the breath of life into his nostrils. He "planted" a garden, "walked" in it in the cool of the day, "called" for the man and "made" coats of skin for him and his wife (2–3).

All these expressions have to do with God's body. But the divine likeness to man goes deeper. He is far from possessing the foreknowledge that was later attributed to Deity. His whole enterprise of creation seems to be conducted experimentally. He first makes man, then provides him a garden, then discovers that he needs a help-meet. To this end He creates the animals, only to find them one by one inadequate. Finally He attains success by creating the woman out of one of the man's ribs (2:5ff). In His further dealings with man He is confronted by apparently unlooked-for situations, which He meets as they arise (3:9ff; 3:22; 6:3). At length the entire human race proves a disappointment and He regrets that He has called man into being (6:6). He resolves to destroy all things living but makes an exception in favour of Noah, by him preserving alive the seed of man and beast. Moved by Noah's sacrifice he resolves never again to curse the ground for man's sake or to smite everything living (8:21). Humanity, again grown strong, presents another problem in the building of Babel, which He meets by separating them into language groups. From one of these He finally calls Abraham to become the father of a nation which shall be blessed above all others (12:2-3).

Not only does He seem to be planning and learning as He goes on; he is also compelled to ascertain what is happening by very human means. "Where art thou?" He calls, when He cannot find the man in the garden. "Who told thee that thou wast naked? Hast thou eaten of the tree?" (3:9ff). "Where is Abel thy brother?" he demands of Cain. "What hast thou done? Hark! thy brother's blood crieth unto me from the ground" (4:9ff). He "comes down" to see the city and the tower that the children of men have built at Babel (11:5). Once more He "goes down" to see whether Sodom and Gomorrah "have done altogether according to the cry of it, which is come unto Him. If not, He will know" (18:21).

He is also moved by human emotions. Man's disobedience evidently angers him (3:11ff). He is "grieved at his heart" by man's corporate wickedness and grimly resolves to wipe him out (6:6-7). He is jealous lest man add immortality to his knowledge of good and evil (3:22) and sharply checks the progress of human achievement at Babel (11:6). He is subject to sudden compunction (8:21) and by supplication is prevailed upon to mitigate punishment (4:13ff; 18:22ff).

But these and other primitive traits in the Yahwist's conception of God should not blind us to its fundamental nobility. To him God's nature was essentially "philanthropic." Having made man, God loved him and set about to meet his needs. In the garden which He planted for man He "made to grow every tree that is pleasant to the sight and good for food." He provided it with abundant rivers and gold and precious stones. He gave man first the animals, then his intimate companion woman (2:9ff). Though the man disappointed Him by disobedience he still took care of him, making for him and his wife coats of skins and giving them a child to gladden them (3:21; 4:1). He reasoned with angry Cain (4:5ff) and continued to watch over him after he had murdered Abel (4:15). He saved Noah and called Abraham. He suffered Israel's disobedience in the wilderness. His punishments of man's sin (except in the case of the flood and of Sodom's overthrow) were severe but not annihilating, His patience great. He understood men's proneness to evil (8:21) and when they worshipped Him was willing to meet them half way.

What He demanded of man was righteousness. Sacrifices indeed pleased Him when those who offered them "did well" (4:5–7; 8:20–21). He made a distinction also between clean and unclean animals (7:2; 8:20). His main concern however was not for ritual matters, but rather that man should obey His commands, exercise self-control (3:17), restrain his pride (11:6), honour his parents (9:22ff), love his wife (2:23), keep clear of murder (4:9ff) and wickedness (6:5). He had no respect for Cain's offering (so the Yahwist implies) because Cain failed to "do well" (4:5ff). His aim in choosing Abraham was that he and his descendants should "do righteousness and justice" (18:19).

A final touch in the Yahwist's portrayal of God needs to be noticed. One may call it the divine *liberality*. Much as Yahweh desired man to remain in a state of innocence He yet placed within his reach the tree of the knowledge of good and evil (2:17). He might remonstrate with Cain but He left him free to go on in sin (4:6). Mankind in general were permitted to make of themselves what they would, though in the end God might despair of them (6:5).

The Yahwist's Interest in Humanity

The central object of God's interest and love, the Yahwist felt, was man. The first thing that God did after making earth and heaven was to create man and provide for his needs. For him were the garden and the animals. It was he who gave each beast its name. For his companionship the woman was formed. His subsequent history constituted the central meaning of the world. To punish him was the ground cursed; and when he failed at last he involved all things in his ruin (2:7ff; 3:17; 6:7). After the flood his renewed worship led God to remove the curse on the ground and to promise continuance of life and seasons (8:20).

This means that the Yahwist himself was interested in humanity. Everything shows that he had thought long and deeply on man, his significance, his nature, his lot. He had pondered upon the amazing pre-eminence of man over the animals, upon the fact that man alone wears clothing and has language and religion. He had asked the reason of human suffering—why briers and thorns grow up the moment laborious cultivation relaxes, why women must endure the agonies of childbirth, why they seem to need men so much more than men need them, why they are in subjection to their husbands, why life is so short, why death awaits all, why the body disintegrates into dust, why men do not all speak the same language, why the nomad is so much worse off than the peasant, why man can count on the return of the seasons, why one people should have so much and another so little, why the Hebrews should be more highly honoured by God than other nations. He had also, as we shall see, given special thought to human sin.

All these matters he looked at from a broadly human point of view, as a man, not primarily as a Hebrew. He believed that the God whom the Hebrews worshipped had been from the beginning the God of all and that He cared for all, even for those whom He set aside in favour of Israel's ancestors. He had brought Lot, the ancestor of Moab and Ammon, out of Sodom and spared Zoar for his sake (19). He had loved the outcast Hagar, showing her water in the wilderness and promising to make of her son Ishmael a "great multitude" (16). In the story of Jacob and Esau one feels that the writer's sympathies were with the defrauded elder brother. Isaac (and therefore Yahweh) had a blessing for this forefather of the Edomites as well as for Jacob himself (27). The Yahwist could never have put into God's mouth the terrible words of Malachi: "I have loved Jacob, but Esau I hated" (Mal. 1:2). No, Yahweh hated none for all were His. He had taken care that from the three sons of Noah all the earth should be overspread (9:19). Like Amos, the Yahwist could have made God say: "Have I not brought Israel up out of the land of Egypt, and the Philistines from Caphtor, and the Syrians from Kir?" (Amos 9:7). St. Paul gave a true summary of the Yahwist's philosophy of history when he said to the Athenians: "God made of one every nation of men to dwell on all the face of the earth, having determined their appointed seasons, and the bounds of their habitation" (Acts 17:26).

This wide interest in humanity continues even after the story narrows itself down to the ancestors of the Israelitish nation. All through the Book of Genesis the treatment of non-Israelites is kindly. The promises to Abraham seem to imply that other peoples

are to benefit by the privileges conferred upon his descendants
(12:3). The relations of the three first patriarchs with the Canaanites are friendly and Jacob rebukes Simeon and Levi sharply for
their violence towards the inhabitants of Shechem (34:30). Joseph
and his family live in cordial harmony with the Egyptians and
the great Israelite serves Pharaoh's interests with fidelity, gladly
permitting Egypt to share in the favour with which he was treated
by God.

But with the Book of Exodus another spirit enters. Egypt becomes a hostile power for whose interest neither Israel nor Yahweh
cares. There are no more heartless words in the Old Testament
than those uttered by Yahweh to the Pharaoh through Moses: "For
now had I put forth my hand, and smitten thee and thy people with
pestilence, and thou hadst been cut off from the earth: but in very
deed for this cause have I made thee to stand, to show thee my
power, and that my name may be declared throughout all the
earth" (Exod. 9:15-16). Hereditary national rancour breathes
through the oracle against Amalek: "Yahweh hath sworn, Yahweh
will have war with Amalek from generation to generation" (Exod.
17:16). As for the Canaanites, they are indeed "bread" for Israel
(Num. 14:9), to be devoured without scruple. Their land is to pass
to the conquerors and they themselves, where not annihilated by
the *herem,* are to become servants of Shem. Sad indeed is the
transformation of the kindly El of Genesis into the War-God of the
Book of Joshua.

What occasions the change? Has the Yahwist's heart narrowed
or is it only his material that is different? Surely the latter is the
explanation. He found this nationalistic strain in the traditions
clustering about Moses and reverently retained it, as he retained
much else that clashed with his own ideas. Here if anywhere we
gain justification for the belief that these later stretches of his narrative no longer furnish us with a true picture of his religion;
the material with which he is dealing is too stubborn for him to
mould it as he could mould the early Genesis stories. To Genesis
therefore we return.

However much the Yahwist might exalt man by making him the
centre of creation he was equally clear that man ought to be kept
low before God. Humanity should not aspire to attain the level of
Yahweh or of the divine beings who served Him. Thus we find
the Yahwist viewing with suspicion all advances of man toward
greater knowledge, power and fame. It was wrong for the woman
to desire the knowledge of good and evil (3:5, 22). Tubal Cain,

by inventing cutting instruments of brass and iron and thus enabling his father Lamech to obtain greater vengeance than God had exacted for Cain, introduced a new and evil era into history (4:22ff). When the cohabitation of the sons of God with the daughters of men gave birth to the race of "the mighty men . . . , the men of renown," humanity lifted up itself still further against its Maker (6:5-6). The Yahwist had a special distrust of cities and high buildings. "Come," said the new people that had been born after the flood, "let us build us a city and a tower, whose top may reach unto heaven, and let us make us a name" (11:4). Such feats were not according to God's plan for man. It may or may not be significant that the first city was attributed to Cain (4:17). To the Yahwist's mind there was something sinister in man's ability to effect new conquests over his material environment. Where would it end? "Behold," he made God exclaim as He examined the new enterprise at Babel, "this is what they begin to do; and now nothing will be withholden from them, which they purpose to do!" (11:6). He goes on to tell with manifest approval how God by confounding their language checked their work: "they left off building the city" (11:8). That was a step in the right direction! This writer would have understood Isaiah when he longed for a "day of Yahweh of hosts upon all that is lifted up . . . upon every lofty tower, and upon every fortified wall, and upon all the ships of Tarshish, and upon all pleasant pictures,"—a day in which Yahweh alone should be exalted (Is. 2:12ff).

The Yahwist's Teaching as to Human Sin

Upon one aspect of man's experience the Yahwist seems to have thought long and painfully. Nowhere else in the Old Testament do we find so profound a study of temptation and sin as in these early chapters of Genesis.

Sin, he believed, was disobedience of God's beneficent will. The commands God laid upon man were not arbitrary but the expression of a friendly purpose. When God forbade man to eat of the tree of the knowledge of good and evil it was because He wished him to remain in a state of happy innocence resembling that of early childhood. When He urged Cain to turn from his anger and "do well" it was that Cain's countenance might be "lifted up" (4:7). In speaking of man's increasing "wickedness" (6:5) before the flood the Yahwist plainly had in mind behaviour that destroyed the "good life." Sin therefore was at once rebellion against God and a defeating of man's true destiny.

How then did sin find an entrance into man's heart? In answering this the Yahwist wrote two stories of temptation, describing just what occurs when man deviates from the known will of God. In the first he represented the evil impulse as coming from without. Eve was approached by the serpent, who first put the thought of disobedience into her childlike mind (3:1). In the second Yahweh speaks of sin as a wild beast "lurking at the door" of Cain's heart, ready to spring upon him (4:7). This latter may be merely a poetic representation but it tends to objectify sin as something distinct from the man himself. Our writer, to be sure, seems to have had no idea of a "kingdom" of evil or of a superhuman "adversary" whose aim it is to pervert man. The serpent (though in the original heathen story it was probably a god) belongs to the lower animal world and the figure of the lurking beast points in the same direction. But the Yahwist was sure that man is *not safe*. He must use all his subtlety (3:1) and all his power (4:7) to avoid sin.

In the narrative of Eve's fall the Yahwist sketches with a master hand the course of her temptation. He knew that before accepted standards can be decisively violated the reason must be induced to revolt against them. He therefore makes the serpent's attack an intellectual one. First, the woman is led to feel ashamed of her naive and unquestioning acceptance. "Hath God actually said, Ye shall not eat of all the trees of the garden?" Childlike trust withers under the cold breath of ridicule. Next she is taught to question. Her prompt reply is met with a sneering denial: "Ye shall not surely die!" Don't be afraid. Nothing terrible will happen to you if you do eat! Then a new freedom and power is promised: "God doth know that in the day that ye eat thereof, then your eyes shall be opened and ye shall be as gods, knowing good and evil." At the same time the woman is brought to see God in an evil light, as actuated by jealousy; His prohibition is only a device to hold man back from self-development! Thus the way is prepared for revolt. And now appetite makes itself felt with sudden force. "The woman saw" (what she had never hitherto permitted her thoughts to dwell on) "that the tree was good for food, and that it was a delight to the eyes, and" (the intellectual in turn reinforcing the sensuous) "that it was to be desired to make one wise." So the cumulated impulses overwhelm what remains of resistance: "she took of the fruit thereof and did eat" (3:1ff).

In the story of Cain he portrays a different kind of temptation. Cain had not been "doing well." Thus the narrative begins with guilt instead of innocence and shows how one sin leads on to another. When as a result of his evil conduct Yahweh withholds from Cain's offering the recognition accorded that of Abel, "Cain was very wroth and his countenance fell." Here however the course of passion is interrupted by a Voice. "Why art thou wroth? And why is thy countenance fallen?" Not anger, but repentance, is required. "If thou doest well, shall there not be a lifting up?" Cain may yet win his way back to divine favour. Continuance in evil, on the other hand, will but hurry him on to further wickedness. "If thou doest not well, sin coucheth at the door: and unto thee shall be its desire!" He is in deadly peril! Now at last an appeal is made to his will. "Do thou rule over it!" There is, the Yahwist believed, only one way to deal with such passions. Cain however refuses to heed the Voice and from wrath goes on to murder (4:3ff).

So far the Yahwist had shown merely the way in which two individuals fell into sin. He had still to answer the question how humanity as a whole became so involved in wickedness that from innocence man passed to a state where the imagination of his heart was evil from his youth (8:21). This he did by revealing the corporate and representative nature of the first transgression.

In the dialogue between Eve and the serpent the plural pronouns are used: "ye" and "we." Both she and the serpent feel that the man is also involved. So her first act after eating the fruit is to "give also unto her husband with her, and he did eat." The consequences forthwith overtake both together. "The eyes of them both were opened and they knew that they were naked." They "hid themselves" from God. Yahweh in administering punishment separates the man from his wife, yet each is treated as representative of his own sex. Their act has involved their descendants in misery. When finally the man is expelled from the garden not only his wife but all mankind suffers the same fate.

The subsequent progress of sin is also corporate. The murderer Cain passes on to his children not only his lot as nomad but also (it is implied) his wickedness. It is from his seed that Lamech and Tubal Cain spring. What finally brings on the flood is the wickedness of the race as a whole. After the flood the single act of pride recorded is a corporate one; man conspires to build the city and tower!

This corporate view of sin is indeed not peculiar to the Yahwist; it belonged to ancient Israel generally. Our writer's pre-eminence lies in his application of it to the beginnings of mankind in such a penetrating and almost philosophical way. It is surprising, on the other hand, that he represents temptation as so entirely a drama in which the individual soul stands alone before the tempter or God, teaching boldly that none needs to succumb to it, and holding that each who does so shall receive his own punishment.

The Yahwist has also a very decided view as to the consequences of sin, especially of the first disobedience which, so to speak, set it in motion among men. Something was thereby lost to man. Had he rejected the suggestion of the serpent he would have remained in the garden, enjoying an innocent and happy intercourse with God, supplied with abundant good things, performing light and pleasant work and cleaving to his beloved wife with a passion of delicate intimacy. Probably he would never have died, though the Yahwist has not made himself quite clear on this. After the forbidden fruit had been eaten the first thing to go was sexual unawareness. "They sewed fig leaves together and made themselves girdles!" Next they discovered that they no longer dared to face God. Then came the woman's punishment—pain in child-bearing, subjugation to the man. The man's followed—laborious toil, scant crops from a blighted ground, death, and a return to dust. Last of all, the man was sent forth from the garden to till the ground and his way back was barred by the angel with the flaming sword. Apparently it is no mere coincidence that the physical consummation of their marriage is not recorded until after the pair began their new and sadder life without the confines of Eden (4:1).

There can be no doubt that the Yahwist meant to portray in this narrative a veritable "fall of man." But the gloom was not unrelieved by hope. God declared that he would put undying enmity between the seed of the woman and the seed of the tempter. Man would never conclude peace with the power that had led him astray. The very prediction of such conflict seems to promise something. The Fathers of the Christian Church were not altogether wrong when they perceived in these words the "first gospel" of the Bible. Not that the Yahwist foresaw a Saviour, but he may very well have caught a glimpse of man's final victory.

Meanwhile man was not helpless before sin. He could still "rule over it" if he would. And some did. Abel's offering was accepted. Noah found favour in the eyes of Yahweh. Towards sinful humanity as a whole God came after the flood to take a mellower and a kindlier attitude (8:21). At last from out their midst He called

Abraham to become the father of a great and blessed nation—and the history of His gracious dealings with Israel began.

The Yahwist's Influence upon Later Religious Thought

If what we have gathered concerning the religious ideas of the Yahwist be true, he must have been a thinker of amazing depth and originality. Coming upon him from a study of such men as Elijah and Elisha we seem to be entering a wider and maturer world. We are suddenly viewing God and man in much the same way as the great prophets of the following century viewed them.[1] Indeed in some respects we have passed beyond the prophets into the humanity and individualism of the wisdom writers.

Obviously such a man must have exercised profound influence on those that followed him, especially after his writing came to be widely received as the true account of God's first dealings with humanity. Others than Christ must have gone to him for instruction as to what had been "from the beginning" (Mk. 10:6).

To trace this influence with any certainty, however, is not easy. Some resemblances between his teaching and that of the prophets are obvious. It may well have been from him that Amos got his conviction that Yahweh is no respecter of nations (Amos 3:2; 9:7ff), Isaiah his exaltation of God over man, Second Isaiah his sublime monotheism. But distinct literary reminiscences of the Yahwist seem to be absent from these writers and the thoughts that they have in common with him are too general, too much in the air of their time, too inevitable, to prove any dependence. In fact, there is little direct evidence that any of the prophets had even read his narrative of the beginnings.

On the other hand we cannot allow ourselves to forget that after all the Yahwist did entertain these thoughts and embody them in matchless literary form before Amos preached at Bethel. There has been too much of a tendency on the part of scholars, in reconstructing the development of Israel's religion, to ignore his contribution and to exclaim over his ideas when they meet them in the prophets as if they were there appearing for the first time. The ninth century B.C. is treated as the age of Elijah and Elisha and its religion measured by them as a standard. The quiet Yahwist is

[1] Professor Simpson writes: "I should say that he had the outlook of a priest, rather than of a prophet, with a priest's concern for the sensibilities of his people, a willingness to take over doubtful legends and use them, where the prophet would be more apt to condemn outright in his enthusiasm."

overlooked. Back of the prophets, therefore, we should ever be feeling the presence of this pioneer thinker.

But if we can say little of his influence upon his immediate successors the case is different when we come down to the days of the apocalyptists, the rabbis[2] and the men of the New Testament. There his early narratives give rise to all sorts of speculations and conceptions, of which space forbids to speak in detail. Suffice it for the Christian to remember that it was from him that Jesus drew his conception of the divine ideal of marriage, St. Paul his teaching of the effect of Adam's sin and his view of Abraham as the prototype of faith.

And what of our own time? Have we outgrown the Yahwist? The present writer cannot think so. Enshrined in the bright colours and quickly changing scenes of these narratives there seem to lie eternal truths that will continue to answer the cravings of the modern man in his quest after the meaning of human life.

[2] For a succinct statement of the effects of the fall in Jewish theology, see Sanday, *Romans*, 136ff.

founder of faith.

CHAPTER XII

AMOS

[*c.* 760 b.c.]

Up to this point the religion of Israel had given evidence of
astonishing strength and persistence, combined with a decided
ethical bent. Its founder, Moses, had forged a people in the fires
of faith, had brought that people into covenant relationship with
the pure and passionate Yahweh, and had stamped upon it a
pattern of burning devotion and lofty ethic. Under his successors
Israel had acquired in the land of Palestine a home in which its
vigorous life might develop, Yahweh being still its inspiration and
bond of union. Before the amazing impulse given by Moses had
spent itself another man of God had arisen in Samuel to restamp
the Mosaic pattern upon the people now fast becoming a nation.
The brilliant David had created that nation and invested its religion
with splendour, giving it an earthly centre in Jerusalem, and pouring into it his own consuming enthusiasm for Yahweh. Through
Nathan the prophet Yahweh had rebuked even His own favourite
and vindicated His outraged moral law against the most powerful
man of the age. In spite of the degeneracy which set in with
Solomon the Mosaic pattern had not dissolved but within a century
had reappeared in a third man of God, Elijah, who turned the
erring people's heart back again. His successor Elisha had domes-
ticated Yahweh, so to speak, bringing the divine helpfulness into
the common life of Israel. At last a thinker had arisen who saw
in Yahweh the creator of heaven and earth, the lover of man and
his teacher in sin and punishment, choosing out Israel to bless the
world.

The real nature of that blessing, however, had as yet scarcely
become evident. There was nothing so far in what Israel's religion
had effected that would have given it significance for mankind.
Now its unique and imperishable contribution was to appear in a
succession of men the like of which history has not known before
or since—the writing prophets. They burst upon us quite unex-

pectedly and follow one another steadily for two hundred years; then disappear as suddenly as they came, leaving behind them a way of thinking about God which later religion has refined and developed but has never really transcended.

And first among them Amos, the herdsman of Tekoa.

The Sources

The sole source for the study of Amos is the Book of Amos. Nowhere else is this prophet so much as mentioned. We can indeed learn a little concerning his time from the Second Book of the Kings and also from the Assyrian monuments. But Amos himself is known to us only through the nine chapters that bear his name.

These however tell us a great deal in a short space. What is more, they are reliable. Scholars agree that the book on the whole reports the genuine words of the prophet. A common view is that he published it after he was expelled from Bethel by Amaziah.

Several passages indeed are rejected by the majority of scholars. One is the doom pronounced in 2:4-5 upon Judah, its expressions regarding Judah's guilt being thought too vague and Deuteronomic. Another is the happy conclusion beginning at 9:8b and continuing to the end. This is attacked on the ground that its message of hope absolutely contradicts the tenor of the rest of the book, and that it also omits the ethical element from its portrayal of the blessed future. A final group is composed of the so-called "nature passages," in which Yahweh's operation in the domain of nature is extolled (4:13; 5:8-9; 9:5-6). These, it is maintained, interrupt the context and have affinities with later literature, particularly Second Isaiah.

While a few scholars of the highest standing dissent from one or more of these conclusions, it is perhaps better to confine our study of Amos to the rich material presented by the rest of the book.

It is only fair to add that other verses have often been rejected also, as 1:9-12; 5:14-15; 8:11-12. But these are so unimportant for the thought of Amos that they may be disregarded.

Taking then the excellent first-hand source presented by the Book of Amos let us see what it has to tell us of the man.

The Israel of Amos' Day

Elisha witnessed in his later years a distressing collapse of northern Israel. Jehu's bloody measures had weakened the little state and the vigorous Hazael, whom (tradition said) Elisha had prompted to seize the throne of Damascus, took advantage of a long quiescence of Assyria to make good his domination not only over Israel but over Judah as well. Neither could resist his victorious armies. The depths of prostration were reached under Jehu's son Jehoahaz, to whom Hazael left only fifty horsemen, ten chariots and ten thousand footmen (II Ki. 13:7). Then a change came. In 805 b.c. Adad-nirari III mounted the Assyrian throne and presently began to bring into subjection the western peoples who under the reign of his harassed predecessor Shamshi-adad V had "rebelled and withheld their tribute." To Damascus he delivered a crushing blow; it was captured and its great wealth seized. The day of its supremacy was over.[1]

The aged Elisha was quick to see that now Israel's chance had come. He encouraged the young king Joash (or Jehoash), Jehu's grandson (798-783 b.c.), to strike at Syria. Joash succeeded in driving out the Syrians from the whole region west of the Jordan (II Ki. 13:25). He also defeated Amaziah of Judah who, flushed with his victory over the Edomites, came north to attack him (II Ki. 14:8ff).

To make the situation yet more favourable, Assyria found itself unable to follow up its capture of Damascus by the reduction of neighbouring states and Joash was left free to deal with his former overlords as he would. He and his son Jeroboam II, who succeeded him in 783 b.c., were able to conquer much of Transjordania (II Ki. 14:25). With military success and enlarged territories prosperity came to Israel. From the Book of Amos we get a picture of the time.

Recent victories had filled people with pride in the army and its accomplishments. They thrilled over the capture of towns like Lo-debar and Karnaim in Transjordania (6:13) and talked enthusiastically about the swiftness and effectiveness of their bowmen and cavalrymen, the strength of their shock troops (2:14ff). Business also was good in spite of frequent agricultural setbacks, outbreaks of pestilence, and earthquakes. Merchants were making money (8:4-5) and one gets the impression that luxury was fairly widespread among the privileged class. They were able to build winter and summer houses and houses of ivory [2] furnished with silk-uphol-

---

[1] T. H. Robinson, *HI*, I, p. 357.

[2] The Harvard expedition has discovered on the site of Samaria many pieces of carved and inlaid ivory inlay, used for the decoration of costly wooden furniture (Albright, *RDBL*, p. 34).

stered couches inlaid (?) with ivory (3:12; 6:3). They enjoyed
plenty of high grade lamb, veal, wine and oil (6:3-6). They had
leisure to carouse and cultivate music (ibid). However badly
distributed, there must have been considerable wealth in the country
to make this possible. Relieved of the pressure from Damascus
the natural vigour of the people issued in greater production and
flourishing commerce.

Prosperity and success were reflected in the national temper.
When reading the pages of Amos one feels himself in an atmosphere
of satisfaction and even elation. Food scarcity, locusts, earthquakes,
and epidemics made little impression upon the general optimism.
No one apparently had any anxiety about the steady encroachments
of Assyria or saw much wrong at home (6:6b).

People were at least outwardly religious. The shrines of Bethel,
Gilgal and Beersheba were visited by great numbers. Sacrifices were
offered freely, tithes paid even more frequently than prescribed
by law (4:4-5; 5:5). Songs accompanied by viols ascended from
their solemn assemblies (5:23). New moons and sabbaths were
scrupulously observed (8:5); the names of the sanctuaries echoed
in their very oaths (8:14). There was much eschatological expectation and longing for the day of Yahweh (5:18).

From this popular religion the note of misgiving was conspicuously absent. Any thought that Yahweh was not well pleased
with them was far from the people's mind. The calamities above
mentioned were explained in some other way, if explained at all.
People do not seem even to have prayed for their removal. At
any rate we hear no cry for help arising from Amos' surroundings.
We must not indeed infer too much from this silence. Possibly
many an Israelite was acutely conscious of his need for divine
assistance and went to the sanctuary with his offering in the hope
of obtaining this aid. And the fact that the day of Yahweh was
desired would seem to indicate a sense that the present was not
proving wholly satisfactory. But certainly such longings did not
lead to any conviction of sin or amendment of life. People had
the unshaken belief that Yahweh was on the side of Israel and saw
in His well-patronized shrines the guarantee of His continuing
favour.

Yet there was enough, if we may trust Amos' testimony, to make
the intelligent observer dissatisfied with Israel's condition. First
and most ominous, the ways in which the well-to-do were acquiring
their wealth were highly anti-social. It was wrung from the poor
by a combination of strong arm methods (3:9) and crooked busi-

ness dealings (8:5), in both of which they were upheld by the courts. A poor man could not obtain justice at law if he brought suit. On the contrary the rich took the aggressive in prosecution, obtaining from him "fines" and "exactions" (5:11). When forced to borrow he must give his very cloak as security and go cold at night, although the law ordered the creditor to return it by evening (2:8). But the law was all against the debtor in these days. Selling into slavery was apparently not uncommon (8:6). As a result, the poor were being pressed downwards economically and their ruin seemed not far distant (8:4).

Another thing that went along with this expropriation of the poor was the effect upon the character of the nation's leaders created by the increase of luxury won in so heartless a fashion. There was a general let-down of inherited *mores*. Plain living had disappeared and in its place had come drunkenness, carousing, extravagant meals, lolling on easy couches, idling days away in music. The women too drank largely and by their expensive manner of life compelled their husbands to increase their extortions from the poor (4:1). And neither men nor women seemed to care what results their conduct was having upon the community (6:6b).

There was also the disquieting character of the worship to which the people were addicted. For all its enthusiasm it had no influence upon behaviour. They did not connect the service of Yahweh with justice and truth and righteousness. Nor did they want to be reminded of those elements in their ancestral religion that emphasized self-denial (2:12). Indeed it was not safe for any one to speak out publicly on behalf of the poor (5:10). The very feasts held beside the altars were provided with wines and cushions at the expense of the defenseless. Unchastity too was present, breaking down the old reverences of the family (2:7). Finally, the forms of worship themselves were open to the charge of idolatry, though Amos is not clear upon this point (5:26).

Amos intervenes on behalf of Yahweh

In the midst of this corrupt and decadent civilization, when it might well have seemed that the pattern left by Moses had ceased to have any influence on men, God was preparing one who was destined to usher in the mightiest spiritual movement of Israel's history. For it was here where society and religion itself were proving bankrupt that the first of the writing prophets came upon the scene. In the little Judean village of Tekoa, some seven miles southeast of Bethlehem, a herdsman named Amos was brooding over the wickedness of his day. Just how he learned of the great world beyond his isolated home we can only conjecture. Perhaps, as G. A. Smith [1] suggested, he was in the habit of making yearly trips into the north to sell the wool of his sheep and so had the opportunity to observe what was going on. In any case, he saw.

But not as the common run of men did he see. In the solitude of the Judean hills he had contemplated the invisible world until it had become to him the supreme reality. "How many men of God, or those who have considered themselves such, have come out of the wilderness, from Moses to the Mahdis of our own time!" [2] Concerning everything that met his eye he asked but one question: "What does Yahweh say to it?" [3]

Then one day Yahweh called him to prophesy.[4] Leaving his sheep in the tangled hills and valleys of Judah he strode northward twenty-five miles till he reached Bethel, the religious centre of Israel. We may picture him in his rough herdsman's dress coming fresh from awful intercourse with deity into the crowded court

---

[1] *BTP* (1901), I, p. 79.

[2] B. Duhm, *Die Propheten*, p. 91.

[3] Kittel, *GMMI*, p. 236.

[4] Amos, like Hosea, tells only the *substance* of his call, not the way in which it came to him (Amos 7:14ff; Hos. 1:2ff). If we may judge from the accounts given by Isaiah (6), Jeremiah (1) and Ezekiel (1:4ff) of their calls, he received it when he was in a psychic condition akin to what we term "ecstasy." The same would be true of the manner in which the "word of Yahweh" was thereafter given to him. Indeed, it is possible that many if not all oracles imparted to a prophet came when he was in ecstasy, when (as Ezekiel expressed it, 3:14, 22; 8:1; 33:22; 37:1) the "hand" of Yahweh was upon him. The realization of this fact has led some scholars to speak of the prophets as "ecstatics." The great exponent of this view is Gustav Hölscher (*Die Profeten*, Leipzig, 1914). T. H. Robinson (*Prophecy and the Prophets*, N. Y., 1923) follows it with reserve. "It does not follow that all their utterances originated in this way (i.e. in ecstasy), yet it is at least possible." When applied in a thoroughgoing fashion the conception of the prophets as ecstatics is apt to lead to very "radical" conclusions, not only in the determination of authentic passages, but also in delineating the prophet's personality. We must be careful, however, to distinguish between these heightened moments and the ordinary tenor of the prophet's life, which gave solidity and continuity to his religious outlook. He did not depend for his intercourse with God upon ecstasy. On the contrary, it seems to have been his normal life of prayer and devotion that determined the character of his heightened experiences (cf. Hempel, *AHL*, p. 62). At any rate, the teaching which the prophet gave was not that of a neurotic but of a clear-eyed man, in deadly earnest, who saw all things from God's point of view, whose only "madness" was an intoxication with God.

of Bethel's famous sanctuary. Something about him makes people
turn as he begins to speak. This is not the usual prophet, but a
man of elemental force.

"Thus saith Yahweh:
For three transgressions of Damascus, yea for four,
I will not turn it away!
Because they have threshed Gilead with threshing instruments of
    iron:
But I will send a fire into the house of Hazael,
And it shall devour the palaces of Ben-hadad.
And I will break the bar of Damascus,
And cut off the inhabitant from the valley of Aven,
And him that holdeth the sceptre from the house of Eden;
And the people of Syria shall go into captivity beyond Kir,
Saith Yahweh."

A thrill of fierce pleasure runs through the listeners; they crowd
about him to hear more. For he is announcing the doom of Israel's
hereditary enemy.

And he goes on in the same vein. Gaza, Tyre, Edom, Ammon,
Moab—those neighbours who in one way and another had gained
Israel's ill will—bow in succession under the rolling thunder of
judgment. What an indictment is entered against them: war-time
barbarities, slave raids, broken covenants, unquenchable hatreds,
sacrilegious outrages! No wonder God will strike!

But suddenly, as they applaud, the prophet turns upon the people
before him:

"Thus saith Yahweh:
For three transgressions of *Israel,* yea for four,
I will not turn it away;
Because they have sold the righteous for silver,
And the needy for a pair of shoes;
They that pant after the dust of the earth on the head of the poor,
And turn aside the way of the meek:
And a man and his father go unto the same maiden,[5]
To profane my holy name:
And they lay themselves down upon clothes taken in pledge
Beside every altar;
And they drink the wine of such as have been fined
In the house of their God!"

   [5] Probably, sacred prostitute.

Yes, Israel, the most privileged of the nations, was the chief offender. All that Yahweh had done for them in the past called forth no gratitude. His best gift had been rejected:

"And I raised up your sons for prophets,
And your young men for Nazirites.
But ye gave the Nazirites wine to drink,
And commanded the prophets, saying, Prophesy not" (1:3–2:12).

The very heathen of Ashdod and Egypt, if they could get a glimpse of the tumults and oppressions going on in Samaria, would be appalled (3:9). Yet all the while these makers of human misery were worshipping Yahweh with enthusiasm as if on the best terms with Him!

"Thus saith Yahweh . . .
I hate, I despise your feasts,
And I will not smell in your solemn assemblies.
Yea, though ye offer me your burnt-offerings
And meal-offerings, I will not accept them;
Neither will I regard the peace-offerings of your fat beasts.
Take thou away from me the noise of thy songs;
For I will not hear the melody of thy viols.
But let justice roll down as waters,
And righteousness as an ever-flowing stream!" (5:21ff).

What would be the end of all this? The Israelites could not see. Many of them were actually longing for the great day when Yahweh would intervene to bring victory and glory to Israel!

"Woe unto you that desire the day of Yahweh!
Wherefore would ye have the day of Yahweh?
It is darkness, and not light. . . .
Shall not the day of Yahweh be darkness, and not light?
Even very dark, and no brightness in it?" (5:18ff).

How confident they were in their army and its petty successes! But the army would collapse in the evil day:

"And flight shall perish from the swift;
And the strong shall not strengthen his force;
Neither shall the mighty deliver himself;
Neither shall he stand that handleth the bow;

And he that is swift of foot shall not deliver himself;
Neither shall he that rideth the horse deliver himself;
And he that is courageous among the mighty
Shall flee away naked in that day,
Saith Yahweh" (2:14ff).

For Yahweh was bringing on His instruments of vengeance:

"For behold, I am raising against you, . . .
O house of Israel, a nation;
And they shall afflict you from the entrance of Hamath
Unto the brook of the Arābāh" (6:14).

"And I will cause you to go into captivity beyond Damascus,
Saith Yahweh, whose name is the God of hosts" (5:27).

No need for Amos to utter the dread name of Assyria; every one understood.

These and many other like things Amos said. How the people received them we do not know, nor how long he continued to utter his oracles in the northern kingdom. Hölscher thinks it possible that the cycle of visions in 7:1ff, which reflects spring, summer and autumn, may indicate an activity extending over some months; and deems it likely that Amos spoke in Samaria and even in various other places, as well as in Bethel. But at last his prophesying was brought harshly to a close.

It was in the temple at Bethel. Amos had been uttering the series of visions above referred to, all of which announced the irrevocable doom of Israel. In the third he saw Yahweh standing by a wall made by a plumbline, with a plumbline in His hand; and the Lord said:

"Behold, I will set a plumbline in the midst of my people Israel;
I will not again pass by them any more;
And the high places of Isaac shall be desolate,
And the sanctuaries of Israel shall be laid waste;
And I will rise against the house of Jeroboam with the sword!"

It was apparently the first time he had spoken the royal name, and his words made a stir. They sounded like the words of Elisha which eighty years before had set in motion the rebellion of Jehu. Serious indeed it was when a prophet announced the rejection of a royal house. Amaziah, the priest of Bethel, jumped to a natural conclusion and sent off a message in hot haste to king Jeroboam in Samaria thirty-five miles away: "Amos hath conspired against thee in the midst of the house of Israel: the land is not able to bear all his words." Then without waiting to get the king's directions he acted on his own account. In all his authority as head of the temple he bore down upon the offender.

"Vision seer," he shouted, "get out! Run for it to the land of Judah; and get your living there, and do your prophesying there. But in Bethel no more prophesying! For *it* is a king's holy place; *it* is a royal house."

It was one of the great encounters of history. We watch them there face to face, the outraged official to whom king and country —to say nothing of his own job—are the biggest things of all, and the poor man from the steppe who can see only God. Little enough did Amos care for kings and royal sanctuaries and "authorities."

"And Amos answered and said to Amaziah: *I* am no prophet, and *I* am no son of a prophet. No, I am a herdsman and a dresser of sycamore trees.[6] And *Yahweh* took me from behind the flock, and *Yahweh* said unto me, Go, prophesy to my people Israel. And now hear the word of Yahweh:

Thou sayest, Prophesy not against Israel,
And drop not thy words against the house of Isaac.
Therefore thus saith Yahweh:
Thy wife in the city shall be a harlot,
And thy sons and thy daughters by the sword shall fall,
And thy land by the cord shall be divided,
And thou upon an unclean land shalt die:
And Israel shall surely go into exile from off their land" (7:10ff).

Then turning to the startled people Amos finished what he had been saying before the interruption, uttering his two final visions of doom:[7]

"Behold, the eyes of the Lord Yahweh are upon the sinful kingdom,
And I will destroy it from off the face of the earth!" (8:1-9:8a).

So he concluded. What happened next we are not told. Probably Amaziah made good his sentence of banishment and Amos retired to his Judean hills to write down and publish his oracles of judgment. He thus became the first of the "writing prophets"

---

[6] That is, I have a job. My reason for being here is not to get a living.
[7] At least the present text gives the impression that he so continued.

and set a precedent which the great prophets who succeeded him
were to follow. To that precedent we owe the preservation of
their "books."

But Amos bequeathed to his successors more than the practice
of publishing their oracles. They took over from him his whole
thought world. Although in several respects he differed from them
yet in general the concepts that dominated his thinking were shared
by them also. We cannot be sure, of course, that they actually got
these concepts from Amos since both he and they may have drawn
them from a common source. But after conceding all that Amos
may have owed to earlier thinkers like Moses, Samuel, Elijah and
the Yahwist he still remains the great pioneer and his book the
creative classic of Hebrew prophecy.

What now were some of his leading ideas concerning God and
man?

Yahweh is the Only God

While Amos does not expressly declare that there is no other god
but Yahweh, we can see on every page that he takes this as a matter
of course. Yahweh has jurisdiction over Damascus, Gaza, Edom,
Tyre, Moab and Ammon. It is before His judgment bar that they
stand, it is His doom that overtakes them (1:3-2:3). The gods
whom they worship—Hadad, Dagon, Melek, Melkart, Chemosh—
are absolutely ignored. Again, it is Yahweh who is about to bring
upon these peoples the common enemy, greater and more remote
than them all—the colossal empire of Assyria. Amos believed also
that it was Yahweh who had conducted the migrations of the past;
He had "brought up the Philistines from Caphtor and the Syrians
from Kir" (9:7). From Yahweh none could escape; not in Sheol,
nor in heaven, nor in the maze of Carmel's thickets, nor in the
bottom of the sea, nor in the distant land of the enemy (9:2ff).
We do not need the support of the disputed "nature-passages" to
prove that in Amos' mind the entire realm of physical phenomena
is under Yahweh's control.

In a sense this was nothing new with Amos. Elijah had already
attained a similar monotheism; but in Amos it takes on a new
range. His world is wider than Elijah's, less centred in Israel.
The doom that Yahweh is about to bring upon the nations has
a vaster sweep than Elijah could conceive. In Amos one begins
to see how the emergence of Assyria compelled the thinkers of
Israel to enlarge their concept of God. Yahweh must now be
great enough to govern that prodigious world empire. And as

Assyria was soon to overwhelm the petty national distinctions of Syria, reducing all to a common servitude, so Yahweh must be conceived as the king of all mankind. Otherwise He must abdicate in favour of the gods of Assyria!

Yahweh Cares for All Nations

This also is not specifically stated by Amos but it is implied in at least three outstanding passages. One is the series of dooms pronounced on the peoples surrounding Israel (1:3-2:3). Back of the indignation at their crimes throbs a sincere desire for their good. Yahweh had wished to see better conditions prevailing among them and had been disappointed. The second is a famous utterance: Yahweh says to the sons of Israel, the whole family which He had brought up out of the land of Egypt:

"You only have I known of all the families of the earth:
Therefore will I visit upon you all your iniquities" (3:2).

Yahweh then will not continue to favour Israel at the expense of other nations. In the last analysis His dealings with all peoples are equal. Greater privileges, greater responsibility. It is the first prophetic enunciation of the conviction that "God is no respecter of persons," or of races (Acts 10:34). It falls into line with the Baptist's warning: "Think not to say within yourselves, We have Abraham for our father: for I say unto you that God is able of these stones to raise up children unto Abraham" (Lk. 3:8). The third is still nobler:

"Are ye not as the children of the Ethiopians unto me,
O children of Israel? saith Yahweh.
Have I not brought up Israel out of the land of Egypt,
And the Philistines from Caphtor, and the Syrians from Kir?" (9:7).

Yahweh has led other peoples in their migrations just as truly as He has led Israel; and fundamentally they mean as much to Him as does Israel. One is reminded of the great universalistic saying of St. Paul in his speech to the Athenians:

"God made of one every nation of men to dwell on all the face of the earth, having determined their appointed seasons, and the bounds of their habitation . . ." (Acts 17:26).

Perhaps Amos was speaking in heightened language and did not actually mean all that his words seem to imply. Yet even so it is a startling utterance to meet in the pages of the Old Testament. It seems to break through from some wider world of the future. The Yahwist had indeed glimpsed the same truth in his stories of the childhood of mankind but he did not quite capture it. That remained for the herdsman of Tekoa who could look out from the barren uplands of Judah upon Philistia with its highroad to Egypt and upon the far off snows of Hermon under which passed the "entering to Hamath," the main route to Assyria and Babylonia.

Yahweh Requires Justice and not Sacrifice

We have already cited the burning passage in which Amos declares that Yahweh rejects the worship of Israel because it is offered by men who oppress their fellow men (5:21ff). Here again he is the pioneer. The thought indeed was not new. It lay implicit in the strong ethical bent that Moses had given to Israel's religion. Samuel had already exalted obedience above sacrifice (I Sam. 15:22) but he had said nothing about justice as being a chief part of obedience. Stern upholders of right like Nathan and Elijah had denounced wrong even in kings but had not brought in any comparison of the values of worship and justice (II Sam. 12:1ff; I Ki. 21). Amos was the first to throw this comparison into such peremptory form that men could not escape its challenge. After him it became a prophetic commonplace.

Amos indeed expressed himself in an extreme way. He seems to speak as if sacrificial worship had played no part in the earlier and purer days of Israel's history. "Did ye bring unto me sacrifices and offerings in the wilderness forty years, O house of Israel?" (5:25). And the present worship at the great shrines he characterizes as "transgression," demanding in Yahweh's name that it be suppressed as an offence to heaven:

> "Come to Bethel, and transgress;
> To Gilgal, and multiply transgression" (4:4).

> "Seek ye me, and ye shall live;
> But seek not Bethel, nor enter into Gilgal,
> And pass not to Beersheba!" (5:5).

In another place he condemns those who swear by the "sin of Samaria"; but here it is possible that he has in mind the bull worship practised there. In that case he would not be denouncing worship as such but only its corrupt form (8:14).

The probability is that Amos in these passages was not rejecting the sacrificial worship of his day in itself but merely expressing his conviction that such worship divorced from justice is an abomination before God. Yet in putting justice first in so uncompromising a fashion he was blazing the trail for the prophets who followed him and (all unconsciously) preparing the way for Christ.

It is characteristic of Amos that he spoke so much of justice. No man of the Old Testament felt more deeply the exploitation of the poor. With what scorching wrath did he burn the well-to-do who were taking advantage of their need!

"Forasmuch therefore as ye trample upon the poor,
And take exactions from him of wheat:
Ye have built houses of cut stone,
But ye shall not live in them;
Ye have planted pleasant vineyards,
But ye shall not drink their wine.
For I know how manifold are your transgressions,
And how mighty are your sins;
Ye that afflict the just, that take a bribe
And that turn aside the needy in the gate" (5:11f).

"Hear this, ye that would swallow up the needy,
And cause the poor of the land to fail,
Saying, When will the new moon be gone, that we may sell grain?
And the sabbath, that we may set forth wheat,
Making the ephah small, and the shekel great,
And dealing falsely with the balances of deceit?" (8:4f).

Quite in keeping with this championship of the poor was Amos' scorn for luxury indulged in at their expense.

"Woe to them that are at ease in Zion,
And to them that are secure in the mountains of Samaria,
The 'notable men' of 'the chief of the nations,'
To whom the house of Israel come. . . .
Ye that put far away the evil day,
And cause the seat of violence to come near;
That lie upon beds of ivory,
And stretch themselves upon their couches,
And eat the lambs out of the flock,

And calves out of the midst of the stall;
That sing idle songs to the sound of the viol;
That invent for themselves instruments of music, like David;
That drink wine in bowls,
And anoint themselves with the chief oils;
But they are not grieved for the affliction of Joseph!" (6:1ff).

He had no patience with people who sprawled on the silk cushions of couches, who had winter houses and summer houses, great houses inlaid with ivory (3:12, 15); with women who were always calling to their husbands for drinks—paid for by the poor (4:1).

Other Prophetic Ideas of Amos

Two other ideas of Amos were to dominate the prophets who followed him. One was, that military preparedness would avail nothing against the evil to come. It belonged with the structures of man's pride which diverted his trust from God and so was not only futile but wicked. Amos does not indeed call it wicked but he implies that it is. We have seen how he poured contempt upon the army in which Israel exulted.

He had thus travelled a long way from the War-God conception which Moses bequeathed to posterity. His mind was quite emancipated from any thought that Yahweh went out at the head of Israel's host to thrust down its enemies. On the contrary, He saw Yahweh bringing on the invading forces of Assyria to punish Israel along with the rest of the wicked peoples of Syria.

The last thing for a prophet of Yahweh to do, therefore, would be to fan the martial ardour of Israel. Let him instead preach the repentance which alone could avert Yahweh's stroke. We get an earlier example of this prophetic attitude in Micaiah ben Imlah when he stood out against the four hundred prophets who encouraged Ahab to march against Jabesh-gilead (I Ki. 22). But Micaiah said no more than that the wicked Ahab could not hope to have Yahweh with him on the field of battle. Amos went much further. To him it was not a question whether a good or a bad king was on the throne; the whole nation was corrupt and any military effort was resistance to the divine will of doom.

The sword, then, was to be left in Yahweh's hand. Perhaps it was in accord with this conviction that Amos abandoned the older prophetic policy of anointing a successor to the reigning king and so stirring up rebellion. The time indeed had gone when a prophet might hope anything from a change of dynasty. But more, to adopt such measures would strike at the root of faith in Yahweh. Let Yahweh attend to punishment! There was no truth therefore in Amaziah's charge that Amos had conspired against Jeroboam. If Yahweh were about to rise against the house of Jeroboam with the sword it would be with the sword of Assyria, not of any Israelitish conspirator.

The other prophetic idea of which we have spoken was that the prophetic work lay in warning the people of what Yahweh was about to do.[1] This of course was not new with Amos but he asserted it with a vigour which brought it clearly into the foreground of men's thought.

"For the Lord Yahweh will not do anything,
Except he reveal his secret unto his servants the prophets.
The lion hath roared; who will not fear?
The Lord Yahweh hath spoken; who will not prophesy?" (3:7f).

This is an amazing statement. It declares nothing less than that knowledge of impending judgments was always available for the Israelite who would listen to the prophets. And Yahweh's habit of communicating His intended acts arose from His *love*. Yes though the acts be punishments of the direst nature, still the fact that He warned of them beforehand showed His desire to help men. The true prophet therefore was always one of His chief gifts to men, an evidence of His grace (2:11). The worst calamity that could happen to Israel would be the cessation of prophecy, when men should run to and fro to seek the word of Yahweh and should not find it (8:12).[2]

Yet this "word of Yahweh" was never a mere word; it fell from the lips of the prophet as a real power, a force that worked towards

[1] For of course Yahweh was *going to do something*. This belief in a God who intervenes in history to effect His will goes back to Moses (see p. 11). It rings through all that the writing prophets uttered. "The prophets experienced Yahweh's nearness, not in mystic absorption, not in beatific vision in the hours of silent transport and high rapture, but in consuming, overpowering will. The consciousness of being seized by Yahweh, accordingly, did not produce a passive attitude of 'still attention, of quietistic contemplation' but 'energetic impulses to active deeds'; and so with them the far-away-in-heaven, placidly-enthroned majesty of Yahweh retreats behind the weight of His action" (Hempel, *GMAT*, p. 104).

[2] Many scholars hold that 8:11–12 is not an utterance of Amos; but the idea contained in it is fundamental to the thinking of the prophets.

its own fulfillment. When Amos chanted that the virgin of Israel was fallen to rise no more (5:2), it was believed that a blighting energy had thereby been released against the doomed people. This idea, so foreign to the modern mind, will meet us often in the prophetic writings. Amos does not express it but he must have shared it. When therefore Amaziah ordered him not to "drop" any more words against the house of Israel (7:16) he wanted to free the land from the malign working of words which were already too much for it to bear (7:10). In a sense then, from his antique point of view, Amaziah was justified in saying that Amos had "conspired" against Jeroboam, though his fellow conspirator might be only God.[3]

So much for the great prophetic ideas that palpitate through the oracles of Amos. It remains to notice a serious omission in his thinking which his successors, with the possible exception of Micah, were later to rectify.

Yahweh Has no Constructive Plan for the Future

It has struck all students of Amos' book that it stops short with punishment. Unless we accept as genuine the promises of 9:8b–15 we find in it no looking forward to a happier day. All thought that Yahweh may yet make something of Israel is abandoned. He has been defeated in His purpose and nothing remains but to bring on the Assyrian. All is to go down in a common ruin and under the wreckage will lie buried the hopes that Yahweh had cherished in the education of His people.

We should expect from Amos' championship of the poor that something would be done for them in the "day of Yahweh." Quite the contrary. They are not to be avenged or helped but simply to be overwhelmed along with their rich oppressors. Now it is probable that the poor were as bad as the rich. Isaiah and Jeremiah found them so (Is. 2:9; Jer. 5:4), and Amos may well have had the same experience. But certainly one gets the impression that his sympathies go out to them, that they would be led by his words to look upon him as their friend. Why does he fail them? Or rather, why is his God powerless on their behalf?

Again, there were the faithful few. Amos does not indeed mention them but they must have existed. Why are they not to be used in building a new community? But we hear nothing from

[3] G. A. Smith, *The Book of the Twelve, ad loc.*

Amos' lips of any pious "remnant" which would furnish material for such an enterprise.

That is the terrible thing about Amos' book. It utters doom without hope; which means the defeat of God. And the worst of it is that Amos seems to find the message congenial! True, he did intercede for Israel twice: "How shall Jacob stand? for he is small" (7:2–5). But when at the third time God forestalls his intercessions he acquiesces and throws himself into God's purpose of destruction with zest (7:7ff).

The question has therefore been raised whether Amos loved. The prevailing answer is that he loved a little, but not enough, not to heart-break; and this answer seems just.

But even though his *love* did not compel him to hope, how could his *faith* allow him to accept the defeat of God? Surely he must have felt that God would succeed in His purpose for men despite Israel's opposition. He must have pictured, however vaguely, a future divine triumph, a kingdom of heaven of some kind rising beyond the Assyrian catastrophe. This feeling has led scholars like Kittel to accept the closing prophecy of promise (9:86ff) as genuine, in spite of its lack of ethical interest and its narrow nationalism. Perhaps he did utter it, although it is hard to see how a future in which his ideals have no real recognition could have interested him. It is more probable however that he did not think the situation through. Had he like Jeremiah lived to see the fulfillment of his dark predictions he would have been forced to ask "What next?" As it was, the doom seems to have absorbed his attention completely.

Amos' Contribution to Religion

Enough perhaps has been said of the heritage which Amos left to his successors the writing prophets. That he came into Israel's religion as an elemental, explosive force which made it for ever after different, more free, more pure, more full of spiritual power, is conceded by all. With him dawns a new era not only for Israel but for mankind. He brought out the things in the Mosaic pattern which were destined to pass over into the higher religion of the future. In him as perhaps in no other we see the strange power of that pattern to burst its own forms and become something new.

What is his value for today? In certain respects we have gone beyond him. His belief that God in a supernatural way reveals to individuals what is about to take place in history does not seem to apply to our time. His vivid sense of God's wrath both shocks us and leaves us cold. His conviction that calamities are to be interpreted as signs of divine displeasure appalls us. His scathing denunciations, though there is that in us which makes us enjoy them, strike us as possibly unfair, probably ineffective and certainly harsh. This same harshness, unrelieved by any tender passages, prevents his book from feeding the inner life; it is exhilarating but not devotional. One does not brood over it on his knees.

And yet it *is* exhilarating. How clearly he puts first things first. There is a lift about this man, a freedom, a throwing off of ordinary human hesitations that acts as a tonic to our sluggish spirits. Amos lives in a vaster world, where wealth and splendour count for nothing, where kings seem small, where the power of the powerful is contemptible and the only things worthy of honour are justice and purity and truth, where what God thinks is the supreme question. He is one of the great emancipated spirits of the race. And he is one of its most passionate champions of the poor. Wherever men have gone to the Bible for encouragement in the long struggle for the liberation of the underprivileged, they have found it chiefly in Amos and in those successors whom he deeply influenced—Isaiah and Micah.

CHAPTER XIII

HOSEA

[AFTER 745 B.C.]

The Sources

As with Amos, so with Hosea, the only knowledge we have of him is drawn from the book that bears his name. Nowhere else in the Old Testament is he even mentioned. But here also the book is a source of the first order. It comes from the pen of Hosea himself or of some one who knew him and his utterances intimately.

The text of the book is in poor condition and in a number of places scholars find it impossible to translate. The Septuagint here and there throws light on obscure passages and modern scholars have also tried to clarify the meaning by ingenious emendations. But in spite of these aids the reader of Hosea is frequently, as Gressmann [1] says, on unsteady ground. Such difficulties however are not serious enough to prevent our getting a true and vivid idea of his thought.

That the book for the most part contains the genuine words of Hosea is not doubted even by radical critics like Marti [2] and Hölscher.[3] Marti goes further perhaps than most in rejecting passages. He believes that the eighth century prophets did not hold out any promises and so he excludes all utterances of a hopeful nature as later interpolations. Hölscher too thinks that Hosea points only to an end, not to a new beginning. The majority of scholars however regard this position as arbitrary and retain most of the hopeful utterances as peculiarly characteristic of Hosea. Another feature of the book that has been questioned is the recurrence of references to Judah. It is thought that in some instances "Israel" may have been in the original text instead of "Judah." We may therefore use the book as a whole with confidence.

[1] *SAT*, II 1, p. 362.
[2] *Dodekapropheton* (Tübingen, 1904), p. 8ff.
[3] *Die Profeten* (Leipzig, 1914), p. 220.

Hosea Looked on the same Israel as Amos, but with Different Eyes

The prophetic activity of Hosea followed that of Amos closely. The dynasty of Jehu was yet occupying the throne when "Yahweh began to speak by him." Not improbably the powerful Jeroboam II was still alive. At any rate the first three chapters of Hosea's book reflect a condition of prosperity that is quite like what we find indicated in the words of Amos.

At last however the long reign of Jeroboam II, which had brought Israel so much outward success, came to a close. In the year 743 B.C. he died and was succeeded by his son Zechariah (II Ki. 15:8ff). And now began a period of more than twenty years in which the royal power passed quickly from hand to hand. Within six months a certain Shallum conspired against Zechariah, killed him "before the people" and seized the throne. His power lasted one month. Then another upstart, Menahem, put him out of the way and reigned in his stead for seven years (II Ki. 15:13ff). In 737 B.C. Menahem's son Pekahiah succeeded him, and within two years he in turn was murdered by "his captain" Pekah the son of Remaliah, who plays a part in Isaiah's story. He reigned from 736 to 730 B.C. (II Ki. 15:23ff). In that year Hoshea the son of Elah conspired against him and after murdering him occupied the throne till 722 B.C. Then Sargon king of Assyria captured Samaria (II Ki. 15:30ff; 17:1ff). All these bloody changes, accompanied as they were by the devastating encroachments of Assyria, must have thrown the nation into increasing confusion. It is often thought by scholars that the frequent mention in Chapters 4 to 14 of robbery, bloodshed, violence and social demoralization shows a condition approaching anarchy, as contrasted with the stable and orderly government of Jeroboam II.

It is doubtful however whether the state of society depicted in these later chapters could be described by such a strong word as "anarchy." Hosea does indeed speak of the land devouring its rulers and attributes the quick displacement of kings to Yahweh's wrath. He also draws a terrible picture of the people's morals, particularly in the matter of violence. But Amos some years earlier speaks of the tumults in Samaria. And we find in Hosea's later as well as his earlier chapters evidence that the prosperity and complacency of Amos' day still prevailed. Israel was like a luxuriant vine, teeming with population, and the land was "good." Therefore Israel could make "goodly pillars" for his shrines (10:1). He was satiated with food and his heart was lifted up and he forgot

Yahweh (13:6). He boasted "I have become rich, I have gotten me wealth" (12:8). He still trusted in the multitude of his mighty men and his fortresses were intact (10:13–14). The principal men still had money enough to drink and carouse (7:5). The people as a whole still thronged the places of worship and enjoyed the round of feasts and observances (9:3–5; 4:14–15). Hosea to be sure speaks of their howling on their beds and assembling themselves for grain and new wine (7:14); but whatever scarcity is meant seems no more to have broken down the general sense of prosperity than did the famine, locusts and epidemics alluded to by Amos. All this did not mean of course that the nation was sound. Hosea declared that it was in a state of decay. Gray hairs were freely sprinkled upon Ephraim. But, as the prophet himself testifies, the people were not aware of it; "he knoweth it not" (7:9). Probably the lawlessness depicted in these chapters interfered little more with the comfort of everyday life than does the "crime-wave" of present day America.

It is safe to say then that Hosea looked out upon substantially the same Israel as did Amos. Certainly whatever changes may have taken place since the time of the earlier prophet had not much altered the ethical and religious characteristics of the people. But Hosea saw different things in the situation. The luxury of the rich (7:5) and the defrauding and oppression of the poor, so bitterly denounced by Amos, did not escape him (12:7f) but he was more shocked by the general disregard of moral obligations, the wholesale lying, murder, stealing, violence, adultery and licentiousness. Like Amos he gave much thought to the popular worship, but its worst feature in his eyes was its adoration of images, to which Amos paid little attention. He noted the way in which the priests misled the laity. He marked the profligacy and drunkenness of the king and his court, their ridiculing of old sanctities, the mutual corruption of prince and people. He saw with aversion the feverish seeking after foreign alliances—a phenomenon apparently new since Amos' day—and the assimilation that was taking place between the Israelites and their heathen neighbours. On the other hand he seems to have given himself no concern over the nations bordering upon Israel—in sharp contrast to Amos' international outlook. Nor does he appear to have estimated clearly the preponderance in vigour of Assyria over Egypt, for he speaks of both empires as equally menacing to Israel.

But the deepest contrast between Hosea and Amos lay not in their different emphases but in the spirit that animated each.

Amos, as we have seen, had thrown himself with a will into the preaching of Israel's doom and was content to stop short with its destruction. Not so Hosea; for he loved Israel.

This may have been due in part to the fact that he belonged to it. Unlike the herdsman of Tekoa he seems to have been a citizen of the northern kingdom and could not view its faults from the outside. But its main cause must be sought in the nature of the man himself, in the mysterious ultimate something that makes each individual what he is.

Hosea's Call

Where Hosea lived, or what was his occupation, we do not know. Only the name of his father, Beeri, has come down to us. In some city or village of the northern kingdom this young man had been watching with burning eyes the wickedness of his people. It must have seemed to him an hour when a prophet was needed; for he had a high conception of the prophet's work. God, he believed, had used prophets from the first to guide His people. Even Moses was not too great to be called by that name. "By a prophet Yahweh brought Israel up out of Egypt, and by a prophet was he preserved" (12:13). Then it was revealed to him that he himself must undertake this task.

The form in which his call came to him was strange indeed. He tells the story in the third person, as if he were describing the experience of another.

"The beginning of Yahweh's speaking to Hosea: And Yahweh said
　　to Hosea,
Go, take thee a wife who is a prostitute and children by a prostitute;
For an utter prostitute is the land, departing from Yahweh.
And he went and took Gomer the daughter of Diblaim" (1:2f).

Does he mean this literally? Impossible, say some scholars. God would never have laid such a monstrous command upon His prophet! Hosea is uttering an allegory. The majority of scholars however refuse to consider his words a mere parable. He is speaking, they feel, of a real woman. Gomer was "no dream, but flesh and blood." [1] But among those who hold to Gomer's reality there is a difference of opinion. Some maintain that at the time when Hosea married her she was no prostitute but a maiden living in her father's home. Only later did he discover that she had proved

[1] G. A. Smith, *The Book of the Twelve* (N. Y., 1901), p. 236.

unfaithful to him. This view is beautifully brought out by G. A. Smith in his incomparable treatment of Hosea. On the other hand some (including the present writer) take the prophet's words as they stand. According to this view Hosea believed that Yahweh had ordered him to marry a prostitute, perhaps one of the "sacred women" attached to a sanctuary. By such an act, so shocking to the people's sense of decency, he was to bring home to them their own "prostitution" from Yahweh. What! A good man marrying a woman like that! Yes, and Yahweh wedded to a harlot nation! Could a more vivid sermon be preached? For of course this would not be done in a corner. A prophet was a public man and Hosea must take care that as many eyes as possible should be fixed henceforth on his home. All this was hard on him, but a prophet's personal happiness did not count!

Presently children came, and each in turn was made a sign of Israel's impending doom.

"Gomer conceived and bore him a son. And Yahweh said to him,

Call his name Jezreel.
For yet a little while,
And I will visit the blood of Jezreel upon the house of Jehu,
And I will cause to cease the kingdom of the house of Israel.
And it shall be in that day,
That I will break the bow of Israel
In the valley of Jezreel" (1:4f).

Such was Hosea's second message to the nation. The wholesale murders by which Jehu stamped out the worship of Melkart must be atoned for. But not only by Jehu's dynasty, whose last great representative Jeroboam II now sat on the throne. Yahweh's vengeance will include the whole people. What a transformation in prophetic thought since Elisha instigated Jehu's rebellion a hundred years before! In Hosea's eyes it is an accursed, not a praiseworthy thing to kill fellow-Israelites, even for the purification of religion. And like Amos he is himself no conspirator against the "house of Jeroboam."

"And she conceived again and bore a daughter. And God said to him, Call her name *Unpitied* (*Lo-ruhamah*). For I will not any more pity the house of Israel; for I have become wholly their enemy.[2]

---

[2] Emending to follow the LXX. V.7 is omitted as probably a later interpolation.

And she weaned *Unpitied,* and conceived and bore a son. And he said, Call his name *Not my people* (*Lo-ammi*); for ye are not my people and I will not be your God [3]" (1:6–9).

Thus the prophet and his whole family became living signs that Yahweh had turned against Israel. But Hosea did not stop with mere signs; he gave an interpretation in poetic words which could not be misunderstood.

Hosea Proclaimed Israel Unfaithful to Yahweh's Love

Israel, said Hosea, was married to Yahweh and the relationship between them demanded the same mutual fidelity and tenderness that should exist between husband and wife. But Israel had violated the bond of love which united them to God. Hosea is the first of the Old Testament writers to apply to Israel's relations with Yahweh this metaphor of marriage, which was later to play its part in the thinking of Jeremiah and Ezekiel. To say this does not mean of course that he invented it, for it must have been current in the popular nature-religion with its exaltation of the sex-principle. But Hosea, as Gressmann [1] truly says, discovered it anew and developed it, thereby making it at home in prophetic literature.

Yahweh had taken Israel to be His wife. Everything that a loving husband could do He had done for her. It was He who had given her the land of Canaan with its agricultural wealth. That was part of His plan, for He wanted her to dwell in peace and plenty. But He also sought from her an answering love and an understanding of His character.

"I desire love, and not sacrifice;
And the knowledge of God more than burnt offerings" (6:6).

Between human beings He hoped to see loving and beautiful relationships. He yearned for a society where people were kind and truthful and chaste.

But Israel had disappointed Him. At first indeed "in the days of her youth, in the day when she came up out of the land of Egypt" (2:15) she had responded to His love; but this had not

---

[3] Emending the text. The present Hebrew text however may be right: *I will not be* to you; thus reversing the name of God given to Moses: *I will be that I will be* (Exod. 3:14).

[1] *SAT,* II 1, p. 364.

lasted. Once in Canaan she had "played the harlot" with its agricultural deities, the local baalim.

"She said, I will go after my lovers,
That give me my bread and my water, my wool and my flax, my oil
    and my drink" (2:5).

This Israel did through ignorance.

"And *she* did not know that it was *I* that gave her
The grain and the new wine and the oil,
And multiplied unto her silver
And gold, which they used for Baal!" (2:8).

But her ignorance did not stop there; she failed also to comprehend the character of Yahweh. Hosea always joins this charge to that of unfaithfulness: Israel did not "know God." The two things went together.

What Hosea meant by "going after the baalim" was probably not only the outright worship of heathen gods but also the worship of Yahweh in a Canaanitish manner. The Israelites had degraded Him in their minds to the level of the local baals and taken over into their service of Him the rites and festivals of the ancient high place with its drunkenness and sacred prostitution. This low conception of Yahweh was to Hosea's thinking summed up in the title *Baali* or "My Baal (Master)" with which the people addressed Him.

A feature of the prevailing cult that specially disgusted Hosea was the adoration of the bull images representing Yahweh. He treated it as a bit of absolute heathenism, refusing to associate such "idols" with the God of Israel. Upon the "calf of Samaria" he poured the bitterest scorn.

"*That!* A mechanic made it! *That* is no god!" (8:6).

So far as we know, no prophet had previously attacked the use of these images.

From the corruption of religion flowed all the evils of Israelitish society.

"Because Ephraim multiplied to himself altars for sinning,
Altars were to him for sinning" (8:11).[2]

  [2] Perhaps we should read:

        Because Ephraim multiplied to himself altars
        They were to him for sinning.

To this cause Hosea in the plainest language ascribed the wide-spread unchastity of respectable girls and women.

"I will not punish your daughters when they play the harlot,
And your brides when they commit adultery.
For *they* [3] go apart with harlots
And sacrifice with the 'sacred women'" (4:14).

What else could the men expect? Hosea implied that the prevalent false swearing, killing and stealing were closely linked with the absence of the "knowledge of God" (4:1ff). Thus a vicious circle was formed. The moral results of such false ideas of God stood in the way of their correction.

"Whoredom and wine and new wine take away the understanding" (4:11).

The people's "doings would not suffer them to turn to their God" (5:4). The very priests to whom Yahweh had given knowledge that they might instruct others had rejected it and "forgotten the law." Instead,

"They feed on the sin of my people
And set their heart on their iniquity" (4:6ff).

Nor was it different with the secular leaders. The nation "made the king glad with their wickedness and the princes with their lies" (7:3).

Two other facts besides Canaanitish worship did Hosea single out as special instances of Israel's departing from Yahweh. One was the prevailing reliance on kings. As we have seen, it was a time of quick changes in the royal power, one dynasty overthrowing another in blood. While these rebellions were carried out by individual adventurers it would be a mistake to think of the people as looking on apathetically. Unless there had been widespread discontent such adventurers could have got no support in their seizures of the throne. Apparently people blamed the king when things went badly, and as they were going more and more badly in these closing days of the northern kingdom each new king had a hard time to keep his subjects with him. When he came

[3] The men.

to power all was hope, and the "day of our king" was celebrated with drunken festivities. But presently it became evident that times were no better and every one began to long for still another king. So they were ready to turn on the ruling monarch with ferocity.

"They are all as hot as an oven,
And they devour their judges;
All their kings are fallen:
There is none among them that calleth unto me" (7:7).

The last line gives Hosea's diagnosis of the trouble. If people would look to God instead of a new king they would not be guilty of such foolish and wicked ways. Yahweh was not responsible for their dynastic changes.

"They have set up kings, but not from me;
They have made princes, but I knew it not" (8:4).

Yet in another sense Yahweh did it, for He let them have their own desire.

"I have destroyed thee, O Israel! Who is among thy helpers?
Where is thy king now, that he may save thee?
Or all thy princes, that they may rule thee?
Those of whom thou hast said, Give me a king and princes.
(Aye) I give thee a king in mine anger,
And I take him away in my wrath" (13:9ff).[4]

The time was coming when they would themselves realize their fatal mistake.

"Surely now shall they say, We have no king!
For we fear not Yahweh; and the king, what can he do for us?"
    (10:3).

Israel's second disloyalty was the seeking of foreign alliances. Aspirants to the throne, looking about them for backing, would not fail to see the possibilities offered by the intervention of Assyria. In the reign of Menahem (745–737 B.C.) Tiglath-pileser had marched against the country and been bought off only by a thou-

[4] G. A. Smith's translation.

sand talents of silver (about two million dollars) which Menahem raised by assessing each well-to-do citizen fifty shekels (about $33). If this statement of II Kings be true it shows that wealth must have been widely distributed, for, to raise the sum required, 60,000 must have contributed (II. Ki. 15:19f).[5] Menahem thus became a vassal of Tiglath-pileser, and the discontent caused by the heavy assessment, aggravated doubtless by yearly tribute, may have helped Pekah in his conspiracy against Menahem's son Pekahiah. If therefore Pekah came to the throne on a program of repudiation of Assyria we can understand why presently he was allied with Rezin of Damascus against the overlord. This insubordination Tiglath-pileser punished by capturing a number of towns in the north and deporting many people from the region round the Sea of Galilee (733–732 B.C., II Ki. 15:23ff). Soon thereafter Hoshea seized the throne (730 B.C.) and although the narrative in II Kings says nothing of it he may have secured the support of Assyria. At any rate Tiglath-pileser's successor Shalmaneser made sure of Hoshea's subjection by marching against him and exacting tribute. Later however Hoshea tried to get the help of So king of Egypt and being apparently encouraged by him stopped his annual tribute to Assyria. This led to the siege and capture of Samaria in 722 B.C., followed by the deportation of 27,290 of its people to Assyria (II Ki. 17:3ff; Barton, AB^7, p. 466).

We can see therefore that during the closing years of the northern kingdom it was forcibly brought into constant contact with the great power on the Tigris. Egypt also seems to have been in men's thoughts. Israel tried to play off the one against the other and to use one or the other in domestic struggles. Senseless indeed was such a policy for it could only plunge the little kingdom deeper into servitude; and Hosea exposed its folly without mercy. But he had a deeper count against it than that for it meant a repudiation of Yahweh, Israel's true help. He was the only power in control of history and thus to offend Him meant ruin.

"Ephraim is like a silly dove, without understanding:
They call unto Egypt, they go to Assyria.
When they go, I shall spread my net upon them;
I will bring them down as the birds of the heavens" (7:11f).

[5] So T. H. Robinson, *HI,* I, p. 374, who however puts the number of contributors at 40,000. It is better to reckon the silver talent at 3000 shekels (Galling, *Biblisches Reallexicon,* Tübingen, 1937, p. 186, on the basis of Exod. 38:25ff), which would make 60,000 contributors. So Sellin, *GIJV,* I, p. 233.

"And Ephraim saw his sickness, and Judah his wound,
And Ephraim went to Assyria, and sent to king Jareb: [6]
But *he* is not able to heal you,
And he will not cure you of your wound.
For *I* will be unto Ephraim as a lion,
And as a young lion to the house of Judah.
I, I will tear and go away;
I will carry off and there will be none to deliver" (5:13f).

All this could have but one end—deportation to the dominions of a conqueror, whoever he might be.

"They shall return into the land of Egypt,[7]
Or the Assyrian shall be their king,
Because they have refused to return" [8] (11:5).

Yahweh must Chastise Israel but could not Let it Go

Israel therefore had broken its marriage vow to God. The people were bent on backsliding from Him. And now the long history of rebellion and disloyalty was approaching its climax. Yahweh must act. Abruptly would He stop His gifts and terminate Israel's pleasant life of "harlotry."

"Therefore will I take back
My grain in its time and my new wine in its season;
And I will pluck away my wool and my flax
For the covering of her nakedness;
And now will I uncover her folly
In the sight of her lovers;[9]
And no man shall save her out of my hand.
And I will cause to cease all her mirth,
Her feasts, her new moons, her sabbaths,
And all her solemn assemblies;
And I will lay waste her vines and her figtrees,
Of which she hath said, These are my hire
Which my lovers gave me;
And I will make them woods
And the beasts of the wild shall eat them;

[6] King Pick-quarrel according to G. A. Smith's translation.
[7] Omitting *not* with the LXX.
[8] That is, to repent.
[9] The baalim.

And I will visit upon her the days of the baalim
Unto whom she burned incense,
And decked herself with her earrings and jewels,
And went after her lovers,
And forgot me, saith Yahweh" (2:9ff).

Deportation, with all its dreadful sufferings, would be deserved!
No one who cared for God and saw with His eyes, as did the
prophet, could fail to be outraged on His behalf.

"The days of visitation are come!
The days of recompense are come!
Israel shall know it!
A fool is the prophet,
Mad is the man of the spirit
Over the magnitude of thy wickedness" (9:7).

No less passionately than Amos did Hosea throw himself into the
proclamation of the doom. But unlike Amos he did not remain
satisfied with doom. For he knew that back of all the divine wrath
lay an unquenchable love.

"How shall I give thee up, Ephraim?
How shall I cast thee off, Israel? . . .
My heart is turned within me,
My compassions are kindled together.
I will not execute the fierceness of mine anger,
I will not return to destroy Ephraim:
For I am God, and not man;
The Holy One in the midst of thee;
And I will not come to consume" (11:8-9).[10]

The impending calamity therefore could not be the end but rather
God's way of winning Israel back.

"Therefore, behold, *I* will allure her,
And bring her into the wilderness,
And speak to her heart.
And I will give her her vineyards from thence,
And the valley of Achor for a door of hope;
And she shall make answer there, as in the days of her youth,

[10] With a slight emendation of the text.

And as in the day when she came up out of the land of Egypt.
And it shall be in that day, saith Yahweh,
That thou shalt call me, My husband,
And shall call me no more, My baal.
For I will take away the names of the baalim out of her mouth,
And they shall no more be mentioned by their name" (2:14ff).

A beautiful new world would open out, of peace between man and beast and between man and man, a world of security and abundance and teeming population. Best of all, the people would have a new heart towards God and each other.

"And I will betroth thee unto me in righteousness,
And in justice, and in lovingkindness and in mercies.
I will even betroth thee unto me in faithfulness;
And thou shalt know Yahweh."

The reconciliation between man and God should be complete.

"I will say unto them that were not my people,
Thou art my people;
And they shall say, Thou art my God" (2:23).

God then would at last succeed in His purpose for Israel, not fail as Amos had thought. And He would succeed because of the perseverance and resourcefulness of love. His punishment would have in it no element of finality; in fact, it would not be punishment so much as discipline, correction, education, always looking forward through some "door of hope" to the day when God could relinquish harshness and speak in His natural tone of tenderness. And it would be the *whole* people that would be restored. Hosea did not distinguish, as did Isaiah later, between a "remnant" and the majority. True, he must have believed that many Israelites would meet their death in the coming disaster, but he laid no stress on this as involving conscious discrimination by God. In spite of losses the unit which returned would be identical with that driven forth into exile. His was indeed a "wider hope."

Thus was the great announcement of doom and restoration set forth in imperishable words. But as at the first Hosea made vivid his words by living signs displayed in his own home, so it was now. Let us return to the story of his relations with his wife.

Up to this time Gomer had been living in Hosea's home, kept

there in spite of the fact that her marriage had not led her to mend her former evil ways. People must have known, as did Hosea himself, that she still had lovers. But this was part of the symbolism. Even so Israel and its children, though these were not Yahweh's, were being maintained with honour and gifts in His house—the land of Canaan. But now something took place which depicted Israel's coming exile. Gomer left Hosea. We infer this from the fact that she was presently in slavery elsewhere or at any rate had to be bought back (3:2). If as seems probable the separation from Hosea's home corresponded in its dramatic features to Israel's impending doom, the prophet must himself have thrust her out. The law gave him the right to do this to an adulterous wife. He might have even caused her to be put to death but he did not wish to destroy her. It is not improbable however that he did sell her into bondage. We wish that the narrative gave us light on this part of the transaction but it loses itself for a while in allegory (chapter 2). We may be sure that Hosea made quite clear to the people the significance of all that was taking place. That is what Yahweh would do to Israel!

But the living parable had not ended. The more Hosea let his thoughts dwell upon God's inextinguishable love for His people, the more he would be prepared for the next command from on high:

"And Yahweh said unto me,
Again go, love a woman
Who loves evil and is an adulteress,
Even as Yahweh loveth the sons of Israel—
And they turning after other gods and loving cakes of raisins!"

There is always an "again" with love. "Love hopeth all things." "So I bought her to me for fifteen pieces of silver and a homer and a half of barley." What a sensation that purchase, carried out doubtless under the public eye, must have caused! How people must have stared to see Gomer taken back home! But they heard a stern sentence pronounced upon her before she entered its doors:

"I said unto her,
Thou shalt abide for me many days;
Thou shalt not play the harlot, and thou shalt not be any
     man's wife:
So will I also be towards thee."

Then, confronting the bystanders, the prophet drove the lesson home:

"For the sons of Israel shall abide many days without king and without prince and without pillar and without ephod or teraphim. Afterward shall the sons of Israel return and seek Yahweh their God and come with fear unto Yahweh and to his goodness in the latter days" (3:1ff).

Thus with a hint of hope for her also Gomer disappeared from view, and so far as we know the parable was concluded. But not so the prophet's messages from God. While we are not expressly told so, some scholars think that he continued to utter oracles for ten years or even longer. It is these oracles that in part at least are contained in his book.

A Comparison of Amos and Hosea

Having concluded our study of the first two writing prophets it would be well to set before us the things in which they agreed and in which they differed. That Hosea shared with Amos his monotheism is evident on his every page, even if like Amos he nowhere expresses it dogmatically. Although emphasizing more than Amos God's peculiar care for Israel he insisted no less sternly that it would be held to strict account. In giving utterance to the divine wrath at Israel's sin he fell no whit below Amos. He expressed with equal clearness the prophetic exaltation of righteousness over ritual. He had the same lofty conception as had Amos of the function of the prophet in the divine plan of history. In general we may say also that he possessed in common with Amos a background of ideas derived from his environment, such as that calamities were a sign of divine displeasure, that the individual did not count for much since Yahweh dealt with the nation as a whole, that there were no rewards or punishments after death, and many others. In these, both were children of their time.

Hosea fell short of Amos in his lack of international outlook. His own people Israel seems to have occupied all his thoughts; to Israel alone he felt himself sent. Hence he did nothing to lead Israel's thought towards universalism. We miss also in his pages the passionate demand for social justice that so distinguished Amos.

He saw however as Amos did not see that dependence on kings and foreign alliances meant disloyalty to Yahweh. Perhaps that was because the evil days which had come since Amos threw these political traits into prominence. He went beyond Amos also in his belief that the relationship between Israel and God was fundamentally one of love. This gave inwardness and unity to his perceptions. And he saw the whole moral life of the nation determined by one thing—its attitude to God; or to use his own words, its "knowledge of God." For him ethics flowed from religion, and he was concerned to make the source pure. That was one reason why he condemned the identification of Yahweh with the baalim. Low sensuous ideas of God could not but corrupt human intercourse. But they were also wrong in themselves, being disloyal to Yahweh. Therefore he poured scorn upon the worship of the "calves" which Amos passed over lightly.

Hosea's Contribution to Israel's Religion

Like Amos Hosea gave an impulse all his own to the thought of succeeding prophets. Isaiah got from him his energetic condemnation of foreign alliances and his promise of a lovely dawn beyond Israel's night. Jeremiah and Ezekiel were influenced by him in a yet deeper way. They appropriated his metaphor of marriage to characterize the relationship between Yahweh and Israel, with its demand for inward devotion and spiritual likeness to God. Hosea's emphasis on the need to know God's character and will made a deep impression upon Jeremiah, who often recurred to it [1] and gave it immortal utterance in the depiction of the new covenant. Jeremiah also re-echoed his teaching of the love of God, and the same theme was set forth with exquisite tenderness and beauty by Second Isaiah. Farther than that one can hardly trace his influence with any definiteness. The thing that he gave Israel lived on, often without being connected with his name. When our Lord sought scriptural justification for putting human need before ritual prescriptions he found it in Hosea's great "summing up":

"Love I desire, and not sacrifice,
And the knowledge of God more than burnt-offerings"
(6:6. Cf. Mt. 9:13; 12:7).[2]

[1] See for example Jer. 2:8; 4:22; 5:4,5; 8:7; 9:3,6,24; 10:25; 24:7; 31:34. Ezekiel constantly uses the phrase: "know that I am Yahweh," but this does not express quite the same idea.

[2] Jesus did not indeed quote the second half of this saying, but it must have been in his mind, for none realized better than he that the love of God and the knowledge of God go together.

Undoubtedly it is in his teaching of the love of God that Christians of today discover Hosea's chief value. It had two corollaries. One was, that suffering for sin, though necessary, is educational; the other, that God never gives up but will have His loving way at last.

CHAPTER XIV

ISAIAH

[PROPHESIED 740–*c.* 700 B.C.]

The Sources

The chief and most reliable source for the study of Isaiah is to be found in chapters 1–32 of the Book of Isaiah.[1] There are also Isaiah narratives in II Ki. 18–20, which are repeated in part in Is. 36–39 and II Chron. 32. In Is. 1–32 there are a number of genuine oracles proceeding from the prophet and some excellent narrative material from him or one of his disciples. Both of these constitute a source of the first order. The same chapters also contain passages which in the opinion of scholars are not from Isaiah, but have been inserted by later hands. Taking the first 39 chapters of the book as a whole we may distinguish three kinds of non-Isaianic material:

1. Passages universally rejected: 13:1–14:23; 21:1–10; 24–27; 34–35; 36–39.
2. Passages rejected by many: 2:1–4; 3:18–23; 4:2–6; 11:10–12:6; 19:18–25; 33.
3. Passages earlier than Isaiah: 15:1–16:12.

The rest of these chapters then would proceed from Isaiah.

The narrative in II Kings tells a vivid story but its reliability is not rated very highly, although some scholars hold that it contains genuine utterances of Isaiah. The narrative proper however seems to be so mixed with legendary elements that it is hard to know how far it may be trusted.

In our study of Isaiah therefore we shall derive our information from the passages that are widely accepted as genuine; though we shall bear in mind that some of these are questioned by certain scholars, particularly the group of passages known as Messianic: 9:2–7; 11:1–9; 32:1–8.

[1] Chapters 40–66 are certainly not Isaianic. They will be considered in the study of Second Isaiah.

Isaiah's Call

From the genuine Isaianic passages we can get a picture of the man who uttered them which is much more detailed and vivid than the pictures we have of Amos and Hosea. Our attention is now directed to the kingdom of Judah instead of its wealthier neighbour to the north. The long and successful reign of Uzziah had just drawn to its end (740 B.C.). Judah, like Israel, was prosperous. A number of people had become rich. Large estates were growing up. Luxuries from abroad were plentiful. Commercial and friendly intercourse with neighbouring peoples had led to the adoption of foreign customs. The land was "full of silver and gold." Horses and chariots, imported doubtless from Egypt for military use, were to be seen everywhere. If there is any truth in the tradition preserved in II Chron. 26 Uzziah had built up quite a military establishment and had strongly fortified Jerusalem. He had also promoted with vigour the pursuit of agriculture and cattle-raising. Religion flourished and the temple courts were thronged with worshippers offering incense and sacrifices. Such at least was the case at a later time (1:10ff) and there is no reason to suppose that it was otherwise in 740 B.C.

Amidst all this teeming prosperity there had grown up a young aristocrat [1] who regarded it with aversion. To judge from his subsequent prophecies he must have known of Amos and have read with burning heart the words he had uttered twenty-five years before against the rich men of Israel and their wives. Taught perhaps by this great predecessor he looked beneath the splendour of the society about him and perceived that it was purchased at the expense of the poor. Wealth went hand in hand with oppression; peasants were being evicted from their farms to make way for large landholdings and fine manor houses; justice was perverted, violence rife. The religious devotion of the people remained a formal thing taken over at second hand from their teachers, devoid of understanding as to the true nature of God and His demands. Along with this soulless service of Yahweh went the actual worship of other gods, and the land was full of idols before which rich and poor alike bowed down. Soothsayers and diviners got many clients. Judah's cosmopolitanism was issuing in a religious syncretism that Yahweh could never tolerate. Through all the national life ran a pride and self-complacence, a satisfaction

[1] This is inferred from the fact that he later had access to the kings of Judah.

in luxury, display, military strength and material wealth which led people to forget their dependence on God.

But Isaiah could not forget Him. Over against the pride and sin of his people he set the thought of Yahweh looking down at it all in wrath. Then one day, in the year that king Uzziah died, he "saw Yahweh." He was in the temple, probably sunk in meditation. Looking up he saw the Lord upon a lofty throne beneath ministering seraphim who cried one to another:

"Holy, holy, holy is Yahweh of hosts;
The fulness of all the earth is his glory" (6:3).

And as the young Isaiah listened amid the shaking of the foundations of the thresholds and the thickening clouds of smoke, his first thought was of the unfitness of himself and his whole people to meet such an awful presence.

"Woe is me! for I am undone;
For a man unclean of lips am I,
And in the midst of a people unclean of lips do I dwell;
For the King, Yahweh of hosts, have mine eyes seen" (6:4f).

When his lips were cleansed by a coal from off the altar he heard Yahweh speak:

"Whom shall I send: And who will go for us?
And I said, Here am I; send me!
And he said, Go and say to this people,
Hear ye indeed, but understand not;
And see ye indeed, but perceive not.
Make fat the heart of this people,
And their ears make heavy, and shut their eyes;
Lest they see with their eyes, and hear with their ears,
And turn again, and be healed" (6:8ff).

Thus Isaiah was accepted and sent forth on his life's mission to speak to a people whom his words would only harden, until desolation and exile should fall on the land again and yet again. Yet after the tree was felled there would remain life to sprout from the stump (6:11ff).

Characteristics of Isaiah's Ministry

The ministry into which the newly commissioned prophet now entered was in important respects different from that of Amos and

Hosea. In the first place, it lasted a whole working lifetime—forty years or more—during which he passed from youth to age, with all the silent changes involved in such a transition. That is a great endurance test for a man's beliefs and enthusiasms, yet we find Isaiah keeping both unaltered to the end. So much the same indeed did his message remain that it would be impossible to distinguish his earlier from his last utterances if the external circumstances mirrored in them did not come to our aid. For Isaiah lived also through vast changes in the Palestinian world. He saw the independence of Judah give place to Assyrian vassalage, he beheld the invasion and final destruction by Assyria of the peoples of Israel and Damascus, he experienced Judah's growing misery as Assyria's yoke made itself felt, the recurring hopes of liberation, the feverish banding together of little states in revolt, and the final punitive expedition of Sennacherib who overran the whole of Judah and almost captured Jerusalem. To what isolation and extremity had the prosperous Judah of his youth been reduced! How the landmarks of many generations had disappeared before the onrush of the devastating flood! How faith after faith had proved powerless! But Isaiah's faith only became the stronger.

Then too he worked these forty years in his own community. He went in and out among the people, speaking to them constantly in places of concourse, making himself and his children a sign, walking once for three years about the streets in the wretched garb of a captive. Every one knew him and had heard him speak. If we had more information about Hosea we might learn that he did the same. But one gets the impression that as Isaiah worked for a longer time, so he was also more in the public eye. Very early we find him confronting king Ahaz and at the end he offered guidance to king Hezekiah. On matters of public policy he uttered divinely given counsel and was evidently a force to be reckoned with.

Finally, Isaiah had Jerusalem and the Davidic dynasty as central facts of his environment. Nothing in the surroundings of Amos or Hosea corresponded to these. Israel had no city about which any particularly sublime associations clustered and no one could cherish much enthusiasm for the royal house of Jehu. Israel indeed had never owned a king to whom a man like Isaiah could look back with any admiration. But Jerusalem was the city of David, of the temple, of a glorious past and (people believed) a yet more glorious future—the city that Yahweh loved. And its king was always a son of David the ideal ruler, though he might be an

Ahaz! Something in that unbroken succession of three hundred years captivated the imagination and held the devotion of man. And the dynasty, like Jerusalem, was a thing of hope. The ideal king would come again! All this affected Isaiah and his hearers profoundly.

Isaiah's Earlier Work

When Isaiah began his activity as a prophet in 740 B.C. the northern kingdom had yet nearly twenty years to run and Judah was still free from Assyrian overlordship. We may picture him as a youth in his early twenties, married to a girl whom he afterwards calls "the prophetess" (8:3), and the father of one son. Following the example of Hosea he had given this little boy a name of portent: *She'ar Yashub,* "A Remnant shall Return." If we may suppose that chapters 3–5 give his earlier prophecies he began at once to denounce the wrongs perpetrated by the strong upon the weak, the luxury, pride and idolatry of the men, the extravagant dress and coquetry of the women. Perhaps the opening of chapter 5 preserves an actual scene. Appearing on the street with a small harp to accompany his voice, he began to sing a song about a well-beloved friend whose vineyard, so carefully tended, had brought forth only wild grapes. A crowd gathered about him listening sympathetically as the crowd had once listened to Amos denounce Israel's enemies. An ungrateful vineyard indeed! Then the singer put the case to them:

"What could have been done more to my vineyard,
That I have not done in it?"

When he went on to describe how he would punish his vineyard by exposing it to the inroads of wild animals, laying it waste and abandoning it to briers, his hearers would have been with him. "Serves it right," they would say. But suddenly he added an ominous touch:

"I will also command the clouds
That they rain no rain upon it."

And while the surprised listeners were asking how he could control the clouds he suddenly thrust his meaning home:

"For the vineyard of Yahweh of hosts is the house of Israel,
And the men of Judah his pleasant plant:
And he looked for justice, but, behold, oppression;
For righteousness, but, behold, a cry!" (5:1ff).

Thus early did the young prophet display the superb command of rhetoric and style which was to win for him pre-eminence among Israel's writers.

He had not been uttering his oracles long before a crisis arose which compelled him to intervene in the public counsels of the nation. The threatening advance of Tiglath-pileser IV in Syria had thrown into a common cause two small powers which had been at each other's throats for a century. Rezin, king of Damascus, and Pekah, who (it will be recalled) had seized the throne of Israel on an anti-Assyrian program, formed an alliance to resist the giant aggressor. The support of Judah seemed to them necessary for their venture and a summons was sent to Jotham king of Judah, or his son and successor Ahaz, to join the league. At least we infer that this was done, and that an unfavourable answer was returned. Judah was quite right in refusing, for acceptance would have aligned it with the weaker side in a death-grapple; and common sense would also warn it against becoming involved with Assyria, which had hitherto let it alone. From Isaiah's point of view likewise the decision was good, for he wished to see Judah rely on God only; but there is no record of his having offered counsel in the matter.

Infuriated by Judah's refusal the allied kings resolved to inflict punishment. With their combined armies they marched south determined to break down the fortifications of Jerusalem and supplant Ahaz with a king of their own making, the "son of Tabeel." When the news reached Jerusalem every one from the king down was thrown into a panic. The heart of Ahaz "trembled, and the heart of his people, as the trees of the forest tremble with the wind."

It was at this moment that Isaiah received a divine command to take his son "A Remnant Shall Return" and go out to meet king Ahaz "at the conduit of the upper pool" whither he had gone, apparently, to inspect the city's water-supply for the impending siege.[1] Thus they came face to face, the harassed king feverishly discussing with his officers what could be done and the young prophet to whom everything was plain, holding the hand of the little boy with the strange name of warning and promise.

As the royal group fell silent Isaiah delivered his message:

"Thus saith Yahweh, Take heed and be quiet; fear not, neither let thy heart be faint, because of these two tails of smoking fire-

[1] The story is told in Is. 7:1ff.

brands, for the fierce anger of Rezin and Aram, and of the son
of Remaliah."

They have a plan against thee but

> "Thus saith Yahweh:
> It shall not stand, neither shall it come to pass.
> For the head of Aram is—Damascus!
> And the head of Damascus is—Rezin! [2]
> And the head of Ephraim is—Samaria!
> And the head of Samaria is—Remaliah's son!"

With what measureless contempt were these names uttered. Played
out little cities and kings, sticks feebly smoking on a dying fire,
setting their intentions up against the purpose of the God of history! The divine assurance concluded with a warning to the
prophet's hearers:

> "If ye will not hold firm, surely ye shall not be held firm." [3]

Ahaz however did not respond. He had in mind to seek what
seemed to him a more certain help than Yahweh could ever be—
the intervention of Tiglath-pileser. Once again then the word of
Yahweh came to him through Isaiah:

> "Ask thee a sign of Yahweh thy God; ask it either in the depth,
> or in the height above."

What amazing faith did this prophet have, that he would thus
undertake for Yahweh to perform anything whatsoever which the
doubting king might call for. But Ahaz had no idea of putting
him to the test. Such a sign would bring with it uncomfortable
obligations! Assuming therefore an extreme humility he replied:

> "I will not ask, neither will I tempt Yahweh."

It was then that the indignation of Isaiah broke upon him.

> "Hear ye now, O house of David; is it a small thing for you to
> weary men, that ye will weary my God also? Therefore the Lord
> himself will give you a sign: behold, a virgin [4] shall conceive, and
> bear a son, and shall call his name "God with us" (*Immanuel*).

---

[2] Omitting v. 8b as a gloss.
[3] That is, if ye will not BELIEVE, make firm the word of Yahweh.
[4] The Hebrew word means "young woman," not "virgin."

Curds and honey shall he eat, until he knoweth to refuse the evil, and choose the good. For before the child shall know to refuse the evil, and choose the good, the land whose two kings thou abhorrest shall be forsaken."

Within three or four years, then, both these enemy kingdoms should be laid desolate. But the evil would not stop with them.

"Yahweh will bring upon thee, and upon thy people, and upon thy father's house, days that have not come, from the day that Ephraim departed from Judah."

The sign accordingly would presage both relief and extreme suffering for Judah. Ahaz' lack of faith would not interfere with Yahweh's purpose against Israel and Aram, but there would be added Judah's own punishment. The "razor" that Ahaz was about to hire "in the parts beyond the River (Euphrates)" would shave Judah itself (7:20).

But what would the sign be? Isaiah's cryptic words, which for centuries were viewed as a prediction of the virgin birth of Christ, have given rise to several differing interpretations. The most probable one (in the view of the present writer) is that he expected a wonderful child to be born within a year of an unnamed young woman, who in anticipation of Yahweh's great deliverance would call him Immanuel. Doubtless he had in mind a royal child of David's line.

Isaiah's intervention in the crisis proved a failure. Ahaz went on with his fatal policy of buying Assyrian aid. It did not arrive in time to prevent the attack of the allies and the capture by Aram of Judah's highly prized sea-port at Elath on the Gulf of Akaba. Jerusalem itself may have been near to capitulation, driving Ahaz to the desperate expedient of offering his own son as a sacrifice to appease Yahweh's wrath (II Ki. 16:3; cf. II Ki. 3:27).

At last however Tiglath-pileser acted, taking and destroying Damascus and deporting the inhabitants of the northern region of Israel. Ahaz got relief, but at the cost of impoverishment and permanent subjection. He seems to have entered with enthusiasm into his new relationship. When summoned to Damascus to pay homage—and tribute—to his overlord he had an Assyrian altar which he saw there copied and the copy set up in the temple court at Jerusalem in place of the old altar, which was removed to one side and used for divination. Thus he yielded with good will the religious subserviency which Assyria demanded of its vassals (II Ki. 16:10ff).

At such an hour there was nothing more for Isaiah to do. Admonished by Yahweh he contented himself with testifying against Ahaz' policy in a striking way. While the success of Israel and Aram seemed imminent he took a large tablet and wrote upon it in conspicuous letters: "The Spoil Speedeth, the Prey Hasteth" (*Maher shalal hash baz*), erecting it in the presence of witnesses in some public place. But this was not enough. When a son was born to him of "the prophetess" he named the baby with the same predictive words, thus declaring that the coming overthrow of the enemy would be due to Yahweh and not to any human means.

Isaiah however did not stand alone; he had the support of the "faithful witnesses" just mentioned and of a group to which he alludes as "my disciples." To them he turned with a reassuring message. They were not to be affrighted by the panic about them, nor to fear the allies.

> "Yahweh of hosts, him shall ye sanctify;
> And let him be your fear, and let him be your dread.
> And he shall be for a sanctuary;
> But for a stone of stumbling, and a rock of offence
> To both the houses of Israel;
> For a gin and for a snare to the inhabitants of Jerusalem.
> And many shall stumble thereon,
> And fall, and be broken,
> And be snared, and be taken" (8:13ff).

And with them for the time did he leave the matter for safe-keeping.

> "Bind thou up the testimony,
> Seal the teaching among my disciples.
> And I will wait for Yahweh,
> That hideth his face from the house of Jacob,
> And I will look for him.

Behold, I and the children whom Yahweh hath given me are for signs and for wonders in Israel from Yahweh of hosts, who dwelleth in mount Zion" (8:16ff).

Isaiah's Later Ministry

For some time after the crisis just described we are given no glimpse of the prophet at work except what we can gather from his oracles. Before the fall of the northern kingdom in 722 B.C. he uttered several against the sins of Samaria (9:8–10:4; 17:1–11; 28:1ff); but it is improbable that he went into its territory to do this. Like his oracles on foreign nations they were "dropped" in Jerusalem, to work themselves out after Yahweh's will. Against Philistia (14:28ff), Moab (16:13f), Damascus (17:1ff), Egypt (19:1–17), Arabia (21:13ff) and Tyre (23) he likewise proclaimed messages of condemnation and doom; but it seems impossible to date these with any exactness.

Meanwhile the progress of Assyrian power went remorselessly on. In 722 B.C. Samaria was taken after a two years' siege begun by Shalmaneser V and completed by his successor Sargon; 27,290 of its people were deported to Assyria, being replaced by colonists deported in turn from the east, and the northern kingdom became an Assyrian province. Ahaz of Judah, who remained faithful to his overlord, may have been rewarded by a strip of Israel's southernmost territory. In 718 B.C. he was succeeded by his son Hezekiah, a vigorous young man who had a longing for the independence of Judah. Seven years later a revolt broke out among the Philistine cities and Hezekiah seems to have taken some part in it, for Sargon speaks of punishing Judah along with Philistia, Edom and Moab. It was in the same year (711 B.C.) that Isaiah was bidden by Yahweh to walk the streets of Jerusalem three years naked and barefoot, thus making himself a living sign of the doom of captivity about to fall upon Egypt and Ethiopia, those powers in which the Palestinian states were placing their trust (20). Sargon's inscription also tells of the rebels bearing pledges to Pharaoh king of Egypt.

After the death of Sargon in 705 B.C. Hezekiah again joined a coalition of neighbouring states to throw off the Assyrian yoke. This was part of a general uprising of subject peoples throughout the Assyrian dominions, headed by an able Babylonian patriot Merodach-baladan (Marduk-apal-iddina). He sent emissaries to Hezekiah, ostensibly to congratulate him on his recovery from an illness, but more probably to enlist his support. The help of Egypt was again sought. Hezekiah seems to have taken a leading part in the movement. Judah probably stood out as one of the most powerful of the little nations of the region, and Hezekiah is said to have accumulated considerable treasure (Is. 39:1f; II Ki. 20:12f). He went ahead with energetic measures of defence. If we may trust the notice in II Chron. 32:5 he strengthened the walls of Jerusalem and increased its stock of arms. It was doubtless at this time that he made a determined attempt to concentrate the worship of Yahweh in the Jerusalem temple by doing away with the "high places" or local sanctuaries scattered over the countryside (II Ki. 18:4ff). This purification of worship probably involved the elimination of Assyrian practices introduced by Ahaz, and so was a gesture of independence.

In this crisis of political affairs the aging Isaiah once more interposed with an uncompromising proclamation of Yahweh's will. Yahweh, he declared, was wholly against the revolt. To seek help of Egypt was futile.

"They carry their riches upon the shoulders of young asses,
And their treasures upon the humps of camels,
To a people that shall not profit them.
For Egypt helpeth in vain, and to no purpose:
Therefore have I cried concerning her,
Rahab that destroys!" [1]

But more, it was wicked.

"Woe to the rebellious children, saith Yahweh,
That take counsel, but not of me;
That pour out a drink-offering, but not (of) my Spirit,
That they may add sin to sin;
That set out to go down to Egypt,
And have not asked at my mouth;
To flee to the stronghold of Pharaoh,
And to take refuge in the shadow of Egypt!
Therefore shall the stronghold of Pharaoh be your shame,
And the refuge in the shadow of Egypt your confusion" (30:1ff).

When the messengers of Merodach-baladan visited Hezekiah Isaiah sternly rebuked the king for showing them his treasures, declaring that these same treasures would for a punishment be carried off to Babylon (II Ki. 20:17).

The program Isaiah advocated was like the course which he had urged on Ahaz a generation before:

"Thus saith the Lord Yahweh, the Holy One of Israel,
In returning and rest shall ye be saved;
In quietness and in confidence shall be your strength" (30:15).

[1] Emending the text slightly. Perhaps we should read instead, *that is destroyed.*

But he could make no impression on king or people. It was an hour when hopes ran high and his assurances and warnings alike were contemptuously brushed aside (30:16).[2]

Then at last his warnings came true. Sargon's successor, Sennacherib, laid hold with vigour. Merodach-baladan and the eastern rebels were overcome in 703 B.C. and he was free to turn his attention to the west. His inscription telling how he did this has been recovered. After capturing Sidon and Ashkelon and restoring Assyrian dominion in those cities he dealt with Judah.

"And as to Hezekiah, the Judean, who had not submitted to my yoke, 46 of his strongholds, fortified cities, and smaller cities of their environs without number, with the onset of battering-rams and the attack of engines, mines, breaches, axes (?) I besieged, I captured. 200,150 people, small and great, male and female, horses, mules, asses, camels, oxen and sheep without number I brought out of their midst and counted as booty. Himself I shut up like a caged bird in Jerusalem, his capital city; I erected beleaguering works against him, and turned back by command every one who came out of his city gate."[3]

It was probably during the harrying of Judah thus described that Isaiah depicted in burning words the isolation and prostration of Jerusalem:

"Why will ye be still stricken, that ye revolt more and more? . . .
Your country is desolate, your cities burned with fire;
Your land, foreigners devour it in your presence,
And it is desolate, as overthrown by foreigners.
And the daughter of Zion is left as a booth in a vineyard,
As a besieged city.
Except Yahweh of hosts had left unto us a very small remnant,
We should have been as Sodom, we should have been like untc
    Gomorrah" (1:5ff).

Finally the forces of the invader closed in upon the capital and the end seemed imminent. One of the means resorted to by Hezekiah to protect the city, now or at some other time, was to bring water by a conduit into a pool within the walls. It is generally believed that the famous Siloam inscription, discovered in 1880 on the wall of the 1700 foot tunnel connecting the spring Ain Sitti Maryam with the pool of Siloam, describes this operation.[4] It was

[2] In 28:7ff is preserved a scene which may well belong to this time.
[3] Barton, *AB*[7], p. 472.
[4] See Barton, *AB*[7], p. 476.

at this hour, when the stoutest-hearted gave way to terror, that Isaiah changed his tone. He who had foretold these fearful consequences suddenly came forward as the one man who had words of hope. The narrative which tells how Hezekiah, on receiving the summons to surrender, turned to him and received exultant assurance that Sennacherib could never take the city, is one of the immortal stories of the Old Testament. It leads the reader breathless through the Assyrian's insolent boasts, the king's despairing confession of helplessness, the prophet's ringing defiance and exposure of the enemy's blasphemous folly, to the striking of the hour of doom and the going forth of the angel of Yahweh in the selfsame night to destroy the Assyrian host. These are the colours laid on by legend. But the utterances of Isaiah which they contain may be genuine. And we have elsewhere in his oracles sayings which may well belong to this hour:

"Woe to the Assyrian! the rod of mine anger,
The staff of mine indignation!
I send him against a profane nation,
And against the people of my wrath do I give him a charge,
To take the spoil, and to take the prey,
And to tread them down like the mire of the streets.
But *he*—he meaneth not so,
Neither doth his heart think so;
But it is in his heart to cut off nations not a few. . . .

Shall the axe boast itself against him that heweth therewith?
Shall the saw magnify itself against him that wieldeth it? . . .
Therefore will the Lord, Yahweh of hosts,
Send among his fat ones leanness;
And under his glory shall be kindled a burning
Like the burning of fire,
And the light of Israel shall be for a fire,
And his Holy One for a flame;
And it will burn, and devour his thorns
And briers in one day" (10:5ff).

This punishment of the Assyrian would mean the safety of Jerusalem.

"For thus saith Yahweh unto me,
As the lion and the young lion growling over his prey,
If a multitude of shepherds be called forth against him,
Will not be dismayed at their voice,

Nor abase himself at the noise of them:
So will Yahweh of hosts come down
To fight upon mount Zion, and upon its hill.
As birds hovering,
So will Yahweh of hosts protect Jerusalem:
He will protect and deliver it,
He will pass over and preserve it" (31:4ff).

The cold reality indeed did not correspond to the glowing promises of the prophet. Hezekiah was forced to buy off the invader
by a staggering ransom. The treasures which he had so proudly
showed Merodach-baladan's envoys were carried off, as Isaiah had
said, but to Assyria not to Babylonia, and in addition he was compelled to cut the gold from the doors and front pillars of the temple
(II Ki. 18:14ff). This statement of the Israelitish historian is confirmed by Sennacherib:

"With 30 talents of gold, 800 talents of silver, precious stones,
rouge, *dakkasi,* lapis lazuli, great *angugmi*-stones, beds of ivory,
stationary ivory thrones, elephants' hide, ivory, *ushu* wood, *ukarinnu*
wood, all sorts of objects, a heavy treasure; also his daughters, the
women of his palace, male and female musicians he sent after me
to Nineveh, my capital city, and sent his messenger to present the
gift and to do homage." [5]

And yet Jerusalem did escape capture. Perhaps its excellent fortifications and the outbreak of other revolts in the east combined to
make Sennacherib offer terms. At any rate he does not boast of
taking it.

So Isaiah was vindicated both in his threats and in his promises.
But the repentance which he demanded of Israel in Yahweh's
name did not come. If, as some think, the oracle contained in
22:1–14 reflects the jubilation of Jerusalem after its frantic efforts
of defence had been rendered unnecessary by Sennacherib's departure, it is a confession of the weary prophet's disappointment:

"And in that day did the Lord, Yahweh of hosts, call
To weeping, and to mourning,
And to baldness, and to girding with sackcloth:
And behold, joy and gladness,
Slaying oxen, and killing sheep,
Eating flesh, and drinking wine:

[5] Barton, *ibid.*

Let us eat and drink, for tomorrow we die.
And Yahweh of hosts revealed himself in mine ears,
Surely this iniquity shall not be forgiven you till ye die,
Saith the Lord, Yahweh of hosts" (22:12ff).

This, so far as we know, was the climax of Isaiah's ministry.
He was now past sixty, and his work cannot have continued
many years longer. In 698 B.C. Hezekiah died and Manasseh, who
succeeded him, abandoned his father's reforming policy. By doing
so he encountered the opposition of the prophets. The Deuteronomic editor of II Kings, who tells this, adds that he shed innocent
blood very much (II Ki. 21:2ff, 16). A late tradition declares
that Isaiah was sawn asunder and it is possible that he met his
death at Manasseh's hands.

One likes to believe with Duhm [6] that at the end of his life he
thought much of the coming of the good king and of the glorious
age to be. But we shall consider his Messianic prophecies in their
due place among his leading religious ideas, to the review of which
we now proceed.

Man is Nothing before God

The Lord whom Isaiah saw in his vision was "high and lifted
up" and that always remained the chief element in his concept of
God. Surrounded by His heavenly hosts Yahweh towered far
above all things earthly. Isaiah loved to apply to Him names significant of this aspect of His being: the "Mighty One of Israel,"
"Yahweh of hosts," "The Lord," "The Holy One of Israel" and
his "Maker." Of course He was the only God: Isaiah did not
trouble himself to assert that. "The fulness of the whole earth is
his glory" (6:3). His was the purpose purposed upon the whole
earth, His the hand stretched out upon all nations (14:26).

The only reasonable and right attitude for man to assume in the
presence of such majesty was one of humility and utter dependence.
Anything that tended to give man confidence in himself, in other
men, or in other gods was not only a delusion, it was impious. For
this reason Isaiah looked with scorn and aversion upon the growing
wealth and luxury of his people, upon their horses, chariots, fortifications and other military resources, upon their leagues with Egypt
and Ethiopia, all of which he classed with their idols, altars, asherim,

[6] *Das Buch Jesaia*[2] (Göttingen, 1914), p. 81. See also *Israels Propheten*[2]
(Tübingen, 1922), p. 79ff.

sun-images and Adonis gardens as offering a false refuge from the Assyrian armies. The qualities of energy, resourcefulness and self-help, which we of today praise as the chief glory of a nation, Isaiah condemned as an attempt of man to "lift himself up" above his Maker. When the vigorous citizens of Samaria refused to be crushed by some disaster that had overtaken them and determined to make a better city rise from the ruins, Isaiah denounced them for their "pride and stoutness of heart." He would doubtless have uttered the same judgment on the citizens of Baltimore or San Francisco who said after their great fires "The bricks are fallen, but we will build with hewn stone" (9:10).

So carried away was Isaiah with this sense of the sublimity of God that he could face the brute colossus of Assyria with equanimity. It was merely the rod in Yahweh's hand with which He would chastise His people. The irony of the situation was that the Assyrian did not comprehend this! (10:5-19).

Thus Isaiah ever thought. His fundamental idea of man's place before God could well be summed up in words that have found a place in his oracles though he probably did not write them: [1]

> "Cease ye from man, whose breath is in his nostrils;
> For wherein is he to be accounted of?" (2:22).

God is Passionately Ethical

When Isaiah saw the lofty God his first thought was of the defilement tainting himself and the society to which he belonged (6:5f). Nothing unclean could survive in God's presence. When he called God again and again the "Holy One," holiness had come to mean for him more than mere divinity; it meant purity also. And the Holy One desired hotly to set forward justice, truth and kindness among men. That had been His aim in all the care that He had lavished on His vineyard, the house of Israel; He looked that it should bring forth grapes, but He had got from it instead the wild grapes of oppression and cruelty (5:1ff). The men responsible for such things were to Him a burden heavier than He could bear.

> "Ah, I will ease me of mine adversaries,
> And avenge me of mine enemies" (1:24).

Like Amos Isaiah condemned most fiercely sins which made the poor suffer. It was for these that God was about to judge the elders and princes.

[1] They are not found in most copies of the LXX.

"It is ye that have eaten up the vineyard!
The spoil of the poor is in your houses:
What mean ye that ye crush my people,
And grind the face of the poor?
Saith the Lord Yahweh of hosts" (3:14f).

He followed Amos likewise in expressing God's hatred of worship
divorced from justice.

"When ye spread forth your hands, I will hide my face;
Yea, when ye make many prayers I will not hear:
Your hands are full of blood!
Wash you, make you clean;
Put away the evil of your doings from before mine eyes . . . ,
Seek justice, relieve the oppressed,
Judge the fatherless, plead for the widow" (1:15-17).

God's Interest is Centred in Jerusalem

The place where Isaiah had his vision of Yahweh was the temple.
That is eloquent of the conviction which he cherished from first
to last regarding Yahweh's connection with Jerusalem. While
Yahweh did not indeed dwell there, His home being in heaven,
He had nevertheless taken it for His own in a peculiar way. Mount
Zion was the "place of the name of Yahweh of hosts" (18:7).

Isaiah's belief in Yahweh's devotion to Jerusalem is simply amazing. He spoke at times as if what God cared for was the spot
itself rather than its inhabitants. Such of course was not his real
meaning. It was the unity of the two that God loved, "His people
that dwelt in Zion." But we have here something quite different
from God's tenderness towards Israel as conceived by Hosea;
which clung to no particular bit of its territory and only in a
vague way to the "land" as a whole. To Isaiah Jerusalem had
become a sacrament. Indeed it was more, being not merely an
"outward and visible sign" of God's presence, but valuable to God
in itself (10:24, 32f; 14:32; 18:4ff; 30:27ff; 31:4f, 8f).

Probably this attitude towards Jerusalem was not new with
Isaiah. It must have been growing up during the three centuries
since David till it had attained a high place in Judah's faith.
Already Amos had spoken of Yahweh as roaring from Zion (Amos
1:2). But among the writings preserved to us in the Old Testament canon those of Isaiah are the first to give it continuous and

rapt expression. If he did not originate it he at least imparted to it a fresh and powerful impulse.

From his belief in God's special care for Jerusalem Isaiah drew the immediate conclusion that the city would be protected. Some of his most beautiful and tender utterances voiced this assurance. One cannot say that he made the inviolability of Zion into a dogma, but he does not seem to have contemplated its possible destruction. In this he differed sharply from his contemporary Micah and left a legacy of confidence against which Jeremiah and Ezekiel had to contend a century later.

In keeping with Isaiah's attitude towards Jerusalem was his narrow nationalism. It was not of course necessary that the two should go together, and if one might regard him as the author of 2:1-4 and 19:19ff one would find him uttering hopes which were anything but narrow and nationalistic. But apart from these doubtful passages it is hard to discover any word of Isaiah which reflects a genuine interest in foreign peoples for their own sake. God was indeed using the Assyrian as His rod, but He would soon break him upon the mountains of Israel (14:25). So it was with the other Gentile nations concerning which Isaiah received divine messages; the reader feels that God really cares for none of them. He was the "Holy One of Israel." He had, to be sure, a purpose for the whole earth, but it was not a purpose of salvation. Towards non-Israelitish mankind He remained indifferent, except where they entered into His plans for His own people. Isaiah seems to have had none of Amos' international sympathy. He could imagine God's love as going no further afield than the neighbouring kingdom of Samaria, which after all was a part of Israel.

In spite then of his many prophecies concerning foreign nations we must seek the heart of Isaiah's message in what he said to the people of both Israelitish kingdoms, and especially to the men of Judah. For them he had a very definite "word" of Yahweh.

God Demands Repentance and Faith

Like Amos and Hosea Isaiah believed that God was about to intervene in men's affairs in a new and startling way. There was to be a "day of Yahweh upon all that was lifted up" (2:12). He was even now standing up to contend and judge His people (3:13). Stroke after stroke would fall, yet His anger would not be turned away, but His hand would be stretched out still (9:12, 17, 21; 10:4; 5:25). At first Isaiah seems to have pictured this punishment as a natural catastrophe combined with a social revolution in which all the leaders would be destroyed and the state lie prostrate under the rule of the mob (3:1ff). But it was not long before the impending doom took the shape of the Assyrian hosts which Yahweh was about to bring upon His unhappy land.

It was time therefore for Judah and Israel to appease Yahweh and avert the coming judgment. Isaiah offered a plain way in which this might be done:

> "In returning and rest shall ye be saved;
> In quietness and in confidence shall be your strength" (30:15).

The first step was to return to God. That meant to "put away the evil of their doings from before His eyes" (1:16). It involved not only the cessation of wrong and oppression but the abandonment of every dependence save that on God. The second step was to wait quietly upon Him in the certainty that He would bring relief and deliverance. On these two things hung Isaiah's whole message.

We have seen how he urged this policy of faith in two crises of Judah's history. It was indeed a heroic faith that the prophet demanded of the commonplace men of his day. To follow it meant to give up not only everything which clashed with Yahweh's requirements but also all the measures which ordinary human foresight would prescribe. It asked them to step out upon the unseen and try whether it would bear the whole weight of the nation's need in a desperate hour. No wonder that he encountered scoffers! The marvel is that he could persuade even a few. But Isaiah, to whom the invisible world was more real than all the world of sense, could not see this.

A Remnant Only will be Saved

The commission given to Isaiah at his call was terrible in its irony:

> "Make fat the heart of this people,
> And their ears make heavy, and shut their eyes;
> Lest they see with their eyes, and hear with their ears,
> And understand with their hearts,
> And turn again, and be healed" (6:10).

Some scholars hold that this saying must be interpreted proleptically; that is, Isaiah on looking back after a disappointed ministry read into his remembrance of his call a foreshadowing of his failure. But one may well question whether this modern view is justified. For the young prophet started his public ministry by naming his child "A Remnant shall Return," indicating that thus early he despaired of the conversion of the people as a whole (7:3). The name would probably be more correctly rendered "A Remnant shall Turn" (be converted). He was not speaking of coming back from future captivity, for he seems not to have contemplated captivity as part of Judah's punishment. The verb "turn" is exactly the same as that in the phrase above quoted, "turn again" (6:10). It appears also as the root of the noun "returning" in the famous saying: "In returning and rest, etc." (30:15). The most natural thing is to believe that Isaiah meant the same process in all three of these passages.

Almost if not quite from the first, then, Isaiah was convinced that his ministry would only aggravate the rebellious disposition of the nation. And as he went on experience proved the truth of this foreboding. Yahweh, whom he offered as a sanctuary, became a stone of stumbling and a rock of offence to both the houses of Israel (8:14). The inexorable conclusion forced itself upon him that the many must perish. He watched this doom fulfilling itself in the march of Assyrian conquest, in the overthrow of Samaria in 722 B.C., in the harrowing of Judah in 701 B.C. Then indeed the "daughter of Zion" was "left as a booth in a vineyard, . . . as a besieged city." Surely the capital and its refugees represented a "very small remnant" of the once populous nation! (1:8f). But it was not yet small enough to be pure; and it may well have been this diminished remainder who after the lifting of the siege called forth Yahweh's indignant sentence: "This iniquity shall not be forgiven you till you die" (22:14).

The Glorious Future of the Remnant

But the doctrine of the remnant had its positive side also. A remnant *shall* return. We should like to know just what Isaiah meant by this. Did he place any hope in the grim process of elimination that he witnessed going on in Samaria and Judah? As each new blow fell did he say to himself, Now the great conversion will take place? If he did, he was disappointed. The few remained as wicked as the many.

Of course! we say. Calamities such as war, earthquakes, hurricanes, epidemics do not discriminate in their victims. What you have after they pass is no purified humanity but a cross-section of a diminished society. Nor is the "moral effect" of the tragedy sufficient to induce the majority of the survivors to change their manner of life.

On the other hand Isaiah, who perceived in Assyria's destructiveness the hand of Yahweh, might well have faced a problem of faith in finding each successive "remnant" as bad as the former whole. That (apparently) he felt no such problem must have been due to his power to project his hopes upon a divinely instituted future. This he conceived in a vague mystical way and the pictures which he drew of it are different one from another, showing that his ideas were far from fixed regarding it. Nevertheless we can assemble some of its features.

Its centre was to be Jerusalem, purified at last from dross and alloy (1.24ff; cf 11:9 "my holy mountain"). The great conversion would have become a reality (10:21). Men would believe in God and lean upon Him, not on human helps or imaginary "gods" (10:20; 17:7ff). King and princes would protect the poor from their oppressors (1:26; 32:1-8).

The Messiah

In two renowned passages Isaiah introduced the figure of a wonderful king through whom the new order would be brought about. Out of the roots of Jesse (after the tree of the Davidic monarchy had been cut down by some catastrophe) would sprout a ruler upon whom the Spirit of Yahweh would rest in fulness. With stern and clear-seeing intervention he would deliver the poor from his persecutors and establish the reign of righteousness and truth. Under him the very wild beasts would grow tame.

> "And the wolf shall dwell with the lamb,
> And the leopard shall lie down with the kid;
> The calf, and the young lion, and the fatling together;
> And a little child shall lead them. . . .
> They shall not hurt nor destroy in all my holy mountain;
> For the earth shall be full of the knowledge of Yahweh,
> As the waters cover the sea" (11:6ff).

In a similar passage Isaiah went further and invested the king with traits which seem to border on the superhuman, if not the divine.

"Unto us a child is born, unto us a son is given;
And the government shall be upon his shoulder:
And his name shall be called
Wonderful, Counsellor, Mighty God,
Everlasting Father, Prince of Peace.
Of the increase of his government and peace there shall be no end,
Upon the throne of David, and upon his kingdom,
To establish it and to uphold it with justice and with righteousness
From henceforth even for ever.
The zeal of Yahweh of hosts shall perform this" (9:6f).

These utterances have been rejected as non-Isaianic by Marti and others, while among scholars who accept them some interpret the epithets applied to the king in 9:6 in a way that leaves out any superhuman connotations: "'wonder of a counsellor, mighty hero, father of booty, prince of peace." But the present writer sees no compelling reason for disputing either their genuineness or their higher meaning. If genuine they would make Isaiah the supreme Messianic prophet of the Old Testament.[1]

Isaiah's Contribution to Israel's Religion

Isaiah transferred the seat of prophecy to Judah. He carried over into that portion of God's people which was destined to survive the sublime inheritance of Amos and Hosea. What he got from these prophets nevertheless became a new thing in his hands for he gave it a fresh and individual expression which in splendour and sheer massiveness of impact far surpassed the work of his predecessors.

Isaiah had also beliefs which distinguished him from Amos and Hosea, beliefs which indeed he did not originate but so took over from his environment into his very self and uttered with such blazing intensity and such compelling beauty that they became henceforth a force to be reckoned with for good or ill.

[1] Among the scholars who accept 9:2–7 as Isaiah's are Sellin (*EAT*[7], p. 83); Hempel (apparently: *AHL*, p. 133); Guthe (*HSAT*); Schmidt (*SAT*, II 2, p. 75, 115f); McFadyen (*IOT*[2], p. 135); Duhm (*HKAT*); Meinhold (*AT*[3], p. 187f); S. A. Cook (apparently: *OT*, p. 163); Procksch (*KAT*); Wade (*WC*); Peake (*PCB*); Elliott Binns (*NCHS*). The following are in doubt, but seem to favour Isaianic authorship: Oesterley and Robinson (*IBOT*, p. 245); Bewer (*LOT*, p. 114ff); Gray (*ICC*). Of these, Oesterley and Robinson, McFadyen, Gray and Peake incline to reject 11:1–10 as non-Isaianic. Meinhold is less sure of it than of 9:2–7. Eissfeldt (*EAT*, p. 357f) is neutral towards 9:2–7 and thinks the scales are weighted against 11:1–10.

Isaiah did more perhaps than any other Old Testament writer to lay stress on the *holiness* of God, including in this quality not only God's "otherness" and transcendence, but also His moral purity. Here he undoubtedly influenced his successors, and the Christian church in its "Holy, holy, holy" still echoes his hymn of the seraphim (6:3).

Developing the tradition of Amos and Hosea he became the father of religious quietism; of the attitude which distrusted and condemned all man's efforts to work out his own destiny and threw itself wholly upon God. This ran out naturally into eschatology and dominated the later apocalyptists, passing over from them into the New Testament world where it left an imposing and intractable deposit quite alien to the temper of modern liberalism.

Isaiah gave powerful impulse to the tendency developing in the southern kingdom to regard Jerusalem as the city of Yahweh's love, the mystic centre of His religion, the sacrament of His presence. After Isaiah this tendency went on apace through Ezekiel, Second Isaiah, the psalmists, the priests, the Levites, the scribes and the apocalyptists straight into the New Testament church, and has left its impress upon the poetry and devotion of the Christian ages.

Isaiah's doctrine of the remnant was also destined to play a conspicuous part in later thought. It tended to break up the solidarity of national religion by distinguishing between two groups within the nation and promising salvation to the righteous alone. Thus it led the way to the individualism of Ezekiel. But it also persisted as a doctrine of pessimism regarding the future of mankind as a whole, and in the familiar form "Many are called, but few are chosen" tinged the pages of the New Testament with a despair against which the prevailing universalism of our day is a spontaneous protest.

Finally, the Isaianic figure of the Messiah fired the imagination of after generations, reappearing now and again in later prophetic writings and in the popular literature of the intra-testamental period, and living on in the minds of the people. In this figure Jesus doubtless saw himself foreshadowed, and from it the New Testament church drew inspiration for its faith in the divine Christ.

To the modern Christian Isaiah makes a unique appeal. The majestic impetuosity and piercing beauty of his diction, his brilliant, ever-changing word pictures, his trumpet-peal of faith, his ringing challenges, his inexorable demands, his white-hot purity, his scorn of all base things, his championing of the poor, his tender assurances, his clear vision of the Messianic age to be, are to be found in their clustered brightness nowhere else in the Bible.

CHAPTER XV

MICAH

[*c.* 730 B.C.]

The Sources

Our sources for the study of Micah consist of the book which bears the prophet's name and a notice concerning him contained in Jer. 26:18-19. This notice is reliable, being found in the material that is usually ascribed to Baruch. Even if Baruch did not write it, scholars are agreed that it proceeds from the age of Jeremiah and preserves a genuine recollection. As to the Book of Micah itself, there is no consensus.

All scholars unite in regarding the major part of chapters 1-3 as utterances of Micah. Only 2:12-13 are generally rejected as later than Micah's time. Some scholars think that these chapters are all that we have of Micah's own words,[1] and they maintain accordingly that we must form our picture of the prophet from these alone.

But perhaps the majority of scholars are not willing entirely to cast out chapters 4-7. They feel that the passages in these chapters which contain denunciation and threats (5:10-15; 6:9-7:6) may be Micah's, though most of them regard the passages containing promises (4:1-5:9; 7:7-20) as of later origin.[2]

In the face of such disagreement the best course would seem to be this: in order to show deference to the scholars who limit themselves to chapters 1-3 let us first see what these have to tell us of Micah. After that we may inquire whether other sections, if genuine, would add anything to our idea of the prophet.

First, then, what do we know of the Micah of chapters 1-3?

[1] E.g. Guthe (*HSAT*, II, p. 53); Hölscher (*GIJR*, p. 110, note 1); and Marti (*KHAT*, p. 262f).

[2] Sellin (*EAT*[7], p. 114f) and Schmidt (*SAT*, II 2, p. 140ff) hold that Micah also wrote the passages of promise contained in 2:12-13; 4:6-5:9. They likewise believe that he took over 4:1-4 from his contemporary Isaiah, whom they regard as its author.

The Micah of Chapters 1-3

The title of the prophet's book tells us that he was a Morashtite (man of Moresheth). Moresheth is identified as a small village in the Shephelah, or low hills, some twenty-five miles southwest of Jerusalem. Those who wish to get a vivid picture of the town and its surroundings should read Prof. G. A. Smith's description in his *Book of the Twelve*. It is generally supposed that Micah, like most Palestinian villagers, was a farmer; and the sympathy he exhibits with the peasants who were being evicted from their holdings points in this direction.

He lived, according to Jer. 26:18, in the time of Hezekiah, but Hölscher thinks that the title of his book draws a sound conclusion when it states that he was active also in the reigns of Jotham and Ahaz. This would make him a contemporary of Isaiah. Whether he came into close contact with that great prophet is uncertain, though Schmidt believes that he was Isaiah's disciple. Like Isaiah he lived through tragic days. His earliest prophecy was directed against Samaria, showing that the capital of the northern kingdom was still standing. Presently he witnessed its investment by the Assyrian army in 725 B.C. and its fall in 722 B.C. Two years later Sargon's army must have passed near Micah's home when it met and defeated Hanno of Gaza and his Egyptian allies. When in 713-711 B.C. a new uprising against Assyria broke out in which Judah, Edom and Moab stood side by side with the Philistines, the Tartan of Sargon (Is. 20:1) came into the same neighbourhood and struck down the rebels, who had been left in the lurch by their Egyptian instigators. Ashdod and Gath (the latter only three hours' walk from Moresheth) were sacked. Ashdod was compelled to receive Assyrian colonists and an Assyrian governor, while Gath sank into obscurity. But the fiery longing for freedom still surged among the Syrian peoples, breaking out after Sargon's death in the great rebellion of 701 B.C. in which Hezekiah took a passionate part. Then came Sennacherib with his resistless host and swept over both Philistia and Micah's own country. This Assyrian monarch in a famous inscription tells us that he took 46 strongholds and other "cities" of Judah, "counting as spoil" 200,150 people, besides unnumbered farm animals. Moresheth may well have been one of these plundered towns. In any case it must have suffered bitterly.

The internal condition of the two kingdoms was no happier than their outward history. We have already seen how in the north

the prosperity of Jeroboam's days had been succeeded by quick
changes of rulers and increasing lawlessness. Within Judah the
dynasty indeed remained secure, but Jotham and Ahaz were weak
kings tolerating both social and religious abuses. Ahaz is even
accused of making his own son "pass through the fire" and of displacing the brazen altar of the temple with a new altar built after
the pattern of one he had seen in Damascus (II Ki. 16:3, 10ff).
It was he also who appealed to Tiglath-pileser for aid against
Samaria and Syria, thus voluntarily bringing Judah into vassalage
to Assyria (II Ki. 16:5ff). Hezekiah indeed introduced a religious
reform in which he endeavoured to do away with the high places
and to purge the temple of impurity. But that popular opinion
was against him is seen by the approval which his son Manasseh
received when he went back to all the practices of Ahaz' time
(II Ki. 21:1ff). It is possible that Micah may have survived till
Manasseh's reign.

In these evils Micah saw the doom of Yahweh upon a sinful
people. Indeed, if his earliest prophecy reads aright, he called not
only Israel but all the nations, the earth and everything in it, to
hear what the Lord Yahweh was testifying against them. In his
prophetic ecstasy he saw Yahweh coming from out His holy place,
the heavenly temple, to tread in judgment upon the high places
of the earth. Under His steps the mountains melted, the valleys
yawned asunder like wax before the fire.

"For the transgression of Jacob is all this,
And for the sins of the house of Israel" (1:5).

It was the religious apostasy of the northern kingdom that cried
aloud for Yahweh's punishment—its graven images, its revenues
derived from sacred prostitution.

"Therefore will I make Samaria as a heap of the field,
And as places for planting vineyards;
And I will pour down the stones thereof into the valley,
And I will uncover the foundations thereof" (1:6).

But the destruction would not stop with Samaria. In accents of
agony he pictures the towns of his own neighbourhood falling one
after another before the invader. Even his native village is not
spared.

"I will yet bring unto thee him that shall possess thee,
O inhabitant of Mareshah" (1:15).

The people of the region have turned to flight, seeking the same desolate refuge that sheltered David long before.

> "Even unto Adullam shall come
> The glory of Israel" (1:15).

And why? In the case of Judah it was not the religious so much as the social evils which excited the divine anger. One thing that outraged the feelings of this farmer was the high-handed way in which the rich were obtaining possession of the houses and land of the poor.

> "Woe to them that devise iniquity
> And work evil upon their beds!
> When the morning is light, they practise it,
> Because it is in the power of their hand!
> And they covet fields—and seize them;
> Houses—and take them away:
> And they oppress a man and his house,
> Even a man and his heritage" (2:1f). . . .
> "The women of my people ye cast out
> From their pleasant houses;
> From their young children ye take away
> My glory for ever" (2:9).

But the violence went further, proceeding even to highway robbery.

> "Of late my people is risen up as an enemy:
> Ye strip the robe from off the garment
> Of them that pass by securely,
> As men averse from war" (2:8).

Fine houses were going up in Jerusalem, at the cost of the lives of the poor.

> "They build up Zion with blood
> And Jerusalem with iniquity" (3:10).

Venality and corruption were everywhere.

> "The heads thereof judge for reward,
> And the priests thereof teach for hire,
> And the prophets thereof divine for money" (3:11).

To the prophet who remonstrated with them they replied with confused cries for silence.

"Prophesy ye not! They are prophesying!
They shall not prophesy of these things!
Their reproaches shall never cease!" (2:6).

What they wanted, Micah commented grimly, was a pleasanter sort of message.

"If a man walking in the spirit of falsehood do lie,
Saying, I will prophesy unto thee of wine and strong drink;
He shall even be the prophet of this people!" (2:11).

But Micah refused to be silenced. He was not like the usual prophets, who thought of nothing but making a living. Upon these he turned with a bitterness that reminds us of Jeremiah a century later:
"Thus saith Yahweh concerning the prophets
That make my people to err:
That bite with their teeth [1] and cry, Peace;
And whoso putteth not into their mouths,
They even sanctify a war against him!"

They shall be punished with the cessation of revelations from on high.

"Therefore it shall be night unto you that ye shall have no vision. . . .
And the seers shall be put to shame,
And the diviners confounded. . . .
For there is no answer of God."

Not such was Micah.

"But as for me, I am full of power
By the Spirit of Yahweh, and of judgment, and of might,
To declare unto Jacob his transgression
And to Israel his sin" (3:5-8).

And what he said to Israel was that they could hope for no peace. The rich dispossessors of the farmer would never enjoy their ill-gotten estates. Do not settle down in them, he warned.

[1] That is, flatter every one that feeds them.

"Arise ye and depart;
For this is not your resting-place;
Because of uncleanness that destroyeth,
Even with a grievous destruction" (2:10).

Nowhere in the Old Testament, that book of blazing denunciation
of all that makes the poor suffer, do we read such invective as this
peasant prophet uttered.

"Hear ye this, I pray you, ye heads of Jacob
And rulers of the house of Israel:
Is it not for you to know justice?
Ye who hate the good and love the evil;
Who pluck off their skin from off them
And their flesh from off their bones;
Who also eat the flesh of my people,
And flay their skin from off them,
And break their bones,
And chop them in pieces, as for the pot,
And as flesh for the caldron!
Then shall they cry unto Yahweh,
But he will not answer them;
Yea, he will hide his face from them at that time,
According as they have wrought evil in their doings" (3:1ff).

Merciless, they shall obtain no mercy.

But he does not let them off with vague threatenings. Plainly
and terribly he announces the exact doom that is to fall.

"Hear ye this, I pray you, ye heads of the house of Jacob,
And rulers of the house of Israel,
That abhor justice,
And pervert all equity. . . .
And they lean upon Yahweh, and say,
Is not Yahweh in the midst of us?
No evil shall come upon us!
Therefore shall Zion for your sake
Be ploughed as a field,
And Jerusalem shall become heaps,
And the mountain of the house as the high places of a forest" (3:9ff).

There it was spoken! What Isaiah had declared would not
happen, what every one in Judah from the least to the greatest

knew was impossible, this poor man from the country announced as the purpose of God: Jerusalem would go down!

A century later men remembered these words and the impression they made. We can dimly apprehend through the notice in Jer. 26:18f the consternation and horror with which they were received. Under a king like Jehoiakim they might well have cost Micah his life. But over Judah at that hour there reigned a nobler monarch. "Did Hezekiah king of Judah and all Judah put him to death? Did he not fear Yahweh, and entreat the favour of Yahweh?" So Micah's proclamation of doom proved a call to penitence (Jer. 26:19).

And was not penitence after all what Micah longed to see? Fierce as was his denunciation, harsh and inexorable as his message of doom, this prophet of the village seems to have found pain rather than satisfaction in the woes that he proclaimed.

> "For this I will lament and wail;
> I will go stripped and naked. . . .
> For her wounds are incurable;
> For it is come even unto Judah;
> It reacheth unto the gate of my people,
> Even to Jerusalem" (1:8f).

Surely the man who said that loved the city whose sentence he was pronouncing. And if we can (with Schmidt, Duhm and others) look on 2:7 as expressing the view of the prophet himself (rather than of his opponents) we have in his preaching a note of pleading.

> "Shall it be said, O house of Jacob,
> Is the Spirit of Yahweh straitened?
> Are these his doings?
> Do not my words do good
> To him that doeth uprightly?" (2:7).

So Micah may well have been among the first to welcome the change of attitude in Hezekiah and the people recorded in Jeremiah.

"And Yahweh repented him of the evil which he had pronounced against them," the Jeremianic notice concludes. In other words, the prediction of Jerusalem's fall did not come to pass. Some scholars see in these words a later explanation of the prophecy's non-fulfilment. But it is possible that some such reassurance came to Hezekiah at the time just as in I Ki. 21:27-29 Elijah's announcement of Ahab's doom was mitigated after he had shown signs of contrition. The tradition seems to imply that Micah himself may have been the medium through whom Yahweh's gracious change of mind was conveyed to the king.

But all this is more or less conjectural. For aught we know, Hölscher is right in finding in Micah only the "austerity and harshness which does not shrink from drawing the ultimate conclusion." [2]

What Chapters 4–7 would Add to our Picture of Micah

First, the "threatening passages" would reinforce our impression of his sternness, and enrich it by several aspects which do not appear in 1–3.

5:10–15 is an outburst of indignation against horses, chariots, strongholds, those symbols of military preparedness which we have met already in Amos, Hosea and Isaiah. Micah opposed them on the same ground as his fellow-prophets, that they made people trust in armaments rather than in God. For that reason he boldly classed them with witchcrafts, soothsayers, pillars, graven images and Asherim, seeing that they were after all a species of idolatry.

"And it shall come to pass in that day, saith Yahweh,
I will cut off thy horses from the midst of thee,
And will destroy thy chariots:
And I will cut off the cities of thy land,
And will throw down all thy strongholds,
And I will cut off witchcrafts out of thy hand,
And sooth-sayers shalt thou have no more;
And I will cut off thy graven images and thy masseboth out of
   the midst of thee;
And thou shalt no more worship the work of thy hands,
And I will pluck up thy Asherim out of the midst of thee;
And I will destroy thy cities."

6:9–10 is directed against "the city" (probably Jerusalem), whose corruptions horrified this man from the country, as a century later they were to amaze the villager Jeremiah (Jer. 5).

"Hark! Yahweh crieth unto the city . . .
Are there yet the treasures of wickedness in the house of the wicked,
And the scant measure that is abominable?
Shall I be pure with wicked balances

[2] *Die Profeten*, p. 256.

And with a bag of deceitful weights?"
For the rich men thereof are full of violence,
And the inhabitants thereof have spoken lies,
And their tongue is deceitful in their mouth. . . ."

Perhaps 7:1–6 is a continuation of this same indictment of the
city, but it may have been addressed to the whole nation. It dwells
more at length upon the universal treachery that the prophet saw
about him.

"The godly man is perished out of the earth,
And the upright among men is no more;
They all lie in wait for blood;
They hunt every man his brother with a net.
Their hands are upon that which is evil to do it diligently;
The prince asketh, and the judge is ready for a bribe;
And the great man, he uttereth the evil desire of his soul;
Thus they weave it together.
The best of them is as a brier;
The most upright is worse than a thorn hedge . . ."

One could not trust those closest to him.

"Put ye not confidence in a familiar friend;
Keep the doors of thy mouth from her that lieth in thy bosom.
For the son dishonoureth the father,
And the daughter riseth up against her mother,
The daughter-in-law against her mother-in-law;
A man's enemies are the men of his own house."

The man who uttered these threatening passages of 4–7 was
surely one of the flaming spirits of the Bible. If he was not Micah
he was at least of the same mind as that passionate champion of
righteousness.

When we come however to 6:1–8 we enter a different atmosphere.
If it be Micah who is speaking here he has "changed his tone."
Or perhaps it would be more accurate to say that certain notes
of tenderness which we imagined might be detected in 1–3 have
here become triumphant, while a hush has fallen upon the trumpet
blasts of wrath.

Once more, as in 1:2, there is to be a law-suit between Yahweh
and His people:

> "Arise, contend thou before the mountains
> And let the hills hear thy voice!"

It is the summons to Israel. And now the judges are put at attention:

> "Hear, O ye mountains, Yahweh's controversy,
> And ye enduring rocks, the foundations of the earth;
> For Yahweh hath a controversy with his people,
> And he will plead with Israel!"

But it is Israel, not mountains or rocks, to whom God speaks:

> "O my people, what have I done unto thee?
> And wherein have I wearied thee?
> Testify against me."

Then, in the usual prophetic fashion, the great things Yahweh has done are rehearsed. The people, overcome with contrition, ask what they shall do to appease God:

> "Wherewith shall I come before Yahweh,
> And bow myself before God on high?
> Shall I come before him with burnt-offerings,
> With calves of a year old?"

Such are the usual sacrifices. But as the people speak of them they realize that these will not be enough. It will take more— much more—to obtain reconciliation:

> "Will Yahweh be pleased with thousands of rams,
> With ten thousands of rivers of oil?"

In vain! But there is still a final dreadful oblation that they might offer:

> "Shall I give my first-born for my transgression,
> The fruit of my body for the sin of my soul?"

Still in vain! And then, as this last cry of agony dies into silence, the prophet tells them what God really wants:

> "It hath been told thee, O man, what is good,
> And what Yahweh doth require of thee:
> Only to do justly, and to love mercy, and to walk humbly
> with thy God!"

If Micah be indeed the author of this remarkable passage we shall have to enlarge our conception of him. The fierce prophet of doom will appear also as a winning evangelist, a yearning and tender pleader with men, able to understand their gropings after God and to see even in the dark rite of child-sacrifice a desire to give God the most precious thing of all. And this evangelist will show himself one of the clearest thinkers among Israel's prophets, able to meet man's questioning as to God's requirements with a single sentence that goes straight to the heart of true religion.

It is probably better that we must stop here in our study of Micah. Criticism, in rejecting the passages that group themselves in 4:11ff about the famous prophecy of the ruler from Bethlehem, has made it unnecessary to paint into our picture of Micah certain nationalistic and warlike features which would harmonize badly with that general prophetic attitude towards war which we now see him sharing. On the other hand, it would do him honour if we could believe that 4:1–5 came from his pen. But we must be content with the results we have already obtained.

Micah's Significance

Such was the peasant prophet of Moresheth in the hill-country of Judah. Let us now ask ourselves what was his significance in the history of Israel's religion.

The one thing that made him stand out in later recollections was, as we have seen, his prediction that Jerusalem would be destroyed. In spite of Isaiah's assurances that this would not be, and their astounding fulfilment when Sennacherib gave up the attempt to take the city; in spite of the fact that inferior prophets were constantly ringing the changes on Isaiah's theme; still the memory of Micah's utterance lived on to remind men that there had been one prophet who had pronounced Jerusalem's doom. What it really meant, of course, was that God cared for righteousness more than for His holy temple—precious as that might be in His eyes. By this Micah became the spiritual ancestor of Jeremiah and Ezekiel, and of him who wept over the Jerusalem of a later day and said that not one stone of its temple should be left upon another.

Micah's sublime utterance as to God's requirements (6:8), though not quoted expressly by any later writer in either the Old or the New Testaments, must have been one of the forces that contributed to build in Israel what we are accustomed to call the prophetic conception of God. Its effect in this direction must have been the greater because the prophets, with all their proclaiming in detail of God's ethical nature, yet produced comparatively few of these summaries ("headings up" to use St. Paul's expression in Rom. 13:9), in which the whole of God's demands and the entire meaning of Israel's religion were "briefly comprehended."

For the rest, Micah proved just one more voice crying in the name of Yahweh against "man's inhumanity to man." His is a particularly poignant voice when he speaks of the wrongs done to the poor. There is no denunciation in the Bible of the oppressing rich more telling than the opening words of his second chapter. And in the age-long struggle of Israel's nobler minds to work out something of that equality between rich and poor which they believed was the will of God Micah played a right manful part.

CHAPTER XVI

THE DEUTERONOMISTS

[*c.* 700–*c.* 500 B.C.]

Midway in the succession of the writing prophets comes a long pause. At its conclusion, when after seventy-five years the youthful Jeremiah had just stepped into the place left vacant by Isaiah, there suddenly appeared in the religious world of Israel an amazing book which brought about a great reform and deeply affected men's thinking about God. We must now interrupt the story of the prophets to consider it.

In the Second Book of the Kings (22:8ff) the story is told of the discovery of "the book of the law" by Hilkiah the priest while repairs were being made in the temple at the command of king Josiah. It was brought to the king and read before him. The effect it produced upon him was profound. He rent his clothes and immediately sent to "inquire of Yahweh" concerning the book, for it proclaimed "great wrath" against him and his people because their fathers had disobeyed its precepts. The messengers went to a prophetess named Huldah, who confirmed the words of the book by an oracle of judgment against Israel. A special oracle addressed to the king, however, assured him that because his heart had been tender towards the words of the book the threatened evil would not come in his days. Josiah then gathered the whole population in the temple area and "read in their ears all the words of the book of the covenant which was found in the house of Yahweh. And the king stood by the pillar, and made a covenant before Yahweh, to walk after Yahweh, and to keep his commandments, and his testimonies, and his statutes, with all his heart and with all his soul, to confirm the words of this covenant that were written in this book: and all the people stood to the covenant" (23:1ff). Thereupon he instituted a most sweeping reform of the worship system of the nation.

What was this book whose discovery had such a profound effect?

Almost unanimously scholars reply: The bulk of our present *Book of Deuteronomy*. The main reason for thinking so is that the details of the reform described correspond almost exactly with the teaching of Deuteronomy, and the story of its discovery is also cast in its own peculiar style.

This theory has prevailed since De Wette first put it forth in 1805. Some fifteen years ago it was sharply challenged from two sides. In 1924 the Scotch scholar Adam Welch [1] maintained that the code of Deuteronomy arose in northern Israel in the early days of the monarchy, as a result of a movement to purify the people from the worship of the baalim. Its aim, Welch held, was not to centralize worship in one place but to confine it to the Yahweh sanctuaries.

Two years earlier Gustav Hölscher [2] argued that Deuteronomy is a product of the post-exilic period. It was produced (not before 500 B.C.) by "the same priestly circles which later showed themselves hostile to Nehemiah." Its laws were quite impracticable and were never really put into operation. It represented therefore a priestly ideal, not an actual program.

Both these attacks on the usual dating of Deuteronomy aroused much controversy [3] but neither has to this time won the support of any large number of scholars. It is better to say, therefore, that the original part of Deuteronomy was the book on which Josiah's reform was based. If so, whence did it come? It purports to be three addresses delivered by Moses to the Israelites on the plains of Moab at the end of his life, together with a body of laws proceeding from him. Why should it be discovered in 621 B.C. six hundred years after Moses' death?

---

[1] *The Code of Deuteronomy,* 1924. Oestreicher (*Das deuteronomische Grundgesetz,* 1923) and Staerk (*Das Problem des Deuteronomiums, etc.* 1924) also advocated an early date. Welch has continued to uphold his theory in two additional works (*Deuteronomy. The Framework to the Code,* 1932; *Post-Exilic Judaism,* 1935). See Barton, "Old Testament Studies" in *HS,* p. 54f).

[2] "Komposition und Ursprung des Deuteronomiums," *ZATW,* XL, 1922, p. 161-255. Similar but less radical views had already been expressed by Berry ("The Code found in the Temple," *JBL,* XXXIX, 1929, p. 44ff) and Kennett (*Deuteronomy and the Decalogue,* 1920). Hölscher's thesis was supported by Horst ("Die Anfänge des Propheten Jeremia," *ZATW,* XLI, 1923, p. 94ff; and "Die Kultusreform des Königs Josia," *ZDMG,* LXXVII, 1923, p. 220ff). See Barton *ibid.*

[3] The controversy up to 1928 is well summed up in a symposium on the "Problem of Deuteronomy," containing articles by Bewer, Paton and Dahl, in the *JBL* (XLVII, 1928, p. 305ff).

The last difficulty is soon cleared away by the proofs advanced by scholars that Moses is not its author.[4]   But who did write it? No certain answer can be given.   In its original form it must have been the work of a remarkable man imbued with prophetic spirit and yet at the same time intent on the purity of worship.   His aim was to purge Israel of foreign rites and to centralize all its worship in one place; but he had also a deeper and more spiritual purpose, to imbue the people's whole life with love towards God. He had made himself master of a prose style whose expressions and cadences gave his writing a beauty quite distinct in the Old Testament.   When and where he wrote we do not know; and what he expected to come of his book, what public he hoped to find, is likewise hidden from us.   Suffice it to say that sometime, somewhere in Israel in the days before 621 B.C. he had composed his matchless work: that it came to be in the temple, where Hilkiah discovered it.

We have spoken as if the author were one man; and doubtless a single creative mind put its stamp upon the book.   But he may have associated with him during his work others of like attitude who soon learned to catch his way of speaking; and in any case additions were made to his book later by men who had learned to write in his style and see with his eyes.   It is because it is so hard to distinguish the work of the first author from that of his "school" that we prefer to group him and his followers together in our study.

The Sources

Scholars generally believe that the book found in the temple contained the central code of laws, Deut. 12–26 and 28.   Many think also that this was from the first preceded by an introductory address, Deut. 4:44–11:32.   The address with which the present book begins, Deut. 1:1–4:43, is universally regarded as a later addition to the original book.   Chapters 29–30, which give a third address of Moses, and chapter 27 are also looked on as secondary Deuteronomic material (D²).   Chapter 31:1-8 and 9-13 (the latter seeming to contain the end of the original code) are probably part of the first book.   The rest of chapter 31 is divided between D² and JE.   The two poems (32:1–43; 33:2–29) are not Deuteronomic, and the rest of the book is pieced together from J, E and P, with perhaps a dash of D².

The Deuteronomic parts of the present book, whether primary

---

[4] For these proofs the reader is referred to any Old Testament Introduction.

or secondary, make upon the reader a unified impression. They breathe throughout one spirit and reflect a pretty consistent view of God and His relations to Israel. We shall therefore use them in our study without discrimination. The central code is of course not Deuteronomic in the sense that the Deuteronomists composed it, for it is largely made up of laws taken from the E code. But the fact that the writers took over these laws, and indeed in some cases modified them, or even added yet other laws not contained in E, shows that the central code must reflect the ideas of the Deuteronomists.

The one thing that we can study in the case of the Deuteronomists is their religious ideas and to these let us now proceed.

Their Lofty and Spiritual Monotheism

"Hear, O Israel: Yahweh our God, Yahweh is one." These words which for more than two thousand years have constituted the creed of Israel were first uttered by the Deuteronomists. Scholars are divided as to the sense in which they were originally meant. Some think that by the one-ness of Yahweh was intended a contrast with the popular idea that the Yahweh of a particular shrine was somehow a different being from the Yahweh of another; as more ignorant Roman Catholics today distinguish between the Virgin of Lourdes and the Virgin of Pompeii, attributing to each a special kind of power. Others believe that the word "one" signifies "unique"; Yahweh is the one and one only. The latter view seems more probable; but in any case there can be little doubt that the Deuteronomists had arrived at a conscious monotheism. "Yahweh, he is God, there is none else beside him" (4:35). "To Yahweh belongeth heaven and the heaven of heavens, the earth and all that therein is" (10:14).

We do indeed meet sayings which on their face seem to reflect the more primitive view that other deities, while subordinate to Yahweh, still have a claim to existence. The expression "other gods" occurs several times (13:2, 6, 13; 18:20; cf. 12:2; 17:3) but this cannot be pressed to mean that the writer took it seriously. In 10:17 Yahweh is called "God of gods, Lord of lords, the great God"; but here too the language implies no real belief that other gods exist. Somewhat different is the declaration (4:19) that Yahweh had allotted the "host of heaven . . . unto all the peoples under the whole heaven." We shall consider later the ethical aspect of this thought, which certainly presents a difficulty. For the present we need only ask whether it conflicts with monotheism, and again our answer must be—No. In all these places the writers are merely using inherited expressions from which nothing can be inferred with any confidence. And it should be added that even if they did look upon the deities of other nations as entities they could still think monotheistically provided they subordinated them enough; just as the New Testament has its angels and demons without infringing on the prerogatives of God. That is what we find in the Song of Moses (32:17); "they sacrificed unto demons (*shedhîm*), which were no God."

This one God the Deuteronomists clothed with sublime and awesome attributes. He is great (3:24; 7:21; 10:17), strong (3:24), terrible (7:21; 10:17); a devouring fire (4:24); to hear His voice out of the fire brings death (4:33). Of course, J and E had said as much. But on one point Deuteronomy transcends them; it revolts against physical anthropomorphisms. "Take ye good heed unto yourselves; for ye saw no manner of form on the day that Yahweh spake unto you in Horeb . . . only ye heard a voice" (4:12, 15). Did the Deuteronomists mean that Yahweh *had* no form? If so, they were going beyond Amos, Isaiah, and Jeremiah, all of whom had visions involving some concept of physical shape. The question is an interesting one. Probably they were merely stressing the fact that Yahweh had not chosen to appear to Israel visibly. But even so they were striking a spiritual note. The practical lesson they drew was that images should not be used in worship.

If Yahweh is the only God He ought (we should say) to be regarded as the God of all men. But like many other thinkers of the Old Testament the Deuteronomists failed to draw this conclusion. For them He remained a national deity. They looked on Him as concerned with Israel mainly; one might almost say, with Israel alone. We shall speak presently of His attitude towards non-Israelites, as they viewed it. Meanwhile however it will be necessary to bear in mind that what is now to be said of Yahweh and His relations with men refers to Him as the God of Israel, dealing with His covenant people. For the Deuteronomists seem to limit their interest to the Israelite.

They Make Love the Central Thing in God's Nature

The vulgar misapprehension that the God of the Old Testament is not a loving God is signally disproved by a careful reading of

Deuteronomy. The Deuteronomists saw in the history of Israel evidence of a divine love. Nowhere in the Old Testament is this familiar idea more beautifully expressed. It was undeserved love that led Yahweh to choose Israel in Egypt. There He intervened to save them, brought them out of their bitter bondage with a mighty hand and an outstretched arm, led them through the wilderness, feeding them with bread that they knew not, suffering all their evil ways, and led them into the good land of Canaan, freely bestowing upon them all its wealth, giving them victory over the inhabitants and standing ready even in the writer's own day to pour blessings upon them. All this was summed up in the covenant that Yahweh had made with them at Horeb, where He undertook to be their God. Here again the Deuteronomists were but repeating in their eloquent way what the Yahwist and Elohist had said before them. But they added the idea of education: Yahweh humbled Israel and suffered him to hunger and fed him with manna

"that he might make thee know that man doth not live by bread alone, but by every thing that proceedeth out of the mouth of Yahweh doth man live. . . . And thou shalt consider in thine heart that, as a man chasteneth his son, so Yahweh thy God chasteneth thee" (8:3ff).

Like their predecessors the Deuteronomists found a special proof of Yahweh's love in the knowledge that He gave Israel of His will. This was imparted through prophets and through laws. Moses was the first prophet and he was able to promise that Yahweh would raise up after him a succession of men empowered to speak authoritatively for God (18:15ff). Of course such intermediaries need not have been necessary. Yahweh, it is implied, would have been willing to speak to the people direct. But they themselves had shrunk from this and it was in answer to their entreaty that He had provided a substitute (5:23ff). Evidently the Deuteronomists thought highly of the prophets and supported them with all their influence. God would require it, they said, at the hand of the man who disobeyed what a prophet uttered in His name (18:19). But what they stressed most was the law. It belongs with the prophetic word because it was given through Moses, but seems to differ from it in that its promulgation had ceased with him. There it stood, once for all delivered, final, perfect. And what a law it was! "What great nation is there, that hath statutes and ordinances so righteous as all this law, which I set before you this day?" (4:8). In the Deuteronomists, with their constant and loving emphasis upon commandments, testimonies, statutes, ordinances, we meet for the first time those enthusiasts for the law that were to stamp their mark upon the piety of later Israel.

The Yahweh who revealed Himself in this law was indeed a God to whom man's heart might well go out in adoration. For He does love people; not only the nation, but its men and women severally. One cannot read the humanitarian provisions that lie in rich profusion upon the pages of Deuteronomy without realizing this fact. Nor does His love stop with human beings; He cares for birds and oxen and even trees.

In return for His tenderness to Israel Yahweh asks an answering affection on man's part. Israel is His holy people (7:6) whom He would have completely devoted to Him. The Deuteronomists were resolutely set to combat any semblance of disloyalty. All that went along with the worship of other gods they abominated. There is no need to dwell upon this.

Then too Israel was to obey Yahweh's laws; that was the practical evidence of affection for Him. The Deuteronomists wanted something more from men than that they should refrain from idolatry and keep the commandments. They aspired to call forth in the human heart nothing less than a passion for God personally. That was to be the central motive of life. "Thou shalt love Yahweh thy God with all thy heart and with all thy soul and with all thy might" (6:5).

No one seems to have said just that until they said it. We have met in the earlier prophets certain great utterances that approach it, but none of these employ the word "love" of man's feelings towards God. They may indeed *imply* it, especially where Hosea is speaking; but the Deuteronomists first expressed it. And so while Jesus quoted Hosea it was in Deuteronomy that he found his great commandment.

Yahweh's Nature Is Ethical, Requiring Ethical Conduct in Men

None of the prophets ever insisted more eloquently on the ethical side of religion than did these Deuteronomists. Their book is crowded with sayings and laws setting forth in generalizations and in searching details their conception of the character of Yahweh and its consequent demands upon Israel. It was the *righteousness* of His law that called forth their devotion (4:8). He is forever against filial impiety (5:16; 27:16; 21:18ff), murder (5:17; 19:11ff), adultery (5:18), sacred prostitution (23:17), theft (5:19), dishonesty (25:13), false witness (5:20; 19:15ff). A rebellious son is to be stoned; he who removes landmarks, or smites another in secret, or takes reward to kill an innocent person, is cursed (27:17ff); he who kidnaps an Israelite shall die (24:7). Lost animals are to be returned to their rightful owners—a significant extension of the eighth commandment (22:1ff). The Deuteronomists dwelt much on the *justice* of God, who "regardeth not persons, nor taketh reward" (10:17). High and low, rich and poor, all stand on an equality before Him. Men must deal in the same way with one another. "Ye shall not respect persons in judgment, ye shall hear the small and the great alike"—so Moses charges the judges he has appointed. "Ye shall not be afraid of the face of man; for the judgment is God's" (1:17). Yahweh is especially interested in those who cannot protect themselves from unfair dealings— the fatherless, the widow, and the alien (10:18; 27:19; 24:17). He commands that the wage-earner, be he Israelite or alien, get his pay when his day's work is over (24:15). Justice must be done to the son of an unloved wife (21:15ff) and to a wife of whom one has grown tired (22:13ff).

It is in the domain of love that we should expect to find the chief ethical contribution of the Deuteronomists, and we are not disappointed. A fellow-Israelite who needs a loan is to be charged no interest (23:19; cf. Exod. 22:25 and Lev. 25:35-37); and at the end of seven years the creditor is to release the debt (15:1ff). This latter provision is peculiar to the Deuteronomists, who add characteristically: "Beware that there be not a base thought in thy heart saying, The seventh year . . . is at hand . . . , and thou give him nought, and he cry to Yahweh and it be sin unto thee. . . . For the poor will never cease out of the land" (15:7ff). They also endeavoured to mitigate the hardships laid upon the debtor in the matter of pledges. "No man shall take the mill or upper millstone to pledge, for he taketh a man's life to pledge. . . . If he be a poor man, thou shalt not sleep with his pledge; thou shalt surely restore to him the pledge when the sun goeth down, that he may sleep in his garment and bless thee. . . . Thou shalt not take the widow's raiment to pledge (24;6, 12f, 17; cf. Exod. 22:26-27). Of these prescriptions the first and third are found only in Deuteronomy.

The poor were further provided for in such commands as that to leave a forgotten sheaf in the field for the gleaner and not to make a thorough job of gathering olives or grapes (24:19ff; cf. Lev. 19:9f); or that to share one's feast of first-fruits and tithes (26:11; 14:27) with the needy, and to include in one's festival dinners the Levite, the sojourner, the fatherless and the widow (16:11). Every third year the whole tithe was to be given outright to these, nothing being consumed by the owner (26:12ff).

The Deuteronomists were interested also in servants. They repeated the law of the Book of the Covenant requiring the release of Hebrew slaves every seventh year (Exod. 21:2–6; Lev. 25:39–43) adding a provision that is peculiarly in their own vein:

"And when thou lettest him go free, thou shalt not let him go empty: thou shalt furnish him liberally out of thy flock, and out of thy threshing-floor, and out of thy wine press. . . . And thou shalt remember that thou wast a bondman in the land of Egypt, and Yahweh thy God redeemed thee; therefore I command thee this thing today" (15:12ff).

This harmonizes with their conclusion of the fourth commandment: the Israelite is to keep the sabbath "that thy man-servant and thy maid-servant may rest as well as thou. And thou shalt remember that thou wast a servant in the land of Egypt" (5:14f). One is reminded also of their use of the same thought in dealing with the alien; "Love the sojourner, for ye were sojourners in the land of Egypt" (10:19). A runaway slave was not to be delivered to his master. The man to whom he came for protection was to keep him safe in his own household, letting him choose his own place and taking no advantage of his helplessness (23:15).

But the Deuteronomists went even further than these humanitarian prescriptions; they included in their book laws that reflect nothing short of what we might call the *considerateness* of God. A certain delicacy of feeling was to be observed in dealing with one's fellows.

"When thou dost lend thy neighbour any manner of loan, thou shalt not go into his house to fetch his pledge. Thou shalt stand without, and the man to whom thou dost lend shall bring forth the pledge without unto thee" (24:10).

And there is a beautiful little passage in which they ordained that before a battle certain classes of men were to be released from the army—those who had built a new house, or planted a vineyard, or betrothed a wife and not taken her; that they might not be killed before they had a real taste of their new hopes and joys! A fourth group was included—any man that was "fearful and faint-hearted," but the motive here was different: "lest his brethren's heart melt in his heart." One is reminded of Gideon's proclamation on mount Gilead (20:1ff; cf. Jud. 7:3).

We must conclude our list of the beneficent laws with a few that reach out to protect other things than man. "Thou shalt not muzzle the ox when it treadeth out the grain" (25:4). If one find a bird's nest with the young birds or eggs in it he may take these but he must let the mother-bird go free (22:6–7). In besieging a city the Israelitish army must spare the fruit-trees. This was partly for motives of prudence ("for thou mayest eat of them"), but it also sprang from a feeling that such destruction was unjust to the trees. "Is the tree of the field man, that it should be besieged of thee?" (20:19f). He who wrote such a sentiment knew what it was to love a tree.

We have cited enough passages to show that the Deuteronomists fell not a whit short of the prophets in their belief that God is ethical and desires to see a human society in which people shall deal with one another kindly, truly, and justly. Indeed, the Book of Deuteronomy far outstrips the prophets in the way in which it works out great moral principles in practical detail. The same may be said of the relation of the Deuteronomic code to those found in Exodus and Leviticus; it coincides with these in its use of some of their finest prescriptions, but it is continually inserting contributions of its own which set it in a class by itself. Driver was certainly right in pronouncing the book unique in its ethical as well as its religious tone. "Nowhere else in the Old Testament do we breathe such an atmosphere of generous devotion to God and of large-hearted benevolence towards man; and nowhere else is it shown with the same fulness of detail how these principles may be made to permeate the entire life of the community." [1]

Yahweh is also Concerned with Matters of Worship and Ritual

Here the Deuteronomists parted company with the prophets, who treated sacrifice and ritual ordinances as subordinate if not negligible. To their mind these things were just as important as ethics. One of the central features of their book is the law of the one sanctuary. Moses is represented as directing that after the Israelites reach Canaan they are to make all their sacrifices and offerings

[1] *Introduction to the Literature of the Old Testament,* p. 79.

in "the place that Yahweh shall choose from all their tribes," i.e. Jerusalem (12:5). There He will put His name and it shall be His habitation. "And thither ye shall bring your burnt-offerings and your sacrifices, and your tithes, and the heave-offering of your hand, and your vows, and your free-will offerings, and the firstlings of your herd and of your flock" (12:6). This was indeed a chief feature of the reformation described in II Ki. 22–23, the impulse to which was given by the newly discovered book of law.[1] Men who insisted so strongly on a provision such as this must have believed that the way in which worship was conducted mattered supremely.

The worship at this central sanctuary was to be punctuated by three great festivals—Passover, Weeks, and Tabernacles—when all males were required to appear before Yahweh in Jerusalem and make their offerings (16). These were to be characterized by feasting and enjoyment. Indeed, the Deuteronomists preserved the ancient idea that worship was to be a happy sociable matter when people made merry with food and drink and the pleasures of companionship, in which the poor were invited to share. This was equally true of the occasions when people went up to the temple between the feasts to bring their tithes or first-fruits or sacrifices of one sort and another; each visit was to be marked by a good time. They wanted worship to be associated with the pleasant moments of life and the temple to become dear through such memories and anticipations.

A corollary of the demand that all sacrifice of animals take place in Jerusalem was the permission (new with the Deuteronomists) to slaughter non-religiously, so to speak, at home (12:20ff). Only the butcher must be careful that the blood was poured out on the ground!

The Deuteronomists were interested to direct the ordinary Israelite in the conduct of his worship. Their book, as has often been pointed out, is no manual for priests but a hand-book of duties for the common man. They told him that he must present only unblemished victims for sacrifice (17:1). They showed him how he must do his tithing (14:22ff; 26:12ff); they gave him a beautiful little office to say when he brought his first-fruits to God (26:3ff). They urged him to take care of the Levites who had no portion of their own but were dependent on the offerings and gifts of the laity (12:19 and elsewhere). The share of these Levite priests in each sacrifice and offering was strictly defined (18:3ff);

[1] Usually identified with the core of Deuteronomy.

and it was further provided that a country Levite coming to Jerusalem was to be admitted to an equal share in the ministrations and the emoluments of the temple clergy (18:6-8). Perhaps this last may have been intended for the admonition of the Jerusalem clergy rather than of the laity; but if so it failed of effect, for the narrative of II Ki. 23:9 tells us that the priests of the high places—the country Levites—did not succeed in establishing themselves in the ranks of the temple clergy.

But it was not only the worship of the temple in which Yahweh was interested. He also insisted upon the people abstaining from "unclean" food, the list of prohibited meats being accurately set forth (14:3ff). The military camp must be kept scrupulously free from ritual defilement (23:9ff). The village that had been the scene of a murder by unknown hands must purge itself by breaking the neck of a heifer (21:1ff). The body of a criminal should not be permitted to remain impaled overnight, lest the land be defiled (21:22f). Leprosy involved ceremonial uncleanness (24:8). Chapters 23 and 24 present a strange mixture in which side by side with noble ethical precepts are found deposits of old taboos and superstitions belonging to the ritual sphere; such as that a man should not sow his vineyard with two kinds of seed, or wear a garment made of mingled linen and wool!

It was this very mingling of ethical and ritual commandments that was destined to characterize the piety of later Judaism. Thus the Deuteronomists proved more successful than the prophets, for Israel retained the ceremonial along with the moral and put both on the same footing. It is only in our age that liberal Judaism has returned to the bold freedom of the prophets and ventured to discard the primitive taboos and rigid ceremonies which have been binding orthodoxy for more than two thousand years.

Yahweh Administers Material Rewards and Punishments

The Deuteronomists held a hard and fast doctrine of retribution, tempered only by a saving belief in the possibility of divine forgiveness. For the nation and the individual alike it was true that what a man sowed that he should also reap. This had its good side, as appeared in their repudiation of the older doctrine that the sins of the fathers ought to be visited on the children. "Every man," they said, "shall be put to death for his own sin" (24:16). But they carried it very far and put it on a decidedly material plane.

Deuteronomy is a book of threats and promises, of curses and blessings. Its writers were constantly holding before Israel the consequences for good or evil that their conduct would bring upon them (4:26; 6:1ff; 7:12ff; 11:26ff; 28:1ff, 15ff; 29:18ff; 30:1ff).

The threats reveal a sinister side of the religion of the Deuteronomists which is strongly at war with the beautiful temper of love exhibited in their ethical idealism. These men were capable of fanatical cruelty in their demands for punishment upon persons who disobeyed Yahweh. Towards idolatry in any form they show no mercy. He who leads others astray in this matter is to be denounced even by his nearest relatives and exterminated (13:6ff). A disobedient and rebellious son is to be punished with death (21:18ff). Adultery is to be punished with death (22:22). A false witness is to be visited with the identical injury that he had intended to bring upon his victim. "Thine eye shall have no pity; life shall go for life, tooth for tooth, hand for hand, foot for foot" (19:21).

Such prescriptions of human penalties however must not be confused with a doctrine of divine retribution. They are mentioned here only to show the temper of the writers when they get into the domain of penalties. The same relentlessness characterized their idea of God's dealings with the sinful. In chapter 28 we find a long and detailed enumeration of the woes that God will bring upon a disobedient Israel.

But it is not the relentlessness of the divine justice that should be emphasized, bad as that is. Still worse is the *material nature* of the penalties involved. All of them have to do with money, possessions, health and honour, which are laid in ruins. Not one touches the spiritual nature of man. Remorse is not mentioned, nor the loss of God's presence, nor the cessation of His word. Only the coarsest fears are used to cow the people into obedience, none that could elevate or arouse nobler emotions.

It is almost the same when the Deuteronomists spread before men the rewards to be expected from serving God. We should expect them to dwell upon the inner happiness of peace with Yahweh, the pleasures of living with Him, of loving Him and being loved in return. They were surely capable of feeling these. But they talked instead of full barns and prolific cattle, of money and children and vanquished enemies (28:7ff).

Of course the prophets had been doing much the same thing when they pictured the woes of foreign invasion and of famine and pestilence, holding out hopes of safety and deliverance through a return to God. But one feels a different *tone* in such prophetic utterances. The material element is not played up, does not stand out so crassly; it never loses its sacramental character of being somehow a vehicle of spiritual realities more weighty than itself. One does not read in the prophets such promises as "Thou shalt lend unto many nations and shalt not borrow. And Yahweh will make thee the head and not the tail" (28:12-13). The Deuteronomists undeniably held out to their countrymen an idea of the profit of piety that savoured of worldliness. Godliness, they said in effect, is a way of gain. Doubtless they spoke here to the rank and file of Israel; that was what the people wanted of religion. But they left an evil legacy against which nobler minds would ever revolt.

Their Lack of Universalism

In reading the pages of Deuteronomy one looks in vain for any of the interest in foreign nations which distinguishes Amos and Jeremiah. God is pictured as caring little or nothing about them. He has no plan for them, does not trouble Himself to govern them, does not crave their worship. He is content to have allotted to them the host of heaven for their devotion (4:19). They figure only as a setting for the history of Israel. If they can contribute to Israel's good they may be tolerated as inferiors, but if they threaten to lead Israel astray they must be summarily exterminated (20:10ff). To the latter class belonged the Canaanites and all other foreigners who lived close by. Towards these the Deuteronomists cultivated a spirit of intense aversion. They dinned into Israel's ears the assertion that these had no right to be living at all; had Israel done its duty they would have been put out of existence long ago! Any adoption of their ways in religion would incur Yahweh's wrath (12:30f). Mixed marriages were specially condemned. "Thy daughter shalt thou not give unto his son, nor his daughter shalt thou take unto thy son. For he will turn away thy son from following me" (7:3-4).

To the Deuteronomists Yahweh was still a War-God. The military camp was holy ground where He was accustomed to walk, and those engaged in warfare were consecrated to Him (23:9ff). The right of conquest was unquestioningly assumed. Yahweh had given Israel a land that was not theirs,

"great and goodly cities, which thou buildedst not, and houses full of all good things, which thou filledst not, and cisterns hewn out, which thou hewedst not, vineyards and olive trees which thou plantedst not" (6:10-11).

It was He who had driven out the Canaanite before them (9:1ff).
He had made Sihon's heart obstinate that he might engage the
Israelites in battle and be delivered into their hand (2:30). He
had forced and delighted in the *herem,* the terrible ban by which
a conquered people were devoted to wholesale destruction (20:16).
The old antagonism towards the Amalekites was perpetuated. "Remember what Amalek did unto thee. . . . Therefore shalt thou
blot out the remembrance of Amalek from under heaven; thou
shalt not forget it" (25:17ff; cf. Exod. 17:8–16). A like ferocity
was prescribed towards the neighbours across the Jordan, the
Moabites and Ammonites: "Thou shalt not seek their peace nor
their prosperity all thy days for ever . . . because they met thee not
with bread and water and because they hired Balaam to curse
thee." Members of these national groups were to be refused ad-
mission to "the assembly of Yahweh" to the tenth generation
(23:1ff).

It is only fair to say that here and there mitigations of this harsh
attitude may be seen. A captive woman was to be treated with
gentleness and consideration (21:10ff). It was recalled that Yahweh
had forbidden the Israelites to attack Edom and Moab on the
march from Kadesh (2:1ff). And perhaps one may see a certain
uneasy questioning as to the morality of the conquest expressing
itself in the theory now first expounded by the Deuteronomists,
that Yahweh drove out the Canaanites because of their wickedness
(9:5). Then too the foreigner who had come into the midst of
Israel as a resident alien relying on the protection of Yahweh became thereby a peculiar object of His care. We have seen the tenderness which the Deuteronomists enjoined in the treatment of the
sojourner.

On the whole however the candid student must admit that the
Deuteronomists threw their influence on the side of a narrow and
bigoted nationalism. The effect of their work must have been to
sharpen the antagonism of the Israelitish people towards their neighbours. Doubtless this had its advantages; perhaps it was the only
way in which the faith of Yahweh could be kept pure and vital.
Certainly we find Ezra and Nehemiah following the Deuteronomists' lead with a right good will. But on the other hand their
book had nothing to contribute to a certain catholicity of outlook
which had been growing in the prophets and was destined to bear
its most perfect flower in Second Isaiah's picture of the Suffering
Servant.

Their Interest in Education

Deuteronomy is the first book of the Old Testament to treat explicitly a matter that was later to assume a place of first importance in Israel: the education of the young in religion. We can be sure that this had not been neglected during the previous ages. The Yahwist had already recorded a traditional command that the story of Israel's deliverance from Egypt was to be repeated to the children at the passover (Exod. 13:14). It stands to reason that this was not an isolated practice. The boys and girls of Israel must have been told the stories of their nation's past and have been inducted in due time into their ceremonial duties as members of Yahweh's people. The ethical precepts embodied in the earlier laws would have been taught them also and many a fragment of religious poetry would have found lodgment in their memory. Probably music had a place in their training and they acquired the ability to "sing unto Yahweh" along with their elders. The very festivals themselves, each with its rich meaning, would have proved educational forces of no small value. Whether there were schools or not is another question; it is likely that in more primitive times the teaching was done by parents or servants.

But of all this effort scarcely an echo remains in the surviving literature. In fact, the books that we have been studying thus far are concerned entirely with adults; children are mentioned only incidentally as part of the adult world. The boy Samuel is a signal exception, but even in his case the narrator was interested in him less as a child than as the prophet that was to be.

The Deuteronomists mark a change. Their eyes were continually resting upon the children; they realized how important they were for the future of Israel. Not that they loved childhood itself. They have nothing to say of the qualities which endear it to the adult heart. Doubtless they were not insensible to these but their thought was all given to something else, the generations yet to be, whose fate lay in children's hands. What they inculcated was the duty of parents to teach their children. No professional teachers seem to be mentioned.

The education prescribed was of the simple transmissive type. What Yahweh had done for Israel, His statutes and ordinances, were to be the unfailing theme of conversation.

"These words which I command thee this day shall be upon thy heart; and thou shalt teach them diligently unto thy children, and shalt talk of them when thou sittest in thy house, and when thou walkest by the way, and when thou liest down, and when thou risest up" (6:6–7).

Thus it was to be done generation after generation. The Deuteronomists were very far from the idea of some modern people that education should foster scepticism and a re-examination of inherited ideas. They did not want their children to think, in this sense. But they did want them to know, to meditate, to remember, to obey and to love; to grow into the kind of men and women who would enjoy talking about God. It cannot be denied that they prescribed a good method for this end. But they did more; they created an atmosphere in which that method could function happily. They suffused their book with a glow of devotion which could warm both teachers and pupils. Centuries later the boy Jesus must have learned to love it; at any rate the man Jesus turned to it unerringly for the truths that he needed in his hour of temptation.

What the Deuteronomists Did for Israel's Religion

The first thing that the Deuteronomists effected was the famous reform of king Josiah. It unquestionably had a great influence in the direction of regularizing and purifying Israel's worship, as well as centring it in Jerusalem. Ezekiel followed much along the lines laid down by them in sketching his worship of the future, although he did not accept their contention that *all* the Levite priests should find a place in the service of the temple. After him the leaders of the early post-exilic church were devoted to the ideals of Deuteronomy for better or worse. The law that Nehemiah tried to enforce seems to have been the Deuteronomic code. Their influence in this field was simply incalculable.

In another field also they moulded the thought of Israel, for the Deuteronomists became the great compilers and editors of the nation's history. For the books of Judges and I and II Kings they supplied the framework and marshalled all facts in the light of their philosophy of history; and they gave something of their colour to the books of Joshua and I and II Samuel. Nor did they refrain from touching up the works of the prophets. Thus they taught Israel to see the past through their eyes.

In the spiritual domain their best contribution was their insistence on the love of God for man and man's duty to love God, his fellow-man and the very beasts and birds. Here they chimed in with Hosea so markedly that some scholars incline to associate that prophet with their work. Jeremiah also sympathized with them; and indeed the publication of their book seems in general to have had a deep influence on his thought as well as on his style.

Looked at in the large, their legacy to Israel was of mixed value. Their book contains some of the loftiest and most spiritual teachings of the Old Testament combined with survivals of the tribal-God idea and a worldly, materialistic temper that exhibits Israel's religion at its worst. It fostered both love and hate, spirituality and worldliness, great-hearted beneficence and fanatical nationalism. It was sublimely ethical and at the same moment intensely in earnest about ceremonial. Perhaps it was this very mixture that made it such a power, for human nature is mixed.

For Bible readers today who will "take forth the precious from the vile" it stands, as it stood for Jesus, among the chief of those Hebrew classics which can bring the soul to God and guide it in the paths of righteousness.

Chapter XVII

JEREMIAH

[prophesied 626–c. 585 B.C.]

The Sources

Jeremiah is twice mentioned in II Chronicles and his writings are cited several times in later books of the Bible; but the only real source for our study of him is to be found in the book that bears his name. It contains two classes of passages which are in the highest degree reliable: (1) prophecies of Jeremiah, probably dictated by himself, (2) narratives concerning him, generally attributed to his friend and scribe Baruch.

Both these classes of material however need to be separated from sections added to the book by later editors. All scholars agree that the Book of Jeremiah contains a certain number of such accretions. The difficulty is to define them. Scholars differ sharply in their conclusions. At the radical extreme we find Duhm, who assigns to Jeremiah only about sixty very short prophetic poems and to Baruch about 200 verses, thus rejecting nearly two-thirds of the book.[1] A conservative like Driver, on the other hand, accepts nearly everything as either Jeremiah's or Baruch's. Between these two extremes range the majority of critics, who unite in condemning Duhm's method and yet reject pretty freely on their own account.

Any designation of non-genuine passages therefore will have to be regarded as more or less tentative. It would be well to divide them into two groups:

1. Passages generally agreed to be later additions: 10:1–16; 17:19–27; 50:1–51:58; 52.

2. Passages held by several scholars to be non-Jeremianic: 3:14–15, 17–18; 16:14–15; 17:12–13; 25:12, 14, 24–38; 30:1–11, 18–23; 31:7–14, 23–30, 35–40; 32:1–5, 17–23, 28–35; 33:1–3, 10–26; 39:1–13; parts of 46; 48; 49.

[1] *Das Buch Jeremia* (Tübingen, 1901), p. xviff.

We can set over against these the passages usually assigned to Baruch's memoirs: 19; 20:1-6; 21:1-10; 26; 28; 29; 34-38; 39:14-18; 40-45.

The remainder of the book would then proceed from Jeremiah himself.

Any such division of the book will of course be unsatisfactory in two ways. It will ignore the many small units—verses or parts of verses—which are questioned in the midst of passages deemed genuine on the whole. It will also fail to note a number of passages which might fairly be called disputed, since some authors of weight reject them. But as a rough and ready guide it will answer our purpose.

In our study of Jeremiah we shall seek our information only from the two latter classes of material: Baruch's memoirs and Jeremiah's oracles. These however are so rich and colourful and supply so many intimate and graphic details regarding the prophet that we know more about Jeremiah than about any other man of the Old Testament, except perhaps David; and the accounts of David fall short of this Jeremianic material in that they present him from the outside, while Jeremiah's inward thoughts lie as open to us as his public words and acts.

Jeremiah's Ministry Coincided with Great Events

Nearly three-quarters of a century separated the work of Jeremiah from that of Isaiah. The latter lived to see Jerusalem spared according to his prediction; but this did not mean release from the Assyrian yoke. Far from it! Hezekiah's successor Manasseh, who came to the throne in 698 B.C., was compelled to pursue a policy of absolute subservience to the great over-lord. It was indeed in Manasseh's long reign of nearly fifty-five years that the empire on the Tigris rose to the pinnacle of its power, subduing Egypt and crushing all revolts from Babylon to Thebes. By the time that Jeremiah began his work as prophet a swift decline had set in. We hear in his pages no echo of the terror which Assyria's name had inspired in Isaiah's age. For a brief period a new storm appeared on the northern horizon—hordes of Scythians which threatened to submerge Judah and all the coastal civilization in a flood of barbarism. Then that suddenly receded and the death-struggle of Assyria began. The Chaldeans, a vigorous Semitic people who had entered Babylonia, combined with the Indo-European Medes from the mountains east of the Tigris to close in upon Nineveh.

In its hour of need Assyria found a helper in Psammetichus of
Egypt, who was determined to prevent a new eastern power from
succeeding to the empire of the weakening over-lord. But the
Chaldeans and Medes finally proved the stronger and in 612 B.C.
Nineveh fell.[1] Ashur-uballit, the Assyrian king, escaped westwards
to Harran in upper Mesopotamia, but was driven out of that city
by the Medes two years later, and together with Necho II, successor to Psammetichus, who had come to his aid with reinforce-
ments, was severely defeated. From that day onward Assyrian
power was a thing of the past.

Necho however returned to the struggle. In 608 B.C. he again
marched northward with an army of which Greek mercenaries
formed a considerable part. Josiah, king of Judah, who undertook
to hold northern Israel against him, was defeated and killed, and
the Egyptian host continued on its way into western Mesopotamia.
There Necho seems to have remained in control for some time.
One use he made of his power was to depose the young anti-
Egyptian king Jehoahaz, set up in Jerusalem as Josiah's successor,
and to place upon the throne his older pro-Egyptian brother
Eliakim, changing his name to Jehoiakim (II Ki. 23:31ff).

But Necho's domination of Syria did not remain long uncon-
tested. In 604 B.C. he was met by a Chaldean army under Nebuchadrezzar and utterly routed.[2] The Chaldeans were now masters of
Syria and the road to Egypt. The victorious Nebuchadrezzar advanced to the very border of Egypt, being prevented from invading
it only by the news of the death of the king, his father Nabopo-
lassar. Having returned to Babylon by forced marches he succeeded peacefully to the throne and then proceeded to make good
his hold on the west. In Judah Josiah's son Jehoiakim renewed
the allegiance he had given earlier, renouncing (at least outwardly)
his alliance with Egypt, which had now become active again.
This was in 600 B.C. Three years later he once more rebelled, and
Nebuchadrezzar moved against Jerusalem. It was saved by the
surrender of Jehoiachin, who had meanwhile succeeded his father
Jehoiakim. This boy-king was deported to Babylonia with his
queen mother, the members of his court, the princes, 7000 of the
best soldiers and a thousand skilled mechanics, leaving behind only
the "poorest people of the land" (II Ki. 24:1ff). On the empty
throne Nebuchadrezzar placed Mattaniah, the twenty-one year old

[1] The prophet Nahum celebrates this fall with grim elation, describing it in
what are perhaps the finest word-pictures to be found in the Old Testament.
[2] For a vivid contemporary description of this rout see Jer. 46.

brother of Jehoiakim, changing his name to Zedekiah. For a while the puppet king remained loyal, but in 590 B.C. the Egyptian Pharaoh Psammetichus II invaded Palestine and its little peoples were stirred up to revolt. Urged by emissaries from his neighbours Zedekiah joined in the insurrection, and in 588 B.C. Nebuchadrezzar appeared and invested Jerusalem. It held out for two years and fell in 586 B.C. Its walls were then broken down, its temple and great houses burned, and all but the lowest stratum of the population deported. Zedekiah, who had attempted to escape, was captured and taken to Riblah in the north. There Nebuchadrezzar killed his sons before his eyes, then blinded him and took him in chains to Babylon (II Ki. 24:20ff). The Davidic monarchy, which had occupied the throne of Judah for four hundred years, was extinguished. The history of Judah seemed to have come to its end.[3]

All these changes Jeremiah witnessed, for like Isaiah he continued forty years as prophet. How different was his last outlook from that of Isaiah! Gone were capital and kingdom and the best of the people, while he himself was hurried unwilling into Egypt by the only considerable group of survivors, there to die.[4]

So much for the course of external history. Meantime, within the tiny nation where, unnoticed by the rest of mankind, the future of the world's supreme religion was being prepared, things of great religious significance had taken place.

First came a popular reaction under Manasseh which swept away Hezekiah's reforms and brought back the Canaanitish ways of the past. Manasseh himself took the lead in reintroducing the cult practised on the high places, with its altars to the baalim, its asherim and all the accompaniments of nature religion. But he went further. Desiring to flatter his Assyrian masters he brought in also the worship of the heavenly bodies prevalent in Nineveh and Babylon, especially that of Ishtar, the "queen of heaven," which speedily became a favourite among the people. The cruel rite of child sacrifice he likewise sponsored, offering up his own son; and this too suited the mood of his subjects. Along with these ritual practices came in the use of augury, necromancy and those other means of controlling destiny which the higher minds in Israel had always condemned and yet had never been able to extirpate (II Ki. 21:1-18).

[3] For an excellent account of these political movements see Olmstead, *HPS*, p. 505ff.
[4] See p. 318.

This went on during Manasseh's reign and that of Amon his son. It prevailed also for the first part of Josiah's time—in all about seventy years. They were years of fundamental misery—the state weak, liberty gone, social relations unhappy. But superficially Manasseh's policy of subjection to Assyria worked for peace and gave the pursuits of ordinary life a chance to go on. Business may well have prospered through the increasing contacts with the wider world opened up by Assyrian domination. On looking back from the agony and prostration succeeding Judah's last hours many saw Manasseh's reign invested with the glamour of a lost prosperity. "Then we had plenty of bread and were well and saw no evil" (Jer. 44:17). Certainly this king had the crowd with him. Those who protested against the turn which religion had taken were ruthlessly silenced. Such at least is the inference naturally drawn from the words of the Deuteronomic historian, who tells us that "Manasseh shed innocent blood very much, till he had filled Jerusalem from one end to the other" (II Ki. 21:16).

But all the while among certain of the priests and prophets and the circles attached to them a suppressed antagonism had been nourished and at last this part of the community found themselves strong enough to effect a sweeping reform. The story is told in II Kings 22 and 23. A book which most scholars identify with the core of the present Book of Deuteronomy having been found in the temple, the young king Josiah proceeded to put its prescriptions into effect. Worship was cleansed of its foreign accretions and centralized in the Jerusalem temple. The noble ethical and social requirements of the new law were held up as an ideal. Much of this was superficial, but Josiah and the promoters of the reform felt they had a right to claim Yahweh's favour for their repentance. Probably Josiah was buoyed up by such confidence when in 608 B.C. he ventured to oppose the northward march of Necho on the plain of Esdraelon.[5]

Josiah's humiliation and death must have dealt the reform movement a serious blow. It is evident that a religious reaction set in which brought back many previous abuses, chief among them the worship of the "queen of heaven" (Ishtar) and child-sacrifice (Jer. 7:18, 31). That king Jehoiakim was in sympathy with the

[5] See p. 302. It has been held by some scholars that Josiah went to Megiddo, on the plain of Esdraelon, not to oppose Necho but in obedience to a summons from his Egyptian over-lord; and that he was there put to death as a punishment for suspected pro-Babylonian intrigues. See T. H. Robinson, *HI*, I, p. 424.

reaction may be gathered from the comment of the Deuteronomic historian: "he did that which was evil in the sight of Yahweh, according to all that his fathers had done" (II Ki. 23:37). After his death and the deportation of the better elements of the people to Babylonia in 597 B.C., matters seem to have gone from bad to worse; that is, if we may trust the picture of Jerusalem's religious practices drawn by Ezekiel (Ezek. 8:1ff; 16:20ff). When finally the Chaldeans burned the temple a man like Jeremiah was justified in feeling grim satisfaction as its roof crashed in. No other fate befitted the mongrel and degenerate religion of Jerusalem.

Of Jeremiah's antecedents nothing is known but what is recorded in the title of his book (1:1). He was the son of one Hilkiah, "of the priests that were in 'Anāthôth." 'Anāthôth was a village situated some three miles north-east of Jerusalem on a hill over-looking the Jordan valley and the Dead Sea.[6] Hither Solomon at the beginning of his reign had banished the priest Abiathar, who had taken part in Adonijah's conspiracy and escaped the death penalty only because of his association with David's early struggles. He settled down in "his own fields" (I Ki. 2:26f) and doubtless acted as priest in the local high place. The priestly family to which Jeremiah belonged may well have claimed descent from this illustrious ancestor.

The young Jeremiah, who seems to have been of warm sympathetic nature, probably grew up as a normal boy in the midst of these priestly surroundings. His family must have possessed some means for Jeremiah was able later to give his whole time to prophesying, and at the end of his life had cash enough to pay outright for a field belonging to the family estate, which he purchased from his uncle's son (32:6ff).

But the pleasant sociable village life which he shared and enjoyed did not prevent the growing boy from thinking upon the wickedness of his people and of all the surrounding nations. If we may judge from his later self-revelation, he had a heart intensely sensitive to divine influences, and the stirrings of conscience would not allow him to feel at home in the world as did his relatives and neighbours. He had read the words of the great

[6] Not on the site of the modern 'Anâta (Blair, *BASOR*, No. 62, p. 18ff). Alt suggested the modern Râs el-Kharrûbeh, about 800 meters SSW of 'Anâta (*Palästinajahrbuch*, XXII, p. 23f), but Bergman who examined the site with Blair in November, 1936, found himself unconvinced (*BASOR*, No. 62, p. 22ff). He argues for el-'Îsâwîyeh (*ibid.* No. 63, p. 22f). Albright however favours Râs el-Kharrûbeh (*ibid.* No. 62, p. 25f, No. 63, p. 23).

prophets before him and had come to look through their clear
suffering eyes upon man's evil and God's disappointment. Add
to this a sense which he must have had from his earliest years that
he was somehow set apart by God for His own ends, and one
sees how he had been made ready for the hour when Yahweh
spoke to him.

Jeremiah's Call

The story of Jeremiah's call (1:4ff) comes from his own lips and
is one of the most intimate, self-revealing documents in all literature. In it we can see the man and his character, as well as his
conception of his whole work.

"The word of Yahweh came unto me, saying,
Before I formed thee in the belly I knew thee,
And before thou camest forth out of the womb I sanctified thee."

There one gets his belief in his personal predestination, his sense
that he himself matters infinitely to God.

"I have appointed thee a prophet unto the nations."

That shows his international outlook.

"Then said I, Ah, Lord Yahweh! behold I know not how to speak;
for I am a child.

Such was his modest, shrinking, tenderly sensitive nature.

"But Yahweh said unto me,
Say not, I am a child;
For to whomsoever I shall send thee thou shalt go,
And whatsoever I shall command thee thou shalt speak."

Thus God had His way with Jeremiah, overriding the hesitations
so congenial to his disposition.

"Be not afraid because of them;
For I am with thee to deliver thee."

Here was the secret of this timid prophet's invincible courage.

"Then Yahweh put forth his hand and touched my mouth; and
Yahweh said unto me, Behold, I have put my words in thy mouth."

Again the intimate relationship between him and God. Here no seraphic intermediary, as with Isaiah, cleanses his lips with a coal from the altar while the ineffable majesty of deity remains high and lifted up above the scene; it is simple, direct, personal, Yahweh and Jeremiah face to face.

> "See, I have this day set thee
> Over the nations and over the kingdoms,"

What a place is accorded the prophet; over, as God is over, the world!

> "To pluck up, and to break down,
> And to destroy, and to overthrow,
> To build, and to plant."

The prophet is to be no mere announcer, he is rather God's agent who by the "word" *accomplishes* what he foretells, whether good or bad. And he is given both kinds of work to do, first tearing down, then building up. His prophecies show him engaged in both activities.

There follow in the narrative two visions, one to show that God is "awake" over His word to perform it—the note of immediacy, God about to act; the other to proclaim that God's action will take the form of bringing in a terrible invader from the north. Probably in 626 B.C. Jeremiah understood this of the Scythians, later of the Babylonians; but it was always from the north that he looked for the boiling cauldron to overflow, never from the south, from Egypt. And he never left off predicting that it *would* overflow.

The call concludes with a characteristic note:

> "And I have made thee this day a fortified city,
> And an iron pillar, and a brazen wall,
> Against the whole land,
> Against the kings of Judah and against the princes thereof,
> And against the people of the land."

Yes, Jeremiah was always "against" them all. At least so it seemed, though in reality no one was so much "for" them as he, had they been able to realize it.

> "And they shall fight against thee,
> But they shall not prevail against thee."

No more did they, though at times it seemed as if he must be overwhelmed.

"For I am with thee, saith Yahweh, to deliver thee."

Again the secret of his strength, the refrain that will echo throughout his life.

It must have been soon after his call or in conjunction with it that Jeremiah received a word of Yahweh which seriously affected his personal life. Hosea had been commanded to marry a prostitute (Hos. 1:2); but Jeremiah was forbidden to marry at all.

"Thou shalt not take thee a wife, neither shalt thou have sons or daughters in this place. For thus saith Yahweh concerning the sons and daughters that are born in this place . . . They shall die grievous deaths: they shall not be lamented, neither shall they be buried; they shall be as dung upon the face of the ground, and they shall be consumed by the sword, and by famine; and their dead bodies shall be food for the birds of the heavens, and for the beasts of the field."

The young prophet then must pass his days without a home, that he might be (as other prophets before him) a living sign of the impending doom which rendered all homes meaningless. But this was not all. Ordinary kindly intercourse with neighbours and friends must be shunned. He dare not be a sympathetic guest either in the house of mourning or in the house of feasting. For Yahweh had taken away His peace from this people, and the prophet as Yahweh's representative must not live in peace with them (16:1ff).

Heavy indeed was the duty of isolation thus laid upon the sociable and very human Jeremiah, but he assumed it sternly and fulfilled it. Like Hosea however he could not stop with such a sign, arresting though it might be. He must also proclaim the word of Yahweh by mouth.

The Sin of Judah Called for its Destruction

There was nothing new in the announcement of doom which Jeremiah uttered. He himself understood that in pronouncing it he was only bringing himself into line with the true prophets who had gone before him (28:8f). Nor did the moral condition of Judah in his day differ from that which Isaiah and Micah had seen around them a century earlier. But to Jeremiah both judgment and sin were horribly real and fresh. There was nothing second-hand in his handling of them; and his emphases were his own.

To begin with the sin. Like his forerunners Jeremiah saw it against the background of God's love. God had been very tender to Israel in the old days, delivering it from Egypt, bringing it into the good land of Canaan. He had planted it there "a noble vine, wholly a right seed." He would have continued to protect it against all its enemies. In fact, there was nothing in all God's dealings with Israel of which the people could later complain.

At first Israel had responded to God's love. Like Hosea, Jeremiah looked back upon the wilderness sojourn as a time of loyalty to Yahweh.

> "I remember thee for the kindness of thy youth,
> The love of thine espousals;
> How thou wentest after me in the wilderness,
> In a land that was not sown" (2:2).

But all too soon the noble vine had become degenerate. Israel forgot Yahweh and left Him for the baalim. Alone among the nations it had changed its gods! And what a change!

> "They have forsaken me, the fountain of living waters,
> And hewed themselves out cisterns, broken cisterns,
> That can hold no water" (2:13).

To the worship of the baalim was added the Assyrian cult of the heavenly bodies.

> "In the cities of Judah and in the streets of Jerusalem the children gather wood, and the fathers kindle the fire, and the women knead the dough, to make cakes for the queen of heaven" (7:18).

It was an affair of the whole family! More sinister than this, child-sacrifice was going on.

> "They have built the high places of Topheth, which is in the valley of the sons of Hinnom, to burn their sons and their daughters in the fire; which I commanded not, neither came it into my mind" (7:31).

Along with these unfaithfulnesses went the old disloyalty of seeking foreign alliances.

> "What hast thou to do in the way to Egypt,
> To drink the waters of the Nile?
> Or what hast thou to do in the way to Assyria,
> To drink the waters of the River?" (2:18).

All this had its ethical consequences. The life of the people seethed with every kind of anti-social conduct. There is no bitterer indictment in all the prophetic writings than Jeremiah's denunciation of Jerusalem in chapter 5.

> "Run ye to and fro through the streets of Jerusalem, and
>   see now, and know,
> And seek in the broad places thereof, if ye can find a man,
> If there be any that doeth justly, that seeketh truth;
> And I will pardon her" (5:1).

But no, among poor and rich, common people, nobles, priests and prophets not one good man could be found.

> "No one repenteth him of his wickedness,
> Saying, What have I done?
> Every one turneth away in his course,
> As a horse that rusheth headlong in the battle" (8:6).

Black indeed was the array of charges brought by the prophet against Israel: adultery, harlotry, injustice, greed, slander, deceit, treachery. The last three of these sins seem to have tortured Jeremiah most of all. Utterly sincere himself, he attributed the same honesty to Yahweh.

> "O Yahweh, do not thine eyes look upon truth?" (5:3).

But Jeremiah saw none of it about him.

> "Take ye heed, every one of his neighbour,
> And trust ye not in any brother;
> For every brother will be an utter Jacob,
> And every neighbour will go about with slanders. . . .
> Thy habitation is in the midst of deceit;
> Through deceit they refuse to know me,
> Saith Yahweh" (9:4,6).

Yet in spite of all this riot of wickedness the public conscience remained untroubled. Again and again Jeremiah cried out against the shamelessness of the people, their unwillingness to admit their wrong-doing. He refused indeed to believe that they could engage in the degrading rites of idolatry without a sense of uneasiness (2:26). But their words were always stout enough. Guilt they absolutely denied. Overtaken by any trouble they would importune Yahweh to save them as if their standing with Him had remained unimpaired (2:27). They never doubted that He would preserve their temple inviolate (7:4).

Yahweh was nearing the end of His patience. Generation after generation He had tried to win the people back. He had sent the prophets, rising up early and sending. He had brought calamities in the hope that they might cause reflection. All in vain. And so we find through Jeremiah's prophecies the note of doom prevailing.

Not indeed entirely. The hope would not down that even now Israel might repent. No prophet uttered more impassioned pleadings for national conversion than this man who is popularly associated with denunciation and woe.

"If thou wilt return, O Israel, said Yahweh,
 If thou wilt return unto me,
 And if thou wilt put away thine abominations out of my sight;
 Then shalt thou not be removed" (4:1).

These words belong to the beginning of his ministry. But even at the end, when so much had been lost beyond recall, he still held out promises that obedience would save *something* from the ruin.

In the main however his thought was that Israel was past repentance: the Ethiopian could not change his skin nor the leopard his spots (13:23). God's wrath therefore could no longer be restrained.

"Shall I not visit for these things, saith Yahweh;
 Shall not my soul be avenged on such a nation as this?" (5:29).

And the punishment when it came would be unsparing. Jerusalem and its temple must go.

"I will do unto the house which is called by my name, wherein ye trust, and unto the place which I gave to you and to your fathers, as I did to Shiloh. And I will cast you out of my sight, as I have cast out your brethren, even the whole seed of Ephraim" (7:14f).

Here Jeremiah ranged himself on the side of Micah and squarely rejected the teaching of Isaiah regarding Jerusalem's inviolability. He could see nothing but its sins.

"Go ye up upon her walls, and destroy, and make an end;
Take away her branches; for they are not Yahweh's" (5:10).

"This is the city to be visited;
She is wholly oppression in the midst of her" (6:6).

Such was Jeremiah's message until the end came.

Jeremiah Against the Whole Land

We have seen in the story of Jeremiah's call that he felt himself destined to oppose his fellow-countrymen. They in turn would "fight against" him—kings, princes, priests, people. There was nothing new in that. Amos had experienced it at the hands of Amaziah. Isaiah was constantly opposed. But in Jeremiah the conflict stands out in unparalleled sharpness. This is partly because we know so much more of his personal trials, partly also because he seems to have been more conscious of the rôle that he was filling. But whatever the reason, the tragedy involved in the struggle was supreme.

It is easy to account for the situation. Both his accusations and his threats roused the anger of people who had a high idea of themselves and their future. We must remember also that according to the view of the time predictions of evil coming from a prophet had a destructive force of their own. Jeremiah believed this intensely. The "word" proceeding from his mouth was like fire, like a hammer that broke the rock in pieces (23:29). He felt that he was "full of the wrath of God" which he would presently "pour out upon the children in the street, and upon the assembly of the young men together" (6:11). He was God's trier who burned out the base metal from the genuine (6:27). His symbolic acts, such as wearing a yoke (27:2; 28:10) or breaking a bottle (19:10f), were looked on as especially potent for ill. Jeremiah certainly thought of himself as an *agent* in Yahweh's work of destruction. In his call he was empowered to cast down and to

destroy, not merely to announce these processes. People therefore
had reason to regard him as an active enemy. And they repaid
his hostility with interest.

The sad irony of the case lay in the fact that Jeremiah's disposition seems to have been companionable and friendly. The last
thing he wanted was to be solitary, much less hated. His message
of doom was none of his own choosing; he had not desired the
woeful day (17:16). In fact, he interceded for the people (11:14;
18:20; 37:3). Much would he have preferred to cry "Peace, peace"
and to hear "Peace" in reply. Instead, he encountered scoffing from
people who refused to credit his threats.

> "I am become a laughing stock all the day,
> Every one mocketh me.
> The word of Yahweh is made to me
> A reproach and a derision all the day" (20:7f).

On all sides he heard imprecations.

> "Woe is me, my mother, that thou hast borne me
> A man of strife and contention to the whole earth!" (15:10).

Nor did his foes stop at ridicule and malediction. In the first
enthusiasm of the Deuteronomic reform the young Jeremiah at
Yahweh's command urged the people to support it (11:1ff). This
he seems to have done not only in Jerusalem but also in the walled
villages ("cities") of the countryside, visiting one after another
for the purpose. By so doing he must have aroused much ill will
among the conservative elements secretly opposed to the reform,
especially the local priests whose high places it was abolishing.
Possibly this helped to infuriate against him the people of his
native village, even his own relatives joining in the outcry behind
his back. The discovery of their treachery was indeed a heavy
blow to Jeremiah, for he had felt secure at home.

It was apparently some years later that he first clashed with
the authorities. In the presence of a group of leading men whom
he had called together for the purpose in the valley of Hinnom
te the south of Jerusalem he solemnly proclaimed Yahweh's sentence of destruction and confirmed the message by breaking before
their eyes an earthen bottle symbolizing the people and the city.
The hostility thus roused presently burst forth when he came up
to the temple court and repeated his words. The priest in charge
of the temple, Pashhur the son of Immer, struck him and put him

in the stocks over night. Jeremiah did not take this indignity lightly, and on his release next morning pronounced a bitter personal sentence from Yahweh upon his persecutor (19:14–20:6).

In the beginning of Jehoiakim's reign a much more serious attack was made upon him. Again standing in the temple court (perhaps on some special day which drew crowds from all the countryside) he ridiculed the people's confidence that the temple of Yahweh would always stand firm. Let them repent and cease to make this place which was called by Yahweh's name a den of robbers! Because of their wickedness God would destroy it as He had destroyed the former sanctuary of Shiloh; and He would cast out into exile the people of Judah as He had already cast out their brethren, the whole seed of Ephraim (7:1ff; cf. 26:1ff).

At the utterance of these destructive words Jeremiah's hearers—priests, prophets and all the people—rushed upon him and seized him. He must die! But the princes of Judah, hearing the uproar from the adjacent "king's house," came up to intervene. Taking their seats of office they listened to the charge brought by the priests and the prophets, the people now relapsing into neutral silence.

"This man deserveth a sentence of death; for he hath prophesied against the city."

Then Jeremiah made his reply to the princes and the people.

"Yahweh sent me to prophesy against this house and against this city all the words that ye have heard. . . . As for me, behold, I am in your hand: do with me as is good and right in your eyes. Only know ye for certain that, if ye put me to death, ye will bring innocent blood upon yourselves, and upon this city, and upon the inhabitants thereof; for of a truth Yahweh hath sent me unto you to speak all these words in your ears."

It was a crucial moment. But the princes saw the truth in Jeremiah's plea and gave their decision, the people concurring.

"This man doth not deserve a sentence of death; for he hath spoken unto us in the name of Yahweh our God."

They supported their decision "before all the assembly of the people" by citing the precedent of Micah, who a hundred years before had likewise predicted the downfall of city and temple.

Hezekiah, the then reigning king, had not put him to death but had repented, thus averting the threatened doom.

So it was settled that Jeremiah had the right to do the same. Yet every one knew that it was only the influence of the powerful Ahikam, one of the princes, which had saved him; for a humbler prophet who followed Jeremiah's example, Uriah the son of She-maiah of Kiriath-jearim, actually did meet death at the hands, not of the priests, prophets and people, but of the vindictive king Jehoiakim himself (26:8ff).

Jeremiah's position was not rendered any more secure by a denunciation which he uttered against Jehoiakim some time during his reign. It was a fearless and outspoken indictment of the unlaw-ful way in which that king had used the forced labour of his subjects (Jeremiah calls them his "neighbours") in building an am-bitious royal house; and it ended with the declaration that he would die unlamented, being "buried with the burial of an ass" (22:13ff). Though this never came true the prediction was left unchanged in the published prophecies, an indication of the honesty of the author.

The final clash between Jeremiah and Jehoiakim came in 603 B.C. A year earlier the prophet had at Yahweh's command dictated to Baruch his scribe all the oracles which he had uttered since his call twenty-two years before. The work seems to have consumed much time, for it was not till the ninth month of the succeeding year that use was made of it. Jeremiah for some unknown reason was restrained from entering the temple; but when a specially proclaimed fast had brought multitudes into the temple courts he sent Baruch to read the roll "in the ears of all the people." Con-sternation followed and the princes intervened a second time, bidding Jeremiah and Baruch hide themselves while the roll was taken to the king. His reception of it was contemptuous. The scene still lives for us: the king sitting in the winter-house, warming himself at a charcoal fire; his princes standing about him; one Jehud reading the roll aloud; Jehoiakim interrupting him after every three or four columns to slash off what had been read with a penknife and toss it into the brazier; three of the princes pleading with him not to burn it, the rest looking on in silence—till, when it was all consumed, a sharp order was given for the arrest of Baruch and Jeremiah. Both eluded arrest and Jehoiakim does not seem to have pressed the matter further. But Jeremiah was not silenced. Commanded once more by Yahweh he dictated another roll containing all that the first had contained and in addition "many like words." This was the basis of our present Book of Jeremiah (36).

Among Jeremiah's most ferocious opponents stood the prophets of prosperity. Always they were contradicting his gloomy words with the brightest of promises.

"They say continually unto them that despise me,
  Yahweh hath said, Ye shall have peace;
And to every one that walketh in the stubbornness of his own
    heart they say,
No evil shall come upon you" (23:17).

Probably these men were sincere. They did but carry on the old tradition of nationalistic prophecy sponsored by Deborah, Samuel and Elisha, not realizing that its day was past. They felt also that their inspiration was as valid as Jeremiah's—indeed, more valid. But we can comprehend the passion with which Jeremiah asserted that they had not "stood in the council of Yahweh," that He had "sent them not, neither spoken to them" (23:18, 21). He accused them also of downright wickedness, adultery, fraud, venality, collusion with the priests, stealing their words from one another. The classic instance of conflict between these men and Jeremiah was his encounter with Hananiah narrated in chapter 28.

It took place in the fourth year of Zedekiah (549-3 B.C.) when the weakened remnant of Judah were brooding over the blow inflicted by Nebuchadrezzar in the first deportation (597 B.C.). For some time Jeremiah had been going about wearing a wooden yoke symbolizing the necessity of submission to the Chaldean overlord. This gave great offence to many, and particularly to the popular prophets whose convictions all ran the other way. On a certain day one of their number, Hananiah, met Jeremiah in the temple court and in the presence of the priests and all the people challenged him by asserting in the name of Yahweh that within two full years the vessels taken to Babylon would be restored to the temple, and king Jehoiachin and all the other captives brought back. Caught unawares Jeremiah could only say Amen. Might Yahweh do so! At the same time he warned Hananiah that in thus predicting "peace" he was going against the uniform precedent of the former prophets, all of whom had foretold doom. Therefore the burden of proof lay upon him, and only the fulfilment of his encouraging message would entitle him to credit. In derision Hananiah caught the yoke from off Jeremiah's neck and broke it, saying that thus within two full years Yahweh would break the yoke of Nebuchadrezzar from off the neck of all the nations.

Jeremiah retired unconvinced, and soon a word of Yahweh came to him. Hananiah had broken the bars of wood, but he had made in their stead bars of iron. Because he was making the people to "trust in a lie" Yahweh would send him away from off the face of the earth.

"This year thou shalt die, because thou hast spoken rebellion against Yahweh."

A curt notice adds that he died in the seventh month.

It was not however till Zedekiah's ill-advised rebellion had at last brought the Chaldean army about the doomed city that the hostility against Jeremiah blazed out in its full intensity. Now that his dark predictions had been fulfilled and the hopes inspired by rival prophets had collapsed, one would have expected credit to be given Jeremiah for having received true "words" of Yahweh. The contrary was the case. When he continued to declare that resistance to Babylon was futile, the princes—inferior successors to the princes now in exile, who had taken his part—were hotly incensed against him. Jeremiah on his part finally went so far as to advise desertion to the Chaldeans as the sole way of saving one's life (21:8ff).

At length the prophet's call to repentance seemed to make some impression on the distracted king and people. In the hope of gaining Yahweh's favour at the last moment Zedekiah made a covenant with all the people to release their Hebrew servants who were being kept in slavery contrary to the Deuteronomic law. This was solemnly ratified, "the princes of Judah, and the princes of Jerusalem, the eunuchs, the priests, and all the people of the land" passing between the halves of a calf which had been cut in two. The slaves in question were thereupon released.

But an unexpected event changed the whole situation. Hearing that the Egyptians were advancing, the Chaldean army suddenly raised the siege of Jerusalem and marched away. The first result was that the owners of the released slaves at once brought them back into servitude again. This called forth from Jeremiah a bitter oracle predicting Yahweh's punishment of the offenders (34:8ff). A second effect was the discrediting of Jeremiah and the feeling that he could now be safely dealt with. As he was leaving the city to collect his share of the family income at Anathoth he was summarily arrested on the charge of deserting to the Chaldeans. He was beaten and in spite of his vehement denials was thrust into prison in the "house of the pit" belonging to Jonathan the scribe—a place so bad that the aged prophet realized that he could not long survive there.

Giving heed to his supplication Zedekiah later transferred him to the "court of the guard" where he could be properly taken care of. But here further trouble broke out. Jeremiah apparently continued to advise desertion to the Chaldeans and the princes resolved to get rid of him. They went to the king with what was in effect a peremptory demand:

"Let this man, we pray thee, be put to death; forasmuch as he weakeneth the hands of the men of war that remain in the city, and the hands of all the people, in speaking such words unto them: for this man seeketh not the welfare of this people, but their hurt" (38:4).

Zedekiah weakly yielded and Jeremiah was thrown into a pit with a miry bottom, to die there of starvation. It was only by the energetic intervention of an Ethiopian servant of the king that he was rescued and brought back to the court of the guard, where he was sustained till the city fell (38:7ff).

Then he was released and kindly treated by the Chaldeans. But he had yet other conflicts before him. The pitiful remnant of people left in Palestine were put under a Jewish governor Gedaliah, a man of high character. To him Jeremiah, who had taken advantage of the conqueror's permission to remain in the land, attached himself and supported his effort to build up again the prostrate national life. Things went well till Gedaliah was murdered, perhaps because of jealousy, by a man of the royal family. Completely discouraged and fearing the Chaldeans' vengeance the people turned their faces toward Egypt as a refuge. Jeremiah was appealed to for a word from Yahweh, and after ten days he uttered it. They were to remain in Palestine and trust in Yahweh. But every one had already decided to go to Egypt, and they turned fiercely on the prophet, accusing him of falsifying the word of Yahweh at the instigation of Baruch. Into Egypt they went, taking with them both Baruch and Jeremiah (42:1–43:7).

There they settled on the eastern edge of the Delta, some going as far south as Thebes. Whether from the influence of their polytheistic surroundings or not, they gave themselves over with one

consent to the worship of the "queen of heaven" which had prevailed so widely in Palestine. And so once more the prophet
of Yahweh was compelled to take up the people's challenge. On
some occasion when both men and women were gathered together
he denounced this idolatry, declaring that it had been the cause
of the disaster which had overtaken the nation, and demanding
in Yahweh's name that it cease. He met with a unanimous refusal. The worship of Ishtar, the people replied, so far from
causing disaster, had brought prosperity in the good old days of
Manasseh. It was the outlawing of this worship by the Deuteronomic reform, and not its practice, that had marked the
beginning of all the nation's troubles.

"As for the word that thou hast spoken to us in the name of
Yahweh, we will not hearken unto thee. But we will certainly
perform every word that is gone out of our mouths, to burn incense
unto the queen of heaven, and to pour out drink offerings unto her,
as we have done, we and our fathers, our kings and our princes,
in the cities of Judah, and in the streets of Jerusalem."

Standing alone against them all Jeremiah hurled back his last
recorded oracle.

"Ye and your wives have both spoken with your mouths and
with your hands have fulfilled it, saying, We will surely perform
our vows that we have vowed, to burn incense to the queen of
heaven, and to pour out drink-offerings unto her: establish then
your vows, and perform your vows! Therefore hear ye the word
of Yahweh, all Judah that dwell in the land of Egypt. Behold,
I have sworn by my great name, saith Yahweh, that my name shall
no more be named in the mouth of any man of Judah in the land
of Egypt. . . . Behold, I watch over them for evil, and not for
good. . . . And all the remnant of Judah, that are gone into the
land of Egypt to sojourn there, shall know whose word shall stand,
mine or theirs" (44).

With this appeal to the verdict of the future the aged prophet
disappears from the stage of history, contending fiercely to the last.

His was a warfare that never ceased. And in all its course we
behold this timid, shrinking, yearning man standing like an "iron
pillar" and a "wall of brass" against the onslaughts of formidable
foes, dashing back every attempt to overwhelm him, uncompromis-

ing, unsilenced, till at last he passes from our view fighting with
undiminished vigour.

What was the secret of such strength? He himself has told us.

Jeremiah was Sustained by his Life with God

"I am with thee, saith Yahweh, to deliver thee."

Such was the promise with which Jeremiah began his ministry,
and he has left us the record of how it was fulfilled. Here we
come to that which is of most value to us in the history of Jeremiah
—his personal religious life. He himself must have written down
from time to time the account of his intercourse with God; or else
have dictated it to Baruch. In the divine providence it has been
preserved to us as perhaps the first Hebrew classic of private devotion.

In it we see that God, by separating Jeremiah from all human
solaces and surrounding him with enemies, had thrown him wholly
upon Himself. The prophet had literally nothing left but God.
To God therefore his burdened soul had recourse in constant
prayer and meditation. These transactions he pictured as dialogues
in which God and he talked freely with one another. Thus he
obtained companionship, relief, encouragement, assurance and all
that he needed in order to go on. In two instances at least we
know how this was done.

The first is contained in chapters 11-12, the original order of
the passage having probably been 12:1-6; 11:18-23. In it we see
that he had been encountering derision. Some particularly flagrant
exhibition of human treachery had called forth his denunciation
and for response he had received ridicule. At any rate, his scorners
had said, we shall outlast him; "he shall not see our latter end"
(12:4). The sting of the words lay in their seeming probability;
for these men were getting along very well and appeared likely
to continue in prosperity. Thus the wound that they inflicted was
aggravated by a doubt of God's just government of the world.

Jeremiah then went to God with his problem.

"Righteous art thou, O Yahweh, when I contend with thee;
Yet would I reason the cause with thee:
Wherefore doth the way of the wicked prosper?
Wherefore are they at ease that deal very treacherously?
Thou art near in their mouth and far from their heart" (12:1f).

Over against their treachery Jeremiah set his own integrity.

> "But thou, O Yahweh, knowest me;
> Thou seest me, and triest my heart towards thee."

What a consciousness of absolute sincerity shines in those words! And what a test of one's purity to be always living in intimacy with God!

Now comes the sufferer's appeal; falling below the Christian ideal, but legitimate enough from Jeremiah's more primitive point of view!

> "Pull them out like sheep for the slaughter,
> And prepare them for the day of slaughter!"

To this impatient cry for vindication God answered:

> "If thou hast run with the footmen and they have wearied thee,
> Then how canst thou contend with horses?
> And if in a land of peace thou fleest,[1]
> Yet how wilt thou do in the jungle of the Jordan?"

It was a stern answer, with no concession in it, not even comfort, but only an iron demand: "Come, let go complaining; *these* enemies are as nothing."

> "For even thy brethren and the house of thy father, even they have dealt treacherously with thee" (12:3ff).

To Jeremiah prayer was evidently no escape from harsh reality; it was a conflict in which the heroic element in his nature conquered self-pity and impatience.

The second instance (15:15-21) shows the same thing. Here again is a prayer for intervention.

> "Thou knowest!
> O Yahweh, remember me, and visit me,
> And avenge me of my persecutors."

Well enough for God to be patient with the wicked, but not at the expense of His servant!

---

[1] Emending the text slightly.

"Take me not away in thy long suffering.
Know that for thy sake I have suffered reproach. . . .
Wilt thou indeed be unto me as a deceitful (brook)?
As waters that fail?"

Once again God replied sternly:

"If thou return, then will I bring thee again,
That thou mayest stand before me;
And if thou take forth the precious from the vile,
Thou shalt be as my mouth."

What Jeremiah needed was to repent, to get rid of this fault-finding; and if he did, then he might—go back to his work! And he would have the strength for it:

"I will make thee unto this people
A fortified brazen wall."

Surely God proved Himself imperious to this man. He was forever ignoring his very human weaknesses and bidding him gird up his loins afresh. He exposed him to the buffetings of hatred, He delayed to make good His own word; and at the same time He peremptorily demanded that Jeremiah trust and obey Him. If for a while Jeremiah refused to speak in His name, then "a burning fire shut up in his bones" compelled him to break silence (20:9). Yahweh was a hard master, one might say.

But Jeremiah did not find Him so. Through struggles like these, through persecutions, loneliness, exhaustion and disappointment Jeremiah tested God and found Him true. Among his complaints and outcries we come upon meditations in which the prophet tells what God is to him:

"O Yahweh, my strength and my stronghold,
And my refuge in the day of affliction,
Unto thee shall the nations come
From the ends of the earth . . ." (16:19).

"Thy words were found, and I did eat them;
And thy words were unto me a joy, and the rejoicing of my
    heart;
For I am called by thy name,
O Yahweh, God of hosts" (15:16).

Jeremiah's International Outlook

As there is but one God, so there is but one divine government for all mankind. This Jeremiah simply assumed. The prophet was set "over the nations" and had a commission to carry out the divine plan upon the whole earth. The hordes of Scythians, the Chaldean armies were but instruments of Yahweh's wide purpose, moving in response to His call (1:15).

That purpose must for the present be punitive. As Jeremiah from his lofty station looked out over mankind he beheld everywhere the same wickedness flaunting itself in the face of God. The picture indeed is blurred; except in the case of Moab (48) he could bring no detailed indictment such as Amos uttered against the peoples surrounding Israel. But of the main fact he was sure. Therefore one fate awaited them all.

"Behold, the days come, saith Yahweh, that I will punish all them that are circumcised in their uncircumcision. . . . For all the nations are uncircumcised and all the house of Israel are uncircumcised in heart" (9:25f).

A cup of the wine of the wrath of God was given into Jeremiah's hand that he might cause all the nations to whom Yahweh sent him to drink it.

"And they shall drink, and reel to and fro, and be mad, because of the word that I will send among them" (25:15f).

And yet they had a chance of escape. It lay in submitting quietly to the Chaldean empire which God had appointed to rule the world. There is a famous scene depicted in Baruch's memoirs illustrating the way in which Jeremiah acted upon this conviction. Early in Zedekiah's reign envoys had come to Jerusalem from the kings of Edom, Moab, Ammon, Tyre and Sidon with the probable intent of persuading Judah to join in a common uprising against Babylon. Suddenly, as they were meeting to discuss this enterprise, Jeremiah appeared before them bent under "bonds and bars" which he had made for his neck, and gave them a charge to carry home.

"Thus saith Yahweh of hosts, the God of Israel, Thus shall ye say to your masters; I have made the earth, the men and the beasts that are upon the face of the earth, by my great power and by my outstretched arm; and I give it unto whom it seemeth right unto me. And now have I given all these lands into the hand of Nebuchadrezzar king of Babylon, my servant. . . . The nation that shall bring their neck under the yoke of the king of Babylon, and serve him, that nation will I let remain in their own land . . . and they shall till it and dwell therein" (27:1ff).

The same advice was given to Zedekiah.

The undeniable friendliness exhibited by Jeremiah towards Nebuchadrezzar strikes one with surprise. It was so different from the hatred which Isaiah felt for Assyria, seeing in that power only the instrument of Yahweh's wrath and exulting over the thought that presently it would itself be broken. Jeremiah on the contrary spoke of Nebuchadrezzar as Yahweh's servant and announced with something very like approval the decree that all were to come under his sway. He did indeed predict that his empire would last only seventy years and that then Babylon would sink to rise no more. But this was uttered without the emotion that accompanied his other prophecies against foreign nations. There is no gainsaying the fact that Jeremiah was what might be called today pro-Babylonian.

Why was this? Our answer can only be that Jeremiah saw in the empire of Nebuchadrezzar a constructive force. True, it was destined by God to work widespread ruin where resisted. But that was only clearing the ground, casting down in order to build. One of the things that had to go was Jewish nationalism. From it Jeremiah had ceased to expect anything. Let it make way for an empire which would order the affairs of the world in discipline and peace!

Now that was a remarkable position for a Jewish prophet to take. Could Jeremiah have had a premonition of the part empires were to play during the coming centuries as developers of civilization? At any rate he was here showing himself a man of the future—a true layer of foundations for structures yet to be.

Small wonder that with such a point of view he came into conflict with the nationalists of his day. We can understand how they regarded him as an enemy of his people. But he was not. He aimed only at Judah's good. He loved his people and his dreams of a greater age to come were confined largely to their part in it. It was not his fault that he helped Nebuchadrezzar's aims and received what must have seemed to most of his fellow-citizens the disgraceful reward of Babylonian favour after the fall of Jerusalem.

And yet there really was in him something which transcended patriotism. His interests were Israel-centred, but they went beyond Israel. To what? It is hard to say. Consciously he does not seem to have been much concerned for the future of mankind as a whole, although sporadic sayings of universalistic import appear in his utterances. One can only feel dimly that he had begun to live in a vaster environment than any of his predecessors. Perhaps it was the domain of the individual.

Building and Planting

We come now to consider the happier side of Jeremiah's work. From the outset he had believed his task to be two-fold, and the first part only a prelude to the second. God's true purpose in the world was creative; destruction came in only as the means to that end.

In building and planting Jeremiah found an activity congenial to his nature. He was at heart a lover of men and he believed God to be the same. That is why all through his prophecies the pleading note kept sounding. If only Israel would give God the chance, what would He not do for them! That was why God had never left off trying to win back His estranged people through the prophets. Israel's doom had now fallen. But that doom only set the prophet free to begin his work of reconstruction—to do what all along his heart had been set upon doing.

Nebuchadrezzar's empire furnished the conditions in which he could hope to build with success. His first enterprise was the future of the Jews deported to Babylon in 598 B.C. In them he set his hope. Contrasted with the worthless remnant still in Palestine they were the basket of "good figs, very good" (24:3). Concerning them he received a word bright with the assurance of divine favour and ultimate restoration, concluding with truly remarkable words:

"And I will give them a heart to know me, that I am Yahweh; and they shall be my people, and I will be their God; for they shall return unto me with their whole heart" (24:4ff).

Later on he addressed to them a letter in which he advised them to settle down in their new home and make themselves a place there, recognizing that Babylon's prosperity meant theirs also. Here he repeated Yahweh's promise to bring them back finally to their own land (29:1ff).

But as the end drew near in Jerusalem he seems to have dropped all distinction between exiles and home-people and to have uttered his conviction of Judah's restoration without limiting it to any one group of the nation. During the last agonies of the siege, when every one else was in despair, it was Jeremiah alone—the prophet of doom—who looked beyond the present blackness to a better day. In his prison he bought his cousin's field at Anathoth and directed Baruch to put the deeds safely away "that they might continue many days."

"For thus saith Yahweh of hosts, the God of Israel; Houses and fields and vineyards shall yet again be bought in this land" (32:6ff).

When once the city had fallen and the wretched train of exiles was leaving on its long bitter march he bade them "set up way-marks" and observe the road carefully, that they might find their way back. It is to this moment that we may perhaps assign the beautiful "restoration prophecies" of chapter 31. Schmidt pictures the train stopping for their first night's halt at Ramah, five miles north of Jerusalem. During the night Jeremiah, who made one of their number, thought he heard the voice of the ancestress of northern Israel wailing from her tomb on a nearby height; and he received a word for her concerning her children that had gone into exile long ago, which embraced in its consolation himself and his fellow-sufferers:

"Refrain thy voice from weeping, and thine eyes from tears;
For thy work shall be rewarded, saith Yahweh;
And they shall come again from the land of the enemy" (31:16).

He was steadfastly looking forward to a day when the scattered captives of north as well as south should be brought home. For like Hosea he believed in the indestructible love of God.

"Thus saith Yahweh,
The people that were left of the sword found favour in the wilderness;
Even Israel, when I went to cause him to rest."

So it had been in the days of Moses and so it would be now.

"Yahweh appeared unto me from afar (saying)
Yea, I have loved thee with an everlasting love:

Therefore have I continued lovingkindness unto thee.
Again I will build thee, and thou shalt be built,
O virgin of Israel . . ." (31:1ff).

Once more, in language that reminds us of Hosea, he hears God say:

"Is Ephraim my dear son? is he a darling child?
For as often as I speak against him, I do earnestly remember
    him still:
Therefore my heart yearneth for him;
I will surely have mercy upon him, saith Yahweh" (31:20).

In all the Old Testament there is nothing tenderer and lovelier
than these restoration prophecies of Jeremiah; and yet in them he
abated not one jot of the stern demand for repentance that he had
been sounding throughout his ministry. For the people of the
future, he perceived, must pass through the gate of penitence.

"I have surely heard Ephraim bemoaning himself (thus),
Thou hast chastised me, and I was chastised,
As a calf unaccustomed to the yoke:
Turn thou me, and I shall be turned;
For thou art my God.
Surely after that I was turned, I repented;
And after that I was instructed, I smote upon my thigh:
I was ashamed and even confounded,
Because I did bear the reproach of my youth" (31:18-19).

It was this necessity for inward conversion that gave rise to
Jeremiah's teaching of the new covenant.

The New Covenant

Yes, Israel must repent. It could not participate in a better order
nor have peace with God until its ethical and religious life under-
went a radical transformation. Hosea and Isaiah had both understood that. Of the two, Hosea seems to have influenced Jeremiah
more, causing him to think of such transformation as inward and
spiritual instead of dwelling, as did Isaiah, upon the outward
alteration of civic life.

Jeremiah's demand had ever been for thoroughgoing conversion
of the inner self. Early in his ministry he had called upon the
men of Judah to "break up their fallow ground and sow not among

thorns"; to "circumcise themselves to Yahweh and take away the
foreskins of their heart" (4:3f). And forty years' experience had
taught him the need for some more radical change in individuals
than had ever yet been seen if God's will was to be done in Israel.
It was for lack of just this that God had hitherto been thwarted in
His dealings with His people.

And so the aged prophet dreamed a great dream.

"Behold, the days come, saith Yahweh, that I will make a new
covenant with the house of Israel, and with the house of Judah. . . .
I will put my law in their inward parts, and in their heart will I
write it: and I will be their God, and they shall be my people:
and they shall teach no more every man his neighbour and every
man his brother, saying, Know Yahweh; for they shall all know
me, from the least of them to the greatest of them, saith Yahweh:
for I will forgive their iniquity, and their sin will I remember no
more" (31:31ff).

Such was the new covenant, which Jeremiah of all Israel's men
of God was the first to conceive. Its notes are five in number:

1. *Inwardness*. Not material blessedness, a changed nature,
plentiful harvests, peace with beasts and men; but something in
the heart, that men should of themselves know and do right.

2. *Fellowship with God*. Again a possession of Jeremiah's own,
for did he not belong to God and God to him?

3. *Immediacy*. Needless for any one to say, Know Yahweh;
intermediaries done away with, priests and prophets no longer
required. How natural for a man who had lived alone with God!

4. *Universality*. They shall *all* know God. The new covenant
would take effect in all without exception. It was to be made
with the house of Israel, and yet in each it would be a personal
sovereign experience, independent of rank and office, the common
man having it as well as the prophet.

5. *Pardon*. Full and final pardon; the sin that had been "written
with a pen of iron and with the point of a diamond" upon hearts
and altars wiped clean forever; life a fresh page whereon to
write better things in a wonderful new day! And sacrifices needed
no longer; for that too seems implied, though Jeremiah says nothing
of it.

This prophecy of the new covenant was one of the sayings which
introduce a fresh era in man's thinking about God. Hereafter it
could not be quite as it had been before these words were spoken.

Not that the ideas they contained were wholly novel. But thus combined and focussed into a single ray they shed an illumination which the world of religion had not hitherto known. They set the norm of expectation for deeply religious souls to which, however long and often it might be forgotten, men must inevitably come back. They were indeed of the nature of a challenge to heaven. Something like this God must some day effect or disappoint mankind.

And they were never superseded. How could they be? There is nothing in the Old Testament more sufficient, more ineluctable and more permanent. Any enduring fellowship between God and man must be built on this foundation or not built at all. Jesus took them over into his thinking and saw them fulfilled in the kingdom that he was initiating. One thing only he added, the thought of the cost: "This cup is the new covenant in my blood" (Lk. 22:20).

Jeremiah the Prophet and the Man

We have now come to the end of our study of Jeremiah. What place shall we accord him in the development of Israel's religion? On this point scholars are fairly well agreed.

Jeremiah was the chief link between the old and the new. He belonged both to the pre-exilic order, in which the nation constituted the unit in religion, and the order now emerging, in which the unit became more and more the individual.

The older order found its consummation in the writing prophets, and Jeremiah was a prophet—some think the greatest of the prophets. He shared the prophets' monotheism, their stern denunciation of national sins, their insistence on obedience rather than sacrifice, their passion for social righteousness, their demand for utter loyalty to Yahweh, for complete trust in Him and in nothing else, their belief that they had received supernatural revelations of God's purpose, their assurance of possessing commission from Him, their sense of responsibility for the people, their prediction of impartial doom, their promise of a blessed future opening out beyond doom for those whom God should deem worthy. As we read his book we know that we are dealing with one who belongs in the company of Amos, Hosea, Micah and Isaiah. Six centuries later, when some people of Galilee saw in Jesus the reincarnation of "one of the prophets," it was Jeremiah to whom their thought went most readily (Mt. 16:14).

And yet he was something else than a prophet. Unlike his forerunners he could not sink his own personality in his message. In this he was perhaps less than they. We cannot but wonder at their power to empty self that God alone might speak through them. To such stern heights of repression Jeremiah failed to rise. The "I" was always breaking through even his public utterances. In reading them we never lose the consciousness that it is *Jeremiah* who is speaking. We may characterize this as a limitation, but we must acknowledge that it gives us something which we do not get in the prophecies of an Isaiah or a Hosea. Behind the voice we feel and touch the man. The heart of his book is undeniably those scenes when he is alone with God, talking about himself, hearing God's answer. More than all the "words of Yahweh" to Israel he left to posterity his life with God.

And what a life with God it was! Even today, with all the succeeding ages of Jewish and Christian devotion for us to draw on, it holds us by its sincerity, its intensity, its surrender, its vigour, its freedom, its intimacy. But the most appealing thing about it is its humanness. The very weaknesses of the man, so simply revealed—his petulance, his timidity, his perplexities, his cries of pain, his calls for vengeance, his desire to give up—bring him close to the common heart. And the way in which he overcame them is what every one knows within himself to be the true way. Here we see the precious being taken from the vile, we watch the very process by which unconquerable resolve is forged in the fires of God. Not all the vile indeed is melted out. Vindictiveness remains to offend the more enlightened conscience of a later day. But those who are large enough to make the necessary allowance can return again and again to Jeremiah's dialogues with God when their own strength runs low.

In all this he belonged to another type of the man of God than the prophet—one destined to play a notable part in Israel and to bequeathe to the world a most precious legacy. Among the psalmists Jeremiah was perhaps the pioneer and the chief.

CHAPTER XVIII

EZEKIEL

[PROPHESIED 592-570 B.C.]

The Sources

Our only knowledge of Ezekiel is drawn from the book that bears his name. It purports to give the utterances of "Ezekiel the priest, the son of Buzi" to whom the word of Yahweh came "in the land of the Chaldaeans by the river Chebar." He states that he was there "among the captives," which must mean those who had been deported along with king Jehoiachin in 597 B.C. (II Ki. 24:10ff). It is to his fellow-exiles therefore that his oracles are ostensibly addressed. They are apparently arranged in chronological order (with few exceptions) and are interspersed with thirteen datings, giving in each case the year, the month and the day, ranging from the first in 592 B.C. to the last in 570 B.C. The first section of the book (1–24) contains repeated threats of the coming destruction of Jerusalem; the second (25–32) is comprised of oracles concerning foreign nations; the third (33–48) tells of the great future awaiting Yahweh's people after the purging of the present.

Until recently most scholars accepted the book as genuine throughout, with perhaps traces of redaction here and there. The usual view was that Ezekiel composed it in Babylonia, and that even the arrangement of the oracles with its precise dating proceeds from his hand. "No critical question arises in connection with the authorship of this book," wrote Driver,[1] "the whole from beginning to end being unmistakably the stamp of a single mind." Even as late as 1933 McFadyen could say: "Corrupt as the text is in many places, we have in Ezekiel the rare satisfaction of studying a carefully elaborated prophecy whose authenticity has, till recently, been practically undisputed. It is not impossible that there are, as Kraetzschmar maintains, occasional doublets, e.g. 2:3–7 and

[1] *ILOT*[9], 1913, p. 279.

3:4-9; but these in any case are very few and hardly affect the question of authenticity." [2]

During the past few years, however, voices have been raised in protest against this almost unanimous view. In 1924 Hölscher [3] maintained that the real Ezekiel, a prophet "standing with both feet on the soil of pre-exilic religion," had uttered only a few brief poems, containing in all 170 verses, the rest of his book having been gradually added by a series of prosaic redactors ending in the fifth century B.C.

A few years later James Smith, [3] a Scotch scholar, advanced the thesis that Ezekiel prophesied both in *northern* Israel and among the Israelitish exiles in *Assyria*, his activity extending from 722 to 669 B.C., thus antedating by more than a century the period usually assigned to it. A redactor later assembled his utterances. About the same time Torrey, [4] writing in America, put forth a still more radical view. The oracles contained in the book of Ezekiel, he declared, were composed as a work of the imagination about 230 B.C. by a man, apparently of priestly rank, residing in Jerusalem, who depicted a prophet of the wicked days of Manasseh inveighing against the corruptions of his time. A later editor introduced the Babylonian setting and altered the original dating to conform to the period of the "captivity." Thus there was really no "Ezekiel" at all! [5]

More moderate is the view sponsored two years later by Herntrich, [6] that Ezekiel prophesied in Jerusalem from 593 to 586 B.C. His prophecies were afterwards given a Babylonian setting by a redactor of the exilic period, who added the final section describing the temple and community of the future (40-48). Oesterley and Robinson in their *Introduction* [7] incline to accept Herntrich's hypothesis and Battersby Harford also endorses it. [8] All of these scholars make much of a difficulty that has long been recognized in interpreting Ezekiel. It is, that while Ezekiel is represented as

[2] *Introduction to the O.T.*, Revised Edition, p. 187. By permission of The Macmillan Company, publishers.

[3] Hölscher, *Hesekiel, der Dichter und das Buch*, Giessen, 1924.

Smith, *The Book of the Prophet Ezekiel*, London, 1931.

[4] *Pseudo-Ezekiel and the Original Prophecy*, New Haven, 1930.

[5] Substantially the same view is upheld by Dahl, "The Crisis in Ezekiel Research," *Quantulacunque: Studies presented to Kirsopp Lake by Pupils, Colleagues and Friends* (London, 1937), p. 265ff.

[6] *Ezechielprobleme*, Giessen, 1932.

[7] *An Introduction to the Books of the O.T.*, N. Y., 1934.

[8] *Studies in the Book of Ezekiel*, Cambridge, 1935.

living in Babylonia his eyes (during the first 24 chapters) are fixed upon Jerusalem, and he speaks of what is taking place there. The usual explanation, that he was gifted with "second sight," they reject as unsatisfactory and insist that his words had no reality unless they were uttered in Palestine.

But these assaults upon the integrity of the book have not convinced several scholars. Spiegel,[9] reviewing Torrey's book in 1931, defends the integrity of Ezekiel as a whole, including the prophet's Babylonian environment. Eissfeldt,[10] though recognizing that the book has been rearranged and touched up by a redactor (especially in 1-3; 8-11; 38-39; 40-48), declares that on the whole it proceeds from Ezekiel. Sellin[11] sponsors substantially the same view. Bertholet[12] maintains the substantial integrity of the book, though allowing for much secondary matter. He feels so keenly, however, that many of Ezekiel's earlier utterances must have been uttered in Judah that he is led to divide the prophet's activity into three periods. The scene of the first period was Jerusalem before its fall; that of the second, some city of Judah not far from the capital (the "other place" of 12:3ff); that of the third, Babylonia, to which he later removed. G. A. Cooke[13] recognizes freely the work of later redactors, but attributes the bulk of the book to Ezekiel himself, and accepts the Babylonian setting as genuine. The only large blocks of material that he regards as secondary are the prophecies concerning Gog of Magog (38:1–39:20) and parts of 40-48, which describe the temple and community of the future, especially 45-48. Here he is more sweeping than Bertholet, who retains most of 45-48 as genuine though he rejects 38:1–39:20. On the other hand, the French scholar Lods[14] seems to accept the great part of the book as Ezekiel's, including even 38:1–39:20 and 45-48.

The tide of criticism, therefore, is returning from the extreme ebb of a few years ago to something like its former level of confidence. Secondary material and rearrangement of genuine portions are indeed recognized, but the book as a whole is believed to be the work of Ezekiel in Babylonia. We are therefore justified in using the bulk of it as a reliable source for our study of the man and his religion. Eissfeldt puts it well: "In spite of the touching

---

[9] "Ezekiel or Pseudo-Ezekiel," *Harvard Theol. Rev.,* Oct. 1931, p. 245ff.
[10] *Einleitung i.d. Alte Testament,* Tübingen, 1934.
[11] *Einleitung i.d. Alte Testament*[7] Leipzig, 1935.
[12] *Hesekiel,* Tübingen, 1936.
[13] *The Book of Ezekiel (ICC),* Edinburgh and N. Y., 1937.
[14] *The Prophets and the Rise of Judaism,* N. Y., 1937.

up by means of spurious elements . . . the book is able to give us
a clear and real (*wirklichkeitsgetreues*) picture of Ezekiel" (p. 426).

Ezekiel's Call

During the middle period of Jeremiah's activity there was growing
up in Jerusalem a boy who was to play a leading part in Israel's
religious future. This was Ezekiel, the son of Buzi, a priest of the
Jerusalem temple. He belonged to the priestly family of the Zado-
kites whom the Deuteronomic reformation had firmly established
as the official hierarchy of the land. Though he never mentions
Jeremiah, the older prophet must have been to him a familiar figure,
and in spite of a radical difference of temper and outlook Ezekiel
must on the whole have sympathized with the lonely man of God,
drinking in his teaching and catching fire from his uncompromising courage.

Then came an abrupt change in his own life. In 597 B.C. the
Chaldeans seized Jerusalem and rounded up the best of its citizens
for deportation. Among these was the young Ezekiel.

So far as we know, he was never to return to his native country.
After the long and exhausting march of three months or more
he settled with his fellow captives in the heart of Babylonia. There
he appears five years later (592 B.C.) living by the "river Chebar,"
or "great river," a wide artificial canal conducting Euphrates water
in a long circuit from the east bank, passing by the ancient city
of Nippur, and returning to the Euphrates again farther down.
Like his fellow Jews of the captivity, he seems to have fared well
enough in outward circumstances. He dwelt with a dearly loved
wife in his furnished house of sun-dried brick, which was large
enough to hold gatherings of the "elders of Israel," and had apparently some leisure at his command. There may have been children
also, but he says nothing of them. In thus living a normal family
life and taking part in social intercourse he was to present a marked
contrast to Jeremiah.

The Jews of the vicinity evidently formed a considerable community. There was at least one town, Tel-abib ("Hill of the Storm-
flood" in Babylonian) where many were settled; and in the later
Book of Ezra we hear of several other "cities" inhabited by Jews.
The impression we get from Ezekiel's prophecies is that they like
himself were fairly comfortable. They were permitted to have their
own clan organization, with elders at its head, to practise their
ancestral religion, to meet freely in houses or to hear a popular

outdoor speaker, and to retain their native Hebrew tongue. This indicates that the policy of the government towards them was enlightened and generous.

All about them throbbed a vast commercial civilization. Trade was the very life of Babylonia, and it had created there a wealth such as they had never witnessed at home. A mixed and teeming population filled the great cities and spread over the countryside. Everywhere was activity. The ancient city of Nippur, not far away, had once been the religious centre of Babylonia for nearly two thousand years. It possessed a large library and a school and, if we may judge from the records of the famous business house of Murashu Sons in the following century, it was also alive with commercial activity. Its stately temple of Enlil, once the supreme deity of Babylonia, maintained a powerful priesthood and imposing ritual. Babylon itself, which some of them may have seen and all had heard of, was unbelievably great, surrounded by almost five miles (8150 metres) of towering walls whose breadth over all was about eighty feet (26 metres), and adorned with palaces and temples passing in magnificence all that they could have imagined.[1] This was indeed the centre of the world. We may well believe that the Jews were quick to avail themselves of its rich opportunities, especially in business, and that some had already begun to accumulate the wealth which was to be at the disposal of the Jewish community in a later generation. It is possible that they may have been aided in establishing themselves by older communities of their fellow-Israelites of the northern kingdom already entrenched in Babylonia; for some of the people transported from Samaria more than a century earlier might well have been settled in the same general neighbourhood.

Stimulating however as were these splendours and activities, tending to throw into shadow all that the Jews had hitherto cherished of culture and religion, the exiled community seems to have remained intensely loyal to their Mosaic heritage. The level Babylonian plain, in spite of its well-irrigated lands, its tree-bordered water-courses, its majestic cities and thriving commerce, had not

[1] There was an outer and an inner wall, the space between them being filled with rubble and levelled on top to make a chariot way. Ninety towers at regular intervals rose from the outer and inner edge of the walls. (L. W. King, *A History of Babylon*, N. Y., 1915.) The length given above is from E. Unger, *Babylon, die heilige Stadt*, etc. (Berlin, 1931), who reports the measurements made by the German Oriental Society. The frontispiece in Unger's book shows Babylon restored, and gives a beautiful picture in colours of a great and stately city.

weaned their hearts from the "mountains of Israel." There all their interest centred and to return thither was all their desire. Both Jeremiah and Ezekiel disclose the fact that such preoccupation with Palestine was taking a sinister form. Among these exiles, as among those left at home, expectancy was running high in the years following the first deportation. Yahweh, it was believed, would soon intervene to break the power of Babylon and bring back the captives with honour and gifts. Here as in Jerusalem self-appointed prophets were stirring up flattering hopes, and we can infer that constant communication was kept up between the home-community and the exiles, fostering a mutual excitement. So intense had the unrest become that the Babylonian police had seized two such prophets as promoters of sedition and had burned them alive (Jer. 29:22).

This was the mental atmosphere in which Ezekiel lived; but he did not share it. Whether because of the influence of Jeremiah or not, he held a deeply pessimistic view of Jerusalem's immediate future. All he could see was that, in spite of the punishment inflicted by Yahweh, Israel had not repented; indeed, its sins were growing worse continually. Nor was his disposition such that he could dismiss this thought lightly. There was in him a vein of sombre brooding, a sense of God's transcendence and awful holiness, an earnestness bordering upon fanaticism, a luxuriant and lurid imagination, which prevented him from forgetting the sin of his people even for a moment.

How long the conflict between his own painful foreboding and the confident hope of his fellow-exiles had been troubling his mind, we can only guess. But at last it reached its climax.[2] On the fifth day of the fourth month of the fifth year of Jehoiachin's captivity (592 B.C.), as he was by the river Chebar, an ecstasy came over him. "The hand of Yahweh was upon him," "the heavens were opened" before his eyes, "and he saw visions of God."

From the north, in a storm cloud pierced by constant flashes of fire, came an apparition which is described in all its weird, complicated details by a mind that loved to elaborate a picture. It was a fourfold living creature combining human with animal faces and parts in the way made familiar to Ezekiel by the hybrid Babylonian statues about him, glittering like burnished bronze, winged, with wheels within wheels, full of eyes, moving hither and thither like a flash of lightning at the behest of the dominating spirit. And over the head of the living creature there was the likeness of a

[2] The story of Ezekiel's call is told in 1:4–3:15.

firmament, like the terrible crystal to look upon, borne on their
wings with a noise like the noise of great waters. Above the firmament was the likeness of a throne, as the appearance of a sapphire
stone; and upon the likeness of the throne was a likeness as the
appearance of a man upon it above.

"And when I saw it (says Ezekiel) I fell upon my face, and I
heard a voice of one that spake. And he said unto me, Son of man,
stand upon thy feet and I will speak with thee. And the Spirit
entered into me, and set me upon my feet; and I heard him that
spake unto me. And he said unto me, Son of man, I send thee
unto the children of Israel, to nations that are rebellious . . . and
thou shalt say unto them, Thus saith the Lord Yahweh. And they,
whether they will hear or whether they will forbear (for they are a
rebellious house), yet shall know that there hath been a prophet
among them. And thou, son of man, be not afraid of them, neither
be afraid of their words, though briars and thorns be with thee, and
thou dost dwell among scorpions. . . .
But thou, son of man, . . . be not rebellious like that rebellious
house: open thy mouth and eat that which I give thee. And when
I looked, behold, a hand was put forth unto me; and lo, the roll
of a book was therein; and he spread it before me: and it was
written within and without; and there were written therein lamentations, and mourning, and woe. And he said unto me, Son of
man, eat . . . this roll, and go, speak unto the house of Israel. So
I opened my mouth and he caused me to eat the roll . . . Then did I
eat it; and it was in my mouth as honey for sweetness" (1:28bff).

So Ezekiel himself described his call; and the narrative, like that
of Jeremiah's call, compresses in itself several things which were
to characterize his ministry. One is, his overpowering feeling of
God's supernal majesty and elevation, exhibited in the grandiose
and fantastic details of the great canvas which he paints. It is full
of the scenery of another order. A second trait is his psychic nature.
He "saw visions of God." There is no other of the prophets who
was so prone to vision, ecstasy and trance as Ezekiel. Again and
again we find him seized by the "hand of God," taken possession
of by the Spirit, struck dumb, lifted up, carried back and forth,
even as far as Jerusalem, shown things taking place at a distance,
inspired to execute sign after sign. A third trait that here appears
is his peremptoriness. "Whether they will hear, or whether they
will forbear, yet shall they know that there hath been a prophet

among them." Such is to be his attitude through the first part of his ministry. Seldom does the note of pleading steal into his utterances, and then only for a moment (as in 18:30ff). His hearers are a "rebellious house," whose words might well dismay the prophet. Yahweh therefore will make his face hard against their faces, his forehead as adamant, harder than flint, against their foreheads. He is not to fear them, but like Jeremiah to wage continual war against them. But again, unlike Jeremiah, he seems to *enjoy* his message of woe; the roll written over with lamentations is sweet in his mouth as honey. It may be unjust to him to say that his heart was not aching for Yahweh's sinful people, for once at least he interceded for them (9:8), and now and then, as we have seen, he expostulated with them. But on the whole his denunciations seem not to have been wrung from him against his will, as was the case with Jeremiah, but to have poured forth in a tide of spontaneous passion.

Finally, he says, he was sent to "them of the captivity." It was among the exiled community that he was to labour, although at first sight it might seem that his message was addressed to the Jews of the homeland, not to those in Babylonia.

But it is time that we consider that message.

Jerusalem Doomed

At once Ezekiel was precipitated into his ministry.

"Then the Spirit lifted me up, and I heard behind me the voice of a great rushing, saying, Blessed be the glory of Yahweh from his place. . . . So the Spirit lifted me up, and took me away; and I went in bitterness, in the heat of my spirit; and the hand of Yahweh was strong upon me. Then I came to them of the captivity at Tel-abib . . . and I sat overwhelmed among them seven days" (3:12ff).

This cataleptic stupour was the first of many signs by which the young prophet arrested the attention of the people. We may imagine the growing interest as day after day passed with no evidence of life stirring in his prostrate body. At last, at the end of seven days, he moved. Rising he got a clay tile of the sort used in writing and traced upon it a map of a besieged city, surrounded by mounds, camps and battering rams. Between himself and this tiny city he set a flat iron plate, emblematic perhaps of Yahweh's iron determination to destroy. All was done in silence, but who could doubt the dreadful import of these divinely guided acts? Jerusalem was doomed! (4:1ff).

This was the beginning of seven years of prophetic work, from 592 B.C. when he received his call to 585 B.C. when word came at last that the city was taken. Through those years his proclamation, like that of Jeremiah's in Judah, remained the same. Sign followed sign. Now he lay first upon his left side for 150 days, then upon his right side for 40 days, signifying the number of years for which Israel and Judah in turn should bear their iniquity (4:4ff); now he weighed himself small quantities of food and water to indicate the famine of the siege (4:9ff); now he cut off his hair with a sharp sword and divided it to show the different fates awaiting the inhabitants of the capital (5:1ff); now he dug through the wall of his house and carried out his furniture on his back, to depict the journey into exile (12:3ff); now he ate his bread with quaking and drank his water with trembling to portray the terror of war (12:17ff); now he executed a sword dance to the accompaniment of a sharp, ringing song of death (21:8ff). When his wife died he made no sign of mourning, for was not Yahweh about to take away from His people the sanctuary that was dearer than even a loved wife? (24:15ff). At times he uttered parables, like that of the useless vine (15), or the two eagles (17), or the whelps of the lioness (19); or he elaborated the metaphor of the faithless wife which he had received from Hosea and Jeremiah (16 and 23). Once, in apocalyptic imagery, he described the abominations of Jerusalem and the slaughter of its inhabitants by heavenly executioners (8–11). At times he employed straight prophetic invective, as when he denounced the venal prophets (13), or presented Yahweh's indictment of the sins of Jerusalem (22), or hurled against it Yahweh's taunt-song (6:11ff). But through all these varied forms of utterance one and the same burden ran: Jerusalem must fall!

The Sin of Jerusalem

Like Micah and Jeremiah Ezekiel declared that the coming doom was due to sin. And this sin was not alone the sin of the present generation; it reached far back to Israel's beginnings. Here Ezekiel outstrips even Jeremiah and Hosea in the gloomy view that he takes of the past. These his fellow prophets had dreamed that in the early days Israel had loved Yahweh purely (Jer. 2:2; Hos. 9:10;

11:1ff); but Ezekiel could see nothing but sin from the very start. While still in Egypt, he asserts, the people had refused to forsake the idols of the land, and had so roused Yahweh's anger that He almost made an end of them there (20:8). And from that time on Israel had rebelled continuously, meriting annihilation again and again (20). Only Yahweh's long-suffering had averted this fate.

Against the Jerusalem of his own time he brings many bitter charges. Some have to do with the worship of other gods, of Israel's idols and its sun-images (6:6,9), of the many forms of creeping things and abominable beasts portrayed with other idols on the walls of a secret chamber in the temple; with the women weeping for Tammuz and the twenty-five men worshipping the sun with their backs to the temple of Yahweh (8:10ff).

But in the terrible indictment of chapter 22, in which he sums up Yahweh's counts against Jerusalem, social wrongs bulk more largely than ritual sins.

"In thee have they set light by father and mother; in the midst of thee have they dealt by oppression with the sojourner; in thee have they wronged the fatherless and widow. . . . Slanderous men have been in thee to shed blood; and in thee have they eaten upon the mountains: in the midst of thee they have committed lewdness. In thee have they uncovered their fathers' nakedness; in thee have they humbled her that was unclean in her impurity. And one had committed abomination with his neighbour's wife; and another hath lewdly defiled his daughter-in-law; and another hath humbled his sister. . . . In thee have they taken bribes to shed blood; thou hast taken interest and increase, and thou hast greedily gained of thy neighbours by oppression, and hast forgotten me, saith Yahweh" (22:7ff).

All classes are alike guilty.

"Thou art a land that is not cleansed, nor rained upon in the day of indignation. There is a conspiracy of her prophets in the midst thereof, like a roaring lion ravening the prey: they have devoured souls; they take treasure and precious things; they have made her widows many in the midst thereof. Her priests have done violence to my law, and have profaned my holy things: they have made no distinction between the holy and the common, neither have they caused men to discern between the unclean and the clean, and have hid their eyes from my sabbaths and I am profaned among them. Her princes in the midst of her are like wolves ravening the prey, to shed blood, and to destroy souls, that they may get dishonest gain. And her prophets have daubed for them with untempered mortar, seeing false visions and divining lies unto them. . . . The people of the land have used oppression and exercised robbery; yea, they have vexed the poor and the needy, and have oppressed the sojourner wrongfully" (22:23ff).

Shall not the "bloody city" be judged?

"And I sought for a man among them that should build up the wall, and stand in the gap before me for the land, that I should not destroy it; but I found none. . . . Therefore . . . I have consumed them with the fire of my wrath: their own way have I brought upon their heads, saith the Lord Yahweh" (22:30f).

It is in the course of these prophecies of doom that Ezekiel brings out two great thoughts which have ever since been associated with his name.

Every Man Responsible for His Own Fate

We have seen how Ezekiel, following Jeremiah, kept bringing up the sin of past generations as something that added to the guilt of the present. It formed indeed no small part of the heavy indictment laid against Jerusalem. But this accusation was now having an unexpected and disconcerting effect. A homely saying was going about: "The fathers have eaten sour grapes, and the children's teeth are set on edge. What is the use of trying? Our generation has no chance. God is not fair."

Such a criticism of Yahweh's dealings would hardly have arisen in an earlier Hebrew, steeped in the sense of the one-ness of his people, past and present. For ages it had been the accepted thing that the sins of the fathers should be visited upon the children to the third and fourth generation. Criminal procedure had followed this rule in the punishment of grave offenders. But two centuries before Ezekiel a breach had been made in this custom when king Amaziah of Judah had refrained from executing the children of the murderers who killed his father (II Ki. 14:6); and recently the book of Deuteronomy had come out boldly for the humaner practice:

"The fathers shall not be put to death for the children, neither shall the children be put to death for the fathers: every man shall be put to death for his own sin" (Deut. 24:16).

Evidently a new ethical concept was emerging; yet God seemed to be operating under the old idea. In an age of catastrophe, when foundations were giving way before frightful calamities, this thought tended, as we have seen, to plunge men in despair and resentment. Jeremiah had been compelled to fight it (Jer. 31:29) by a sweeping denial. But it remained for Ezekiel to demolish it once and for all.

"As I live, saith Yahweh, ye shall not have occasion any more to use this proverb in Israel. Behold, all souls are mine: the soul that sinneth, *it* shall die (18:3f). . . . The righteousness of the righteous shall be upon him, and the wickedness of the wicked shall be upon him" (18:20).

"All souls are mine." That is, each stands before God in its own right, unaffected by what any other soul may have done. Ezekiel develops this in detail, picturing a good father succeeded by a bad son and *vice versa* over three generations, and affirming that neither goodness nor wickedness involves him who follows. Every child that is born starts free of inherited guilt or credit, builds his own character and draws on his own destiny.

But Ezekiel goes further. No man is tied even by his own past! The moment he ceases to be what he has been, whether bad or good, that moment God's attitude and treatment changes towards him.

"If the wicked turn from all his sins that he hath committed, and keep all my statutes, and do that which is lawful and right, he shall surely live, he shall not die. None of his transgressions that he hath committed shall be remembered against him: in his righteousness that he hath done he shall live. Have I any pleasure in the death of the wicked? saith the Lord Yahweh; and not rather that he should return from his way, and live?"

The stern converse is also true:

"But when the righteous turneth away from his righteousness, and committeth iniquity . . . shall he live? None of his righteous deeds that he hath done shall be remembered: in his trespass that he hath trespassed, and in his sin that he hath sinned, in them he shall die" (18:21ff).

What could be more fair?

"Yet ye say, The way of Yahweh is not equal. Hear now, O house of Israel: Is not my way equal? are not your ways unequal?"

And it is not only fair: it opens the door to hope. Here the harsh prophet breaks suddenly into pleading:

"Return ye, and turn yourselves from all your transgressions; so iniquity shall not be your ruin. Cast away from you all your transgressions . . . and make you a new heart and a new spirit: for why will ye die, O house of Israel? For I have no pleasure in the death of him that dieth, saith the Lord Yahweh: wherefore turn yourselves, and live" (18:30ff).

Of course, this is a one-sided utterance. It ignores the fact that one man's sin inevitably affects others and often drags them down with him into misery. It also seems to leave out any idea of individual *character,* built up by all the actions of the past and carrying over into the present, so that one cannot wipe the slate clean by simply leaving off evil. And finally, it promises more than human experience warrants, for bad men do not always meet calamity, nor do the good invariably prosper. But it none the less enunciates a great emancipating truth. God plays no favourites. Because all souls are His, He holds wide open to every man at every moment the door to repentance and to life.

The Prophet a Watchman

This is the second great thought which Israel owes to Ezekiel. Because he saw so vividly that every man's fate lay in his own hands he believed himself called by God to perform the duty of a watchman on behalf of his fellows. The watchman's responsibility is to announce the approach of an enemy. In his hand is a trumpet which he must blow in warning.

"So thou, son of man, I have set thee a watchman unto the house of Israel; therefore hear the word at my mouth, and give them warning from me. When I say unto the wicked, O wicked man, thou shalt surely die, and thou dost not speak to warn the wicked from his way; that wicked man shall die in his iniquity, but his blood will I require at thy hand. Nevertheless, if thou warn the wicked of his way to turn from it, and he turn not from his way; he shall die in his iniquity, but thou hast delivered thy soul" (33:7ff; cf. 3:16ff).

Here, it appears, is something new in the religion of Israel. The prophets before Ezekiel recognized that Yahweh had sent them to warn men of impending doom; but they seem always to have thought of themselves as sounding a *general* alarm, directed to the people as a whole. Ezekiel is the first to picture the alarm as addressed to the individual. He must take care that each one hears for himself.

Nor is his duty confined to warning; it includes encouragement. Around him were depressed people who were saying: "Our transgressions and our sins are upon us, and we pine away in them; how then can we live?" For these God's pity had a heartening message:

"Say unto them, As I live, saith the Lord Yahweh, I have no pleasure in the death of the wicked; but that the wicked turn from his way and live: turn ye, turn ye from your evil ways; for why will ye die, O house of Israel?" (33:10ff).

He who speaks thus is something like a shepherd of souls; and not unjustly has Ezekiel been called the first pastor in Israel.

The Doom Fulfilled

What was the effect of these threatening prophecies upon the people? Of that Ezekiel tells us little. From his brief words as to "briers and thorns," "scorpions," intimidating "words" and "looks," the "rebellious house," a "hard forehead and stiff heart" (all of which occur in the account of his call) we may perhaps infer that he was met with hostility. But in his actual prophecies there is no hint of persecution. On the contrary, the elders of Israel (or Judah) are said to have visited his house on three occasions to receive through him a communication from Yahweh (8:1; 14:1; 20:1). When he carried out his symbolic actions before the people they were apparently interested (cf. 12:9; 24:19), and do not seem to have molested him or even to have ridiculed him. But neither were they convinced. As the years wore on and Jerusalem remained intact their feeling deepened that Ezekiel's threats would not be fulfilled—at least in their time. "The days are prolonged, and every vision faileth" (12:22).[1] "The vision that he seeth is for many days to come, and he prophesieth of times that are far off" (12:27).

All the more passionately, however, did the stern prophet continue his warnings. At last Zedekiah definitely revolted and the

---

[1] Ezekiel tells us that this was said "in the land of Israel," but he implies that the exiles in Babylonia shared the same feeling.

punitive machinery of Babylonia was set in motion. Nebuchadrezzer was on the march westward. In one oracle Ezekiel pictured
him as pausing at the parting of the ways to determine by sacred
lot and by divination whether he should first attack Rabbah of
Ammon or Jerusalem, the lot pointing to Jerusalem (21:18ff).
Later there came to the prophet a revelation that the blow was
about to fall. On the tenth day of the tenth month of the ninth
year (January 588 B.C.) he heard the divine command: "Son of
man, write thee the name of the day, of this selfsame day: the king
of Babylon drew close unto Jerusalem this selfsame day" (24:2).
But the impending disaster was to be brought home to him in a far
more personal way.

One morning he made a strange announcement to the people:

"Son of man (thus Yahweh had spoken), behold, I take away
from thee the desire of thine eyes with a stroke: yet thou shalt
neither mourn nor weep, neither shall thy tears run down. Sigh,
but not aloud, make no mourning for the dead: bind thine headtire
upon thee, and put thy shoes upon thy feet, and cover thy lips, and
eat not the bread of men" [2] (24:16ff).

That evening his wife died. How much she meant to him is
disclosed by the two words [3] with which he describes her. It was
indeed a "stroke" that God had dealt him. But faithful to the
command he sternly refrained from any sign of grief. When the
people asked him why, he told them:

"Thus saith the Lord Yahweh: Behold, I will profane my sanctuary, the pride of your power, the desire of your eyes, and the pity
of your soul; and your sons and your daughters whom ye have
left behind shall fall by the sword. And ye shall do as I have done.
. . . Ye shall not mourn nor weep; but ye shall pine away in your
iniquities, and mourn one towards another" (24:21ff).

"Thus," he added, "shall Ezekiel be unto you a sign." Once more
a prophet was called to empty out his own happiness and become a
mere vessel of Yahweh's purpose.

From that moment Ezekiel was stricken by Yahweh with dumbness and physical prostration. So at least think several scholars,

[2] Probably the food offered the bereaved by sympathetic friends to console
them (cf. Jer. 16:7).

[3] *Mahmadh 'eneka*, "the desire of thine eyes."

who transpose to this passage the divine inhibition described in the beginning of his book:

"Son of man, they (possibly, I) shall lay bands upon thee, and shall bind thee with them, and thou shalt not go out among them: and I will make thy tongue cleave to the roof of thy mouth, and thou shalt be dumb, and shalt not be to them a reprover; for they are a rebellious house" (3:25f).

In the months that followed he remained silent indoors. How the cessation of the prophetic voice must have added to the forebodings of the people! It was the hush before the catastrophe.

At last it was broken.

"And it came to pass in the twelfth year of our captivity, in the tenth month, in the fifth day of the month [4] that one that had escaped out of Jerusalem came unto me, saying, *The city is smitten!*" (33:21).

With those tidings ended Ezekiel's prophecies of doom.

The Restoration of Israel

The fatal news had very different effects upon Ezekiel and upon his fellow exiles. To them it brought the death of all their high hopes. Jerusalem and its temple were gone; many of the survivors were now on the way to captivity; those that remained were a miserable remnant from whom nothing could be expected in spite of their own confidence in themselves. Babylon which had crushed the nation remained in command of the world. Israel and its God were done for. Over the exiled community settled a black despair. "Our bones are dried up," men were saying, "and our hope is lost; we are clean cut off" (37:11).

Not so Ezekiel. To him the news came as a liberation.

"Now the hand of Yahweh had been upon me in the evening, before he that was escaped came; and he had opened my mouth, until he came to me in the morning; and my mouth was opened, and I was no more dumb" (33:22).

The judgment of God having been carried out upon His sinful people, there was no further need of warning. The way was open

---

[4] Jan. 585 B.C., according to Cooke.

for a proclamation of hope. And Ezekiel could give such a proclamation. Like Jeremiah in distant Palestine he refused to succumb to the prevailing despair; for he believed in God. Once more, therefore, he put the trumpet to his lips and sounded the eternal call of expectation. From chapter 34 onwards his book is full of the mighty future that is to be. These prophecies are not dated [1] and we shall review them briefly in the order in which they now stand.

First Ezekiel declared that Yahweh Himself would now take charge of His people. Their human shepherds, the king and the other rulers, had failed them. In one of the great ringing utterances of the Old Testament he denounced these shepherds for feeding themselves instead of the flock. He turned also on the well-to-do and charged them with despoiling the poor.

"Seemeth it a small thing unto you to have fed upon the good pasture, but ye must tread down with your feet the residue of your pasture? and to have drunk of the clear waters, but ye must foul the residue with your feet? And as for my sheep, they eat that which ye have trodden with your feet, and they drink that which ye have fouled with your feet" (34:18ff).

But Yahweh will permit all this no more.

"I myself, even I, will search for my sheep, and will seek them out. . . . And I will deliver them out of all places whither they have been scattered in the cloudy and dark day. And I will bring them from out the peoples . . . and will bring them into their own land; and I will feed them upon the mountains of Israel (34:11ff). But the fat and the strong will I destroy; I will feed them in justice" (34:16).

Israel shall have a ruler who cares for the weak.

"And I will set up one shepherd over them, and he shall feed them, even my servant David; he shall feed them, and he shall be their shepherd. And I, Yahweh, will be their God, and my servant David prince among them; I, Yahweh, have spoken it" (34:23f).

Next Ezekiel thundered against the Edomites who were now expecting to get possession of the territory of the two kingdoms of Israel (35); and went on to console the "mountains of Israel" for

[1] Chapters 40–48 are not here included.

the scorn now poured upon them by their enemies and would-be inheritors. True, the land was blighted by desolate wastes and forsaken cities;

"But ye, O mountains of Israel, ye shall shoot forth your branches, and yield your fruit to my people Israel; for they are at hand to come. For, behold, I am for you, and I will turn unto you, and ye shall be tilled and sown; and I will multiply men upon you, all the house of Israel, even all of it; and the cities shall be inhabited, and the waste places shall be builded; and I will multiply upon you man and beast; and they shall increase and be fruitful; and I will cause you to be inhabited after your former estate, and will do better things unto you than at your beginnings: and ye shall know that I am Yahweh" (36:8ff).

But what would become of the sins which had brought the doom on Israel? Had they been repented of? Not yet; but in the blessed time of restoration even that wonder will be performed by God.

"And I will sprinkle clean water upon you, and ye shall be clean: from all your filthiness, and from all your idols, will I cleanse you. A new heart also will I give you, and a new spirit will I put within you; and I will give you a heart of flesh. And I will put my Spirit within you, and cause you to walk in my statutes, and ye shall keep my ordinances, and do them" (36:25ff).

This indeed is not quite repentance; it is rather regeneration. Full repentance will not come till after renewed Israel shall receive from God's hand marvellous abundance of food and good things.

"Then ye shall remember your evil ways, and your doings that were not good; and ye shall loathe yourselves in your own sight for your iniquities and for your abominations" (36:31).

God, then, will not wait for Israel's repentance; He will anticipate it by Himself working a change in their heart and by pouring material gifts upon them. It is all His free gift, not their desert!

"Not for your sake do I this, saith the Lord Yahweh, be it known unto you: be ashamed and confounded for your ways, O house of Israel" (36:32).[2]

[2] This spiritual conception of God's course with future Israel is a favourite with Ezekiel (6:9; 16:61ff; 20:43).

At another time Ezekiel had a vision of the restoration of the people. Overcome by a prophetic ecstasy he was brought in the Spirit of Yahweh and set down in the midst of a valley full of dry bones—a picture of devastated Israel. Admonished by the divine voice he prophesied and suddenly the bones formed into bodies without animation. Admonished a second time, he called for the Spirit, and now they lived and "stood upon their feet, an exceeding great army." So to the hopeless nation came a word of reviving:

"Thus saith the Lord Yahweh: Behold, I will open your graves, and cause you to come up out of your graves, O my people; and I will bring you into the land of Israel" (37:12).

A final oracle proclaimed the reunion in Palestine of the two long separated kingdoms. For Ezekiel, like Jeremiah, was content with nothing less than the restoration of the north as well as the south. He was to take two sticks inscribed with the names of "Judah and the sons of Israel his companions" and of "Joseph and all the house of Israel his companions," and join them into one stick in his hand, thus explaining his action:

"Thus saith the Lord Yahweh: Behold, I will take the sons of Israel from among the nations . . . and bring them into their own land: and I will make them one nation in the land . . . and one king shall be king to them all; and they shall be no more two kingdoms, neither shall they be divided into two kingdoms any more at all. . . . Moreover I will make a covenant of peace with them; it shall be an everlasting covenant with them; and I will place them, and multiply them, and will set my sanctuary in the midst of them for evermore. My tabernacle also shall be with them; and I will be their God, and they shall be my people. And the nations shall know that I am Yahweh that sanctifieth Israel, when my sanctuary shall be in the midst of them for evermore" (37:15ff).

Ezekiel the Prophet

With this oracle of reunion the prophecies of Ezekiel may be said to come to an end. The rest of his book belongs to a different kind of utterance, which we shall consider in a moment. In the oracles thus far reviewed Ezekiel moves in the familiar world of history. Only the grandiose vision of the "glory of God" intrudes upon the earthly scene. Like his older contemporary and the prophets before him he pronounces doom upon Israel for its sin and expects that doom to take the well-known form of invasion by hostile armies. So after the blow has fallen he pictures restoration taking place by means of the divine manipulation of historical factors, in some vague fashion which he describes only in its results. God's grace indeed is there, as seen in the new-created hearts of His people, but it operates within the accustomed frame of history. Even the wonderful productivity of the mountains of Palestine will be but an augmenting of the natural processes.

Only one point seems to differentiate him from the other prophets. He is for the most part speaking over the heads of his fellow-exiles to distant Jerusalem. It is this indirection which, as we have seen, has led several scholars to maintain that Ezekiel did not prophesy in Babylonia but in Palestine, and to pronounce the so-called "Babylonian setting" of his oracles a device of a later hand. We must, however, remember two things. One, that (as has been said) the exile community needed above all else to have its extravagant hopes of immediate restoration punctured. The other, that Ezekiel must have said much to his fellow-exiles which is not recorded in his book. This seems to be indicated by the twice repeated "watchman" passage, which implies that he urged his hearers constantly to turn from their sins; and by another passage in which he describes his popularity as a preacher.

For apparently he did become popular. Doubtless this took place after his note changed from doom to hope, for as we have seen there are indications that he was anything but popular during the first part of his ministry.

"And as for thee, son of man, the children of thy people talk of thee by the walls and in the doors of the houses, and speak one to another, . . . saying, Come, I pray you, and hear what is the word that cometh forth from Yahweh. And they come unto thee as the people cometh, and they sit before thee as my people, and they hear thy words, but do them not; for with their mouth they show much love, but their heart goeth after their gain. And lo, thou art unto them as a very lovely song of one that hath a pleasant voice, and can play well on an instrument; for they hear thy words, but they do them not" (33:30ff).

Here it is implied that Ezekiel gave practical admonitions to his hearers of the sort that they might well fulfil, but did not because they were too much occupied in making money.

Ezekiel, then, did speak to the people around him. Indeed we have one utterance in which he charges the elders of Israel who wish to consult him with taking "their idols into their heart" and putting "the stumbling block of their iniquity before their face" (14:1ff). Again, in his denunciation of lying prophets (13) he seems to have in mind persons in the exile community as well as in Jerusalem. On the whole, however, he looks with much more favourable eyes upon the exiles than upon the people left in Palestine, sometimes taking the part of the former against the latter (11: 14ff; 33:23ff). He agrees with Jeremiah in regarding the captives as the Israel of the future (cf. Jer. 24). But this favourable attitude does not diminish the reality of what he says to them.

In all this Ezekiel shows himself the prophet. But, as has been said, there is another side to his utterances which seems to leave prophecy behind.

Ezekiel the Apocalyptist

Two sections of Ezekiel's book do not fit into the frame of history. In them the phenomena of men's familiar world drop away and the reader finds himself moving in the midst of entities that transcend earth. There is a hint of this in the vision of the "glory of God" vouchsafed him at the time of his call. But that heavenly apparition is no more supernal than the seraphim which Isaiah saw (Is. 6). When, however, we come to chapters 8–10 we enter a transcendent world. In September 591 B.C., as Ezekiel was sitting in front of the elders in his house, the "hand of Yahweh fell upon him." In his trance he beheld a fiery figure who seized him by a lock of his head and transported him "in the visions of God" to Jerusalem, setting him down at the north entrance of the inner court of the temple. There he perceived alongside of the "image of jealousy" the same apparition of the "glory of the God of Israel" which he had seen at the time of his call. The fiery being then proceeded to show him the abominations of heathen worship which were polluting the temple: seventy elders of Israel in a secret chamber burning incense to reptiles, unclean animals and other idols painted upon the wall; women weeping for Tammuz; twenty-five men with their backs to the temple adoring the sun in the east. Because of these things (so Ezekiel's conductor announces) and because of the violence with which men have filled the land, the hour of doom is at hand.

Then with a loud voice he summons "them that have charge over the city." Six superhuman beings draw nigh, each with his slaughter weapon in his hand; and in the midst of them a man "clothed in linen, with a writer's inkhorn by his side." They take their stand by the brazen altar. At the same moment the "glory of the God of Israel" leaves the "cherub whereupon it was" [1] and pauses upon the threshold of the house. God is about to depart from His temple. The divine scribe is now ordered to pass through the city and set a mark upon the forehead of all who lament the wickedness of the nation. After him are to follow the armed beings, slaying without pity every one of every age and sex who is not marked with the mark. By express command they begin with the elders that are east of the house, and the temple courts are polluted with corpses. Then they go out and Ezekiel is left with the dead bodies and his conductor. Falling on his face he implores mercy for the "residue of Israel," but in vain. Presently the scribe returns and reports: "I have done as thou hast commanded me."

Next the order comes to take coals from between the whirling wheels, from between the cherubim, and scatter them over the city. As Jerusalem burns the glory mounts up from over the threshold and borne by the cherubim stands at the east gate of Yahweh's house. Finally it moves out from the city and stands upon the mount of Olives, prepared to take flight eastward. At that moment Ezekiel is transported back to Chaldea and the vision ends.

So Yahweh left His city. But there was a happy sequel to the cosmic story. Nineteen years afterwards (572 B.C.) the hand of Yahweh was again upon His prophet, now in later middle life. For the second time he was transported to the land of Israel; not to the Israel of the present, with its ruined capital and devastated temple, its unrestored villages and thinly inhabited countryside —mere shell of the nation that had once been; but to the Israel of a vaster future.

"In the visions of God brought he me into the land of Israel, and set me down upon a very high mountain, whereon was as it were the frame of a city on the south. And he brought me thither; and, behold, there was a man, whose appearance was like the appearance of brass, with a line of flax in his hand, and a measuring reed; and he stood in the gate. And the man said unto me, Son of man, behold with thine ears, and set thy heart upon all that I shall show thee. . . . Declare all that thou seest to the house of Israel" (40:1–4).

[1] The ark and the holy of holies?

Then before him was disclosed the temple of the coming age, its dimensions so carefully measured by the heavenly ministrant that it is possible today to draw a sketch of the complex of buildings.[2] This done, Ezekiel was brought to the east gate, to behold a joyful sight: Yahweh returning to His house which He had abandoned many years before:

"Behold, the glory of the God of Israel came from the way of the east: and his voice was like the sound of many waters, and the earth shined with his glory. And it was according to the appearance of the vision which I saw . . . when I came to destroy the city. . . . And I fell upon my face. And the glory of Yahweh came into the house by way of the gate whose prospect is to the east. And the Spirit took me up, and brought me into the inner court; and, behold, the glory of Yahweh filled the house.

And I heard one speaking unto me out of the house; and a man stood by me. And he said unto me, Son of man, this is the place of my throne, and the place of the soles of my feet, where I will dwell in the midst of the children of Israel for ever" (43:1ff).

The chapters that follow must be treated with caution for, as we have seen, they are thought by scholars to contain much secondary material. We are justified, however, in using them to fill out tentatively the rest of Ezekiel's vision.

With an attention to ecclesiastical detail which reminds us of the priestly description of the tabernacle in the Book of Exodus he records the divine provision for the worship of the temple and for its ministers. Land adjoining the temple is set apart for the priests and Levites and for the city, the whole comprising a "holy oblation" to Yahweh. On each side of this oblation is reserved land for the "prince," who is to have his own revenues and thus to be free of the temptation to oppress the people. His work is to maintain justice and honesty in the land and to procure the gifts to be offered in the temple.

The holy oblation is to be a strip running east and west in the centre of the land and is to contain a square city where the people are to live, next to the priests and Levites. North and south of the oblation are the portions reserved for the twelve tribes, seven on the north, five on the south. Thus the whole land converges towards the temple as its centre.

[2] Montet prints such a sketch made by Perrot and Chipiez (*Histoire du Peuple d' Israël,* Paris, 1926, p. 149).

From under the threshold of the temple door Ezekiel saw in his vision waters issuing, flowing east and speedily increasing till they became "a river that could not be passed through" (47:1ff). Upon its banks on either side were "very many trees" of marvellous kind, bringing forth new fruit every month, the fruit being for food and the leaves for healing. Neither fruit nor leaf ever fails. The river passed down into the Arābāh, emptying into the Dead Sea, which because of it was no longer dead, but swarmed with as many kinds of fish as were to be found in the Mediterranean. Only the marshes remained briny, to supply salt to men.

All this is apocalyptic. The prophet moves amid apparitions of another order. What is done is done without human hands. Divine beings slay the wicked, destroy city and temple and then rebuild both in a refashioned land overlooked by a very high mountain and watered by a mystic river of God, with trees of wonder on either side. The scene indeed is still Palestine, and the people Israelites. Human society still needs its prince to preserve justice. Buying and selling, sowing and reaping, marrying and giving in marriage (it is implied) still go on. Even the central divine activity of worship has experienced no essential change, and is carried on in the temple not built with hands by the familiar priests and Levites. But the *atmosphere* has changed; the air is translucent with radiance from beyond earth.

Apocalyptic probably did not begin with Ezekiel. But he is the first of the writing prophets to employ it freely and his great name must have given it increased currency. From now on it holds an authoritative place in the Old Testament scriptures.

Ezekiel and the Gentile World

It was the rise of the great empires that called forth the writing prophets. The Israelitish people could no longer ignore the Gentile world but must bring it somehow into their religious thinking; and the prophets responded by the bold declaration that Yahweh was supreme over all nations. All were accountable to Him and to all He had His word to say through the prophets. But this did not mean that the prophets necessarily became internationally minded. They might still shut out the Gentiles from the love of Yahweh and depict Him as caring only for Israel. What was Ezekiel's attitude on this matter?

Like Isaiah and Jeremiah he uttered oracles concerning other nations. Chapters 25–32 contain a series of such prophecies dealing with Ammon, Moab, Edom, the Philistines (25); Tyre, including Sidon (26–28); and Egypt (29–32). Chapter 35 also is directed against Edom. In these oracles, especially those concerning Tyre and Egypt, we find some of his most daring and imaginative writing; they abound in startling pictures and memorable sayings, and many of them are clothed in the poetic form that is rather rare in Ezekiel. But they do not make pleasant reading. Not a single generous note is heard; bitterness and hostility reign supreme.

Of course there was some justification for the prophet's animosity. During the last agonized days of the Jewish state the peoples round about gave themselves over to cruel delight at the humbling of Yahweh's chosen nation; and after the fall of Jerusalem they pushed in to seize its territory, taking vengeance upon the wretched survivors for past grievances (cf. 25:3, 8, 12, 15). The Tyrians rejoiced that the profitable business done by Jerusalem "the gate of the peoples" would now revert to them (26:2). Egypt, for its part, had encouraged Judah to lean upon it and then had broken under pressure, "rending all their shoulders" (29:6f). All were alike insufferable in their arrogant self-gratulation (cf.28:2ff; 29:3). It was quite human in Ezekiel to dwell with grim satisfaction on the picture of their coming doom.

And apparently it was to be doom unrelieved by hope. For in the blessed future of Israel the Gentiles were to have no share. Ezekiel might behold in his vision a very high mountain on whose side lay Yahweh's house, full of worshippers; but these were all Israelites. Unlike the nameless prophet whose oracle is preserved in Is. 2:1ff and Mic. 4:1ff he did not conceive the elevated temple of Yahweh as the goal of converging multitudes of Gentiles, nor contemplate Yahweh as establishing peace and plenty for a war-torn world. Indeed, if one regards chapters 38–39 as the work of Ezekiel, he predicted instead a future invasion of restored Israel by shadowy hordes from the land of Magog, and gloated over their destruction on the mountains of Israel by a divine stroke. But happily these chapters, which are among the worst examples of Jewish nationalism in the Old Testament, can now be attributed to a later hand.

Towards one Gentile power, indeed, Ezekiel exhibited undeniable friendliness. In chapter 17 he pictures Nebuchadrezzar as a great eagle with kindly intentions towards Israel, and condemns Zedekiah for breaking faith with him; and in his latest prophecy (29:17ff) he sympathizes with Nebuchadrezzar's failure to capture Tyre, promising him in Yahweh's name Egypt as a recompense.

Evidently he shared Jeremiah's view that the Chaldean empire was a beneficent instrument in Yahweh's hand for accomplishing his purposes towards Israel. But that is all. While no doom is pronounced upon Babylon, neither is any future held out before it.

To say, however, that Ezekiel's hostility to foreign nations was natural enough is not to acquit him before the bar of history. If other prophets in bitter days could rise to universalistic dreams, why could not he? If he himself could charge Jerusalem with worse sins than the surrounding nations (5:6f) or even ancient Sodom (16:48), why could he not envisage forgiveness and restoration for these contemporary nations as well as for Israel? That he did not records a failure.

Other Limitations of Ezekiel

If Ezekiel failed to think of God as caring for the Gentiles he displayed another lack in his depiction of the divine attitude toward Israel. For more than any other of the writing prophets he attributed to God the motive of vindicating His own honour. This comes out especially in Ezekiel's review of Israel's history in chapter 20. From the sojourn in Egypt onwards Israel had rebelled against Yahweh, but again and again He had been restrained from destroying it because by doing so He would have discredited Himself (20:8f, 14ff, 21f, 44). Again, in chapter 36 Ezekiel ascribes Israel's restoration to Yahweh's desire to vindicate His own reputation. Israel's miserable fate had given the world the impression that Yahweh was powerless: "These are the people of Yahweh," men were saying, "and they are gone forth out of his land" (v. 20). He would therefore bring them back, yet

"I do not this for your sake, O house of Israel, but for my holy name, which ye have profaned among the nations whither ye went. And I will sanctify my great name . . . and the nations shall know that I am Yahweh, when I shall be sanctified in you before their eyes" (vv. 22f).

Ezekiel to be sure did not originate this interpretation of God's goodness to Israel, for it lay ready to his hand in the JE stories of Moses' intercession (Exod. 32:12ff; Num. 14:13ff; cf. Deut. 9:28). He employed it also for the same purpose as did the earlier writers. He wished to humble his fellow Israelites and make them realize their own unworthiness: "Be ashamed and confounded for your ways, O house of Israel" (36:32). Nor did it express all his mind. For Ezekiel was perfectly aware that God had also saved Israel because He loved it. We have seen that he could plead with the unrepentant (18:25ff; 33:10ff) and that now and again his restoration prophecies throb with a feeling which approaches even tenderness (cf. 34:11ff; 36:8ff; 37:11f). Nevertheless, he did express the motive of divine self-vindication in a peculiarly crude way.

This trait does not stand alone but is part of a general temper that pervades Ezekiel's prophecies. We may describe it perhaps as harshness. In spite of many relieving touches the reader senses it throughout. He misses a genuine human sympathy for man's weakness; he misses warmth. Fire is there, certainly, but somehow it is a cold fire. We have already noticed Ezekiel's peremptoriness and a certain congeniality in his nature with his message of woe. And yet in saying this we must again remember that Ezekiel's written words may leave out much which was present in his spoken utterances. There must after all have been in him a warmth which drew his hearers (33:30).

It is a common view today that Ezekiel helped to remove God from man by his overpowering sense of the divine transcendence and particularly by his introduction of intermediaries between himself and God in his visions. This however seems to the present writer an exaggeration. Ezekiel makes no more of the awful majesty of God than does Isaiah, though the way in which he elaborates his vision of the glory of God may not appeal to us as much as the self-restraint with which the earlier prophet confines his picture to a few strokes. The intermediate beings appear only in the apocalyptic sections and even there do not really make God Himself more remote. They only bring in the sense that God is not alone in the supernal world but is served by ministrants greater than man; which is no new idea in the Old Testament.

Finally, Ezekiel differs from the prophets who preceded him in that he gives the worship of the temple a central place in his thought. They had boldly declared that God desires lovingkindness and not sacrifice. He, on the other hand, regards sacrifice and the whole ritual side of religion as of equal value with the ethical. This stands out most plainly in the apocalyptic sections, especially the closing chapters of his book. When after years of brooding he was vouchsafed the vision of restored Israel he beheld the new temple as the centre of the whole land and its life. Now this fact of itself ought not to set him apart from the other prophets, for it may well be that they also, had they been in his place, would have thought of the future Israel in the same way. But the temple would not have been so vital to them as to Ezekiel. Their emphasis would have been instead upon the social relationships of the people and their common life. Ezekiel hardly mentions these, though he does indeed presuppose that they will be sound and happy. His attention is all devoted to what we may call the ecclesiastical aspect of the picture. The temple is provided first of all; then its worship is cared for. Priests and Levites are to be dominant figures in the restored community.

To his mind, God is tremendously concerned for the maintenance of physical *holiness*. All sorts of precautions must be taken to insure against its violation or misuse. The priests, for instance, must eat the "most holy things" in "holy chambers" and minister in the holy place wearing special garments, which are to be laid off when they go out to mingle with the people (42:13f). God is so antagonistic to physical defilement that He insists upon the whole top of the temple mountain being kept "most holy." He will in the future avoid the offence that was given Him in the past by the fact that the king's house was next His own (43:8). Many more illustrations of this could be cited if we could treat chapters 44-48 as certainly from Ezekiel's hand; but inasmuch as these are in many parts, if not entirely, viewed with suspicion by scholars, we ought not to construct our idea of Ezekiel from them. But enough can be found in chapters 40–43 to justify us in making much of the priestly and ritual element in Ezekiel's teaching.

Now that element has its rightful place in religion. Ezekiel, as a priest, naturally valued it and did well to stress it; for man needs it. To the Israel of his day, deprived of its temple and sacrificial worship, his vision of both restored supplied a very tangible hope and gave it something to tie to in its thoughts of the future. But it cannot be denied that in equating it with the ethical side of religion he lacked the sense of proportion.

Ezekiel's Contribution to Israel's Religion

Ezekiel in Babylonia, like Jeremiah in Palestine, saw Israel die. But like Jeremiah he refused to take that death as death. The No of the present he met with the Everlasting Yea. For he believed in God. When men around him perceived only dry bones he beheld also the Spirit of God which would make them live. To the power and splendour of the empire that had crushed his people he opposed the "glory of Yahweh" who moves with majestic certitude through history towards His own appointed ends. Therefore he also was a planter and builder of the greater future.

Faith and hope were his; but did he also possess love? At first, it seems not. The shell of this man's nature had a bitter taste. But within was a devotion to his contemporaries which fell nothing short of the devotion of an Isaiah or a Jeremiah. In a certain practical way Ezekiel even surpassed them, for he became (as we have seen) the first pastor of souls.

Perhaps this bitter quality fitted him for his work. The melting tenderness of Second Isaiah might have been out of place in his situation. His very harshness may have supplied a needed tonic to invigorate flabby spirits and to inculcate a heroism such as the future demanded.

Beyond question he divined aright the direction that future would take. In the restored community worship was destined to assume a new importance. For this Israel was to be organized with a rigour unknown in past ages. The priest and the Levite were to dominate the national life. The law was to become the marshalling force of the whole community and its expounder, the scribe, was finally to displace priest and Levite in leadership. Apocalyptic also was to flourish more and more.

For all this Ezekiel unquestionably prepared the way, especially in his great concluding vision, which was to be eagerly elaborated by younger men as they drew the nation farther and farther along the path pointed out. It was a path which in important aspects does not appeal to Christians of today. It was not, we believe, the final path marked out by God for man (although millions of orthodox Jews are still taking it). But it was probably the path best fitted to conduct Israel through the next five centuries.

Nor must we forget that within the ecclesiastical and ritual frame of the life now beginning were to flower Hebrew wisdom with its autonomy of the individual and the marvellous personal religion which we meet in the psalms. To the individual Ezekiel in his retribution dogma (18) issued a basic charter of freedom. Psalmody, indeed, he did not inspire. But in supplying the setting for it he built with true instinct. For after all his was a deeply religious nature. He desired for Israel not only outward restoration but inward regeneration and that social righteousness without which man cannot attain peace with God. When he saw the coming temple gather into itself the life of the new Israel it meant to him that God was dwelling in the midst of His people forever.

"And the name of the city from that day shall be, *Yahweh is there*" (48:35).

Chapter XIX

SECOND ISAIAH

[*c.* 540 B.C.]

Ezekiel has shown us that the eyes of the Jews in Babylonia were turned towards the land of Israel and the great future which should there come to be. So long however as the Chaldean power remained unshaken these hopes could never find fulfilment. For twenty years after Ezekiel's last recorded prophecy (dated 570 B.C., Ezek. 29:17ff) nothing disturbed the empire bequeathed by Nebuchadrezzar to his successors. During this period the Jewish exiles slowly struck root in the alien soil of their captors.

Then a storm-cloud arose on the eastern horizon and spread rapidly over the north and north-west. In 553 B.C. Cyrus king of Anshan, a vassal state of the Medes, revolted from his over-lord, and in 550 B.C. made himself king of Persia. Next he marched westward into Asia Minor and subdued the domain of Croesus king of Lydia, taking Sardis in 547 B.C. Up to this time he was probably posing as a friend of the Chaldeans. But now he threw off the disguise. In 546 B.C. he entered north Babylonia and established a Persian governor in Uruk, the chief city of the south. Every one knew that his next objective was Babylon itself. Through the subject peoples groaning under the Babylonian yoke ran a thrill of hope, and among the Babylonians themselves a strong priestly party, angered by their king's neglect of the great god Marduk, began to turn to the outsider as a deliverer.[1]

In 540 B.C. Cyrus renewed his attack. By two successful battles he crushed the Chaldean resistance and opened the way to Babylon. That vast fortress, which the foresight of Nebuchadrezzar had rendered practically impregnable, might have held out against him indefinitely. But the disaffected elements within its walls proved so strong that in 539 B.C. they were able to open its gates to Cyrus' general Gobryas, who entered it without a struggle. Its last king Nabu-naid became a prisoner and the Chaldean empire gave place

[1] Olmstead, *HPS*, p. 547ff.

to the Persian.[2] Thus began the Persian period of Israel's history, during which the people remained under the dominion of Cyrus and his successors for two hundred years. At last in 332 B.C. the Macedonian Alexander shattered the Persian power for ever.[3]

It was at some moment after Cyrus had appeared on the horizon as a conquering hero but before the collapse of the Chaldean rule became certain to every one, that the last of Israel's great prophets began to speak to his fellow-Jews in exile. His name is not preserved, but because his oracles are found at the close of the Book of Isaiah he is today known universally as Second Isaiah.

The Sources

The Book of Isaiah has long been divided by scholars into two great sections, 1–39 and 40–66. The first section contains all that we have of the genuine prophecies of Isaiah, although much of it is not from his hand. The second section in its entirety proceeds from a later age than Isaiah's and from other hands than his. This has been the belief of scholars for three generations, and indeed it was suspected long before that. When the separation was first clearly made, the opinion of scholars was that the whole of chapters 40–66 was the work of a single man, whom they called Second Isaiah. But after a while critics began to question its unity and in 1892 Berhard Duhm came forward with the theory that chapters 56–66 proceed from a different prophet, whom he named the Third Isaiah. This idea found acceptance in the scholarly world and today the large majority of scholars regard the division into Second and Third Isaiah as established. Duhm's thesis, however, has been modified in an important detail. "Third Isaiah" is not usually looked upon as a single person, but chapters 56-66 are broken up into a number of separate poems from various hands and assigned to various dates.

The prevailing view therefore is that chapters 40–55 were uttered by a great anonymous prophet of the exile somewhere about 540 B.C. This date is arrived at by inference. The prophet speaks of Cyrus as a well-known conqueror, yet his capture of Babylon is still in the future. Now Cyrus probably got the notice of the world by his victories over Croesus, king of Lydia, in 547–546 B.C., and so these utterances would have followed that date. He took Babylon in 539 B.C. and therefore they must have been given forth before

[2] Olmstead, *HPS*, p. 551.
[3] See p. 557.

that. Did the prophet live in Babylonia? Most scholars think that he did, at least while he was composing chapters 40–48, for in them he seems to be addressing exiles in Babylonia. Chapters 49–55, however, reflect a Palestinian rather than a Babylonian background, and he may have written them in the homeland.

Not all, indeed, of 40–55 is attributed to Second Isaiah. The process of analysis has been at work upon these chapters also, and a number of smaller passages are regarded by many scholars as "secondary," especially the description of idol-making in 44:9–20. This is set aside on the ground that it is prose, while Second Isaiah wrote always in poetry. Again, many have followed Duhm in discovering a group of "Servant Songs" (42:1–4; 49:1–6; 50:4–9; 52:13–53:12) which, it is said, interrupt the context and portray a figure not elsewhere to be found in Second Isaiah's writing. These "Servant Songs" are usually ascribed to a follower of Second Isaiah who composed them and inserted them into his master's work. Others think that Second Isaiah himself wrote them, but as a separate group of utterances.

So much for the view that is almost universal among scholars today. It has been sharply contradicted by Torrey in his masterly book *The Second Isaiah*.[1] He maintains that chapters 40–66 are not to be dismembered, but together with 34–35 form a splendid whole, containing twenty-seven poems by one of the noblest thinkers and sublimest poets of mankind. He repudiates the common idea that in 56–66 the style degenerates, and has by his own superb rendering endeavoured to show that it continues unimpaired to a glorious climax in 66. Throughout these nineteen chapters, declares Torrey, a single commanding genius is speaking, and all his utterances are manifestly parts of a whole, written in a comparatively short period and arranged in their present order by the author himself; chapters 34-35 having been separated from their fellows by a block of narrative material having to do with Isaiah (36–39) because the editor who added these poems to the book of Isaiah wished to tie them on to it in a close way.

The date of this work of genius Torrey puts at about 400 B.C. In order to do this he is compelled to regard as interpolations the mention of Cyrus in 45:1 and 44:28, and the names "Babylon" and "Chaldea" in 43:14; 48:14 and 48:20. These, he believes, all mar the metre and were inserted by a later hand to make the prophecies fit into the picture of a Babylonian "exile" painted by the Chronicler. As a matter of fact, he declares, the prophecies

[1] Scribner's, 1928.

have to do with Jews in Palestine at a much later period and the "exile" they speak of is a figure for the Jewish dispersion which had then reached alarming proportions.[2]

So revolutionary a theory has naturally gained few adherents. Its weak point lies in its need to expunge from the text names that are attested by all manuscripts and versions. If only Torrey could have let these stand his contention for the unity of 40–66 might carry greater weight. As he translates and interprets these chapters they fit into a single imposing whole, and the reader finds 56–66 no less marvellous than those preceding them.

More recently L. Glahn has argued at length that chapters 40–66 are all the work of Second Isaiah, 40:1–56:8 being composed in Babylonia after 540 B.C. and 56:9–66:24 in Jerusalem, whither he returned in 538–7 B.C.[3] Albright (*APB*, p. 218) also agrees with Torrey in regarding the whole of Is. 40–66 as the work of one man, but unlike Torrey he places him between 540 and 522 B.C. (in round numbers). The present writer inclines to follow Albright here.

In our study of Second Isaiah we shall follow the usual view that his work stops with chapter 55, and confine ourselves to the material which can be drawn from 40–55. Yet it will be well for the reader to bear in mind that in the opinion of some recent scholars we should also include 56–66.

In regard to the minor question of the authenticity of the "Servant Songs" we shall be more sceptical. There is no convincing proof that they form a separate group of writings, and certainly none that they proceed from another pen than that of Second Isaiah. We shall therefore take the position that they are really part of the chapters in which they are found, having been composed by Second Isaiah himself in their present context. So far from being alien to his thought, they are essential to it, and constitute indeed its very crown.

Second Isaiah Spoke Comfort to an Israel that had Lost Heart

We know nothing of the man whom we call "Second Isaiah" except what we may glean from his words addressed to Israel. Of himself he says little if anything. We are told neither his name,

[2] Barton (*Haverford Symposium on Archaeology and the Bible,* p. 61) and Dahl (*Journal of Biblical Literature,* No. 48, p. 362ff) accept Torrey's view in substance).

[3] *Der Prophet der Heimkehr,* Vol. I (Giesen, 1934). Reviewed by J. A. Montgomery, *ATR,* July 1934, p. 217f.

his parentage, his home, his status, his age, whether he was married and had a family, nor a single incident out of his experiences. He remains for us—to use a word of his that he employed with a different meaning—a voice. But from that voice we can gather much regarding him who uttered it. And first we can perceive the conditions which prevailed about him. "Comfort ye, comfort ye my people" he begins; and that at once gives us the setting. For the Israel of his day needed comfort. They were a broken and despairing people.

What made them so? Unquestionably it was the fall of their national state and especially of Jerusalem with its temple. The fatal year 586 B.C. marked a change in the temper of the Hebrew people. Before that it was only the prophets who had talked of ruin; the majority continued stout-hearted, hoping in spite of repeated disasters that the tide would yet turn in their favour. After 586 B.C. it was the prophets who hoped, while those about them were plunged in despondency. Let us now try to form a picture of the situation which confronted Second Isaiah.

The land of Palestine, or at least the former kingdom of Judah, lay very largely in ruins. Second Isaiah speaks of the "desolate cities" (54:3), the "desolate heritages" (49:8); "the waste and desolate places, the land that hath been destroyed" (49:19).[1] Jerusalem was "heaps," and as for the temple its foundation must be relaid if it was ever to rise again (44:28). The people also were terribly diminished in number and strength. He calls Zion a widow bereaved of her children (49:19ff) or a barren mother without offspring (54:1).

"There is none to guide her among all the sons that she hath
    brought forth;
Neither is there any that taketh her by the hand among all the
    sons that she hath brought up.
These two things are befallen thee; who shall bemoan thee?
Desolation and destruction, and the famine and the sword; how
    shall I comfort thee?
Thy sons have fainted, they lie at the head of all the streets, as an
    antelope in a net;
They are full of the wrath of Yahweh, the rebuke of thy God"
    (51:18–20).

[1] Albright, *APB*, p. 171ff, who has made a study of the surface remains of Judaean mounds, declares that many of them exhibit no remains later than the Babylonian exile (Early Iron II), thus proving that there was extensive devastation of Judah by the Chaldeans.

The cause of the sparseness and wretchedness of the population is in part clearly indicated by these words: many had been killed in war,[2] many had starved by reason of the interruption of agriculture. The rest were weak and dispirited. Any hope of their "taking Jerusalem by the hand" and rebuilding it was out of the question. Of course, there were people still living in Judah and even in Jerusalem. They had made some sort of quarters for themselves amid the stone of the fallen houses and were supporting themselves as best they could. But they were not enough to count. And in many instances no doubt the desolate cities were actually uninhabited.

But sword and famine were not responsible for *all* the thinness of population. A wide *scattering* had taken place. Second Isaiah seems to speak especially of the exiles in Babylonia but he manifestly had more than these in mind in many of his utterances. North, south, east and west all possessed some of Yahweh's people (43:5; 49:12, 22). How had these Israelites come to be so far from home? Partly by deportation. Ever since Tiglath-pileser in 733 B.C. had carried inhabitants of Gilead, Galilee and Naphtali captive to Assyria one deportation after another had taken place. In 722 B.C. Sargon had removed 27,290 inhabitants of the northern kingdom to Assyria. These, it is true, were not people of Judah, but their loss was none the less keenly felt by their brothers of the southern kingdom (cf. Jer. 31:20), and the dispersed state of "Jacob" lay heavily on the minds of men in Second Isaiah's day (49:5ff). Then Judah had suffered. Sennacherib tells us that in 701 B.C. he took no less than 200,150 prisoners from the towns surrounding Jerusalem—an unbelievable number; and some of these may have been deported. Finally, in 597 B.C. and 586 B.C. had come the deportations from Jerusalem and Judah at the hands of the Chaldeans. Slave-raids also from the time of Amos down had accounted for the transportation of many individuals to remote lands (Amos. 1:6,9) and Israelites were doubtless continually getting into slavery from debt and thus running the risk of being sold to foreigners (cf. Neh. 5:8).

But not all had left home by compulsion. We recall how a considerable group in Jeremiah's last days had migrated to Egypt voluntarily, in the hope of escaping war and famine (Jer. 42:14). Less than a hundred years after Second Isaiah there was a large and flourishing colony of Jews at Elephantiné far up the Nile, as

[2] Clashes with hostile neighbours must have been frequent after the great slaughter by the Babylonian armies.

the recently discovered papyri show.[3]   There is no reason why the commercial relations with other peoples fostered by Solomon should not have given rise to a steady migration of enterprising Hebrews in search of better business opportunities in other lands. After the fall of Jerusalem (586 B.C.) this migration would have been much augmented because of the deplorable conditions at home.

But whatever may have been the reason for the scattering, many Israelites took it deeply to heart. Second Isaiah was one of these. In his eyes it was a monstrous abnormality, an unmitigated calamity, to be rectified only by the reassembling of all dispersed Israelites in the home-land.

And these scattered Hebrews were in misery. It is indeed possible that here and there Jews had attained prosperity, especially in rich trading centres, but the picture we get from Second Isaiah's words is not one of well-being. Wherever he turned he saw his people plunged in wretchedness. Much of what he says in his earlier chapters applies probably to the exiles in Babylonia, but he makes no distinction between them and Hebrews elsewhere.

The chief hardship was exile itself: they were not "let go free" (45:13). But there was more than that. Second Isaiah makes Yahweh accuse Babylon of pitilessness:

"I gave them into thy hand: thou didst show them no mercy;
Upon the aged hast thou very heavily laid thy yoke" (47:6).

He says again:

"This is a people robbed and plundered, they are all of
    them snared in holes,
And are hid in prison houses:
They are for a prey, and none delivereth; for a spoil, and
    none saith, Restore" (42:22).

Just what this means we cannot say, for we are dealing with a poet who uses figures of speech freely; but it seems to indicate that the Israelites were undergoing oppression. A number may have been actually in prison. Poor king Jehoiachin had been kept in confinement for thirty-seven years (II Ki. 25:27) and perhaps the same treatment had been meted out to others. Jeremiah speaks of two Hebrew agitators being barbarously punished (Jer. 29:22). But even where unmolested by the government these Jews were not given adequate protection. No one cared about them, and the

[3] Albright, W. F., *APB*, p. 169f.

people of the country must have been quick to see that they could be roughly handled with impunity. The general attitude towards them seems to have been hostile. Second Isaiah speaks of "them that are incensed against thee," "them that strive with thee" (41: 11); of men "gathering together against thee" (54:15). The Jews lived in constant dread of violence and even death. They "feared continually all the day because of the fury of the oppressor, as though he made ready to destroy" (51:13). It reminds us of situations all too familiar in our own day.

One of the hardest things they had to bear was wide-spread contempt. They were nobodies, their nation dragged in the dust. Insults came from every quarter. They dreaded not only blows but taunts; they "feared the reproach of men, and were dismayed at their revilings" (51:7). Jacob was a "worm" (41:14).

> "They have said to thy soul, Bow down, and let us pass over;
> And thou hast made thy back as the earth, and as the street,
>   to them that passed over" (51:23).

Small wonder, then, that our prophet used words of pity to describe their condition:

> "The poor and needy seek water, and there is none, and their
>   tongue faileth for thirst" (41:17).

The effect of all this upon the mind of Israel had been unhappy. Instead of bringing out their courage and their faith in God it had done just the reverse. We have already seen how they lived in apprehension; and fear has a devastating influence upon the character. They had also turned against God. Had he not cast them off? "My way is hid from Yahweh," Israel said, "and the justice due me is passed away from my God" (40:27). "Yahweh hath forsaken me, and the Lord hath forgotten me" (49:14). He had divorced their mother (Israel) and had sold them to his creditors (50:1). Some were declaring that Yahweh was played out; He had become faint and weary (40:28). His arm was shorter than it used to be; His ancient power to deliver had not proven equal to the new time with its greater needs (50:2). Some were openly defiant, angrily (45:24) taking Him to task for His conduct towards Israel (45:9) and stoutly disobeying His laws (46:12), making their obstinate neck as an iron sinew, and their brows brass (48:4).

On the other hand, the despairing people were taking refuge

in idolatry. Whether it was the splendour of heathen worship that they saw about them, the prestige of Babylon's great world-conquering gods, Bel and Nebo, that led to this we cannot tell. But Second Isaiah's attacks upon the folly of idolatry leave small doubt that it was widely practised among the Jews. Images of deity—whatever the deity might be—seem to have been bought if not actually made by Israelites, and to have been worshipped in the usual way (44:17). Whenever fortune smiled upon them they attributed it to their idol (48:5). It was the same way of thinking that Jeremiah had encountered among the survivors of the catastrophe of 586 B.C., when in response to his reproaches they told him frankly that they intended to go on in the worship of the queen of heaven, for it was to her favour that the nation had owed the prosperity of the good old days of Manasseh (Jer. 44:17ff).

Such was the time in which our prophet found himself. But it had no such effect upon him as upon his contemporaries. Instead of depressing it elated him; for he saw in its very prostration a call for Yahweh to intervene. Like Moses in the desert he heard the approach of divine footsteps hastening to save. The heavier the clouds of disbelief about him, the fiercer blazed his own fire of faith. Now was the hour for Israel to fulfil its mission in the world! Then came the heavenly command to himself. He has left us no story of how he received it, but come it did. He must speak to Israel!

And what must he speak? With God-given insight he apprehended the task that lay before him. It was, as we have said, different from that of his earlier predecessors. No longer could he say with Micah:

"As for me, I am full of power by the Spirit of Yahweh,
    and of judgment, and of might,
To declare unto Jacob, his transgression, and to Israel his
    sin" (Mic. 3:8).

True, Israel was sinning, and he must not let it go unrebuked. But as he moved among the depression and apostasy of his time he saw that the fundamental need of Israel was not to be upbraided. It had lost heart, lost belief in its God and in its destiny. Unless it could be restored to confidence it would fail in its mission to mankind. What it wanted was comfort, and comfort he could give, for he possessed it in overflowing measure. So he set the trumpet to his lips and blew mightily.

Israel's God is in Control of the World

"Comfort ye, comfort ye my people, saith your God" (40:1). The first thing that made the situation full of hope was the fact of God Himself. For He, Yahweh, the God of Israel, stood supreme over nature and men. The universe had doubtless widened bleakly for these Israelites; they felt themselves in the midst of a vaster environment than they had realized in little Palestine. The world stretched over immeasurable distances; the stars above them looked down on multitudes of nations and peoples; the heavens were no longer familiar and protecting but alien and indifferent. Yet their God was over all! He was the *creator* of heaven and earth and men. Again and again Second Isaiah kindled to that thought. "I am Yahweh, that maketh all things; that stretcheth forth the heavens alone: that spreadeth abroad the earth (who is with me?)" (44:24). "I form the light, and create the darkness: I make peace and create evil: I am Yahweh that doeth all these things" (45:7 cf. 45:12, 18; 48:13; 51:13, 15; 54:16).

> "Lift up your eyes on high, and see who hath created these,
> That bringeth out their host by number, he calleth them
>   all by name;
> By the greatness of his might, and for that he is strong in
>   power, not one is lacking" (40:26).

Such a God was raised incomparably above the proud empires of earth; they were all in His hand, to do with them what He would.

> "Behold, the nations are as a drop of a bucket, and are
>   accounted as the small dust of the balance;
> Behold, he taketh up the isles as a very little thing . . .
> All nations are as nothing before him; they are accounted
>   by him as less than nothing and vanity. . . .
> It is he that sitteth above the circle of the earth, and the
>   inhabitants thereof are as grasshoppers. . . .
> That bringeth princes to nothing; that maketh the judges
>   of the earth as vanity. . . .
> Yea, they have not been planted; yea, they have not been
>   sown; yea, their stock hath not taken root in the earth;
> Moreover he bloweth upon them, and they wither, and the
>   whirlwind taketh them away as stubble" (40:15ff).

By the side of God nothing human had any permanence:

> "The voice of one saying, Cry. And one said, What shall
>   I cry?
> All flesh is grass, and all the goodliness thereof as the
>   flower of the field:
> The grass withereth, the flower fadeth, because the breath
>   of Yahweh bloweth upon it; surely the people is grass.
> The grass withereth the flower fadeth; but the word of our
>   God shall stand forever" (40:6ff).

It was Yahweh therefore who directed the course of history. This
was proven by the fact that He had predicted through His prophets
what would happen; He could foretell because He knew what
He would do!

> "I have declared, and I have saved, and I have showed; and
>   there was no strange god among you:
> Therefore ye are my witnesses, saith Yahweh" (43:12).

And He was directing history now. Second Isaiah saw this especially in the recent victories of Cyrus, from whom he hoped great
things.

> "I have raised up one from the north, and he is come;
> From the rising of the sun one that calleth upon my name"
>   (41:25).
> "Who hath raised up one from the east, whom he calleth
>   in righteousness to his foot?
> He giveth nations before him, and maketh him rule over
>   kings;
> He giveth them as the dust to his sword, as the driven
>   stubble to his bow.
> He pursueth them and passeth on safely, even by a way
>   that he had not gone with his feet.
> Who hath wrought and done it, calling the generations
>   from the beginning?
> I Yahweh, the first, and with the last; I am He" (41:2ff).

How absurd, then, to think of Yahweh as played out!

> "Hast thou not known? Hast thou not heard?
> The everlasting God, Yahweh, the Creator of the ends of
>   the earth

Fainteth not, neither is weary; there is no searching of
his understanding.
He giveth power to the faint; and to him that hath no
might he increaseth strength.
Even the youths shall faint and be weary, and the young
men shall utterly fall:
But they that wait for Yahweh shall renew their strength;
they shall mount up with wings as eagles;
They shall run, and not be weary; they shall walk, and
not faint" (40:28ff).

No, Yahweh's hand was not shortened that it could not redeem;
He still had power to deliver! (50:2).

What utter folly then did they exhibit who turned from Him
to the protection of idols! For there was no God but Yahweh.
Here we come upon a theme which peals through the earlier
prophecies of Second Isaiah like a refrain.

"Thus saith Yahweh, the King of Israel, and his Redeemer,
Yahweh of hosts:
I am the first, and I am the last; and besides me there
is no God" (44:6).

"I am he:
Before me there was no God formed, neither shall there
be after me.
I, even I, am Yahweh; and besides me there is no Saviour"
(43:10; cf. 44:24; 45:6,18,21; 46:9; 48:11f).

Yahweh had no intention of sharing His divinity with any rival:

"I am Yahweh, that is my name;
And my glory will I not give to another, neither my praise
unto graven images" (42:8).

To think of making an image of God!

"To whom then will ye liken God? Or what likeness will
ye compare unto him?
The image—a workman hath cast it, and the goldsmith
overlayeth it with gold,
And casteth for it silver chains.
He that is too impoverished for such an oblation chooseth
a tree that will not rot;

He seeketh unto him a skilful workman to set up a graven
image, that shall not be moved.
Have ye not known? have ye not heard? hath it not been
told you from the beginning?
Have ye not understood from the foundation of the earth?"
(40:18ff).

Yes, Israel should know better! For of what use were these idols?
They could not even *move!* Imagine praying to a piece of wood
for help! (44:17). Much less could they (like Yahweh) control
the course of history. In a dramatic scene Yahweh is represented
as challenging them to this test:

"Produce your cause, saith Yahweh,
Bring forth your strong reasons, saith the King of Jacob.
Let them bring forth and declare unto us what shall happen:
Declare ye the former things, what they are, that we may
consider them,
And know the latter end of them; or show us things to come.
Declare the things that are to come hereafter, that we may
know that ye are gods:
Yea, do good, or do evil, that we may be dismayed, and
behold it together!
Behold, ye are of nothing, and your work is of nought; an
abomination is he that chooseth you!" (41:21ff).

Yes, even the mighty idols of Babylon, which were borne in solemn
pomp along the sacred way, would be carted off ignominiously
as plunder!

"Bel boweth down, Nebo stoopeth; their idols are upon the
beasts and upon the cattle:
The things that ye carried about are made a load, a burden
to the weary beast.
They stoop, they bow down together; they could not deliver the burden,
But themselves are gone into captivity" (46:1f).

Second Isaiah also took a passing fling at the magical practices and
the astrological forecasts for which Babylon was famous; neither
magic nor star-reading can accomplish anything against God!

"Stand now with thine enchantments, and with the multitude of thy sorceries,
Wherein thou hast laboured from thy youth;

If so be that thou shalt be able to profit, if so be thou
    mayest strike terror.
Thou art wearied in the multitude of thy counsels: let them
    now stand up,
And save thee—the dividers of the heavens, the star-gazers,
Those who predict by the new moon—from the things
    that shall come upon thee!" (47:12f).

In all this Second Isaiah proved himself a worthy successor of the
earlier prophets. Like them he saw the living God so plainly that
he could see nothing else. He even went beyond them in the
incisive way in which he insisted on Yahweh's uniqueness, His
sole Godhead. None of them uttered this truth with the same
definiteness, made it stand out so sharply as did he. Indeed some
scholars have held that it is in Second Isaiah that we first meet
ethical monotheism. Such is not the case, as we have abundantly
seen. But he is its greatest exponent in the Old Testament.

Because he was so convinced that Yahweh was the only being
who could be called God, he could regard the deities of the heathen
as absolutely non-existent. They were not even subordinate entities,
demons, "powers" of any sort! The only things that did exist
were the images, and these were just wood, silver, gold—manufactured articles, standing fast indeed, but only because they stood
where they were nailed! (41:7).[1] He understood indeed that the
idol-worshippers believed in beings whom these images were intended to represent, but having swept such beings out of existence
he could fairly ridicule the idols as inanimate things. In this he
showed himself more mature than the fathers of the early church,
who commonly looked upon idols as representatives of real demonic
forces.

Israel's God, then, was in control of the world. But that was
only the first thought of comfort. Of what use to dwell on
Yahweh's greatness if he had indeed cast off his people? But He
had not!

Yahweh Still Loves His People

It is true, Second Isaiah declared, that Yahweh had been angry
with Israel and for punishment had given them into the hands
of Babylon just as in the past they had suffered oppression from
Egypt and Assyria (52:4). And our prophet was very frank in
stating the reason: It had been because of Israel's sin:

[1] Torrey has pointed out the humour of this passage, p. 185.

"Behold, for your iniquities were ye sold, and for your transgression was your mother put away (50:1).

Thy first father sinned, and thy interpreters have trans-
gressed against me.
Therefore I profaned the holy princes, and made Jacob a
curse, and Israel a reviling" (43:27f; cf. 48:1ff).

But wrath and chastisement were now a thing of the past, for
Yahweh had freely forgiven his people:

"Speak ye to the heart of Jerusalem, and cry unto her,
That her warfare is accomplished, that her iniquity is
pardoned,
That she hath received of Yahweh's hand double for all
her sins" (40:2).

He seems to have felt that this could not be too much insisted on
for he returns to it again and again:

"I, even I, am he that blotteth out thy transgressions for mine
own sake; and I will not remember thy sins" (43:25).
"I have blotted out as a thick cloud thy transgressions, and
as a cloud thy sins" (44:22; cf. 48:9; 51:22; 54:6ff).

If we inquire what ground Second Isaiah gave for this free pardon
we find that he rested it mainly on Israel's *misery*. Babylon had
gone too far in punishment and called forth a revulsion of feeling
in Yahweh (47:6). Jerusalem had indeed paid the penalty twice
over (40:2). And therefore Yahweh forgave her, both because
He loved her and for His own sake, to redeem His own reputation
before the world (48:9ff). It was not, strange to say, because
Israel had repented. At least, Second Isaiah said nothing of any
repentance on their part, and certainly did not give it as a reason
for God's change of attitude. He did not tell them, "Your sufferings have brought you to a better mind and so God has forgiven
you." Why did he thus leave out the one condition of divine
favour on which the prophets of the past had insisted? Doubtless
it was because he felt that God's generosity was the thing needed
to bring the people to repentance. He may have hoped with
Ezekiel that after the great restoration they would at last "loathe
themselves" for all they had done. But for whatever reason he did
not make it a condition of pardon.

Yes, Yahweh had forgiven and now He desired his prophet to
"speak to Jerusalem's heart," which is the beautiful way the

Hebrews expressed it. And that Second Isaiah could do, for his own heart overflowed with tenderness towards his unhappy people. Both he and God were now able for once to let go sternness and pour forth what was really in their souls. Nowhere in the Bible do we meet such surges of love and pity as in these chapters. To use a picture taken from a late writer whose utterances are found also in the Book of Isaiah, it is as if God were wiping the tears from off the face of a suffering child (Is. 25:8).

Over and over God repeated endearing names for Israel, assuring them that they were not abandoned:

> "But thou, Israel, my servant, Jacob whom I have chosen,
> The seed of Abraham my friend,
> Thou whom I have taken hold of from the ends of the
>   earth, and called from the corners thereof,
> And said unto thee, Thou art my servant, I have chosen
>   thee and not cast thee away" (41:8f).

Now it was "my servant," now "Jeshurun" (upright one), now "my chosen," now "my people" or "my nation" (44:1,21; 51:4,16). Each single Israelite was God's "servant," called by His name (43:7; 44:5; 54:17).

God likewise spoke of Himself by names that inspired comfort and trust: "thy Redeemer" (41:14; 44:24; 47:4; 54:5), "thy God" (41:10; 43:3), "the Holy One of Israel" (41:14; 43:3; 45:11; 47:4; 54:5), "thy Saviour" (43:3; cf. 45:21), "thy Maker," "thy Creator," "He that formed thee" (43:1; 44:24; 45:11; 51:13; 54:5), "thy husband" (54:5). He reminded them that He had carried them from birth, and would carry them through old age (46:3f). He told them how precious they were in His sight, how honourable—more precious than any of the nations (43:3f). How could they imagine that he had forgotten them?

> "Can a woman forget her sucking child, that she should not
>   have compassion on the son of her womb?
> Yea, these may forget, yet will I not forget thee.
> Behold, I have graven thee on the palms of my hands; thy
>   walls are continually before me" (49:15f).

Israel must not fear:

> "Fear thou not, for I am with thee; look not anxiously [1]
>   about, for I am thy God . . ." (41:10).

[1] Torrey's rendering.

Let them remember that their God is stronger than men!

> "I, even I, am he that comforteth you: who art thou, that
> thou art afraid of man that will die, and of the son
> of man that shall be made grass?" (51:12 cf. 41:10;
> 54:4,14).

Yahweh pitied their suffering, their weakness, hunger and thirst,
and told them over and over what He would now do for them.
Like a good shepherd He would feed them, gathering the lambs
in His bosom, and gently leading those that had their young (40:
11). He would open rivers on the bare heights, and fountains in
the midst of the valleys, that they might drink, and make lovely
trees to grow in the wilderness to shade them (41:17ff; cf. 44:3;
49:9ff). He would bring the blind by a way that they knew not
(42:16); He would loose the prisoners (49:9); He would hold their
right hand (41:13); strengthen, help, support them (41:10,14);
bring them safe through overflowing waters and consuming fire
(43:2); give them triumph over their enemies (41:11,15).

> "O thou afflicted, tossed with tempest, and not comforted.
> Behold, I will set thy stones in fair colours, and lay thy
> foundations with sapphires.
> And I will make thy pinnacles of rubies, and thy gates of
> carbuncles,
> And all thy border of precious stones.
> And all thy children shall be taught of Yahweh;
> And great shall be the peace of thy children" (54:11ff).

Nor would God's favour come any more to an end:

> "For the mountains may depart, and the hills be removed;
> But my lovingkindness shall not depart from thee, neither
> shall my covenant of peace be removed,
> Saith Yahweh that hath mercy upon thee" (54:10).

He who was intrusted with such a message as this would surely
find a welcome; for it was indeed a "gospel" [2] (40:9).

[2] The author is indebted to Professor C. B. Hedrick for the following comment: The New Testament term "gospel" owes its origin and its distinctive connotations to Second Isaiah (see G. Kittel, *Theologisches Wörterbuch zum N.T.*, Stuttgart, 1935, II, p. 706; also Burrows, "The Origin of the Term Gospel," *JBL*, XLIV, 1925, p. 22). The linguistic link between the two is the verb to "bring" or "proclaim good tidings" found in Is. 40:9; 52:7; 60:6; 61:1. But the connection is far more than linguistic. It extends

"How beautiful upon the mountains are the feet of him that
    bringeth good tidings,
That publisheth peace, that bringeth good tidings of good,
    that publisheth salvation,
That saith to Zion, Thy God reigneth" (52:7).

Those keeping guard on Zion's walls would break forth into singing when the messenger came and the waste places of Jerusalem
would join in the chorus;

"For Yahweh hath comforted his people, he hath redeemed
    Jerusalem!" (52:9).

And along with the good news came a gracious invitation:

"Return unto me, for I have redeemed thee" (44:22).
"Ho, everyone that thirsteth, come ye to the waters, and he
    that hath no money; Come ye!
Buy and eat; yea, come, buy wine and milk without money
    and without price. . . .
Wherefore do ye spend money for that which is not bread,
    and your labour for that which satisfieth not?
Hearken diligently unto me, and eat that which is good,
    and let your soul delight itself in fatness. . . .
Seek ye Yahweh, while he may be found; call ye upon him
    while he is near:
Let the wicked forsake his way, and the unrighteous man
    his thoughts;
And let him return unto Yahweh, and he will have mercy
    upon him; and to our God, for he will abundantly
    pardon" (55:1ff).

These promises, however, were somewhat vague. What was it
more exactly that God would do for Israel? Second Isaiah made
it quite plain, though even here he spoke in the glowing pictures
of the poet rather than with the sober precision of the man of
science.

to all that makes Second Isaiah distinctive among the prophets of the Old
Testament, and especially to the spring-like joy that pervades the whole of
his book—a joy which is inherent in the very nature of the message. God
and God's gracious breaking into history to bless and save are the ground of
this joy in both cases. Note, for example, the direct application to himself
and his mission which Jesus makes of Is. 61:1f, according to Lk. 4:16–21.
Compare also St. Mark's conscious sense of parallelism between the beginning of his message and that of Second Isaiah (Mk. 1:1–3; Is. 40:3).

Israel is to be Exalted over the Nations

In the past Yahweh had intervened with majestic power to save
Israel, especially when He brought it out of Egypt. But that
would all be forgotten in the great new thing which He was
about to do; "now shall it spring forth; shall ye not know it?"
(43:19; 48:6; cf. 51:9). It would be something that had not entered
Israel's mind, so startling and unexpected it would prove.

The exiles should be released from Babylonia. That seemed
incredible, for the vast Chaldean empire appeared to be standing
impregnable, and it had no intention of letting its captives go.

"Shall the prey be taken from the mighty, or the captives
of the terrible [1] be delivered?
But thus saith Yahweh,
Even the captives of the mighty shall be taken away, and
the prey of the terrible shall be delivered;
For I will contend with him that contendeth with thee,
and I will save thy children" (49:24f).

Second Isaiah had a very definite idea of how this would come
to pass. He had, as we have seen, been stirred by the news of
Cyrus' conquests in Asia Minor, and his faith leaped to the conclusion that the Persian monarch was to be Yahweh's instrument
in liberation. Perhaps he had heard of Cyrus' high character and
magnanimity. At any rate, he boldly proclaimed his view of the
world-situation:

"Thus saith Yahweh to his anointed, to Cyrus, whose right
hand I have holden, [2]
To subdue nations before him, and I will loose the loins
of kings;
To open the doors before him, and the gates shall not be
shut:
I will go before thee, and make the rough places smooth;
I will break in pieces the doors of brass, and cut in sunder
the bars of iron;

[1] Thus the ancient versions read.
[2] Cyrus in his well-known inscription says of the Babylonian god Marduk:
"Through all lands he made his way, he looked, he sought a righteous prince,
a being whom he loved, whom he took by the hand. Cyrus, King of Anshan,
he called by name and designated him to rule over all lands . . ." (Barton,
AB[7], p. 484). These ideas were plainly in the air at that time.

And I will give thee the treasures of darkness, and the
hidden riches of secret places,
That thou mayest know that it is I, Yahweh, who call thee
by thy name, even the God of Israel.
For Jacob my servant's sake, and Israel my chosen,
I have called thee by thy name: I have surnamed thee,
though thou hast not known me" (45:1ff).

Brought onwards by Yahweh's irresistible might Cyrus would
sweep upon Babylon and capture it, wreaking upon the doomed
city Yahweh's vengeance for its oppression of Israel. As Second
Isaiah pictured this he displayed a side of his nature which seems
strangely out of keeping with usual wide-heartedness.

"Come down and sit in the dust, O virgin daughter of
Babylon;
Sit on the ground without a throne, O daughter of the
Chaldeans:
For thou shalt no more be called tender and delicate.
Take the mill-stones, and grind meal, remove thy veil,
Strip off the train, uncover the leg, pass through the rivers.
Thy nakedness shall be uncovered, yea, thy shame shall be
seen:
I will take vengeance, and will spare no man, saith our
Redeemer . . ." (47:1ff; cf. 43:14; 46:1f; 48:14).

Cyrus then would fall heir to Babylon's captives, "taking the
prey from the mighty," and moved by Yahweh would let His
exiles go free (45:13). In exultation the prophet called his fellow-
Israelites to leave the hated city:

"Go ye forth from Babylon, flee ye from the Chaldeans" (48:20).
"Depart ye, depart ye, go out from thence, touch no unclean
thing;
Go ye out of the midst of her; cleanse yourselves, ye that
bear the vessels of Yahweh!
For ye shall not go out in haste, neither shall ye go by
flight:
For Yahweh will go before you, and the God of Israel will
be your rearward" (52:11f).

Yes, it would be a triumphal march. Cyrus would restore the captured vessels of the temple and send them forth honourably. And

now behold a wonder! The scorching wastes which years before
their fathers had traversed on the road to exile would become a
green and level way, shaded by trees and refreshed by abundant
springs of water. Such at least seems to have been the prophet's
expectation, though he might have been speaking only in figures:

> "I will even make a way in the wilderness, and rivers in
> the desert" (43:19; cf. 40:3f; 47:21).

Yahweh would lovingly lead the pilgrims, and with them enter
Jerusalem—from which He had so long been absent! (40:9ff).

Then would take place a rebuilding of fallen Jerusalem and all
the desolate cities of Judah (44:26ff). The temple would rise upon
a new foundation and Zion would be adorned with incomparable
splendour (54:11f). Second Isaiah believed that this would be
undertaken by the royal conqueror himself at Yahweh's behest
(45:13).

And in the newly constructed cities would dwell a multitudinous
people. Zion would have children!

> "For, as for thy waste and desolate places, and thy land that
> hath been destroyed,
> Surely now shalt thou be too strait for the inhabitants,
> and they that swallowed thee up shall be far away.
> The children of thy bereavement shall yet say in thine ears,
> The place is too strait for me; give place to me that I may
> dwell.
> Then shalt thou say in thy heart, Who hath begotten me
> these?
> Seeing I have been bereaved of my children, and am soli-
> tary; and who hath brought up these?
> Behold, I was left alone; these, where were they?" (49:19ff).

Whence indeed would they come? Partly by natural increase, for
Yahweh would give abundant productivity:

> "I will pour my spirit upon thy seed, and my blessing upon
> thine offspring:
> And they shall spring up among the grass, as willows by
> the watercourses.
> One shall say, I am Yahweh's, and another shall call
> himself by the name of Jacob;
> And another shall subscribe with his hand unto Yahweh,
> and surname himself by the name of Israel" (44:3ff).

But there would also be a vast gathering of Israelites from out all the lands whither they had been scattered. This is a theme on which Second Isaiah loved to dwell.

> "I will bring thy seed from the east, and gather thee from
> the west;
> I will say to the north, Give up; and to the south, Keep
> not back;
> Bring my sons from far, and my daughters from the ends
> of the earth" (43:5f; cf. 49:12; 51:11; 55:12 etc.).

The face of nature would be transformed to provide for these myriads. When Second Isaiah speaks of such a transformation it is hard at times to tell whether he means the enrichment of the deserts over which the exiles must pass on their way home or whether he has Palestine itself in mind. But there are passages that seem to refer to the latter.

> "I will open rivers on the bare heights, and fountains in the
> midst of the valleys;
> I will make the wilderness a pool of water, and the dry
> land springs of water.
> I will put in the wilderness the cedar, the acacia, and the
> myrtle, and the oil-tree;
> I will set in the desert the fir-tree, the pine, and the boxtree
> together . . ." (41:18f).
> "For Yahweh hath comforted Zion; he hath comforted all
> her waste places,
> And hath made her wilderness like Eden, and her desert
> like the garden of Yahweh . . ." (51:3; cf. 55:13).

Every one therefore would have enough. But Yahweh would also spread a spiritual feast for his people. He Himself would return to Zion, and be seen "eye to eye."

> "And all thy children shall be taught of Yahweh; and great
> shall be the peace of thy children" (54:13).

To crown all, the now despised Israel would be exalted as chief of the nations. Yahweh would make his people a "new sharp threshing instrument having teeth" to thresh the mountains—meaning probably its enemies; beating them small as chaff, for the wind to whirl away (41:15). All its foes would be humbled (41:11) and made powerless (54:15). Foreigners would no longer force themselves into the holy city to profane and destroy it (49:17; 52:1). Israel's freedom would be purchased by the enslaving of proud nations, which Yahweh would give as its ransom (43:3). Whoever should speak against Israel would be condemned by God's manifest judgment (54:17). All mankind would acknowledge its vindication:

> "Yahweh hath made bare his holy arm in the eyes of all the
> nations;
> And all the ends of the earth have seen the salvation of our
> God" (52:10).

But more, it would have dominion over the world: "Thy seed shall possess the nations" (54:3). Here, as in his exultation over Babylon's punishment, Second Isaiah shocks us by his nationalistic spirit:

> "Thus saith Yahweh,
> The labour of Egypt, and the merchandise of Ethiopia, and
> the Sabeans, men of stature,
> Shall come over unto thee, and they shall be thine: they
> shall go after thee; in chains shall they come over,
> And they shall fall down unto thee, they shall make sup-
> plication unto thee,
> Surely God is in thee; and there is none else, there is no
> God" (45:14).

In another scene he depicted the nations as slaves carrying home the dispersed Israelites:

> "Thus saith the Lord Yahweh,
> Behold, I will lift up my hand to the nations, and set up
> my ensign to the peoples;
> And they shall bring thy sons in their bosom, and thy
> daughters shall be carried upon their shoulders.
> And kings shall be thy nursing fathers, and their queens
> thy nursing mothers:
> They shall bow down to thee with their faces to the earth,
> and lick the dust of thy feet" (49:22f.).

Such is the program Second Isaiah sketched for the immediate future. But he did not rest content with the picture of a dominant and prosperous Israel. With noble inconsistency he went on to tell of a still higher destiny that was reserved for Israel or at least for one supreme Israelite. It was here that he burst the bands of nationalism and revealed a heart as wide as all mankind.

The World is to be Saved Through the Servant of Yahweh

In these chapters there appears from time to time a mysterious figure who is called the "Servant of Yahweh." Let us leave to one side for the moment the question of his identity and inquire first what work is assigned to the Servant, especially in the so-called "Servant Songs." We come upon him suddenly in 42:1ff, where Yahweh speaks:

> "Behold, my servant, whom I uphold; my chosen, in whom
>   my soul delighteth:
> I have put my Spirit upon him; he will bring forth justice
>   to the Gentiles.
> He will not cry, nor lift up his voice, nor cause it to be
>   heard in the street.
> A bruised reed will he not break, and a dimly burning
>   wick will he not quench:
> He will bring forth justice in truth. He will not burn
>   dimly nor be bruised,
> Till he have set justice in the earth: and the isles shall wait
>   for his law."

At once we see that the work of this Servant was to go beyond Israel. It was indeed the purpose of God to use him on behalf of His own chosen nation; but that would not be enough, as the Servant himself declares. For Yahweh said to him:

> "It is too light a thing that thou shouldest be my servant
>   to raise up the tribes of Jacob,
> And to restore the preserved of Israel: I will also give thee
>   for a light to the Gentiles,
> And that thou mayest be my salvation unto the end of the
>   earth" (49:6).

His was to be a universal mission, to express the tenderness of God for mankind. He would set justice in the earth, bringing it forth in truth (42:3, 4). Wheresoever men were oppressed or suffering he would come as liberator (42:7). The hungry and thirsty he would guide by springs of water (49:10), shielding them from the heat of the sun. Himself taught by God, he would know how to sustain with words them that are weary (50:4). No wonder that the isles—the coastlands of the Gentile world—would wait for his law! (42:4).

But this service would not be forced upon men. Very meekly and self-effacingly would the Servant go about his work. Although clothed with power from on high, he would use it gently. He would encounter hostility, but not resist. Yes, the mission entrusted to him involved maltreatment, but even from this he would not draw back; for he was not rebellious. He would give his back to the smiters and his cheeks to them that pluck off the hair; he would hide not his face from shame and spitting (50:5,6).

Such gentle humility, however, did not mean weakness. He would not "burn dimly" or "be bruised" till he had seen his work through (42:4). Confident that the Lord Yahweh would help him, he would set his face like a flint (50:7). At times, indeed, he might complain to God that he was receiving less than justice from the divine hand (49:4), but he would be restored to courage by a renewed glimpse of his sublime destiny and the certainty of vindication from heaven.

At last, however, he would seem to be overwhelmed. The hand of God would strike him down, crowning the sufferings and ignominy of his life with a shameful death. In derision men would give him a criminal's burial.

And then God would step in to reverse the sentence of man! His life would go on uninterrupted, he would succeed in carrying out God's will, and contemplating the result of his suffering would be fully satisfied (53:10ff).

Here there enters the poet's interpretation of the Servant's suffering, an interpretation that may well astound those who are familiar with the usual thought of the Old Testament, so new and startling is it. With consummate art he does not utter it directly, but puts it into the mouth of those who had witnessed the fate of the Servant. These were not obscure persons, for the tragedy had been enacted on a vast world stage. The spectators had been kings and nations of the earth. As they watched his agonies and death they found these suddenly illuminated by an amazing significance.

This is set forth in the matchless passage that for many constitutes the very heart of the Old Testament (52:13-53:12). It is well to let it tell its own story:

(Yahweh speaks)

"Behold, my servant shall deal wisely, he shall be exalted
and lifted up, and shall be very high.
Like as many were astonished at thee,
(His visage was so marred more than any man, and his
form more than the sons of man,)
So shall he startle many nations; kings shall shut their
mouths because of him:
For that which had not been told them shall they see; and
that which they had not heard shall they understand.

(The Gentiles speak—or perhaps Jews and Gentiles together)

Who hath believed our message? and to whom hath the
arm of Yahweh been revealed?
For he grew up before him as a tender plant, and as a root
out of a dry ground:
He hath no form nor comeliness; and when we see him
there is no beauty that we should desire him.
He was despised and rejected of men; a man of sorrows
and acquainted with grief:
And as one from whom men hide their face he was de-
spised; and we esteemed him not.
Surely he hath borne our sicknesses, and carried our
sorrows;
Yet did we esteem him smitten of God, and afflicted.
But he was wounded for our transgressions, he was bruised
for our iniquities;
The chastisement of our peace was upon him; and with his
stripes we were healed.
All we like sheep have gone astray; we have turned every
one to his own way;
And Yahweh hath laid on him the iniquity of us all.

He was oppressed, yet when he was afflicted he opened not
his mouth;
As a lamb that is led to the slaughter, and as a sheep that
before his shearers
Is dumb, so he opened not his mouth.

From oppression and judgment he was taken away: and as
for his generation, who among them considered
That he was cut off out of the land of the living for the
transgression of my people to whom the stroke was
due?

And they made his grave with the wicked, and with a rich
    man [1] in his death;
Although he had done no violence, neither was there any
    deceit in his mouth.

Yet it pleased Yahweh to bruise him; he hath put him to
    grief (or, made him sick);
When thou shalt make his soul an offering for sin, he shall
    see his seed, he shall prolong his days, and the pleasure
    of Yahweh shall prosper in his hand.
He shall see of the travail of his soul and shall be satisfied.

(Yahweh speaks)

By the knowledge of himself shall my righteous servant
    make many righteous; and he shall bear their iniquities.
Therefore will I divide him a portion with the great, and
    he shall divide the spoil with the strong;
Because he poured out his soul unto death, and was num-
    bered with the transgressors:
Yet he bare the sin of many, and made intercession for the
    transgressors."

The great truth, then, that dawned upon mankind after the
Servant's sufferings and death was just this—that these had been
vicarious. At first men thought that he was being punished for
his own sins, and they despised him; but at last they perceived that
it was they who had been the sinners, while he, the innocent, had
borne the penalty of their transgressions. While they were deriding
and crushing him he was making intercession for them.

And God had heard his intercession, had accepted his sin-offering
on their behalf. Through his chastisement peace with God had
come to them, through his stripes healing. They the erring sheep
had been brought back and freely forgiven. By the knowledge
of himself God's righteous servant had made many righteous.

This had all been willed by God; it was the divine plan of
human restoration. And the Servant had accepted it, whatever the
cost to himself. Therefore God's love went out to him; for did
not he and God stand side by side over against sinful men?

And God had seen him through! After the suffering had been
fulfilled the triumph had come. The Servant divided the spoil with

---

[1] Perhaps we should read *evil-doers* instead of a *rich man*.

the strong; and his spoil was men won to God, forgiven, healed, made righteous. And not a few, but many—he saw his seed, and they were a vast throng of the redeemed. He had become God's salvation to the end of the earth (49:6). So was he satisfied, and mankind, now at last understanding the meaning of his sufferings, rose up to bless him. A peaceful, happy earth waited for his teaching (42:4). He lived on and on, the pleasure of Yahweh prospered in his hand, and justice reigned among men (42:4).

Such was to be the work of the Servant of Yahweh. In all the Old Testament there is nothing quite like it. Its dreams for the future of mankind resemble those to be found in Is. 2:1ff (Mic. 4:1ff) and Is. 25:6ff; and the unique relation of the Servant to God is something like that of the coming king in Is. 9:6f; 11:1ff, and of the one like unto a son of man in Dan. 7:13f. But nowhere else is the redemption of mankind attributed to the *vicarious sacrifice* of the innocent for the guilty.

Who was this Servant? That question has perplexed men from the days of the Ethiopian eunuch (Acts 8:34) to the present. The question is too much involved to be discussed here. The view of the present writer is that none of the individuals with whom the Servant has been identified was vast enough to fulfil the role assigned him; and that the traditional Jewish interpretation is correct when it sees in the Servant the martyr people of God, Israel, made a spectacle to the world by its sufferings, yet by these redeeming it.

But after all the prophet's picture of the Servant and his work remains equally stupendous, whoever he might have been. With the Servant therefore we bring to a close our study of Second Isaiah, and pass on to consider what is this prophet's contribution to religion.

Second Isaiah's Contribution to Religion

When we ask how Second Isaiah affected the religious thought of Israel we are met at once with the difficulty that because of the very profundity and beauty of his ideas his influence is hard to trace. That he did exercise a marked influence is evident from the fact that his book has been preserved and placed in the canon of Scripture. It is easy of course to perceive many echoes of his thought and diction in the later writings of the Old Testament, particularly in the so-called Third Isaiah, if indeed Is. 56–66 comes from a different hand than his. But his fundamental thinking probably diffused itself over that of his successors in so pervasive a way that it cannot be confidently pointed out. To monotheistic belief he must have given a powerful impulse; so also to the idea of God's love and tenderness, the divine qualities which inspire hope and courage in faltering men. Though his glowing promises as to the future found only a pitiable fulfilment in actuality, his faith and enthusiasm could not but kindle ever afresh men's feeble energies in the "day of small things" that followed him. His universalism too continued to live on in nobler minds. His concept indeed of the suffering Servant who ministered to men, who died that they might be forgiven and lived on to possess a reborn humanity, seems to have obtained no real hold on Israel's thought for (with the exception of the doubtful Third Isaiah, cf. Is. 61:1ff) it does not reappear in the Old Testament. But here again the very fact that it was preserved shows that some must have cherished it.

But when we ask what this supreme genius of the Old Testament has given to the religious life of mankind in general it is easier to return an adequate answer. Men in all ages have gone to him for satisfaction of many needs, and have found what they sought. Several things seem to stand out clearly.

As one reads his poems one feels borne in upon him the *transscendence* of God. Nowhere in the Old Testament, not even in the oracles of Isaiah himself, does one meet more vividly the sense of God's infinite aboveness, and see the proudest of things human shrivel more helplessly in the breath of the Almighty. If we seek "creature-feeling" we find it here at its intensest.

But this transcendent God is not removed from men's world. He is grappling with it to bend it to His will. And so Second Isaiah is pre-eminently the prophet of *expectation*. The great acts of God in the past are not enough; God will do a new thing—now shall it spring forth! And it will be nothing less than a new earth wherein dwelleth righteousness. The kingdoms of the world will become the kingdom of God. For this reason Second Isaiah is the prophet of *comfort*. But we ought to understand that word in its earlier sense of encouragement, not its later meaning of mere consolation. For Second Isaiah does not console; he blows a trumpet, that the fainting and weary may revive and play the man.

In the portrait of the Servant of Yahweh he has put before men the ideal of service. It lay implicit in the lives of Israel's greatest before his time, but it was he who first gave it clear expression. When our Lord stood up to read in the synagogue at Nazareth he chose out of all the roll of Isaiah a passage which, though not included by most scholars in the "Servant Songs," might well be of their number—61:1ff. For in the mission there claimed by the Servant he saw the meaning of his own work—to preach good tidings to the meek, to bind up the broken-hearted, to proclaim liberty to the captives, and the opening of the prison to them that are bound (Lk. 4:18). It seems quite clear that he found the philosophy of his life illustrated in Second Isaiah, if he did not actually take it from Second Isaiah: "I am among you as he that serveth" (Lk. 22:27); "The Son of man came not to be ministered unto but to minister" (Mk. 10:45).

And finally, Second Isaiah has challenged us forever with his bold assertion of the truth of vicarious sacrifice. The Servant "bare the sin of many" (53:12). There are some modern minds to which the whole conception of atoning sufferings and death is offensive. For them Isaiah 53 is a survival of primitive religion which we ought long ago to have outgrown.

There can be no reasonable doubt, however, that our Lord is on the side of Second Isaiah here. Indeed, it was in this same chapter that he found the meaning set forth, not only of his work but of his death. He was to "give his life a ransom for many" (Mk. 10:45).[1] Through this he came to the firm conviction that "it was written" that he should suffer; and, we may add, that he should rise again. One cannot say indeed that it was Second Isaiah who first suggested this to his mind, although such may well have been the case. But if he conceived the necessity of his death independently, he yet must have been strengthened in his conviction by brooding over the depiction of the Servant's fate.

And many of us, though we live in the modern world, still hold to the truth which Second Isaiah here set forth and Jesus made historical reality on Calvary. Explain it how we will, the cross of Christ is to us what it was to St. Paul—an atonement. Others may account this interpretation of it foolishness; but to us it remains "the power of God and the wisdom of God" (I Cor. 1:24). And so to us the Servant Songs, and especially their climax in 52:13–53:12, seem the deepest place in the Old Testament.

[1] Some scholars think that this saying was not uttered by Jesus but is the creation of the early Christian church. The present writer, however, remains unconvinced by the arguments given in support of this view.

Chapter XX

HAGGAI AND ZECHARIAH

[520 B.C.]

The Sources

Our sources for the study of Haggai and Zechariah are the books that bear the name of these two prophets. The Book of Haggai contains four prophecies uttered by "Haggai the prophet" (his father's name is not given) from August to December 520 B.C. The first eight chapters of the Book of Zechariah (the remaining six chapters are from a later hand) give a series of prophecies and visions of "Zechariah the son of Berechiah" from November 520 B.C. to December 518 B.C.

Scholars are practically unanimous that these collections contain throughout the genuine words of the two prophets. We have therefore the best sort of first-hand sources available.

In addition to these books we have the first six chapters of the Book of Ezra, which purport to give a history of the return from the Babylonian captivity and the rebuilding of the temple (537–516 B.C.). The Books of Ezra and Nehemiah are a continuation of the Books of Chronicles and form the conclusion of the Chronicler's extensive history of Israel. Is the section with which we now have to do (Ezra 1–6) reliable? Scholars differ sharply in their answers. Some—perhaps the majority—follow the traditional view that these chapters are in the main trustworthy. Such is the position maintained in the two most recent German histories of Israel, by Kittel and Sellin. On the other hand, the late H. P. Smith, whose *History of Israel* is still a standard work, and Torrey in his *Ezra Studies* and elsewhere, follow Kosters in discarding Ezra 1–6 as a fabrication of the Chronicler and refuse to use it as a source for the history of this time. A middle ground is taken by Oesterley in his *History of Israel* [1], who pronounces the chapters unreliable but holds that at their base are various documents which contain valuable in-

[1] Vol. II, p. 81.

formation, although these have been mixed up and altered by the Chronicler. Lods' position is about the same.[2]

Who is right? The burden of proof lies (as always) upon those who reject the testimony of the document. In the opinion of the present writer they have not sustained this burden with definite proofs. He feels that their arguments, while not without weight, have been answered convincingly by those who uphold the general historicity of these chapters. The Ezra narrative, moreover, makes upon him a strong impression of reliability. This is of course a matter of individual judgment. Probably neither view will ever be *proved* unless new archaeological finds throw light upon the matter. Our best course is therefore to use Ezra 1-6 as reliable, but always to bear in mind that there are outstanding scholars who do not so regard it.

What now can these sources tell us of Haggai and Zechariah?

Haggai and Zechariah Faced a Time of New Beginning

With these two prophets we enter a new era in the history of Israel. We have seen it about to break in the prophecies of Second Isaiah; now it is here. The Jews refer to it as "the second commonwealth," but the usual term employed by scholars to describe it is "the post-exilic period."

It was brought about by the new policy of Cyrus, the Persian conqueror, who in 538 B.C. took Babylon and succeeded to the world empire of the Chaldeans. For the thrilling story of how this came about the reader must consult a history of Israel. It is enough for us to review the change of policy that made such a difference to the Jewish people.

It will be recalled that the policy of the Chaldean Empire towards rebellious states such as Judah was to deport their leaders, thus depriving them of those who would naturally build up the intellectual, economic and political life of the state, and to lay in ruins any temples, palaces and houses that might keep up the pride and spirit of those who remained in the homeland. Along with this went the carrying away of the gods of the conquered people to Babylonia, thus insuring that the former temple sites would be no longer centres for their worship. In the case of Yahweh there was no image that could be deported and the conquerors had to content themselves with taking to Babylon what sacred vessels were not broken up (II Ki. 25:13ff). As a corollary of this policy it would

[2] *PRJ*, p. 185ff.

follow that the exiles would be prohibited from returning and the people at home from rebuilding to any considerable extent.

This policy had proven successful. The leadership of the Jewish people passed from Palestine to Babylonia, which became the religious, intellectual and economic centre of the nation. The ruins were not restored; Jerusalem and Judah lay wasted. Yahweh had departed from the land of Israel, at least so far as His favour was concerned.

Cyrus on his accession to the imperial power at once changed the attitude of government. It was his policy to conciliate vassal states. One chief way of doing this was to recognize and honour their national deities, bringing them back where necessary to their original seats of worship. In the Cyrus Cylinder he glories in the fact that he had done this for many gods.[1] Such a course would involve the rebuilding of their sanctuaries, whether by the efforts of the worshippers alone, or with his aid. It would also necessitate giving permission to the exiles to return to their homes. What a wonderful thing this new policy must have been to the prostrate peoples kept under foot by the successors of Nebuchadrezzar! It marked indeed the dawn of a better day. Oesterley is right in saying of Cyrus: "His considerate treatment of the subjects of his vassal-states, and his broad-minded toleration of every form of worship, mark him out as one of the most enlightened rulers the world has ever seen." [2]

The Chronicler tells us that he gave a decree concerning the Jews, permitting them to return and to build their temple. The form in which this decree is reported in Ezra 1:2ff is open to question, particularly as the Chronicler himself gives it in a different version in Ezra 6:3ff. But that there was such a decree is likely. To reinforce his gracious edict Cyrus caused the captive vessels of Yahweh's house to be handed over to the newly appointed governor of Judah, Sheshbazzar (Ezra 1:8ff).

The permission was not in vain. If with Kittel [3] and Sellin [4] we hold that the list of Ezra 2 (= Neh. 7) gives the record of those who returned, more than 42,000 persons joined the caravan. Even if, like Oesterley,[5] we think the number of those returning was not large we may still believe that many hundreds threw in their lot

[1] Oesterley, *HI*, II, 75; Barton, *AB*⁷, p. 484f.
[2] *Ibid.*, p. 65. Quoted with permission of The Clarendon Press.
[3] *GVI*, 3/2, p. 334ff.
[4] *GIJV*, II, p. 85.
[5] *HI*, II, p. 79.

with the new venture.[6] It was a courageous thing thus to leave the life that had grown familiar to them through half a century, to give up the business or the land by which they had supported themselves, to turn their backs upon the rich opportunities, cultural and economic, now enjoyed in the world's great centre, to sever their connection with the Jewish community of Babylonia where the best of their people were to be found, and embark upon an enterprise sure to involve hardship and privation in a land which however endeared to them by the traditions of the past was really a strange country; among a people also who, though their brethren, were on a lower plane of religious and economic culture. But the pull of Jerusalem was enough. Most of the returning group must have been men of energy and enthusiasm. Of course it is possible that along with them went some who had not made a success in Babylonia and hoped for better things in the new surroundings. But the majority must have been of the pioneer type.

The long journey of the caravan is passed over in silence by our source. We can picture it in imagination, its leader Shesbazzar, to whom had been committed the responsibility of the undertaking, and associated with him twelve men, two of whom were to play an important part in the coming activities, Zerubbabel, a scion of the house of David, and Joshua or Jeshua the chief among the priests; the Levites, singers, temple servants; the hundreds (perhaps thousands) of lay-people; the following of servants; the line of burden-bearing animals—horses, mules, camels, asses—all wending their way along the glaring desert tracks through endless days. But hope ran high and eager resolve made the march less wearisome. Doubtless the singers would break forth now and then into "one of the songs of Zion" and the long line would take up the melody. There would be sabbath halts, with worship and exhortations. To us, looking back across the centuries and knowing its significance for the after world, it is an impressive sight. For these are the rebuilders of Jerusalem!

With their arrival at Jerusalem the post-exilic community came

[6] Albright, *APB*, p. 172, thinks that the list includes both the returned families and the inhabitants of the villages around Jerusalem who had remained in the land. Welch, *PEJ*, p. 140f, holds that the list gives the names of those who, up to the time when it was drawn up, had arrived from Babylonia, and could prove their right to be enrolled among the children of Israel. Eleven leaders prior to Ezra are mentioned as having led up returning exiles, Ezra himself not being included (Ezra 2:2). The list was drawn up (according to Welch) to determine the men who had the right to take part in some assembly in the "seventh month" (Neh. 7:73).

into being. Very different it was from the community of pre-exilic times, a shadow of former glory. What did the returning exiles find?

For one thing, they found people inhabiting the country. In spite of the heightened language of Second Isaiah and Zechariah we must not think of it as deserted. Just how large a population it was supporting we can only guess, but human life was going on there. Houses were dwelt in, land was cultivated. Yet the general aspect of the landscape was one of desolation. The "cities" of Judah, completely devastated by the Chaldean armies, had in many cases been permanently abandoned.[7] Multitudes of demolished stone houses and other buildings formed large stretches of ruins. Many fields must have grown up in the "thorns and briers" which in Palestine take the place of our weeds and brush. The old stone walls enclosing them would have fallen into disrepair. There would be a lack of cheerful olive and fig orchards and vineyards.

All this was evidence of a scanty and dispirited population. We have seen how with the deportations of 597 and 586 B.C., if not earlier, an outward tide of emigration had set in heavily until now Israel was a nation scattered over the whole known world. The result showed plainly in Palestine. Nor were the new-comers sufficiently numerous to make good the deficiency. From now on one of the chief complaints recurring in the literature is fewness of men.

The territory of Judah, too, had shrunk. Gone were the Negeb [8] and the Shephelah [9] and whatever districts to the north of Jerusalem the last kings had recovered of the ancient domain of the northern kingdom. There remained only a small area around Jerusalem, estimated by Kittel to have been about forty miles square, including Jericho. How pitiful a contrast to the wide domains of a David or a Solomon! Here is the ground of a second longing that meets us in the post-exilic writers—the cry for more land.

A third fact, which has been already indicated, was poverty. The luxury and magnificence which had been increasing through much of the pre-exilic period had passed with the "great houses" that lay in heaps. The peasants left in Palestine were fortunate if they could keep body and soul together. Abroad Jews had evidently

---

[7] Cf. Albright, *APB*, p. 171ff.

[8] The territory south of Hebron.

[9] The lower hills west of the central ridge. It is of course possible that the extent of early post-exilic Judah may have been greater than the estimate of Kittel (*GVI*, 3/2, p. 341ff), which is followed here. Cf. Lods, *PRJ*, p. 192.

come to riches, and the newly arrived caravan brought with it some silver and gold and other wealth (Ezra 1:6); but we can see from what Haggai says that this was by no means enough to raise the economic level to anything like comfort. Poverty, then, was the condition in which the destinies of the post-exilic community were to be worked out; and the sighing for money and abundance is another feature of the literature of the period.[10]

A fourth change from the older time was the absence of the monarchy. No Davidic king now lent dignity and hope to Jerusalem. In his place a Persian governor ruled—an emblem of their servitude!

The temple, too, lay in ruins. Just how much of it had been demolished is not clear. The notice in II Kings 25:9 mentions burning only. This would have destroyed the wood-work, including the roof and panelling, and probably have seriously injured the stone-work as well. Both Haggai and Zechariah show that stones had to be put into place (Hag. 2:15; Zech. 4:7) and a foundation laid (Zech. 4:9). Probably much of the former building still stood, but in such condition that it had to be reconstructed from the foundation up. It must have presented a dismal and heart-rending sight!

A final misery lay in the attitude of the neighbouring peoples. Jerusalem's prostration was interpreted by them in the only possible way: as a proof that Israel had been cast off and forsaken by Yahweh; or perhaps that Yahweh Himself had been powerless to prevent the disaster. They contrasted this with their own comparative "ease" (Zech. 1:13ff). As a consequence insolent contempt filled their minds. In times past Israelitish pride, to say nothing of Israelitish oppression of subjected populations, had incurred their hostility and now they could give it full rein. The Edomites particularly had taken advantage of Judah's weakness to occupy the former Jewish territory to the south. The literature of the period is poisoned with impotent maledictions against this hereditary enemy.

Such were the discouragements. On the other hand they had for the first time in centuries a favourably disposed government. Imperial oppression seems to have disappeared. They had the long discipline of the captivity behind them, their religious ideas had

---

[10] This fact of poverty is confirmed by archaeology. "It is increasingly clear that the population of the new Judaea remained poor and small until the Greek conquest, since it is only then that we begin to find solidly constructed dwellings and abundant pottery remains." Albright, *Haverford Symposium, etc.*, p. 34.

been purified, and their enthusiasm for Yahweh deepened. They had hope and faith in Yahweh and the pertinacity which later ages have learned to associate with the Jewish character. Looking back we can see that the faith was justified; the Power that shapes history was indeed on their side.

We wish we might know more of the way in which the returned exiles adjusted themselves to their fellow-Jews whom they found in the land. The account in Ezra reads as if these latter were a negligible factor; as if the new-comers assumed charge of the situation without difficulty. In fact, no mention is made of resident Jews. It is not surprising that the Chronicler omits all reference to them, for he undoubtedly took no account of them in his own mind. But it is strange that both Haggai and Zechariah, speaking only fifteen years later, say nothing of any adjustment and make no distinction between the returned and the residents. This fact has led some scholars to deny that there was any return worth recording. We can only infer that the residents welcomed the returned gladly and allowed them to assume leadership.[11] From henceforth the two groups formed one community though differences in outlook continued to exist.

One thing was now uppermost in all minds: the temple must be restored. For this purpose the exiles had returned, bearing the permission of Cyrus to rebuild. Soon after their arrival (in the early autumn of 536 b.c.) the whole countryside assembled in Jerusalem to undertake the task. The Chronicler tells us that the first act was to set the altar upon its base; which was done by the priests under the leadership of Joshua. The daily sacrifices were begun again and the whole calendar of feasts observed, starting with the feast of tabernacles. Money was contributed in preparation for the work of building and turned over to carpenters and masons. We ought not indeed to infer from this statement of the Chronicler that sacrificial worship had entirely ceased during the period of the exile; for we get a glimpse of men carrying meal-offerings and incense to the "house of Yahweh" shortly after its destruction in 586 b.c. (Jer. 41:4ff), and it is probable that animal sacrifices also continued in some fashion. This would require an altar and a priesthood, the latter being perhaps recruited from the Levites of the

---

[11] According to Welch, *PEJ*, p. 158, the Book of Ezra gives the official record published by the returned exiles, who after they had at last got control of the new Jewish state projected that slowly won control back to the very beginning of the post-exilic community. In reality, however, they had had no such exclusive power at the first.

country shrines, since the Jerusalem priests may have been largely carried into captivity. The returning exiles would have found this worship in operation. If so, the Chronicler may have ignored it deliberately, feeling that both it and its altar were "invalid" and unclean.[12] In any case, it was probably desultory, slovenly and unimpressive, and the new arrivals thought better to make an entirely fresh start.

The actual construction began the following spring, under the oversight of the Levites.

"And when the builders laid the foundation of the temple of Yahweh, they set the priests in their apparel with trumpets, and the Levites the sons of Asaph with cymbals, to praise Yahweh. . . . And they sang one to another in praising and giving thanks unto Yahweh, saying, For he is good, for his lovingkindness *endureth* for ever toward Israel. And all the people shouted with a great shout, when they praised Yahweh, because the foundation of the house of Yahweh was laid. But many of the priests and Levites and heads of fathers' houses, the old men that had seen the first house, when the foundation of this house was laid before their eyes, wept with a loud voice; and many shouted aloud for joy: so that the people could not discern the noise of the shout of joy from the noise of the weeping of the people; for the people shouted with a loud shout, and the noise was heard afar off" (Ezra 3:8ff).

This happy inauguration of the work was soon to be followed by its cessation. When the news of the undertaking spread through the northern districts it roused in the descendants of the northern Israelites the desire to have a share in it. The Chronicler in telling his story calls them "the adversaries of Judah and Benjamin," probably because they presently became hostile. But at first they seem to have been friendly enough. They approached Zerubbabel (who had apparently succeeded Sheshbazzar as governor) and the "heads of the fathers' houses of Israel" with a petition: "Let us build with you; for we seek your God, as ye do; and we sacrifice unto him since the days of Esar-haddon king of Assyria, who brought us up hither." This latter clause is possibly a malicious thrust of the Chronicler, who wanted to make it appear that the northern Israelites of his day (then called "the Samaritans") were of foreign

[12] So Welch, *PEJ*, Ch. IX, who suggests that Haggai in Hag. 2:10ff was speaking of the defilement caused by this worship and its altar.

ancestry. The probability is that they were mainly of Israelitish and Canaanitish stock.[13]

This petition opened two possible courses before the restored community. They might be comprehensive or exclusive. The whole future of the Jewish religion depended on their choice. Apparently they did not debate the matter but gave a prompt and abrupt answer:

"Ye have nothing to do with us in building a house unto our God; but we ourselves together will build unto Yahweh, the God of Israel, as king Cyrus, the king of Persia, hath commanded us" (Ezra 4:1ff).

As might have been expected, this rebuff turned friendliness into hostility.

"Then the people of the land weakened the hands of the people of Judah, and troubled them in building, and hired counsellors against them, to frustrate their purpose, all the days of Cyrus king of Persia, even until the reign of Darius king of Persia" (Ezra 4:4–5).

It was the sort of tactics that Nehemiah had to combat nearly a century later. These rejected petitioners were neighbours of the old residents and connected with them by many ties of friendship, marriage and business. Living near by and having free access to Jerusalem, they stood about and watched the slow painful process of rebuilding, ridiculed the whole idea, argued against it, made threats, used political pressure. And there was no Nehemiah to defy them! They had on their side the immense difficulties of the task, which naturally tended to discourage the workmen, and the prevailing poverty. Perhaps they employed the argument that Haggai later had to combat, that the immediate thing to do was to provide for individual needs. Why should the Jews neglect the obvious requirement of rebuilding their own houses and cultivating their own fields to labour at an unproductive enterprise like restoring a temple? Let the temple wait a while!

[13] Welch, *PEJ*, p. 154f, thinks that those who requested to take part in the rebuilding of the temple were the loyal Israelites of the north, who had remained true to the worship of Yahweh in Jerusalem. Their petition was repulsed by the authorities because the permission to rebuild was given only to the local community, and it would be unwise to awaken suspicion by making it a wider enterprise. This of course is reading into the Chronicler's words quite a different meaning from that which he intended.

But whatever means they used, the hostile neighbours were successful. The Jews gave up the attempt. "Then ceased the work of the house of God, . . . and it ceased until the second year of Darius king of Persia" (520 B.C.)—that is, for something like fifteen years [14] (Ezra 4:24).

Instead, the people went about building their own houses. The stone walls were erected or repaired and roofs snugly fitted over (Hag. 1:4). Fields were worked and orchards tended. But prosperity did not come. The usual rains did not fall; blasting, mildew and hail made inroads into the scanty crops. Unemployment became chronic. Disappointment and misery led to ill-feeling. Every one turned against every one else and tried to ~h him. Perjury and theft were common, violence made daily ... unsafe. To all these things was added the hostility of the populations bordering on Judah and holding constant intercourse with it (Hag. 1:11; 2:16f; Zech. 5:3f; 8:10, 16f).

Small wonder that the people became discouraged. It seemed as if no change had taken place, as if the indignation of Yahweh were continuing unabated after seventy years (Zech. 1:12). There seems to have been talk from time to time of beginning the reconstruction of the temple but the prevailing depression made delay appear imperative.

[14] Elsewhere one of the Chronicler's sources speaks of the foundation having been laid by Sheshbazzar and asserts that the building work continued till 520 (Ezra 5:16). We have told the story of the laying of the foundation as it appears in the Book of Ezra. But the prophet Haggai (Hag. 2:18) speaks as if the foundation was laid fifteen years later, in 520 B.C. Possibly the two statements can be reconciled. If not, we must follow Haggai as the more reliable witness, and conclude that the Chronicler got his dates mixed. This is the view of Lods, *PRJ*, p. 187, who holds that his story is his personal reconstruction of events in the distant past. Welch on the other hand, *PEJ*, p. 103, believes that the foundation was laid by Sheshbazzar, whom Cyrus sent up alone as governor, and that the real building began in 520 after the arrival of Zerubbabel and the returning exiles (for Welch places the return in 520). Horst (*Die zwölf kleinen Propheten, HAT*, 1938), agrees with Welch that Sheshbazzar came up alone, the exiles under Zerubbabel returning in the reign of Cambyses (529–522); but that Sheshbazzar did nothing to carry out his commission to rebuild the temple. Oesterley, *HI*, II, p. 89ff, suggests as his reconstruction that when the exiles under Sheshbazzar came up in 537 they found the temple still standing, though in a dilapidated condition, and sacrifices being offered on the altar. But nothing was done to rebuild until Haggai and Zechariah, accompanied by Zerubbabel and Joshua, led up another band of Jews from Babylonia early in the reign of Darius I. It can be seen from this selection of recent views how the disagreement of the sources renders certainty impossible.

It looked as if the great dream of a restored sanctuary was fading out; as if the high hopes of the return were dwindling away; as if the new community were settling down to a feeble acquiescence in defeat .... only result in the final disappearance of their religion as a force upon earth.

Then came Haggai.

Haggai Summoned the Jews to Restore the Temple

We know nothing about the man who intervened to save the situation, except what we can glean from his utterances. Not even his father's name is recorded; he comes before us simply as "Haggai the prophet, Yahweh's messenger." Had he been an exile, and if so had he returned with the caravan of 537 B.C.? Why then had he not spoken long ago? Perhaps he was like the men mentioned in Zech. 6:9ff, a recent arrival. How old was he? Perhaps he had been too young hitherto to take part in public affairs. We can return no answer. He steps upon the stage of Israel's history at a moment of crisis, speaks four times within five months, and disappears.

As he looked on the misery and failure about him he felt that he understood the reason for it. There was one thing that needed to be done and people were not doing it! Until it were done nothing would be right! Then on the first day of the sixth month (August-September), in the second year of Darius the king (520 B.C.) the word of Yahweh came unto him. We may picture him as striding forth from his place of solitary communing with deity into some forlorn open space of Jerusalem, where people were discussing their troubles amidst the intermittent activities of business, and proclaiming his message to their startled ears:

"Thus speaketh Yahweh of hosts, saying, This people say: The time is not come for Yahweh's house to be built. . . . Is it a time for you yourselves to dwell in your ceiled houses, while this house lieth waste?"

Here is the cause of all your poverty!

"Consider your ways. Ye have sown much, and bring in little; ye eat, but ye have not enough; ye drink, but ye are not filled with drink; ye clothe you, but there is none warm; and he that earneth wages earneth wages to be put into a bag with holes" (1:2ff).

Do you not see?

"Consider your ways. Ye looked for much, and lo, it came to little; and when ye brought it home, I did blow it away. Why? saith Yahweh of hosts. Because of my house that lieth waste, while ye run every man to his own house!"

What then is to be done?

"Go up to the hill-country, and bring wood, and build the house; and I will take pleasure in it, and I will be glorified, saith Yahweh" (1:8).

The effect of this abrupt demand seems to have been immediate.

"Then Zerubbabel . . . the governor of Judah . . . and Joshua the high priest, with all the remnant of the people, obeyed the voice of Yahweh their God and the words of Haggai the prophet . . . and the people did fear before Yahweh."

Preparations for the task were made with an earnestness that satisfied even the impetuous prophet. He on his part was prompt to meet their response with a new message:

"Then spake Haggai Yahweh's messenger unto the people, saying, I am with you, saith Yahweh."

Encouragement added to their zeal.

"And Yahweh stirred up (their) spirit; and they came and did work on the house of Yahweh of hosts, their God, in the four and twentieth day, in the sixth month."

Three weeks after Haggai's initial utterance the enterprise of restoration was under way! (1:12ff).

But a beginning is only a beginning. From Haggai's next utterance a month later (2:1ff) we can infer that people were realizing their poverty and lack of resources to complete their undertaking worthily. The prophet met the growing discouragement boldly:

"Who is left among you that saw this house in its former glory? and how do ye see it now? is it not in your eyes as nothing? Yet now be strong, O Zerubbabel, saith Yahweh; and be strong, O Joshua . . . the high priest; and be strong, all ye people of the land, saith Yahweh, and work: for I am with you, saith Yahweh of hosts . . . fear ye not. For thus saith Yahweh of hosts: Yet once, it is a little while, and I will shake the heavens, and the earth, and the sea, and the dry land; and I will shake all nations; and the precious things of the nations shall come; and I will fill this house with glory, saith Yahweh of hosts. The silver is mine, and the gold is mine, saith Yahweh of hosts. The latter glory of this house shall be greater than the former . . . and in this place will I give peace (prosperity), saith Yahweh of hosts" (2:3ff).

The discouragement however continued to appear. It was apparently aggravated by disappointment; the prophet's glowing promises of better times gave no sign of materializing. People were beginning to grumble. In December therefore Haggai was impelled to a third utterance, this time in a sterner tone. On the 24th day of the ninth month he reminded the people bluntly that as long as the temple stood uncompleted their worship could not please Yahweh. By dramatic questioning he elicited from the priests an enunciation of the principle that uncleanness was more infectious than holiness, then pointed the moral: "So is this people, and so is this nation before me, saith Yahweh; and so is every work of their hands; and that which they offer there is unclean." He seems to mean: "You cannot expect too much! But go on and it will come." He then reviewed the situation as it had existed before the rebuilding had started, recalling the constant set-backs they had experienced—yet without learning the needed lesson: "ye turned not to me, saith Yahweh." That past is still affecting you! It is the cause of your having no seed in the barn, no fruit products laid up for the winter. But the promises hold good. Mark this 24th day of the ninth month: "from this day will I bless you" (2:10ff).

On the same day he uttered a message to Zerubbabel personally. The governor seems to have been in special need of heartening, and Haggai knew a way to meet his need. Repeating his former declaration that Yahweh was about to shake heaven and earth, overthrow the armed power of all nations and cause them to perish in mutual conflict, he added the significant words: "In that day, saith Yahweh of hosts, will I take thee, O Zerubbabel, my servant, . . . and will make thee as a signet; for I have chosen thee, saith Yahweh of hosts" (2:20ff).

After that we hear no more of Haggai. Meanwhile there had begun to speak another prophet, Zechariah the son of Berechiah.

Zechariah Called the Jews both to Rebuild and to Repent

Like Haggai Zechariah is only a voice, although that voice is perhaps more revealing of the personality behind it. He may have come recently from Babylon, or been one of the original returning band, or a child of Jews who had all along remained in Palestine. Apparently he too had done nothing to rouse the people from their lethargy before the autumn of 520 B.C., nor is there any evidence that he joined with Haggai in sounding the first call to rebuild. He had doubtless viewed with entire sympathy the enterprise instituted by his colleague and later he was to help in carrying it through. But when the word of Yahweh came to him in November 520 B.C. (a month after Haggai had sounded his call) it struck quite a different note—the old prophetic summons to repent:

"Yahweh was sore displeased with your fathers. Therefore say thou unto them, Thus saith Yahweh of hosts: Return unto me . . . and I will return unto you. . . . Be ye not as your fathers, unto whom the former prophets cried, saying, Thus saith Yahweh of hosts, Return ye now from your evil ways, and from your evil doings: but they did not hear. . . . Your fathers, where are they? and the prophets, do they live for ever? But my words and my statutes . . . did they not overtake your fathers? and they turned and said, Like as Yahweh of hosts thought to do unto us, according to our ways, and according to our doings, so hath he dealt with us" (Zech. 1:2ff).

Here he stands in marked contrast to Haggai. Haggai did indeed pronounce the whole nation unclean (2:14) but he seems to have been speaking of the defilement caused by neglect of the temple. Now that the people were remedying this, Yahweh will bless them. That was enough for Haggai!

But not for Zechariah. In spite of the people's zeal for temple restoration he saw as he looked about him things that warned him all was not well. Not for nothing had he read and reread the prophets of a former day. Accepting their philosophy of history as vindicated by the events (1:6)—that Israel's fall had been due to its sin—he saw the same sin today threatening to bring the same doom.

In his oracles that followed there are recurring indications that the sin of Judah lay heavily on his mind. Joshua clothed in filthy garments (3:3), the flying roll of curse passing over the whole

land and cutting off every one who steals or swears falsely (5:2ff),
the woman Wickedness sealed within an ephah and carried away to
Shinar (5:5ff), show that his visions were tinged with the thought.
In spite of the frequent fasts observed during the past seventy
years of humiliation the people had not really given themselves to
Yahweh: "Did ye at all fast unto me, even to me?" It was the
same with their festivals: "And when ye eat, and when ye drink,
do ye not eat for yourselves, and drink for yourselves?" (7:5f).

In thus brooding over the sin of his people Zechariah was, as
we have said, carrying out the tradition of "the former prophets."
Their ideas found in him a receptive mind—so receptive that he
was in a certain sense fettered by them. One feels in reading his
utterances that his originality as a writer suffered from his mind
being saturated with the classics of the past. Again and again one
catches in his pages an echo of earlier passages. They are indeed
reshaped by his genius, but they remain echoes none the less.

And yet in a practical way he did show himself original. Had
he copied their *method* he would have remained content with a call
to repentance, reinforced by fierce denunciation and threatening.
But unlike the pre-exilic prophets he had a second responsibility—to
encourage the people in rebuilding their fallen state, a gigantic
physical task. We have seen how Amos and his successors found
no place for the construction of a material civilization; indeed they
regarded all efforts in this direction as futile and impious, seeing that
Yahweh's purpose was to throw down. To use a modern phrase,
they conceived themselves to be living under a *sin economy,* where
the right attitude was one of welcoming doom as a just punishment. To the mind of Zechariah, as of Second Isaiah, the sin
economy had now given place to an *economy of divine favour,* and
the prophet was confronted with the task of actual physical construction. If he had denounced too fiercely he might well have
interfered with this by lowering the morale of the people and
perhaps leading them (as did Jeremiah) to despair (Jer. 2:25). He
must balance the two requirements nicely, fostering repentance and
energy at the same time. His way of doing this displays real originality.

On the one hand, he made no peace with wickedness but held
before the people the inexorable divine demand for righteousness.
Nothing but thoroughgoing moral reformation would bring prosperity and success. He did this at times in a somewhat indirect way,
by holding up their father's sin and doom or by allusions in his
visions. Thus he could make the old prophets speak again to his

contemporaries, pleading for the widow, the fatherless, the alien, the poor, warning against mutual wrongs (7:8ff; cf. 1:2ff). At other times however he talked plainly to them of themselves, telling them their sin (7:5), and holding before them Yahweh's requirements. But in so doing he stressed the positive side of *hope* rather than the negative side of *threatening*. Thus in 8:14ff he first reminded them of Yahweh's changed attitude, how He now intended to do good to Jerusalem, how they were not to fear; and then he went on: "These are the things that ye shall do: Speak ye every man the truth with his neighbour; execute the judgment of truth and peace in your gates; and let none of you devise evil in your hearts against his neighbour; and love no false oath: for all these are things that I hate, saith Yahweh." Again, after announcing that the fasts are now to be turned into "cheerful feasts" he added: "Therefore love truth and peace."

On the other hand he was forever sounding the note of encouragement. He dwelt on Yahweh's altered disposition. "Good words, comfortable words" came to him from out the unseen (1:13) and he passed them on to his people with an overflowing tenderness that reminds us of Second Isaiah: "Thus saith Yahweh: I am returned to Jerusalem with mercies; my house shall be built in it . . . and a line shall be stretched forth over Jerusalem" (1:13ff; cf. 2:8; 8:2, 11). He loved that idea of Yahweh's coming back after being so long absent, and making the land once more His own (2:12; 8:3). This would bring all blessings in its train—the restoration of the house, the raising of Jerusalem and the cities of Judah upon their ruins, overflowing prosperity (1:16), nature never failing to yield its increase (8:12), every man able to invite his neighbour under his own vine and his own fig-tree (3:10), the return of the scattered Jews from far countries to help build the temple (6:15), Jerusalem not large enough for its inhabitants (2:4). One of the loveliest bits in the Old Testament is his picture of the future Zion:

"Jerusalem shall be called The city of truth; and the mountain of Yahweh, The holy mountain. Thus saith Yahweh of hosts: There shall yet old men and old women sit in the streets of Jerusalem, every man with his staff in his hand for very age. And the streets of the city shall be full of boys and girls playing in the streets thereof" (8:4f).

This reveals his humanness; but it also shows what we might expect from him, that the ethical note would not be lacking from his dream. "Wickedness" was to be carried away from the land (3:9; 5:5ff). As a result of all this, Israel and Judah would be restored to honour among the nations (8:13) and become no longer a curse, but a blessing.

Like Haggai, Zechariah threw himself into the enterprise of restoring the temple. He pledged his credibility as a prophet on the truth of his recurring assertion that Zerubbabel would finish the task he had begun (4:9; 6:12). True, it was a "day of small things," but not therefore to be despised. Insuperable difficulties would be overcome; "Who art thou, O great mountain? Before Zerubbabel thou shalt become a plain; and he shall bring forth the top stone with shoutings of Grace, grace, unto it" (4:7). He had indeed special messages for the hard-pressed leaders, Zerubbabel and Joshua, and he did his best to hold up their hands and the hands of the priests associated with Joshua. In one vision he saw Joshua (perhaps the representative as high priest of the whole community) freed from the accusations of the Satan, clothed in clean garments and given access to the heavenly courts along with authority to rule the earthly temple (3:1ff). In another he saw Zerubbabel and Joshua supplied with divine power in a constant stream (4:12). An oracle bade him make a crown for "the Branch" and set it upon Joshua's head in token that the Branch should rule with Joshua at his right hand (6:9ff as usually altered).

Two years later, in December 518 B.C., when the task of rebuilding was only half done and the people had apparently begun to grow disheartened again, he came forward with a message for them all. Its refrain is, Fear not, . . . let your hands be strong (8:9, 13, 15). It was then that he uttered some of his brightest promises and especially one which held out a world-challenge to the Jewish nation. But of that presently. Thus long after Haggai's voice had fallen silent we still hear him encouraging his fellow-Jews to carry through the enterprise they had undertaken.

Both Haggai and Zechariah Looked for the Exaltation of Jerusalem through a World-Catastrophe.

As we have seen in our study of Amos, Isaiah, Jeremiah and Ezekiel, it was nothing new for prophets to take a world-view. Did not Yahweh's purpose embrace the whole earth; was not His hand stretched out upon all the nations? (Is. 14:26). But in these prophets of the tiny restored community, with its experience of being emptied from vessel to vessel (Jer. 48:11), with its brethren

scattered through all lands, the world-prospect was even more pronounced. Zechariah felt himself in the presence of the Lord of the
whole earth (4:14; 6:5), saw His eyes and His winds running to and
fro through the nations (4:10; 6:7). All that happened within little
Judah was big with universal importance, gave meaning to the vast
drama of human history.

To Haggai, and probably also to Zechariah, this drama was about
to culminate in a great divine intervention; not a change from one
empire to another, but a catastrophe bringing all earthly dominions
to a close, and ushering in the rule of Yahweh, the kingdom of
God. Yahweh was to shake the heavens and the earth and the sea
and the dry land and all nations (2:6f, 21f). "Be silent, all flesh,
before Yahweh," cried Zechariah; "for he is waked up out of his
holy habitation" (2:13).

This would mean the exaltation of Jerusalem. Haggai saw the
precious things of all nations coming into its gates, and their silver
and gold making the house of Yahweh glorious (2:8f). Yahweh
would overthrow the throne of kingdoms and destroy the strength
of the kingdoms of the nations, their chariots and those that ride
in them, every one by the sword of his brother, and then would
come the day of the Jews (2:22f). Zechariah looked forward to
the time when the horns of the nations lifted up against Judah
should be cast down, when Yahweh would shake His hand over
the nations and the Jews would despoil those whom they had
served (1:21; 2:8f).

It would also mean the manifestation of the Messiah. And both
prophets were agreed that the Messiah would prove none other
than Zerubbabel, the governor, scion of the house of David. Haggai
said so plainly: "In that day, saith Yahweh of hosts, will I take thee,
O Zerubbabel, my servant, the son of Shealtiel . . . and will make
thee as a signet; for I have chosen thee, saith Yahweh of hosts"
(2:23).

Zechariah seems to have had the Messiahship in mind when he
told his vision of Zerubbabel and Joshua standing by the Lord of
the whole earth as "anointed ones" (sons of fresh anointing oil),
receiving the constant supply of divine power. It is interesting to
note that he associated the high-priest with the Davidic scion in
this dignity (4:11ff). When a number of Jews arrived from Babylon bringing rich offerings for the temple, Zechariah, who doubtless saw in their coming an earnest of the great gathering about
to be, received a divine command to take of them silver and gold
and make a crown for Zerubbabel's head. He was then to say

unto him: "Thus speaketh Yahweh of hosts, saying, Behold, the man whose name is the Branch; and he shall grow up out of his place; and he shall build the temple of Yahweh . . . and he shall bear the glory and shall sit and rule upon his throne; and a priest shall be at his right hand (LXX); and the counsel of peace shall be between them both." The crown was then given to the men from Babylon to be kept for a memorial in the temple against the day of fulfilment (6:9ff). Here again the office is conceived as a double one. Joshua receives the crown, yet apparently not for himself, but for the Branch, to whom it is not yet given—perhaps for the sake of caution. The Branch is to have a priestly colleague with whom he works in utmost harmony.

One wonders what effect these pointed utterances had upon Zerubbabel himself. Did they encourage him to tread ambitious paths? Did they, as some think, lead to his displacement as governor? Certainly they must have been heady wine; and it is not at all unlikely that Zechariah had to warn him against plans to seize power by worldly means. "This is the word of Yahweh unto Zerubbabel, saying, Not by an army, nor by power, but by my Spirit" (4:6). The angel's admonition in the third vision may have been aimed at his aspiration to fortify the capital:

"Jerusalem shall be inhabited without walls. . . . For I, saith Yahweh, will be unto her a wall of fire round about her, and I will be the glory in the midst of her" (2:4f).

If Zechariah had said no more than what we have recorded above he would have to be placed alongside Haggai in the ranks of Israel's nationalistic prophets. For merely looking out over the whole world and believing that one's God rules all peoples does not prevent one from being a nationalist. We see that in Haggai, who had no further interest in other nations than to get their money! As for themselves, let them kill each other off (2:22). Of course, he probably did not mean this literally, but the significant thing is that he made for them no place in the happy future soon to dawn. And Zechariah, as we have just seen, talked at times in much the same strain. He was enraged at the peoples surrounding Judah, at their prosperity when Judah was prostrate, at their adding to Judah's misery in whatever way they could (1:15). He cherished an especial enmity towards Babylonia for its long cruelty to his people (2:8) and with grim satisfaction witnessed the woman Wickedness being transported to the "land of Shinar" where she would build her a house! (5:9ff). "And when it is established, she shall be set there in her own place." That was where she belonged! Not even the fact that Persia now ruled in Babylon checked his hatred. Indeed one of the surprising things in him, as in Haggai, is that he had no good word for Persia, in spite of the benignity of its policy. One would have expected him to regard the reigning emperor as Yahweh's appointed regent, as Jeremiah and Ezekiel regarded Nebuchadrezzar. Had not Second Isaiah proclaimed Cyrus as Yahweh's servant? But no. He was too full of dreams of Yahweh's coming dominion and Israel's autonomy to welcome even the comparatively mild yoke of Persia.

But there were two sayings in Zechariah's prophecies that transcended nationalism. Both depict the destiny of the Gentiles in the glorious future. The first is found in 2:11: "And many nations shall join themselves to Yahweh in that day, and shall be my people." The other concludes the beautiful series of oracles in chapter 8:

"Thus saith Yahweh of hosts: It shall yet come to pass, that there shall come peoples, and the inhabitants of many cities; and the inhabitants of one city shall go to another, saying, Let us go speedily to entreat the favour of Yahweh and to seek Yahweh of hosts: I will go also. Yea, many peoples and strong nations shall come to seek Yahweh of hosts in Jerusalem, and to entreat the favour of Yahweh. Thus saith Yahweh of hosts: In those days it shall come to pass, that ten men shall take hold, out of all the languages of the nations, they shall take hold of the skirt of him that is a Jew, saying, We will go with you, for we have heard that God is with you" (8:20ff).

Now it must be granted that in a sense these sayings are nationalistic, for they make the Jews and their worship the object of world-wide desire and thus feed the pride of the hearers. Very flattering it was for a people now universally despised and shunned to think that soon they would be sought out by multitudes all over the world. What is more, the Gentiles must become converts to Judaism. But none the less there is an international ring about the passages, as there is about the great saying from which the second seems to draw its inspiration (Is. 2:2ff = Micah 4:1ff). For the Gentiles are not to be coerced; they will come of their own free will, come because they see the need of divine help, come with love and expectancy. And they will be welcomed, will be made

Yahweh's people just as much as the Jews themselves. True, there will be an exaltation of the Jew, but a noble one. For the saying lays on him a responsibility; if they wish to go with him he must receive them, must teach them and make room for them. He dare not be selfish; he must share his God with all peoples.

With this utterance Zechariah's book comes to an end.

But though he and Haggai seem to have uttered no further oracles, the work went on. Two years later (516 B.C.) the second temple stood completed (Ezra 6:15).

Reflections on Haggai and Zechariah

The two prophets whose work we have been reviewing are not towering figures in Israel's history. When one contrasts them with Amos, Isaiah, Jeremiah or Second Isaiah they seem small indeed. So was every one else in the new commonwealth. It was a day of small personalities, as of small things. And yet they, like their community, had a greatness of their own. For they stood (and they sensed it) between a mighty past and a yet mightier future. That was their significance. And standing just there they and their contemporaries had to fulfil a certain definite task—to carry the past over into the future. This they did.

As we have seen, that task imposed upon them a responsibility such as rested on none of the giant prophets of the past. A material civilization must be painfully reared; in particular, a sacred building must be restored; and they must inspire their fellow-Jews to do this. What impresses us in Haggai is that he perceived this so clearly. He was a man of one idea, one objective.

It was indeed a narrow one. That is why he alone of the prophets may be said to have succeeded in carrying the people with him. He did not ask them to make any radical change in their lives, but only to throw off their lethargy and start rebuilding the temple. That was not much more of an undertaking than for a modern parish to erect a church or a parish house, or even to put through a successful every member canvass!

But it was a necessary one. The whole future of the Jewish religion was being held up for the lack of a temple which people could love and respect. It might be a small matter compared to the deep things of the Spirit, but it had to be attended to at once. Such situations do arise, and when they do a leader like Haggai is needed—a leader who can (though perhaps only temporarily) concentrate on the single task before him.

A leader is needed also who can see in the feeble present the sublime future. And that takes faith. What faith these two men had! To Haggai's vision the unpretentious structure now beginning to arise need not fear comparison with the remembered splendour of the past. Was it not Yahweh's house? And to Yahweh belonged the future. "The latter glory of this house shall be greater than the former" (2:9).

Greater than the former! Had we been there and heard him utter those words amid the fallen stones of that tiny city in a corner of the Persian empire, we should have deemed them fantastic. And yet he was right.

He wanted material glory—silver and gold and pleasant things. It did not come as soon as he expected, or in the same way, but it did come. Five hundred years later there was to stand on this very site a temple that in its marble and gilt, its spacious courts and long colonnades would be one of the wonders of the world. To that temple yearly were to come unnumbered thousands of the faithful from all countries bringing the pleasant things of the nations as an offering. Rich men would cast their gifts into its treasury; people would exclaim over its goodly stones and offerings. Yes, Haggai was right.

And yet—for this must be added—just because he thought mainly of the material glory he missed the meaning of it all. For the true glory of Israel's future lay in a realm which he did not mention— the spiritual. The modest second temple now arising was to become the centre of the amazing religious life which we meet in the psalms. From Herod's temple were to go out the world's two supreme religions to bless mankind. While as for the material glory, that would pass. The time would come when not one stone would be left upon another, and the religion of Israel would be thrust forth homeless into history, homeless to remain.

Haggai did the work that was essential; but his influence was thrown on the side of two tendencies that were destined to bear evil fruit in post-exilic Judaism. One was the tendency towards a narrow nationalism. The other was the tendency to think that he who did the will of Yahweh was justified in expecting material rewards. Haggai plied this motive boldly and without reserve. In no other writing of the Old Testament is the *quid pro quo* more brazenly proclaimed.

When we turn to Zechariah we are sensible of a different atmosphere. He did indeed hold out material rewards as an incentive (8:11ff) but he also dwelt on the love of God and gave voice to moral aspiration. He blew the harsh trumpet of nationalism, but put it from his mouth to utter the wooing call of an all-embracing hope. In spite of his devotion to the material needs of his hour his heart remained set upon the greater things. We have seen how, unlike his predecessors, he had to shoulder a dual responsibility—for reconstruction and repentance—and undeniably he lost something thereby. He did not utter in its blazing simplicity the eternal "Either . . . Or." But he did give forth a ringing "Both . . . And."

In this he showed himself nearer our own age than were the former prophets. Their attitude of indifference or hostility towards material enterprises is an impossible one if it be widely held in any community. Zechariah, on the other hand, was interested in building not only a temple to God but houses for people to live in. We may not care for the fantastic visions in which he clothes his thought; his Messianic expectation and his prediction of world-catastrophe may leave us cold; his little book may be full of foreign and antique touches; but when he talks of old people sitting in the sun and boys and girls playing in the streets; when he bids men to be strong and fear not, but build; when he welcomes all nations to God's house; when he speaks of loving truth and peace and looking out for the widow, the fatherless, the alien, the poor—then we understand him. He was very human and his influence made for humanity. He had his limitations but he was on the side of the angels—the angels with whom he used to talk.

Chapter XXI

MALACHI

[*c.* 500 B.C.]

The Sources

Our only source for the study of Malachi is the little book that bears his name. This is accepted by scholars as genuine throughout. It contains a number of utterances grouped under the general caption: "The burden of the word of Yahweh by Malachi." Though Malachi does not adhere to the usual prophetic style his words were evidently intended by himself to be received as prophecy. In any case they supply us with a first-hand source from which we may gather something of what he thought, though they tell us absolutely nothing about him directly; not even his name, for "Malachi" (my messenger) is not really a name.

Nor do we know just when he lived. It must have been in the Persian period, for he uses the word "governor" (*pehah*) to denote the official in charge of the district, a term employed elsewhere of Persian officers. The temple is evidently standing, so we must place him after 516 B.C., the date of its rebuilding. He complains of marriages with heathen women and stinginess towards the temple services, both of which evils were attacked by Nehemiah and Ezra; and so it is customary among scholars to set him shortly before the Nehemiah-Ezra reforms—say about 460 B.C. But we must remember that this is not a certain date. Unlike the books of Haggai and Zechariah his book contains no dating of its own. In any case, it seems likely that it was published before the priests' code became authoritative, for it speaks (as does Deuteronomy) of the priests as the sons of Levi, not of Aaron, while the priests' code derives them from Aaron as ancestor.

Malachi Lived Among a Complaining People

It was a time of economic depression. Farming was going badly, and most of the people seem to have been dependent on farming.

413

A succession of parasites had attacked the crops, and the vines were casting their fruit prematurely (3:11). This was interpreted in the usual way, as a sign of Yahweh's disfavour. Yet the people could not understand why He should be harsh with them. They felt that they had served Him faithfully. No gross breach of duty was on their consciences; they were paying tithes and bringing animals to sacrifice (1:6ff; 3:7ff). Yahweh's ordinances were being observed, and they had humbled themselves before Him in mourning and doubtless in fasting, that they might avert His wrath (3:14). All in vain. The misery continued. And it was aggravated by the prosperity of persons who made no pretence of caring for Yahweh but openly derided religion and talked with insolent contempt of God. Their conduct was in open defiance of His righteous laws. Yet nothing happened to them! (2:17; 3:15). All this led to discontent with Yahweh. Why did He not give evidence of His love; why did He not intervene to vindicate His righteous government? Not that the people were rebellious. They continued to serve Him and to give Him their allegiance. But they did complain among themselves of His slackness (3:16).

And indeed their religious faith was being severely tested. Had there not been definite promises made by Haggai and Zechariah as to the prosperity which would come if the temple were only restored? Had they not been told by Second Isaiah and by Zechariah that Yahweh's attitude had changed from anger to favour, that they might expect a new age of blessing? Yet He was still afflicting them!

Some one was needed to speak for Yahweh and he now appeared.

Malachi Came Forward as Yahweh's Advocate

Into the midst of the malcontents and their grumbling came one who addressed them abruptly, without the customary introductory formula of the prophets. In Yahweh's name he boldly asserted the very truth that they were denying: "I have loved you, saith Yahweh." Then, in a way all his own, he let them answer back: "Yet ye say, Wherein hast thou loved us?" He was ready for their challenge:

"Was not Esau Jacob's brother? saith Yahweh:
Yet I loved Jacob; but Esau I hated,
And made his mountains a desolation,
And gave his heritage to the jackals of the wilderness" (1:2f).

It was a strange answer, to our thinking. He seems to have been pointing to some disaster that had recently overtaken the Edomites —perhaps the invasion by the Nabatean Arabs. Edom, Judah's hated enemy, had suffered somewhat the same fate that had come to Judah at the fall of Jerusalem in 586 B.C. Malachi saw in this an evidence of Yahweh's love to Israel! And the divine favour was further shown by the assertion that Yahweh did not intend to let the Edomites rebuild! So that men would call them "The border of wickedness," and "The people against whom Yahweh hath indignation for ever." "And your eyes shall see, and ye shall say, Let Yahweh be magnified beyond the border of Israel" (1:4f).

Certainly this was not a happy exordium. Malachi was playing upon one of the most sinister passions of his people—their execration of Edom. The conception of Yahweh to which he was giving utterance was vicious. And moreover his reply was not convincing. After all, men want some more satisfactory evidence of divine favour than the sight of calamity befalling their enemies.

But this prophet had better things to say. He next turned on the priests.

"A son honoureth his father, and a servant his master:
    If then I am a father, where is mine honour?
    And if I am a master, where is my fear?
    Saith Yahweh of hosts
    Unto you, O priests, that despise my name" (1:6).

To their indignant question: "Wherein have we despised thy name?" he replied by charging them with offering worthless animals on the altar. The lay-people were cheating God by bringing to sacrifice the poorest beasts they possessed; and the priests were allowing it. This was due in part to their fear of offending the offerers, when they were people of influence (2:9), and in part to their own mental attitude towards the temple services. Malachi charged them with nothing less than contempt of the table of Yahweh (1:7). "Ye say, The table of Yahweh is polluted, and the fruit thereof, even its food, is contemptible. Ye say also, Behold, what a weariness is it! and ye have snuffed at it, saith Yahweh of hosts" (1:12f).

Why should not Yahweh be offended? Would the governor accept such animals in payment of dues? Could they expect Yahweh to receive them? "And now," went on the prophet ironically, "entreat I pray you, the favour of God, that he may be gracious

unto us!" What! With such priests? "This hath been from your
hand (all this trouble): will he accept any of your persons? . . .
Oh that there were one among you that would shut the doors that
ye might not kindle fire on mine altar in vain!" Contrast this
with what is going on in the Gentile world.

> "For from the rising of the sun even unto the going down
>   of the same
> My name is great among the Gentiles;
> And in every place incense is offered unto my name, and
>   a pure offering:
> For my name is great among the Gentiles,
> Saith Yahweh of hosts" (1:11).

Now that is an astounding thing to hear from the lips of an
ancient Jew, especially one who had just spoken with such bitterness of Edom! For it seems to mean nothing less than that Malachi
looked on the worship of the heathen world as offered to Yahweh;
offered also in a purer way than by His own priests in His own
temple.[1] True, this meaning does not appear in the American
Revised Version, which follows an old Christian tradition in putting
the verbs in the future tense. Read thus, Malachi was merely predicting that in the time to come the world would turn to Yahweh.
But the Hebrew points to the present tense and is so understood
by modern scholars generally. The usual interpretation is that
Malachi was thinking of the noble worship of Ahura Mazda, the
Persian "God of heaven," and saw in this an unconscious honouring
of Yahweh.

It is easy to see what led Malachi to insist upon such a wide
and catholic view of non-Jewish religion. Priests and people were
suffering from an oppressive sense of the *smallness* of the Jerusalem
temple and its services. It seemed to count for so little in the world;
that was why they had come to think slightingly of it. Malachi
wanted to bring home to them the immensity and majesty of the
Being whom they served; "I am a great King, saith Yahweh of
hosts, and my name is terrible among the Gentiles" (1:14).

Unless you amend and give glory to my Name, said Malachi
to the priests, I will strike you in your most vulnerable spot—I will
"curse your blessings" (diminish your income)! Indeed, Yahweh
had cursed these already. And naturally; for the popular disregard

[1] Eichrodt, *TAT*, p. 222, regards this as coinciding with the P code idea
that in the Noachic covenant God gave a constitution (*Ordnung*) to all
mankind (cf. Ezek. 5:6f).

of obligations and lowering of standards in offerings had made itself felt in decreased revenues. And Yahweh would further humiliate them before the people, to teach them the true meaning of their office. Here Malachi reminded them of the high ideal of their vocation, as it appeared in Yahweh's dealings with their ancestor Levi.

> "My covenant was with him of life
> And peace, and I gave them to him
> That he might fear; and he feared me,
> And stood in awe of my name.
> The law of truth was in his mouth,
> And unrighteousness was not found in his lips:
> He walked with me in peace and uprightness,
> And turned many away from iniquity.
> For the priest's lips should keep knowledge,
> And they should seek the law at his mouth;
> For he is a messenger of Yahweh of hosts" (2:5ff).

Forgetting this the priests had themselves fallen into contempt.
  But it was not the priests alone that he attacked on this score of worship. Boldly he confronted the laity with their dishonesty. "Cursed be the deceiver, who hath in his flock a male, and voweth, and sacrificeth unto the Lord a blemished thing!" (1:14). When to his call for repentance they responded, "Wherein shall we return?" he replied that they had robbed God in tithes and offerings (3:8). Like Ananias and Sapphira (Acts 5:1ff) they had been keeping back part of their dues!

> "Ye are cursed with a curse,
> For ye rob me, even this whole nation.
> Bring ye the whole tithe into the store-house,
> That there may be food in my house,
> And prove me now herewith . . .
> If I will not open you the windows of heaven
> And pour you out a blessing,
> That there shall not be room enough to receive it" (3:9f).

Here Malachi fell back on the motive already used by Haggai and Zechariah and made the same promise of material well-being; adding that all the other nations would then bless Israel, seeing its prosperity!
  Dishonesty in rendering dues to God, however, was not the only

charge that Malachi brought against the religious people of his day. He was outraged by their frequent practice of divorcing the wives with whom they had been living for years, and taking other women in their place. The passage in which he attacks this (2:10ff) is obscure, and it is not clear what wives were thus being put away—whether Jewish wives set aside in favour of Gentile women, or Gentile wives divorced because of religious scruples. The former view is more commonly held by scholars and seems to be the more likely one. We shall therefore follow it here.[2]

Malachi brought two counts against this practice. The first was that it profaned the holiness of Yahweh by introducing into the community the daughter of a foreign god. Yahweh's aim was to have a "seed of God" (2:15), a holy people; and these heathen women constituted an alien element of the population which could not but injure its religious purity. And what of the children of such a union? Would they not grow up under heathen influence? Apart from this, the physical integrity of the race was threatened, and that meant much to Malachi. The deed, to his mind, was an "abomination" before Yahweh, to be punished by the extermination of the guilty family (2:11f). Yahweh loved His holiness and would tolerate no infraction of it.

The second count was what we should call ethical as distinguished from ritual—although Malachi probably made no such separation in his own thought. Such divorces were a betrayal of a sacred obligation to the first wife. Here Malachi struck a note that is unique in the Old Testament:

> "Have we not all one father? hath not one God created us?
> Why do we deal treacherously every man against his
> brother,
> Profaning the covenant of our fathers? . . .
> And this ye do: ye cover
> The altar of Yahweh with tears, with weeping and with
> sighing,
> Because he regardeth not the offering any more,
> Neither receiveth it with good will at your hand.
> Yet ye say, Wherefore?

[2] Kittel, *GVI*, 3/2, p. 556; Marti, *HSAT;* Nowack, *HKAT;* Heller, *SAT,* II, 3, p. 114; J. M. P. Smith, *ICC;* Grieve, *PCB;* Horst, *HAT,* take the view that those divorced were Jewish wives. Sellin, *GIJV,* II, p. 128, excises verses 11 and 12 as a later prosaic addition and thinks that Malachi is condemning divorce in general, even of Philistine and Canaanitish wives. Oesterley, *HI,* II, p. 108, seems to have the same view as Sellin.

Because Yahweh hath been witness between thee and the
 wife of thy youth,
Against whom thou hast dealt treacherously
Though she is thy companion, and the wife of thy cove-
 nant. . . .
Take heed in your spirit,
And let none of you deal treacherously against the wife
 of his youth.
For I hate putting away, saith Yahweh, the God of Israel,
And him that covereth his garment with violence. . . .
Therefore take heed in your spirit, that ye deal not treach-
 erously" (2:10ff).

Finally, Malachi threw back into the people's teeth their very
complaining against God.

"Ye have wearied Yahweh with your words.
 Yet ye say, Wherein have we wearied him?
In that ye say, Every one that doeth evil is good
In the sight of Yahweh, and he delighteth in them;
Or where is the God of justice?" (2:17).
"Your words have been stout against me. . . .
Ye have said, It is vain to serve God;
What profit is it that we have kept his charge? . . .
And now we call the proud happy;
Yea, they that work wickedness are built up;
Yea, they tempt God and escape" (3:13ff).

Malachi realized that this sort of talk voiced a real difficulty.
It was not the godless that spoke "thus" (LXX 3:16) but they that
feared Yahweh, in their own pious circle. Indeed, it is what we
hear in many of the psalms, and the Book of Job justifies its hero
in his passionate utterance of the same complaint. But our prophet
had his answer ready. He made three points:

1. This talk is in itself wrong, it shows a mind that is "stout"
 against Yahweh, and it wearies Him.

2. It is unjustified. The God of justice is at hand, and you will
 presently see Him.

"Behold, I send my messenger, and he shall prepare the way
 before me;
And the Lord, whom ye seek, will suddenly come to his
 temple;

And the messenger of the covenant, whom ye desire,
Behold, he cometh, saith Yahweh of hosts.
But who can abide the day of his coming?
And who can stand when he appeareth?
For he is like a refiner's fire, and like fuller's soap" (3:1ff).

He will begin with the priests, purging them, refining them, till they shall offer unto Yahweh offerings in righteousness! But he will not stop there;

"I will come near to you to judgment:
And I will be a swift witness
Against the sorcerers, and against the adulterers, and
    against the false swearers,
And against those that oppress the hireling in his wages,
The widow and the fatherless,
That turn aside the sojourner from his right, and fear not
    me,
Saith Yahweh of hosts. For I, Yahweh, change not;
Therefore ye, O sons of Jacob, are not consumed" (3:5f).

What did Malachi mean? Did he imply that among the godly people who were impatient for Yahweh's intervention there were those who were committing grave social wrongs, as well as using magic? It seems so. There is no mistaking the warning tone of his words. He was taking up the old theme of Amos: "Wherefore would ye have the day of Yahweh?" (Amos 5:18). At any rate, he wanted them to look into their own lives. "Who may abide the day of his coming?" Better be thinking of that, instead of asking "Where is the God of justice?"

3. For those who can stand the test, that day will be all that
    you hope. For God is not forgetting; He is listening to all
    that His lovers say among themselves, and recording it.

"And they shall be mine, saith Yahweh of hosts,
Even mine own possession, in the day that I make;
And I will spare them, as a man spareth
His own son that serveth him.
Then shall ye discern between the righteous and the
    wicked,
Between him that serveth God, and him that serveth him
    not" (3:17f).

No trouble then about God's favouring the God-tempters, the proud, the bad!

"For behold, the day cometh, it burneth
As a furnace, and all the proud,
And all that work wickedness, shall be stubble;
And the day that cometh shall burn them up . . .
That it leave them neither root nor branch.
But there shall arise upon you, O ye who fear my name,
The sun of righteousness with healing in its rays;
And ye shall go forth, and gambol as calves of the stall."

But this lovely picture is marred by the conclusion:

"And ye shall tread down the wicked; for they shall be ashes
Under the soles of your feet
In the day that I make, saith Yahweh of hosts" (4:1ff).

There follow three verses which are regarded by many scholars as a later addition. They urge men to remember the law of Moses and declare that God in his mercy will send Elijah before the great and terrible day to restore unity to a divided people, turning the hearts of fathers and children to each other, lest Yahweh coming should smite the earth with a ban, destroying all that lives (4:4ff). If Malachi wrote them, he concluded with the thought of man's sin and God's forbearance—a forbearance without which man would have no hope.

This third point that Malachi made shows that he understood the grumblers' need of *comfort*. Their words called for rebuke, their self-confidence for warning, but neither rebuke nor warning were enough. And so, "changing his tone" like St. Paul (Gal. 4:20), he broke forth in tender assurance. Do not be distressed. God loves you. He knows that you are serving Him, that your very words of complaint show your loyalty. He will make everything right. Only trust Him, and keep His commandments, and He will give you your hearts' desire. One is reminded of the father's tenderness to the indignant elder brother in the parable: "Son, thou art ever with me, and all that I have is thine" (Lk. 15:31).

An Estimate of Malachi

Malachi had his distinct limitations. He appealed to Jewish hatred of Edom, projecting this back upon God. He invited the pious to gloat over the coming downfall of the wicked whom they would tread under foot as ashes. He insisted frankly on the dogma of material retribution and played upon the motive of worldly self-interest.

Some say that he also exalted the ritual side of religion too highly; that he was more interested in the presentation of unblemished victims for sacrifice and the payment of tithes in full than in man's relations with man. There may be some truth in this but on the whole it seems unjust. In the first place, he was deeply concerned over divorce, which was a matter of social ethics; and he sounded the old prophetic note against the violators of the great social duties. But in the second place, he had good reason to make much of the fraud being practised by priests and people in temple gifts and dues. The moral effect of such trifling with God could not but prove injurious. Looked at in the light of Israel's historic mission it was of supreme importance that the Jews should take the worship side of religion seriously. Malachi saw clearly that disrespect towards God in ritual matters struck at the very root of those relations with the Unseen that were Israel's peculiar treasure. Nor have modern Christians outgrown the necessity for reverent and pure worship. Wherever this is threatened (as it was in the days before the Oxford Movement in England and America) Christian leaders are compelled to give it the same attention as did Malachi, till it be restored. And since even today there is ever present in the church a tendency towards slovenliness and easy-going ways in worship, Malachi's book continues to be timely.

Especially challenging is the high ideal of the priest which he enunciated (2:4–7). Awe before God, sincerity, high character, knowledge, responsibility for other men's amendment, a conviction of divine message, trustworthy teaching, walking with God in peace and uprightness—these are qualifications that can still cause men to seek the law at his mouth. One can truly say that Malachi here summed up all that was implicit in the attitude of the best Old Testament thinkers towards the priesthood. For we must remember that when they were uttering their severest condemnation of priests the prophets did but reveal their own lofty estimate of what the office should mean if worthily represented. And when our Lord spoke of a priest passing the wounded traveller without helping him (Lk. 10:31), he too was pointing a contrast between many actual priests of his day and the ideal implied in their sacred calling.

A second contribution of Malachi was the amazing catholicity which led him to look on the worship of the Gentiles as offered to Yahweh (1:11). Too much stress ought not to be laid upon this, as the passage *may* be open to another interpretation. But as it is usually read by scholars it seems to be without its like in the Old Testament.[1]

But there can be no doubt that Malachi enriched Old Testament religion in a third way—by his use of the idea of God as Father. Apparently this term was in common use among his contemporaries, for he was throwing back their own words to them when he said: "If I am a father, where is mine honour?" (1:6). But it was Malachi who used the concept to enforce human brotherhood. "Have we not all one father? hath not one God created us? why do we deal treacherously every man against his brother?" (2:10) Now it is true that by "father" he may have been referring to the common ancestor of the race, Jacob, or Abraham; but scholars usually think that he meant Yahweh.[2] The utterance is not indeed universal, for he was speaking of Jews (unless Sellin and Oesterley be right).[3] But it was much to have the fatherhood of God and the brotherhood of man enunciated even within the limits of the nation.

He employed the same idea in his words of comfort to the godly (3:17). You are God's children and He will spare you as a man spares his own son that serves him. We have seen how this thought is used with great tenderness, reminding us of the New Testament. Malachi was thinking of individual sonship rather than national, how each one of the godly shall be God's own possession. Is not his personal name written down in God's book of remembrance? And here it is to be noted that the comfort offered by Malachi rested ultimately not on the hope of worldly prosperity but on the sense that God cares.

Finally, Malachi's conception of the marriage relation was singularly beautiful. A man enters into a covenant with his wife when she is young and fair and he must keep true to it after she has faded with advancing years. She must still be his companion, bound to him by intimate and sacred ties. She has trusted him and he must not deal treacherously with her by turning from her and seeking a younger face. Something of what Malachi said in this matter has been obscured by corruption of the text; but it seems likely that he looked on the divine purpose in instituting marriage

---

[1] Even Is.19:19ff refers to the future, not the present.
[2] So Grieve, Marti, Nowack, Haller, J. M. P. Smith, Sellin, McFayden, etc.
[3] See p. 418, note 2.

as aimed at securing a seed of God, i.e. children consecrated to Him. Wedlock was under God's special protection, and the preservation of the home His passionate concern: "I hate putting away, saith Yahweh." Evidently Malachi rejected the "liberality" of the Deuteronomic provision for divorce (Deut. 24:1ff) which permitted a man to let his wife go "if she find no favour in his eyes, because he hath found some unseemly thing in her"—and when could a man not find such unseemliness if his heart was set on it? Malachi's sympathies were all on the side of the woman. And so, he believed, were God's. No use in weeping and groaning over the altar so long as this wrong remains unrighted! For "Yahweh is witness between thee and the wife of thy youth."

Thus there are two great sayings of our Lord that Malachi in a real sense anticipated. The one was that in which he gave his interpretation of the Deuteronomic provision: "For the hardness of your heart Moses wrote you this commandment. . . . What God hath joined together let not man put asunder" (Mk. 10:5ff). The other had to do with offering gifts to God when one has broken the peace with his brother: "Leave there thy gift before the altar and go thy way; first be reconciled to thy brother and then come and offer thy gift" (Mt. 5:23). The latter thought is indeed a prophetic commonplace; but to Malachi alone among Old Testament writers belongs the honour of having given utterance to the former. Christ, to be sure, did not quote him in his reply to the Pharisees, but Malachi's words could not have been without their influence upon him.

Chapter XXII

THE PRIESTLY WRITERS

[*c.* 550–450 B.C.]

The Priestly Document, or Priests' Code

"In the beginning God created the heavens and the earth." The story of creation thus introduced is the first of a long series of passages couched in the same peculiar style which constitute one of the main strata of the Pentateuch. Since this stratum exhibits a deep interest in the ceremonial and priestly side of religion it has been given the name of the Priestly Writing or the Priests' Code.

Its style is well described by Driver. "If JE—and especially J— be free, flowing and picturesque, P is stereotyped, measured and prosaic. The narrative, both as a whole and in its several parts, is articulated systematically; the beginning and close of an enumeration are regularly marked by stated formulae. The descriptions of P are methodical and precise. When they embrace details, emphasis and completeness are studied . . . . Metaphors, similes, etc., are eschewed, and there is generally an absence of the poetical or dramatic element, which is frequently conspicuous in the other historical books of the Old Testament." [1]

For a long time scholars considered this remarkable document as the most primitive part of the Pentateuch. This was due in part to its seemingly archaic language and in part to the fact that it provides a framework into which the whole Pentateuchal narrative is fitted. But Graf [2] and Wellhausen [3] convinced the scholarly world that it is really the latest strand of the Pentateuch and this view has prevailed ever since. Today the document is placed generally in the sixth or fifth century B.C. Every one realizes however that it contains much reliable priestly tradition which goes back to more ancient times. It is now no longer regarded as a unit

[1] *Introduction to the Literature of the Old Testament*[9], N. Y., 1913, p. 129f.
[2] K. H. Graf, *Die geschichtlichen Bücher des AT*, 1866.
[3] J. Wellhausen, *Prolegomena zur Geschichte Israels*, 1878.

and a current view considers it a weaving together of two strands of narrative, the later of which has definitely a more priestly character than the earlier.[4] This composite character however does not involve it in inner contradiction, except in details. If we cannot go as far as Sellin when he says that "it certainly now bears the impress of a single mind"[5] we recognize that the group or school who produced it were so unified in their point of view that we can treat them as one.[6]

The document that these priestly writers produced is indeed a challenging one. First, because of its place at the beginning of Holy Scripture. For more than two thousand years it has said the first word to Bible readers.

Secondly, because of its bulk. It contains over 100 pages of the American Standard Revised Version, as against the 96 pages of Chronicles-Ezra-Nehemiah, the 67 of the Kings, the 66 of Samuel and the 62 of Jeremiah. It is the largest block of material in the Bible.

Thirdly, because of its style, content and point of view, so utterly different from what we meet in almost all the rest of the Bible and so alien on the whole to modern ideas of religion.

Fourthly, because of its significance to the Jewish religion. It constituted the great mass of legislation in the Law, or *Torah,* Judaism's most sacred and binding division of the Scriptures. It provided also an important element of the background of Christianity. The Christian church found in its sacrificial system a foreshadowing of the atonement of Christ.

It cannot be without interest therefore to inquire who wrote it and with what aim it was produced. In answering these questions we are compelled to rely upon the reconstruction sketched by a majority of present day scholars, since the Bible does not even mention the priestly writers, much less distinguish their work from the rest of the Pentateuch. But since this reconstruction has withstood all assaults for two generations we may look upon it as correct in its main outlines.

One word more needs to be said here. The priestly writing contains a long section which is generally recognized to be of a

---

[4] E.g. Von Rad, *Die Priesterschaft,* 1934, cited by Eissfeldt, who accepts his view (*EAT,* p. 233f). Sellin however differs from von Rad in regarding the so-called second strand as merely a series of additions by a later hand to the main P narrative (*EAT*[7], 1935, p. 52).

[5] *EAT*[7], p. 51.

[6] Cf. Oesterley and Robinson, *IBOT,* p. 43.

different nature from the rest—the so-called Law of Holiness (Lev. 17–26). This is manifestly an earlier block of material which the priestly writers took over and incorporated into their work. It resembles the more ancient codes, the Book of the Covenant (Exod. 20:22–23:33) and the laws of Deuteronomy (Deut. 12–26 and 28), and breathes a spirit that is much more akin to them than to the rest of the priestly writing. In studying the priestly writers therefore we shall not make much use of it as a source but confine ourselves to the main bulk of homogeneous material that bears the characteristic priestly stamp. On the other hand we must bear in mind that they would not have so incorporated it unless they had been in sympathy with its ideas.

The Priestly Writers Aimed to Perpetuate and Develop the Inherited Ecclesiastical Institutions of Israel

We have already seen how the Deuteronomic reforms carried out in 622 B.C. by king Josiah (II Ki. 22–23) had displaced the local sanctuaries throughout his kingdom and centred all sacrificial worship in the Jerusalem temple. For more than thirty-five years thereafter the Zadokean priesthood which controlled the temple enjoyed a commanding position in the nation. Ignoring a Deuteronomic injunction (Deut. 18:6ff) they refused to accept on equal terms the now unemployed priests of the local sanctuaries and insisted that these occupy an inferior status at the central shrine. Ezekiel, himself a Zadokite priest, boldly supported this ungenerous policy, declaring that the local priests deserved to be deprived of their office because of the corruptions in worship they had practised in the past (Ezek. 44:10ff). Such an opinion may have had some justice on its side. The Jerusalem priesthood seems on the whole to have fostered a greater purity of worship than prevailed in the high places. But whether rightly or wrongly, this group now monopolized the priestly functions of Israel. The people came to look to them for instruction and leadership in all matters pertaining to the ritual side of religion.

When however Nebuchadrezzar first took Jerusalem in 597 B.C. some priests must have been torn rudely from the temple and deported to Babylon. We know that this happened to Ezekiel and there is no reason to suppose that he was the only one of his order to undergo such a fate. But the crowning catastrophe took place eleven years later, when at the second capture of the city the temple was destroyed and its sacred vessels appropriated. Probably many of its priests were also carried away to join the exiles already in Babylonia.

The sacrificial worship with all its glories came thus to an abrupt termination. If maintained at all it remained only a shadow of its former self. The Zadokean priests therefore were faced with a tragic situation. They were now themselves dispossessed. However much of their priestly prestige they might retain, their supreme function was gone. It was not possible, had they desired it, to build another temple in Babylonia, as the Jewish colony of Elephantiné was later to do in Egypt, for Deuteronomy had declared illegitimate all sanctuaries but the Jerusalem temple. Nor was it only the future of their order that gave them concern. What was to be the fate of the Jewish religion itself? For they could hardly have conceived it as permanently existing without the temple and all that the temple stood for.

Ezekiel has already shown us what answer they returned to such questions. This was not the end! God would soon restore Israel to its land, the temple would be rebuilt in new splendour and its worship would be resumed. Believing this they determined that when the good time came it would not find God's people unprepared.

Here, they conceived, lay their own work. It was to provide against the loss of Israel's churchly heritage. Ecclesiastical institutions like the sabbath, circumcision, the recurring feasts and fasts, the laws prescribing ritual cleanness, the distinction between permitted and forbidden foods, must not be allowed to lapse, for all these could be kept up in the foreign and "unclean" land of their exile. But above all the special function of the priesthood must be held before the people, that Israel might be ready to resume the sacrificial worship of the temple as its chief work whenever God opened the way. For the present crisis provided an opportunity to give such institutions a more commanding place in the life of the nation. Into the enterprise of accomplishing this the priestly writers threw themselves wholeheartedly. How well they succeeded is attested by more than two thousand years of Jewish history.

Their method probably included oral instruction and to this end they *may* have fostered assemblies for worship and teaching—which proved the beginnings of the synagogue. On this point we have no information: the origin of the synagogue is shrouded in obscurity.[1] But they also devoted themselves to writing. They set

[1] Cf. Oesterley, *A Fresh Approach to the Psalms* (N. Y., 1937), Ch. IX.

about collecting, systematizing and enriching the body of priestly tradition that had come down to them from the past. None could do this better than they. In former ages it had been a special duty of the priests of each sanctuary to teach the people resorting thither the history of the shrine and the ways in which God wished to be worshipped there. When the Jerusalem temple displaced the other sanctuaries this scattered lore had probably been brought to he central shrine and incorporated into the Jerusalem tradition. The Jerusalem priests were therefore in a position to give the nation a fairly complete and rounded corpus of ritual law. The result of their labours, carried on over several generations, was the massive priestly writing of the Pentateuch.

The Priestly Writers Composed a History of the Origins of Israel's Ecclesiastical Institutions

In order to understand the priestly writers we must remember that they were chiefly interested in ecclesiastical institutions. Loving these with all the devotion of their hearts they desired to inculcate the same passion in the people at large. But to kindle such popular affection more was needed than the mere drawing up of a corpus of laws. Experience had taught them that people must be told *stories* of the origin of shrines and rituals. They set out accordingly to write a history of God's dealing with man from the creation of the world to the conquest of Canaan, showing how the various divine institutions came to be given. With characteristic systemization they represented God as proceeding from step to step in an ordered scheme of progress until the climax was reached. These steps took the form of four successive dispensations or "covenants," in which God accorded man certain privileges and enjoined upon him certain ceremonial ways or institutions.

The first came at the creation, when God after bidding man multiply gave him dominion over all animals, but confined his food to vegetables. This dispensation was marked by the ordinance of the *sabbath,* which God himself observed after His six days of creative activity (Gen. 1:28ff). The second (the "Noachic Covenant") followed the flood. By it God permitted Noah and his sons to eat animal flesh ("every moving thing that liveth") but commanded that the blood must first be drained from the carcase. This, the priestly writers taught, was the origin of the immemorial custom of *eating bloodless meat.* God added yet other injunctions. Men should be fruitful and multiply, they should dominate by fear all lesser animals, they should shed the blood of any who shed the blood of another human being. Finally God promised never again to destroy the earth by a flood (Gen. 9:1ff). In these first two dispensations God was known simply as "Elohim." The third was the "Abrahamic Covenant," by which God undertook to make Abraham a father of many nations, giving to his descendants the land of Canaan and imposing the rite of *circumcision* upon all the males of his family as a sign of their relationship to Himself (Gen. 17). Abraham was now taught to call God *"El Shaddai."* All these led up to the exodus, marked by the institution of the *passover, unleavened bread,* and the *dedication of the first-born* (Exod. 12:1-20; 13:1f); and to the final covenant on mount Sinai, in which God (probably after taking Israel to be His people) commanded Moses to make the *ark* and the *tabernacle* with its furnishings and imposed the whole body of *Levitical legislation* (Exodus 25-31; 35-40; Leviticus; Numbers, in part). Now God was revealed to Moses as *Yahweh* (Exod. 6:2ff). The history closed with the complete conquest of Canaan and the settlement of the tribes in their allotted territories (Joshua). For the priestly writers had a passion for the *land,* which was the home of the church and the scene of its worship. That was why they told in such detail how Abraham purchased the field of Mamre (Gen. 23): it was an earnest of Israel's future possession of the whole country.

The history thus composed was of course not history in the sense that it correctly represented the past; it was rather an interpretation. While it did portray *existing* institutions with some faithfulness (and not a few of these dated from ancient times), its accounts of their *origin* were largely erroneous. Its stories often rested upon actual tradition but this tradition had been so altered in priestly circles that it retained little of its original form. The greatest unreality of the narrative however lay in its *perspective,* which caused things ecclesiastical to assume grotesque proportions and permitted other things to drop largely out of sight.

But if it was not history, neither does it provide entertaining reading today. True, it has its fine passages. The creation story moves with majestic rhythm from day to day, the very repetition of formulae adding to its impressiveness—a noble prose poem (Gen. 1-2:4a). It is to the priestly writers that we owe the picture of Moses' shining face (Exod. 34:29) and the glory of Yahweh coming as a cloud from the wilderness to still the murmurings of the people (Exod. 16:10; Num. 14:10). But *human interest* is after all necessary to make a good story and that is just what the priestly writers lacked. Neither the people of whom they told nor the men and women for whom they wrote seem to have mattered much to them as human beings; they viewed them chiefly as institutors and practisers of an institutional system. Thus with a few exceptions their characters are colourless. Even Moses their ideal is but a draped statue compared with the titanic Moses of the earlier narratives of J and E. It is significant too that the priestly writers did not permit him to act alone but always had Aaron at his side to help him—Aaron being the incarnation of the priesthood.

If the stories of the priestly writers are dull, how much more their statistical matter—genealogies, lists, specifications, laws, page on page of rubrics! It is these chiefly that make the bulk of their work such a dreary waste. Yet in passing judgment on this kind of material we must bear in mind the writers' purpose. It was to preserve institutions. Now institutions are ways of doing things and these ways, if they are to be preserved, must be taught, generally in dull detail. But when *practised* they cease to be dull and make an impressive transaction, often full of dignity, beauty and meaning, fraught with emotion and capable of exercising a vital influence on those who participate in them. Such doubtless were the rites prescribed by the priestly code. They were vehicles of a nation's religious devotion. We cannot appreciate the prescriptions of Leviticus apart from its institutions as they were actually practised any more justly than we can estimate the rubrics of the Book of Common Prayer apart from the actual services of the church. The same can be said of the directions for the tabernacle given in Exod. 25ff. These, like the architect's specifications for a church, make prosy reading; but carried out by the builder they produce a noble structure which lifts the soul to heaven. Our parents delighted to translate them into a picture, and a very charming one they made in illustrated Bibles. Who does not remember with pleasure the stately tent, the altar with the smoke of sacrifice arising from it, the spacious enclosure—and the representations in colours of Aaron in his high-priestly robes, turban, breastplate and all! The absence of this *portrayal* in modern books on the Old Testament is a distinct loss.

But after all the true value of ecclesiastical institutions is to be judged by the ideas of God which they foster. Back of the ceremonies and structures lay a conception of God, and to this we now turn.

The Priestly Writers' Conception of God

To the priestly writers the God of Israel was the only God. All scholars agree in praising their lofty monotheism. It appears strikingly in their creation story (Gen. 1:1–2:4a), especially when we remember that this was based on the Babylonian account of creation.[1] Here there is no hint of the warring, mutually jealous gods that appear in the original. God is the sole mover of the enterprise. He has associated with Him indeed some sort of heavenly council whom He addresses: "Let us make man in our image" (Gen. 1:26). But these beings are wholly subordinate, not gods in the same sense that Yahweh is God.

It is true that the priestly writers, unlike the Yahwist and the Elohist, twice speak of the struggle preceding Israel's exodus from Egypt as a contest between Yahweh and the gods of Egypt (Exod. 12:12; Num. 33:4); but these passages are isolated and must not be pressed. Long after monotheism became established in Israel people still talked of "other gods" (e.g. Ps. 95:3). So the priestly writers probably thought that other gods were real beings, but they never doubted that Yahweh was in complete control of the universe.

The one God was endued with unutterable majesty and transcendence. How finely the creation story brings this out: "In the beginning God . . ." There is God's eternity. "Created the heavens and the earth"; i.e. out of nothing. He is the source of the universe. "And God said, Let there be light, and there was light." He needed but to speak. Not like the primitively conceived God of J, who worked with His own hands, moulding man out of clay, blowing the breath of life into his nostrils, planting a garden, etc. It was this power to effect by word only that so impressed the psalmist:

> "He spake, and it was done;
> He commanded, and it stood fast" (Ps. 33:9).

Akin to the sense of the divine majesty is the priestly writers' repeated introduction of the "glory of Yahweh" which comes in the form of a cloud and rests on the tabernacle.

Another thing that stands out in the creation story is the idea of what the Greeks called *cosmos*: God is a God of order. Day followed day, each with its work according to the divine plan. And

[1] For the Babylonian account see Barton, *AB*⁷, p. 279ff.

so ever after God developed in orderly sequence His plan for man. Nor was this mere order; like cosmos it was invested with beauty. For it cannot escape the reader that below the specifications and rubrics of the priestly writers there throbbed a passion for the beautiful. God would have Aaron clothed in his priestly garments "for glory and for beauty" (Exod. 28:2). He called Bezalel and filled him with His Spirit to produce articles of exquisite craftsmanship (Exod. 35:30ff). It was this conception of God that made the priestly writers patrons of sacred art.

Yet for all His transcendence this God of the priestly writers was still very like men. He displayed human traits, being pleased when He saw that His works were good (Gen. 1:31) and taking a rest from His labour on the seventh day (Gen. 2:2). After the flood He set the bow in the cloud to remind Him of His covenant with all flesh not to destroy it again (Gen. 9:16). Later He appeared to Abraham, talked with him and "went up" from him (Gen. 17:1,22). He prescribed that Aaron wear golden bells on his skirts, lest coming unheard into the holy place he surprise God and die for it (Exod. 28:33ff). In general the priestly writers joined with the rest of the men of the Old Testament in picturing God as a Person who thinks, acts and speaks as do human persons. Indeed they declared boldly that God had made man in His own image (Gen. 1:26ff). It has been maintained by some that this last phrase denotes a spiritual rather than a bodily likeness. But we suspect that the priestly writers were no more emancipated than the prophets from the idea that God had a body like man's.

It followed from this kinship that man held a special place in God's affections. He was the climax of creation, given dominion over all living things. From the first God looked out for his needs, providing him with food and clothing and leading him onward according to a benevolent plan. At the outset this plan embraced the entire race; then owing to man's sin it was narrowed down to Noah. After the flood there came a fresh covenant with humanity and indeed with all living creatures (Gen. 9:9ff), which has remained unbroken ever since. Then from the descendants of Shem God singled out Abraham as father of a favoured nation which He proceeded to bless by special dispensations. All through we meet touches of God's philanthropy. He saved Noah, set the bow of promise in the cloud, made promises to Abraham, gave him Isaac when Abraham was content to have Ishmael only (Gen. 17:18f), delivered Lot for his sake (Gen. 19:29), heard the groaning of the Israelites in Egypt (Exod. 6:5), led them out by Moses, delivered them at the Red Sea (Exod. 14), gave them manna in the wilderness even when they murmured against Him (Exod. 16), allowed Himself to be entreated on their behalf by Moses and Aaron (Num. 16:20ff), took them for His own at Sinai, imparted to them the ordinances by performance of which they might have intercourse with Him (Exod. 25ff; Lev.; Num. in part), and finally gave them the land of Canaan (Josh.). However harsh He might be, as we shall see later, He was fundamentally a God of love.

Thus far the God of the priestly writers was much the same as the God of the other men of the Old Testament. It is when we come to examine His interests and His demands upon men that we see the difference arising. For He not only asked of men ritual performance as well as ethical conduct: He seemed to lay chief stress on the former.

Here we find a startling difference between the priestly writers and the prophets. The prophets had declared in many an imperishable utterance that Yahweh desires lovingkindness and not sacrifice (e.g. Hos. 6:6). Some of them had gone very far, affirming that God hates Israel's worship and its church year (Is. 1:11ff; Amos 5:21ff). Jeremiah and Amos had actually taught that sacrifices had no place in the original Mosaic legislation (Amos 5:25; Jer. 7:21ff). The priestly writers on the contrary conceived God as caring deeply for ecclesiastical ordinances, even those of a purely formal and seemingly mechanical nature. God could not admit to intimate intercourse with Himself any who did not observe them. They were valuable to Him *in themselves,* and not merely because they proved a "means of grace" to men.

When it came to matters of ceremonial they pictured God as rigidly exacting. No latitude was allowed; no human considerations could excuse one from observance. When Nadab and Abihu offered strange fire before Yahweh they were consumed (Lev. 10:1ff). Aaron and his sons were not to interrupt their consecration to mourn for these slain brethren (Lev. 10:6). For sins "with a high hand" (Num. 15:30) there was no forgiveness. These would include any approach to God by one who knew himself to be unclean and had not taken the trouble to be purified (e.g. Num. 19:13). Indeed the frequency with which death was prescribed as a punishment in these laws is amazing. True, it was an ideal rather than an actual penalty; but it shows at least what the priestly writers desired in theory.

This rigidity and even harshness characterized their portrayal of God throughout. They saw something peremptory in the divine nature. The God of the priestly writers did not "strive with man," nor show Himself "merciful and gracious, slow to anger, and abundant in lovingkindness" (Exod. 34:6). In the JE narratives, for all His wrath, Yahweh is prevailingly patient towards the rebellious Israelites; but in the priestly writing He strikes down offenders in the moment of their sin with an almost automatic wrath.

Again the God of the priestly writers was so preoccupied with ritual and sacrifices that He seemed to have little interest to spare for the vast areas of human life extending beyond it, where people get their living, marry, rear children, maintain homes, pursue ambitions, build the structure of civilization. He seemed indeed to be little concerned for history, unless it were the history of institutions. His plan was a plan for the church, not for the nation in its varied life. Nay, He viewed the nation largely as a church. He was accordingly satisfied with a future in which the church might "serve Him in all godly quietness." It is a question how far the priestly writers shared the prophets' dreams of a wonderful time to come. Composing as they did the story of the origins, they did not describe God's purpose for the ages following Joshua. They did indeed imply that the Solomonic temple had been the successor of the tabernacle, and as we have seen they doubtless shared with Ezekiel the passionate hope of its restoration.[2] But beyond this they do not seem to have gone. All they asked was that the ecclesiastical system, restored, amended and embellished but still substantially unaltered, might continue for ever. Their God was the God of the churchly *status quo*. Last but not least, He was a God who exalted the priest as the chief officer of the nation, who would have all power placed in priestly hands and priestly revenues insured in rich profusion. For the priestly writers in their thought of God were apparently not able to rise above the corporate self-interest which in all ages has tended to characterize the hierarchy of both Jewish and Christian churches.

It would however be a mistake to imagine that the priestly writers regarded ethics as unimportant. Now and again in their history they portrayed God as demanding righteousness. When men corrupted their way on earth and filled it with violence He destroyed

---

[2] Eissfeldt, *EAT*, p. 231, holds that P's laws have even more significance for the future than for the present. "For P is a creation of the time of exile, intended to serve as a legal foundation for the rebuilding of the people and the worshipping church, so fervently longed for. To this extent it is like the programmatic sketch of laws at the end of the Book of Ezekiel, except that it is projected back into the past."

them, saving only Noah who was righteous and perfect (Gen. 6: 9ff). To Abraham He said, "Walk before me and be thou perfect" (Gen. 17:1). Such moral obligation was assumed in all the ritual legislation. A trespass-offering was provided for a witness who concealed the truth (Lev. 5:1ff), for one who swore rashly to do evil, for those who dealt falsely with a neighbour in a matter of deposit or of a bargain or of robbery, or who had oppressed a neighbour, or found what was lost and kept it (Lev. 6:1ff). Special stress was laid upon the duty of restoration, adding one fifth of the value.

It is important to keep in mind also that the priestly writers incorporated into the Levitical legislation the strongly ethical "Law of Holiness" (Lev. 17-26). This code, to be sure, was not completely ethical, for like the other ancient codes of the Book of the Covenant and of Deuteronomy it mingled ritual prescriptions with moral demands. But it proclaimed in clear and ringing tones the great duties of reverence for parents and the aged, generosity toward the poor and the foreigner, honesty, truth, fairness to employees, respect for the handicapped, impartiality in judgment, freedom from oppression and slander, from bearing grudges and taking vengeance. Chapter 19, which contains most of these ethical injunctions, went beyond the other early codes in calling for fundamental attitudes of the heart which would spontaneously bring forth the desired conduct. "Ye shall be holy; for I Yahweh your God am holy" (v. 2). "Thou shalt love thy neighbour as thyself" (v. 18). The two went together. The Israelite, imitating God in the midst of the profane nations of the world, must love his brother as himself because God is like that. "I am Yahweh" (v. 18).

Just as the priestly writers throughout their massive history presupposed the ethical injunctions of the earlier laws, so they must have known and embraced the sublime moral teachings of the prophets, many of which were in circulation in their day. The reason why they did not make more of the ethical was not that they regarded it lightly but that they wished to *supplement* it by setting forth another aspect of religion which they deemed vital. This was the element supplied by the system of ritual and sacrifice.

Now that system, with all its faults (so obvious to us), did bring home to those who used it certain profound truths. For one thing, its ritual made men feel the ineffable majesty of God. He was a Being with whom one dared not be familiar. In dealing with Him formality was required, a formality punctilious, exacting, costly. A man must cleanse himself, must have his person and all about him scrupulously pure, must be on his good behaviour. Even innocent proceedings of natural life—marital intercourse, menstruation, child-birth, a skin eruption, death—shut out those who were connected with them from the divine presence until the required purification was made. Then too there were holy things which only specially consecrated persons might handle, functions which the ordinary layman might not perform, sacred areas which he might not enter, a most holy place into which none but the high priest might go, and he only once a year. All this heightened the sense of God's "holiness," of the awful chasm between Him and man. The very non-rational, non-ethical, rigidly mechanical element in the ritual removed God from the plain and the reasonable, from what could be included in the categories of man's thinking, and emphasized His "otherness." And yet strangely enough all of it made men feel closer to Him. For much of the ritual brought Him into their ordinary life, kept Him in their thoughts, gave them a means of uniting themselves with Him whereby they became "holy as He is holy."

Deeper still, its sacrifices spoke to man's sense of sin. They taught that there were many things which interrupted man's harmony with God in so serious a way that the propitiation of blood was required to restore the relationship. One could not take for granted that if one repented and made amends one would be right with God. Even confession and the plea for pardon was not enough. A sacrifice must be offered, atonement made. This gives the legislation of Leviticus a peculiarly solemn tone. A shadow seems to brood over the book—at least in its first part—which reaches its darkest in the prescriptions of the annual day of atonement (Ch. 16).[3]

There it is told how Aaron was directed by God to come once a year into the holy place with one sacrifice for himself and his family and another for the people. The blood he must sprinkle on the mercy-seat, thus making atonement for the holy place; then with the same blood he must atone for the tent of meeting and the altar "because of the uncleanness of the children of Israel, and because of their transgressions, even all their sins" (v. 16). After that he must lay his hands on the head of the scapegoat, confess over it "all the iniquities of the children of Israel, even all their sins," and send it away into the wilderness to "bear upon it all

[3] Ch. 16 is probably one of the latest sections of the Levitical code, but it must not therefore be excluded as a source for the religion of the priestly writers. On the contrary, their whole system here finds its climax.

their iniquities unto a solitary land" (v. 20ff). Finally, leaving in the tent of meeting the sacred linen garments in which he had entered the holy place, he must bathe his flesh in water in a consecrated spot, to remove the intense holiness contracted within, put on his usual garments and come out to "offer his burnt-offering and the burnt-offering of the people, and to make atonement for himself and for the people" (v. 24). But only the fat was burnt upon the altar; the carcases so offered, laden as they were with the sins of man, were "carried forth without the camp" and totally consumed by fire (v. 27). That day was to be observed for ever as "a sabbath of solemn rest" in which men were to afflict their souls (v. 31).

But in the shadow there brooded light, for the ultimate meaning of the sacrificial system was one of comfort. Sin *could* be covered, atonement had! And so the priestly writers offered the people the way of peace. True, it was costly. Individuals had to pay heavily for the victims required in their own case, and upon the community at large lay the constant expense of maintaining the public sacrifices. But this very costliness made men respect the God who exacted it and enhanced the value of the atonement so obtained. Thus in the bosom of the law was hid a gospel.

We may therefore easily overstress the difference between the priestly writers and the prophets, not only in the domain of ethics but also in that of the ritual law. The prophets likewise proclaimed sin and its doom, and held out assurance of restoration to the penitent. Both priests and prophets were aiming at substantially the same goal—a righteous, or holy, people living in fellowship with God. The dissimilarity lay in their conceptions of the way to that goal. The prophets insisted that God required only true repentance and that He forgave freely because of His own righteousness and love. Thus they seemed to deny the necessity and the adequacy of the sacrificial atonement, while the priestly writers maintained both. But the disagreement was not absolute. Probably neither group failed to recognize that there was truth in the teaching of the other. And their difference in emphasis led apparently to no open clash. In all the priestly document we find no slighting word regarding the prophets. The prophets on their part never condemned priests as such, but only unfaithful priests, and these no more than unfaithful prophets.

These two ways of viewing sinful man's relationship to God had probably existed side by side in Israel for several centuries. A plain example is the parallel ministries of Jeremiah and Ezekiel, the former of whom represented the prophetic, the latter the priestly outlook. But the same situation doubtless obtained in the time of the earlier prophets also.[4]

The prophetic view and the priestly view were in fact complementary each to the other. Of neither could it be said that it contained the whole truth about God. Both were necessary to the fulness of Israel's religion.

The Legacy of the Priestly Writers

The effect of the priestly writers upon the subsequent religion of Israel was profound and enduring. In their day Israel was becoming a people of the law, and most of the law was to be found in the priests' code. As long as the temple stood this law was carried out more or less in its entirety; and even after the destruction of the temple in 70 A.D. considerable portions of the priests' code remained in practice. Today orthodox Judaism gets the laws concerning the sabbath, circumcision, *kosher* food, the Day of Atonement and the annual feasts, partly or entirely from this document. Its spirit of conscientious precision also passed over into Jewish legal study, making it a by-word through the ages.

In presenting the institutional side of religion at such length and in such detail the priestly writers were meeting and fostering a real craving of their nation. Israel then desired, as perhaps never before, the security and dignity imparted by divinely imposed institutions with their ritual and worship and sacraments. These alone seemed to offer the support it required to carry out its destiny in the face of poverty and insignificance.

But these institutions met still deeper needs. As we have seen, they made man feel the awful transcendence and holiness of God, yet at the same time His oneness with faithful Israel. They brought home to man his sinfulness and need of redemption and provided him with atonement and restoration to divine fellowship.

The priestly writers had therefore a real mission to fulfil. Without what they brought the precious thing which is Judaism might not have been preserved to the world. We must remember this when we find them attributing too high a place to institutions in the religious life. Nor must we condemn them over-hastily for being absorbed in the details of ritual. If ritual is to be used at all, it should be mastered thoroughly. But we may well believe that the priestly writers, if they came to carrying out ritual details, did not set their minds on ceremonial. It sank into the background,

[4] Cf. Davidson, *The Theology of the Old Testament*, p. 157.

becoming a *means* through which their souls apprehended God in mystical devotion. We see it performing this function in Ps. 42–43 and Ps. 84, in the Deuteronomic account of the dedication of Solomon's temple (I Ki. 8) and in the Chronicler's story of Ezra's reading the law (Neh. 8); and it is only reasonable to picture the same thing happening in countless priestly rites. The Psalter, with its wealth of personal and corporate devotion, must have had the sanction of the temple-priesthood, and not a few of its lovely songs may have been composed by priests. Nor is the priestly writing itself completely barren of spiritual verdure, as we have seen; and once it blossoms out into the beautiful priestly blessing:

"Yahweh bless thee, and keep thee:
Yahweh make his face to shine upon thee, and be gracious
      unto thee:
Yahweh lift up his countenance upon thee, and give thee peace"
      (Num. 6:24ff).

They who recorded this must have had at their command other material of like nature, excluding it only because of the self-imposed limits of their work. For we must again remind ourselves that the priestly writing was not intended to stand alone, but to supplement the very human laws and narratives of the earlier documents. It also presupposed the teaching of the prophets. Its authors were probably more interested in the common life than it would lead us to imagine.

The influence of the priestly writers upon Christian thought has been profound. It is evident that the 19th chapter of Leviticus was much in the mind of Jesus, for he enjoined upon his disciples the two fundamental attitudes of heart for which it called. When in the sermon on the mount He described how the law must be carried out in its inward spirit and not only in its letter, He gave this reason for holding his followers up to such an heroic standard: "Ye therefore shall be perfect, as your heavenly Father is perfect" (Mt. 5:48). This seems to be an echo of the Levitical demand, "Ye shall be holy, for I Yahweh your God am holy" (Lev. 19:2).[1] And again, when challenged to point out the great commandment of the law he replied by taking two utterances, and only two, from the whole Old Testament. One of these came from this same chapter: "Thou shalt love thy neighbour as thyself" (Lev. 19:18).

[1] The word "perfect" which Jesus substituted for "holy" was also peculiarly characteristic of the priestly writers. Cf. Gen. 6:9; 17:1; Lev. 1:3,10 and elsewhere.

But it was not only on the ethical side that the priestly writers affected Christianity. From the Levitical law the church later caught the spirit and the beauty of institutional worship, with its priesthood and rites and its richly varied church year. Around the central sacrament of the altar, as around the altar of the ancient temple, was raised a majestic fabric of liturgy, music and symbolic art, by help of which the faithful, in the midst of the changes and chances of the world, drew near to the abiding Source of life eternal.

This influence of the Levitical law, however, extended yet deeper into the heart of Christianity. For, as has been said already, the church from the beginning saw in its sacrificial system a fore-shadowing of the atonement of Christ. When St. Paul wrote to the Corinthians "Christ our passover was sacrificed for us" (I Cor. 5:7), he seems to have been alluding to a wide-spread identification of Christ with the lamb offered up at the passover, according to the directions recorded by the priestly writers.[2] But the chief relationship of Christian thought to the sacrificial system was an indirect one, mediated through Second Isaiah. When that prophet depicted the vicarious suffering of the Servant of Yahweh he was making use of concepts derived, not indeed from the priestly writers (who came later), but from the system of sacrifices which they inherited and set forth. In fact, he actually employed one of its technical terms, "guilt-offering" (Is. 53:10), to describe the significance of the Servant's death. Our Lord plainly had this Levitical concept in mind when he interpreted his own approaching death in the light of the Isaianic passage: "the Son of man came not to be ministered unto, but to minister, and to give his life a ransom for many."[3]

Christian thought therefore was far from rejecting the priestly writers' fundamental idea of atonement for sin. It welcomed it as preparing for Christ. Nowhere is this so beautifully and fully expressed as in the Epistle to the Hebrews. And yet it is this epistle which brings out most clearly the Christian criticism of the sacrificial system of the Old Covenant: it failed to provide the very atonement which it promised. For after all its temple was built by

[2] Exod. 12:1ff. It is interesting to note that the Yahwist recorded similar directions (Exod. 12:21ff). This fact makes us wonder whether the earlier documents J and E may not have contained yet other parallels to P's ritual and sacrificial ordinances, which the compiler of the Pentateuch did not think it necessary to embody in his work.

[3] Mk. 10:45. Cf. p. 389.

man, not God. Its high-priest was only a man, compassed with infirmity, needing year by year to make propitiation for himself as well as for the people, never abiding but always giving place to a successor. And the blood it had to offer was only the blood of bulls and of goats, which could never take away sin. Therefore, "at the end of the days," God had provided the perfect High-Priest, who through his own blood entered in once for all into the holy place not made with hands, having obtained eternal redemption for us (Heb. 9:11f and elsewhere).

CHAPTER XXIII

NEHEMIAH

[ACTIVE IN JUDAH 445–*c.* 432 B.C.]

The Sources

Our knowledge of Nehemiah is derived from an excellent first hand source which the Chronicler has embodied with little change in his great work on the history of Israel. This source is the so-called memoirs of Nehemiah, written by his own hand. It begins in Neh. 1:1b and extends through 7:73a. It is resumed in 11:1 and continues to the end of the book. This latter section is thought by many scholars to be less reliable and to contain lists and other materials that may have been inserted later. The sections 11:1–2 and 13:4–31, however, bear the marks of Nehemiah's own style, and should be accepted as an authentic part of his memoirs. The narrative in 12:27–13:3, though derived from Nehemiah's memoirs, has apparently been worked over by the Chronicler and must therefore be used with more caution.

This memoir is indeed a remarkable piece of writing. No other man in the Old Testament (with the exception of Ezra, to be considered later) has left us a continuous narrative of his own deeds and thoughts. Some of the prophets, it is true, give glimpses of themselves here and there, particularly Jeremiah and Ezekiel. But these passages are apt to be brief, fragmentary, often merely a setting for their oracles. Nehemiah, on the contrary, tells a story that enables us to follow him from the beginning to the end of his enterprise. He does so with a straightforward simplicity and a frankness that reveal his motives throughout. For this reason we know him as we know few others of the Old Testament personalities. His narrative is fresh and rich in colour and holds the reader by its unconscious charm.

It is an autobiography, yet it is free from gross egoism. The writer does indeed call attention to his own unselfishness and devotion and utters several naïve prayers that God will remember them

443

to his good. One feels however that he is not writing to display himself but to tell of the great work that has been accomplished by his hand.

We shall now try to glean from this memoir the situation that confronted Nehemiah, how he met it, what manner of man he was, what was the value of his accomplishment for Israel.

Nehemiah Learns that Jerusalem is in Ruins

About the year 445 B.C. there was living at the court of king Artaxerxes in Shushan, Persia, a Jew who had attained to high position. We know nothing of the past life of Nehemiah before the beginning of his memoir, when he introduces himself to us as the cup-bearer of the king (1:11). He was a man of large wealth and high in favour with the king, whom he served in an intimate capacity. To judge from the address and practical ability he displayed in what followed, he probably was active in the affairs of government.[1]

But for all his success he could not regard Persia as his true home. His heart was in Jerusalem, "the place of his fathers' sepulchres" (2:3), and in the Palestinian community that had survived the devastating blow of the "captivity" more than a century before. He was an enthusiast for the law of the Lord and had about him a company of those who "delighted to fear His name." Apparently however he had not been closely in touch with conditions at home. He was now to learn about them more fully.

Things had not been going well in Judah since the days of Haggai and Zechariah. The high hopes entertained when the temple was rebuilt in 516 B.C. had given place to disappointment. Malachi had been compelled to plead for God with a discontented people. And now, seventy years after the rebuilding, misery still prevailed. True, there seems to have been some progress. Nothing is said in Nehemiah's memoir of ruined villages in Judah. People were living in towns over a wide area from Beersheba to Hazor and from Jericho to Ziklag. Nor does he complain of scanty population. Indeed in one passage (5:2) large families are expressly mentioned: there were plenty of "sons and daughters." Crops were apparently undamaged by pests, and while there is an allusion to a time of dearth (5:3) Nehemiah makes nothing of it.

---

[1] From the fact that he was permitted to stand in the presence of the queen (2:6) it has been inferred that Nehemiah was an eunuch: but nothing else in the story supports this view.

We can infer however that lax ways prevailed in the religious life of the community. Though the temple was still standing its worship was conducted in so slovenly a fashion that Nehemiah later had to establish it on a new basis. Mixed marriages were frequent, especially in high circles, and foreign influences were making themselves felt. Apparently the sabbath was loosely observed.

But the crowning wretchedness lay in the condition of Jerusalem. Its walls and gates were still in ruins and the area within was covered with heaps of rubbish in which the stones of former buildings were buried. As for population, it had none to speak of.

All this lowered the prestige of the Jews among their neighbours. The prevailing attitude of the non-Jewish populations surrounding Jerusalem was one of contempt. This was all the more felt because they freely came and went through Judah and not a few Jews were living among them in the outlying regions.

As a result despair had settled down over the Jewish community, augmenting the demoralization. If this went on there could be but one end—disintegration. Doubtless there were those who longed for a vigorous reform but they lacked the power to effect it. A leader was required strong enough to win favour at court, overcome hostile forces in the environment and rally the people.

It is very possible that in this hour the eyes of such faithful men turned to Nehemiah. His high position at court may well have been known in Palestine, along with his piety. If this was so we may suppose that the "certain men out of Judah" mentioned by Nehemiah in 1:2 had come on a definite mission to secure his help. At any rate (through Hanani, a relative of Nehemiah) they were introduced to him. "I asked them," he writes, "concerning the Jews that had escaped, that were left of the captivity, and concerning Judah."

He got a dismal answer. "The remnant that are left of the captivity there in the province are in great affliction and reproach: the wall of Jerusalem also is broken down, and the gates thereof are burned with fire."

This news came as a terrible shock to Nehemiah. Probably he had known in a general way that things were not going too well, but the true extent of the desolation was now finally brought home to him.[2]

---

[2] It is a common idea among scholars that the ruins reported must have been *recent* and therefore they connect them with a supposed attempt of Ezra to rebuild the walls (cf. Ezra 4:11ff). But nothing in Nehemiah's story bears this out.

He was completely overcome. "When I heard these words I
sat down and wept and mourned certain days; and I fasted and
prayed before the God of heaven" . . . (1:4). His prayer, as given
in the memoir, is generally thought to be worked over, but through
it still breathes a passionate confession of sin followed by an appeal
to God to help. It was during this time of mourning that his own
course was made clear.

Nehemiah Appointed Governor of Judah with Commission to Rebuild Jerusalem

What Nehemiah saw was that he himself must go to Jerusalem
and take vigorous hold of the situation. To do so he must be
governor, clothed with the authority of the king. His position at
court was such that he might reasonably expect to obtain this
appointment, yet to make the request involved serious risk. Artaxerxes might be offended at the desire of a trusted and useful officer
to leave his presence on a distant and lengthy errand, and Nehemiah might not only fail to gain his petition but might fall from
the royal favour as well. Such a course also involved great personal
sacrifice on his own part; for who could wish to relinquish a
successful life amid familiar surroundings in the centre of the
empire to undertake a hard and costly mission in a distant and
wretched province? Prosperous Zionists of the present day, for
all their ardour, sometimes prefer remaining in New York to
colonizing Palestine.

But Nehemiah was of the same stuff as Moses and the prophets.
Once the call of God came [1] personal considerations must be
brushed aside and dangers boldly faced. And "the God of heaven"
would be with His emissary; for Nehemiah shared the *faith* of the
prophets. All this was confirmed by prayer. "Prosper, I pray
thee, thy servant this day (his prayer concluded) and grant him
mercy in the sight of this man."

Thus fortified he went into the royal presence to make the venture. In a few words (2:1ff) he tells the story of the interview.
He took up the wine, as his custom was, and gave it to the king.
The king, noting his unaccustomed melancholy, asked him the
reason of it. It was a moment of intense fear, but Nehemiah made
the plunge. "Let the king live for ever: Why should not my coun-

---

[1] Nehemiah, indeed, does not speak of any divine command given him
ʌy revelation, as did the prophets, but he evidently felt that in undertaking
the enterprise he was doing God's will.

tenance be sad, when the city, the place of my father's sepulchres, lieth in waste, and the gates thereof are consumed with fire?" No burst of royal anger came; instead the king said: "For what dost thou make request?" Flashing a silent prayer upward Nehemiah answered roundly: "If it please the king, and thy servant here hath found favour in thy sight, that thou wouldst send me unto Judah, unto the city of my fathers' sepulchres, that I may build it."

It was indeed a bold request. Nehemiah implies that the presence of the queen operated in his favour. At any rate the reply of the king showed that he was considering it sympathetically. "For how long shall thy journey be? And when wilt thou return?" Nehemiah promptly set him a time and asked further for a safe-conduct and timber from the royal forest for the rebuilding. "And the king granted me, according to the good hand of my God upon me" (2:8).

He set out with an escort of "captains of the army and horsemen" and in due time presented himself at Jerusalem as its new Persian governor (2:11). Along with him must have gone a fair-sized company of assistants from the Jewish communities at Susa and elsewhere in Persia.

The Walls Rebuilt in Fifty-two Days

He had come as a friend of the discouraged Jews in Judah. That was recognized not only by the Jews themselves but by two non-Jews who were to play a prominent part in the events that followed—"Sanballat, the Horonite" (now shown by the papyri to have been the governor of Samaria) and "Tobiah, the servant, the Ammonite," closely connected by marriage with leading Jewish families. "It grieved them exceedingly, for that there was come a man to seek the welfare of the children of Israel" (2:10). But as yet he had told no one his intention of rebuilding (2:12). Evidently he did not trust the leaders of the Jewish community or even his own entourage. He must first see for himself the condition of Jerusalem.

Three days after his arrival he went out by night with a few companions and surveyed the walls.[1] He found them as ruinous as had been reported, yet saw that they could be repaired. Now he was ready to disclose his purpose. Calling an assembly [2] of the

[1] See "Nehemiah's Tour of Inspection," by Millar Burrows, BASOR, No. 64, p. 11ff.
[2] This is implied in 2:17ff.

priests, the nobles, the rulers and "the rest that did the work" (i.e. the common people) he addressed them. " 'Ye see the evil case that we are in, how Jerusalem lieth waste, and the gates thereof are burned with fire: come, and let us build up the wall of Jerusalem, that we be no more a reproach.' And I told them of the hand of my God which was good upon me, as also of the king's words he had spoken unto me." The effect of the speech was immediate. "And they said, Let us rise up and build. So they strengthened their hands for the good work" (2:17ff).

What a man Nehemiah must have been, thus to carry with him a whole discouraged community to undertake what for their slender resources must have been a stupendous work! One is reminded of the day seventy-five years earlier when Haggai roused the people to restore the temple. But there are two manifest differences: first, the task was now much greater: second, Nehemiah was no prophet furnished with divine oracles of promise. He did not deal in miraculous apocalyptic futures but in the facts of the present situation. He won his compatriots by his faith in God, his burning energy, his determination and (not least) by the influence he had acquired with the king.

There follows the amazing story of the rebuilding. In Ch. 3 he gives the list of the groups that did the work with the portion of the wall that each repaired.[3] Foremost among the workers was Eliashib the high-priest who with his brethren the priests builded the sheep-gate (3:1). Other priests were busy elsewhere (3:22,28). Rulers of districts and half districts laboured side by side with Levites (3:17), Nethinim (3:26), merchants (3:32), perfumers (3:8), gold-smiths (3:8,31), and the bulk of the peasant farmers. Men of many towns and villages, some as distant as Beth-zur, Keilah, Hazor, Jericho, had come to do their part.

Serious obstacles were now encountered. Sanballat, Tobiah and one Geshem "the Arabian" had no intention of permitting the walls of Jerusalem to go up if they could help it. At first they tried ridicule: "What is this thing that ye do? Will ye rebel against the king!" Nehemiah parried with a proud assertion of national faith: "The God of heaven, he will prosper us: therefore we his servants will arise and build: but ye have no portion, nor right, nor memorial in Jerusalem" (2:19-20). Later however when news came to Sanballat that the rebuilding was actually progressing he

[3] Burrows, *ibid*. p. 20, thinks that the list is not from Nehemiah but inserted later in his work. "Possibly it did not originally refer to Nehemiah's work, though we cannot take that for granted."

hurried down in anger with "his brethren and the army of Samaria" —probably a small but not negligible band of followers—and attempted again to put an end to the enterprise by pouring scorn upon it. Standing nearby (we gather) he addressed his audience of retainers: "What are these feeble Jews doing? Will they fortify themselves? Will they sacrifice? Will they make a day's job of it? Will they pull the stones that the fire has ruined out of the heaps of rubbish and make them come to life?" Tobiah here put in his contribution: "If a fox should go up on their stone wall, he would break it down." We may be sure that loud guffaws rewarded the speakers.

Nehemiah was stung: "Hear, O our God," he exclaimed: "for we are despised: and turn back their reproach upon their own head . . . for they have provoked thee to anger before the builders" (4:1-5).

The last phrase is significant, for it reveals Sanballat's real purpose—he wished to destroy the morale of the people who were doing the work. And here we pause to consider a second obstacle facing Nehemiah. In spite of the seeming whole-heartedness with which "the Jews" responded to his call, elements of disaffection existed among them. It is plain from the narrative that an influential group, including some of the nobles and the priests, were much more friendly disposed than Nehemiah to their non-Jewish neighbours. Such a fact seems hard to reconcile with the contempt showed the Jews by these neighbours, but present day conditions can help us to understand it. These people were not in sympathy with his separatist program and they probably saw that the rebuilding of the walls, though it would indeed add to the prestige of the Jews and hence of themselves, tended to the exclusion of non-Jews. The nobles of Tekoa actually stood aloof from the whole enterprise (3:5). Others may have felt that they would like to follow their example. At any rate there would be in the minds of many a sense of being only half persuaded. The attempt to rebuild might easily be made ridiculous in their eyes; and it was on this that Sanballat and his associates seem to have been counting.

It is a commentary on the weakness of the Jewish community in the eyes of outsiders that Sanballat and his friends had expected ridicule alone to check the victorious course of Nehemiah's leadership. But it failed to do so. Presently the many groups of builders had so filled in the breaches that the wall ran continuous up to half its height. "For the people had a mind to work" (4:6). The conspirators now perceived that they had not taken Nehemiah seriously enough; more drastic means must be employed. They agreed to assemble with an armed force outside Jerusalem and by sudden attacks here and there to keep the builders in a state of confusion (4:8). This situation was complicated by a rising tide of discouragement among the workers.

"And Judah said, The strength of the bearers of burdens is decayed, and there is much rubbish." Evidently the magnitude and difficulty of the task was becoming daily more apparent. "We can never build the wall," people were saying. Jews from outlying districts where they lived in close proximity to non-Jewish neighbours kept coming to Jerusalem and urging the builders to go back home [4] (4:7ff).

Nehemiah met the new attack with his usual faith and decision. "We made our prayer unto our God and set a watch against them day and night, because of them." Back of the wall he posted guards ready armed, and he exhorted "the nobles, the rulers and the rest of the people" to take heart. "Be not ye afraid of them: remember the Lord, who is great and terrible, and fight for your brethren, your sons, and your daughters, your wives and your houses" (4:14).

News that the Jews were prepared put an end to the project of their enemies and the people were able to return to their work. But the danger of assault had not been removed and Nehemiah made provision for continued preparedness. His description of the measures taken is not clear but it seems that the bulk of the workers went about their labours girt with swords, while half of his own employes were detailed to hold the heavier armour in readiness. The trumpeter accompanied Nehemiah constantly that an alarm might be sounded at any moment, the people having instructions to run together to the place whence the blast emanated. So the work proceeded from dawn to dark. Nehemiah also commanded the workers from the surrounding country to lodge in Jerusalem, thus providing a guard by night. During these tense days neither Nehemiah himself nor his associates nor his employes nor the men of the guard that followed him were able to put off their clothes (4:15ff). All this had its effect. No attack was made.

But now came an internal dissension that threatened to destroy all co-operation. "There arose a great cry of the people and of their wives against their brethren the Jews." It was the poor, complaining of the exactions of the well-to-do. Some demanded food for their large families; some asserted that they had been compelled to mortgage fields, vineyards and houses to obtain food in

_____
[4] This is the probable sense of the mutilated text in 4:12.

a time of famine; some that they had borrowed to pay the king's tax on their land, had lost fields and vineyards and were now being forced to sell their children as slaves to discharge the debt (5:1ff).

It is unlikely that this misery was a new thing, caused by the neglect of agriculture during the building of the walls. On the contrary the borrowing by the poor seems to have been going on for a long time, the present situation merely bringing it to its climax. Nehemiah's words imply that he had been giving it little attention, doubtless because he was immersed in his immediate enterprise. But the time had come when it could no longer be ignored.

Thus confronted with the situation Nehemiah showed himself imbued with the best tradition of Israel's ethics. "I was very angry when I heard their cry and these words."

There could be no doubt as to which side he, the governor, would take. Asking advice from no one he attacked the nobles and rulers for demanding interest from brother Jews, and in order to bring the pressure of public opinion to his aid "held a great assembly against them." There in the hearing of the whole community he declared that while he and his associates had been buying back, so far as they were able, Jews sold into slavery to the heathen, these men had actually been selling fellow-Jews into slavery for Nehemiah and his friends to redeem! Thus confronted they could make no answer and he went on, "The thing that ye do is not good: ought ye not to walk in the fear of our God, because of the reproach of the nations our enemies?" He then stated that he, his friends and employes, had been lending money and grain without interest [5] and appealed to them to join him in a reform. "I pray you, let us leave off the usury." He also asked them to return immediately to the debtors their real property and one per cent of the money and produce exacted of them. Whatever their feelings may have been the creditors acceded and Nehemiah, to make the transaction sure, called the priests and had them confirm their agreement with an oath (5:6ff).

At this point of his narrative Nehemiah, having revealed the fact that he bought back Jewish slaves, pauses to recount another instance of his generosity. All the time that he was governor (445–433 B.C.) he refused to impose the usual tax for the governor's support, not only living at his own charges but feeding at his table a hundred and fifty of the Jews and the rulers "besides those that came unto us from the nations that were round about us." He

[5] This is the probable meaning of the Hebrew.

would not "demand the bread of the governor," he says, "because the bondage was heavy upon this people." And he adds: "Remember unto me, O my God, for good all that I have done for the people" (5:14ff).

Presently the news reached Sanballat and his friends that the wall was complete; it remained only to set up the gates. Reduced to desperation they now tried to lure Nehemiah out to the plain of Ono under the pretence of a conference. His answer was: "I am doing a great work, so that I cannot come down: why should the work cease, whilst I leave it, and come down to you?" After four unsuccessful attempts to entice him Sanballat finally sent him an open letter saying that according to report Nehemiah and the Jews were planning to rebel and Nehemiah was aspiring to the kingship, prompting prophets to speak of him as king. Sanballat professed uneasiness on Nehemiah's account lest Artaxerxes hear of this, and renewed his invitation to a conference. Nehemiah refused to be intimidated. He sent back a curt denial of the charges and pressed on with the work, praying God to strengthen his hands (6:1ff).

But the resources of his enemies were not exhausted. They now bribed several prophets in Jerusalem to work on his fears through supposedly divine oracles. One of them named Shelemiah urged him to take refuge with him in the temple as a precaution against assassination. Such a step on Nehemiah's part would doubtless have been used to show that he himself was in a panic, thus creating demoralization among the people. At first Nehemiah seems to have regarded the message as sincere: yet he declined peremptorily: "Should such a man as I flee? and who is there, that, being such a man as I, would go into the temple to save his life? I will not go in." Presently however the whole plot became evident to him and he invoked the punishment of God upon both the prophets and those who set them on (6:10ff).

At last the work was done: the wall stood completed in the incredibly short space of fifty-two days. Nehemiah takes a pardonable pleasure in picturing the discomfiture of his enemies on receiving the news: "They were much cast down in their own eyes: for they perceived that the work was wrought of our God." Sanballat and Geshem seem now to have given up the struggle but Tobiah did not cease his efforts. Letters came and went between him and the nobles of Judah, many of whom were his sworn friends because of his close connection by marriage with the Jewish nobility. These nobles on their part were always praising Tobiah to Nehemiah and reporting back to Tobiah whatever Nehemiah might say (6:15ff). It is not clear what Tobiah was trying to accomplish; possibly he wanted to be reconciled with Nehemiah and taken into the Jewish community as a recognized member. The marital alliance of his family with the Jews seems to show that he liked the Jews. Later he took advantage of Nehemiah's absence to obtain living quarters in the temple itself (13:4ff).

It remained to dedicate the walls and the story of how this was done is told in 12:27ff, a passage that bears the marks of having been worked over by the Chronicler; yet the outline of the ceremony is still visible. Nehemiah divided the princes of Judah into two groups and caused them to lead the way in opposite directions around the top of the wall, each group followed by a "great company of people." It was a joyful procession, uttering thanksgivings and enlivened by the music of cymbals, psalteries and harps and the chanting of the singers. The two companies came together at last in the temple enclosure and stood there, the music bursting forth in triumphant gratitude while "great sacrifices" were offered, providing a feast partaken of with shouting and gladness, the treble of the women's and children's voices mingling with the deeper tones of the men "so that the joy of Jerusalem was heard even afar off."

Further Measures of Nehemiah

It was not possible however for Nehemiah to remain content with the completion of the wall. He does indeed devote most of his memoir to this enterprise, as if it were the chief goal he aimed at. Its very accomplishment at once raised the Jewish community to a respected position. Yet after all it was but the means to an end. What use would he now make of it? The scanty notices that enable us to answer this question reveal the true elements of Nehemiah's policy.

Jerusalem was to be established in glory as the centre of a worshipping community. To effect this it must be provided with inhabitants who would construct houses for themselves in its now empty spaces. Nehemiah caused the princes of the people to make their homes there, thus insuring its social and economic prestige, and had a tenth of the outside population chosen by lot to dwell there. Popular enthusiasm for the enterprise seems to have run high and a number volunteered to make the move, receiving as their reward the blessing of the people (11:1f). Apparently the repopulation was accomplished, for Nehemiah says nothing more of it.

Again, Nehemiah was concerned for the racial purity of the Jewish community no less than for the re-establishment of the holy city. We have seen how he denied all share in rebuilding the walls to Sanballat, Tobiah and Geshem (2:20). "Ye have no portion, nor right, nor memorial in Jerusalem." The moment the wall and gates were complete he chose two men whom he could trust for their religious zeal, Hanani his "brother" and Hananiah the governor of the castle, and put them in charge of the city, giving them strict orders to keep shut the gates during the hours of darkness. This meant a close watch on those entering the city and the exclusion of all possible "enemies." By "enemies" he seems to have meant the surrounding non-Jewish population, without making any discrimination (5:9). Jerusalem was now to be for Jews only.

But even the Jewish community itself needed purification in his eyes. He tells how God put it into his head to gather together the nobles and the rulers and the people that they might be reckoned by genealogy (7:5). Here there is inserted in his narrative (7:6ff) what purports to be a list which he found of "them that came up at the first." It is a duplicate of the list cited by the Chronicler in Ezra 2, and some scholars maintain that it gives, not the exiles returning in 537 b.c. but the members of the Jewish community about a century later. A genuine list of some period it is, however. Its aim was to establish the racial rights of those included and its use by Nehemiah was in the interests of racial purity. Strenuous exclusiveness was now to be the rule. Probably intermarriage with foreigners also was condemned (cf. 13:23ff).

But what in Nehemiah's mind was to be the activity of the community thus purified? Our source gives us an answer that may be too much coloured by the Chronicler, but in the main point it is probably reliable. Nehemiah provided for a continuous daily worship in the temple, enriched by the services of Levites and singers (7:1). He tells nothing of the condition of the temple worship before his arrival, but if we may draw an inference from what took place after his departure (13:10) we may well believe that it suffered through lack of support by the community (Mal. 1:6ff). This he would rectify by insuring the regular revenues for priests, Levites and singers. It also goes without saying that he would purge the temple precincts of all contamination by the presence of non-Jews (cf. 13:4ff). Another institution for which

he would zealously care was the sabbath (cf. 13:15ff). His ideal
was a people resting according to the commandment on the seventh
day. We may infer from 13:15ff that the Jews had been very lax
in this matter.

The economic condition of the people likewise would engage
Nehemiah's attention. He himself continued to do without the
"bread of the governor" and kept open house with a lavish hand.
We may feel sure that he held the nobles of Judah to their oath,
preventing the charging of interest, the alienation of the lands of
the poor and the selling into slavery for debt.

We may thus picture his governorship as a period of comparative
well-being, strongly contrasting with the time before and after it.
Nehemiah indeed was powerless to remedy the fundamental poverty of the people or to lift from them the oppressive yoke of a
foreign power. But we cannot go wrong in supposing that he
would do all that a conscientious, energetic, deeply religious governor could do to alleviate these miseries and inspire the community
with national pride and devotion to its God. His was a rigorous
regime, under which not a few would be restless; but it would
work for the benefit of the majority.

This continued for twelve years (13:6). Doubtless Nehemiah
had not originally intended to remain so long a time and had
been compelled to ask of the king an extension of his leave. It
is a tribute to his influence with Artaxerxes that he was able to
obtain this and keep the royal confidence through so many years
of absence, in spite of the false reports and intrigues against him
that must have emanated from his enemies. At last in 432 B.C.
he returned to the king, but not for long. "After certain days
asked I leave of the king and I came to Jerusalem" (13:6, 7). He
felt that his presence there was still needed.

Nor was he mistaken. Matters had not been going well during
his absence. Eliashib the priest had permitted Tobiah, with whom
he was connected by marriage, actually to occupy a large room in
the temple which had been previously used as a store chamber for
offerings. The outraged Nehemiah lost no time in throwing his
furniture out of doors and returning the room to its legitimate use
(13:4ff). Worse still, the temple stood empty of its ministers. On
inquiry he learned that the Levites and singers, not receiving the
support due them, had been compelled to go back to their lands
to make a living. Nehemiah at once placed the responsibility for
this on the rulers. "Why is the house of God forsaken?" he demanded. He then saw to it that the Levites and singers were called

together and restored to their place in the temple, while "all Judah" were forced to pay up their tithes. To insure proper distribution of these Nehemiah appointed treasurers over the stores, men who could be trusted to disburse them faithfully to their colleagues (13:10ff).

The sabbath too was disregarded. Nehemiah to his amazement saw some men on the sabbath treading wine presses, bringing in sheaves and leading asses which carried foodstuff and other burdens into Jerusalem. Men from Tyre also brought in fish and all manner of wares for the same purpose. Here again he laid the blame on the nobles of Judah, who must indeed have had a very uncomfortable time these first days after Nehemiah's return. "What evil thing is this that ye do, and profane the sabbath day? Did not your fathers thus, and did not our God bring all this evil upon us, and upon this city? Yet ye bring more wrath upon Israel by profaning the sabbath" (13:15ff).

He then attempted to put a stop to such violation by keeping the gates of Jerusalem closed over the sabbath, except for pedestrians, and preventing any of these from carrying a burden in or out. The Tyrian merchants, clever business men that they were, merely moved their market outside the gates. This went on for a week or two, when Nehemiah intervened with the threat that he would "lay hands on them" if they came again. They did not. To insure against further violations Nehemiah put the gates in charge of Levites especially purified for their duty as wardens (13:19ff).

His attention was directed also to another evil, "the Jews that had married women of Ashdod, of Ammon and of Moab." He found that their children spoke a mixture of tongues, and could not use the Hebrew language. This roused him to a high pitch of anger. "And I contended with them, and cursed them, and smote certain of them, and plucked off their hair, and made them swear by God. Ye shall not (I said) give your daughters unto their sons, nor take their daughters for your sons, or for yourselves. Did not Solomon king of Israel sin by these things? Yet among many nations there was no king like him, and he was beloved of his God, and God made him king over all Israel: nevertheless even him did foreign women cause to sin. Shall we then hearken unto you to do all this great evil, to trespass against our God in marrying foreign women?" (13:23ff).

We can imagine his indignation when he discovered that the practice had invaded the sacred precincts of the priesthood. A grandson of Eliashib the high priest had married a daughter of Sanballat and yet was apparently going on calmly with his sacred duties. Nehemiah promptly expelled him from his office and apparently from Judah. "Remember them, O my God," cries the outraged purist, "because they have defiled the priesthood, and the covenant of the priesthood, and of the Levites" (13:28f).

It was after these measures apparently [1] that Nehemiah effected a corporate act of purging. On a certain day the people were assembled to hear the "book of Moses" (i.e. Deuteronomy). "And therein was found written that an Ammonite and a Moabite should not enter into the assembly of God for ever.[2] And it came to pass, when they had heard the law, that they separated from Israel all the mixed multitude" (13:1ff). How this was carried out is not reported.

"Thus," Nehemiah concludes his memoir, "cleansed I them of everything foreign, and appointed charges for the priests and for the Levites, everyone in his work, and for the wood-offering, at times appointed, and for the first fruits. Remember me, O my God, for good" (13:30f).

This is all we know of his story.

An Estimate of Nehemiah and His Work

It is impossible to ponder on Nehemiah's account of his work without yielding him admiration. There were indeed things about him that repel us. His bitterness towards non-Jews, his narrow nationalism, his lack of any feeling that God belongs to mankind at large, his insistence on genealogies, race-purity and the whole ceremonial side of religion, his uncompromising rigorism, his ruthless discipline of others, all are against him. And yet the total effect of his personality is pleasing. Though a layman, making no pretence of being a man of God, he shared with the great spiritual leaders of Israel's history the capacity to lose himself in the service of God and his people. He was interested, not in personal gain, but in something much wider, something in which the individual was merged—the religious destiny of Israel. We have noted the absence of egoism from his memoir. His life also was free from

[1] Cf. 13:4, "before this." The chronological notices however may not be in proper succession. And the whole paragraph (13:1–3) is thought by some scholars to have been worked over by the Chronicler.

[2] In Deut. 23:3ff the words "for ever" are qualified by adding "even unto the tenth generation."

it. With this pervading unselfishness were blended other qualities
—simplicity, transparent sincerity, courage, directness, intense faith
in God and in prayer, untiring energy, reliability, dogged persistence, imagination to see the possibilities of a desperate situation
and daring to make them real. He was a leader, able to carry
men with him in the accomplishment of a stupendous undertaking.

We have spoken of him as a rigorist and stern disciplinarian
but we should be mistaken if we pictured him as forbidding in
manner. He could indeed fly into a passion and speak with terrific
bluntness, not stopping short at times of personal violence (cf.
13:25). But he had all the power to win men that characterizes
the true leader. Artaxerxes seems to have cherished for him a real
affection; his "brethren" and "servants" were devoted to him, willing to make any sacrifices to carry out his policy. He knew how
to put heart into a whole despairing community and despite the
murmurings of the disaffected and the ridicule and threats of
enemies carry them with him through fifty-two days of exhausting
labour to the completion of a colossal undertaking. Though he
"contended" with the nobles on more than one occasion and made
very hard demands upon them, he obtained in each instance at
least their outward co-operation. All this would have been impossible had he not possessed unusual charm.

Part of his ability to lead lay undoubtedly in his knowledge of
men. He had something of David's power to see through a situation (cf. II Sam. 14:19) and meet it in just the right way. He
was also quick to make decisions and fearless in carrying them
out. This was why he depended in crises on his own judgment
and took counsel of no one. He may often have asked advice at
other times, but it is significant that he nowhere speaks of doing
so. He could hardly trust the "nobles" or priests, while his
"brethren" and "servants" were more fitted to follow than to point
the way. For the most part he was compelled to decide alone.

One of the beautiful traits of Nehemiah was his care for the
poor. From the hour of his appointment he resolved to take nothing for his expenses. This course, as we have seen, he maintained
for twelve years at a cost that must have reduced his personal
wealth to almost nothing. He also checked the propensity of his
governmental employes to play the petty tyrant, as had been done
in the past to the misery of the people. All this, he tells us, was
due to his "fear of God" (5:15). It sprang also from his compassion: "because the bondage was heavy on this people" (5:18).
From the same motives, we may be sure, proceeded the expendi-

tures for ransoming Jewish slaves and the loans to the poor which
characterized him and his friends. At the "cry" of the poor he
felt the age-old indignation of the ideal Old Testament ruler and
intervened fearlessly on their behalf. One gets the impression
that Nehemiah tended to stand with the common people as against
the powerful monied groups. This was not strange, for it was
among the aristocracy that disaffection most showed itself. And
yet there was a deeper religious reason. For the Mosaic law on
the whole takes the side of the poor and Nehemiah was steeped
in the law (especially, it seems, the Book of Deuteronomy). From
the same source he imbibed a certain democratic spirit that pervades his memoir. Imperious though he was by nature he did
not use his power as governor in an autocratic way. For each
important step he sought and won general co-operation and we
may well believe that the "great assembly" which he speaks once
of calling (5:7) was not the only one he held (cf. 2:17).

This strong enforcement of social ethics must be remembered
when we consider his zeal for such things as the sabbath, the sacrificial worship and race-purity. Nehemiah's piety included both the
ethical and the ceremonial side of religion. Herein he was a true
child of Deuteronomy and it is to that book that we must go if
we wish to understand him. For Deuteronomy, as we have seen,
represented both the prophetic and the priestly traditions in Israel's
thought. Judged from our standpoint it fell below the prophets
in its emphasis upon the ritual and the ceremonial and Nehemiah
did but follow Deuteronomy. It was from Deuteronomy in particular that he derived his antagonistic attitude towards the surrounding non-Jewish populations and his lack of any sense of
Israel's world mission. From the same source he drew his conception of God as the military champion of Israel, a conception
so decisively rejected by the prophets. So it was with his use of
material means. Unlike the prophets Nehemiah favoured "fortified
towers," city walls, spears, swords, bows, shields, coats of mail.
He could not have understood Zechariah's angel when he forbade
the erection of a city wall on the ground that God would be a
wall of fire round about Jerusalem (Zech. 2:5). Nehemiah believed in the wall of fire, certainly, but he thought the wall of stone
very essential too! True, he did not build it primarily for a military purpose, for he was not interested in making war. It was to
be used to fence off Jerusalem from contamination, not to resist
the siege of armies. Yet it could repel attacks from hostile neigh-

bours if need be. And this was in harmony with the spirit of Deuteronomy.

A final difference from the prophets may be noted. Nehemiah expected God to work in the ways of this familiar order, through common means. He looked for no vast irruption of the divine into history, no day of the Lord with its catastrophic overwhelming of established things. The duty of the faithful, to his mind, was not to wait for such supernatural events but to build whatever was needed in the here and now—with God's help, of course. Ezra had the same attitude. Here both of them were in harmony with the law, which is non-eschatological.

All this reminds us that Nehemiah did not come to the Jews of his day as an innovator. His memoir shows that the teaching of the law was known and accepted by the people with whom he dealt, and it was to the law that he made his appeal in reasoning with them. They were not indeed living up to the law, but when confronted with its demands they could make no answer. It is important to realize this fact in our effort to comprehend Nehemiah's story. It shows that a great educational work had been somehow accomplished in the centuries preceding. And in this Deuteronomy and the men who followed the Deuteronomic tradition must have had a large share. Nehemiah never could have succeeded unless the ground had been so prepared.

Nehemiah was in short a sort of incarnate conscience for the Jewish community, holding up each of its groups to the ideals prescribed for them by the law. They might not like it but they could not very well resist openly. And there must have been a number who really welcomed it—persons specially devoted to the law, enthusiasts for it, men who, to use Nehemiah's own phrase, "delighted to fear God's Name" (1:11). Such were many members of his own household and the circles from which the messengers had gone to him in Persia to seek his help. On these he could depend.

This inner conformity of Nehemiah's mind to the patterns already impressed upon the Jewish people will help us correctly to estimate his work. The piety of the law was destined to prevail in the ages that followed. For good or ill, the Jews were henceforth to become more and more the people of the law, rigidly exclusive (except to proselytes who accepted the patterns of the law), equating the ritual with the ethical precepts as complementary parts of the one will of God in the performance of which lay Israel's peace. Nehemiah sensed that destiny. He saw that for its fulfilment a wall must surround Jerusalem and the holy city must be rebuilt, peopled, glorified. The cult, for which the city really existed, must be established on a permanent and worthy basis. The inroads of foreign culture must be checked, the race kept pure, the sabbath, Judaism's chief distinguishing mark, rigidly observed. Upon the task of accomplishing all this he threw himself with his whole strength. His wealth, personality and long governorship enabled him to give a decisive push in the direction that the development of his people was taking. He built a fence about them, leaving them free to grow within it towards their destiny. Had he not built the wall and ruled them vigorously for many years their development might have faltered and stopped. But after his work this was not likely to occur. They might indeed relax from his strenuous ways, but they could not go back utterly. Thus humanly speaking it was due to Nehemiah that four centuries later there existed a Jewish community with a Jewish religion in which he could grow up who was to mediate that religion to the Gentile world.

himself with his whole strength. His wealth, personality and long

CHAPTER **XXIV**

EZRA

[397 B.C.(?)]

The Sources

The sources for which we depend for our knowledge of Ezra
are contained in the Books of Ezra and Nehemiah, which form
part of the Chronicler's great historical work. The collection of
Apocrypha contains two books which bear the name of Ezra, but
one of these (I Esdras) simply repeats material found in our Ezra-
Nehemiah, and the other is a late apocalypse (II Esdras) in which
no historical data appear. The canonical Ezra-Nehemiah give us
first a narrative purporting to have been written by Ezra in the first
person (Ezra 7:27–9:15, and possibly 7:11–9:15). Prefixed to this, or
forming its opening section, is what claims to be a letter from king
Artaxerxes clothing Ezra with certain authority (Ezra 7:12–26); it
is in Aramaic while the memoir proper is in Hebrew. This entire
section is often referred to as the "I" narrative. Second, there is an
account of Ezra in the third person, the so-called "He" narrative
(Ezra 10; Neh. 8–10—though Neh. 10 may belong to another group
of material and not refer to Ezra at all). Finally, there are three
lists (Ezra 8:1–14; 10:18–44; Neh. 10:1–27) which may be treated as
component parts of the sources in which they are found, though
there is some doubt about the genuineness of the third list.

Most scholars accept the "I" narrative as a genuine memoir of
Ezra. Some who do so also regard the Aramaic letter as genuine,
while others look upon this with suspicion. Scholars who accept
the "I" narrative are apt to look upon the "He" narrative as derived
from the Ezra memoir, the Chronicler having changed the first
person into the third and otherwise worked over the material. Or
he may have got it from still another source. According to this
school of historians we can form a pretty trustworthy picture of Ezra
and his work.

A few scholars on the other hand reject these documents as creations of the Chronicler and declare that we know little about Ezra. Torrey [1] and Hölscher [2] go so far as to deny that the man Ezra existed, asserting that he is a figment of the Chronicler's imagination. Some colour is given to this extreme view by the fact that Ben Sirach (about 175 B.C.) in enumerating Israel's famous men does not mention Ezra at all (Ecclus. 49:11ff). It has however found little acceptance to date.

For a discussion of the question, the reader is referred to any good Introduction to the Old Testament. So far as we here are concerned the view that Ezra never existed may be set aside. The burden of proof resting upon it is too heavy even for Torrey's able arguments. Of the sources available the "I" narrative seems genuine and we shall follow it with confidence. Nor is there any reason why we should not use the "He" narrative in its main outlines, although we must recognize that here we fall short of certainty. The same may be said of the brief introduction to the "I" narrative in Ezra 7:1-10 or 11. The Aramaic letter of Artaxerxes may also be treated as genuine, though it raises doubts in so many quarters that we should not rest upon it heavily.

The sources, then, can be depended on sufficiently to form a generally correct idea of Ezra and his work. And here we must mention a divergence of view among scholars as to the *date* of Ezra. The Chronicler tells us (Ezra 7:7) that Ezra went up to Jerusalem in the seventh year of Artaxerxes the king. Now there were two kings of Persia bearing that name. If the first is meant the date is 458 B.C., and in the past historians have put Ezra's enterprise in that year. This would make him a precursor and contemporary of Nehemiah. If such be the case the outline of events would be as follows: Ezra instituted his reforms about 458 B.C., then perhaps fell into disfavour with the government because he went beyond his commission and undertook to rebuild the walls of Jerusalem. This rebuilding was stopped by royal order, as recounted in the Aramaic narrative preserved in Ezra 4:7-23. Then followed the intervention of Nehemiah who had heard of the misfortune, and so Ezra and Nehemiah were in Jerusalem together, mutually co-operating. Such was the Chronicler's own idea, for he definitely connects them in his story (Neh. 8:9; 12:26, 36).[3]

In recent years however the view has found favour in some quar-

---

[1] *Ezra Studies.* Chicago, 1910.
[2] *GIJR*, p. 140.
[3] Neh. 12:26 may however have been inserted by a later hand (Eissfeldt, *EAT*, p. 596).

ters that Ezra's work should be put in 397 B.C. under the second Artaxerxes (*Mnemon*), our old friend of Xenophon's *Anabasis*.[4] The chief reason for doing so is that (apart from the two instances above cited) neither Ezra nor Nehemiah mentions the other. Nor does there seem to be room for them both on the stage at the same time. As we have seen, Nehemiah's memoir does not presuppose any recent reform by Ezra nor any recent attempt to rebuild the city walls; nor does Ezra's later work take into account any activities of Nehemiah (Neh. 8–9). The scholars who uphold this view think it much more probable that Ezra followed Nehemiah after an interval of a generation, during which Nehemiah's reforms had time to fall into non-observance. That is the view taken in this chapter. The passages connecting the two men are accordingly set aside as harmonizing insertions by the Chronicler or a later redactor.

Ezra Led a Second Mass Movement of Babylonian Jews to Jerusalem

Something like a generation had passed since Nehemiah's governorship came to an end. Deprived of his leadership the rigoristic party in Judah had lost ground and the former laxity was showing itself, especially in the matter of mixed marriages. Over in Babylonia great dissatisfaction existed in the Jewish community concerning the state of religion in Palestine. Let us pause for a moment to fix our attention on that community, for it was now about to intervene a second time in the course of Jewish history.

Since the first Jewish captives had settled in Babylonia in 597 B.C. the number of Jews in that district had grown by other deportations and doubtless by voluntary accretion until presently they formed a substantial community. If the list in Ezra 2-Nehemiah 7 is correct they were able in 537 B.C. to furnish some 42,000 people for the return to Palestine. Even if these figures be set aside there is reason to believe that the caravan of that memorable year comprised several thousands. And now in 397 B.C. they were able to send up about five thousand with Ezra.

There is nothing improbable in this assumption if we consider the tendency of the Jewish race in later ages to congregate in great centres of population. Nor again can we go wrong in supposing

---

[4] For a good statement of the reasons for this view see Oesterley, *HI*, II, p. 114ff. Several scholars, however, who put Ezra's work after Nehemiah's, date it about 430 B.C. E.g. Albright, Batten, Bertholet, Haller.

that the same Jewish ability to accumulate wealth showed itself
then as now. In Palestine, an agricultural country, the Jews as a
people had remained poor although there were even in pre-exilic
days many complaints of growing wealth. Some were turning to
business and making money by sharp practices. In Babylonia however they would find abundant scope for their business talent. The
Chronicler tells us that in 537 B.C. they were able to make wide-
spread contributions towards rebuilding the temple, and after allowing for his weakness in recounting splendid offerings we may still
believe that not a little money was given. A little later Zechariah
mentions three men having arrived in Jerusalem from Babylon with
silver and gold for Yahweh's service (Zech. 6:10). We have seen
how Nehemiah must have been a man of ample means. And now
when we come to the time of Ezra an ability to make even magnificent offerings manifests itself. We may therefore picture the
Babylonian Jews as having attained something of the financial
position that their race was to enjoy in subsequent history, together
with the power that money always confers upon its possessor.

But prosperity had not weaned their hearts from Yahweh and
His city Jerusalem. True, there must have been a number who
succumbed to the atmosphere surrounding them and followed the
ways of their Gentile neighbours. But on these "forsakers" of God
(Ezra 8:22) the bulk of the community looked with aversion. For
the fact is that here in Babylonia rather than in the home-land
was to be found the most burning zeal for Yahweh's religion.
From the outset these Jews of the captivity had been of a better
stamp than those left in Palestine (cf. Jer. 24:2). In their number
must have been many of the party that had favoured the Deuteronomic reforms—men with a high ideal of prophet and priest.
Ezekiel had lived and taught among them in the early days and
there must have been a succession of lesser men to take up his
work. Absence from Jerusalem and the pressure of a foreign
population served but to intensify their devotion to things Jewish.
Many apparently gave themselves to the study and editing of the
law and the writings of the prophets, including the history of their
people. Learning flourished; the scribe, or student of the law,
became an important figure. The enthusiasm of the leaders spread
among the community at large. Thus Nehemiah, a layman, counted
himself as one of those that delighted to fear the name of God
(Neh. 1:11), and his retainers were animated by the same spirit.

But these enthusiasts were not content to have Babylonia the
centre of fervent Jewish piety. Their eyes were always on Jeru-

salem and what they were doing looked to the home-land for its
consummation. At the time our story opens two elements in the
Palestine situation seemed to require their intervention.

One was, that the temple still stood unadorned. We recall how
its bareness had weighed upon the older men of Haggai's day who
remembered the glory of the first temple (Hag. 2:3). Haggai
had indeed consoled them with the assurance that presently Yahweh
would shake heaven and earth and bring the gold and silver of the
nations into His house, so that it would excel the former house in
glory. But this promise remained unfulfilled.

Now the lack of such "glory" was a serious thing to the Babylonian lovers of the law. In their work of editing and expanding
its priestly sections they had made a great deal of the way in which
the tabernacle of the wilderness was beautified. This, they thought,
was important to God Himself, for had He not occupied much of
the forty days spent by Moses on the mount in prescribing exactly
how the sanctuary and its furniture should be made? And did
not the sacred narrative tell with the same detail how the people
had responded to God's requirements with wonderful gifts which
were used for beautifying the tabernacle? (Exod. 25-31; 35-40).
It was therefore high time that they themselves did the same for
the present house!

The second need of the Palestine community was to know and
keep the law. The laxity of which we have spoken would be reported to these Babylonian Jews, causing them pain and anxiety.
But they felt they had just the remedy required. Their labours on
the law had come to such completion that there was now ready
a "book of the law" which might be taken to Judah and put into
force there. We do not know just what this book of the law comprised, but it certainly contained much of the latest stratum of the
Pentateuch, the so-called priestly writing (P), in a developed form
not yet published in Palestine.

At the head of the Babylonian enthusiasts stood a man whose
name was to play a great part in the traditions of later Judaism,
Ezra the son of Seraiah. He is introduced to us by the Chronicler as
a priest (of course of the Aaronic succession) and a "ready scribe
in the law of Moses" (Ezra 7:1ff). How he had obtained his position of leadership we do not know, but we find him carrying the
community along with him in a remarkable manner. A single
purpose animated him. "He had set his heart to seek the law of
Yahweh, and to do it, and to teach in Israel statutes and ordinances"

(7:10). This meant that he intended to lead a caravan to Jerusalem and to take charge of affairs there.

In order to do this it was necessary to obtain the authorization of the king. A deputation of Jews, apparently headed by Ezra,[1] obtained an audience with Artaxerxes and laid before him their plan. As a result they secured from him a "letter" which gave Ezra large powers (7:12–26)—so large, indeed, that some scholars, as we have seen, regard the document as fictitious. It commissions Ezra to "make an investigation concerning Judah and Jerusalem, according to the law of thy God which is in thy hand," to appoint judges over the Jews living west of the Euphrates with the duty of enforcing the law under severe penalties and of teaching it to those who did not know it. Ezra was further authorized to take up with him any Babylonian Jews who might volunteer for the expedition and to solicit free-will offerings from the Jewish community for the temple worship, conveying these, along with the offerings made by the king and his counsellors, to the proper officials in Jerusalem. He was also directed to provide for worthy worship in the temple, drawing on the king's treasurers to a generous extent if need be. Finally the document ordered that the clergy of the temple be free of taxation.

Why, we may ask, was the Persian king willing to confer such wide authority on a leader of the Jews? The most probable answer is that he needed their support. In his loosely knit empire elements of disaffection were continually making themselves felt. It had been but a few years before that his younger brother Cyrus had marched with Greek mercenaries to the very doors of Babylon and all but succeeded in wrenching the sceptre from his hand. The subsequent escape of the ten thousand Greeks had shown how little the forces of the government could effect against modern troops from the west. The province beyond the Euphrates moreover had always been of the utmost concern to the Persian monarchs, for beyond it lay Egypt to the southwest and Asia Minor to the northwest—both breeders of revolt. In the Jews with their energy, ability and growing compactness he saw a welcome ally, provided he could win their support. At that time their chief concern was their national religion, and the law of their God was calculated to make them quiet and peaceable, so long as they were free to follow it. In promoting its observance he could obtain their gratitude without any risk to his empire.

Ezra acted promptly on the authority given him and presently

[1] Ezra uses the plural: "we had spoken unto the king" (8:22).

assembled on one of the canals of Babylonia ("the river Ahava") a
caravan of about 1500 males, or perhaps 5000 persons in all, including priests and Levites (8:1ff). The contributions of the king and
his officials and the offerings of the Jewish community itself,
amounting to a large sum of money, together with a number of
splendid vessels for the temple, were collected at the same place.

All was now ready, and Ezra found himself facing the responsibility of conducting so numerous a caravan with its freight of costly
gifts through the perils of the long journey. The king, if asked,
might have furnished a force of soldiers and horsemen to protect
them, but Ezra was ashamed to make the request—"because," he
says with charming frankness, "we had spoken unto the king, saying, The hand of our God is upon all them that seek him, for
good." Instead, he threw himself upon God. "Then I proclaimed a
fast there at the river Ahava, that we might humble ourselves before
our God, to seek a straight way for us, and for our little ones,
and for all our substance. . . . So we fasted and besought our God
for this: and he was entreated of us" (8:21ff).

This done, Ezra turned over to twelve of the chiefs of the priests
the gifts for the temple, weighing them all accurately. The priests
undertook to deliver them intact to the temple authorities. It must
have been a long and tedious transaction (8:24ff).

The caravan set out on the 12th day of the first month. Of the
four months' journey Ezra records only that it was made in safety.
"The hand of our God was upon us, and he delivered us from the
hand of the enemy and the lier-in-wait by the way. And we came
to Jerusalem." The arrival occurred on the last day of the fifth
month, in the late summer. For the next three days they rested, and
on the fourth the vessels and silver and gold were duly handed over
to a committee of priests and Levites in the temple. Then the
returned company offered up an imposing array of animals as sin-
offerings and burnt-offerings in recognition of God's goodness and
for their own purification. The commissions from the king had
meanwhile been delivered to the satraps and the governors beyond
the River and they, obeying the king's command, "furthered the
people and the house of God" (Ezra 8:31ff).

How much all this must have meant to the poor and struggling
community of Palestinian Jews! To receive an accession of five
thousand new colonists, not a few of them men of influence and
personal force, bringing both enthusiasm and amazing gifts; to see
their beloved temple taking on the splendour of which they had
vainly dreamed; to feel in this very practical way what a powerful

and wealthy support they had in their brethren beyond the desert—must have raised them to a high pitch of gratitude and joy. Of course there would be some—and these mainly among the leading clergy and laity—who looked with apprehension on the new-comers, seeing in their presence an impending attack upon the laxities in which they had become involved. But the sequel shows that the majority were overwhelmingly favourable. Thus was created the best possible atmosphere for the carrying out of the second part of Ezra's task; and to that we now turn.

Ezra Brought the People into a Covenant to Keep the Law [1]

It would not long remain unknown that Ezra had brought with him a book of the law which was more complete than any now in circulation. This fact, even if not officially announced, was bound to leak out. Ezra meanwhile kept his treasure hidden. This was good strategy for delay increased expectation. At length curiosity and interest issued in a wide-spread popular demand for him to "bring the book of the law of Moses which Yahweh had commanded to Israel" (Neh. 8:1).[2]

Ezra complied in a most solemn and impressive manner. On the first day of the seventh month (September-October), when the people had gathered as one man for the purpose, he mounted a pulpit of wood erected for this special occasion and in the presence of a vast concourse of men, women and older children assembled in the broad place before the water-gate on the east of the city, with six Levites standing on his right and six on his left, opened the book high above them all. Spontaneously the whole assembly rose to their feet. "And Ezra blessed Yahweh, the great God. And all the people answered, Amen, Amen, with the lifting up of their hands: and they bowed their heads and worshipped Yahweh with their faces to the ground" (Neh. 8:5ff).

The reading then proceeded. Ezra seems to have read for a while himself and when his voice failed to have given place to the assisting Levites. Along with the reading went an interpretation conducted by the Levites, who "gave the sense, so that the people understood the reading" (Neh. 8:8). Perhaps it was found neces-

---

[1] We pass now to Neh. 8–10, which seems to belong between Ezra 8:36 and Ezra 9:1.

[2] Welch, *PEJ*, Ch. XIII, regards the account in Neh. 8 as composite. Its original part (v.7–12) pictured a group of thirteen men starting the new custom of interpreting the law. The origin of this custom was later ascribed to Ezra by the editor, to give it authority.

sary to translate into Aramaic for the benefit of those not sufficiently familiar with Hebrew. But in any case some sort of explanatory comment was deemed advisable. The people meanwhile continued standing.

It is not known what part of the law was read, but probably Ezra had made his selections beforehand with a view to the prevailing laxities. If so, he succeeded in awaking his auditors to penitence. The people broke forth into lamentation. Then Ezra and the Levites, having obtained their aim, interposed to remind them of their duty to rejoice. "This day is holy unto Yahweh your God; mourn not, nor weep. . . . Go your way, eat the fat and drink the sweet, and send portions unto him for whom nothing is prepared . . . for the joy of Yahweh is your strength" (Neh. 8:9ff). The people obeyed and the mourning was turned into "great mirth"; for after all, had they not understood the words that were declared unto them?

Next day a small group of leading men met to hear more of the law. This time the passage read was that part of the so-called Law of Holiness which gives directions as to the observance of the feast of tabernacles (Lev. 23:34, 40, 42). At once measures were taken to carry them out. The people, summoned by proclamation throughout the countryside, went up on the hills and brought back boughs of various trees which they used for the erection of the booths. So many were needed that not only the roofs and courts of houses but the courts of the temple and the broad places of the water gate and the gate of Ephraim were requisitioned for space. The people thoroughly enjoyed it: "there was very great gladness." Thus were fulfilled the appointed seven days of the feast, crowned by the holy convocation on the eighth day. And on each day Ezra read in the book of the law to the people. This must have been done in a joyful strain to comport with the atmosphere of the feast. Emphasis would be laid, not on the penal side of the law, but on the goodness of Yahweh in giving it to Israel (cf. Neh. 8:12). In this manner he was able to introduce large sections of the book to the people generally (Neh. 8:13ff).

In thus following out the prescriptions of Leviticus the leaders seem to have been enriching the observance of the feast of tabernacles hitherto prevailing. The Chronicler tells us that the children of Israel had not done in this fashion since the days of Joshua the son of Nun (Neh. 8:17). The allusion to Joshua is due to the Chronicler's theory that what was new in the priestly legislation really dated back to an early time; and this is undoubtedly what

Ezra and his contemporaries believed also. But his words if credible show that an innovation of some sort was made. Possibly it consisted in the erection of booths and in the assemblies on the first and eighth days. We see here the kind of new departure that the adoption of Ezra's book involved.

And the people liked it! No wonder! For the narrative reveals a side of Ezra's religion which is too often overlooked. Rigorous though he might be in enforcing the law he regarded himself as an evangelist. What he brought was joy. If only one took pains to carry out the will of God as disclosed in the law he would experience the gladness of a dutiful child in the presence of his loving Father. Therefore Ezra would have no grieving on the day when the law was first introduced. Far as they might have wandered from Yahweh's ways they yet had His law, and that in itself ought to make them glad. Moreover, the day had been consecrated to Yahweh for the purpose of reading the law and nothing but joy had place on a "holy day." We may well picture Ezra's face, when he stilled the people's weeping, as alight with joy.

Thus the feast had right of way; sins might remain for the moment in the background. But they must presently be reckoned with; and so a fast was proclaimed for the 24th day of the month. Again the people assembled, this time "with fasting and with sackcloth and with earth upon them." Sternly they separated themselves from all foreigners, abandoning the easy way of intermingling which had characterized their past; and then standing they "confessed their sins and the iniquities of their fathers." For three hours the book of the law was read and for three hours they confessed and worshipped Yahweh their God. Then chosen Levites stationed on "the stairs of the Levites" summoned the congregation to stand and bless Yahweh. The words of the beautiful prayer that follows (Neh. 9:6ff) are probably a composition of the Chronicler, but we may well believe that they give the sense of what was uttered. Yahweh's mercies in time past were reviewed, the constant ingratitude and disobedience of the fathers, their punishment, the recurring forgiveness of God, the final catastrophe, in which however God did not make a full end of His people, the present condition of servitude and heavy taxation. This led up to a transaction, doubtless well prepared for beforehand: [3] "And because of all this we make a sure covenant, and write it; and our princes, our Levites and our priests seal unto it." One by one the leaders came forward

[3] Welch, *PEJ*, p. 69ff, has advanced the theory that the pact narrated in Neh. 10 took place more than a century earlier, during the exile.

and set their seals to the agreement. The rest of the people, including priests, Levites, door-keepers, singers, Nethinim and the laity in general, men, women and older children, ratified what the nobles had done. They "entered into a curse and into an oath, to walk in God's law, which was given by Moses the servant of God, and to observe and do all the commandments of Yahweh our Lord . . . , and that we would not give our daughters unto the peoples of the land, nor take their daughters for our sons; and that if the peoples of the land bring wares or any grain on the sabbath day to sell, that we would not buy of them on the sabbath, or on a holy day; and that we would forego the seventh year, and the exaction of every debt" (Neh. 9–10).

But this was not enough. In order that the continual round of temple services might be maintained they agreed to assess each person a third of a shekel annually. The upkeep of the wood-offering was apportioned by lot and prompt payment of first-fruits, first-born animals and tithes was pledged for the support of priests and Levites, including the door-keepers and the singers. This is the first recorded instance of a practice that was to characterize Judaism in the centuries to come—adding to the law to insure its observance.[4]

Thus Ezra had obtained his end. The entire congregation stood committed to observe the law. They had come to this decision of their own free will. Ezra indeed had led them, but without compulsion; the procedure had been democratic throughout. In the drawing up of the supplementary ordinances just recorded he had apparently voted as one, associating himself with the other leading men; "we imposed upon ourselves obligations," he says.[5] The brilliance of his leadership in bringing this about is equalled by the modesty with which he tells the story.[6]

Ezra Took Action against Mixed Marriages [1]

It must have been an hour of elation for Ezra and his supporters but they were probably experienced enough to know that their

[4] Cf. Moore, *Judaism* (Cambridge 1927), I, p. 30.

[5] Cf. Moore, *ibid*.

[6] Welch, *PEJ*, p. 278f, however, thinks that the early documents (which do not include, in his view, Neh. 8–9) represent Ezra merely as a devoted Jew who held fast loyally to the institutions of his people, but originated no new polity under which the Jews were to live. That is why he is not mentioned by Ben Sirach in his praise of famous men (Ecclus. 44–50).

[1] We return now to Ezra 9:1ff.

task had only begun. It was one thing for the people in a moment of repentance and mass emotion to pledge observance of the law, and quite another to carry out the pledge in cold blood after old ways had begun once more to assert themselves. Not two months had passed since the great day of ratification when a serious situation was brought to Ezra's attention. A number of the princes approached him with the information that a chief item of the agreement was not being carried out. "The people of Israel and the priests and the Levites have not separated themselves from the peoples of the lands, according to their abominations . . . , for they have taken of their daughters for themselves and for their sons . . . ; yea, the hand of the princes and rulers hath been chief in this trespass" (Ezra 9:1f).

Possibly this was no news to Ezra. Indeed, as Kittel thinks, he might himself have planned the whole scene. If so he could hardly have gone about the matter in a more effective way. "And when I heard this thing," he writes, "I rent my garment and my robe and plucked off the hair of my head and of my beard, and sat down confounded" (Ezra 9:3). This took place "before the house of God" (Ezra 10:1), probably in the court east of the temple, and so in the eyes of the public. The effect upon the witnesses must have been overwhelming. The news spread and soon a crowd had gathered. It was made up, he tells us, of those who "trembled at the words of the God of Israel"—that is, those who took the law in earnest. They stood about his prostrate form in silence.

Hours passed and still he remained motionless. Then, he writes, "at the evening oblation I arose up from my humiliation, even with my garment and my robe rent; and I fell upon my knees, and spread out my hands unto Yahweh my God." Wonderful is the prayer that follows, expressing (however much the work of the Chronicler it may be) something of what Ezra must have poured out to God in the agony of his soul (Ezra 9:6ff). It was a confession of despair. After all their sins and punishment God had given them a little hope of something better, had helped them in their slavery by granting them favour with the kings of Persia, restoring the temple and building the walls—and yet even now they were breaking His explicit command by mingling with the heathen. What had they to expect? "Behold, we are before thee in our guiltiness; for none can stand before thee because of this" (Ezra 9:15).

While Ezra thus "prayed and made confession, weeping and casting himself down before the house of God," the crowd about him had increased until it was "a very great assembly of men and women and children." The sight of their beloved leader—hitherto so full of hope and joy—plunged into despair, the vicarious agony with which he took the sins of the people upon himself, brought home to them as nothing else could the enormity of their transgression. On a small scale it was not unlike the effect of Ghandi's fasts upon the Indian people. Their remorse found passionate expression in lamentations that were added to his own: "the people wept very sore" (Ezra 10:1).

At last one Shecaniah, probably a noble, spoke out on behalf of them all: "We have trespassed against our God," he said to Ezra, "and have married foreign women of the peoples of the land: yet now there is hope for Israel concerning this thing. Now therefore let us make a covenant with our God to put away all the wives, and such as are born of them, according to the counsel of my lord, and of those that tremble at the commandment of our God; and let it be done according to the law. Arise; for the matter belongeth unto thee, and we are with thee: be of good courage and do it!" (Ezra 10:2ff).

Ezra immediately accepted the challenge. Rising from the earth, he summoned "the chiefs of the priests, the Levites, and all Israel to swear that they would do according to this word." They complied. Feeling that he had set things in motion, he now retired to the chamber of Jehohanan, grandson of the Eliashib who had been high priest in Nehemiah's time, and there continued to fast and to mourn because of what he deemed the people's trespass. Meanwhile the princes and the elders issued a proclamation throughout Judah and Jerusalem that all "the children of the captivity" (the Chronicler's phrase for the Jews) should assemble within three days at Jerusalem on pain of confiscation of goods and loss of citizenship (Ezra 10:5ff).

At the appointed time "all the men of Judah and Benjamin gathered themselves together unto Jerusalem." It was the 20th day of the ninth month, somewhere in early December, and the cold rains had come on. They squatted miserably in the broad place before the temple, shivering from apprehension and wet clothes. Ezra, who had been given charge of the matter by common consent (Ezra 10:4), stood up and addressed them, accusing them of increasing the guilt of Israel by their mixed marriages and demanding that such unions be dissolved. A deep cry of assent came from the multitude. A discussion seems to have followed in which four men were bold enough to oppose Ezra's demand; but they stood alone. The separation was agreed upon; but it was pointed out that it would take much longer than one or two days to put it into effect, since mixed marriages were wide-spread. The decision therefore was to appoint the princes a commission on behalf of all the assembly that they might pass from village to village and hold sessions to which local offenders might come with the elders of the place. This was duly carried out and completed by the 1st day of the first month (Ezra 10:9ff).

The Chronicler (drawing probably on a contemporary record) gives the list of those who were thus compelled to dissolve their marriages with foreign women (Ezra 10:18ff). It includes 17 priests, 6 Levites, one singer, 3 door-keepers and 86 laymen.[2] Some of them had children by these wives and such children were also disowned (Ezra 10:3). If the list is complete the number of offenders was not large; but it contained not a few men in prominent position whose example must have had a demoralizing effect on the small Palestinian community. That these were unable to offer a successful resistance shows the influence Ezra had acquired with the bulk of the population. Nothing is said of any compensation given the victims of this measure—the women and children thrust out from their homes and the community; but it is not impossible that something was done for their support. Fairness would call for such an arrangement and nothing in the law forbade it. But if it took place Ezra (or the Chronicler) did not feel it important enough to record.

At this point the history of Ezra concludes. Later Jewish tradition represents him as remaining in Jerusalem and (with the help of the imaginary body called "the Great Synagogue") continuing his labours for the law, making supplementary ordinances and regulations as they were found necessary and promulgating them with authority.[3] Probably he did spend the rest of his life in the holy city, establishing on as firm a foundation as he could the work which he had so successfully begun. At any rate this work was destined to be permanent. Ezra and his group, following Ne-

[2] Welch, *PEJ*, Ch. XIII, believes that the small number of persons found guilty of mixed marriages, and the fact that they are referred to as "they of the captivity," indicate that the offenders were not people already in the country at the time of Ezra's arrival, but members of Ezra's own caravan. This consisted chiefly of males, and there may not have been enough Jewish wives to go round. It is a mistake, in Welch's judgment, to think (with Schäder, Sellin and Kittel) that the extent of the mixed marriages threatened the loss of the community's Jewish character.

[3] Moore, *Judaism*, I, 31ff.

hemiah, impressed upon Judaism the stamp that it was to bear through all the ages to our own time. Let us now try to estimate what he accomplished.

Ezra and His Work

The story just told brings clearly before us the character of its hero. Much in Ezra reminds us of Nehemiah. They both showed energy, initiative, power of leadership; both were selfless men, devoted to a cause. Both had intense faith in God and in prayer. Both were rigorous almost to the point of fanaticism, yet they possessed great personal charm.

Their aim was essentially the same—to make Israel a people of the law. But they carried it out in different ways. Nehemiah as a practical layman built the wall and organized the worship. Ezra as priest and scribe came with the "book of the law in his hand" seeking a spiritual end—the people's agreement to follow it. In carrying out their methods both were democratic, winning rather than driving the people. Ezra went beyond Nehemiah in this for he looked to the women and older children as well as to the men, showing his appreciation of the part these had to play in forming the religious life of the nation. His supreme work, as he conceived it, was to teach. To this end he read the law to the congregation day after day. As teacher he was true to both the offices united in him. From time immemorial the priest had instructed the people in the inherited customs of ritual and ethics. Whatever the scribe may have done in the past, from now on he was to study the law and expound it. He was the coming man, destined one day to supersede the priest as the leader of Israel though now he exalted the priest and increased his authority.

It was to make glorious the priestly side of religion that Ezra brought treasures for the temple's adornment. This fact should always be present in our picture of Ezra. We should see him moving against the background of a beautiful sanctuary where richly tinted hangings set off gleaming vessels of silver and gold. He and his group were patrons of sacred art. And art means love. He must have loved the temple as some of the psalmists loved it:

"One thing have I asked of Yahweh, that will I seek after;
   That I may dwell in the house of Yahweh all the days of
      my life,
   To behold the beauty of Yahweh,
   And to consider his temple" (Ps. 27:4).

And this sense of the "pleasantness" of the Lord was to characterize the Judaism of later ages. We must not forget that behind the bearded rabbis of after centuries, poring over their dusty tomes, is always the synagogue with its sweet weird music and its perpetual lamp burning before the veiled ark of the law; always the Jewish home with its sabbath lights shining down from their silver candlesticks upon the white table-cloth and the sabbath feast.

And here we should recall how prominent in Ezra's religion was the note of joy. "Eat the fat and drink the sweet . . . for the joy of Yahweh is your strength" (Neh. 8:10). Along with this went his insistence on brotherhood: "Send portions unto him for whom nothing is prepared" (*ibid*). When the solemn covenant to keep the law was drawn up for princes and people to swear to it, it expressly mentioned—besides the obligation to avoid mixed marriages and to observe the sabbath—the duty every seventh year of letting one's land lie fallow for the sake of the poor and of releasing one's debtors (Neh. 10:31). Here too he resembled Nehemiah. All this tends to brighten and sweeten our idea of Ezra's religion and of subsequent Judaism.

One thing about Ezra that repels the modern reader is the harshness he displayed in breaking up marriages with non-Jews. In this he went even further than the rigorist Nehemiah. Of course such a policy was not new with him; it went back to the earlier law (e.g. Exod. 34:16; Deut. 7:3) and he accepted it as the revealed will of God. Nor was it peculiar to the Jews.[1] Wedlock in ancient times was looked on as a community matter and whenever a community felt the necessity of preserving its separateness marriages had to fall into line.[2] But this does not annul the fact that such harshness was part of Ezra's religion, however he came by it. We do not like it.

This question leads us naturally to essay an appraisal of Ezra's work as a whole. Even more than Nehemiah he established upon an enduring basis what we have come to call "legalism." By "legalism" we mean the religious attitude which regards life as governed by a revealed code expressing the "will of God." The Jewish code, following a tradition that went back to Moses, included ritual prescriptions along with moral ordinances. Both together formed the one indivisible divine will.

The prophets had broken away from this traditional fusing of ritual and ethical and had told men that God cared only for the

---

[1] Moore, *Judaism*, I, 19f, gives instances of even harsher laws of the same sort among the Romans and the Athenians.

[2] As in some modern countries and in some of our states.

ethical: "What doth Yahweh require of thee, but to do justice, and to love mercy, and to walk humbly with thy God?" (Mic. 6:8). They had had their day—though not unopposed by the followers of the older tradition—and had failed. However mighty their influence on succeeding ages they had not been able to bring the nation to their view; and they acknowledged it.

The priests and scribes kept on with the older way, and they did in measure succeed. Nehemiah, Ezra and the men of the law who followed them gradually made Israel a people that at least *outwardly* observed the law. And so the question arises: Were they not more practical than the prophets? Was not the ritual needed as a vessel in which to preserve the ethical and the mystical? For the ethical and the mystical, as we have seen in the case of Ezra and Nehemiah, were always there. This is something that ought to be pondered over in our day, so empty of ritual and the discipline that ritual inevitably compels. Compare the life of an ordinary American Protestant Christian, for whom religious customs tend towards the vanishing point, with the life of an orthodox Jew, coloured by such customs from morning to night. Which is apt to be reminded of God oftener?

And yet, the fusing of ritual and ethics in one single will of God has two weaknesses, both of which are illustrated in the experience of Judaism. The first is, that it blurs the sense of proportion. The rabbis spent as much time over the ritual commandments as over the ethical—if not more! Why not? Are they not both parts of the one will of God? Hillel was as much interested in ceremonial problems as in ethics and deemed them fully as important.[3] The second weakness is, that by binding religion so firmly to ceremonial it prevents it from being thought of apart from ceremonial. Liberal Judaism in our day is trying to relax this inherited bond and to identify religion with the great simplicities of the prophets. Jesus did the same by his summary of the law (Mk. 12: 29-31). Nor can Christianity forget its debt to that great Pharasaic thinker who came to perceive that Christ is the end of the law unto righteousness to every one that believeth (Rom. 10:4).

[3] Cf. Klausner, J., *Jesus of Nazareth* (Engl. transl. N. Y., 1925), p. 225. "The same Hillel who popularized the principle 'what is hateful to thyself do not to thy neighbor' was likewise the author of the 'Seven rules of Hermeneutics' . . . by which he laid the basis for the whole of Pharisaic Judaism." Quoted by permission of The Macmillan Company, publishers.

CHAPTER XXV

THE CHRONICLER

[*c*. 350 B.C.(?)]

The Sources

We come now to the study of one of the most unique men of the
Old Testament, who has left us a great work quite unlike any other
writing of the Bible. We call him "The Chronicler" from the title
of his work, his name being unknown to us. Our only source for
the study of the man is what he has written—a history comprising
the four books, I and II Chronicles, Ezra and Nehemiah.[1] Next
to the priestly writing it is the longest composition in the Bible,
covering almost 100 pages of the American Standard Revised
Version.

In spite of its division into smaller books, this is a single work,
conceived and executed by one man[2] and bearing the impress of
his personality. His work was later much added to and altered,
but without obscuring the essential outlook of its original writer.

It was not however his free composition. He made use of older
sources, copying from them at times very faithfully. A list of

[1] Welch, *PEJ*, Ch. XI, holds that the author of the Book of Ezra is a very
different man from the author of I and II Chronicles, with a different attitude and aim. Most scholars, however, think that the same man wrote both
books.

[2] Cf. Eissfeldt, *EAT*, p. 613. On the other hand, Sellin, *EAT*[7] (1935), p.
156; Meinhold, *AT*[3] (1932), p. 303; and Oesterley and Robinson, *IBOT*, p.
116, all accept the theory of Rothstein-Hänel (*Das erste Buch der Chronik*,
1927) and Von Rad (*Das Geschichtsbild des chronistischen Werkes*, 1930).
Meinhold in effect sums up this theory: The complete work proceeds, not from
one, but from at least two principal authors, who lived not long after 400 B.C.
The first followed in his depiction and view-point the priestly writing of the
Pentateuch (though not exclusively). The second, writing not much later,
leaned more heavily on Deuteronomy. Eissfeldt, however, maintains that the
differences in the material hardly warrant such decided pronouncements, and
speaks throughout of "The Chronicler" as of a single person.

these is given by Oesterley and Robinson in their *Introduction*[3] and we shall here mention them only briefly.

1. The Biblical books of the Pentateuch, Joshua, Samuel and Kings. Since we can verify at once the passages taken from these, it would be helpful for the student to mark them with a red marginal line, following Driver's excellent analysis in his *Introduction*.[4]

2. Possibly some earlier sources used by the writers of our books of Samuel and Kings.

3. A work which he calls the "midrash to the book of the kings" (II 24:27), probably an independent edifying commentary, which possibly contained the narratives concerning the prophets to which he so constantly refers.

4. Lists and genealogies drawn probably from official documents.

5. The book of Isaiah (II 26:22).

6. The memoirs of Ezra.

7. The memoirs of Nehemiah.

8. What purport to be official documents in Aramaic (in Ezra only).

The fact that the Chronicler used these sources makes it of course more difficult for us to isolate his own views. Yet the latter are continually showing through in several ways:

1. From what he selects from the Samuel-Kings sources which we now possess. This will indicate what he deemed significant and interesting.

2. From what he omits as unimportant or objectionable.

3. From what he alters or adds. There is a great deal of this, and it is very revealing. Examples of all three items will appear as we proceed with our study. The third item is of special value, as it enables us to infer the kind of alterations and additions he would be likely to make in his use of the sources now lost to us. Thus we can discern throughout his book certain characteristic touches and embellishments which are probably his own free composition and therefore reveal his mind quite clearly.

Finally, the work in its totality makes a decided impression as to its writer. As we have said, it is unlike any other portion of the

---

[3] Pp. 112ff; pp. 125f.

[4] 9th Ed., N. Y., 1920, pp. 519ff.

Old Testament. We can feel therefore that the Chronicler can be known from his writings. What do they tell us of him?

The Chronicler Wrote a History of the Jewish Church as Viewed by a Levitical Singer

The man we are studying was evidently a Levite and a temple singer.[1] This is the prevailing conclusion of scholars, drawn from his preponderant interest in Levites and temple music, which will be considered in another paragraph. We know nothing of his outward circumstances and his date can be inferred only from slight indications in his book. Scholars now date this some time after the work of Nehemiah and Ezra was concluded, which would be 350 B.C. or later if one thinks Ezra succeeded Nehemiah,[2] and shortly after 433 B.C. if Ezra came first.[3] The fact that the Chronicler does not mention the Samaritan schism and the building of the rival temple on mount Gerizim seems to show that he wrote before that event, although the bad relations between Jews and Samaritans which led up to the schism are much in evidence in his book. His work seems to proceed from a time of comparative peace, when religion was characterized by a joyous note, and the relations with the government were rather favourable. At any rate, he had abundant leisure to write and he availed himself of it. It is evident that none of the histories of Israel current in his day satisfied him. He felt that there was need of a new history which would put the really important things in their true place. As he saw the past and present one man, one city and one building occupied a central position, and one aspect of the national life was chiefly significant. He would show how *David* founded the Jewish church, made the *holy city* his own, planned its *temple* and instituted the *temple worship,* leaving behind him a dynasty assured of divine favour forever; how Solomon built the temple and ordered it according to David's plan; how therefore he prospered; how after his death the self-will of Jeroboam brought on the great schism whereby northern Israel fell away from Yahweh's true

---

[1] Albright, however, *APB,* p. 218, thinks that Ezra himself was the Chronicler.

[2] E.g. Oesterley and Robinson, *IBOT,* p. 111. But other scholars who accept this sequence put Ezra about 430 B.C. E.g. Albright, Batten, Bertholet, Haller. See p. 464.

[3] Eissfeldt, *EAT,* p. 612f. Sellin places the first redaction about 400 B.C., the second about 350 (*EAT*[7] [1935], p. 156). Meinhold puts both not long after 400 B.C. (*AT*[3] [1932], p. 303).

religion and ceased to count as a factor in the national church; how the kings of Judah prospered whenever they adhered to the Davidic institutions but suffered through each disloyalty, till at last accumulated transgressions brought about the destruction of city and temple and the captivity of the people; how under Cyrus a great number of faithful Jews returned from captivity and rebuilt the temple, but mingling with the profane people of the land did not prosper; how Nehemiah the governor rebuilt the walls of the city with the help of the people, provided Jerusalem with residents, introduced reforms and restored the full Levitical worship of the temple; how finally Ezra the priest and scribe brought with him the law of Moses from Babylon and induced the people to undertake its observance, putting an end to the marriages of Jews with aliens and establishing the temple worship on a sufficient basis. Throughout this new history the importance of the Levites, and particularly their service of music and praise, should be portrayed. Due honour should be given also to priests and prophets, the Davidic dynasty should be extolled as the nation's guarantee of blessing, and in general non-ecclesiastical interests should relapse into the insignificance that was properly theirs.

The conception of this great work was carried out with enthusiasm and ability. Of course, what the Chronicler composed was not sober history. In spite of his copious use of sources he succeeded in making his book a heroic interpretation of the past in the light of his own ideas. It does indeed contain much reliable information and we are especially indebted to him for preserving the priceless memoirs of Nehemiah and Ezra. But where we cannot check him by his sources we can never be sure just which of his statements is trustworthy. And the general effect of the picture he has drawn is quite untrue to reality.

But he has told a good story. Apart from the lists and genealogies the narrative is full of movement and interest. What is more, he has written a *religious* book, containing many passages of real devotional value. In both these respects he rises superior to the priestly writers, whose work displays an equal ecclesiastical interest.

Let us now consider in detail some of the characteristic ideas and traits revealed in the Chronicler's book.

The Chronicler Pictured David as the Founder of the Jewish Church

No one can read the First Book of the Chronicles without being struck by the extravagant position occupied by David and the radically different portrayal of his character, when compared with the David of Samuel and Kings. David has become more than Israel's greatest king, whose genius stamped itself upon the nation in many ways; he is now the divinely inspired creator of an ecclesiastical entity—the Jewish church—and the giver of its constitution, temple and worship. In short, he occupies much the same place in Judaism that Moses, according to the priestly writing, held in the religion of Israel. He might be called a second Moses, were it not that the Chronicler almost lets Moses drop out of sight. Of course, the Chronicler accepted Moses as "the man of God" who instituted the origins of Israel's religion. He presupposed the whole account of the priestly writers; but he stopped there. For him the significant thing was how his own Jewish church came into being, and here David was the sole figure of importance.

David's chief work, in which his whole life culminated, was the planning for the temple. Beginning with the story of II Samuel 7 the Chronicler told how David conceived the idea of building a temple to Yahweh, but was held back from doing so by a divine message, which deferred the enterprise till his son's day (I 17). He then altered the Samuel account and related how when David, at the command of Yahweh conveyed through the seer Gad, had erected an altar on Ornan's threshing-floor, Yahweh answered his sacrifices by fire from heaven. "Then David said, This is the house of Yahweh God, and this is the altar of burnt-offering for Israel" (I 21:18ff). The site being thus determined, David set about preparing materials and assembling workmen, charging Solomon to carry out the project and commanding all the princes of Israel to help him do so (I 22:2ff). As his end approached he gathered together all the great men and military leaders of the nation and in their presence handed over to Solomon the plan of the temple, its courses of priests and Levites, its work of service and its furniture. "All this, said David, have I been made to understand in writing from the hand of Yahweh, even all the works of this pattern" (I 28:1ff). In other words, just as Moses received the plan and specifications for the ark and tabernacle on mount Sinai, so David got those for the Jerusalem sanctuary by an equal revelation. One of his principal concerns was the ordering of the temple music (I 25:1ff) and the regulation of the Levites; "for by the last words of David the sons of Levi were numbered" (I 23:27) and assigned their duties. David also took the lead in making princely offerings for the temple construction, which upon his invitation were generously supplemented by the leaders of the nation (I 29:1ff). It was David who dreamed the dream of the temple's future greatness: "The house that is to be builded must be exceeding magnificent, of fame and glory throughout all countries" (I 22:5).

Almost all of this comes from those sections of the Chronicler's book that are not based on the Biblical books of Samuel and Kings. One is tempted to imagine that he composed not a little of it out of his own fancy. Yet we must always bear in mind the fact that he used older sources, and it may well be that this legend of David as a second Moses was not his invention, but had grown up over a long period and already embodied itself in Levitical writings before the Chronicler's time. In any case, however, he embraced it ardently and passed it on to posterity.

Nor did his metamorphosis of David cease here; he so used the Samuel-Kings material as to make it conform to the new Levitical picture. He omitted everything that seemed to him unimportant or unworthy of the supreme churchman, or disconcerting to his own view of history. Thus he left out the whole story of David's earlier life, with its rich variety of incident, and began the king's history with his elevation to the throne of united Israel. He told nothing of David's revenge on Michal for her cutting words (II Sam. 6:21f), of his kindness to Mephibosheth, his sin with Bathsheba, Amnon's outrage on Tamar, Absalom's revenge and rebellion, David's reinstatement to his lost kingdom, Sheba's rebellion, the sacrifice of Saul's sons to satisfy the Gibeonites, and the events of David's last days which led up to Solomon's accession. He excised David's "Song" and "Last Words" (II Sam. 22; 23:1ff) and his death charge to Solomon to do away with Joab and Shimei (I Ki. 2:5ff); substituting for the last the exhortation to build the temple (I Chron. 28:9ff). In nothing indeed is the David of the Chronicler so unlike the earlier David as in the thoughts that occupied him on the approach of death.

On the other hand, the Chronicler deemed important and worthy of insertion the account of David's being made king over all Israel, his capture of Jerusalem and bringing up of the ark to his new capital, his friendship with Hiram, his taking more wives, his wish to build the temple, his justice and his court, his numbering of the people and the pestilence that followed, his purchase of Araunah's (Ornan's) threshing floor, and above all else his military prowess, his mighty men and his victories.

It was thus a magnified and a white-washed David that the Chronicler presented. Yet the whitewashing in one respect did not go far enough—to our thinking—for David still remained the successful warrior, who in at least one instance treated his prisoners of war with barbarous cruelty (I 20:3). And in another respect it went much too far, for it washed over all the colours of the richly tinted David of Samuel-Kings and effaced the outlines of his noblest traits, his unconquerable spirit in adversity, his high heroism, his magnanimity, his readiness to forgive, his kindness. We no longer see him sparing Saul or hear the strains of his exquisite elegy over the slain hero. His love of Jonathan is gone, his heart-broken cry over the dead Absalom has fallen silent. Even the glaring faults and the weaknesses that disfigure his character are sorely missed, for it is they that make David more human.

The fact is, the Chronicler had little interest in the human side of David. For him the great king had become the founder of the church, occupied with ecclesiastical concerns rather than with political affairs and the welfare of his people. Only his military glory was retained, for the Chronicler, as we shall see, had no difficulty in mixing things military with things ecclesiastical.

David possessed for him one other value. Through his personal standing with God he was able to guarantee the divine favour not only to his own house but to the nation forever. This was no new thought with the Chronicler, for the Deuteronomic editors of the books of the Kings had already expressed it clearly. The Chronicler indeed was not quite so explicit regarding it as they. But none the less it lay at the base of his whole view of the history of the Jewish church. It was in the air of his time, as a number of the psalms testify. He must have accepted with fervour the glowing words of Second Isaiah: "I will make an everlasting covenant with you, even the sure mercies of David" (Is. 55:3).

No wonder that Sellin has termed this new way of regarding Israel's religious history, whereby the figure of Moses was overshadowed by that of David, a "David-religion." [1] And its chief exponent among Bible writers was the Chronicler.

[1] *GIJV*, II, p. 175.

The Chronicler exalted the Levitical Order and the Temple Music

In reading the Chronicler's book one cannot fail to notice how prominently the Levites appear on all occasions. There is reason to believe that he himself is responsible for this, having inserted such passages into the narrative as told by his sources. We can see that he did this with the Samuel-Kings material. For instance, the Samuel account of the bringing up of the ark to Jerusalem (II Sam. 6) told how first it was carried on a cart driven by Uzzah and Ahio, Abinadab's sons, one of whom was struck down by Yahweh because he rashly took hold of it to prevent its falling; and how later it was borne, apparently on men's shoulders, nothing being said of these bearers. The Chronicler altered this. He told how after the first tragedy David decreed that none ought to carry the ark but the Levites. Them he bade sanctify themselves for the duty, saying, "Because ye bare it not at the first Yahweh our God made a breach upon us, for that we sought him not according to the ordinance" (I 15: 2,13). Again, in the Kings account of the dedication of the temple (II Ki. 8) the Levites were not mentioned. The Chronicler remedied this by telling how after the priests came out from the holy place "the Levites also, who were the singers, all of them . . . arrayed in fine linen, with cymbals and psalteries and harps, stood at the east end of the altar . . . and the trumpeters and singers were as one, to make one sound to be heard in praising and thanking Yahweh; and . . . they lifted up their voice with the trumpets and cymbals and instruments of music, and praised Yahweh, saying, For he is good; for his lovingkindness endureth for ever. . . ." He then proceeded with the rest of the Kings account (II 5:11ff). This is the sort of thing he must have done with his other sources; though at times he overlooked an opportunity, as when in Nehemiah's narrative of the building of the walls he left unaltered Nehemiah's very casual mention of the part taken by the Levites (Neh. 3:17).

But he did more than play them up in his story; he raised them to a much higher position than they had been given in the priestly writing. The priestly writers (though exalting the Levites above the laity) had kept them in a very subordinate place, giving them only menial functions and making them mere assistants to the priests. They were to carry and set up the tabernacle, encamp around the sanctuary and keep account of the gifts offered for its construction. The holy place they might not enter, nor look upon its furniture. The grim story of Korah's rebellion, in which the

Levites were blasted by divine fire for claiming the right to offer incense, was intended to shut them out forever from "seeking the priesthood" (Num. 16). The Chronicler, however, turned the attention of his readers from the priests to the Levites. He did indeed recognize the exclusive prerogatives of the former to enter the holy of holies, to offer sacrifice and bless the people. But he associated the Levites with the priests, as essentially their brothers (I 23:32; II 5:11ff; cf. Neh. 9:38; 10:34). He represented the Levites as bearing the ark with the priests (I 15:14), indeed as the sole proper bearers of the ark (I 15:2); as having free access apparently to the holy place (I 23:32), as assisting the priests in offering sacrifices, as caring for the shew-bread, purifying all holy things, keeping charge of the holy place (I 23:28ff); as killing the paschal lambs and handing the blood to the priests (II 30:16f; 35:6). They had now a responsibility, along with the priests, for teaching the people (II 17:7f; 35:3) and it was they who interpreted the law to the congregation when it was read by Ezra, joining with him in admonishing the hearers not to weep but to keep the feast joyfully (Neh. 8:7ff). They were also said to have been appointed by David over the treasures of the house of Yahweh and "for the outward business over Israel, for officers and judges" (I 26:22, 29). Zerubbabel and Joshua, said the Chronicler, gave them oversight over the building of the second temple (Ezra 3:8). Certain of them were assigned by David responsible duties as gatekeepers of the temple (I 26). Their numbers he represented as very large (I 23:3, 38,000). Their revenue was assured (Neh. 12:47; 13:5; cf. 13:13) and they were exempted from taxation along with the priests (Ezra 7:24).

One function of the Levites seems to have stood out prominently in the Chronicler's mind. It was their duty to lead the congregation in praise and prayer. He told how David appointed certain of the Levites to minister before the ark of Yahweh and to celebrate and to thank and praise Yahweh (I 16:4). Among their other responsibilities assigned by David was that of standing every morning and evening to offer this service to God (I 23:30). Though he did not mention many instances of their carrying out this duty the Chronicler seems to have implied that they were thus occupied throughout his story. And when he came to the great covenant of Ezra's day, by which the people solemnly bound themselves to keep the law, he gave free rein to his favourite idea, telling how the Levites "stood upon the stairs of the Levites and cried with a loud voice unto Yahweh their God," exhorting the people to stand

and bless Yahweh their God, and leading their devotions in a long utterance of praise and petition (Neh. 9).

This of course involved their service of music, for much of their praise seems to have been expressed in song accompanied by musical instruments. Like their service of prayer and praise, this too went back to David, who had bidden the chief of the Levites "appoint singers with instruments of music, psalteries and harps and cymbals, sounding aloud and lifting up the voice with joy." With what enthusiasm did the Chronicler narrate how this was carried out! How Heman, Asaph and Ethan (familiar names in the psalms) were appointed with cymbals of brass to sound aloud; others with "psalteries set to *Alāmôth*"; others "with harps set to the *Shĕmînîth*, to lead"; how Chenaniah, chief of the Levites, was over the "lifting up"; how he "instructed about the lifting up because he was skilful" (I 15:16ff). Plainly it was a musician who related all this! It was a musician also who told how God gave Heman fourteen sons and three daughters, all of whom were "under the hands of their father for song in the house of Yahweh, for the service of the house of God"; how a great choir of 288 voices was "instructed in singing unto Yahweh" (it seems to have included women's voices as well as men's); how in this fraternity of musicians things were democratic, for "they cast lots for their offices, all alike, as well the small as the great, the teacher as the scholar" (I 25:1ff); how "the singers, heads of fathers' houses of the Levites, were employed in their work day and night" (I 9:33), being set free from all other duties and living in the chambers of the sanctuary; how the dedication of Solomon's temple (II 5:11ff; 7:6), the laying of the foundation of the second temple (Ezra 3:10), the dedication of the walls under Nehemiah (Neh. 12:27) and all great celebrations were made glad by strains of music; how once a vast host of invaders was thrown into mutual slaughter on the approach of the Jewish army headed by a choir of singers in holy array chanting praises to Yahweh (II 20:20ff). In no other book of the Bible except the Psalms does the reader so constantly catch the echo of melodious hymns to God. And all this music came from Levites, with one exception; the Chronicler freely conceded to the priests the privilege of blowing the trumpets! (I 16:6 and elsewhere).

Yet other touches might be added to show how the Chronicler exalted the Levites. He told how they included men of wealth (I 26:6,32); how they furnished 4600 men of war (I 12:23ff); how they engaged the attention of other kings than David, ordinances concerning them being made by Solomon (II 8:14ff), Hezekiah (II 31:2) and Josiah (II 35:3ff), as well as by Nehemiah, the governor (Neh. 7:1); how Ezra thought them indispensable for his enterprise, going to great pains to secure even a few of them (Ezra 8:16ff). In one instance he went so far as to praise them to the disadvantage of the priests, declaring that in the day of Hezekiah's reform they were "more upright of heart to sanctify themselves" (II 29:34). This passage is indeed unique, for his general treatment of the priests was friendly. He seems to have realized that priests and Levites stood or fell together, and his ecclesiastical interest also led him to put the former in a high place. But no one can read his book without feeling that after all the Levites are continually in the centre of the stage, while the priests, the main actors in the priestly writing, are bowed courteously to one side.

Friendliness characterized also the Chronicler's treatment of the prophets. They appear constantly in his book, and always in a favourable light. Nehemiah, it is true, spoke slightingly of them (Neh. 6:14), but in repeating this the Chronicler was merely following his source. His own kindly view is plain. Yet in adopting the prophets he altered them somewhat; they became *ecclesiastical*. Their messages had to do with worship more than with the great social duties that the ancient prophets were ever proclaiming. Only once did he strike this ethical note, when he told how Elijah wrote a letter to Jehoram of Judah denouncing him for killing his brethren (II 21:13) as well as for making high places in the mountains. Indeed, he transferred prophetic activity into his own favourite order, declaring that David and the captains of the host set apart certain of the sons of Asaph, Heman and Jeduthun to "prophesy with harps, with psalteries and with cymbals" (I 25:1). He seems to have viewed inspired outbursts of song during the temple service as actual prophecy; and he doubtless had in mind the sort of prophetic utterances that meet us in some of the psalms (e.g. Psalms 2:7; 81:5, etc.). He also on one occasion introduced a Levite as prophet into his story (II 20:14), Jahaziel of the sons of Asaph.

Finally, the Chronicler was on good terms with the lay potentates of the nation. We have seen how he exalted David. Many other kings fared well at his hands. Military leaders and "heads of fathers' houses" he treated with respect. His attitude towards the Persian government was not unkindly. Of course the lay people, however powerful, must keep to their allotted place. An Uzziah must not be allowed to usurp the priestly function of burning incense (II 26:16ff). But if they recognized the superiority of the clergy they were to be treated as allies. The Chronicler's book contains no hint of any disaffection towards the controlling classes of the community. Was not a king the founder of the church, the guarantor of its blessing forever? And if, as several modern scholars now think, the house of David was the most commanding among the leading lay families of his own time, he would be the last to question their prerogatives.

Thus the Chronicler, with all his devotion to his own order, lived in harmony with other powerful groups within the church. His condemnation was reserved for those who had left the fold.

The Chronicler Believed that the Jewish Church Alone was Sanctioned by God, and Excluded Northern Israel from Yahweh's True Religion

No one can read the book of the Chronicler without noticing his animus against the northern kingdom before the exile and the Samaritans after the return. He began his history with the death of Saul, which, he pointed out, was due to his sin in consulting the medium instead of Yahweh, and to his general disobedience (I 10:13f). Plainly, Saul the Benjamite did not count! We wonder what the Chronicler thought of the period before Saul, the days of the Judges. Possibly one passage throws light on his attitude: "Now for a long season Israel was without the true God, and without a teaching priest, and without law; but when in their distress they turned unto Yahweh, the God of Israel, and sought him, he was found of them. And in those times there was no peace to him that went out, nor to him that came in; but great vexations were upon the inhabitants of the lands. And they were broken in pieces, nation against nation, and city against city; for God did vex them with all adversity" (II 15:3ff). It is of course not certain of what period the Chronicler was speaking, but in any case we can see that for him the time before Saul, and Saul's own reign, were negligible. The history of the true church began with David's call to be king over all Israel (I 11:1ff). Here was the right combination: the dynasty and the whole of the people. This continued through the great age of Solomon, to the happiness of all.

Then came the rebellion of northern Israel under Jeroboam, by which it cut itself off from its divinely appointed sovereign and from Yahweh's true religion (II 10:1ff). This the Chronicler narrated very fairly, adhering closely to the Kings story (I Ki. 12), in which the sympathy of the writer plainly lay with the rebels. But having done so he went on to tell how Jeroboam expelled the priests and Levites from the offices they had hitherto occupied in the north, substituting his own priests "for the high places, and for the he-goats, and for the calves which he had made" (II 11:13ff). Here he went beyond the already prejudiced account of I Ki. 12:25ff, affirming the total eradication of the Levitical priesthood and the total departure from the Yahweh religion. Henceforth these were to be found only in Judah! His point of view is disclosed in the utterance of Abijah the prophet, which he reported in this context:

"Hear me, O Jeroboam and all Israel: Ought ye not to know that Yahweh, the God of Israel, gave the kingdom over Israel to David for ever, even to him and his sons by a covenant of salt? Yet Jeroboam . . . the servant of Solomon the son of David rose up and rebelled against his lord. And there were gathered unto him worthless men, base fellows, that strengthened themselves against Rehoboam the son of Solomon, when Rehoboam was young and tender-hearted (i.e. feeble in intelligence) and could not withstand them. And now ye think to withstand the kingdom of Yahweh in the hand of the sons of David; and ye are a great multitude, and there are with you the golden calves which Jeroboam made you for gods. Have ye not driven out the priests of Yahweh, the sons of Aaron, and the Levites, and made you priests after the manner of the peoples of other lands? . . . so that whosoever cometh to consecrate himself with a young bullock and seven rams, the same may be a priest of them that are no gods. But as for us, Yahweh is our God, and we have not forsaken him; and we have priests ministering unto Yahweh, the sons of Aaron, and the Levites in their work, . . . for we keep the charge of Yahweh our God; but ye have forsaken him" (II 13:4ff).

The conclusion that the Chronicler drew from all this he expressed through another prophet on a different occasion: "Yahweh is not with Israel, that is, with all the children of Ephraim" (II 25:7). From the days of Jeroboam northern Israel ceased for him to play any part in the plan of God for his people. That is why the Chronicler paid no further attention to their history, except where it threw light upon that of the true church, the southern kingdom. This view he supported by a gross misrepresentation of their religion, as we have just seen, and an insistence that Judah, in spite of its many apostasies, was somehow better: "in Judah there were good things" (II 12:12).

Such a thorough-going rejection of northern Israel carried with it two logical consequences, both of which the Chronicler drew with heartiness.

One was that the north was now a missionary field whence converts might be won back to the true church and the true God. The priests and Levites who fled to Jerusalem in Jeroboam's time were but precursors of many lay-people whose homesickness compelled them to return to the bosom of the church under later kings: Asa (II 15:9), Jehoshaphat (II 19:4), Hezekiah (II 30:11) and Josiah (II 35:17f). Jehoshaphat and Hezekiah indeed did not wait for volunteers but extended a cordial invitation, the former actually going in person among the people from Beersheba to the hill-country of Ephraim and bringing them back to Yahweh, the God of their fathers. Hezekiah contented himself with sending letters, which unfortunately were on the whole not very well received!

The second consequence drawn by the Chronicler was that Judah must have no dealings with the schismatic north. The good Jehoshaphat was sternly rebuked for his alliance with Ahab (II 19:2), whereby he helped the wicked and loved them that hated Yahweh. When he failed to profit by this lesson and entered into a ship-building project with Ahaziah, he suffered the loss of his ships before they could set out on their first voyage (II 20:35ff). When Amaziah hired a hundred thousand auxiliary troops "out of Israel" he was peremptorily bidden by a man of God to send them back at once (II 25:5ff).

Yet the Chronicler was not always able to maintain such an adamantine exclusiveness. Now and again he was betrayed into something very like recognition of good in Israel, even of true religion. His hostility to Ahab led him to insert the story of the true prophet Micaiah (II 18) and to commend Jehu for "executing justice" upon Ahab's house (II 22:8). He told how Oded, a prophet of Yahweh in Samaria, persuaded his fellow-countrymen to a noble clemency (II 28:9ff). And he actually reported a letter of Elijah to a king of Judah, Jehoram, in which the prophet boldly rebuked the king's wickedness! (II 21:12ff). But these were only momentary aberrations.[1]

Thus he led up to the situation following the exile. When the Jews that returned from Babylon began to rebuild the temple the descendants of the apostate northerners asked to be admitted to a

[1] Welch, however, concludes from instances such as these that the Chronicler did not regard the nation of northern Israel, with its leaders, as apostate, but only condemned the northern kingdom, *as a kingdom,* because of the schism it had made in the unity of the nation (*PEJ,* p. 205).

share in the enterprise (Ezra 4:1ff). But now the Chronicler was not willing even to admit that the same racial stock persisted in Samaria. With what may have been a malicious twisting of his sources he represented them as acknowledging themselves foreigners, descendants of the colonists settled there by Esarhaddon (II Ki. 17:24ff), who had learned to sacrifice to Yahweh only after their arrival. Their petition was of course rejected: "Ye have nothing to do with us in building a house unto our God." This turned them into enemies who did all they could to hinder the rebuilding both of the temple and (in the days of Nehemiah) of the walls of the city. One of Nehemiah's most determined opponents was Sanballat of Samaria, whom Nehemiah counted a foreigner, declaring that marriage with his daughter by a priest defiled the priesthood (Neh. 13:28ff). One would never gather from the account of the Chronicler that the Samaritans were devoted adherents of the law of Moses, as was the fact! He simply perverted history in the interest of an ecclesiastical dogma. He was not alone in this, to be sure, for we find the same process beginning in the books of the Kings; he did but express with a will what too many of his fellow-Jews were already thinking. His arrogant exclusiveness, his ignoring of all good in the north, his "David-religion" with its overshadowing of Moses, his extravagant idea of Judah and Jerusalem, were sadly typical and help us to understand why presently the Samaritans seceded definitely from all adherence to the Jerusalem temple, and taking with them the law of Moses as their only Scripture built their own sanctuary on mount Gerizim.

Thus far we have been considering some of the outstanding characteristics of the Chronicler's thinking. Back of these lay a theology, and it is time that we turn our attention to this.

The Chronicler's Idea of God

On the whole the Chronicler thought of God as did the other men of the Old Testament, especially those of a later age; but there are some features of his theology that distinguish him, or at least make his total picture of God peculiarly his own. He believed of course that Yahweh, the God of Israel, was supreme in heaven and earth; "great is our God, above all gods" (II 2:5). Indeed, He was the only God, for the expression "above all gods" in later Old Testament writers was generally but a poetic survival of earlier language. Being so great, Yahweh could not be contained by any house (II 2:6). Solomon's temple was only for the purpose of worship, "to burn incense before him."

At the same time, the temple was not unimportant: indeed, it was perhaps the central thing in the divine mind and purpose, at least so far as human history was concerned. God ordained that Solomon should build it, setting aside David as unsuitable (I 28:2ff). And it must be built and furnished in exactly the right manner. So insistent was God on this point that he took the pains to deliver to David in writing the plan and specifications, not only for the building and furniture, but for the courses of the priests and Levites who were to minister in it, and for "all the work of the service of the house," that is, for the way in which worship was to be offered (I 28:11ff).

He was therefore a God who really cared about such things; a "liturgically-minded" God, we should call Him. In this He differed widely from the God of the prophets, who required of man nothing but to do justly and to love kindness and to walk humbly with Him (Mic. 6:8). He was like the God of the priestly writers. Yet a divergence is to be noted also. For to the priestly writers God's mind was centred in sacrifices. The Chronicler had got beyond that. He did indeed take as a matter of course that God required sacrifices, but he did not dwell upon this. What he delighted to tell was how the Levites and singers offered up praises, thanksgiving and prayer, for these were what God craved most. But they must be offered by the accredited persons and in the prescribed way. If music were used, as it generally was, to convey the church's devotion heavenwards, it must be good music rendered by skilled performers and trained voices. God was very particular about that!

God also—and here the Chronicler agreed with the priestly writers—set much store by liberal contributions towards the building and furnishing of the sanctuary and the maintenance of the clergy. Like Moses of old, David called for free-will offerings from the leaders of the people, having first, as a great monarch should, made a kingly gift himself (I 29:1ff); and the princes responded lavishly—a good example to the laity of the Chronicler's day! David thereupon poured out his joy in a beautiful offertory prayer whose cadences still re-echo in the Book of Common Prayer (I 29:10ff).

To the Chronicler God could be known and worshipped only through the Jewish church; *extra ecclesiam nulla salus*. This alone had God's approval. No temple was valid but the Jerusalem temple, no ministrants but the Jerusalem priests and Levites. The same was true of Jerusalem's kings; the Davidic dynasty ruled by divine right over *all* Israel, whether acknowledged or no. It was God's insistence on validity that made Him so careful about genealogies and successions.

The Chronicler's God was therefore not a wide-hearted God. No single passage in this writer's long book revealed the divine good will towards mankind which meets us in rudimentary form even in the priestly writing. The nations appeared only as a public before which the glory of Yahweh's house might be exhibited (I 22:5) or a Jewish king exalted (II 32:23). Not a word of either temple or king being *for* all peoples! With the exception of Hiram (II 2:11ff), Pharaoh Neco (II 35:20ff) and Cyrus (Ezra 1:1ff), to whom Yahweh seems to have been friendly, the divine attitude towards foreigners was one of aversion. Solomon's Egyptian wife must not dwell in the house of David, because the places were holy whereunto the ark had come (II 8:11). The seed of Israel must separate itself from all foreigners when it approached Yahweh (Neh. 9:2), and intermarriage with them must be sternly forbidden (Ezra 10:1ff). The only use for foreigners was to be conquered by Judah's righteous kings, such as David (I 18-20), or Jotham, whose faithfulness Yahweh rewarded by enabling him to make Ammon tributary (II 27). Reliance on foreign powers for military aid was a thing displeasing to Yahweh, for was He not Judah's true stay? (II 16:7; 28:16ff). Here the Chronicler sounded a genuine prophetic note.

If such were Yahweh's feeling towards the nations generally, how much more did He turn against those in Israel who had wilfully abandoned His saving ordinances and set up for themselves unauthorized, invalid and corrupt ordinances out of their own heart! The Chronicler, as we have seen, believed that Yahweh was not with Israel, that is, with all the sons of Ephraim (II 25:7).

Within the Jewish church Yahweh was kind to all save those who exhibited disloyalty to Him. These He commanded to be put to death (II 15:13). The rest He embraced in His good will, not only the clergy, but the laity. The part played by the congregation, though subordinate, was important (I 29:20; Neh. 8:2ff) in the eyes of God, even the women and children sharing in the responsibility of worship and solemn undertakings (II 20:13; Neh. 10:28). Those who returned from out northern Israel were welcomed and on one occasion a ritual requirement was relaxed that they might take part in the passover (II 30:18ff). "For Hezekiah had prayed for them, saying, The good Yahweh pardon every one that setteth his heart to seek God . . . though he be not cleansed according to the purification of the sanctuary."

Yet one cannot avoid the impression that the Chronicler's God was interested in His people mainly as a *congregation,* a churchgoing body, and had none too much care for their life outside church, their daily toil, their laughter and their tears, their ambitions and their anxieties. Perhaps we are doing the Chronicler an injustice in saying this, but the way in which he passed over the human side even of God's favourite David points to such a conclusion.

Nor apparently did the Chronicler think of God as having much concern for individuals. David of course was an exception, for God lavished on him all kinds of love and favour. The kings that followed also engaged the divine attention. God dealt with them on a system of prompt retribution, rewarding their faithfulness and punishing their disobedience without delay. A striking feature of the Chronicler's book is just this rigid scheme of recompense, wherein every royal misfortune is accounted for by previous evildoing, even where the latter (we suspect) had to be invented (II 12:1ff; 16:12; 20:35ff; 21:1ff; 24:23ff; 25:14ff; 26:16ff; 27:1ff).

It is in keeping with his general point of view that the Chronicler did not stress the ethical demands of God. The sins for which the kings were punished were mostly in the domain of man's relation to God—corrupt worship, seeking other gods, depending on foreign alliances (in one case on physicians, II 16:12) instead of on God, and the like. Only once was a crime against a fellow-man avenged—Jehoram's murder of his brethren (II 21:13). Perhaps another instance would be the killing of the prophet Zechariah ben Jehoida, in which Joash was involved (II 24:20ff). In telling the latter story the Chronicler related Zechariah's prayer for vengeance, "Yahweh, look upon it and require it," as one that evidently had the divine approval.

A final aspect of the Chronicler's idea of God must be mentioned. He was a stout believer in Yahweh as a God of war. We have seen how one kind of material which he selected from his Samuel sources regarding David had to do with the great king's mighty men and military successes. He even added from another source a list of the mighty men who came to David to Ziklag (I 12:1ff). Military leaders figured prominently in David's councils; indeed it was with the advice of the captains of the host that David set apart Levites to prophesy with musical instruments

(I 25:1). Plainly they stood high in God's esteem and their authorization gave a flavour of its own to ecclesiastical appointments. It was to David as a man of war that God's favour was shown. True, David was not permitted to build the temple because he had been a man of war, but (to judge from the Chronicler's whole attitude) this prohibition rested on some ritual incongruity and not upon any ethical disapproval of war. Of succeeding kings the Chronicler loved to tell how the good kings built fortifications and prepared armaments (II 1:14; 8:3ff; 11:5ff; 14:6ff; 17:13; 26:6ff; 27:3f; 32:5; 33:14). In spite of all the prophets had said, he looked on such activity as pleasing to God. Of his own beloved order, the Levites, he told proudly that they contributed 4600 mighty men of valour to David's forces (I 12:26).

Such are some of the chief traits of God, as the Chronicler saw Him. They fit in well with his own characteristics and enable us to perceive the kind of religion that he cherished and tried through his book to pass on to others. Let us now ask what is its value.

The Chronicler's Contribution to Religion

It is quite possible that the Chronicler's impressive book had great effect upon the Jewish church of his day. The Levitical group to which he belonged would naturally welcome it as a confirmation of their claims, and the community at large probably found it acceptable. At any rate it was preserved and eventually made its way into the canon of holy Scripture. It must have tended to intensify the racial exclusiveness of the Jews, especially towards the Samaritans, and to foster enthusiasm for the "David-religion" with its exaltation of the Levites and of sacred music. But all this is speculation, for the Old Testament itself tells us nothing of the influence exerted by the Chronicler's history.

What significance has the Chronicler for our own time? Those who have read his long book with sympathy and appreciation may well find that he has something of real value to give. For in it he has presented a necessary side of religion, the side that has to do with things churchly and with worship. In this he is like the priestly writers, but he differs from them in two ways. He stresses the prayer and praise element in worship rather than the offering of sacrifices, and is thus more spiritual. He is superior to them also in that he has incorporated into his book much devotional material, giving it warmth and colour and religious emotion, qualities in which their work was conspicuously lacking. His love for the music of the church further enriches his narrative. One of the loveliest traits he displays is his pervasive note of joy, which of course is a well-spring of praise.

The Chronicler's book will therefore always have value for those who crave a beautiful and stately church service in a historic church with its ancient orders of the ministry and its ages-old liturgy. But even for these it will suffer under serious limitations.

For like the priestly writers the Chronicler sins against the true proportions of religion. He thinks of God as concerned chiefly for things ecclesiastical rather than for the "weightier matters of the law, justice and mercy and faith" (Matt. 23:23). And in so doing he falls into *unreality*. For it is unreality that characterizes his book from beginning to end. Not only the unreality arising from its unhistorical character, its perversion of the past; but the deeper unreality which divorces it from actual human life. It is as if the reader were always confined within the walls of a church and could not get out into the streets and fields, the homes and the market-places of men. Now a church is a holy place where one draws apart from the world and feels the presence of the Unseen. And this experience within the church is essential. But it finds its interpretation only when we go out from the church to mingle with people amid the common occupations of society. The Chronicler however would have his reader stay within and contemplate life as it is portrayed in the stained-glass windows. And often the windows are not very beautiful or edifying. There are, for instance, too many soldiers! There are also too many caricatures of heretics and schismatics.

For on the ethical side the Chronicler is far from satisfactory. Much as he makes of prophets he seems to have learned little from the mighty men of old who bore that name. Royal wealth and splendour, which they abominated, he delighted in. Military preparedness, which they denounced, he extolled. But it is most of all in his silences that he stood over against them. He is ever speaking of kings, but when does he say anything about their duty to govern well? He glories in the beauty of the temple services, but lets fall no word concerning clean hands and a pure heart. He is strong for valid orders, but omits mention of the moral responsibilities of the ministry. His most unlovely trait—his ecclesiastical narrowness—betrays a completely non-ethical way of judging, an absolute inability to ask the kind of questions concerning opponents that the prophets would have asked.

Yet after all it is not our duty to pass judgment upon this man.

He may have been more interested in ethics than the scope of his book permitted him to show. If he were anything like the later psalmists, who seem to reflect his love of the temple worship, he was not devoid of care for the poor and oppressed. Let us take him with his limitations and get from him what we can.

Chapter XXVI

THE WISE MEN OF THE BOOK OF PROVERBS

[MAINLY AFTER 586 B.C.]

From an early age there existed in Israel men who gave themselves to the study of what was called "wisdom." This wisdom was not peculiar to Israel but was found throughout the ancient east, especially in Babylonia, Egypt and Edom. Solomon, as we have seen, became its patron in Israel and was credited with having attained great proficiency in its pursuit. Partly by the aid of his powerful name it won a place in the Hebrew Scriptures, appearing in a number of psalms and in three remarkable books which are popularly called "wisdom books"—Job, Proverbs and Ecclesiastes.[1]

The Sources

Of all the examples of wisdom literature that have come down to us from ancient Israel the most typical are the collections contained in the Book of Proverbs. It is here that we see the *usual* work of the wise men, as contrasted with such unique utterances as the books of Job and Ecclesiastes (Qoheleth). For our study of these teachers it is not necessary to distinguish the several collections nor concern ourselves with their dates. The book may be taken as a whole. In it we have the best sort of primary sources, since here the wise men speak for themselves.

The Wise Men Sought to Win the Individual to Wisdom

The moment one begins to read the Book of Proverbs he is struck by the fact that he is being addressed personally. "My son, hear the instruction of thy father (1:8) . . . My son, if thou wilt receive my words (2:1)." How different from the prophets! There everything was directed to Israel or Judah as a people. The unit was

[1] To these might well be added the Apocryphal books Ecclesiasticus (Ben Sirach) and The Wisdom of Solomon.

500

the nation or the city Jerusalem or at times the king, the princes, priests or prophets. Only now and then did some individual receive a message, and then he was singled out for a special reason, as Amaziah, Shebna, Hananiah, Baruch. But in the Book of Proverbs the nation has disappeared from view. Its public functionaries, with the exception of the king, are forgotten and attention is concentrated upon the ordinary citizen. Yet he is no longer regarded primarily as a citizen, or even a Jew. What is said to him is applicable to any one, whether Jew or Gentile, ancient or modern. That is, in the main. Once and again things peculiar to Israel are alluded to; and of course the name given to God is Yahweh. But the whole idea that Israel is in unique covenant relation with God, involving special privileges, responsibility and destiny, lies below the horizon. The reader is nowhere appealed to on the ground that he belongs to a favoured group or has any part to play in the world because of it. He is just a man. The wise men are interested in him for his own sake, because he personally— as every one else—is worth while.

And they really *are* interested. They have no axe to grind, no institution such as the nation or the priesthood to promote, no advantage of their own to seek. They are concerned entirely with the good of the reader, or hearer, as the case may be. To be sure, they look beyond him to other individuals, whose happiness they would foster as well as his own. For while, as Toy says, they show no recognition of society as an ethical cosmos or unified whole,[1] no one can fail to see that they want human relations in general made beautiful and fruitful. They are ever looking at the individual as one of many to whom both he and they have responsibilities. He is a father, a son, a husband, a neighbour, a friend, a business man, a subject; and they would so guide him in all these relations that he may be a blessing to himself and to others.

Their approach to him is fatherly. It is not, "Thus saith Yahweh," as with the prophets. They do not command, like the legislators. The only authority to which they lay claim is that naturally conferred by age, experience and learning. They speak in their own name only, and aim to win the hearer to wisdom by persuasion. They appeal to inherited beliefs, common sense, his own observation and right feeling. They tell him plainly what is best for him, give their reasons, and urge him with all the compulsion of friendliness to follow it. The course to which they would win him they call "wisdom."

[1] *Proverbs*, p. xiv.

Wisdom is Ethical Conformity to God's Creation

Throughout most of the Book of Proverbs wisdom is plainly a human quality; but the wise men, being deeply religious, felt the necessity of giving it a higher sanction and origin. For they began their thinking with God. He was the kind of God whom the prophets had declared—a Person, possessing intelligence, character and purpose. He had created the world with a plan conformable to His own nature, and this plan they named Wisdom, looked at from its divine side. In an eloquent passage the author of the first collection introduces Wisdom herself as saying: "Yahweh formed me in the beginning of his way . . . before the earth was. . . . When he established the heavens I was there, . . . when he marked out the foundations of the earth . . . I was by him as a master workman" (8:22–30). Wisdom therefore was wrought into the constitution of the universe. It was independent of men, though in a real sense it existed specially for them. "My delight," Wisdom adds, "was with the sons of men" (8:31).

Man's wisdom was to know this divine Wisdom—plan, order— and attune his ways to it. For him wisdom began by acknowledging the primary reality of the cosmos—God. "The fear of Yahweh is the beginning of knowledge" (1:7). "Trust in Yahweh with all thy heart and lean not upon thine own understanding: in all thy ways acknowledge him and he will direct thy paths" (3:5–6). Like all things else, wisdom came from God. It was apparently conceived, to use Toy's words [1] as "a life common to God and man, breathed into man by God," and thus is "parallel to the Old Testament idea of 'spirit.'"

In human life therefore wisdom meant conforming to the divine constitution of the world. One must find out what it is, then order himself accordingly. Of course this was but another way of saying that one must do the will of God. But the wise men tended always to look on that will as taking effect in an orderly path of causation. While they spoke at times as if the thought of God watching over each act of man and meting out His response to it were present in their minds, yet in the main they expressed their observations in terms of natural law. They had the strong feeling that whatever runs counter to these laws is unsound, crooked, doomed to collapse—just as Ezekiel called prophecy opposed to God's will "building with untempered mortar" (Ezek. 13:11ff).

[1] P. xvii.

Now since God is ethical in His inmost nature the constitution of the universe must be ethical also. We find therefore that wisdom in the Book of Proverbs is largely identical with ethics. To be sure, one occasionally runs across maxims of what we might term mere prudence, but these are rare in comparison with those that have a distinctly moral tone. The fundamental assumption is that virtue is the only sound way of life.

The standard of ethics that they set was high. The divine plan calls for a society in which people work hard, observe each other's rights, respect each other, treat the less fortunate kindly, have concern for the poor, maintain an atmosphere of general friendliness, enjoy the pleasures of moderation, love their families and homes, are sincere, modest, self-controlled, temperate, reliable, chaste, willing to listen and learn, forgiving, considerate, discreet, kind to animals, sweet-tempered, liberal, yet withal prudent and keeping an eye to their own welfare. Such an ideal, though falling short as we shall see in several important ways, is certainly one which if carried into effect would make the world a not unlovely place.

It will be seen from this that wisdom to these men was a very practical thing. It had to do with life more than with thought. Indeed one could hardly call the wise men thinkers in the sense in which we apply that word to Socrates or even to the Hebrew Qoheleth (Ecclesiastes). Certainly they were no philosophers inquiring into the nature of reality and endeavouring to define common-sense concepts. They took over their view of the universe ready-made from their predecessors. Only once was any question raised, and then it quickly died into silence (30:1–4). In their ethical sayings no attempt was made to discuss the nature of right and wrong, or to strike a balance between apparently conflicting duties. All was simple, direct, dogmatic, traditional. Nor can we say that the wise men were even profound observers of human life. They did indeed perceive many truths regarding it; but their vision was so clouded by the inherited dogma of retribution that they simply refused to look at great masses of facts which contradicted it.

This dogma formed a central part of their interpretation of life and it is time that we now consider it.

Wisdom Infallibly Brings Happiness

God has so ordered the world, taught the wise men, that the exact reward of each man's conduct is sure to be meted out to him before he dies. There was nothing new in such a belief. Ezekiel had formulated the doctrine that the sinning soul—and no other—would die for its iniquity, while the righteous soul would live (Ezek. 18). Back of Ezekiel the prophets and Deuteronomists had made the same claim regarding God's dealings with the nation. Sin brought doom, repentance delivered from death. The wise men assumed it as a truism which needed only to be asserted over and over again but never to be established by argument. "Behold, the righteous shall be recompensed in the earth: how much more the wicked and the sinner" (11:31).

It is easy to see that this was a corollary to their deep conviction that God is just and that His universe is fundamentally ethical. Since they could not fall back upon a future life in which accounts would be evened, they must posit retribution this side the grave. For that God could be satisfied to allow wickedness to go unpunished and virtue unrewarded was unthinkable.

They developed the dogma of retribution in great detail. One need but open the Book of Proverbs at random to find saying after saying in which threats alternate with promises. "Treasures of wickedness profit nothing; but righteousness delivereth from death." "He becometh poor that worketh with a slack hand; but the hand of the diligent maketh rich." "The memory of the righteous is blessed; but the name of the wicked shall rot" (10:2, 4, 7). Many of these convictions could have been arrived at empirically by noticing the usual results of different kinds of conduct. They do little more than describe the working of ordinary cause and effect. But many of them are pronouncements of faith in the moral order, in the light of which actual happenings are read, and to which they are somehow made to conform. And always behind the sayings based on experience lay the same vigorous faith, ready to reinforce them if at any point they seemed to fail.

Wisdom is Open to All who will Learn It

Along with this retribution dogma went the tacit assumption of free will. Every man had the ability to insure happiness through wisdom, if he would but use it. There was equal opportunity for all. Nothing was said of handicaps of environment and education, of differing temperaments and mental capacities, or of the weakness of the will to which all are so prone. The attitude of the wise men was: "It lies with you. If you pay the price you can live to a good old age in excellent health, gain a competence, rear a family of children in whom you will take pride, enjoy the good will of your fellow men and leave an honourable name behind you."

It need not surprise us therefore to find them harsh towards the man who refused to learn wisdom. In their eyes he was indeed a "fool." When he got into trouble as the result of his ways they wasted scant sympathy upon him. Wisdom had warned him beforehand that such would be the case. "Because ye have set at nought all my counsel . . . I also will mock when your fear cometh" (1:25f). The wise men were not the ones to help a poor fellow out of the ditch.

The Educational Method of the Wise Men

However open wisdom might be to all men, it would not come to any spontaneously. It could be acquired only through education.

Here it was that the function of the wise men came in. They looked on themselves as able and ready to impart wisdom to those who sought it, especially the younger generation. The Book of Proverbs shows us how they went about their task. Not that it tells us much explicitly regarding their method; but viewed as itself the great illustration of their teaching it furnishes rich material from which we can draw inferences.

We see from it that they aimed to carry on and improve a tradition. It did not occur to any one of them to question it or strike out on a new path for himself. Their material was inherited from those who had gone before them. What they had to impart was really the funded experience of mankind regarding human life.

Inherited likewise was the vehicle by means of which this experience was handed on. The "proverb" or aphorism (*māshāl*), as it here appears, was not a genuine folk-saying but the product of conscious and laborious art. By generations of striving there had been worked out a literary form of singular beauty and incisive power into which each writer endeavoured to throw his own contribution. Of course, the aphorism gave place at times to flowing sentences developing a theme at some length, but it remained none the less the unit of style and constituted the bulk of the older part of the book. Evidently the wise men believed in its effectiveness. It challenged the attention, provoked thought, could easily be retained in memory by reason of its poetic rhythm and trenchant brevity, and tended to unfold as the imagination dwelt upon it into a wealth of concrete detail. Its very beauty also acted as a charm to win men. To judge from the perfection attained, the wise men must have laboured very hard over this literary form.

Having made ready the material they desired to inculcate they next set out to find their pupils. These they sought from the general public, making their appeal as wide as possible. It was no esoteric doctrine that they had to reveal, confined to some picked group, but plain and wholesome good sense for the ordinary man. "Doth not wisdom cry? . . . On the top of the high places by the way, where the paths meet, she standeth; beside the gates, at the entry of the city, at the coming in at the doors, she crieth aloud: Unto you, O men, I call. . . . Whoso is simple, let him turn in hither. . . . Come, eat ye of my bread" (8:1-4; 9:4f). Stripped of its poetic personification, this seems to mean that the wise men did not wait till they were visited by inquirers but themselves went out into the "streets and lanes" of the city with a genuine evangelical spirit, teaching on corners and in public squares and uttering impassioned calls to the passing throngs. Theirs was a genuinely democratic enterprise.

Surrounded as a result of these efforts by a group of pupils, they taught by means of maxims. These must have been uttered with all the impressiveness at their command. They would avail themselves of the corporate influence of the class to which they belonged and also of any personal prestige the individual may have acquired. For their aim was to carry the hearer along with them, to convince him and induce him to action, and the weight of the speaker was an important factor in attaining this result. Such a bearing, combined with their genuinely affectionate interest in the individual, would be reinforced by the telling style of their diction and the manifest truth of what they uttered.

Their purpose, as has just been said, was practical. Almost every one of their aphorisms was intended to lead straight to some sort of action. Teaching was tied to life. Therefore they made themselves masters of the art of playing upon motives. What these motives were we shall consider in the next section.

It is a significant fact that the wise men did not argue. Their method was to assert, not to prove. All through the book we get intimations that some of the community repudiated the assumptions on which their teaching was based, but nowhere do we find them disputing with these "scoffers"; they met such opposition only by sweeping denials and a mixture of condemnation and threatening. The idea of the Greek "dialogue," in which the exponents of differing views confront each other as equals and have the right

to a full examination of their respective claims in the court of reason, was evidently quite foreign to these sages—as indeed to the
men of the Old Testament generally. Similarly, when they were
talking to their pupils and others who sympathized with their
beliefs, they nowhere sought to establish these on the foundation
of reason. If asked why argument was unnecessary they would
probably have pointed first to the authority of tradition. All this
has been settled long ago, they would have said. Then they would
have appealed to men's own observation of the results of various
kinds of conduct. But always they would have met any further
pressing of difficulties by simple dogmatic affirmations. Such at
least was the course of Job's friends, who seem to represent the
view-point of the Book of Proverbs very faithfully.

Naturally therefore they required from their pupil an attitude of
receptivity. They aimed to promote those mental activities by
which the tradition would be passed on most surely and effectively
—unaltered. Great stress was laid on the value of attention. In
this activity memory played an important part. "My son, forget
not my law; but let thy heart keep my commandments. . . . Let
not kindness and truth—i.e. the chief element of my teaching—
forsake thee; bind them about thy neck; write them upon the tablet
of thy heart" (3:1ff). Nothing was further from their desire than
to "teach their pupil to think." To be sure, they did provoke
thought of a certain sort. They wanted him constantly to revolve
in his mind the aphorisms they uttered and enrich them by appli-
cations of his own. They would encourage him to produce
aphorisms for himself—a strenuous mental exercise. But the search-
light of his scrutiny must always be kept away from the foundations upon which the structure of wisdom rested, unless it were to
admire and extol. Anything like independence of reflection was
anathema. "Seest thou a man wise in his own conceit? There is
more hope of a fool than of him" (26:12).

Such a method of education had its obvious drawbacks. It
tended to close the mind against new views of truth. It made for
rigidity and intolerance. It left its product quite unprepared to
meet unlooked for situations, changing needs. If one should find
that its dogmas were insufficient to explain his experience, it might
lead to a collapse of his whole religious faith. But on the other
hand it did succeed in preserving and strengthening a tradition
that after all was a noble one. It freed the plain man—so far as it
succeeded—from hesitancy and the bewilderment of conflicting
ideas. It engendered solidarity, enthusiasm, power.

Nor must we lay too much stress on its dogmatic element. Along with affirmations of dogma we meet in Proverbs an abundance of observations, the self-evident truth of which is as inescapable today as when the wise men first uttered them.

A few other things may be said of their way of teaching. They realized the importance of moulding lives while yet they retained their plasticity. With this in view they called in the aid of parents as teachers of young children, provided them with material, and reinforced their influence with all the means at their disposal. How frequent are the exhortations to young people to heed what they have learned from father and mother! The home and the school thus co-operated towards the common end. Upon fathers they urged what they felt was a wise severity in dealing with their sons. "Withhold not correction from the child; for if thou beat him with the rod, he will not die" (23:13). "Chasten thy son, seeing there is hope; and set not thy heart on his destruction" (19:18). They themselves sought especially the young man, presumably at the age when he would look beyond the home for his ideas. They tried to win him to a life-decision in favour of wisdom, and when that was done to provide for his "increase in learning" through the means outlined above, and also (apparently) by association with wise men. The company of "fools," loose women and others who disregarded wisdom's dictates, was to be sedulously avoided (13:20). Nor did they hesitate to go to him with sharp rebukes if it seemed necessary (17:10).

The Wise Men Addressed Themselves to Various Motives

Nothing is of more importance in education than the motives which are called into play. First of all, it is necessary to excite motives of some sort if one expects to obtain results in human lives. That was well understood by the wise men, who learned to work constantly upon the desires of their pupils. Another thing that they knew very well was that the mind is swayed by a rich variety of motives, all of which may be called in to promote a given course of action. They avoided in consequence the mistake of over-simplicity in their appeal; and it is not uncommon to find that within the compass of a few aphorisms desires of quite different sorts are stimulated. Let us now ask ourselves into what classes these various motives fall.

1. By far the largest number of direct appeals was made to self-interest. The wise men frankly assumed that a controlling motive

in man's mind is and ought to be his desire for personal happiness. Therefore they strove by all sorts of approaches to inculcate in the pupil the conviction that the individual most concerned in his choice between good and evil was himself. "If thou art wise, thou art wise for thyself; and if thou scoffest, thou alone shalt bear it" (9:12). They pictured wisdom as laden with rewards for her devotee. "Length of days is in her right hand, and in her left hand are riches and honour. Her ways are ways of pleasantness and all her paths are peace. She is a tree of life to them that lay hold upon her, and happy is every one that retaineth her" (3:16–18). It is hardly necessary to enumerate the many different goods which they held up to him as obtainable through wisdom. They range all the way from health, money and the satisfaction of hunger, through popularity, good reputation, a blessed memory, the prosperity of one's children after one, power over others, to such things as service, truthfulness, the glory of self-control, the enjoyment of married love, a place in the affection of others, the favour of Yahweh.

This note of self-interest is struck so often in the Book of Proverbs that one might get the impression from a cursory reading that no other incentive is there held out to virtue. But closer examination reveals frequent exceptions.

2. Interest in others was also used as a motive by the wise men. For they realized very well two things: one, that to say "thou alone shalt bear it" is untrue, since every man's life is bound up with that of others; and second, that people are swayed by a desire to give these others pleasure, not pain. And so they appealed to what we may call natural good feeling, quite apart from self-interest. It is here that we find most of the loftiest utterances of the book. The sages hold out as lovely and desirable such actions as to gladden one's father and mother (23:25), one's husband (12:4) and indeed any one else, to brighten the heavy-hearted (15:23; 12:25), to avoid causing sorrow (12:18), to give life to others (10:11), to feed many with satisfying words (10:21), to prove faithful to the trust of others (11:13), to promote peace and pour forth forgiveness (10:12), to guide one's neighbour (12:26), to exalt one's city (11:11) and one's nation (14:34) by one's character.

Because however motives of this altruistic sort are mingled with others of an egoistic nature, some readers of the book have felt justified in merging the former in the latter, and pronouncing all such appeals as addressed to self-interest. But this does not seem fair. They stand out sharp and clear and should not be confused because of mere proximity with appeals to personal happiness. For the book here is true to life. In any individual motives are generally mixed—that is, different motives co-operate towards the same result. The same may be said of the other two classes of motives upon which the wise men played.

3. One of these was the love of wisdom for its own sake. Who can read the impassioned praise of wisdom in the first section of the book and not feel that altogether apart from any of her external rewards these men loved her with an ardent devotion? She was at once an ideal to inflame the affection and a possession to feed the mind with inner joy. "Then shalt thou understand righteousness and justice, yea, every good path. For wisdom shall enter into thy heart and knowledge shall be pleasant unto thy soul" (2:9-10). "Happy is the man that findeth wisdom, . . . for the gaining of it is better than the gaining of silver, and the profit thereof than fine gold. She is more precious than rubies, and none of the things that thou canst desire are to be compared unto her" (3:13-15). Of course this was not what we should call intellectual curiosity; it was not the love of knowledge or learning for its own sake. It was more akin to ethical and religious passion. But to class it with the desire for money and a long life or any of the external goods that one can get out of the pursuit of wisdom is a confusion of terms.

4. Finally, the wise men appealed to the love of God; or more exactly, the desire to please Him and be loved by Him. This is more difficult to prove by actual citations than even the third class of motive. God is not mentioned often in the book, and comparatively few things are said which would reveal explicitly the deeper attitude of heart which the wise man had towards Him. It is true that He is spoken of a number of times as the rewarder and punisher of men; and this thought is always present as a background. But there is a background behind that—an ultimate repose in Him as man's guide and friend, who gives meaning to life and the universe, making both good—if one conforms to His purpose. The constantly recurring admonition to trust Yahweh surely had in mind something more than the mere reliance on Him to provide riches and honour and length of days. To trust Yahweh with all one's heart was first of all to feel Him *there* and be glad. The resolve to avoid those things that He abominated and follow what He loved sprang from a deeper motive than the desire to play safe. Once in a great while this longing to be at one with Him found definite expression. "My son, despise not the chastening of Yahweh, neither be weary of his reproof; for whom Yahweh loveth

he reproveth, even as a father the son in whom he delighteth"
(3:11–12). "His friendship is with the upright" (3:32). But on
the whole it was just an atmosphere in which the wise men lived
and would have their pupil live also.

A Comparison of the Wise Men and the Prophets

That there was much in common between the wise men and the
prophets is plain to the thoughtful reader of the Book of Proverbs.

It is customary to say that the great contribution of the prophets
was ethical monotheism. In this the wise men followed them
faithfully. To the writers of Proverbs God was "supreme and absolute in power, wisdom and goodness." [1] Even lesser supernatural
beings, such as angels or demons, are not there mentioned. All
thought was concentrated upon Yahweh alone. And He was conceived as demanding ethical conduct from men as the chief thing.
Apart from righteousness no act of worship pleased Him. "To
do righteousness and justice is more acceptable to Yahweh than
sacrifice" (21:3). "The sacrifice of the wicked is an abomination:
how much more, when he bringeth it to atone for wickedness!"
(21:27). "He that turneth away his ear from hearing the law, even
his prayer is an abomination" (28:9). So far as the idea they contain is concerned, these sayings might have emanated from an
Amos or an Isaiah.

The wise men followed the prophets also in stressing the social
side of ethics. For the poor they believed God had an especial
care. "Rob not the poor because he is poor; neither oppress the
afflicted in the gate: for Yahweh will plead their cause, and despoil
of life those that despoil them" (22:22). Cheating, lying, slander-
ing, bearing false witness, shedding innocent blood, were all things
that fell under the divine displeasure.

Again, they echoed the prophetic teaching of faith. In spite of
all their counsels of worldly prudence, the wise men kept bringing home to their pupils the solemn truth that "the way of man is
not in himself." The only wise attitude is to commit one's life to
God. "Roll thy works unto Yahweh and thy purposes shall be
established" (16:3). He alone is man's refuge. "The name of
Yahweh is a strong tower; the righteous runneth into it and is set
on high" (18:10).

On the whole the reader of Proverbs gets the impression that the
men who framed these sayings were pulling with the prophets

[1] Toy, *Proverbs,* p. xv.

rather than against them. One might say the same also of their attitude towards the ancient law of Israel, such as is contained in the Book of the Covenant and in Deuteronomy. They were helping to enforce its aims and principles. As Cornill remarks, the Book of Proverbs, "taking its stand on the pure and lofty plane of the religious and moral ideas attained by those two potent forces, mints the good metal of Prophecy and Law into current coin." [2]

This indeed was the chief service rendered by the wise men— to apply to the life of the ordinary individual the great words uttered by these men of old to the nation. No one can deny that they performed it well. In some respects they even went beyond anything that we find in law or prophets. One example of this is their beautiful teaching as to the treatment of an enemy; another, their continual exhortations to act lovingly, sympathetically, gently, covering the faults of others and forgiving those who injure one; a third, their personal interest in the individual.

And yet in this very process of dividing the massive ore of prophetic utterance into useful smaller coin something has been lost.

To begin with, the nation has disappeared below the horizon; and with it the sense of corporate responsibilities, enterprises, failures and accomplishments. The individual no longer sees himself as part of a whole in whose relation to God his own religion finds a wider significance. Isaiah's cry, "I am a man of unclean lips, and I dwell in the midst of a people of unclean lips" could scarcely meet a response from these sages who with all their sense of one's responsibility to others still made the ego the unit of religion. They seem to have had no ability to take wide and sweeping glimpses of human phenomena. They possessed no sense of what we today call "conditions," meaning facts that generally prevail in a community, requiring community action.

In the second place, God has become less vivid. It is true that the wise men frequently bring Him into their teaching, speaking of Him as a Person of strong emotions, who has indignation, hates, abominates, loves, watches, protects, avenges, counsels, guides. But they often allow Him to drop out of sight behind the operation of natural laws; and when He is mentioned His presence does not burn and palpitate as in the pages of the prophets. Above all else, God has ceased to be the Intervener, the One about to do. Gone is "the purpose that is purposed upon the whole earth, the hand that is stretched out upon all the nations." One no longer waits in

[2] C. Cornill, *Introduction to the Canonical Books of the Old Testament* (N. Y., 1907), p. 444.

breathless suspense for the onleaping of the lion, the crash of the divine tempest, the fall of doom, the coming of deliverance. The "word of Yahweh" with its trumpet blast of warning is heard no more. The day of theophanies and mighty burstings in of the divine upon the human is past. Nothing particularly new is going to happen in these times. God confines Himself to visiting upon individuals the due reward of their conduct and lets the course of history pretty much alone. For His "word" He has substituted "wisdom." Faith in God now means following Him along well-worn paths, not launching out with Him upon the deep. Nor does God any more call men, as He called the prophets, to leave all and go forth on a mission terrible, sublime, and lonely.

A third change is akin to this, the cooling down of the emotional temperature. The prophets were constantly getting excited; the wise men are calm. They persuade, plead, threaten, rebuke with a great deal of feeling, but they never lose control of themselves or cry out or weep or hurl denunciations. Life for them is on the whole a placid affair, a stream flowing gently between its banks, not a roaring torrent plunging down from the heights and sweeping all before it. The "great waters" have passed away. One wonders what place there would be for a man like Jeremiah in this comfortable, negotiable little world of the wise men, where the good settle down, make money, marry, have children, enjoy their friends, dispense philanthropy, live peacefully and depart in a mellow old age! How harsh and discordant would his words to Baruch strike across the kindly assurances of its teachers: "Thus saith Yahweh: Behold, that which I have built will I break down, and that which I have planted will I pluck up; and this in the whole land. And seekest thou great things for thyself? seek them not; for behold, I will bring evil upon all flesh, saith Yahweh; but thy life will I give unto thee for a prey in all places whither thou goest" (Jer. 45:4-5).

One is led to reflect, finally, that the very concept of wisdom as the chief good involves religion in a deficiency from which the prophets did not suffer. For wisdom is essentially a matter of personal acquisition, of self-culture. However enthusiastic its devotees may grow over it, it can never take a man outside of himself as can the thought of God and the passion for righteousness. And it is of God and righteousness that the prophets were ever speaking. Make these a matter of wisdom, and forthwith they shrink into something smaller, cooling as they contract. Perhaps that is why the Book of Proverbs, with all its nobility, somehow falls short of a great message.

The Wise Men Could not Have the Last Word

Life is after all too big, too passionate, too unpredictable to be confined within the limits of the ordered, everyday scheme drawn up by the sages. While their sayings would prove a fairly satisfactory guide in the usual course of human life, occasions were bound to arise when a man would find himself deserted by them, and that when he most needed help. Or again, he might begin to look out over the sufferings of humanity and discover that the dogma of retribution was quite inadequate to explain them. We shall now consider a man to whom both these things seem to have happened—the writer of the Book of Job.

CHAPTER XXVII

THE WRITER OF THE BOOK OF JOB

[*c.* 400 B.C. (?)]

About the time when Ezra was carrying out his reforms one of the world's greatest classics was being written by a nameless Jew whom we know only as the author of the Book of Job. In it he grappled with the problem of undeserved suffering which has tormented men in all ages and reached a conclusion which is perhaps as satisfactory today as it was then.

The Sources

The sources for the study of this great thinker are those parts of the Book of Job which may safely be considered the product of his pen. Let us therefore pass in review the sections that are questioned by scholars, after which we may make our own selection.

The prologue and epilogue (1–2; 42:7–17) were thought by Duhm to be the work of an earlier writer giving the traditional story of a righteous man who was tempted to renounce God by his misfortunes but remained steadfast in loyalty. From this *Volksbuch,* as Duhm [1] called it, the author of our book took only the opening and closing sections, substituting for the account of Job's talk with his friends a composition of his own; namely, the poetic portion of our book. Duhm does not therefore consider either prologue or epilogue as a reliable source for the religion of the writer.

Chapter 28 is viewed by most scholars as a later insertion, since it interrupts the course of the dialogue.

The Elihu speeches (32–37) also are questioned by many on the ground that they contribute nothing new and seem to be ignored by the rest of the dialogue, as well as by the prologue and epilogue. They contain also more Aramaisms than the other parts of the book.

[1] *Das Buch Hiob* (Freiburg, 1897), p. viiff.

515

A few scholars have doubted the genuineness of the Yahweh speeches (38–41); but the majority accept them, excluding only the descriptions of behemoth and leviathan (40:15–41:34). This latter section is almost universally regarded as a later addition on the ground that its florid language falls far below the majestic but restrained style of our author.

A reasonable conclusion would seem to be this: to exclude from our consideration the passages widely rejected: Chapter 28, the Elihu speeches (32–37) and the last-mentioned descriptions (40:15–41:34). As to the prologue and epilogue, they had better be looked upon as an integral part of the book. Very possibly our author did take them over from an earlier tale, but in so doing he made them his own. At the same time, one feels that they should be more cautiously used in our study than the poetic portion. The Yahweh speeches on the other hand should be accepted without hesitation as embodying the author's thought. They are quite on a level with the dialogue in poetic grandeur and fit into the development of its thought in a very satisfying way.

Having now determined which parts of the book we shall attribute to the author, we can go on to ask ourselves by what method we shall try to come at his thought. The obvious answer is, through a study of his chief character. Job may not indeed be an autobiographical figure; our author may not have gone through personally any such terrible experience as his hero. But one cannot resist the feeling that somehow Job speaks for him. On the other hand, Yahweh sets Job right at the end of the book; and we must view the Yahweh speeches as our author's criticism of what Job had been saying up to that point. Job himself admits their truth in his concluding words. Let us inquire then what Job experienced, how he met that experience, and what Yahweh said to him after he had uttered all his heart.

Job, the Ideal Wise Man, Saw his Life Suddenly Broken Past Mending

All scholars agree that the Book of Job was written as a criticism of the teaching of the wise men of Proverbs and their like. We must therefore begin from that teaching. The wise men had urged upon their disciples a high standard of ethics. They were true to the prophets in maintaining that what Yahweh desires of men is righteousness more than ritual; although they spoke respectfully of the cult side of religion. As an incentive to such high living they held out the promise of earthly reward. The hope of material blessings was not indeed the only motive to which they appealed, but it was a chief one. They came back to it again and again, affirming retribution to be one of the surest facts of God's government. "Behold, the righteous shall be recompensed in the earth; how much more the wicked and the sinner" (Prov. 11:31).

Having this in mind our writer introduces his Job as the faultless pattern of the wise man; he was "perfect and upright, and the one that feared God, and turned away from evil" (1:1). These epithets are taken straight from the Book of Proverbs. Just what he meant by them can be seen from Job's own description of his life as he reviews it in chapters 29 and 31.

> "I delivered the poor that cried,
> The fatherless also that had none to help him.
> The blessing of him that was ready to perish came upon me;
> And I caused the widow's heart to sing for joy.
> I was eyes to the blind,
> And feet was I to the lame.
> I was a father to the needy:
> And the cause of him that I knew not I searched out.
> And I brake the jaws of the unrighteous,
> And plucked the prey out of his teeth" (29:12-17).

In his personal morality he also aimed high.

> "I made a covenant with mine eyes:
> How then should I look upon a virgin?" (31:1)

Falsehood and deceit he shunned (31:5-8). His neighbour's wife he let absolutely alone (31:9-12). Towards his servant he observed scrupulous justice in any dispute. "Did not he that made me in the womb make him?" (31:13-15). With him the traveller found entertainment (31:32). Even towards his enemies he kept good will.

> "If I have rejoiced at the destruction of him that hated me,
> Or lifted up myself when evil found him:
> (Yea, I have not suffered my mouth to sin
> By asking his life with a curse) . . ." (31:29-30).

On the whole we may say that the ethical standard attributed by our author to Job is as high as any we find in the Old Testament.

Nor did Job neglect religious observances. When the days of his children's feasting "were gone about . . . Job sent and sanctified them, and rose up early in the morning and offered up burnt-offerings according to the number of them all: for Job said, it may be that my sons have sinned, and renounced God in their hearts. This Job did continually" (1:5). No one could have been more careful in performing all possible ritual obligations. From the seductive worship of the heavenly bodies he kept himself free.

> "If I have beheld the sun when it shined,
>   Or the moon walking in brightness,
>   And my heart hath been secretly enticed,
>   And my mouth hath kissed my hand . . ." (31:26–27).

Nor did he allow his wealth to come between him and God.

> "If I have made gold my hope,
>   And have said to the fine gold, Thou art my confidence;
>   If I have rejoiced because my wealth was great,
>   And because my hand hath gotten much . . ." (31:24–25).

Towards God and towards men therefore Job proved himself all that the noblest of the wise men could have asked. How then did their promises of material reward turn out in his case?

For long years these came true. Job was blessed with thousands of cattle, many slaves, good health, honour, children, "so that this man was the greatest of all the children of the east" (1:2–3). His sons and daughters found life a perpetual feast (1:4). Job himself later described the happiness of this period as he looked back upon it.

> "O that I were as in the months of old,
>   As in the days when God watched over me;
>   When his lamp shined upon my head,
>   And by his light I walked through darkness;
>   As I was in the ripeness of my days,
>   When the friendship of God was upon my tent;
>   When the Almighty was yet with me,
>   And my children were about me;
>   When my steps were washed with butter,
>   And the rock poured me out streams of oil!
>   When I went forth to the gate unto the city,
>   When I prepared my seat in the street,

The young men saw me and hid themselves,
And the aged rose up and stood;
The princes refrained from talking,
And laid their hand on their mouth;
The voice of the nobles was hushed,
And their tongue cleaved to the roof of their mouth.
For when the ear heard me, then it blessed me;
And when the eye saw me, it gave witness unto me"
(29:2–11).

So far therefore Job exemplified in his person everything that had been said by the wise men.

But suddenly a terrible change came. In one day he lost all that he had, sons, daughters, slaves, cattle. Hardly had this come home to him when he himself was seized by a loathsome and fatal disease, marked by swellings and ulcers over his whole body—elephantiasis, as it is usually pronounced by scholars. The reader now beholds him seated upon the refuse heap of the village, scraping his sores with a piece of broken pottery to relieve their intolerable itching. His reputation was gone, for every one saw in his sufferings the condemnation of God. Instead of the respect to which he was accustomed ridicule and mockery became his lot. The very outcast did not hesitate to spit in his face! (1:13ff; 2:7ff; 30:1ff, and elsewhere).

It was because of this tragic change in Job's fortunes that his three friends came to visit him. "They made an appointment together to come to bemoan him and to comfort him." The impression that his altered appearance made upon them was overpowering. "And when they lifted up their eyes afar off and knew him not, they lifted up their voice and wept; and they rent every one his robe, and sprinkled dust upon their heads towards heaven. So they sat down with him upon the ground seven days and seven nights, and none spake a word unto him; for they saw that his grief was very great" (2:11–13).

Thus the stage was set for the great dialogue. The question was, what would they four make out of these wholly unlooked for sufferings of the ideally wise and happy man? For they did not know, as does the reader, that God is not punishing Job for sin. He is merely permitting the Satan to test Job's sincerity (1:12; 2:6).

Both Job and His Friends Interpreted His Calamity by the Light of the Wise Men's Retribution Dogma

As one reads the dialogue he at first gets the impression that Job and his friends are at fundamental disagreement. For what the latter maintain with monotonous repetition throughout three cycles of speeches is something that Job indignantly repudiates. Job, they believe, must have done evil to bring upon him these visitations of God. At first they only hint this. The opening speech of Eliphaz has often been pointed to as a model of courtesy. All men sin, he says in effect; they cannot be just before God. Job therefore makes a mistake in crying out against God's chastisement. The wise course would be to turn to God in penitence.

"As for me, I would seek unto God,
And unto God would I commit my cause" (5:8).

For just as Job caused his own calamity, so its removal lies in his power. Let him humble himself under the just and mighty hand of God and all will be well again.

"Behold, happy is the man whom God correcteth;
Therefore despise not thou the chastening of the Almighty.
For he maketh sore and bindeth up;
He woundeth and his hands make whole" (5:17-18).

But as Job's defiance increases the tone of the friends changes until the blunt Zophar presently tells him: "Know that God exacteth of thee less than thine iniquity deserveth" (11:6); and even Eliphaz finally breaks out into definite charges of the most serious nature.

"Is not thy wickedness great?
Neither is there any end to thine iniquities.
For thou hast taken pledges of thy brother for nought,
And stripped the naked of their clothing.
Thou hast not given water to the weary to drink,
And thou hast withholden bread from the hungry. . . .
Thou hast sent widows away empty,
And the arms of the fatherless have been broken.
Therefore snares are round about thee . . ." (22:5-10).

Against these insinuations and open indictments Job with increasing passion maintains his innocence. True, he may have sinned as all men sin. He is far from claiming to be just before God in any absolute way. What is more, God is too powerful to argue with even when one is conscious of his rectitude. But what he vehemently denies is that he has done any wrong that would account for God's singling him out for disaster. To give in to his friends on this matter would be to stultify his sense of truth.

> "Surely my lips shall not speak unrighteousness,
> Neither shall my tongue utter deceit.
> Far be it from me that I should justify you:
> Till I die will I not put away mine integrity from me.
> My righteousness I hold fast and will not let it go:
> My heart shall not reproach me so long as I live" (27:4-6).

As we look deeper however we see that with all his protestations against his friends' charges Job does not challenge their assumption that calamity *ought* to be the punishment of sin. His ideal of God's government is still that expressed by the retribution dogma. If God is just, He should see to it that righteousness is rewarded by prosperity and wickedness visited by adversity. What outrages Job is that God has failed to do this in his own case. And as he looks about him with eyes sharpened by his personal experience he perceives that such failure is nothing exceptional.

> "How oft is it that the lamp of the wicked is put out?
> That their calamity cometh upon them?
> That God distributeth sorrows in his anger?
> That they are as stubble before the wind,
> And as chaff that the storm carrieth away?" (21:17-18).

It is this wholesale miscarriage of what he feels to be justice that forces him to question the goodness of God. And that is indeed a fearful misgiving to entertain.

> "Even when I remember I am troubled,
> And horror taketh hold on my flesh" (21:6).

Nor does Job deny the truth of his friends' contention that God has condemned him. He assumes in much that he says that God means to make him out a sinner. He can find no other significance in his sufferings than that God is angry with him.

> "He hath torn me in his wrath, and hated me;
> He hath gnashed upon me with his teeth:

> Mine adversary sharpeneth his eyes upon me . . .
> Thou hast made desolate all my company.
> And thou hast shrivelled me up—a witness against me!
> And my leanness riseth up against me,
> It testifieth to my face" (16:7-9).

We thus see emerging behind the question in dispute between Job and his friends—whether or no Job has sinned—a second question of which Job is not yet conscious—whether the assumption of the retribution dogma which involves such fearful consequences can be correct.

Job Maintained (as Against His Friends) the Right of Remonstrating with God for His Cruelty and Injustice

One of the things that strikes the reader in the dialogue of the Book of Job is the unrestrained freedom with which the hero spoke his mind to God. Such was not the case in the prologue where his words were few and submissive. On hearing how he had lost all he "arose, and rent his robe, and shaved his head, and fell down upon the ground, and worshipped"; and he said,

> "Naked came I out of my mother's womb,
> And naked shall I return thither:
> Yahweh gave, and Yahweh hath taken away;
> Blessed be the name of Yahweh" (1:20-21).

To his wife's bitter words after his sickness had fallen upon him he replied:

> "Shall we receive good at the hand of God,
> And shall we not receive evil?" (2:10).

Quite justly does the writer make comment: "In all this did not Job sin with his lips" (2:10).

But with the opening of the dialogue (3:1ff) Job's attitude had changed. Whether the strain of continued suffering was too much for him or whether the sympathy of his friends turned him to thoughts of self-pity, his first words after the long silence were anything but respectful or restrained. He cursed the day in which he was born and cried out for death as a blessed release. While he did not as yet make any definite charge against God, he asked angrily:

> "Wherefore is light given to him that is in misery,
> And life unto the bitter of soul?" (3:20).

In chapter 6 he repeated this cry:

> "Oh that I might have my request;
> And that God would grant me the thing that I long for!
> Even that it would please God to crush me!" (6:8–9).

Presently he went further. After letting his thoughts dwell upon the briefness and hopelessness of his lot, he turned to face God.

> "Therefore I will not refrain my mouth;
> I will speak in the anguish of my spirit;
> I will complain in the bitterness of my soul.
> Am I a sea, or a sea-monster,
> That thou settest a watch over me?" (7:11–12).

In answering Bildad he fell to what Davidson[1] declared to be the lowest depth of his alienation from God: God, he said, was too powerful to argue one's case against Him. He had it all His own way:

> "Though I be righteous, mine own mouth shall condemn
>   me:
> Though I be perfect, it shall prove me perverse."

Then came a burst of wild defiance:

> "I am perfect: I regard not myself;
> I despise my life.
> It is all one; therefore I say,
> He destroyeth the perfect and the wicked.
> If the scourge slay suddenly,
> He will mock at the trial of the innocent.
> The earth is given into the hand of the wicked;
> He covereth the faces of the judges thereof:
> If it be not he, who then is it?" (9:20–24).

He went on to demand that God should cease to silence him.

> "Let him take his rod away from me,
> And let not his terror make me afraid:

[1] A. B. Davidson, *Job* (*CB*, 1899), p. 72.

> Then would I speak, and not fear him;
> For I am not so in myself" [2] (9:34–35).

But even so he refused to be silenced.

> "I will say unto God, Do not condemn me;
> Show me wherefore thou contendest with me.
> Is it good unto thee that thou shouldest oppress,
> That thou shouldest despise the work of thy hands,
> And shine upon the counsels of the wicked?
> Hast thou eyes of flesh?
> Or seest thou as man seeth? . . .
> That thou inquirest after mine iniquity . . .
> And searchest after my sin,
> Although thou knowest that I am not wicked,
> And there is none that can deliver out of thy hand?"
>   (10:2–7).

He then charged God with having shown him favour with the express purpose of turning it into calamity:

> "Thou hast granted me life and lovingkindness;
> And thy visitation hath preserved my spirit.
> Yet *these* things thou didst hide in thy heart" (10:12–13).

At the end of this long outcry he repeated the petition already made in his second speech:

> "Are not my days few? cease then,
> And let me alone, that I may take comfort a little,
> Before I go whence I shall not return" (10:20–21).

God, Job declared again and again, was now his enemy. We have seen already how he hurled this charge in God's face, and always with the assertion that he had given no cause for such divine malignity. When he talked thus Job on his side appeared not unlike an enemy of God, meeting oppression with defiance. Nowhere else in the Old Testament do we find such language used by man towards God. The psalmists are many of them very free in their address to Him, but they always keep within certain bounds; they come very near at times to upbraiding Him for His inaction, but they make no angry charges against Him. Jeremiah, the pioneer in this liberty of speech with God, went no

---

[2] I.e. that I should fear Him.

further than argument. But Job stood up hotly as the accuser of the Almighty and stormed against Him to His face.

No wonder then that the pious friends were scandalized by what they heard him utter. Eliphaz declared that the vexation and indignation displayed in his opening speech were unworthy of one who had sustained others in affliction (4:2ff) and fraught with peril for Job himself (5:2). But his later words seemed to Eliphaz to cut at the root of all religion: ·

> ". . . Thou doest away with fear,
> And hinderest devotion before God."

Eliphaz could explain them in only one way:

> "For thine iniquity teacheth thy mouth,
> And thou choosest the tongue of the crafty.
> Thine own mouth condemneth thee, and not I;
> Yea, thine own lips testify against thee" (15:4–6).

He remonstrated with Job for what he was doing:

> "Why doth thy heart carry thee away?
> And why do thine eyes flash,
> That against God thou turnest thy spirit,
> And lettest words go out of thy mouth?" (15:12–13).

Job on the other hand maintained that it was the friends, not he, who were really offending God; for in their attempt to make Job out a sinner that God might be absolved from the charge of injustice, they were employing falsehood on God's behalf.

> "Will ye speak unrighteously for God,
> And talk deceitfully for him?
> Will ye show partiality to him?
> Will ye contend for God?
> Is it good that he should search you out?
> Or as one deceiveth a man, will ye deceive him?
> He will surely reprove you,
> If ye do secretly show partiality.
> Shall not his majesty make you afraid,
> And his dread fall upon you?" (13:7–11).

There lies the heart of Job's conviction: one must above all things else be *honest* with God. If one does not like the way He is doing, one must not suppress his dissatisfaction, but come out with it! That is what God wants.

Another thing. God understands that a man does not mean all that he says under the strain of great torture.

> "Oh that my vexation were but weighed,
> And all my calamity laid in the balances!
> For now it would be heavier than the sand of the seas;
> Therefore have my words been rash" (6:2-3).

He feels that the friends should have understood this also.

> "Do ye think to reprove words,
> Seeing that the speeches of one that is desperate are
>   as wind?" (6:26).

What he wanted from them was sympathy, not lectures:

> "To him that is ready to faint kindness should be
>   showed from his friend;
> Even to him that forsaketh the fear of the Almighty"
>   (6:14).
> "Have pity upon me, have pity upon me, O ye my friends;
> For the hand of God hath touched me.
> Why do ye persecute me as God,
> And are not satisfied with my flesh?" (19:21-22).

In saying this he implied his belief that God would supply the pity that the friends failed to give. And that leads us to our next point.

In Spite of His Remonstrance, Job Turned to God as His Only Friend

No, Job did not mean all that he said when he was defying God. He was not really hostile. In the midst of his outcries his heart was reaching out to God. That is what one feels through the whole course of the dialogue. It was Job, far more than the friends, who loved God. And we can see this love breaking through the storms of his indignation in a beautiful way. There are six places where this occurs.

In his second speech he checked his lament over his miserable days now passing swiftly to the grave and made a sudden appeal to God:

"Oh, remember that my life is a breath:
Mine eye shall no more see good.
The eye of him [1] who seeth me shall behold me no more;
Thine eyes shall be upon me, but I shall not be" (7:7-8).

Here he was speaking almost like a hurt child to God: "You
will be sorry when I am gone."
In his reply to Bildad he uttered another such childlike cry
to God:

"Thy hands have framed me and fashioned me
Together round about: yet thou dost destroy me.
Remember, I beseech thee, that thou hast fashioned me as clay;
And wilt thou bring me into dust again?" (10:8-9).

At the close of the first cycle of speeches comes a famous passage
where Job looked for a moment at the possibility of intercourse
with God beyond the grave. He had been dwelling in language
of pathetic beauty upon life's brevity and wretchedness and death's
finality. Unlike a tree, man when cut down will not grow again.
Then came a fleeting glimpse of something different:

"Oh that thou wouldest hide me in Sheol,
That thou wouldest keep me secret until thy wrath be past,
That thou wouldest appoint me a set time, and remember me!
If a man die, shall he live again?
All the days of my warfare would I wait,
Till my release should come.
Thou wouldest call, and I would answer thee:
Thou wouldest have a desire to the work of thy hands"
     (14:13-15).

There one sees Job's "heart's desire." What he wanted most
was God, the restoration of fellowship with God. He was not saying that he would get this—indeed, he despaired of it the next
instant. But the ravishing thought was destined to reappear.
In his next speech he definitely turned from his friends to God.
They had proved themselves "miserable comforters." How differently would he have treated them if their cases had been re-
versed! He would have "strengthened them with his mouth and
with the solace of his lips would have assuaged their grief" (16:5).
Instead, they had believed him guilty! Then he cried suddenly:

[1] I.e. God.

> "O earth, cover not thou my blood,
> And let my cry have no resting-place.
> Even now, behold, my witness is in heaven,
> And he that voucheth for me is on high.
> My friends scoff at me:
> But mine eye poureth out tears unto God,
> That he would maintain the right of a man with God,
> And of a son of man with his neighbour" (16:18–21).

The same conviction came back to him in victorious completeness in his answer to Bildad that followed. After his appeal to
the friends to have pity upon him he relinquished all hope from
that quarter and threw himself upon the thought of some vindication after he should have been long dead. At first this took the
form of a writing which would outlast him.

> "Oh that my words were now written!
> Oh that they were inscribed in a book!
> That with an iron pen and lead
> They were graven in the rock for ever!"

Then a better way flashed upon him:

> "But as for me I know that my Redeemer liveth,
> And at last he will stand up upon the earth:
> And after my skin, even this body, is destroyed,
> Then without my flesh shall I see God;
> Whom I, even I, shall see on my side,
> And mine eyes shall behold, and not as a stranger.
> My heart is consumed within me." [2]

> "If ye say, How we will persecute him!
> And that the root of the matter is found in me;
> Be ye afraid of the sword:
> For wrath bringeth the punishments of the sword,
> That ye may know there is a judgment" (19:23–29).

Here Job knew, if only for an instant, that it was to God he must
look for his vindication, not to men; and that this hope would not
disappoint him. Scholars are divided as to whether he was speaking of something to take place after his death. The present writer

[2] For joyous longing?

has accepted that view as the most natural reading of the words "from my flesh"; but it makes no difference for the point he is making whether the "post-mortem" or the "ante-mortem" interpretation be correct. In either case Job turned to God only, and to God as his champion, vindicator, redeemer.

This was the clearest vision attained by Job. But even later in the dialogue he gave utterance to his longing to reach God:

> "Oh that I knew where I might find him!
> That I might come even unto his seat!" (23:3).

True, his object in finding God was (he said) to set his cause before Him; but the confidence with which he contemplated such a pleading shows how (as Peake says) his thought of God had softened from its original defiance:

> "I would know the words which he would answer me,
> And understand what he would say unto me.
> Would he contend with me in the greatness of his power?
> Nay; but he would give heed unto me.
> There the upright might reason with him;
> So should I be delivered for ever from my judge. . . .
> For he knoweth the way that I take;
> When he hath tried me, I shall come forth as gold" (23:3–7, 10).

When we come therefore to the last passionate declaration of innocence which Job seemed to hurl into God's very teeth, we must remember these tenderer passages that have gone before.

> "Oh that I had one to hear me!
> (Lo, here is my signature, let the Almighty answer me;)
> And that I had the indictment which mine adversary hath
>   written!
> Surely I would carry it upon my shoulder;
> I would bind it unto me as a crown:
> I would declare unto him the number of my steps;
> As a prince would I go near unto him" (31:35-37).

Can we be wrong in taking these as a mixture? in feeling that to defiance they add confidence, to indignation love?

So far only men had spoken. It remains to inquire what God had to say.

Yahweh when He Appeared Rebuked Job for His Retribution Dogma but Acknowledged Him as a Friend

At last Yahweh, whom Job had so often challenged and invoked, whom Zophar had wished might open His lips against Job (11:5), made His voice heard. "Then Yahweh answered Job out of the whirlwind and said . . ." (38:1). The reader waits in tense expectation: What did He say? For here if anywhere will be found the writer's own appraisal of his hero.

God's first words were a rebuke:

"Who is this that darkeneth counsel
By words without knowledge?" (38:2).

So Job had been mistaken: in what?

"Gird up now thy loins like a man;
For I will demand of thee, and declare thou unto me.
Where wast thou when I laid the foundations of the earth?
Declare, if thou hast understanding. . . ."

There follows a series of ironical questions aimed to bring home to Job his lack of "wisdom"; that is, of the knowledge and power necessary to create and sustain the world. And the point of them all is plainly that Job had gone beyond his capacities in criticizing God's government of mankind. He had been talking as if he knew exactly what God ought to do if He were a just God. That was what the retribution dogma involved. Prosperity, it said, *ought* to follow goodness, and calamity overtake sin. God's answer was to direct Job's attention from his own life and from human society in general to the divine ordering of nature and the divine provision for animals.

"Who shut up the sea with doors? . . .
Hast thou commanded the morning since thy days began? . . .
Hast thou entered into the springs of the sea? . . .
Where is the way to the dwelling of light? . . .
Who hath cleft a channel for the waterflood? . . .
Canst thou bind the clusters of the Pleiades? . . .
Canst thou lift up thy voice to the clouds,
That abundance of waters may cover thee? . . .
Canst thou hunt the prey for the lioness? . . .
Who hath sent out the wild ass free? . . .
Hast thou given the horse his might? . . .
Is it by thy wisdom that the hawk soareth? . . ." (38–39).

Then, after Job had acknowledged himself unable to answer, Yahweh went on to challenge him in the particular sphere of the divine activity where Job had found matter of complaint. Let Job essay to punish the wicked!

"Deck now thyself with excellency and dignity;
And array thyself with honour and majesty.
Pour forth the overflowings of thine anger;
And look upon every one that is proud, and abase him.
Look on every one that is proud, and bring him low;
And tread down the wicked where they stand.
Hide them in the dust together;
Bind their faces in the hidden place.
Then will I also confess of thee
That thine own right hand can save thee" (40:10–14).

This, the poet declares, reduced Job to complete silence.

"Then Job answered Yahweh and said:

I know that thou canst do all things,
And that no purpose of thine can be restrained,
Who is this that hideth counsel without knowledge?
Therefore have I uttered that which I understood not,
Things too wonderful for me, which I knew not."

Henceforth all he asked was to learn of God:

"Hear, I beseech thee, and I will speak;
I will demand of thee, and declare thou unto me."

Job's criticisms had been based on second-hand information only —now proven utterly inadequate:

"I had heard of thee by the hearing of the ear;
But now mine eye seeth thee:
Wherefore I abhor myself,
And repent in dust and ashes" (42:1–6).

At first sight Job seems inconsistent here. Had he not continually asserted that he recognized God's *power*, but that power did not make right God's injustice? Why was it that the divine reply satisfied him, seeing that it stressed God's power without meeting Job's complaints of injustice? As when, for instance, God said:

"Wilt thou even annul my judgment?
Wilt thou condemn me, that thou mayest be justified?
Or hast thou an arm like God?
And canst thou thunder with a voice like him?" (40:8-9).

Why did not Job reply: "No, but what of it?" Why did he say instead:

"I know that thou canst do all things"?

But as one reads Yahweh's words more attentively he perceives that their real emphasis is on Job's ignorance rather than on his weakness. "Hast thou comprehended the earth in its breadth? Declare, if thou knowest it all!" (38:18). And it was this ignorance that now seemed to dawn upon Job for the first time. Hence his contrition.

But perhaps the most striking thing about God's rebuke of Job is that it stopped at this point. Not a word was said of what the friends were waiting for so anxiously—Job's sin previous to his calamity. The reader is not surprised to have Job's main contention thus agreed to by God, for he has known all along that Job was innocent. But he may well be startled to note that God ignored also Job's hard words towards Himself. True, these had been presumptuous in view of Job's ignorance; but insolent they had not been. So Job was vindicated in his assumption that God welcomed freedom of speech!

And finally, God talked to Job as to a friend. He might indeed speak out of the whirlwind and say stinging things; but it was not in wrath. His "terror" did not make Job afraid, though His "hand" was still laid upon him. Instead, He reasoned with the caviller and not unkindly. One feels that in the whole transaction there was recognition and vindication. Despite the rebuke it was an honour that was being done Job. He was being singled out as alone worthy of being thus talked to by God. They two were on the heights together, the rest of men lost to sight beneath them.

And Job was satisfied. There can be no slightest doubt of that. True, he was now in dust and ashes, but that is just where all along he wanted to be—if only he honestly could! All his words of seeming rebellion had come from a bleeding heart. Now his heart was healed. He had been shown how he could humble himself before God in adoring love and he took this posture of soul in peace; it was natural to him.

Nor did it matter to him that God's hand was still laid upon him; that his fatal disease was not taken away nor his possessions, children and honour restored. This was not necessary. He had seen God on his side and not as a stranger. It was enough.

For after all, the great loss that had been weighing on Job was the loss of God's friendship. God had been the supreme love of his life. Once assured that God had loved him all along, he needed nothing else.

But the writer was not content to leave the situation thus. He added an epilogue telling how God made good the outward losses of his faithful servant. Eliphaz and the other two friends were rebuked: "For ye have not spoken of me the thing that is right, as my servant Job hath." They were advised to seek Job's intercession that God's wrath might be averted from them. And when Job prayed for his friends God "turned his captivity" and gave him (along with restored health, it is implied) "twice as much as he had before." His brothers, sisters and acquaintances, won back by his returning prosperity, came to him with comfort and with gifts. Children were born to him, and at last he died in a ripe old age (42:7ff).

This picture has offended the taste of some scholars, for they find in it a falling back from the high plane reached at the end of the Yahweh speeches; so they maintain that the writer stopped his work short with Job's words of humility (42:2–6) and attribute the epilogue to another hand. But it seems better to accept it and to regard Yahweh's outward beneficence as both an act of justice and an expression of love.

What Did the Writer Himself Think?

We have now come to the point where we may try to summarize the thoughts of the author on the basis of his portrayal of Job's religion. In so doing we must bear in mind that scholars differ widely on this matter. It is not indeed possible, for lack of space, to pass in review the various opinions that have been entertained as to what the author intended to be the real teaching of his great book. But certain things seem fairly clear.

1. He believed the retribution dogma to be quite inadequate. It can explain with satisfactory completeness neither human suffering nor human happiness. Moreover it is presumptuous, for it assumes that it can lay down the principles on which God should govern the universe. As a matter of fact, prosperity and adversity

have no necessary connection with goodness and wickedness. God's dispensations towards individuals cannot be interpreted as rewards or punishments.

It is in line with this that the writer did not lay stress on what might happen after death to redress seeming injustices this side the grave. For while he does seem to have touched longingly, and even perhaps with some conviction, upon the thought of God's friendship in a beyond, he certainly did not fall back upon it as a delayed vindication of the retribution dogma. That is a role too often played by the hereafter in the popular religion of today.

Nor did his conclusion of Job's story with its restored "health, happiness and success" indicate a relapse into the old faith. We have seen how prologue and epilogue must be used with caution in our inquiry after the writer's religious ideas. In them he did not speak with freedom, being hampered by the outlines of the traditional story which he there reproduced. It is far better to interpret them by the Yahweh speeches, as we have tried to do above, and find in these latter the true expression of the poet's thought.

Thus he set aside the retribution dogma. What a release that must have been for those who could follow him! How it would take away from suffering the fearful thought of guilt! And from prosperity any sense of complacence!

2. But the writer saw in the dismissal of the dogma yet another liberation. While it held sway no one could ever be sure that he was "fearing God for nought." Perhaps God Himself could not be sure. The sneer of the Satan (1:9) would always have some colour. This must have been an aspect of the religion of the wise men that seriously disquieted our author; and with reason. He felt in his heart that the only true love for God was a disinterested love. And he welcomed a philosophy which dropped the idea of reward and punishment.

3. God, he believed, is too great and too understanding to be offended by wild words. Indeed, these may well be more "right" concerning God than the most decorous of apologetic orthodoxies employed to suppress the doubtings of a tormented soul. What God wants from men is honesty. The real wrong is to disguise one's difficulties before Him. By making Job talk in so defiant and shocking a fashion to God the author brought home to his readers man's charter of free speech in the presence of the Almighty. And he made people see how mistaken it is to condemn what is uttered under the stress of pain instead of pitying and sympathizing.

4. God therefore does not want a man to confess sin where he does not see his sin. Job was right in refusing to do this. He *never did retract* his assertion of integrity, yet his end was peace. Of course, he freely admitted human frailty and stain; he knew that man must rely on God's willingness to overlook much. But he went no further nor did God call on him to do so. There is a striking absence here of the Pauline thought that all men are under the wrath of God. Job was not. He needed no atonement, no reconciling sacrifice to put him right with God, for he had not been wrong. This then was a possible state for man, according to our author's thinking. Was he merely shallow here? Was Jeremiah's belief the deeper one: that the heart is deceitful above all things, and desperately wicked—"who can know it?" (Jer. 17:9).

5. Did he have any answer to the question, Why must the righteous suffer? In Job's case, according to the prologue, it was to prove his disinterestedness. But did our author present that as the general answer? Did he even put the question? Probably not. At any rate, Yahweh's speech seems to imply that man cannot understand nor make over the course of the world so far as it affects his own fortune. He must simply accept it and go on. But this was not (as a recent writer has declared) [1] an impersonal solution. For if we can be sure of anything about our author it is that to him God is a Person. And what he feels is not merely acceptance—it is a great love.

The Writer's Contribution to Israel's Religion

One would expect that such a shattering blow as was dealt to the retribution dogma by this poet would have discredited it forever in the thought of Israel. The contrary however proved true. That dogma continued to be the working faith, not only of the rank and file, but of the leaders in Israel's religion. The Book of Psalms, which reveals the inward thought of earnest Israelites over several centuries, is dominated by it: and many of the psalms must have been written after the publication of the Book of Job. To one reading the later writings of the Old Testament it often seems as if the latter work had made no impression at all. Yet had such been the case it would not have been preserved. The very fact that it lived on and was finally taken into the canon of Holy Scripture proves that it was working as a leaven within the lump of Israel's religious thought. There must have been here and

[1] Walter Lippmann: *A Preface to Morals* (New York, 1929), p. 214ff.

there perplexed but voiceless souls who found in it just what they needed.

So to this day it has remained a book for the few rather than for the many. Now as in ancient Israel the many who believe in God go through life fairly well with the old retribution dogma. But to the few who do not the writer of the Book of Job still offers a philosophy which can at length bring release and healing.

QOHELETH: THE PREACHER

[*c.* 250 B.C.]

The Sources

Perhaps a century and a half after the writer of the Book of Job had composed his criticism of the retribution dogma another Israelitish thinker attacked it in a different way. His little treatise has come down to us under the title *Qôhĕlĕth,* i.e. one who speaks in an assembly (*qāhāl*). The Greek translators rendered this by *Ecclesiastes,* St. Jerome by *Concionator* and our English Version by *The Preacher.* Following a literary custom of his day he put forth his reflections under the great name of Solomon, who had come to be a symbol for all wisdom and oratory. His own name is unknown to us, nor does he tell us directly anything about himself. Whether he was old or middle-aged or young, whether he lived in Palestine or Egypt, we can only conjecture. But for all its pretence of representing Solomon his book is a revelation of his own soul's pilgrimage. We have only to strip off the trappings of royalty and we see the figure of Qoheleth.

All that we know of Qoheleth is drawn from his own book, Ecclesiastes. It purports to be the reflections of Solomon as he reviewed his life's experience, but scholars are unanimous that this representation is fictitious. The author was a Jew of the Greek period (which began about 332 B.C.) and had been considerably influenced by Greek ways of thinking, although there seems to be no evidence that he had made any real study of Hellenic philosophy. He also used literary devices derived from the wisdom literature of Egypt, but the spirit of his book is not Egyptian.[1]

In the book there is no discernible development of thought and it seems often to contradict itself. Attempts to reduce it to unity and logical order have led to somewhat violent critical reconstructions, one scholar (Siegfried) having gone so far as to find in it

[1] Eissfeldt, *EAT,* p. 557.

the work of six hands.[2]   A more moderate procedure is to maintain that Qoheleth's original writing has been added to by two inter-polators, one an earnestly religious man (*hāsîdh*) and the other a "wise man" (*hākām*).[3]   The prevailing tendency today however is to regard the book as the product of one mind in its varying moods, except for small additions, especially at the end.[4]

The date of the book is generally put at about 200 B.C. or a little earlier.   Its advanced stage of thought, its use of Aramaisms and the affinity of its language to the Hebrew of the Mishnah all point to a time well on in the Greek period.

Qoheleth's Experience and Character

"Vanity of vanities, saith the Preacher; vanity of vanities, all is vanity!" (1:2).   Such was the conclusion to which Qoheleth finally came, but it was not his belief when he began. Life then seemed to him to possess many values and he was determined to appropriate them. He started out, he says (1:13), to "search out by wisdom all that is done under heaven."   It was a wide ambition, involving a study of the whole universe, but particularly of man's activities. He "applied his heart to see the business that is done upon the earth" (8:16). And he did this not only to satisfy his intellectual curiosity; he wanted also to obtain a practical understanding of life, to "see what it was good for the sons of men that they should do under heaven all the days of their life" (2:3).

Nor apparently did he at first doubt that wisdom would bring him to this desired goal. Probably he took the promises of the wise men of Proverbs at their face value, and believed that the seeker of wisdom would find not only the "knowledge of God" (and so, of the world) but also personal happiness.

The method he employed however was different in one important respect from that of the wise men. They started from dogma, he began with the facts. For the make-up of his nature was quite unlike theirs. This man had a passion for observation. He insisted on seeing *everything,* while the wise men kept their eyes con-veniently closed to happenings which could not be reconciled with their faith. In the same way Qoheleth made *experiments* in dif-

---

[2] D. C. Siegfried, *Prediger und Hohelied* (Göttingen, 1898), p. 2ff.

[3] McNeile, Barton, Podechard, Oesterley and Robinson(?).

[4] Odeberg, Hertzberg, Galling, Allgeier, Sellin, Meinhold, Eissfeldt. Eiss-feldt, *EAT,* p. 558, finds the following interpolations: 2:26; 3:17; 7:26b; 8:5,12b,13a; 11:9b; 12:7b, 12–14.

ferent life-policies "till he might see what it was good for the sons
of men that they should do" (2:3). The wise men apparently
never thought of doing this. Being sure that one path only led
to human happiness they walked in it resolutely, nor did they
make any honest effort to learn from people who followed "foolish" courses what satisfaction these gave to those who tried them.

The result of Qoheleth's pursuit of wisdom proved a disappointment. He discovered that the study of the world—and he seems
to have been an ardent student—brought weariness instead of pleasure, while the accompanying increase of knowledge increased pain
rather than joy. Wisdom gave its possessor no ultimate good, for
he had to die like the fool. Nor indeed is any adequate knowledge of the universe attainable. For the facts reveal no dependable
moral order but only a cycle that makes all hope of progress
illusory (1:2ff).

Convinced that wisdom was empty, Qoheleth (like Dr. Faustus)
next made trial of enjoyment. Not that he went to excess, for his
heart yet guided him with wisdom. Indeed, he seems to have been
a man of naturally pure tastes and moderate desires, as can be seen
from the picture of the life of pleasure sketched by his pen. Nor
did he have that levity of disposition which would have enabled
him to forget himself in play. A Hebraic seriousness pervaded his
mind and characterized his very quest of pleasure. Along with
the delights of banqueting, music and love he gave rein to his
constructive impulses, planting and building and increasing wealth.
Of course he lays on the colours heavily in his description, to keep
true to his assumed role of Solomon; but in a more modest way
he must himself have followed out these lines of experiment
(2:1-10).

But accomplishment, construction, possession and enjoyment alike
proved empty. One thought that weighed hard upon him had to
do with his work, in which he took the creator's pleasure. It was
the reflection that he must die and leave it to some successor of
unknown capacity—very likely a fool who would dissipate all its
fruits. That was continually happening in the world! (2:19). For
Qoheleth had little confidence in men, and none at all in women
(7:28).

The effect of all this disillusionment was that he began to "hate
life" and "all his labour wherein he laboured under the sun" (2:
17-18). Unutterable weariness descended upon him (1:8) and he
"turned about to cause his heart to despair concerning all the labour
wherein he had laboured under the sun" (2:20). That is a very

human confession. Such a giving up meant a revolution in his life. He "turned about" with the same sort of hopelessness with which Saul relinquished his pursuit of David after he had escaped into the land of the Philistines: the word "despair" is the same in both passages (I Sam. 27:1). What an acknowledgment that he had not always been the preacher of "vanity"!

It is significant that this resolve of Qoheleth was apparently not the outcome of any bitter personal experience. His case was not like that of Job, on whom Yahweh permitted the Satan to lay so heavy a hand. Quite the contrary. For so far as we can see Qoheleth's lot was unusually favoured. It was rather the great setting in which his individual life was placed that crushed his hope. He saw himself as but a part of a general situation. Job here and there attained to a similar breadth of view (e.g. Job 21) but with Qoheleth it is continuous. This it was that involved his personal disappointment in unrelieved shadow. One is reminded of the outcry of Tennyson:

"That loss is common would not make
    My own less bitter, rather more.
    Too common! Never morning wore
To evening, but some heart did break."

What longings lay back of his disappointment? What did this man really want from the universe? We can gather it from his complaints. On the surface, so to speak, of life he desired to see injustice, oppression and wickedness in high places done away— that those who weep should have a comforter, that none should have power over another to his hurt, that every one should have the health to enjoy his goods, that none should be lonely. He wanted to believe in men and women. He longed to be remembered. But down below the surface he asked to find a meaning for the world and men, to discover a moral order by which one might plan for the future with some confidence; above all, to feel that we are getting somewhere, that the individual can share in the progress, that he can really add something new to the sum of things. Along with this went the desire for permanence—for something that would endure amid the coming and going of phenomena; yes, that the enjoyment of their fleeting beauty might somehow last.

It was such hopes and longings that he saw denied, baffled. Therefore he despaired. And his despair, however calm, was passionate. He was no "gentle cynic" who could smile good-naturedly upon life. He was no Epicurean Horace urbanely accepting the universe. Enjoy it indeed he did; but only because there was "nothing better." He remained the undeceived rebel, the hater of life and work. The hater, because the lover; the lover of life, of his own work, of "everything," seeing that it is beautiful in its time. And the weariness that hangs like a pall over his book is not that of satiety but of disappointment.

The question arises, Was Qoheleth selfish? The answer will depend on the feeling of the reader, on his idea of the atmosphere that pervades the book. The present writer takes the contrary view. It was not Qoheleth's own sorrows but the "tears of things" that took away this man's hope. If he had been able to see light in the lot of mankind would he have cared greatly what happened to him personally? It seems not.

Again, why did he write his book? Was it merely to find in utterance relief from his despair? The present writer cannot think so. It was rather that he felt he had something to give which would help others.

> "And further, because the Preacher was wise,
> He still taught the people knowledge;
> Yea, he pondered, and sought out, and set in order many
>   proverbs.
> The Preacher sought to find out words of delight,
> And that which was written uprightly, words of truth"
>   (12:9f).

It may seem that what he had to give was of doubtful value. Certainly it was not "wisdom" as the great tradition understood it. But Qoheleth felt it was the truth and that men ought to have it. For their sakes he made it as beautiful as he could, seeking to find out "words of delight."

But this is surmise. When we seek certainty we must recognize that we cannot *know* why he wrote. For there is no man in the Bible who so eludes the reader. Thus he who was the baffled became in turn the baffler.

Let us now consider his thought more in detail.

Qoheleth's Criticism of the World

It is well to begin with this, for it constitutes the chief element of his book. He is above all things else a critic, a sceptic who insists on examining and analyzing the world and especially that aspect of it which has to do with human life. As a result of this analysis he pronounces it valueless. Vanity of vanity, all is vanity— breath, nothingness. For in spite of its illusive promises, which had apparently for a time deceived even himself, it has fundamental defects that cancel out its goods and leave—nothing!

The first of these is that there is no real progress possible to man. "What profit hath man of all his labour wherein he laboureth under the sun?" (1:3). The word means "something left over," a "surplus." After all his efforts man never has, never will have, anything to show as their product. The reason for this is now plain to Qoheleth: all moves in a cycle. "That which hath been is that which shall be; and that which hath been done is that which shall be done" (1:9). In language of great beauty and pathos he shows how this is true not only in the life of man but in the course of nature.

> "One generation goeth and another generation cometh;
> But the earth abideth for ever. . . .
> All the rivers run into the sea,
> Yet the sea is not full;
> Unto the place whither the rivers go,
> Thither they go again" (1:4,7).

No gain, no "remainder." "The sea is not full." So with the constant flow of sensations into the human mind.

> "The eye is not satisfied with seeing,
> Nor the ear filled with hearing" (1:8).

Never anything acquired!

A corollary of this is that "there is no new thing under the sun." All the sense of freshness, change, novelty that stimulates activity and enjoyment is illusion.

> "Is there a thing whereof it may be said,
> See, this is new!—
> It hath been long ago
> In the ages that were before us" (1:10).

The only reason that we can cheat ourselves into greeting any experience as new is that we have forgotten!

And that very forgetfulness is in itself one of the poignant evils of man's life.

> "There is no remembrance of the former generations,
> Neither of the later generations that are to come
> Will there be any remembrance
> Among those that shall come after" (1:11).

How much this weighed upon Qoheleth may be seen from his returning to the same theme again and again. He gives two instances which had specially brought it to his attention. A poor young man had supplanted an old king who had come to the point where he did not know how to take advice any more. The popularity of the new monarch was astounding.

> "I saw all the living
> That were under the sun,
> That they were with the youth, the second,
> That stood up in his stead."

Yet even this popularity, reflected Qoheleth, would not outlast his death.

> "They that come after shall not rejoice in him" (4:13ff).

Often indeed oblivion overwhelms a public benefactor long before he dies. A little city had been saved from the attack of a great king by the wisdom of a poor man who lived in it; "yet no man remembered that same poor man" (9:13ff). However much we labour and accomplish, it shall be presently as though we had never been.

Another consequence of the world's unending cycle is that there is nothing permanently good or bad.

> "For everything there is a season,
> And a time for every purpose under heaven."

Qoheleth chants a long and intentionally monotonous series of particular activities and emotions of which this is true. Life's constructive, joyous, hopeful energies inevitably give place to their opposites; only for a while indeed, but long enough to cancel both out. Then the process is ready to start again. Qoheleth probably did not have ethical good and evil specifically in mind; he is speaking of the whole of human effort, including ethics. But he considers it a great indictment of the world that one can believe in no absolutes of conduct and aim. The most that one can say of anything is that it is good *now;* and he cannot be sure of that! (3:1ff).

For a fifth count against the universe is just this *inscrutability.*

Qoheleth, who has spent years trying to understand "all that is done under heaven" (1:13) has felt himself baffled everywhere by the veil that lies over phenomena. "It is not known what man is" (6:10). No, nor what is to his advantage. "Who knoweth what is good for man in his life, all the days of his vain life which he spendeth as a shadow?" And one chief reason is the impenetrability of the future. "Who can tell a man what shall be after him under the sun?" (6:12; cf. 8:7; 11:5–6).

Looked at as a whole, human life is a burden. Other things besides those mentioned tend to make it so. One is the irrepressible impulse to know where no real knowledge is possible. Qoheleth himself is a good example of that. Another is the kindred desire to obtain success, to accomplish some work, to accumulate wealth, only to die and let all go to a successor who will quite possibly squander it like a fool. Again, the frequent inability of the successful to enjoy what they have won strikes Qoheleth as a bitter irony (6:1f). Solitariness too happens to men; they have no one for whom to work, yet they keep on getting money at the cost of great privations (4:7ff). The widespread oppression of the defenceless (3:16; 4:1; 5:8–9), the hierarchy of graft in the government that renders justice impossible for the poor (5:8), the power of the exploiting class (4:1) all combine to make one "praise the dead that have been long dead more than the living that are still alive" (4:2). A canker eating at the root of all experience is the absence of satisfaction and contentment (1:8; 6:7).

"All things are full of weariness;
Man cannot utter it" (1:8).

And this joylessness will deepen as one goes down into old age. Then indeed the evil days come, and the years "wherein thou shalt say, I have no pleasure in them" (12:1). Finally death awaits each. That is the chief of evils for with it comes the loss of everything in which the living has taken delight: "there is no work, nor device, nor knowledge, nor wisdom, in Sheol, whither thou goest" (9:10). And its shadow lurks everywhere; one never knows when it will cross his path.

"Man knoweth not his time:
As the fishes that are taken in an evil net,
And as the birds that are caught in the snare,
Even so are the sons of men snared in an evil time,
When it falleth suddenly upon them" (9:12).

Yes, man's lot is evil indeed. And man, involved within it, finds himself powerless to alter it. "That which is crooked cannot be made straight" (1:15). He cannot "contend with him that is mightier than he" (6:10). He must take everything as it comes.

> "If the clouds be full of rain,
> They empty themselves upon the earth;
> And if a tree fall toward the south or toward the north,
> In the place where the tree falleth, there shall it be" (11:3).

In particular, he cannot by all his efforts avert the last calamity.

> "There is no man that hath power over the spirit, to retain
>   the spirit;
> Neither hath any power over the day of death" (8:8).

Has Qoheleth Discovered Any Values in the World?

If all is empty, is there anything worth while? Qoheleth would answer: No, if one seeks permanent values. But if one will reconcile himself to the partial and the fleeting he can still get a great deal out of life. Here are some of the goods that he finds:

In spite of all that he has said against it *life itself* is not a thing to be despised. Its very briefness counsels us to take what it offers.

> "Truly the light is sweet,
> And a pleasant thing it is to behold the sun.
> Yea, if a man live many years,
> Let him rejoice in them all;
> And let him remember the days of darkness,
> For they shall be many" (11:7-8).

This was spoken in one of Qoheleth's more expansive moods. But even when his vision grew dark, he could still see that life had one great advantage over death.

> "To him that is joined with all the living
>   There is hope;
> For a living dog is better than a dead lion.
> For the living know that they shall die,
> But the dead know not anything" (9:4ff).

Life gives something to look forward to (however uninteresting!) and it gives *awareness*.

This brings us to Qoheleth's second good: *wisdom*. By this term he seems to mean the same practical sagacity and understanding of life that the wise men praised. Now wisdom, it is true, will not confer any ultimate benefit upon its possessor, and Qoheleth had often asked how he who had acquired it had any advantage over the fool, seeing that death and forgetfulness overtake both. But he is quite clear that *meanwhile* wisdom can do much for one. To begin with, it puts eyes in his head. He can at least see the facts of life, however melancholy they may be. It makes all the difference between moving in light and in darkness (2:13f). Moreover it helps him to live safely and comfortably. It is a defence, even as money is a defence: it preserves the life of him that has it (7:12). It makes a man's face to shine (8:1). In many ways it proves useful. The community gains by it, as we have noticed in the story of the poor wise man who delivered the city (9:13ff). This had impressed Qoheleth very much: "it seemed great unto me," he tells us. Wisdom is also of great value when one determines to make trial of pleasure (2:3).

For Qoheleth boldly recommends *pleasure* as about the best thing open to man. This was the conclusion he had arrived at after long experiments with life.

"There is nothing better for a man than that he should eat and drink, and make his soul enjoy good in his labour" (2:24).

To this advice he comes back again and again as to something comparatively solid and secure (3:12, 22; 5:18–20; 8:15; 9:7ff; 11:8–10).

> "Go thy way, eat thy bread with joy
> And drink thy wine with a merry heart;
> For God hath already accepted thy works.
> Let thy garments be always white
> And let not thy head lack oil.
> Live joyfully with thy wife
> Whom thou lovest
> All the days of thy life of vanity" (9:7ff).

Man deserves this as a reward for his toil. "That is thy portion in life, and in thy labour wherein thou labourest under the sun." One can almost find here the thought that it is man's *destiny*— so far as Qoheleth feels that he has one! He adds to this picture the joy of *occupation* which as an industrious man he prized so highly himself: "whatsoever thy hand findeth to do, do it with thy might" (9:10). One can see from the idyllic nature of Qoheleth's portrayal that his idea of true pleasure was far removed from that of the profligate.

Another good is *contentment*. Qoheleth is very strong against anything that upsets one's equability. Avarice, for instance:

> "He that loveth silver shall not be satisfied with silver;
> Nor he that loveth abundance, with increase. . . .
> When goods increase, they are increased that eat them;
> And what advantage is there to the owner thereof
> Save the beholding of them with his eyes?" (5:10f).

One's desire for righteousness also can be carried too far, as well as his ambition for wisdom.

> "Be not righteous overmuch;
> Neither make thyself overwise:
> Why shouldest thou destroy thyself?" (7:16).

Nor should one worry over the contrast between the present and the past.

> "Say not thou, what is the cause that the former days
> Were better than these?
> For thou dost not inquire wisely concerning this" (7:10).

Nor should he bother about posterity. "Who shall bring him back to see what shall be after him?" (3:22). After all, there is no sense in trying to set the world right. "Consider the work of God: for who can make that straight, which he hath made crooked?" (7:13). Don't be looking for trouble; ignore a great deal for the sake of peace.

> "Take not heed unto all words that are spoken,
> Lest thou hear thy servant curse thee" (7:21).

In general avoid the crowding of life with activities. "A dream cometh with the multitude of business" (5:3). And don't try to keep pace with successful people.

> "I saw all labour, and every successful work, that for this a man is envied of his neighbour. This also is vanity, and a striving after wind. . . . Better is a handful with quietness, than two handfuls with labour and a striving after wind" (4:4,6).

To this counsel of easy-going moderation Qoheleth adds (if we may attribute them to his pen) a number of prudent observations as to how one can keep clear of trouble and obtain the modicum of well-being possible to man. One should realize the value of association with others, for "two are better than one" (4:9). In his dealings with the king and with God he should be circumspect, for both have power to injure him (10:4, 20; 5:1–7). Liberality will bring great return (11:1–3); a good name is better than precious oil (7:1); and the like. All of these imply that there are things in life worth while, whose pursuit is prompted by wisdom. Qoheleth is far from recommending despair with its accompanying paralysis of effort.

> "Whatsoever thy hand findeth to do,
>   Do it with thy might" (9:10).
> "In the morning sow thy seed
>   And in the evening withhold not thy hand;
>   For thou knowest not which shall prosper,
>   Whether this or that,
>   Or whether they both shall be alike good" (11:6).

Where Does God Come In?

God is in control of the world; of that Qoheleth is convinced. The universe is personally governed by its Author and all that takes place is His doing. Whatever Qoheleth says therefore in criticism of the world reflects upon God by implication. But there are a number of utterances in which he goes beyond implication and lays the responsibility expressly at God's door.

God is the great Baffler of men.

> "He hath made everything beautiful in its time;
>   Also he hath set eternity in their heart,
>   Yet so that man cannot find out
>   The work that God hath done
>   From the beginning unto the end" (3:11).

Much is contained in this pregnant sentence. First, God has established the unceasing cycle of phenomena, with all its results. Next, He has made men love the fleeting because of its beauty. To possess its goods they are driven to unending toil. Yet He has also put into their hearts a desire for eternity, "duration"—in a world where nothing endures! Akin to this is their longing to *know* the meaning of it all; a longing that He deliberately disappoints from first to last! Of all this fruitless endeavour to possess the unpossessible and to know the unknowable Qoheleth says bitterly: "I have seen the travail which God hath given to the sons of men to be exercised therewith" (3:10). Finally—another way of saying the same thing—He has doomed man to complete helplessness.

> "I know that
> Whatsoever God doeth, it shall be forever;
> Nothing can be put to it, nor anything taken from it" (3:14).

"Man cannot contend with Him that is mightier than he" (6:10).

Within this sad lot which God has assigned to men there are indeed gleams of kindness. God is the Author of such *joy* as is attainable. He gives not only riches and wealth and other goods but also the power to enjoy them.

"For he answereth a man in the joy of his heart" (5:20).

That is, He takes sympathetic pleasure in His creature's gladness. Qoheleth seems to believe that such happiness is man's normal "portion" from God (9:9). This measured beneficence Qoheleth freely acknowledges.

And yet it has its dark obverse. For often possessions prove a mockery.

"There is an evil which I have seen under the sun, and it is heavy upon men: a man to whom God giveth riches, wealth and honour, so that he lacketh nothing for his soul of all that he desireth, yet God giveth him not power to eat thereof, but an alien eateth it; this is vanity, and it is an evil disease.

> If a man beget a hundred children,
> And live many years,
> So that the days of his years are many,
> But his soul be not filled with good,
> And moreover he have no burial;
> I say, that an untimely birth is better than he" (6:1-3).

But there is a darkness deeper than this, into which Qoheleth enters. It is where he gives over entirely the thought of God's personal treatment of men, whether good or bad, and sees the world ruled by *chance*. God, he declared at times, exercised no more

supervision over men than over beasts. That was why injustice and
wrong prevailed.

"And moreover I saw under the sun,
    In the place of justice, there was wickedness;
    In the place of the righteous, there was the wicked.[1]

I said in my heart: It is because of the sons of men, that God
may prove them, and that they may see that they themselves are
but as the beasts; for it chanceth to the sons of men as it chanceth
to the beasts; one chance happeneth to them (both): as the one
dieth, the other dieth, and everything hath one spirit; and man hath
no superiority over the beasts; for all is vanity. Everything goeth to
one place. Everything is of dust, and everything returneth to dust.
Who knoweth the spirit of man, whether it goeth upward, and the
spirit of the beast, whether it goeth downward to the earth?"
(3:16ff).

The word Qoheleth uses here for "chance" (*miqreh*) signifies
something that "just happens" as contrasted with a personal pur-
poseful act of God (cf. I Sam. 6:9). He means that neither man
himself nor anything that comes to him has any significance or
purpose. Like the beasts, man is but a part of nature—from dust,
to dust—and so meaningless. All is vanity. Man's supposed
uniqueness, over which the priestly writers and the author of
psalm 8 had grown so eloquent, is illusory. Man dies like the
beasts; and death is—dust. Those who in Qoheleth's day were
venturing to maintain that at death the human spirit ascended
had no real proof of it. Who knoweth?

With this abandonment of everything to chance all belief in a
discriminating government of the world disappears.

"There is one chance to the righteous, and to the wicked;
    To the good, and to the bad;
    To the clean, and to the unclean;
    To him that sacrificeth, and to him that sacrificeth not.
    As is the good, so is the sinner;
    As he that sweareth, so is he that feareth an oath" (9:2).

Thus the retribution dogma, already pierced in a score of places by
the boring of Qoheleth's criticism, finally crashed to the ground.
But what a difference between Qoheleth's refutation and that of
the writer of Job! The latter found his way to the peace of a

[1] Omitting v.17 as an interpolation.

complete trust in God. Qoheleth ended by losing the sense of God's providence altogether. The facts as he saw them forced him to this conclusion, but he had no joy in it.

"This is an evil in all that is done under the sun, that there is one chance to all . . ." (9:3).

What then was Qoheleth's religion? What value did God possess in the thinking of this man for whom He had ceased to give a meaning to life? Here we see the very human inconsistency of Qoheleth. He could not rest in utter scepticism for the faith of his childhood still had a real hold over him. Atheism he would have found impossible. The name of God was constantly on his lips, and he still kept his religious faith—in a measure. Practically however the thought of God gave him little happiness or comfort or strength. God had become to him simply the personal Maker and Controller of the universe, insisting on being treated with respect (one's vows must be scrupulously paid!), His relations with men lit up by a fitful benevolence (though of this Qoheleth was not sure), but fundamentally man's Disturber and Disappointer, if He took the trouble to do even as much as that!

As for intercourse with God, that must be circumspect. Qoheleth's dominant feeling for God was fear (he no longer looked up to His character). God was like the king; the less one called oneself to His attention the better! Qoheleth had apparently ceased to pray, nor does he mention thanksgiving. His heart might be bleeding at the sight of the world's wretchedness, but he did not try intercession. The desire to know God, to seek Him, to throw oneself upon Him amid the heartbreaks of life, to pour one's soul out to Him, as did the psalmists, Qoheleth did not experience. Perhaps he had never been anything of a mystic. Certainly he did not bewail, as did Job, the loss of God's friendship.

The fact is, Qoheleth had come to the point where he could let his idea of God fade away without any real deprivation. Possibly he would have been better off after it vanished, seeing it was what it was. And yet he was not really irreligious. Except for a possible lack of mysticism in his nature, he possessed many of those feelings which God—and God alone—is fitted to satisfy.

Qoheleth's Influence on Israel's Religion

Qoheleth's book seems to have attained great popularity. Its haunting melancholy beauty, its bitter sweetness, its glimpses of the "solemn horizons of man's ways," its ineluctable pathos, its refusal to ignore unwelcome facts, all spoke direct to human hearts. But it appealed to different people for different reasons.

Here and there must have been men who read it with the sense that its author was speaking their own thoughts. Perhaps he helped them to retain something of their early belief in God. Most of these would be quiet men who kept their misgivings to themselves. There must also have been others who used his book as an excuse for rejecting all inherited sanctities and restraints, boldly embracing a heartless profligacy which was the opposite of his own position.[1]

The main stream of Israel's religious development however continued to follow the Mosaic pattern of unconquerable faith and affirmation. In the upholders of the "great tradition" Qoheleth's philosophy could have excited no feeling but that of loathing. But pious hands soon retouched his book so that its real thought was obscured and the Preacher of emptiness became a champion of God's discriminating providence. Thus the orthodox also found delight in it and in spite of uncomfortable doubts it was accorded a place in the canon of holy Scripture.

For this reason the influence of Qoheleth's actual philosophy upon Israel's religious life was probably negligible. Its chief service may well have been a challenge to call forth the ringing *credo* of God's people. To its despairing "Vanity of vanities" they made answer with the psalmists' halleluia chorus, "For his mercy endureth for ever."

To modern Christians its presence in the Bible is an unmixed gain. For alone among the men of the Bible [2] Qoheleth saw the *difficulties* of belief in God. He raised the fundamental questions that in our darker seasons trouble us. The writer of the Book of Job, for all his profundity, did not go so deep; for he asked only whether God governs cruelly or lovingly. Qoheleth asked whether God really governs at all; and as a corollary, whether man has any significance. The two questions inevitably go together.

The answer that he gave likewise finds an echo in our minds. His scepticism, his denial of man's significance, his refusal to think that man is getting anywhere, all harmonize with the temper of an age which influences us because we live in it. It is somehow a

---

[1] The writer of the Book of the Wisdom of Solomon may have had this effect of Qoheleth's philosophy in mind in his attack on such profligates in his day (Wisd. 2:1ff).

[2] With one possible exception: the writer of Prov. 30:1-4.

relief to come upon one who at least faces the worst. We yield ourselves to his "words of delight" and while borne along by their music unexpectedly find stirring afresh within us the undying energy of faith.

Chapter XXIX

THE WRITER OF THE BOOK OF DANIEL

[WROTE 166–165 B.C.]

The last man whom we shall study is the author of a book that because of its strangeness has ever exercised a weird fascination upon Bible readers. Under the scrutiny of modern research it has lost its function as a storehouse of millennarian prediction but has acquired for compensation a heroic and comforting message for the faithful in this or any age.

The Sources

The only source from which we draw our knowledge of the writer of the Book of Daniel is the book itself. There are other sources which throw light on the situation in which he found himself but they tell us nothing of him personally.

The Book of Daniel is unique in the Old Testament. Other books contain short sections which remind us of it, but as a whole it stands alone. It purports to come from a captive Jew who rose to prominence in one empire after another during the changing sixth century B.C. The first half recounts incidents in which this Daniel and his associates figured; the second half discloses visions that were vouchsafed to him concerning the "time of the end." These he was commanded to seal until the end should come. It is written partly in Hebrew, partly in Aramaic, without any apparent reason for the transition from the one language to the other.

The ancient view of the book, held by both Jews and Christians, was that it contained genuine prophecies written by Daniel, who received revelations as to the course of history from about 600 B.C. to about 167 B.C., or even later.[1] This view still has its able exponents.

[1] It became general in the early Christian church to regard the prophecies of the "time of the end" as pointing to the Roman Empire, although some placed this age in the days of the Seleucid kings.

It is safe to say however that the almost universal judgment of modern scholars rejects the ancient view and holds that the book was written in the midst of the persecution of the Jews by Antiochus Epiphanes beginning in 168 B.C., and that its author was a faithful Jew who wished to strengthen his people to resist the persecutor boldly. The reasons for this view are briefly as follows:

The writer makes palpable mistakes as to the history of the sixth century B.C., but depicts in detail the history of the early second century through the first stages of the Antiochian persecution, and then stops abruptly.

The language of both the Hebrew and Aramaic portions is declared by experts to come from a later age than the sixth century. The use of Persian and Greek words points in the same direction.

The apocalyptic character of the book points to a later date.

The theology is much more developed than we should expect in the sixth century.

Finally, the book is plainly *aimed* at the situation created by the Antiochian persecution. This seems to indicate that the writer himself faced that situation. Of course it is conceivable that he might by a supernatural revelation have foreseen it across five centuries, but there is no need to suppose such a miracle. Moreover, if that were the case, the book would be the only example in the Bible of a genuine detailed prediction of events centuries in advance.[2]

Those who are interested in knowing more about the question of date may consult the commentaries and introductions and articles in Bible dictionaries where it is treated at length. We shall, without further discussion, assume the correctness of the modern view. The author was not Daniel, but some unidentified Jew living in the terrible days of the great persecution who put this message into the mouth of Daniel. We naturally dislike such a deception but in his age it seems to have been considered legitimate, for a number of other "pseudepigraphic" works, as they are called, have come down to us from the same period. And we must remember that he was really no deceiver, but a true man with a true message about which he was in deadly earnest.

So effectually did he hide himself behind his famous hero that he escaped notice till modern scholarship discovered him, as it did the Yahwist, the priestly writers and the Second Isaiah. And it finds him in his book.

---

[2] The prediction regarding Josiah in I Ki. 13:2 is generally regarded as unhistorical.

Yet even here a question arises, Is the whole book from his hand? Some scholars say no. There is at present a disposition in some quarters to regard the *narratives* of the first six chapters as older by several generations than the *visions* of chapters 7–12. This may be true. But even if the author did use older material he made it his own. Other scholars hold that the book is a unity proceeding from the pen of one man. In either case therefore we are justified in using the whole book as a source for our study of the author.

When we come to the situation which the author confronted we are not limited in the data furnished by the book. We have other accounts of the Antiochian persecution in I and II Maccabees and in Josephus. All of these we shall use in the following paragraphs.

The Author of the Book of Daniel Wrote to Sustain his Fellow-Jews under the Antiochian Persecution

Before we can comprehend the situation in which the author wrote we must turn our gaze from the little Jerusalem community, which up to this point has been the centre of our interest, to the great west.[1] Hardly had the Chronicler done his work when a revolution took place in the ancient world. There arose in Greece a movement which was destined to affect the whole course of human history from that day to this and to have the most momentous consequences not only for Judaism but for Christianity.

In a sense this movement was the personal achievement of two amazing personalities, Philip of Macedonia and his son Alexander. The story of their advance from the half barbaric kingdom of Macedonia to the conquest, first of Greece, and then of the vastest empire hitherto known to man, must be sought in the various historical works that treat this period. We can here review it only in the briefest outline.

In 338 B.C. Philip made himself master of Greece by his victory at Chaeronea. Two years later he was murdered and his son Alexander, then only twenty years of age, succeeded to the throne. Though sprung of a line of rude northern chieftains this young man had from his earliest years been nurtured in the thought-world of Greece. No less a man than Aristotle, perhaps the greatest all-round empirical investigator and thinker the world has known, was his tutor. Alexander conceived a passion for Hellenism, not only

[1] In the following description of the rise of Hellenism the author has drawn freely on an unpublished lecture by his colleague, Prof. C. B. Hedrick.

on its warlike side as represented by his favourite classic, the *Iliad,* but on its humanistic side as well. Under its impulse he deliberately set himself to conquer and Hellenize mankind.

After firmly establishing the Macedonian power over Greece itself he turned his face towards the ancient East where for two centuries the empire of Persia had held sway. The battle of Granicus in 334 B.C. opened Asia Minor to him. His victory at Issus in 333 and his subjection of Tyre and Gaza in 332 gave him Syria and the road to Egypt. Egypt was taken and Alexandria founded. Thence in 331 he pressed on towards Mesopotamia, which was opened to him by his great victory at Arbela, and occupied the Persian summer and winter capitals, Susa and Babylon. With scarce a pause he pushed into Persia and before the end of 330 penetrated to the confines of what is now Afghanistan. In 327 he entered the plains of India and in 326 made himself master of the Punjab. Next year he started back, reaching Susa early in 324. Then suddenly in 323, while he was occupied with plans for conquering Arabia, he died in Babylon before attaining his thirty-third birthday.[2]

He left no heir and upon his death his leading generals constituted themselves his successors, presently calling themselves kings. This resulted after some years in the establishment of four dynasties, two of which divided the orient between them: the Ptolemies in Egypt and the Seleucids in Asia. Both were Macedonian, carrying on Alexander's tradition of the Greek culture. Consider for a moment what this meant.

Alexander had been an "apostle of Hellenism." Wherever his arms penetrated he brought Greek civilization. This was what made his conquests significant. "It was his proud distinction," says Fairweather, "to revitalize by the alchemy of Hellenism the countries he subdued." [3] Hellenism Bevan describes as a body of ideas, a way of thinking about the world, which had arisen among the Greeks and had no parallel elsewhere.[4] It transformed the ancient world into something different, and brought in an absolutely new era. What was it?

At its heart lay an appreciation of man and his capacities, especially his reason and intellect and sense of beauty. In relation to the rational life of mankind, says Bevan,[5] it was analogous to the

[2] W. Fairweather, *Jesus and the Greeks* (Edinburgh, 1924), p. 15ff.
[3] *Ibid.,* p. 17.
[4] *Jerusalem under the High Priests* (London, 1912), p. 18.
[5] *Ibid.,* p. 19.

appearance of Jesus in the religious life of man. It recognized the worth of the individual and the value of individual liberty, including the right of private judgment, freedom from tradition, and the spirit of free critical inquiry (the "scientific spirit"). It was marked by a sense of proportion and fitness, and so by a love of the beautiful in art and literature and the human body.

But it was not purely individualistic. It possessed also an appreciation of man as a social being and of the richness and value of a well-ordered community life, of what we call "civilization." It regarded the world as the *oikumené,* the sphere of human society. Rostovsteff remarks that the conception of humanity (*humanitas*) dates from this age.[6]

Along with the conversion of the world to Greek culture and inseparable from it went the adoption of Greek as a world language. Mankind became bilingual and everywhere the traveller went he could converse not only with the educated but also with the shop-keepers of the bazaars in the tongue that a century before had been almost unknown outside the small Hellenic world. And this common language—the *koiné* as it came to be called—though altered somewhat to fit new times and wider needs remained still substantially the Attic Greek of Xenophon, Thucydides, Socrates and Plato. A language cannot but express the thought-world of a people and the speaking of Greek inevitably made men at home in Greek thinking.

Then too there arose everywhere the Greek cities, sometimes newly-founded, sometimes old cities made over. Each contained buildings and institutions that were new to mankind—theatres, baths, palaestrae, market-places, gymnasia, musea, arcades, even universities, all in the Greek style of architecture. In these buildings centred a new kind of city life where men enjoyed pleasures, excitements and enrichments hitherto unknown. In Alexandria, the supreme Hellenistic city, where the Ptolemies showed themselves unique patrons of art and learning, this cultural life assumed a splendour that won world fame. Other centres like Antioch and Tarsus attained something of the same glory. A crowning grace of the Greek city was its freedom, for it was permitted a large degree of popular government.

As this Hellenic culture rolled its bright waves over the world it was inevitable that it should dash itself against the more austere structure of thought that had for centuries found its home in the Hebrew people. At first the contact seems to have been friendly

[6] *History of the Ancient World* (Oxford, 1926), I, p. 381.

enough. Jewish legend told how the great Alexander, passing down the coast to attack Gaza, had honoured Jerusalem with a visit and made obeisance to the high priest as the representative of the true and only God. But it soon became manifest that the humanistic outlook of Hellenism, at its best, could not but dissolve Israel's God-centred view of the universe. Thus the instinct of self-preservation roused the Jew to oppose it. Nor was this all. The new civilization had a darker side also, to which the ethically sensitive Jew was keenly alive. For all its seeming democracy and liberty it was based on human slavery, nor did its passion for the beautiful keep it from deep moral degradation. Profoundly as it comprehended the human mind, it remained blind to the corruption of human nature; it lacked the sense of sin. Fairweather has compared it to the sick man lying at the beautiful gate of the temple.[7] Therefore the Jew turned from it in loathing.

But not every Jew. Those who had made their home in the regions outside Palestine—the far-flung settlements of the Diaspora —had naturally to come to terms with it. Living in Greek cities, they must to a certain extent follow Greek ways. And not a few went further, embracing Hellenic culture with ardour. These liberal Jews were in many instances men of high character who in spite of their love of Hellenism remained true to the faith of their fathers. But always there were some who tended to give up Jewish customs and even to adopt the immoralities of the heathen.

Nor was this true only of the Diaspora. In Judah and in the holy city itself such Hellenizers began to appear. Naturally they excited bitter antagonism. Between them and the rigorists, who loved the law with increasing passion, there could be no peace. It is held by some scholars that the denunciations of the "ungodly" in the psalms are an echo of the conflict between the poorer "saints," or strict adherents of the law, and the more powerful Hellenizers who generally belonged to the wealthier class and so were able to "oppress" their opponents. Be that as it may, Hellenism made such progress among the Palestinian Jews that shortly before the publication of the Book of Daniel it had come to exercise a decisive influence upon the nation.

In order to understand the situation which thus arose we must briefly survey the fortunes of the Palestinian community under the Macedonian dynasties. The Ptolemies early gained control of Palestine and retained it for over a century, ruling on the whole with mildness and consideration. Then the Seleucid Antiochus

[7] *Ibid.*, p. 114.

III (the Great) wrested it from Egypt by his victory at Panion in 198 B.C. For a time the change of masters made little difference to the Jews although they were now divided into the Egyptian and Syrian parties. Antiochus III laid no new burden upon them. His successor Seleucus did indeed—so runs the legend—send his chancellor Heliodorus to rob the temple of its trust funds; but when the latter was driven back from his impious attempt by angelic avengers he made no further effort to carry out the sacrilege. In 175 B.C. however there came to the throne a king who was destined to bear a sinister name in Jewish annals—Antiochus IV, *Epiphanes*.

Hardly had he assumed the crown when he was approached by a leading Hellenizer of Jerusalem with a petition to be appointed high priest. This was Jason, the son of the late Onias III (a high priest known for his "godliness"), who now attempted to supplant his brother Onias IV in the supreme ecclesiastical dignity. To this end he offered Antiochus a huge bribe which he expected to pay out of the temple revenues. But he tendered at the same time another request: that he might be allowed to build for him in Jerusalem a Greek gymnasium and form a body of youths (*ephebi*) to be trained in it; and at the same time to register the inhabitants of Jerusalem as citizens of Antioch (II Macc. 4:7ff).

This request was exactly of the sort to please Antiochus, who was an enthusiastic Hellenist. Combined with the bribe it proved irresistible and Jason was duly constituted high priest. His appointment was a severe blow to the stricter Jews, who now beheld an avowed Hellenizer in the most sacred office of the church. The Hellenizers on the other hand were emboldened to push their cause vigorously. Under the leadership of the new high priest they brought in a new tide of Greek manners. A gymnasium was erected under the citadel itself. Young men began to wear the Greek cap and to follow Greek fashions. Even the priests caught the fever, so that they no longer had any interest in the services of the altar; "but despising the sanctuary and neglecting the sacrifices they hastened to enjoy what was unlawfully provided in the palaestra, after the summons of the discus; making no account of the honours of their fathers and thinking the glories of the Greeks best of all" (II Macc. 4:12ff). So far did Jason proceed that he actually sent envoys to the quinquennial games at Tyre with a substantial offering to be expended in sacrifices to Herakles. This was too much even for the bearers, who diverted the money to the equipment of the galleys (II Macc. 4:18ff).

Matters went from bad to worse. Jason was soon displaced by

Menelaus, another Hellenizer not even of high-priestly descent, who promised Antiochus a greater bribe. This was a supreme outrage to the feelings of the rigorists. We cannot go into the sordid details of what followed. Suffice it to say that violence at last broke out against Menelaus, who promptly appealed to Antiochus. To the Syrian king it looked as if a turbulent people were flouting his royal authority. Marching to Jerusalem he inflicted upon it bloody punishment. Two years later he revisited it with renewed vengeance. This time he built a fort south of the temple area and in it the Hellenizers took refuge. Sallying forth from time to time they attacked those engaged in the temple worship, shedding blood freely. It was an intolerable situation.

But Antiochus had a yet severer blow to deal. He decided to make an end of Judaism altogether. The story is best told in the horror-charged words of the Jewish historian (I Macc. 1:44ff).

"And the king sent letters by the hand of messengers unto Jerusalem and the cities of Judah, that they should follow laws strange to the land, and should forbid whole burnt-offerings and sacrifices and drink-offerings in the sanctuary; and should profane the sabbaths and feasts, and pollute the sanctuary and the holy persons; that they should build altars and temples and shrines for idols, and should sacrifice swine's flesh and unclean beasts; and that they should leave their sons uncircumcised, that they should make their souls abominable with all manner of uncleanness and profanation; so that they might forget the law and change all the ordinances. And whosoever shall not do according to the word of the king, he shall die."

Steps were at once taken to carry this decree into effect. On the fifteenth day of Chisleu (December) 168 B.C. a small heathen altar was erected on the altar of the temple, thus defiling it (I Macc. 1:54). On the 25th of Chisleu heathen sacrifices were offered upon this new altar (I Macc. 1:59). The temple itself was rededicated to Zeus Olympios. In the cities of Judah small altars consecrated to heathen deities were reared on every side. At the doors of houses and in the streets incense was burned. Where books of the law were found these were torn up and burned, while their possessors were executed. Acknowledgment of loyalty to the law brought death. Where children had been circumcised the mothers and all who participated in the ceremony were executed. These measures were enforced by systematic visitation of villages and districts. All were compelled to sacrifice to heathen deities, to eat swine's flesh and to observe the pagan festivals (I Macc. 1:54ff).

Thus was instituted the first religious persecution the Jewish people had ever known. In the past many woes had come upon them but never before had they been faced with the alternative of denying their religion or undergoing tortures and death. They met it in different ways. Those who had already lost all real hold on Judaism found no difficulty in complying with the king's demands. "From the people," says the historian bitterly, "were gathered to them (the Greeks) many, every one that had forsaken the law" (I Macc. 1:52). Others fled from the danger. Many must have yielded against their consciences. But there remained a considerable number who stood fast.

"And many in Israel were fully resolved and confirmed in themselves not to eat unclean things. And they chose to die, that they might not be defiled with the meats, and that they might not profane the holy covenant; and they died" (I Macc. 1:62f).

So far the only alternatives to apostasy were flight or death. But still another choice was to present itself. One day the king's officer commissioned to enforce the decree came to the little village of Modin in the Shephelah (the low hill-country west of the central range) and summoned the people to comply. Mattathias, the chief man of the village, was first appealed to: let him set an example of obedience and win rich rewards! He had scarcely finished an impassioned speech of refusal when some Jew, thinking to gain favour, stepped forward to sacrifice on the altar. The sight proved too much for Mattathias. In a transport of rage he ran upon the offender and killed him upon the altar, then killed the astonished king's officer, pulled down the altar, and summoning all who were zealous for the law to follow him made for the mountains accompanied by his five stalwart sons. The die was cast. From now on it was to be war! Little did he realize that by this one wrathful act he had inaugurated the "wars of the Jews," and set his people on the course which was to lead straight through two centuries of bloodshed to the final downfall of Jerusalem in 70 A.D.!

It was not long thereafter, when the resolute band of Maccabees had won some initial successes in arms, that the writer of Daniel put forth his book. He was one of the "godly" who had watched the growing inroads of Hellenism with horror. When the persecution broke out he found himself among those who were resolved to remain true to the law, come what might. Thus far he had escaped. But he stood ready.

Meanwhile his heart yearned over his brethren who like him had come under the shadow of mortal danger. He saw that they were unable to comprehend the fiery trial which had overtaken them. To their minds it was a manifestation of the "wrath" of God brought on by their sins. And so however brave their resolve they might falter.

They needed encouragement—the blowing of trumpets. They needed also a philosophy of martyrdom to make it all clear. And he could provide both! A message was stirring within him which he believed came direct from God. Yet if he put it forth in his own name, or anonymously, it would not be listened to as divine. For what claim had he to speak for God, seeing that the line of the prophets had long since come to an end? And so he boldly chose to present it as coming through a great Jewish saint of an earlier age, Daniel the man of God.

The Writer Inflamed his Fellow-Jews by Heroic Stories of the Past

First, he blew the trumpet. By a series of thrilling narratives he endeavoured to rouse the flagging spirits of his compatriots and inspire them to meet the trial of their faith heroically. It is not possible here to review in detail these incomparable stories. Let us rather look at them as a whole and try to understand how they met the need of God's people in this critical hour.

1. The writer wished to make men feel that the imposing power of the Seleucid empire was insignificant in comparison with the vast dominions of old. Hence he painted the human setting of his narratives on a grandiose scale. This is seen particularly in the case of Nebuchadnezzar, who in the first four chapters represents the power of the world. He was the "head of gold" (2:38), superior to all the rulers who succeeded him. His colossal image of gold set up in the plain of Dura (3:1) put to shame the puny idols of Antiochus' day; the prodigious assembly of his officers (3:3) set over the peoples, nations and languages (3:4) eclipsed anything the Seleucids could show; the tortures now threatening the Jews paled before the terror of his burning fiery furnace (3:6). What city could now be shown comparable to his "great Babylon" (4:30)? No wonder he fancied he could maintain his will even against divine interference: "who is the god that shall deliver you out of my hands?" (3:15). Even when he had passed away the splendour

of empire remained. We see Belshazzar making a feast to a thousand of his lords (5:1) and Darius setting one hundred and twenty satraps over his wide dominions (6:1). Yes, that was the day of great things!

2. And yet these stupendous potentates shrank into nothingness before the awful majesty of Israel's God—the "God of heaven" (2:18), the "Most High God" (3:26). All their splendour came from Him; they and their multitudes were in His hand. He knew all secrets (2:28) and could reveal to Daniel the king's forgotten dream. He created the stone without hands which smote the image of worldly empire and became a mountain that filled the whole earth (2:31ff). When Nebuchadnezzar's heart was lifted up, the divine sentence fell upon him and he was driven with vacant mind and naked body to dwell among the beasts "till he knew that the Most High ruleth in the kingdom of men, and giveth it to whomsoever he will" (4:25). When Belshazzar and his lords and concubines made light of such a God, the fingers of a man's hand wrote his doom upon the wall (5:5)—a doom fulfilled in that very night (5:30). All through the stories God's praises are ringing and their song is a song of victory:

"Blessed be the name of God for ever and ever: for wisdom and might are his. And he changeth the times and the seasons; he removeth kings and setteth up kings; he giveth wisdom unto the wise, and knowledge to them that have understanding; he revealeth the deep and secret things: he knoweth what is in the darkness, and the light dwelleth with him" (2:20ff).

How shall He not show Himself victor against this lesser foe?

3. It was faith in such a God that led Daniel and his friends to keep truth with Him, and hold fast His law in the face of death itself. The fair youths refused to defile themselves with the king's dainties (1:8) though only the friendliness of the prince of the eunuchs prevented the serious consequences which might have ensued. How heartening now to those who are ordered to eat swine's flesh! The three stood unbending when the whole world fell upon its face before the golden image of Nebuchadnezzar, and to the fury of the king opposed their claim faith.

"O Nebuchadnezzar, we are not careful to answer thee in this matter. If it be so, our God whom we serve is able to deliver us from the burning, fiery furnace; and he will deliver us out of thy hand, O king. But if not, be it known unto thee, O king, that we will not serve thy gods, nor worship the golden image that thou hast set up" (3:16ff).

Thus it was also in the day when men were forbidden to pray to any but the king. Daniel, knowing the consequences, "went into his house" and with windows open toward Jerusalem "kneeled upon his knees three times a day, and prayed, and gave thanks before his God, as he did aforetime" (6:10). If he despised the den of lions surely we can despise the terrors of this hour! Let us also continue in prayer.

4. And God, in whom these men of old believed, proved worthy of their trust. He gave health to the youths who lived on pulse and water (1:15). He answered the prayer of Daniel and his friends, revealing the king's dream (2:17ff). He sent His angel and saved the three in the fiery furnace (3:28). He stopped the mouths of the lions before Daniel (6:22). Be sure therefore that He will not forsake his people now. True, His power may not intervene to save them from torture and death: but that is only because He has some better plan for them. Trust Him.

5. It was not only the Jews who thus experienced the might of God and confessed His glory. So marvellous were His works in the days of old that those great monarchs freely acknowledged His supremacy over all gods. Thrice did Nebuchadnezzar make such a confession (2:47; 3:28; 4:1ff). He, the supreme ruler of the modern age, knew well that he was in the hands of God (though at times he forgot it) and nobly proclaimed this fact to men. His son Belshazzar tacitly admitted it when he honoured Daniel (5:29). Darius the Mede, after his efforts to save Daniel had proven fruitless, commended the confessor to God's power: and when the deliverance came he issued a decree like those of Nebuchadnezzar proclaiming the God of Daniel as the "living God, and steadfast for ever, whose kingdom shall not be destroyed" (6:25ff). What therefore Nebuchadnezzar and Darius acknowledged, the "little horn" Antiochus will be forced to confess. Resist him boldly.

6. Finally, the writer in these stories represented the Jews as constantly attaining success and honour. Not indeed because of their own natural powers: Daniel had made that plain to Nebuchadnezzar (2:30). It was only because their God worked with them that they seemed to accomplish so much more than other men. Yet none the less they did get forward. The fair youths proved themselves ten times better than all the magi of Babylon (1:20). Daniel could reveal a secret that baffled all his non-Jewish

colleagues (2:30). The three who could not worship the idol suc- ceeded in "changing the king's word"—an undreamed of thing (3:28). Daniel alone could interpret Nebuchadnezzar's second dream (4:19ff) and read the writing on the wall to Belshazzar (5:25ff). His high character and ability pointed him out under two empires as the one man to rule a realm (2:48; 6:3). These abilities and services actually led to promotion and rewards. In one passage the writer almost permitted divine honour to be offered to him (2:46). He and his associates enjoyed the favour of monarchs and earned the envy of disappointed rivals. On the whole Nebuchadnezzar and Darius were represented as friendly to these Jewish leaders, whose services they were glad to use.

We can see how such a glorification of Jews met the need of the persecuted faithful in the writer's day. All the world seemed to be turning against them; contempt and injury crushed their self-esteem. How insignificant, how weak we are! must have been their thought. No, our writer reminded them, your past has been among the great—so will your future be. And your enemies will be put to shame!

Thus he blew the trumpet. Then he met their second need—to understand the meaning of this persecution.

He Promised Them Speedy Divine Intervention

The present trial, our author believed, could be understood only when it was contemplated as part of the great sweep of history. By this he meant, not the entire past of Israel, but what for him was the modern age, beginning with the exile in 586 B.C. and now about to end. Taking Jeremiah's prediction that the exile would continue 70 years (Jer. 29:10) he reinterpreted it as meaning 70 weeks or hebdomads (i.e. 490) of years. This however gave him only the *period*. He filled it up with his grandiose scheme of four kingdoms, as set forth completely in Nebuchadnezzar's dream of the great image (2:31ff) and Daniel's dream of the four beasts (7:2ff) and of the man (7:13ff), partially in Daniel's vision of the ram and the he-goat (8:2ff). Worldly dominion, he believed, was all of one piece whoever exercised it: hence the single image seen by Nebuchadnezzar (2:31).

Like an image, it was man-made, not divine, though its power was given it by God. It was represented by a succession of empires portrayed as beasts, each poorer, more sinister, more destructive than its predecessor.

The first had been the Chaldean, represented chiefly by Nebuchadnezzar, the "head of gold" (2:38), the beast like a lion, having eagle's wings (7:4). This was by far the best of them all, rising actually to the human level: for "it was lifted up from the earth, and made to stand upon two feet as a man; and a man's heart was given to it" (7:4). We have already seen how our writer inclined to magnify Nebuchadnezzar and idealize his friendship for the Jews.

The second kingdom had been that of the "Medes," which the writer erroneously supposed to have intervened between the Chaldean and the Persian empires. It was the breast and arms of silver (2:32), the beast like a bear raised up on one side with three ribs in its mouth between its teeth (7:5). In Daniel's vision it appeared as the shorter horn of the ram (i.e. the Medo-Persian empire, 8:3). Its representative was "Darius the Mede," who likewise appears in a favourable light in the narratives. The prowess of this kingdom was indicated by the supernal command given to it: "Arise, devour much flesh" (7:5) and by the pre-eminence of the ram.

It had been followed by the Persian kingdom—the "belly and thighs of brass" (2:32). In the dream of the beasts it was pictured as like a leopard with four wings and four heads (7:6), agile, intelligent, cruel, occupying the four corners of the earth. Again, it is seen as the second and higher horn of the ram, which pushed west, north, south; and no beasts could stand before him (8:4). This is doubtless a reminiscence of the wide conquests of Cyrus: "He did according to his will, and magnified himself."

The fourth and worst empire was that of the Greeks (2:32f). It was the "legs of iron" (Alexander) and the feet, part of iron, part of clay (Alexander's successors). In the writer's description we can still catch an echo of the terror excited by the armies of the young Macedonian conqueror. He was as "strong as iron," breaking in pieces, subduing all things (2:40). He alone of the beasts was likened to no known animal, but pictured simply as "a fourth beast, terrible and dreadful, and strong exceedingly: and it had great iron teeth: it devoured and brake in pieces, and stamped the residue with its feet" (7:7). He was the great horn of the goat that "came from the west over the face of the whole earth, and touched not the ground" (8:5), before whose fury the ram collapsed; "and there was none that could deliver the ram out of his hand" (8:7). Then came his death ("when he was strong, the great horn was broken") and the division of his kingdom (2:42) among the four notable horns (the Diadochi, 8:8).

From this point onward the portrayal of events becomes more vivid as the writer nears his own time. We see the divided realm of the Diadochi, its toes, part of iron, part of clay (2:42), its ten horns (the successive rulers, 7:7), its struggles between the Ptolemies and Seleucids (11:5ff); till last of all there rises "a contemptible person" who seizes the kingdom by flatteries (11:21), a "little horn, with the eyes of a man and a mouth speaking great things" (7:8). He is "a king of fierce countenance, and understanding dark sentences" (8:23), "who through his policy shall cause craft to prosper in his hand; and he shall magnify himself in his heart" (8:25). In other words, Antiochus Epiphanes.

In Antiochus world empire reaches the height of its effrontery. He magnifies himself even to the Prince of the host (8:11), speaking words against the Most High (7:25). He takes away from Him the continual burnt-offering (8:11), profanes His sanctuary and sets up "the abomination that maketh desolate" (11:31). His heart is against the holy covenant (11:28). He thinks to change the times and the law (7:25). To this end he makes war with the saints (the faithful Jews) and prevails against them (7:21). They fall by the sword and by the flame, by captivity and by spoil. Thus he wears them out (7:25). On the other hand, he makes profane by flatteries such as do wickedly against the covenant (the apostate Jews, 11:32).

What is the reason for all this? Why does God permit it? The author gives in part the customary answer: God is angry at the sons of Israel (implied in 9:16; 8:19: it is a "time of indignation"). But he adds something of deep significance: it is also to *prove the saints.* The people that know their God are now revealed in their true heroism (11:32), and turn many to righteousness (12:3). Though some of the teachers are struck down it is to refine them, to purify and make them white, even to the time of the end.

For the end is at hand! Even while the little horn is strutting across the front of the stage of history uttering great words, preparations are being made behind him for the final judgment. Thrones are placed. One that is ancient of days takes His fiery seat. The innumerable hosts of heavenly attendants assemble. The books are opened (7:9-11). Give Antiochus a few moments more! We are in the midst of the 1150 last days foretold by the holy one to Daniel long ago (8:14)—the time, times and a half made sure by celestial oath (12:7). Only three and a half years, and these partly spent!

Then shall the fourth beast be slain—little horn and all—and its body destroyed (7:11). Nay, the whole image of worldly dominion shall be broken by the stone cut out without hands (2:34f). For God will bring in the fifth kingdom—the kingdom of the saints of the Most High (7:27). It is symbolized by one like unto a son of man coming with the clouds of heaven (7:13), a human figure, displacing the beasts. All the peoples and nations and languages shall serve him: his dominion is an everlasting dominion which shall not pass away (7:14). This stone will become a great mountain and fill the whole earth (2:35).

His coming will precipitate agony in the world. When Michael, the great prince who stands for Israel, shall stand up, there shall be a time of trouble, such as never was since there was a nation even to that same time. But the faithful of Israel need have no fear. "At that time thy people shall be delivered, every one that shall be found written in the book." Nor are those who have already perished to be forgotten—whether faithful or apostates.

"Many of them that sleep in the dust of the earth shall awake, some to everlasting life, and some to shame and everlasting contempt. And they that are wise shall shine as the brightness of the firmament; and they that turn many to righteousness as the stars for ever and ever" (12:1-4).

By such a philosophy of history and martyrdom did our author comfort his fellows.

His Idea of God

From what we have already seen we can perceive that the writer of the Book of Daniel was possessed by the thought of the greatness of God and the littleness of man. This appears in the titles that he gives to God: "the God of heaven" (2:18), "the Most High God" (4:2), "the living God" (6:20), "the God of gods and Lord of kings" (2:47); in his picture of God as "one that was ancient of days," from whom, as he took His place upon His throne of fiery flames, a fiery stream issued (7:9f); and in the doxologies in which God is extolled in language of adoration and awe (e.g. 2:20ff). God is the "Prince" of the heavenly host (8:11): thousands of thousands minister unto Him, and ten thousand times ten thousand stand before Him (7:10). These angels are so terrible in appearance that they strike down even the godly Daniel (10:9); how much more fearsome must be the God whose service they perform!

It is indeed the angels who come out from the invisible world into the sight of Daniel; God himself remains (with the one exception just cited, 7:9ff) behind the scenes. Or better, He is exalted above man's gaze in remote transcendent majesty. Nowhere does He speak. We hear the supernal voices of watchers, holy ones, angels, "men," but never God's.

For the most part God does His work in the world through angelic intermediaries. It is they who watch over the course of history and intervene to pronounce sentence in due time (4:13ff). Through them God helps and teaches the saints. Their chieftains fight for Him against the princes of Persia and Greece, since not all superhuman beings are obedient to His will (10:20ff). It seems to be the idea of the writer that each nation has its celestial advocate, or prince, who contends for it in the regions above; and according as this upper conflict results, so earth's history is determined. The advocate of Israel is Michael, who is having a hard struggle in this final hour with the advocate of Greece.

But he will prove victorious. In spite of stubborn resistance in heaven and earth God's purposes will be accomplished; for God is in control of history. His doom has fallen once and again ere this, on Nebuchadnezzar (4:31f) and on Belshazzar (5:26ff); and as then the part of the hand was sent from before Him to write the *mené tekel* upon the wall, so now He is but waiting. Presently He will bring judgment and break into pieces forever the kingdoms of the earth (2:44).

Since God is so highly exalted, it follows that no sin of man is deadlier than pride. Because of his pride was the great Nebuchadnezzar driven to dwell among the beasts till he knew "that the Most High ruleth in the kingdom of men, and giveth it to whomsoever he will" (4:32). So at this final hour, when the thrones are being placed, the judgment set and the books opened, the crowning irony of the scene lies in the insolence of Antiochus, the "mouth speaking great things" (7:8ff).

Yet to the saints this majestic God is not terrible. He keeps covenant and lovingkindness with them that love Him and keep His commandments (9:4). He has been the God of their fathers in days gone by (2:23). Work though He may through angels, He is not distant from them, but His ear is quick to receive their prayers (2:18; 9:21). The machinery of intermediary angels causes but a little delay in His answer (9:23); and at times He even reveals secrets personally—through a dream (2:19). Though His people may fall into sin He does not give them up, but is ready to hear the intercession of Daniel. The confession of the saint, whose fasting, sackcloth and ashes vouch for his earnestness, moves God profoundly (9:3ff). For He loves Daniel greatly (9:23; 10:11), and however He may bring wrath upon them He is on the side of His saints.

It is indeed a chief lesson of the book that God never fails His own. Transcendent though He be, He provides angelic help for them in the time of need. He sends His angel to deliver His servants that trusted in Him and to walk with them in the midst of the burning fiery furnace (3:28); or again, to shut the mouths of the lions when Daniel was cast into their den (6:22). An angel reassures the terrified saint and explains to him the hidden divine counsel (9:21ff; 10:10ff; 12:5ff). One gets from the book a feeling that man is surrounded by an invisible society of beings who sustain him in peril and co-operate with his striving after the good. This goes some way towards compensating for the loss of God's nearness. The saint is not alone; he is in the midst of celestial friends.

The loving care of God makes itself evident in the way in which the saints get along in the present world. We have seen how Daniel and his associates prospered and outdistanced all competitors in the royal favour. Such success was indeed no occasion of pride, for all that distinguished the saints came from God. Yet it did give them a pleasant place in the sun.

And such earthly splendour is but an earnest of greater glory to come; for God will soon deliver over to the saints an everlasting dominion (7:14, 27). Those who remain true in the present trial need not fear death, for they shall awake from their sleep in the dust to everlasting life (12:2). And if they have been among the leaders who instruct others and sustain them in their faithfulness they shall receive pre-eminent honour (12:3).

So much indeed does God love the saints that He treats in friendly fashion even non-Jews who befriend them. An unmistakable cordiality pervades the narratives regarding Nebuchadnezzar and Darius. The former He vouchsafes to teach in rough but kindly fashion (4:1ff) and He wins the gratitude of the latter by preserving Daniel (6:25ff). Even towards the enemies of His people He displays forbearance (cf. 7:12) and when punishment falls upon them there is no disposition to gloat over it. In spite of the intensity of the conflict reflected in the book, it is singularly free from vindictiveness. The end of Antiochus is portrayed with a brevity which almost disappoints the reader (7:11; 11:45). Only once does the spirit of revenge flare up (6:24) and that but for a moment. Nor is it too much to say that through the book there runs an

implied universalism, which in one passage trembles on the verge
of utterance (7:13ff). The kingdom of the saints is not for the
saints alone but for all mankind. All peoples and nations and languages shall serve the "one like unto a son of man"; and his
dominion will not be like the dominion of the beast-powers which
preceded him—terrible, oppressive, brutal—but man-like and
humane, bringing to the world a peace which shall not pass away.

Such was our writer's idea of God. It had its serious limitations,
to be sure, for he wrote as a rigoristic Jew who believed that the
ceremonial side of the law was as important to God as the ethical,
and that Israel—or at least the saints of Israel—were dearer to
Him than all the rest of the world put together. But on the whole
it is a noble concept of the divine nature that meets us in this book
of bitter conflict, and one that was worthy to sustain the persecuted
in succeeding ages.

It is to this God that our writer looks and to no other help. The
brilliant resistance already being offered by the arms of the Maccabees does not divert his attention from God, the true source of
deliverance. Their military prowess is indeed helping the saints
with a little help, and he is grateful for that (11:34); but already
they are paying the price of success in that insincere men are joining their movement. And in any case it is not by the weapons of
man nor on this earthly scene that Israel's salvation is to be worked
out. For already history is drawing to its close and God is seated
on His judgment throne; why waste thought and hope on men?

The Writer's Contribution to Religion

Such was the effort of our writer—to interpret the present fiery
trial to his fellow-Jews, and inspire them to meet it bravely. How
well he succeeded we do not know. The fact that his book was
preserved indicates that it must have proved helpful.

There can be no doubt however of its influence on succeeding
ages. The figure of the "one like unto a son of man" evidently
seized upon the imagination of apocalyptic thinkers, for we find it
reappearing in the Similitudes of Enoch written perhaps a century
later. Here the Son of man has become a person, a heavenly
being, the Elect One of God, who seated on the throne of his glory
will judge mankind (Enoch 45, 46, 62, etc.). Somewhere about
80 A.D. the Jewish writer of Second Esdras again employed the
figure to portray the Son of the Most High who should blast the
wicked and deliver the saints (2 Esdras 13).

But it is the adoption of the title "Son of man" by our Lord that most interests us. He had evidently pondered deeply upon its use in the Book of Enoch and when he called himself thus he seems to have identified himself with the heavenly Man whom God had chosen to judge and rule mankind forever. This significance he read back into the Daniel passage, which became for him the key to the mystery of his person, just as the Servant Songs of Second Isaiah revealed the philosophy of his death. In his great confession before the high priest he blended the words of Daniel with his own: "Ye shall see the Son of man sitting at the right hand of power, and coming with the clouds of heaven (Mk. 14:62).

Along with the Son of man passage Jesus seems to have applied the whole book to his own time. The "abomination of desolation" standing where it ought not (Mk. 13:14) was for him not the heathen altar erected by Antiochus upon the altar of the Lord (Dan. 9:27; 11:31; 12:11), but some nameless horror presently to appear. The "tribulation such as there hath not been the like from the beginning of the creation" (Mk. 13:19) had not spent itself in the final struggle with the "contemptible person" of 167 B.C. (Dan. 11:21; 12:1), but was even now lowering like a storm upon the horizon. For our Lord shared with the writer of Daniel the conviction that he was standing at the end of history: he too saw upon the wall of time the handwriting of eternity.

Certainly there was no other book in the Jewish Bible that in this respect so met his apocalyptic mood. The ancient prophets had spoken of a coming day of the Lord when God would intervene to punish, to save and to renew. But where else than in Daniel could he find the whole sweep of history so envisaged, empire succeeding empire in its mad pride, only to fall before the strokes of the divine doom which now approaches its consummation? Where else so clear a looking through the final break-up of the world to the resurrection of the faithful and the coming of the eternal kingdom of God?

And just here perhaps lies the value of the writer of Daniel for modern Christians. In many things we have left him far behind. But amidst the antique and often grotesque imagery of his book we catch sight of something that does not pass—something without which religion cannot live. It is the "scenery of eternity." Imposing indeed are the colossal states of our own day; resistless seems their power. The world is given into their hand. Yet here we see beyond them; we behold the four winds of heaven breaking forth upon the great sea—the sea from whence they came: thrones are placed, and one like unto a Son of man takes his seat by the Ancient of Days. And then we know that after all these states are but a passing thing in the presence of our Lord; that the forces of the world, which often seem to be carrying all before them, cannot prevail. For he will have the last word.

> "So be it, Lord; thy throne shall never,
> Like earth's proud empires, pass away:
> Thy kingdom stands and grows forever,
> Till all thy creatures own thy sway."

A CONCLUDING WORD

As the writer reviews this study of Israel's leaders three things stand out in his mind. One is, that the religion of Israel, on which so much depended for mankind, was itself dependent on a succession of leaders extending over a thousand years. It was because these leaders somehow came as they were needed and added in each case just the impulse that was required to carry on and develop this religion that it continued its course. Their coming was no chance; it was the plan of God. The second is, that the progress of Israel's religion was always contrary to human probability. Perhaps at no moment in those thousand years would an unprejudiced onlooker have expected it to amount to much in history. The future actually before it was always unbelievably greater than its present. Again and again, especially in the forlorn beginnings after the exile, one might have concluded that it had spent its force. But new force kept coming into it, largely mediated through new leaders. This too was of God.

Yet—and here is the third thing—these leaders did not work in a vacuum. At the outset our study of Moses reminded us that they could have done nothing apart from those they led—the people—the mass of men and women who followed. Among these were indeed too many who dragged the leaders back by their sheer inertia, some even who opposed them; and at times disaffection seized upon all, even the best. But for the most part enough honest and convinced followers existed to carry with them the whole people. It was these who gave the pattern of the leaders concrete embodiment and a society in which it found expression. Their names are lost to us, but we should never forget them. More even than the leaders they built of the people a *church*. In that church the religion of the Old Testament lived; out of it came the leaders and in it they did their work. By it the very remembrance of the leaders was handed down to posterity.

This Old Testament church has always been regarded by the Christian church as its precursor, and Christians have liked to think that the saints of the Old Covenant belong to them also, as well as to Israel after the flesh. The festival of All Saints includes them,

575

just as their nameless followers find a place in the festival of All Souls. Both together constitute no insignificant part of the great cloud of witnesses with which we are compassed about as we run the race that is set before us.

All this has a lesson for our time. Unless God has changed He will continue to provide the necessary leaders for mankind. And as long as there come leaders who recall men to the ideal—that is, to the purpose of God—so long humanity will go on towards that ideal. The "seven thousand" to follow will not be lacking. No hour of history, however dark, should blot out confidence in God's purpose for men. In Israel's experience those were right who like Jeremiah and Ezekiel met the No of the present with the everlasting Yea. Ours is a time of disillusionment, when many who have given up belief in God and in man have exchanged the modern idea of "progress" for a cynical despair. To the believer such an attitude, viewed in the light of Israel's history, seems unrealistic. "Progress," meaning an automatic increase of human welfare apart from God, is indeed a myth. But the true alternative is not despair; it is hope in the living God.

CHRONOLOGY

(The dates indicate the period of activity)

Moses,	13th century B.C.(?)	
Joshua,	Late 13th century B.C.(?)	
Deborah,	c. 1150 B.C.	
Gideon,	After 1150 B.C.	
Samuel,	c. 1050 B.C.	
Saul,	1036(?)–1016 B.C.	
David,	1016–976 B.C.	
Solomon,	976–936 B.C.	First temple completed, 966 B.C.
		Israel divided into two kingdoms, 936 B.C.
		Assyria becomes active in the west, c. 850 B.C.
Elijah,	c. 850 B.C.	
Elisha,	After 850 B.C.	
The Yahwist,	c. 850 B.C.	
The Writing Prophets,	c. 760–c. 500 B.C.	
Amos,	c. 760 B.C.	
Hosea,	After 745 B.C.	
Isaiah,	740–c. 700 B.C.	Fall of Samaria, 721 B.C.
Micah,	c. 730 B.C.	
The Deuteronomists,	c. 700–c. 500 B.C.	Law-book found in the temple, 621 B.C.
Jeremiah,	626–c. 585 B.C.	Chaldeans succeed to world-empire, 605 B.C.
Ezekiel,	592–570 B.C.	Fall of Jerusalem, destruction of temple, 586 B.C.
		Beginning of the exile
Second Isaiah,	c. 540 B.C.	Persians succeed to world-empire, c. 540 B.C.

Haggai and Zechariah,	520 B.C.	Second temple completed, 516 B.C.
Malachi,	c. 500 B.C.	
The Priestly Writers,	c. 500–c. 400 B.C.	
Nehemiah,	445–c. 432 B.C.	
Ezra	397 B.C.(?)	
The Chronicler	c. 350 B.C.(?)	Greeks succeed to world-empire, 331 B.C.
The Wise Men of Proverbs,	Mainly after 586 B.C.	
The Writer of Job,	c. 400 B.C.(?)	
Qoheleth, the Preacher,	c. 250 B.C.	
The Writer of the Book of Daniel,	166–165 B.C.	Maccabean revolt, 167 B.C.

A BRIEF SUMMARY OF SOME RECENT VIEWS AS TO THE DATE AND MANNER
OF THE CONQUEST OF CANAAN

See Footnote 10 on page 47.

Kittel (*GVI*[5.6], I, p. 439f, 1923). Before Joshua, for several centuries, a number of tribes and clans which by blood and a common past stood close to those coming out of Egypt under Moses, had found a nest in the land—partly by the sword, partly by treaty. These immigrants formed the *bulk of the non-Canaanitish population*. Then, under Moses, a union of clans had been created which penetrated into Canaan in two divisions: 1) Judah and Simeon, with parts of Levi, pressed into the south. 2) Separated from these, but united with them by the Moses-league, the house of Joseph under Joshua established itself on mount Ephraim. The attitude of the earlier immigrants to these Israelitish new-comers varied. The more the former had come into friendly relations with the Canaanites, the more they would stand off from the Israelites. On the other hand, the more others such as Asher, Zebulon, Naphtali, Issachar, Dan and Gad, had retained their old individuality, the more friendly they would be to the Israelites. More and more they may have joined the confederacy of the tribes allied under Moses and of the Joshua-league. It is an appealing supposition that in *Shechem* the brotherhood was from time to time sealed anew, and that here their allegiance to Yahweh and His ordinances was again confirmed.

Sellin (*GIJV*, 1923, I, p. 96). There were two invasions of Canaan: 1) An older immigration of the Habiru (or the first Israelitish clans) in the region of Adam, aiming at Shechem, in whose vicinity lay a Gilgal sanctuary, and eventually capturing Jericho. This invasion has been amalgamated in the present Book of Joshua with: 2) Joshua crossed the Jordan opposite Jericho in the vicinity of the later Judahite Gilgal, defeated the men of Jericho in a battle, captured Ai and Bethel, made a league with the Gibeonites, won a victory over the confederated kings of the south and successfully established the "house of Joseph" (i.e. Joshua's followers) in mount Ephraim. Joshua of course found in Canaan the Israelitish clans that had previously come in. Shechem was in their possession. These clans did not worship Yahweh, for He had been revealed only to the Israelites who had come out of Egypt with Moses and were at present under Joshua's leadership. Joshua now made use of a festal assembly of *all* the clans at Shechem (where the clans of Israel had probably been previously holding their confederate assemblies) to win the pre-Joshua clans to the worship of Yahweh. These for the first time entered into the Yahweh covenant. Thus Joshua, and not Moses, was the real founder of the national cultic Yahweh religion.

Lods (*Israel*, 1930, translation 1932, p. 331ff). While the ancient narrative no doubt gives a picture of the settlement of the nomad Hebrews in Canaan that is accurate in its main outline, the actual advance was more diversified, irregular and unorganized than the Biblical sources portray it. One section of invaders entered from the east, fording the Jordan at either Jericho or Adam. The southern group however probably came in from the south (Judah, Simeon, Kenites, Kenizzites (Caleb) and Jerahmeelites), being stopped by the line of Canaanitish strongholds running west from Jerusalem. Within Canaan itself there were migrations, and the territory of the several tribes was apt to change. Hebrew tribes also entered Canaan peacefully, making leagues with the residents. In the end Hebrews and Canaanites merged into one another. (Lods apparently says nothing of any union of the invaders with Hebrews already resident in the country.) Joshua, "if he is an historical personage," was merely the chief of the house of Joseph.

Garstang (*JJ*, 1931) seems to picture only one general invasion, in the time of Joshua (whom he places about 1400 B.C.), lasting into the Amarna age and taking in the encroachments of the Habiru mentioned in the Amarna letters. (This date was also advocated by J. W. Jack in 1936: *PCB Supplement*, p. 7.)

T. H. Robinson (*HI*, I, 1932, p. 77ff) had come independently to a chronology similar to that of Garstang. Rather tentatively he dates the exodus in the early part of the fifteenth century (p. 80), and the invasion later in the same century. He seems inclined to identify the Israelite invaders with the Habiru of the Amarna letters, but takes no decided stand on the question. Following the earlier Bible sources as reliable in their main outlines he holds (p. 118ff) that there were three invasions of Canaan: 1) Judah, Simeon, and some of the Kenites, acting quite independently, pressed in from the south. With this attack Joshua had nothing to do. 2) The second wave of invasion was led by Joshua and consisted chiefly by the Joseph tribes. 3) There was finally a third wave which after Joshua's day entered by one of the fords north of the Sea of Galilee and seized with some amount of success the northern hill-country. By the end of the thirteenth century Palestine was occupied but not yet conquered. The three sections of Israelites, though loosely connected, were bound together by traditions of a common descent and a common worship, as is shown by the song of Deborah. "Whatever Moses had done or had not done at Sinai, he had given to all the tribes a common God, valid for themselves and for all who should unite with them in after days, and it was this devotion to a single deity, which, above all else, made Israel a nation." [1]

---

[1] Quoted by permission of The Clarendon Press.

Olmstead (*HPS*, 1931, p. 197ff) identifies the Biblical Joshua with the Joshua (Iashuia) mentioned in an Amarna letter along with two other men bearing Hebrew names, Job, king of Pella, and Benjamin. He was then east of the Jordan. He later crossed the Jordan and invaded Palestine, the steps of his conquest being recorded in the "epic" preserved in the Biblical sources. Jericho was captured, Ai taken, an alliance concluded with a Gibeonite confederacy, the kings of the southern counteralliance were defeated, Luz (Bethel) was captured, perhaps Shechem. "Joshua was the hero of the tribe of Ephraim, which took its name from the wild bull it had worshipped in the desert, and thus found little difficulty in accepting the Canaanite bull-cults at Bethel and the neighbouring shrines." It was not till later that the religion of Yahweh was brought into northern Israel from the south. Yahweh was the God of Judah, who had been accepted by the Simeonites, and by the Levites, who became his priests (p. 270).

Meek (*HO*, 1936, p. 24f) gives a similar reconstruction. The Hebrew invaders came down from the north, took territory east of the Jordan about 1400 B.C., captured Jericho not much later, then gradually occupied the highlands of Ephraim, seizing Bethel about 1300 B.C. or a little later, and thence pressing down to the edge of the coastal plain. They were a mixed group, perhaps mainly Aramean (cf. Deut. 26:5). In course of time Joshua formed some of these loosely organized tribes (at first probably only the Joseph tribes) into a confederacy. This took place at Shechem (cf. Josh. 24), where a covenant was entered into and a simple code of laws put forth. Here was the beginning of the "Israel" of later days. The tribes of the far north, Asher, Dan, Naphtali, Issachar and Zebulon, all being more native than Hebrew, were not drawn into the Hebrew confederacy until a common peril arose, beginning about the time of Deborah. Joshua's conquests completed the invasion of the Hebrews of which the Amarna tablets reflect the beginning. Meek sees no ground for identifying the Amarna Joshua with the Joshua of the Bible, since the Canaanitish kings mentioned in the two instances are different.

Most of the Hebrew hordes, however, found it impossible (p. 28) to enter Canaan, so they went around to the Negeb (the south), mingling there with a number of pastoral groups such as the Calebites, Jerahmeelites and others. Some of the tribe of Levi entered Egypt by permission and were later oppressed there by Ramses II. Many of these made their way out under Moses about 1200 B.C. and rejoined their kinsfolk in the Negeb (p. 33f). When the grazing lands of the Negeb no longer sufficed for all, Moses led out a group which he organized into a confederacy, making Yahweh, the old tribal God of Judah, the God of the league, bringing the people into covenant with Him and collecting laws to govern them. This confederacy gradually pushed northwards and finally dominated all of Canaan south of Jerusalem. This was early in the twelfth century. Judah then proceeded (p. 108) to extend its Yahweh cult northwards into the earlier Joshua confederacy, until in David's age it had won the north and Yahweh became the national God of united Israel.

Vincent (so far as the present writer knows) gives no explicit statement of his views regarding the conquest, but it can be inferred from two of his articles in the *Revue Biblique* (XLIV, 4, Oct. 1935, p. 602: XLVI, 2, April 1937, p. 262f) that he adheres to the substantial historicity of the *JE* account in Joshua. Jericho's fall he places at ± 1250 B.C. The ancient ruin of Ai (see p. 52, n. 1) was next taken, and the entrance into the hill-country thus obtained was followed by the league with the Gibeonites, the victory over the five kings, etc.

Albright (*BASOR,* No. 58, April 1935, p. 14ff), on the basis of recent archaeological data, concludes that there were two invasions: 1) That of the House of Joseph, whom he identifies with Habiru of the Amarna letters and the Shasu of the inscriptions of Sethos I, took Jericho (± 1360–± 1320 B.C.) [2] and later Bethel-Ai (± 1300–± 1250 B.C.). He also mentions "more remotely related Hebrew groups such as those which were later called 'sons of the concubines'," who (he implies) likewise found a foothold in the land. 2) That of the tribal group which followed Moses. Leaving Egypt about 1290 B.C. they conquered Sihon's territory before 1250. They then presumably united in a confederacy with kindred Hebrew groups such as the House of Joseph and the "sons of the concubines," the confederacy being called "Israel," and under the leadership of Joshua first subdued the Gibeonite tetrapolis, then defeated the Canaanite city-states of the Shephelah of Judah, and afterwards—"if we accept the tradition in Joshua"—a group of Canaanite city-states in Galilee. Lachish, in the south, was taken by the Israelites about 1231 B.C. or somewhat later (*BASOR,* No. 68, December 1937, p. 24). Joshua's campaigns he dates between ± 1235 and ± 1200 (No. 56, p. 18). Megiddo, on the southern edge of the plain of Esdraelon, was destroyed by the Israelites shortly after 1150 (No. 68, p. 25). Joshua's confederacy was established in western Palestine before Menephthes (Merneptah) boasted on his stele of having "desolated" and exterminated Israel there in 1231 (Barton, *AB*[7], p. 376).

Albright also points out that the excavations at Bethel (No. 56, p. 11) show a sharp break in culture following the destruction of the city in the thirteenth century. The culture that succeeded was much poorer, as evidenced by the masonry, building-plans and pottery (p. 9). This inferior pottery, which can now definitely be identified as Israelitish, is found also at Shechem, Shiloh, Ai, Gibeah, Beth-zur and Megiddo (No. 68, p. 25).

It can thus be seen that in spite of very definite new data furnished by archaeology, and the improvement in historical method introduced by Alt (cf. Albright, *BASOR,* No. 58, p. 14) in 1925, the situation which

---

[2] These datings have now been extended by Albright to 1375-1300 B.C. (*BASOR,* No. 74, April, 1939, p. 20).

was described by Alt in his memorable monograph of that year still to a real extent prevails: "In the same proportion in which the completeness of (each scholar's) picture (of the conquest) increases, its reliability decreases. In almost every new portrayal the hypothetical connecting lines are drawn in still a different fashion, and the general ways of looking at it come out in correspondingly varied form." (*Die Landnahme der Israeliten in Palästina*, Leipzig, 1925, p. 1.)

"These problems are very elusive!" declares Albright.[3] "I suspect that when the truth is known (if ever), we shall find that all our reconstructions diverge farther from historical fact than does the Israelite tradition itself, though some alteration through tradition and compilation *must* be assumed."

It is pleasant to place such a high testimony to the value of the Bible tradition over against the extreme view of Noth (not included in the summary above) that this tradition is almost completely unreliable (cf. Albright's criticism of Noth's methods in *BASOR*, No. 74, p. 12ff).

[3] In a letter dated March 20, 1939.

THE HALE LECTURES

The Rt. Rev. Charles Reuben Hale, D.D., LL.D., Bishop of Cairo, Bishop Coadjutor of Springfield, was born in 1837, consecrated Bishop on July 26, 1892, and died on Christmas Day in the year 1900.

In his will he bequeathed to Western Theological Seminary, now Seabury-Western Theological Seminary of Evanston, Illinois, a fund to be held in trust "for the general purpose of promoting the Catholic Faith, in its purity and integrity, as taught in Holy Scripture, held by the Primitive Church, summed up in the Creeds, and affirmed by the undisputed General Councils, and, in particular, to be used only and exclusively for . . . the establishment, endowment, printing, and due circulation of a yearly Sermon . . . and . . . of Courses of Lectures."

The subjects of these Lectures were to be:

(*a*) Liturgies and Liturgics.
(*b*) Church Hymns and Church Music.
(*c*) The History of the Eastern Churches.
(*d*) The History of National Churches.
(*e*) Contemporaneous Church History: i.e. treating of events happening since the beginning of what is called "The Oxford Movement," in 1833.

The Trustees of the Seminary accepted the generous bequest of Bishop Hale and have endeavoured faithfully to carry out its provisions. A full list of the Hale Lectures thus far delivered and published appears at the front of the present volume.

BIBLIOGRAPHY

What follows is not a bibliography for the whole Old Testament field, but one limited to the scope of the present study of the personalities of Israel. It is designed to suggest books in English for the clergy and others who would like to read further along this line. It makes no claim to be exhaustive, but aims rather at selection from a larger number of good books. A few outstanding books in German have been added, but those who desire to read more extensively in German are referred to the excellent selection of German works up to 1933 in the bibliography of Professor Bewer's *The Literature of the Old Testament*. In general his much more comprehensive bibliography may be used with profit as a supplement to the present list. It is specially valuable for its comments upon the books listed.

The present bibliography also contains comments on a few books. The absence of comment, however, in no way implies that a book is less valuable. An asterisk indicates books of great usefulness, which are recommended to those who may wish to acquire a small working library on the personalities of the Old Testament.

The classifications employed here are not mutually exclusive, and books listed under one title may contain material belonging to another. The titles History, Religion, Culture, Origins are specially prone to overlap.

BIBLIOGRAPHICAL AND OTHER ABBREVIATIONS

These apply to footnotes throughout the book as well as to the Bibliography.

Note: A small figure placed after the title of a book (e.g. EAT^7) signifies the number of the edition.

AB	*Archaeology and the Bible.* G. A. Barton.
ABC	*The Abingdon Bible Commentary.* Eiselen, Lewis, Downey, Editors.
AHL	*Die Althebräische Literatur und ihr hellenistisch-jüdisches Nachleben.* J. Hempel.
APB	*The Archaeology of Palestine and the Bible.* W. F. Albright.
ASOR	The American Schools of Oriental Research.
AT	*Einführung in das Alte Testament.* J. Meinhold.
BA	*Biblical Archaeology.*
BASOR	*Bulletin of the American Schools of Oriental Research.*

BHS	*The Bible for Home and School.*
BTP	*The Book of the Twelve Prophets.* G. A. Smith.
c.	about.
CB	*The Cambridge Bible for Schools and Colleges.*
Cent. B.	*The New-Century Bible.*
cf.	compare.
Ch.	Chapter.
Clar. B.	*The Clarendon Bible.*
EAT	*Einleitung in das Alte Testament.* O. Eissfeldt.
EAT	*Einleitung in das Alte Testament.* E. Sellin.
Ecclus	Ecclesiasticus.
e.g.	for example.
f, ff	and following (singular, f, plural, ff).
GIJR	*Geschichte der israelitischen und jüdischen Religion.* G. Hölscher.
GIJV	*Geschichte des israelitischen und jüdischen Volkes.* E. Sellin.
GMAT	*Gott und Mensch im Alten Testament.* J. Hempel.
GMMI	*Great Men and Movements in Israel.* R. Kittel.
GVI	*Geschichte des Volkes Israel.* R. Kittel.
HAT	*Handbuch zum Alten Testament.* O. Eissfeldt, Editor.
HDB	*Hastings' Dictionary of the Bible.* Scribner.
HH	*History of the Hebrews.* R. Kittel.
HI	*History of Israel.* Oesterley and Robinson.
HKAT	*Handkommentar zum Alten Testament.* W. Nowack, Editor.
HO	*Hebrew Origins.* T. J. Meek.
HPS	*History of Palestine and Syria.* A. T. Olmstead.
HR	*Hebrew Religion: Its Origin and Development.* Oesterley and Robinson.
HS	*Haverford Symposium on Archaeology and the Bible.* E. Grant, Editor.
HSAT	*Die Heilige Schrift des Alten Testaments.* Kautzsch and Bertholet, Editors.
ibid.	in the same passage, or book.
IBOT	*An Introduction to the Books of the Old Testament.* Oesterley and Robinson.
ICC	*International Critical Commentary.*
i.e.	that is.
ILOT	*Introduction to the Literature of the Old Testament.* S. R. Driver.
IOT	*Introduction to the Old Testament.* E. Sellin.
JBL	*Journal of Biblical Literature.* E. R. Goodenough, Editor.
JJ	*Joshua and Judges.* J. Garstang.
JPOS	*Journal of the Palestinian Oriental Society.*
KAT	*Kommentar zum Alten Testament.* E. Sellin, Editor.

KHAT	*Kurtzer Hand-Commentar zum Alten Testament.* K. Marti, Editor.
LOT	*The Literature of the Old Testament.* J. A. Bewer.
LXX	The Septuagint, or Greek translation of the Old Testament.
NCHS	*A New Commentary on Holy Scripture.* Gore, Goudge, Guillame, Editors.
OTR	*Old Testament Religion, in the Light of Its Canaanite Background.* E. A. Leslie.
passim	here and there
PCB	*Peake's Commentary on the Bible.* A. S. Peake, Editor.
PEJ	*Post-Exilic Judaism.* A. C. Welch.
PRJ	*The Prophets and the Rise of Judaism.* A. Lods.
RB	*Revue Biblique.*
RDBL	"Recent Discoveries in Bible Lands." W. F. Albright. In *Young's Analytical Concordance.*
SAT	*Die Schriften des Alten Testaments.* Gressmann, etc., Editors.
SCM	Student Christian Movement.
SPCK	Society for the Promotion of Christian Knowledge.
TAT	*Theologie des Alten Testaments.* W. Eichrodt.
WC	*Westminster Commentary.*
Wisd.	Wisdom of Solomon.
ZATW	*Zeitschrift für die Alttestamentlichen Wissenschaft.* J. Hempel, Editor.
ZDMG	*Zeitschrift der deutschen Morgenländischen Gesellschaft.*

THE OLD TESTAMENT STORY

Bowie, W. R., *The Story of the Bible.* Abingdon, 1934.

TRANSLATIONS OF THE OLD TESTAMENT

American Revised Version: Standard Edition. International Council of Religious Education, Chicago, 1901. (A new edition is in preparation.)

Smith and Goodspeed, *The Bible: an American Translation.* Univ. Chicago Press, 1935.

The Holy Scriptures According to the Massoretic Text. Jewish Publication Society, 1917.

Kent, C. F., *The Student's Old Testament.* See under Literature.

Moffatt, J., *The Old Testament,* 2 vols. Doran, 1924.

THE STUDY OF THE OLD TESTAMENT, PARTICULARLY OLD TESTAMENT CRITICISM

Barton, G. A., "The Present State of Old Testament Studies," *Haverford Symposium* (*HS,* see under Archaeology), pp. 47-78.

Colwell, E. C., *The Study of the Bible.* Univ. Chicago Press, 1938. Describes the field and method of Bible study.

Cook, S. A., *The Old Testament. A Reinterpretation.* Macmillan, 1936.

Fosdick, H. E., *The Modern Use of the Bible.* Macmillan, 1932. May be regarded as an introduction to *A Guide to the Understanding of the Bible* (see under Theology of the Old Testament).

Gunkel, H., *What Remains of the Old Testament.* Macmillan, 1928.

Peake, A. S., Ed., *The People and the Book.* Clarendon Press, 1925. A collection of essays by British scholars.

Robinson, T. H., "The Methods of Higher Criticism," in *The People and the Book.*

INTRODUCTION TO THE OLD TESTAMENT

Driver, S. R., *An Introduction to the Literature of the Old Testament* (*ILOT*). 9th edition, Scribner, 1913. A classic. Though out of date in its critical data and opinions, it is permanently valuable for its appreciation of the literature.

Eissfeldt, O., *Einleitung in das Alte Testament* (*EAT*). Tübingen, 1934. Comprehensive, judicious, clear, a monument of scholarship.

*Oesterley and Robinson, *Introduction to the Books of the Old Testament* (*IBOT*). Macmillan, 1934. The best recent Introduction in English. An excellent complement to Driver.

Robinson, H. W., *The Old Testament: its Making and Meaning.* Cokesbury Press, 1937. A brief, popular book by a competent scholar.

Sellin, E., *Introduction to the Old Testament* (*IOT*). Doran, 1923. By a brilliant but sometimes eccentric German scholar. It needs to be supplemented by the 7th German edition, Leipzig, 1935.

LITERATURE OF THE OLD TESTAMENT

*Bewer, J. A., *The Literature of the Old Testament* (*LOT²*). Columbia Univ. Press, 1933. Not exactly an Introduction, since it treats the literature in the order of its growth, with comment and full citations, bringing in critical and historical questions as subsidiary. Written with deep aesthetic and religious appreciation. Perhaps the best single book on the Old Testament.

Dinsmore, C. A., *The English Bible as Literature.* Houghton Mifflin, 1931. Excellent.

Eiselen, F. C., *The Books of the Pentateuch: their Origin, Contents and Significance.* Methodist Book Concern, 1916.

The Prophetic Books of the Old Testament: their Origin, Contents and Significance, 2 vols. Abingdon, 1923.

The Psalms and Other Sacred Writings. Methodist Book Concern, 1918.

Fowler, H. F., *A History of the Literature of Ancient Israel from the Earliest Times to 135 B.C.* Macmillan, 1912.

Gordon, A. R., *The Poets of the Old Testament*. Hodder & Stoughton, 1912.

The Prophets of the Old Testament, Doran, 1916.

Kent, C. F., *The Growth and Contents of the Old Testament*. Scribner, 1925.

Macdonald, D. B., *The Hebrew Literary Genius, an Interpretation: being an Introduction to the reading of the Old Testament*. Princeton Univ. Press, 1933.

Moore, G. F., *The Literature of the Old Testament*. Holt, 1913.

Oesterley, W. O. E., *Ancient Hebrew Poems; metrically translated, with Introductions and Notes*. Macmillan, 1938. Has an excellent brief introduction on the nature of Hebrew poetry.

HISTORIES OF ISRAEL

Bailey and Kent, *History of the Hebrew Commonwealth*. Illustrated. Revised edition, Scribner, 1935. Elementary but useful.

Baron, S. M., *A Social and Religious History of the Jews,* 3 vols. (Biblical history in Vol. I.) Columbia Univ. Press, 1937.

Barton, G. A., *A History of the Hebrew People*. Century, 1930.

Baynes, N. H., *Israel amongst the Nations*. 2d edition, S.C.M., 1928.

Blunt, A. W. F., *Israel in World-History*. Illustrated. Oxford Univ. Press, 1927.

Cornill, C. H., *History of the People of Israel*. Open Court, Chicago, 1917.

Foakes Jackson, F. J., *The Biblical History of the Hebrews*. Heffer, 1921.

Kent, C. F., *The Historical Bible,* 4 vols. (3 by Kent). Scribner, 1908-1911. Tells the story in words of the Bible, interspersed with excellent comment.

A History of the Hebrew People, 2 vols.

A History of the Jewish People.

Kittel, R., *History of the Hebrews* (*HH*) (to the Exile), 2 vols. Williams & Norgate, 1895-6. Old but valuable. By the outstanding German historian of ancient Israel (who died recently). It needs to be supplemented by the 7th German edition, last revision (*GVI*), Stuttgart, 1932; and also by Vol. III, containing Israel's post-exilic history, Stuttgart, 1927 and 1929.

Knopf, C. S., *The Old Testament Speaks*. Illustrated. Nelson, 1933. Good. Contains profuse suggestions for further study.

Lods, A., *Israel, from its Beginnings to the Middle of the Eighth Century*. Illustrated. Knopf, 1932. An encyclopaedic work by a learned French scholar.

The Prophets and the Rise of Judaism (*PRJ*), Dutton, 1937. Equally good.

*Oesterley and Robinson, *A History of Israel* (*HI*), 2 vols. Clarendon Press, 1932.

Vol. I. *From the Exodus to the Fall of Jerusalem, 586 B.C.* By T. H. Robinson.

Vol. II. *From the Fall of Jerusalem, 586 B.C. to the Bar-Kokhba Revolt, A.D. 135.* By W. O. E. Oesterley. A standard work by two leading British scholars. Judicious, full, readable.

Olmstead, A. T., *History of Palestine and Syria (HPS).* Illustrated: Scribner, 1931. Especially valuable for the light it throws upon Israel's culture and international environment.

Sellin, E., *Geschichte des israelitischen-jüdischen Volkes (GIJV),* 2 vols. Leipzig, 1924 and 1932.

Smith, H. P., *Old Testament History.* Scribner, 1903. Still valuable.

Wade, G. W., *Old Testament History.* 12th edition, Methuen, 1934.

Wardle, W. L., *The History and Religion of Israel.* Clarendon Press (*Clar. B.*), 1936.

HEBREW ORIGINS

Barton, G. A., *Semitic and Hamitic Origins, Social and Religious.* Univ. Penna. Press, 1934.

Duncan, J. G., *New Light on Hebrew Origins.* S.P.C.K., 1936.

Meek, T. J., *Hebrew Origins (HO).* Harper, 1936. Presents challenging views.

ARCHAEOLOGY AND THE OLD TESTAMENT

Albright, W. F., *The Archaeology of Palestine and the Bible (APB).* 2d edition, Revell, 1935 (out of print).

"Recent Discoveries in Bible Lands" (*RDBL*). *Young's Analytical Concordance,* Funk & Wagnalls, 1936. A recent survey at some length of the field of Biblical archaeology by a recognized authority.

"The Present State of Syro-Palestinian Archaeology." *Haverford Symposium,* pp. 1–46. Briefer than the above, but more recent.

*Barton, G. A., *Archaeology and the Bible (AB).* 7th edition, American S.S. Union, 1937. Contains a wealth of archaeological material throwing light on various parts of the Bible. Profusely illustrated.

The Biblical Archaeologist. Edited by C. E. Wright, under the direction of the Board of Editors of the *Bulletin.* Quarterly. Same address. Illustrated. More popular than the *Bulletin.*

Bulletin of the American Schools of Oriental Research (BASOR). Edited by W. F. Albright. Published quarterly by the Schools, 409 Prospect St., New Haven, Conn. Illustrated. Aims to keep the reader abreast of the outstanding results of Biblical archaeological research.

Grant, E., Ed., *The Haverford Symposium on Archaeology and the Bible (HS).* ASOR, New Haven, 1938. A series of papers covering the results to date in the various fields of Biblical archaeology,

with surveys of the present state of OT and NT criticism. By nine
American scholars.
See also Olmstead, *HPS;* Lods, *Israel;* Cook, S. A., *The Religion of
Ancient Palestine in the Light of Archaeology,* British Academy,
London, 1930; and the books on Israel's culture.

CULTURE OF ISRAEL

Bertholet, A., *A History of Hebrew Civilization.* Harrap, 1926. A stand-
ard book.
Cook, S. A., "The Religious Environment of Israel," in *The People and
the Book.*
Graham and May, *Culture and Conscience. An Archaeological Study of
the New Religious Past in Ancient Palestine.* Univ. Chicago Press,
1936. Excellent.
Harris, C. W., *The Hebrew Heritage. A Study of Israel's Cultural and
Spiritual Origins.* Abingdon, 1935.
Montgomery, J. A., *Arabia and the Bible.* Univ. Penna. Press, 1934.
Very good.
Pedersen, J., *Israel: its Life and Culture.* Oxford Univ. Press, 1926. The
work of a richly stored, original and luminous mind.

See also treatments of the archaeological background in books on
Israel's history, origins and religion, especially Lods, *Israel,* Meek, *HO,*
Leslie, *OTR,* and Olmstead, *HPS.*

GEOGRAPHY

Smith, G. A., *Historical Atlas of the Holy Land.* 2d edition (contains
few changes). Hodder & Stoughton, 1936.
  The Historical Geography of the Holy Land. 26th edition, brought
up to 1931. Harper, 1931. Delightful and illuminating.
The National Geographic Society's Map: "Bible Lands and the Cradle
of Western Civilization," 25 x 53 inches. With Index. 1939.

RELIGION OF ISRAEL

Barton, G. A., *The Religion of Israel.* 2d edition. Univ. Penna. Press,
1928.
Budde, K., *The Religion of Israel to the Exile.* Putnam, 1899. A standard work.
Burrows, M., *Bible Religion: its Growth in the Scriptures.* Abingdon,
1938. Very brief, but good.
Cheyne, T. K., *Jewish Religious Life after the Exile.* Putnam, 1898.
Hempel, J., *Gott und Mensch im Alten Testament (GMAT).* 2d edition, Stuttgart, 1936.

James, Grant, Easton, Hedrick, *The Beginnings of Our Religion*. Macmillan, 1935. The OT portion gives a briefer treatment by the present author.

Kautzsch, E., "The Religion of Israel." *Hastings' Dictionary of the Bible*, Scribner, 1904. Methodical, exhaustive, still useful.

Kittel, R., *The Religion of the People of Israel.*. Macmillan, 1925.

Leslie, E. A., *The Old Testament Religion in the Light of its Canaanite Background*. Abingdon, 1936. Excellent.

Löhr, M., *A History of Religion in the Old Testament*. London, Nicholson & Watson, 1936. New York, Scribner.

*Oesterley and Robinson, *Hebrew Religion; its Origin and Development*. 2d edition. Macmillan, 1937.

Pace, E., *Ideas of God in Israel; their Content and Development*. Allen & Unwin, 1924.

Peters, J. M. P., *The Religion of the Hebrews*. Harvard Univ. Press, 1923 (copyright, 1914).

Smith, H. P., *The Religion of Israel*. Scribner, 1925 (copyright, 1914).

Smith, W. R., *Lectures on the Religion of the Semites*. 3d edition, with introduction and additional notes by S. A. Cook. Macmillan, 1927.

Histories of Israel often contain sections treating of the religion of the various periods.

THEOLOGY OF THE OLD TESTAMENT, ETC.

Cadbury, H. J., *National Ideals in the Old Testament*. Scribner, 1920.

Davidson, A. B., *Old Testament Theology*. Scribner, 1904. By a profound scholar of the past generation, comprehensive, clear, readable and deeply religious. A book that has not grown old.

Fosdick, H. E., *A Guide to Understanding the Bible. The Development of Ideas within the Old and New Testaments*. Harper, 1938.

Knudson, A. C., *The Religious Teaching of the Old Testament*. Abingdon, 1918.

Robinson, H. W., *The Religious Ideas of the Old Testament*. Scribner, 1927.

COMMENTARIES, ETC., ON THE WHOLE OLD TESTAMENT

Czarnomska, E., *The Authentic Literature of Israel*, 2 vols. Macmillan, 1924.

The Clarendon Bible (*Clar. B.*), edited by the Bishop of Oxford, Bishop Wild and Canon Box. Clarendon Press, Oxford.

Vol. I. Wardle, W. L., *The History and Religion of Israel*, 1936.

Vol. II. Binns, L. E., *From Moses to Elisha*, 1929.

Vol. III. Robinson, T. H., *The Decline and Fall of the Hebrew Kingdoms*, 1926.

Vol. IV. Lofthouse, W. F., *Israel after the Exile: Sixth and Fifth Centuries,* 1928.

Vol. V. Box, G. H., *Judaism in the Greek Period,* 1932.

The Abingdon Bible Commentary (*ABC*), Eiselen, Lewis, Downey, editors. Abingdon, 1929.

A New Commentary on Holy Scripture (*NCHS*), Gore, Goudge, Guillaume, editors. Macmillan, 1928.

A Commentary on the Bible (*PCB*), Peake and Grieve, editors. Nelson, 1920.

Peake's Commentary on the Bible, Supplement, Grieve, A. J., editor, 1936.

Kent, C. F., *The Student's Old Testament.* 6 vols. Scribner, 1904–1927. Very helpful.

Die Schriften des Alten Testaments (*SAT*), Gunkel, Staerk, Volz, Gressmann, Schmidt, Haller, editors. 7 vols. Göttingen, 1911–1921.

Die Heilige Schrift des Alten Testaments (*HSAT*), Kautzsch and Bertholet, editors. 2 vols. Tübingen, 1922.

*The student is advised to own one of the three one-volume commentaries (*ABC, NCHS, PCB*).

GENERAL BOOKS ON THE PERSONALITIES

Bowie, W. R., *Great Men of the Bible.* Harper, 1937.

*Dahl, G., *The Heroes of Israel's Golden Age: from Samuel to Micah.* Macmillan, 1923. Excellent.

*Fowler, H. T., *Great Leaders of Hebrew History.* Macmillan, 1920. (From Jeremiah through Job.) Excellent.

Jordan, W. G., *Ancient Hebrew Stories and Their Modern Interpretation.* Hodder & Stoughton, 1922.

*Kittel, R., *Great Men and Movements in Israel.* Macmillan, 1929. A sketch of Israel's outstanding personalities, written in a more popular style than the *History of the Hebrews,* and much more recent. A most useful book.

Mead, F. S., *Two Hundred and Fifty Bible Biographies.* Harper, 1934. These "thumb-nail sketches" are often excellent, but too brief to be of much value for serious study.

Rogers, R. W., *Great Characters of the Old Testament.* Methodist Book Concern, 1920. Brief but good.

*Wood, I. F., *The Heroes of Early Israel* (before Samuel). Macmillan, 1920. Very good.

Several older books may be mentioned, for they treat the personalities with a freedom and religious insight not always found in books of the present critical era.

Ewald, H., *The History of Israel.* 5 vols. London, 1869. Still valuable

for its portrayal of character, though as a history it is completely
out of date.

Matheson, G., *Representative Men of the Bible*. 2 vols. Armstrong,
1902(?)–1907.

Maurice, F. D., *The Prophets and Kings of the Old Testament*. New
York, 1871.

Stanley, A. P., *Lectures on the History of the Jewish Church*. 3 vols.
New York, 1868, 1869. A classic of English prose, telling the story
of Israel with freshness, charm, fulness of detail and religious
warmth. Can often be picked up second-hand. Based on Ewald,
and similarly out of date.

Histories of Israel, and of its religion, often have sections dealing with
the period and work of Old Testament personalities, while commentaries also throw much light upon them. One should likewise
consult articles under their names in Hastings' *Dictionary of the
Bible,* the *Encyclopaedia Biblica,* the *Jewish Encyclopaedia,* the several editions of the *Encyclopaedia Britannica,* and other standard
works of reference.

Beginning with the "Yahwist," Bewer (*LOT,* Ch. Vff) has illuminating treatments of the personalities.

In the detailed list that follows the aim is to suggest a few additional
sources of information for the study of each personality, besides
those indicated in the general lists.

MOSES

Burrows, M., *Founders of Great Religions*. Scribner, 1931. Ch. VII.

Charles, R. H., *The Decalogue*. T. & T. Clark, 1923.

Gressmann, H., *Mose und seine Zeit*. Göttingen, 1913. A monumental
work.

Die Anfänge Israels (in *Die Schriften des Alten Testaments*), Göttingen, 1914.

Smith, J. M. P., *The Origin and History of Hebrew Law*. Univ. Chicago Press, 1931.

Volz, P., *Mose und sein Werk*. 2d edition. Tübingen, 1932. A monograph of great value, giving a true appreciation of the uniqueness
of Moses.

Commentaries on Exodus: Bernett, undated, *Cent.B;* Driver, 1911, *CB;*
McNeile, 1908, *WC*.

Commentaries on Numbers: Binns, 1927, *WC;* Gray, 1903, *ICC;* Kennedy, undated, *Cent.B;* McNeile, 1911, *CB*.

JOSHUA

Blaikie, W. G., *The Book of Joshua*. Armstrong, 1893. *Expositor's
Bible*. Outdated in many ways, but it does treat Joshua the man
appreciatively from a religious point of view.

Garstang, J., *Joshua and Judges (JJ)*. Illustrated. Smith, 1931.

Smith, G. A., *Historical Geography of the Holy Land*. See index under names of places associated with Joshua.

Commentaries on the Book of Joshua: Cooke, 1918, *CB;* Robinson, undated, *Cent.B.*

See also articles, etc., referred to in footnotes and text, and p. 579ff.

DEBORAH AND GIDEON

Garstang, J., *Joshua and Judges* (see under Joshua).

Commentaries on the Book of Judges: Burney, 1918, Rivington; Cooke, 1913, *CB;* Moore, 1895, *ICC* (the standard work on *Judges*); Thatcher, undated, *Cent.B;* Watson, 1896, *Expositor's Bible* (for character study).

SAMUEL, SAUL AND DAVID

Commentaries on the Books of Samuel: Blaikie, 1888 and 1898, *Expositor's Bible* (for character study); Driver, *Notes on the Hebrew Text and Topography of the Books of Samuel*, Clarendon Press, 1913. 2d edition; Kennedy, undated, *Cent.B;* Kirkpatrick, 1930, *CB;* Smith, 1904, *ICC.*

Smith, J. M. P., "The Character of King David." *JBL*, April, 1933, p. 1ff.

SOLOMON, ELIJAH AND ELISHA

Commentaries on the Books of the Kings: Barnes, 1908, *CB;* Burney, *Notes on the Hebrew Text of the Books of the Kings,* Clarendon Press, 1903; Skinner, undated, *Cent.B.*

Peake, A. S., "Elijah and Jezebel. The Conflict with the Tyrian Baal." In *The Servant of Yahweh* (see under *Second Isaiah*).

THE YAHWIST

Brightman, E. S., *The Sources of the Hexateuch*. Abingdon, 1918. Ch. I.

Gordon, A. R., *Early Traditions of Genesis*. Clarke, 1907.

Gunkel, H., *The Legends of Genesis*. Open Court, 1901.

James, A. G., *Creation Stories of Genesis: their Relation to Modern Thought*. S.C.M., 1927.

Jordan, W. G., *Ancient Hebrew Stories and their Modern Interpretation*. Hodder & Stoughton, 1922. Chs. II–VI.

Commentaries on the Book of Genesis: Driver, 1904, *WC;* Skinner, 1910, *ICC.*

Books on Introduction, while they do not treat the Yahwist as a personality, have something to say of his theology and style. Books on the history of Israel, and of its religion, also generally give some space to the Yahwist. Bewer's treatment (*LOT,* Ch. V) is very fine.

THE PROPHETS (GENERAL)

Blunt, A. W. F., *The Prophets of Israel.* Clarendon Press, 1929.

Cornill, C. H., *The Prophets of Israel.* Open Court, 1895. Brief, illuminating, genuinely religious.

Davidson, A. B., *Old Testament Prophecy.* T. & T. Clark, 1904. "Prophecy and Prophets." *HDB.*

Duhm, B., *Israels Propheten.* 2d edition. Tübingen, 1922. A deeply religious book, by a great scholar and thinker.

Gordon, A. R., *The Prophets of the Old Testament.* Doran, 1916.

Graham, W. C., *The Prophets and Israel's Culture.* Univ. Chicago Press, 1934.

Gunkel, H., *Die Propheten.* Göttingen, 1917.

Hölscher, G., *Die Profeten.* Leipzig, 1914. Develops at length the idea that the prophets were ecstatics.

Knudson, A. C., *Beacon Lights of Prophecy.* Methodist Book Concern, 1914.

Lods, A., *The Prophets and the Rise of Judaism.* Dutton, 1937.

McCown, C. C., *The Promise of His Coming.* Macmillan, 1921.

Micklem, N., *Prophecy and Eschatology.* Allen & Unwin, 1926.

Robinson, T. H., *Prophecy and the Prophets in Ancient Israel.* Scribner, 1923.

Smith, J. M. P., *The Prophet and his Problems.* Scribner, 1914.
The Prophets and their Times. Univ. Chicago Press, 1925.

Smith, W. R., *The Prophets of Israel.* Revised with introduction and notes by T. K. Cheyne. Black, 1897.

Welch, A. C., *Prophet and Priest in Old Israel.* S.C.M., 1936.

Wells, U., *Pioneer Prophets.* Macmillan, 1929.
Prophets of Judah. Macmillan, 1931.

Histories of Israel, and of its religion, generally contain studies of the individual prophets. In another way, the books on the literature of the Old Testament do the same, especially Bewer (*LOT*, Chs. VIIff).

COMMENTARIES ON THE MINOR PROPHETS

Duhm, B., *The Twelve Prophets.* Black, 1912. A translation, with brief introductions and a very few notes.

Horton, R. F., *The Minor Prophets.* Jack, *Cent.B,* undated.

Robinson, T. H., and Horst, F., *Die zwölf kleinen Propheten.* Tübingen, 1936 and 1938.

Sellin, E., *Das Zwölfprophetenbuch.* Leipzig, 1928.

Smith, G. A., *The Book of the Twelve Prophets.* 2 vols. *Expositor's Bible.* New and revised edition, Hodder & Stoughton, 1928. A superb classic, indispensable for any student of the Minor Prophets.

AMOS AND HOSEA

Commentaries: Brown (Hosea), 1932, *WC;* Cheyne (Hosea), 1913, *CB;* Cripps (Amos), 1929, S.P.C.K.; Driver (Joel and Amos), 1915, *CB;* Edgehill (Amos), 1914, *WC;* Harper (Amos and Hosea), 1905, *ICC;* Longacre (Amos), 1921, Abingdon; Smith, J. M. P. (Amos, Hosea and Micah), 1914, *BHS.*

Morgenstern, J., "Amos Studies, I." *Hebrew Union College Annual,* XI, 1936, pp. 19-140.

ISAIAH

Commentaries on the Book of Isaiah: Box, 1909, Macmillan; Gray, 1912, *ICC;* McFadyen, 1910, *BHS;* Skinner, 1900, *CB;* Smith, G. A., 1927 (2d edition), *Expositor's Bible;* Wade, 1911, *WC;* Whitehouse, 1905, *Cent.B.*

Driver, S. R., *Isaiah, His Life and Times.* Randolph, 1893. Still about the best brief book on Isaiah, the man.

Glazebrook, M. G., *Studies in the Book of Isaiah.* Clarendon Press, 1910.

Jefferson, C. E., *Cardinal Ideas of Isaiah.* Macmillan, 1925.

MICAH

Commentaries: Margolis, 1908, Jewish Publication Society; Smith, J. M. P. (Amos, Hosea and Micah), 1914, *BHS;* Wade, 1925, *WC.*

THE DEUTERONOMISTS

For the problem of the date and unity of Deuteronomy, see books and articles listed in the footnotes; and also works on Introduction.

Commentaries: Driver, 1895, *ICC* (a work of the highest order); Jordan, 1911, *BHS;* Reider, 1937, Jewish Publication Society; Robinson, H. W., 1907, *Cent.B;* Smith, G. A., 1918, *CB.*

JEREMIAH

Calkins, R., *Jeremiah the Prophet: a Study in Personal Religion.* Macmillan, 1930.

Commentaries: Binns, 1919, *WC;* Driver, 1906, Scribner (very brief); Peake, 1910, *Cent.B.*

Gordon, T. C., *The Rebel Prophet.* Harper, 1932.

Lofthouse, W. F., *Jeremiah and the New Covenant.* S.C.M., 1925.

Longacre, L. B., *A Prophet of the Spirit.* Methodist Book Concern, 1922.

Robinson, H. W., *The Cross of Jeremiah.* S.C.M., 1925.

Skinner, J., *Prophecy and Religion. Studies in the Life of Jeremiah.* Cambridge Univ. Press, 1922. Probably the best book on Jeremiah.

Smith, G. A., *Jeremiah*. 4th edition, revised and enlarged, Doran, 1929.
Welch, A. C., *Jeremiah, His Time and His Work*. Oxford Univ. Press, 1928.
Werfel, F. V., *Hearken unto the Voice*. Viking Press, 1938.

THE EXILIC AND POST-EXILIC PERIOD (GENERAL)

Bevan, E., *Jerusalem under the High-Priests*. Arnold, 1912. Excellent.
Cheyne, T. K., *Jewish Religious Life after the Exile*. Putnam, 1898.
Cook, S. A., *The Old Testament*. Macmillan, 1936. Chs. XI–XII.
Duff, A., *A History of the Religion of Judaism 500–200 B.C.* Clarke, 1927.
Lods, A., *The Prophets and the Rise of Judaism*. Dutton, 1937.
Torrey, C. C., *Ezra Studies*. Univ. Chicago Press, 1910, Ch. X (for Torrey's reconstruction of the period's history).
Welch, A. C., *Post-Exilic Judaism (PEJ)*. Blackwood, 1935.

Most of these books have something to say about the personalities of the period. See also the appropriate sections in histories of Israel, and of its religion, as well as in other books covering the Old Testament field.

EZEKIEL

For the critical problem of the Book of Ezekiel see references in the footnotes.

Commentaries: Cooke, 1937, *ICC* (excellent); Davidson-Streane, 1916, *CB;* Lofthouse, undated, *Cent.B;* Redpath, 1907, *WC.*
Lofthouse, W. F., *The Prophet of Reconstruction. A Patriot's Dream for a New Age*. Clarke, 1920.

SECOND ISAIAH

Commentaries: Levy, 1925, Oxford Univ. Press; Skinner, 1898, *CB;* Smith, G. A., 1927 (2d edition), Hodder & Stoughton; Torrey, 1928, Scribner (a masterly commentary, embodying Torrey's views); Whitehouse, undated, *Cent.B.*
Jordan, W. G., *Songs of Service and Sacrifice*. Clark, 1924.
Oesterley, W. O. E., *Studies in Isaiah 40–66*. Scott, 1916.
Peake, A. S., *The Servant of Yahweh*. May, 1931.
Robinson, H. W., *The Cross of the Servant*. S.C.M., 1926.

HAGGAI, ZECHARIAH AND MALACHI

Commentaries: Barnes, 1917, *CB;* Mitchell (Haggai and Zechariah), 1912, *ICC;* Smith, J. M. P. (Malachi), 1912, *ICC.*

NEHEMIAH AND EZRA

Commentaries: Batten, 1913, *ICC;* Davies, undated, *Cent.B;* Ryle, 1893, *CB.*

THE PRIESTLY WRITERS

See under the Yahwist, Moses and Joshua for commentaries on the Hexateuch. Also commentaries on Leviticus in the one-volume commentaries on the Bible.

THE CHRONICLER

Commentaries on the Books of Chronicles: Curtis-Madsen, 1910, *ICC;* Elmslie, 1916, *CB;* Harvey-Jellie, 1906, *Cent.B.*

Torrey, C. C., *Ezra Studies,* Univ. Chicago Press, 1910, Ch. VII.

HEBREW WISDOM WRITERS (GENERAL)

Bruce, W. S., *The Wisdom Literature of the Old Testament.* J. Clarke, 1928.

Cheyne, T. K., *Job and Solomon.* Whittaker, 1887.

Davison, W. T., *The Wisdom-Literature of the Old Testament.* 4th edition. Kelly, 1912.

Dillon, E. J., *The Sceptics of the Old Testament.* Isbrister, 1895.

Genung, J. F., *The Hebrew Literature of Wisdom.* Houghton Mifflin, 1906. Excellent.

Harvey-Jellie, W. D., *Where shall Wisdom be Found?* J. Clarke, 1928. *The Wisdom of God and the Word of God.* Pilgrim Press, 1911.

Macdonald, D. B., *The Hebrew Philosophical Genius. A Vindication.* Princeton Univ. Press, 1936.

Rankin, O. S., *Israel's Wisdom Literature; its Bearing on Theology and the History of Religion.* T. & T. Clark, 1938. Largely concerned with religious ideas.

Ranston, H., *The Old Testament Wisdom Books and their Teaching.* Epworth Press, 1930.

THE WISE MEN OF THE BOOK OF PROVERBS

Commentaries on the Book of Proverbs: Martin, 1908, *Cent.B;* Oesterley, 1929, Dutton; Toy, 1916, *ICC* (the two latter are excellent).

Warschauer, J., *The Way of Understanding.* Pilgrim Press, 1913. A series of 25 sermons.

THE WRITER OF THE BOOK OF JOB

Commentaries: Ball, 1922, Clarendon Press; Barton, 1911, *BHS;* Buttenwieser, 1922, Macmillan (rearranges the text drastically); Davidson-Lanchester, 1918, *CB;* Driver and Gray, 1921, *ICC;* Gibson, 1899,

Macmillan; Peake, 1905, *Cent.B;* Strahan, 1914 (2d edition), T. & T. Clark.

Jastrow, M., *The Book of Job.* Lippincott, 1920.

Jordan, W. G., *The Book of Job; its Substance and Spirit.* Macmillan, 1929.

Kraeling, E. G., *The Book of the Ways of God* (contains 8 illustrations by Blake and 8 original poems). Scribner, 1939.

McKechnie, J., *Job: Moral Hero, Religious Egoist and Mystic.* Doran, 1927.

Robinson, H. W., *The Cross of Job.* S.C.M., 1917.

QOHELETH

Commentaries on the Book of Ecclesiastes: Barton, 1908, *ICC;* Genung, 1904, Houghton Mifflin; McNeile, 1904, Cambridge Univ. Press; Martin, 1908, *Cent.B;* Odeberg, 1929, Upsala.

Jastrow, M., *A Gentle Cynic.* Lippincott, 1919.

THE WRITER OF DANIEL

Commentaries: Charles, undated, *Cent.B;* also 1929, Clarendon Press; Driver, 1900, *CB;* Montgomery, 1927, *ICC.* The last three excellent.

Rowley, H. H., *Darius the Mede and the Four World Empires . . . A Historical Study of Contemporary Theories.* Univ. Wales Press, 1937. Deals with the critical and historical questions mainly.

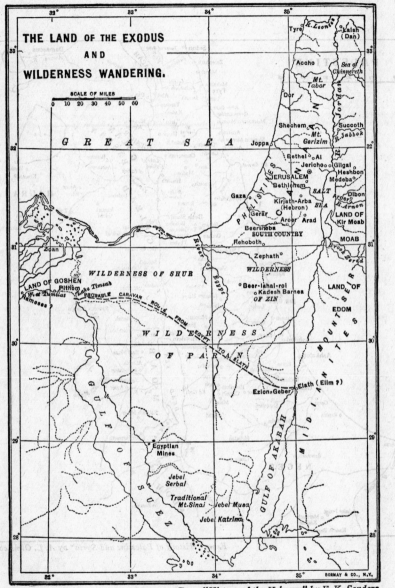

THE LAND OF THE EXODUS
AND
WILDERNESS WANDERING.

SCALE OF MILES
0 10 20 30 40 50 60

From "History of the Hebrews" by F. K. Sanders

601

From "History of Palestine and Syria" by A. L. Olmstead

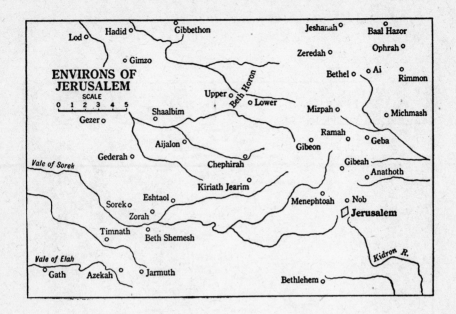

ENVIRONS OF JERUSALEM

SCALE

0 1 2 3 4 5

Lod   Hadid   Gibbethon   Jeshanah   Baal Hazor

Gimzo   Zeredah   Ophrah

Bethel   Ai   Rimmon

Upper   Beth Horon   Lower

Shaalbim   Mizpah   Michmash

Gezer

Ramah   Geba

Aijalon   Gibeon

Gederah   Chephirah   Gibeah   Anathoth

Vale of Sorek   Kiriath Jearim

Sorek   Eshtaol   Menephtoah   Nob

Zorah   Jerusalem

Timnath   Beth Shemesh

Kidron R.

Vale of Elah

Gath   Azekah   Jarmuth   Bethlehem

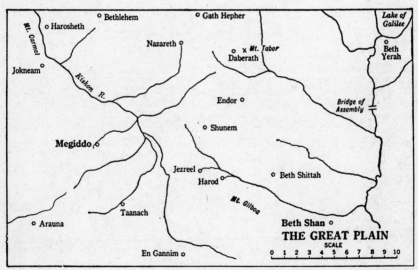

Mt. Carmel   Haросheth   Bethlehem   Gath Hepher   Lake of Galilee

Nazareth   Mt. Tabor   Beth Yerah

Daberath

Jokneam   Kishon R.

Endor   Bridge of Assembly

Shunem

Megiddo

Jezreel   Beth Shittah

Harod

Mt. Gilboa

Taanach

Arauna   Beth Shan

THE GREAT PLAIN

SCALE

0 1 2 3 4 5 6 7 8 9 10

En Gannim

From "History of Palestine and Syria" by A. L. Olmstead

603

From "History of Palestine and Syria" by A. L. Olmstead

INDEX OF OLD TESTAMENT PASSAGES

605

INDEX TO OTHER PASSAGES

INDEX OF NAMES AND SUBJECTS